Building Service Provider Networks

Howard Berkowitz

Wiley Computer Publishing

John Wiley & Sons, Inc.

Publisher: Robert Ipsen
Editor: Carol A. Long
Assistant Editor: Adaobi Obi
Managing Editor: Micheline Frederick

Text Design & Composition: North Market Street Graphics

Library of Congress Cataloging-in-Publication Data:

ISBN 0-471-09922-8
Printed in the United States of America.

10 9 8 7 6 5 4 3 2 1

Wiley Networking Council Series

Scott Bradner
Senior Technical Consultant, Harvard University

Vinton Cerf
Senior Vice President, MCI WorldCom

Lyman Chapin
Chief Scientist, NextHop Technologies, Inc.

Books in the Series

Howard C. Berkowitz, *WAN Survival Guide: Strategies for VPNs and Multiservice Networks* 0471-38428-3

Tim Casey, *ISP Liability Survival Guide: Strategies for Managing Copyright, Spam, Cache, and Privacy Regulations* 0-471-37748-1

Jon Crowcroft & Iain Phillips, *TCP/IP and Linux Protocol Implementation: Systems Code for the Linux Internet* 0-471-40882-4

Bill Dutcher, *The NAT Handbook: Implementing and Managing Network Address Translation* 0-471-39089-5

Igor Faynberg, Hui-Lan Lu, & Lawrence Gabuzda, *Converged Networks and Services: Internetworking IP and the PSTN* 0-471-35644-1

Russ Housley & Tim Polk, *Planning for PKI: Best Practices Guide for Deploying Public Key Infrastructure* 0-471-39702-4

Geoff Huston, *Internet Performance Survival Guide: QoS Strategies for Multiservice Networks* 0-471-37808-9

Geoff Huston, *ISP Survival Guide: Strategies for Running a Competitive ISP* 0-471-31499-4

Elizabeth Kaufman & Andrew Newman, *Implementing IPsec: Making Security Work on VPN's, Intranets, and Extranets* 0-471-34467-2

Dave Kosiur, *Understanding Policy-Based Networking* 0-471-38804-1

Mark E. Laubach, David J. Farber, & Stephen D. Dukes, *Delivering Internet Connections over Cable: Breaking the Access Barrier* 0-471-38950-1

Dave McDysan, *VPN Applications Guide: Real Solutions for Enterprise Networks* 0-471-37175-0

Henry Sinnreich & Alan Johnston, *Internet Communications Using SIP: Delivering VoIP and Multimedia Services with Session Initiation Protocol* 0-471-41399-2

James P.G. Sterbenz & Joseph D. Touch, *High Speed Networking: A Systematic Approach to High-Bandwidth Low-Latency Communication* 0-471-33036-1

Dedication

To friends and colleagues who have left this layer
of existence during the writing of this book:

To a protege whose utter unwillingness to quit, and her drive to
learn, is an inspiration: Heather Allan

To Curt Freemyer, Beckey Badgett, and the rest of the team at Gett:
Thanks for all the support. You all have a role in this book.

Abha Ahuja, routing area director, IETF

Lynn Acquaviva, a dear and inspirational friend

Contents

Networking Council Foreword

The Networking Council Series was created in 1998 within Wiley's Computer Publishing group to fill an important gap in networking literature. Many current technical books are long on details but short on understanding. They do not give the reader a sense of where, in the universe of practical and theoretical knowledge, the technology might be useful in a particular organization. The Networking Council Series is concerned more with how to think clearly about networking issues than with promoting the virtues of a particular technology—how to relate new information to the rest of what the reader knows and needs, so the reader can develop a customized strategy for vendor and product selection, outsourcing, and design.

In *Building Service Provider Networks* by Howard Berkowitz, you'll see the hallmarks of Networking Council books—examination of the advantages and disadvantages, strengths and weaknesses of market-ready technology, useful ways to think about options pragmatically, and direct links to business practices and needs. Disclosure of pertinent background issues needed to understand who supports a technology and how it was developed is another goal of all Networking Council books.

The Networking Council Series is aimed at satisfying the need for perspective in an evolving data and telecommunications world filled with hyperbole, speculation, and unearned optimism. In *Building Service Provider Networks* you'll get clear information from experienced practitioners.

We hope you enjoy the read. Let us know what you think. Feel free to visit the Networking Council web site at www.wiley.com/networkingcouncil.

Scott Bradner
Senior Technical Consultant, *Harvard University*

Vinton Cerf
Senior Vice President, *MCI WorldCom*

Lyman Chapin
Chief Scientist, *NextHop Technologies, Inc.*

Acknowledgments

Many have contributed to my growth in learning to build networks. It's hard to count the number of colleagues in the North American Network Operations Group and Internet Engineering Task Force who have helped me understand issues and with whom I brainstormed issues. Thanks to Sean Donelan, Susan Harris, Sue Hares, Vijay Gill, Kevin Dubray, Yakov Rekhter, Frank Kastenholz, Lyman Chapin, Scott Bradner, Sean Doran, and Geoff Huston.

Major support came from my employer, Gett Communications and Gett Labs.

My previous employer, Nortel Networks, gave me many opportunities for thinking about, arguing about, and screaming about provider issues. Let me thank colleagues including my immediate team of Francis Ovenden, Kirby Dolak, and Silvana Romagnino. Other valuable insight came from Nortel colleagues including Avri Doria, Elwyn Davies, Fiffi Hellstrand, Ken Sundell, Ruth Fox, and Dmitri Krioukov.

The BGP convergence team in the IETF Benchmarking Working Group was another strong sounding board, where I am delighted to credit Padma Krishnaswamy, Marianne Lepp, Alvaro Retana, Martin Biddiscombe, and (again) Elwyn Davies and Sue Hares. There are too many people on the Babylon research team to give individual credit, but let me single out Loa Andersson, Tove Madsen, and Yong Jiang, and again Avri Doria.

CertificationZone.com, and Paul Borghese's site and mailing list groupstudy.com, have been an excellent forum to understand the learning process. Let me thank Paul, as well as other contributors including Chuck Larrieu, John Neiberger, Peter van Oene, Erik Roy, and Priscilla Oppenheimer.

My home life stayed sane through a fourth book largely through the skill of my housekeeper and assistant, Mariatu Kamara, and my distinguished feline editorial assistant, Clifford—even if he did have a hairball on the copy edit of Chapter 10.

Carol Long of Wiley has been incredibly supportive in this project and throughout my publishing career. This is my fourth full book, and the first one where the production and copy editors have made the process better rather than more frustrating. Thanks to production editor Micheline Frederick and copy editor Stephanie Landis for adding value to the book.

Finally, I cannot sufficiently praise the contributions of Annlee Hines, my peer reviewer on this book.

Introduction

Arthur C. Clarke defined any sufficiently advanced technology as indistinguishable from magic. A great many network service customers seem to believe in magical solutions, and, unfortunately, too many salespeople are willing to promise magical solutions.

Service provider engineers often face the need to meet a less than logical requirement. Their customers might have posed more logical requirements had they read my *WAN Survival Book*, which focuses on the customer side of the WAN service relationship. Nevertheless, many customers and their sales representatives have not done this, so this book needed to be written.

Building Service Provider Networks could perhaps have been titled *Engineering Design of Magic Networks*. It gives approaches for implementing the provider side of a network offering with a service level agreement (SLA) without being afraid to mention technologies that, to put it politely, are just solidifying from conceptual vaporware. It will mention when arguments for certain technologies are at least partially based on fear, uncertainty, and doubt (FUD).

Overview of the Book and Technology

Systematic communications systems involving the transfer of messages without the need to handle paper have certainly been with us for at least two centuries, going back to Napoleonic semaphore systems. Less systematic remote communications go back to smoke signals.

Electrical communications began in 1844, and were in regular commercial use by the late nineteenth century. Electrical and electronic communications were largely controlled by technical monopolies, so innovation was paced by the operational needs of the major carriers and their ability to absorb and deploy new technology. When telecommunications divestiture and widespread deregulation began in the 1970s, the rate of new technology introduction increased dramatically, interacting with customer perceptions to create incredible demand for both feasible and infeasible services.

This book will constantly balance business requirements, administrative relationships, and technical capabilities in guiding readers through their networking decisions.

How This Book Is Organized

In general, the book is organized into three main parts. Chapters 1 through 5 deal with
defining customer requirements and the abstract provider architecture. Chapters 6
through 8 deal with building and extending carrier facilities and transmission systems.
Chapters 9 through 13 deal with the intelligent communications systems overlaid onto
the physical structures, which to varying extents involve Internet Protocol (IP)–based
control planes, and possibly IP forwarding.

As in all my books, Chapter 1 begins with my mantra: "What is the problem you are
trying to solve?" It focuses on perceived customer requirements, including the serene
assumption that appropriate incantations exist to bring implementation magic into
being. However, deployment of these services in all or part depends on the existing
telecommunications infrastructure, the architecture, limitations, and capabilities of
which are introduced in Chapter 2.

Chapter 3 begins the translation of customer desires into technical requirements,
with special emphasis on service level agreements. This translation becomes more formal with the introduction of policy specification language in Chapter 4, and an extensive discussion of obtaining and managing address space in Chapter 5. Case studies
illustrate the increasing amount of detail each step brings to the technical specification.

Chapter 6 marks a strong transition from the world of conceptual requirements to the
very real facilities of telecommunications carriers, dealing with the practical requirements for "carrier-grade" equipment, buildings, and network operations centers. In Chapter 7, facilities-oriented discussion moves to the physical and data-link facilities at the
increasingly complex provider edge, from the first meter through the first 100 meters,
first mile, and second mile. Chapter 8 deals with core transmission technologies.

The modern provider network is intelligent. Historically, telephony networks only
achieved appreciable scalability when they separated their control (call setup) from
their forwarding (voice transfer) functions. This separation became blurred with the
early introduction of data networking, but has returned as a basic architectural idea.

A favorite Dilbert-style T-shirt of mine says, "the beatings will continue until morale
improves." In this context, let me emphasize the beatings will continue until it is realized that Multiprotocol Label Switching (MPLS) does not replace IP routing, but complements it. MPLS especially complements IP routing in the forwarding plane, but is
also representative of what is now termed the sub-IP control plane. IP routing still is the
brain of the control plane of every new transmission technology.

Chapter 9 begins with a discussion of the functionality of the Border Gateway Protocol, Version 4 (BGP-4) and its applicability to specific customer requirements. The
approach I take in this chapter differs from that of other BGP books: It deals first with
the problem to be solved, then identifies the mechanisms to solve it—including the latest extensions in development. It does not, however, focus on the commands to configure and troubleshoot specific routers, but complements books that do.

Chapter 10 moves to the provider side of the edge between customer and provider,
introducing other routing mechanisms and concentrating on the design of the carrier

point of presence (POP). Chapter 11 then moves to the intraprovider core, which has undergone revolutionary changes in scalability with the introduction of MPLS and other technologies.

Chapters 12 and 13 involve extending the network beyond a single provider. Specifically, Chapter 12 deals with interprovider connectivity, while Chapter 13 involves virtual private networks (VPNs). In VPNs, there are interesting problems of extending provider responsibility into the enterprise networks, of developing private extranets among multiple enterprises, and of interprovider VPNs.

Who Should Read This Book

The ideal reader needs to make decisions about wide area network (WAN) requirements and technologies or guide others in making such decisions. You could be making these decisions from the perspective of the WAN service provider or the customer. This book focuses on the service provider network, and ideally will be read in concern with the more customer-oriented *WAN Survival Guide*. It is not aimed at protocol implementers, although it does present alternatives between techniques in development. If a reader finishes the book and is disappointed that he or she did not become utterly familiar with bit-level techniques, I have succeeded in my goals! There are many excellent sources for dealing with protocol mechanics, but a shortage of sources for pinning down problems and selecting solutions.

CHAPTER 1

What Is the Problem to Be Solved?

What is the difference, Grasshopper, between a network sales representative and a seller of used cars named Honest Joe?

I know not, my Master.

(1) The seller of used cars knows when he is lying.

(2) The seller of used cars usually knows how to drive.
—Heard at a trade show

The long-term maximization of return on investment requires technical correctness. Unfortunately there is often a lot of arbitrage by people with very short-term goals. Sadly, some of the worst technologies are the ones that get lots of short-term interest.
—Sean Doran, NANOG List, March 16, 2001

Again, men desire what is good, and not merely what their fathers had.
—Aristotle

Students of human culture rather frequently find, regardless of their particular field of study, that humanity has an annoying tendency to split into two or more cultures. C.P. Snow contrasted science and government. Art versus technology is a recurring theme. This chapter emphasizes important technical cultural differences, as well as the broadest characteristics of user requirements. We will deliberately take a "10,000 foot" view in order to define the problem without the details. The next chapter will begin to delve into the technical details.

Networking cultures differ in the traditions of the users of the networks and of the people who build the networks. A principal problem in today's "Internet" is that there is no generally agreed-upon definition of which networking technologies are inside or outside the "Internet" scope—or, indeed, if anything is included. This book uses a working definition that includes services enabled using Internet Protocol (IP) and the IP architecture, where the service either is offered to outside subscribers or forms part of the service provider's infrastructure. I focus on the generic Internet Protocol service provider (IPSP), of which a subset is involved in the public Internet. Many IP-based services cannot be delivered with production quality in a public environment.

To confuse things further, there is a common technology called the Internet Protocol. While the public Internet is based on IP, so are private networks with performance guarantees. This is good for realizing economies of scale with common equipment and technologies, but less good when naive users equate the public Internet, and its pricing, with the necessarily higher pricing of higher-performance, higher-availability services also based on IP.

Do not confuse the existence of private networks with an assumption that resources are dedicated to the specific customer only. The reality is that large resources with significant economies of scale are partitioned into subsets serving public and private customers. Think of a physical highway, where lanes can be committed to carpools or to general traffic.

The User Culture

Major user versions of what we loosely call the Internet include [Berkowitz 2001a]:

- A collaborative environment for networking research. This is the original model for the ARPANET. While it is important in the work of many researchers, it is not expected to be of production quality—the reliability on which I'd stake a project's existence. It includes various research overlays, such as Mbone and 6bone, which again are not of production quality. It is public, but with controlled access to various experimental services.

- A distributed environment for sharing information among individuals and organizations. This is quite achievable within the public Internet. Again, it isn't what I'd call production quality. An environment that includes people without much network or system administration experience, or the resources required for fault tolerance, is good for informal sharing. Insisting on production quality would constitute an economic bar to entry. Again, I think this falls into your usage.

- Commercial services characterized by having a known set of public servers, but without the clients/users being predefined. This is the basic model for business-to-consumer applications. Servers and their access networks need to be of production quality to be reliable. This category blurs into a range of applications where clients can reach servers from arbitrary locations, but the client has to establish a relationship with the provider before application processing can begin. Think of online banking or investing.

- Commercial services with both clients and servers known before communications begin, with assumptions about security (for example, that it is a closed environment) and possibly about quality of service. This is the domain of intranet and extranet virtual private networks. While these services use the Internet Protocol, and indeed may share parts of the same provider infrastructure used by public applications, they are in the domain of IP service providers rather than Internet service providers (ISPs).

The Implementer Culture

When dealing with the builders and operators of networks, I find there are four significant cultures:

1. *Mainframe, or more recently management information system (MIS) computing.* The network exists to serve the central computer(s). "When we desire the opinion of users, we will tell them what it is."

2. *Distributed, or more recently local area network (LAN)-centric, computing.* The network is a means to the end of interconnecting the bright and glorious user-driven applications in LAN-connected hosts. "Users are in total control."

3. *Old-time Internet computing.* Hosts are a test program for the wonders of the intelligent network and the infrastructure that makes it up. "Users are test programs for hosts."

4. *Traditional telecommunications.* Networks are plumbing systems for carrying bitstreams. We will tell the network what it is to do. "Users are irrelevant. They have been assimilated."

It is the goal of this book to describe an environment in which the positive aspects of all these cultures can thrive, in which people who grew up in one of the cultures can work with the others, and in which the no longer useful aspects of the cultures can enter graceful retirement.

Precisely how the social, business, and political factors will create this environment, often called the eighth layer of Open System Interconnection (OSI), is, however, beyond the scope of this book. As my colleague Annlee Hines put it, Zeus gave up after the first headache. These goals stop short of massively increasing government services while cutting taxes; authors must know their limits.

CROSS-CULTURAL CONFLICT

Some years ago, I was teaching the introductory Cisco router software configuration course in a very nice classroom at a DEC training center in the Boston area. Around the midpoint of the course, one of my students screamed "I can't take it any longer," hurled his course notebook into the air, and ran out of the room.

It was one of those moments where no one had the slightest idea what to say. Calling a coffee break, I went out in search of the student and found him trembling on a couch in a break area. We chatted a bit, as I used every skill I had learned in counseling workshops. Whether or not medical intervention was called for was, indeed, crossing my mind.

It turned out that the student was a very nice and competent IBM systems programmer. The realization that his users could change addresses without his knowledge, consent, and blessing with a new sysgen (system generation, a massive process) had truly struck home, and it was too alien a concept for him to cope with. Eventually, he calmed down and continued the course.

Later on, he shared his feelings with the class, and some of the LAN-oriented students learned about sysgens (and, for the picky among my readers, VTAMgens and NCPgens). Some of the LAN people had been complaining that Cisco configurations, as I taught them from experience rather than the simple book examples, were too lengthy and complex. When they realized that the full output of a sysgen process might be a foot-thick pile of paper, and they could write their "complex" router configurations on the side of that stack, there was a moment of cross-cultural understanding. Much rejoicing followed, birds sang, church bells rang, etc.

The perspective of this book is taken from that of the service provider. You will not see the term *service provider* mentioned explicitly in any of the exaggerated cultural descriptions we just discussed, but it is always implicit. Someone always must pay for service, and someone must provide that service because they are paid to do so. In our popular culture, this reality occasionally is obscured by the way in which the global Internet came into being: as a subsidized academic and research network. Some users of the Internet have not been aware of these subsidies, and have formed a subculture of entitlement whose central tenet is that the Internet should be free.

What Services Do Users Want?

Let's approach this question in a very basic way. The most basic model concerns the simple relationships of endpoints that will communicate. Such a model is far more basic than one that considers the quality of service (QoS) requirements of voice versus data, but is a prerequisite for any more specific discussions. For this discussion, I will use a client/server model in which the client initiates a request for service and a server responds to a service request. These are asymmetrical relationships, but you will find peer-to-peer, symmetrical relationships to be special cases of the client/server modeled cases.

Clients and servers are end hosts on the network, most often operated by a customer of the service provider. Service providers may contract to operate certain of these hosts, but such contracts are separate from basic network service contracts. Axiomatic to any communication between client and server is that each has to have an *identifier* defining, in machine-readable terms, who it is rather than where it is. Knowing identifiers is necessary to establish the endpoints of a communication. Once the endpoints are known, it is necessary to determine the *locators* of the endpoints: where those points are and how they can be reached. It also may be necessary to know the locators of intermediate points on the path between the endpoints, such as routers or the growing class of *midboxes* (network address translators, caches, proxies, and so on). Let's examine the main categories of user communication from the perspective of identifiers.

Sites and Communities of Interest

As shown in Figure 1.1, an enterprise may have one or more sites. Sites traditionally have been defined geographically by traditional telecommunications carriers as locations at which all hosts are interconnected by transmission facilities under the control of the enterprise (for example, campus LANs). Such sites, in turn, are linked by the traditional wide area network (WAN) carrier architecture (Figure 1.1). However, with the advent of virtual private networks (VPNs), sites may be defined virtually as a set of users and servers with common information interests: a *community of interest* (COI). Figure 1.1 contrasts these two views.

Separating Customer and Provider Responsibility

Data terminal equipment (DTE) is the last point of full customer responsibility, *data circuit terminating equipment* (DCE) is the carrier's interface to the customer, and *data switching equipment* (DXE) is internal to the carrier. In recent years, with increasing deregulation, the function of the DCE—the point of demarcation of the responsibility between subscriber to provider—has changed. Since either the customer or the provider may own the demarcation function, the term *customer premises equipment* (CPE) has come to mean a demarcation device owned by the subscriber, while *customer location equip-*

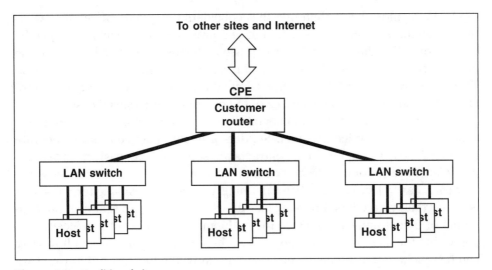

Figure 1.1   Traditional site.

ment (CLE) is owned by the carrier. These edge functions are discussed further in Chapter 7.

The traditional model involves the DTE connecting to DCE at various physical sites, and information automagically flowing through the provider's "cloud," the details of which (Figures 1.2 and 1.3) are invisible to the subscriber. Some models of virtual private networks, however, have the concept of a virtual site: A set of hosts or users that have met some authentication criterion, independent of their physical location (Figure 1.4).

TWO PEOPLES SEPARATED BY A COMMON LANGUAGE, PART 1

Carriers make an important distinction between the customer network and the provider network, and the point of demarcation between. Mainframe MIS people, or people used to LANs, think of one network. Carrier people think of many.

The Internet confuses both sides. Mainframe and LAN people are used to owning all resources and being able to control quality by implementing the correct amount of resources.

Telecommunications people also believe that appropriate allocation of resources can ensure quality, even if multiple organizations own the resources. What confuses telecommunications people is that in the classic Internet, they may not know which organizations even form the path, and that this path changes. In the public Internet, there is no way to keep resources committed.

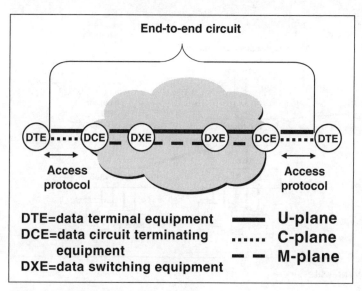

Figure 1.2 Traditional carrier model.

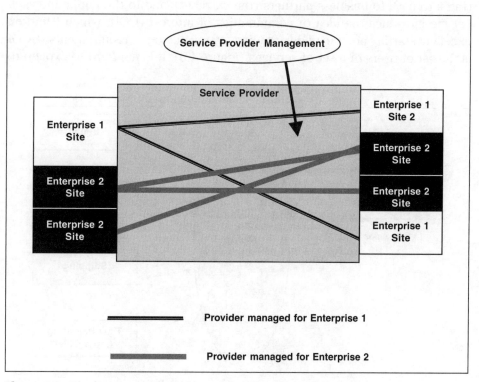

Figure 1.3 Site interconnection with traditional carrier model.

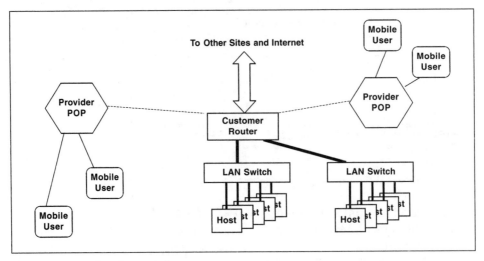

Figure 1.4   Real and virtual sites.

Communities of Interest

The role of the service provider is in interconnecting the sites to one another (the intranet), to business partners (the extranet), and to the public Internet. Let me introduce the idea of communities of interest (COI), which I find an excellent starting point in understanding overall customer requirements. A COI is the set of users of a set of services (Figure 1.5). It is not hard to explain to

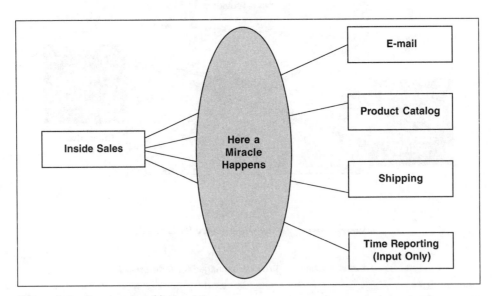

Figure 1.5   Community of interest.

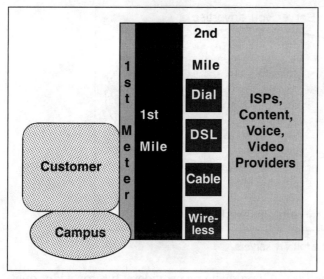

Figure 1.6 New provider model.

nontechnical people, but it is definitely a good start for the formal requirements definition discussed in Chapter 3.

A COI may further be broken down if certain users of the same set of servers have different availability, security, or performance requirements than other users. At this stage of the discussion, assume all users within a class have the same requirements. This differs from the traditional model of the carrier largely as a point-to-point, or series of point-to-point, links between customer data terminal equipment (DTE).

This model has gone through substantial revision, as providers literally transform themselves into service providers and specialize in different parts of the problem. Figure 1.6 shows the basic role of many of these specializations. Access providers are a special focus of Chapter 7, while IP service providers are detailed in Chapters 8 through 12. Content provider services are in Chapter 13.

Known Clients to Arbitrary Servers

In the typical case of web surfing for enterprise users, your clients' identifiers are known but the identifiers of their desired server destinations are not known until the clients actually request service. You have a level of trust in the client identifiers, which may be based on their connecting from a trusted location, or you may trust that they come in from random locations but have passed authentication criteria (see Figure 1.7).

While the "popular wisdom" speaks of telephone systems as monolithic in comparison with data networks, for all practical purposes they have always

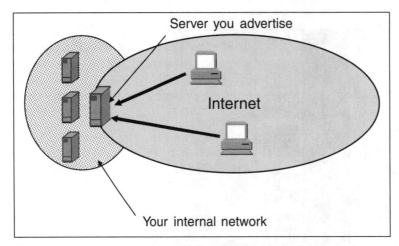

Figure 1.7   Known clients to arbitrary servers.

been divided into local access and long-distance providers. Interprovider operation is an everyday part of the telephone culture, actually to a greater degree than it has been a part of the non-Internet data culture. The public Internet, however, not only involves the cooperation of multiple connectivity providers but involves a wide range of content providers.

Known Servers to Arbitrary Clients

To do business on the Internet, the server owner makes it accessible to clients that are not known prior to the interaction. If the interaction is simply to pro-

PRICING IMPLICATIONS OF CONVERGED NETWORKS

The somewhat technically unfortunate term *converged networks* has come into use to describe networks that provide data, video, and voice services. The known client to arbitrary server case is not that dissimilar from the model of telephony, where enterprise telephone users expect to be able to connect to any telephone in the world (see Figure 1.8).

An important differentiator for this model is its price sensitivity. Not that any customer is immune to price, but this case is also the basic application for residential Internet users. Residential users typically want very low price, but when the network carries voice or entertainment video, consumers are more willing to pay premium prices than for Internet access. There is a greater expectation of reliability for these services. The higher price tolerance is an incentive for carriers to provide multiple services, which in turn motivates broadband connectivity to the residence. See Chapter 2 for a discussion of traditional telephony architecture.

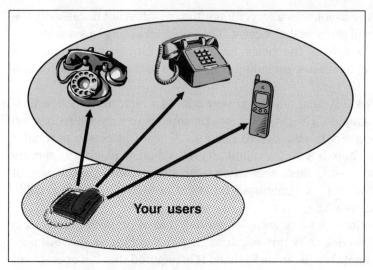

Figure 1.8   Telephony metaphor.

vide public content (for instance, getting news headlines from CNN), the only level of identification needed is that which is required to return a response to the client (Figure 1.9).

When the application involves credit card charges or other sensitive information, authentication is needed. The content provider's security policy needs to make clear whether the authentication is of the human being using the identified host (for example, verifying a credit card number) or if the client host needs also to be authenticated as part of audit controls.

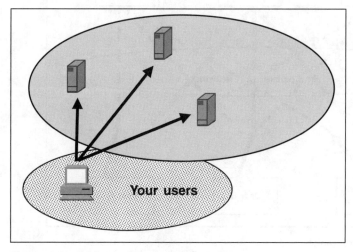

Figure 1.9   Arbitrary client to known server.

Remember that the client sees a server identifier, which is not necessarily the actual server that will process the request. The potential ability to separate virtual from actual servers is the basis for many performance-enhancing or resource-conserving functions, including web caches and content distribution services.

Figure 1.10 shows a typical television scenario, in which the broadcasters' transmissions are simplex. The broadcasters (analogous to servers) receive no feedback from receivers (analogous to clients). A client selects a particular channel to receive. There is a distinct similarity to a cnn.com placing its servers on the Internet and making them accessible to arbitrary clients. In the case of the Internet, minimal duplex communications are needed simply for reliable transmission of the web data.

Figure 1.11 introduces a more complex model, that of premium services in television. In this model, it is not required that the content sources know which particular clients are listening to them. It is required that the operator of the access control devices either enable subscription service or authorize and collect pay-per-view services. It is not unreasonable to make an analogy between the access control providers for pay-per-view and the micro-cash-transfer services (for example, PayPal) evolving to provide paid passwords to specific Internet services. Paying for specific passwords is subtly different than the next case of having pre-established relationships between clients and servers.

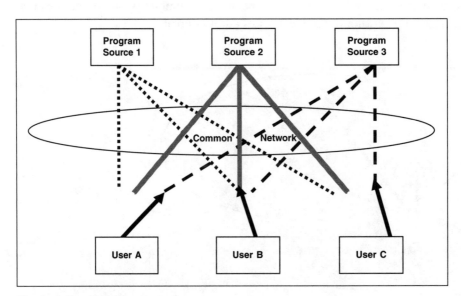

Figure 1.10   Television metaphor.

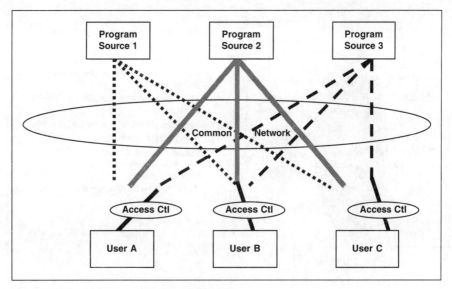

Figure 1.11 Premium television metaphor.

Known Clients to Known Servers under Common Administration

Traditional enterprise-operated networks fall under this category, as do a variety of models in which the operation of some services is outsourced to providers. Even the traditional model, however, involves a certain amount of operational outsourcing when the customer does not operate their own wide area links. When multiple sites interconnect, the wide area transmission facilities among the sites are assumed to be under the control of a service provider. In other words, there is an administrative boundary between the customer and provider. Some technologies, such as asynchronous transfer mode (ATM), can be used both within and between sites, so it proves more useful to distinguish between site and wide area services with respect to administrative models rather than technologies.

In principle, the service provider is responsible for its own network, both its facilities and their administration. Figure 1.12 shows that the service providers may have many customers, whose traffic flows over shared resources under provider control. The provider has an operational support network for controlling these resources. In Figure 1.12, there are sites that belong to the intranet of one enterprise only or to the extranet of either or both of enterprises 1 and 2. See the next section for a discussion of intranets and extranets.

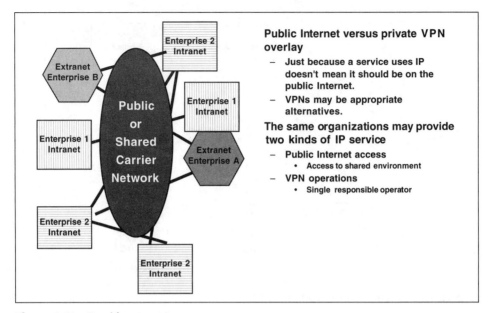

Figure 1.12   Provider structure.

Introduction to VPNs

Managed service models still require significant customer involvement in defining requirements for connections between sites, the technical details of interconnection devices, and so on. A model that reduces customer involvement is the intranet VPN (Figure 1.13).

No single, universally accepted definition of a VPN yet exists. When I taught Cisco University seminars for resellers that would offer VPNs to their customers, I observed that it had long been traditional for network sales to sell products that didn't exist. Since VPNs didn't have actual existence—if they did, they obviously wouldn't be virtual—then sales should be able to sell infinite numbers of VPNs.

In this book, I define a VPN as a set of endpoints that are interconnected over shared facilities operated by a single contractually responsible service provider. The customer has the illusion that it has a private network, and indeed different customers on the VPN are isolated from one another. The shared infrastructure *may* be the public Internet. If any appreciable performance/service guarantees are needed, however, it is quite unrealistic for the customer to expect any guarantees if the provider has no control of the underlying transmission facilities.

There are many vendor-specific interpretations of VPNs. It is not meant as a criticism that vendors tend to emphasize their core competence in their definition of VPNs. Those concerned with packet transport tend to emphasize the

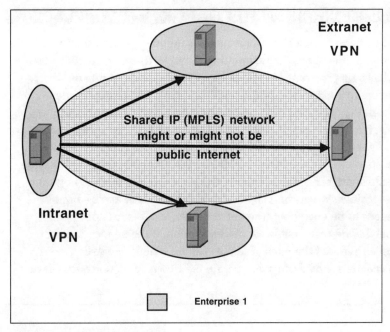

Figure 1.13 Intranet VPN.

networking aspects, while those who make security products tend to define VPNs with respect to security. But what if the customer needs connectivity to the Internet? There are two main requirements for Internet connectivity, known clients to arbitrary servers and known servers to arbitrary clients. Both may be needed by a given enterprise.

Personally, the only way I have been able to make sense of the chaos of VPNs is to separate the issues of requirements and implementation technology. User requirements include a minimal set of core requirements and an assortment of optional capabilities. VPNs with only the core requirements tend to be uninteresting and not extremely useful. Almost any VPN will need some of the optional

TWO PEOPLES SEPARATED BY A COMMON LANGUAGE, PART 2

Many LAN-oriented people don't really get the sense that adding capacity to a WAN system is more than just throwing in a new cable or switch port. Many WAN-oriented people don't recognize that just because traffic is IP, it probably should not go over the public Internet if QoS guarantees are important. QoS is achievable in VPNs, but not in the random public Internet of today. Provider-provisioned VPNs can be operated by one carrier on its own facilities, or by one organization that subcontracts for capacity to other facilities providers.

ROLES FOR PUBLIC-INTERNET-BASED VPN

There are applications in which customers may make reasonable use of public Internet facilities as the shared infrastructure of a VPN. These applications are characterized by being tolerant of the quality of service and capable of managing the security exposures of the public network. The customer may operate these, or they still may be provider-provisioned. A wise provider, however, may give guarantees of availability, but never QoS, for such a network.

Consider a light-demand application such as overnight uploading of sales receipts from stores to headquarters. As long as the upload takes place at some point during the night, service is adequate. The data being uploaded, however, is financially sensitive. Whenever sensitive data is being sent across a public network, it needs to be encrypted. The network interface device does not necessarily need to be responsible for the encryption. If the application host does file-level encryption, the encrypted files can be transferred over unencrypted channels. Hosts can also operate their own communications-level encryption.

---

capabilities, but the set needed by any arbitrary enterprise needs to be defined for that specific enterprise. To meet a given set of user requirements, the designer needs to specify who belongs to the VPN, how the VPN is mapped on to the underlying transport, and the characteristics of the transport. See Chapter 13 for a discussion of VPN deployment.

Introduction to Managed Networks

In the early 1980s, data networks outside academic and research centers were most commonly found in Fortune 500 companies. The great majority of such enterprises usually had a staff of qualified network engineers. The talent pool from which these engineers came was of limited size then, and has been growing more slowly than the need for it. As data networking became far more widespread, the talent pool did not grow as quickly, and smaller firms quickly found they could not justify full-time networking staffs. Even when they could afford them, they often simply did not have enough interesting work to retain qualified staffs.

A stopgap solution came with equipment vendors moving their small and medium business (SMB) sales principally to value-added resellers (VARs) rather than directly to enterprises. VARs could retain qualified staff but spread the people across many projects. Typically, the VAR effort was most intense during design and initial implementation. While the VAR might have a continuing maintenance contract, most commonly the VAR would document the operation of the system in a manner that could be executed by low-level staff of the enterprise. A wise enterprise also bought maintenance contracts with the original hardware vendors.

Obtaining VAR support for installation did not solve the problems of success, in which the enterprise network grew significantly but the enterprise variously could not, or did not know how to, build an appropriate staff. Expertise in hardware resellers emphasized equipment, not wide area networks. WAN support remained the province of carriers, although there often was finger-pointing between VAR/enterprise and carrier.

Another way that the equipment reseller model did not fit larger networks was that resellers rarely had 24 hour per day, 7 day per week (24/7) operations centers. While some large VARs were exceptions, only two kinds of organizations normally had 24/7 support: carriers and data centers. Neither of these organization types was ideal for supporting distributed enterprise networks or Internet connectivity, simply because their knowledge bases were from one culture: telecommunications or MIS. The carriers were intimately familiar with keeping telecommunications facilities operating, but they were very short of people who could take user reports phrased with respect to applications services and troubleshoot servers as well as the network proper. Data centers had the reverse problem, that of not necessarily being able to analyze problems involving remote computers or distant network problems.

In the 1990s, the virtual corporation trend gained momentum, with enterprises retaining staff only for their core competencies and outsourcing all other functions. Networking is not a core competency for most enterprises, and financial managers sought ways to outsource routine networking. Both carriers and data centers learned they could augment their skill sets and offer *managed network services* (Figure 1.14). While this occasionally means putting full-time personnel at major customer sites, the form it usually takes is granting the service provider remote privileged access to enterprise components being managed. In a managed services model, the customer still orders—perhaps with the provider's guidance—the same wide area links as before. However, the customer contracts for the provider to do the day-to-day operations, including working with the device that connects sites to the provider networks as well as networking devices inside the site. The customer might even outsource the operation of certain servers, if the provider understands application management as well as network management. Managed network services often include application and infrastructure (for example, directory) servers, as well as campus networking components such as LAN switches. When they include the full range of components, from user to server, they offer the benefit of a single point of contact for troubleshooting, upgrades, and changes.

Not every enterprise, however, wants to grant an outside provider total access to its information system components. Other enterprises feel they cannot afford the usually significant cost of managed services. When the enterprise connectivity requirements primarily involve connectivity among its own sites

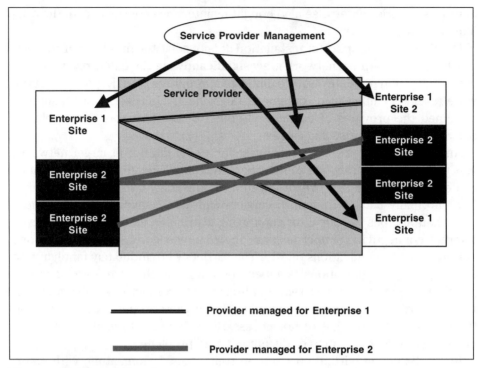

Figure 1.14   Managed services.

and mobile users (intranet) or predefined external partners (extranet), virtual private networks (VPN) services may offer a reasonable compromise.

Known Clients to Known Servers under Different Administration

Strategic partnerships; outsourcing; virtual corporations; extranets: All these terms describe networking relationships among a set of enterprises. In such relationships, the parties are known before any communications can occur (Figure 1.15). To what extent do the activities of these organizations need to be coordinated? To what extent can and will they cooperate directly? Is it politically acceptable to have one of the enterprises take a lead role and coordinate such things as address assignments?

Business management theorists increasingly emphasize "virtual corporations" or other forms of partnerships among different organizations. Outsourcing everything except an enterprise's "core competencies" has become extremely popular among managers concerned with the immediate bottom line. While such outsourcing may or may not be in the long-term interest of an enterprise—and I confess to increasing annoyance with outsourced administrative services that have no idea what the people with core competency actu-

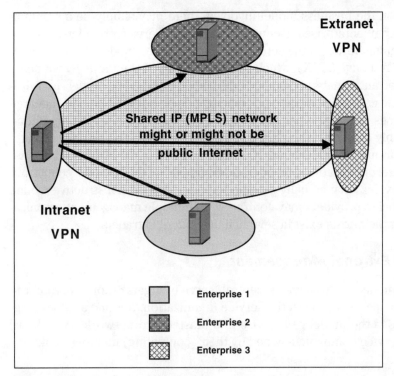

Figure 1.15   Extranet business models.

ally do or need—it certainly represents an opportunity for providers. In dealing with their customers, of course, providers should be cautious about enterprises that outsource their outsourcing function, and thus become the management equivalent of a cosmological black hole.

In general, a network where services run between a predefined set of servers and clients in different organizations is an *extranet*. Extranets are commonly, but not always, implemented as VPNs.

Distributed Extranet Management

Does there, in fact, need to be a specific extranet, or will a specific set of technical specifications, such as those of the Automotive Network Exchange (ANX) (see "Federated Extranet Management") suffice? *Distributed management* characterizes the type of extranet where all participants negotiate and deploy their bilateral connectivity.

Federated Extranet Management

In certain cases the participants may be generally cooperative, but still need a coordinating body to avoid, for example, name and address overlaps. This sort of *federated management* is characteristic of interservice military networks.

Depending on the business model involved, there may simply be a common model for different enterprises to connect to arbitrary service providers, without centralized administration of the actual service. This is the model of the Automotive Network Exchange (ANX), which specifies technical standards by which its members will arrange bilateral communications. Other business models may designate a specific enterprise as network manager. Such a model implies a degree of trust that does not exist when the linked enterprises are active competitors, but that certainly can exist when the dominant enterprise is a customer, or supplier, of the various other elements. It is not uncommon, for example, for managed healthcare organizations to operate extranets to the various contracted healthcare providers that actually provide services. This is an instructive model, because healthcare providers may contract with multiple management organizations such that their hosts exist in several independent extranets.

Centralized Extranet Management

Yet another model is to have a central service organization operate the extranet. Participants deal with the service organization, not one another (Figure 1.16). This is the model of the Visa and MasterCard networks, which are operated by service companies owned by their (competing) member banks.

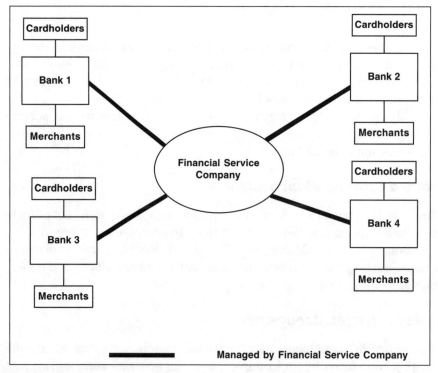

Figure 1.16 Centrally managed extranet.

Central service organizations solve many problems at the political layer of OSI, providing a diplomatic way for competitors to cooperate. It never can be certain with whom a given network will want to cooperate. In the Gulf War, there was little problem in the NATO countries communicating, since NATO had expended extensive engineering effort on developing interoperable networks. More difficult was working with coalition partners that had been near-enemies the week before, such as Syria, but the problem was solved with liaison officers and text messages. The true challenge was communicating the massive Air Tasking Order between the U.S. Air Force and the U.S. Navy, which eventually was solved by flying magnetic media from Air Force headquarters to aircraft carriers.

Mixed Dedicated Extranet Networks

A given customer may be best served by a mixture of VPN and dedicated network technologies. One of my clients provided a specialized service in the healthcare industry. The primary customers were hospitals and physicians, who were connected to my client's data centers through redundant frame relay links. Certain portions of the work on this application were outsourced to independent contractors who received access through an Internet-based VPN. All of the data potentially applied to individual patients and thus needed stringent security (Figure 1.17).

From the enterprise-side perspective, the firm could be considered either an extranet or a specialized Internet service provider. An extranet model did not fit as well as a service provider model, because the customers never shared data. These customers ranged from small professional offices to large institutions with extensive networks of their own. Some used private address space, while

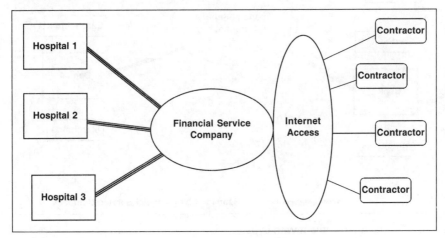

Figure 1.17 Hybrid access in a healthcare application.

others had registered addresses. At the customer sites, we placed a router and specialized servers. Normally, the router connected to our data center with Frame Relay, but Integrated Services Digital Network (ISDN) and Internet backup were being introduced. We needed to virtualize a consistent address space for our network. At each customer site, we configured network address translation (NAT) to translate the customer space into our registered provider space. While this worked for many applications, we did have problems with Windows Internet Naming Service (WINS) and Domain Naming System (DNS), and had to obtain application-level gateway functions.

Under current U.S. healthcare regulations, as defined by the Health Insurance Portability and Accountability Act (HIPAA), medical data must be encrypted when traveling over the Internet or dial facilities. While the Frame Relay circuits technically did not need to be encrypted, the customer backup links did. Since we would rather err in encrypting than not encrypting, we chose to use IP Security Protocol (IPSec), with preshared keys, both for the dedicated and backup links (Figure 1.18). Contractor access was a different problem. At the time of implementation, we did not have an affordable and reliable IPSec client for PCs, and the cost of digital certificates and the certificate authority was prohibitive. A realistic compromise was to use Secure

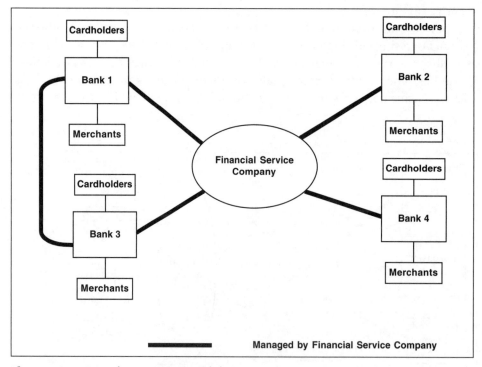

Figure 1.18   Central management with bypass.

Sockets Layer (SSL) for the contractors, terminating on a security gateway in the data center. The operational network, therefore, used both IPSec and transport layer security. Security and availability were the key requirements for this customer. Another client, in the financial services industry, was extremely concerned with performance, specifically the response time of automatic teller machines and credit card authorization terminals. The model here was centrally managed, but with premium services deformed from the central operations organization. The central organization, not the participants, decided whether bypass links were necessary to get the desired performance level (Figure 1.18). This decision was based on whether or not the service provider organization felt it could meet service level agreements (SLAs) only by incurring the extra cost of bypassing bottlenecks or having to add extra capacity in major parts of the core network.

I saw a different economic model for bypass when I worked with one of the major centrally managed credit card authorization networks (Figure 1.19). This network charged a per-transaction fee to merchants and member banks. Two large banks, which were both major credit card issuers, realized that perhaps a third of their transactions were with each other. When they multiplied their

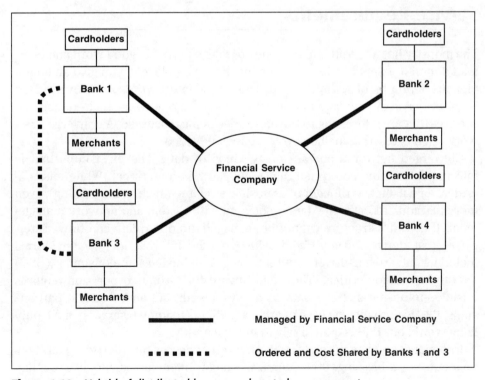

Figure 1.19   Hybrid of distributed bypass and central management.

total bilateral transaction volume by the per-transaction charge, they realized they could save a substantial amount of money by running direct links between them. Their application routing policy was to use the direct link to the other bank as long as it was up, and to use the common network to get to other banks and as backup. They were not at all concerned with reducing the cost of the central network, as in the previous example. Notice that the topology in Figure 1.19 is exactly the same as in Figure 1.18, but that different organizations are responsible for the bypass links.

Belonging to Multiple Extranets

In the U.S. healthcare system, it is quite common for healthcare providers, such as physician offices and hospitals, to belong to multiple managed care services and other payers, such as insurance companies or government programs. It would not be physically practical to have rows and rows of workstations in a small billing area, each on a different extranet.

Responding to New and Converged Service Requirements

The industry has a regrettable tendency to take a perfectly good word and overload it until it essentially has no meaning. For example, can you give an unambiguous definition of *switch* or *hub?* One of the latest words to be overloaded is *convergence.* A converged network seems to be a network that contains all services that are interesting to the enterprise being discussed. A converged network often is one that includes voice, data, and video.

Converged networks contain many kinds of data. The most important is internal data of the enterprise that is judged mission-critical. While mission-critical data usually is thought of as business-related (such as accounting), even more mission-critical is the data associated with system and network management. If the infrastructure cannot be managed, no other data can flow. Enterprises that derive revenue from selling on the Internet in its many forms including advertising-driven content also find business-to-consumer (B2C) data to be mission critical. The trend toward the virtual corporation requires business-to-business (B2B) data to allow outsourcing and strategic partnerships. B2C is normally the case of arbitrary clients to known servers on the public network, but B2B is quite likely to involve a VPN.

Depending on the enterprise, general Internet access by enterprise staff may be a curse or a blessing. It is a curse when staff members spend 40% of a day downloading pornography, music, and, for that matter, pornographic music. It is a blessing when development engineers can use the Internet to acquire the latest relevant research and speed the time it takes to make products ready for market. It is a boon if when the availability of e-mail makes an enterprise more accessible and responsive to its customers.

Long before individuals had to justify whether they needed a computer to do their work—which no longer needs explicit justification—it was accepted that members of the staff would be telescopes. Of course telephony remains a critical application. Using IP telephony has both operational and cost advantages. Operational advantages include the ability to move telephones and telephone extensions simply by unplugging them in one place and plugging them in in another. No longer do employees have to wait a week for an internal private branch exchange (PBX) or a telephone company work order.

An interesting range of applications falls under various headings of video and imagery. Video often is equated to television, but that assumption approaches a given only in the residential entertainment marketplace. Even in residential applications, there are perfectly valid uses for less-than-broadcast-quality video, such as the ability to watch one's children in their own beds or in a day care center. Perhaps even more pervasive than full-motion video are imagery applications. As a teleworker, I routinely use collaborative software such as NetMeeting to mark up documents with my coworkers.

Both moving and fixed images have tremendous value in healthcare delivery. Requirements both for resolution and for speed of motion (if any) vary considerably with the application. Mammograms, for example, need high resolution but are not moving images. An orthopedist or physical therapist evaluating a patient's walk needs to see motion, but not necessarily fine detail.

Not all cost-effective telemedicine applications are obvious. Dermatologists sometimes are thought of as the Rodney Dangerfields of medicine, not quite getting respect. The classic reason to become a dermatologist is "your patients never die, they never get well, and they never get you up at night." However, experienced dermatologists have excellent visual memories, and with a glance can often diagnose and prescribe effective therapy, where a more generally trained physician might experiment for months. High-resolution color images of rashes are obviously needed, but a slow-motion capability also is required. The dermatologist may need to see how color returns to skin after it is pressed, or may ask to have the patient's body turned so light hits the rash from the side rather than above.

The lesson here is to listen to the user about requirements, and, if the requirements are excessively expensive, propose workable alternatives. One hospital with which I worked moved its radiologists' offices to a building a short distance from the campus, keeping the x-ray and other machines in the hospital. The radiologists demanded instant viewing of images, but that would have required bandwidth that was not affordable. I asked if the real issue was needing to see the image as it was taken, or to be able to retrieve it quickly when the radiologist was ready to interpret it. (Incidentally, the radiologist was present in the hospital for those studies that actually required the doctor to touch the patient.) Agreeing that the issue was efficient retrieval, and that in the real world it might be several days until a nonurgent MRI might be interpreted, we arranged for the images to be recorded onto optical disks, put into a box, driven to the radiology offices, and loaded onto the image retrieval system overnight. Not an elegant network service provider solution, but very worthwhile to the client.

Fundamental Principle 1: Don't Break What Already Makes Money

Equipment vendors and service providers love to enter into mating dances with venture capitalists, seeking funding for "disruptive paradigms" or "greenfield operations." Disruptive paradigms, regarded favorably, are examples of "out-of-the-box" thinking, which offer radical and useful new approaches to problem solving. The World Wide Web, for example, was an effective disruptive paradigm vis-à-vis earlier methods of using networked computers for information retrieval. If you question this, have you used a gopher or Wide Area Information Server (WAIS) interface recently? In a less favorable manner, a disruptive paradigm is just the sort of thing that, if implemented and not resulting in the showering of riches onto the enterprise, leads to shareholder suits.

Many "distruptive paradigm" vendors tout Internet connectivity without the availability or quality issues common in low-cost Internet services, but ignore that price dominates many market segments, such as the residential. A corollary, however, is that services have to make money to continue to operate.

I LOVE MBA JARGON. I REALLY DO.

Greenfield operations imply that the new business is being built in a virgin forest, although images of ecological disaster are not what their proponents wish to invoke. Personally, I'd prefer to think of them as I do my garden, with well-prepared soil waiting for careful spring planting. Rich with compost, the waiting ground is a brownfield or even blackfield.

Affordable Business-to-Consumer Internet

There is an established market for low-price services, and it certainly can be a challenge to operate profitably in this area. Proposals to make the entire Internet "business-quality" fly in the face of this market reality. There are markets for business-grade services with business-grade pricing. New service delivery approaches do reduce the cost of service and still can offer economies.

Hosting Centers

Highly fault-tolerant networked servers need expensive physical facilities (Chapter 6) and multiple network connections. Meeting these needs, however, may be beyond the financial resources of small and medium businesses. Even large businesses may decide that highly available servers and networks are not part of their "core competence." There are technical realities that make it difficult for an enterprise that has a small number of Internet-visible servers to manage its own public Internet visibility. Current fault-tolerant routing schemes assume that a multihomed organization will use substantial amounts of routable address space.

One option is for organizations without large amounts of address space to place their servers into a colocation facility and advertise their servers as part of the colocation provider's address space. Doing so can have many political, security, and technical implications. Organizations may find that placing their servers in one or more shared hosting centers brings both economies of scale and the availability of expertise that a nonnetwork organization cannot support. On the other hand, placing servers in a shared facility gives up a degree of control that some organizations' cultures cannot tolerate, or the servers may be so business-critical that it is inconceivable that the enterprise or government agency will not do whatever is necessary to maintain the required resources in-house. Consider American Express or Amazon.com deciding their computing resources are not business-critical, or the North American Air Defense Command moving out of Cheyenne Mountain into a commercial facility.

People from the traditional telecommunications carrier culture often fall into a trap of believing you must be a carrier to require infrastructure of appreciable size. Yet there are hosting centers that require the bandwidth of metropolitan areas and generate revenue in excess of $1 billion per month. Carrier-grade solutions need to be responsive to this market, which often differs from that of single enterprises. There is, of course, a spectrum of enterprise requirements. The criticality of Internet accessibility for Amazon.com is rather different than for the Hidden Hollow Municipal and Independent Library, although they are both single enterprises. Such hosting centers are carrier-grade in the sense of environmental hardening, security, 24/7/365 staffing, emergency power, and so on. See Chapter 6 for a discussion of building such facilities. Large hosting centers also can justify the cost of being attached to redundant high-capacity WAN backbones, with appropriate redundancy both with respect to physical connectivity and to IP routing.

New Service Provider Models

The term *hosting center* generally refers to a facility shared among enterprise servers. Carrier hotels are similar, except their customers are not enterprises but other carriers. A carrier hotel, for example, may be a point of presence (POP) for several ISPs in a locality, with shared high-speed uplinks. See Chapter 7 for discussion of the emerging roles of specialized access providers versus IP service providers and content providers. Carrier hotels may also contain part of the internal core network of a widely distributed network provider. Another variant is the cooperative local exchange, where ISPs and enterprises may cooperate to avoid sending traffic destined across the street by way of a major carrier hub hundreds of miles away. (See Chapter 12.)

A hosting service that literally hosts hundreds or thousands of B2B and B2C virtual sites can no more afford downtime than can a major telephone company. Such services, however, usually are quite aware that they need to budget for such high availability. Individual sites may not be willing to budget in such a way. High availability does involve economies of scale. Ironically, it may be the carrier or carrier-oriented equipment vendor that lumps small enterprises and large hosting centers together and does not see the hosting centers as special vendor opportunities.

SOME THINGS SEEM NEVER TO CHANGE

Again and again I've seen people with a bright idea do a proof of concept to their venture capitalists using a quick prototype on a LAN, using NetBIOS/NetBEUI browsers and other techniques that simply do not scale even to private WANs, much less the Internet. They do not pay much attention to backup and recovery, which isn't extremely important in the prototype. By caving in to the pressure of the financial people and putting their prototype into production, they are setting themselves up for service interruptions without appropriate backup—and, even worse, for success. A small LAN system simply will not scale to large size.

Fundamental Problem 2:
Keep Everything Scalable

Traditional experience is not only a trap for the telecommunications culture, but can be equally alluring for people who know the enterprise culture well. Just because a given technology works for 100 or 1,000 devices doesn't mean it will work for 100,000 or more. Scalability, in the broadest sense, means that an infrastructure can support all of the continuing requirements of growth. These requirements are more than increasing numbers of users. Before we get into the specifics of scalability, let's agree on some terminology.

Challenge for Service Providers:
Keep it Scalable within the
Changing Industry Paradigms

The days are long past when providers could say, "trust us, we're the phone company." The days are also long past when there was a single dominant provider that could dictate interconnection standards to other providers.

A key difference between "consumer-grade" and "business-grade" service offerings is that business grade services are intimately involved with service level agreements. This intimacy comes, in large part, from customer expectations. The term *service level agreement* came into prominence in the mainframe culture. Originally, its usage was limited to performance characteristics, such as the delay components that make up response time and throughput for bulk data transfer. Since there can be no useful performance if a service is not available, SLAs have broadened to include availability requirements.

Table 1.1 summarizes the first considerations in understanding customer requirements. Again, LAN people tend not to think of scalability in large WAN-based services. I have seen too many cases where a worthwhile concept was prototyped on a LAN and demonstrated to venture capitalists. The VCs immediately wanted to see revenue, so the prototype servers, protocols, and so on were connected to WAN facilities without redesign. Enormous and preventable performance, reliability, and scalability problems ensued.

Other factors involve not just the enterprise, but the overall scalability of the Internet, assuming public Internet connectivity is a requirement. Will the hosts be reachable given the relevant addressing (Chapter 5) and enterprise connectivity (Chapter 9)? Is the desired level of performance and availability realistic to achieve over the public network, or is the application more appropriate for the tighter controls possible with a VPN?

Table 1.1   User Requirements for Project Scalability

Enterprise-wide	Total clients
	Total servers
	Total mobile users
	Total fixed sites
	Security policy
Per site	Total users per site
	Availability/redundancy requirements
	Support capabilities (or outsource)
Per application	Number of users
	Quality of service requirements
	Sites needing the application
	Security
	Mobile user requirements

Relationship to Transmission System

Traditional telecommunications carriers have a strong experience base with transmission systems. This experience base includes an intense concern with high availability. They also have substantial experience with the interconnection of transmission systems operated by independent service providers (Figure 1.20).

Transmission networks, however, rarely support topologies as complex and as fast-changing as IP networks (Figure 1.21).

Interprovider Connectivity

It's something of an urban legend that the top-level providers perform significant traffic exchange at the exchange points. At that level, they are far more likely to have private peerings over direct OC-3 or faster links. Exchange points, however, are useful for medium-level providers in a given urban or geographic area. Indeed, there is an ever-growing trend toward having metropolitan exchange points among cooperating ISPs in small cities.

Depending on the type of service provider you are, you may need to connect with access providers or bandwidth providers (Chapter 7), or with other IP service providers (Chapter 12).

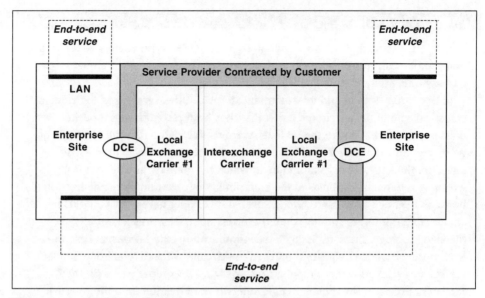

Figure 1.20 Traditions of telephone interprovider connectivity.

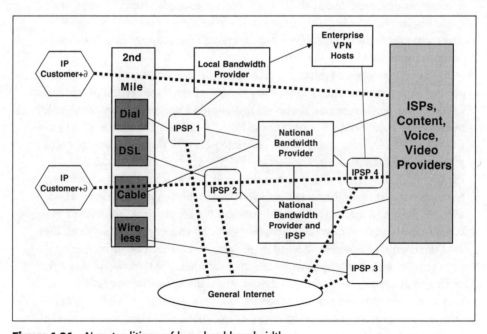

Figure 1.21 New traditions of long-haul bandwidth.

PACKET? OR PACKET

Both transmission and IP people speak of packets. Over the years, I've learned that the two cultures may be using the word *packet* in quite different contexts, and assuming they have consensus when none exists.

In the 1970s, both IP and telecommunications cultures recognized the value of statistically multiplexed, shared networks. They both recognized that packets, as units of information above the bit level, were useful to describe the elements of work the network needed to distribute. IP architecture, however, progressed based on the end-to-end assumption, in which the greatest intelligence (for example, retransmission) was at the endpoints, there was no strong distinction between user and provider networks, user and provider networks would use comparable (router) technology, and there was not necessarily a centrally planned topology. The contrasting telecommunications model was, at first, the X.25 protocol, whose behavior mimicked the circuit-switched telephone network, but sending packets rather than digitized speech. X.25 proper was a protocol family for access to the provider edge, and was not intended for internal provider use. The separate but related X.75 protocol implemented interprovider connectivity. The network, not the end hosts, was responsible for retransmission.

While we called both X.25 and IP networks "packet switching," the internals of provider networks were quite different. While IP was consciously independent of the underlying transmission system, X.25 was intended to deal with the speed, delay, and error performance characteristics of analog transmission systems. Incidentally, I still find niche applications for X.25 in special cases, such as high-frequency radio or telephone systems in developing countries, where these performance characteristics still apply. X.25 is by no means something to be discarded.

As carrier networks moved to digital and optical transmission systems, their performance characteristics changed to a model where it was accepted that errors would be extremely rare, and that endpoint-oriented retransmission, much as in IP, was more appropriate. The broadband ISDN (B-ISDN) architectural effort gave us ATM, ISDN, and frame relay. These technologies, with respect to user services provided, were generically called *fast packet.* They remained fundamentally circuit-switched services; they were packet-switched only in the sense that they supported statistical multiplexing and were fast in the sense that they had less protocol overhead than X.25. They did not have the topological flexibility of IP. When many telecommunications people speak of providing packet services, they are thinking about a model such as Frame Relay, not routed networks.

In parallel with the telecommunications evolution, the IP world realized that certain applications needed much more control than traditional routing provided. They initiated various schemes that permitted traffic engineering, such as Multiprotocol Label Switching (MPLS). These schemes have significant similarities to traditional circuit switching, but with more internal control and topological flexibility.

Looking Ahead

In the next chapter we set more background for the concepts of providing service. These include even more of a perspective on scalability and on the ever-evolving definition of routing and control. Chapter 3 deals with the more quantitative definition of SLAs, while Chapter 4 discusses the translation of customer SLAs into provider technical policies, the basis for detailed design.

Before going on to the next chapter, if your background is in data, think of the seemingly strange views that telephone people seem to have. If you are from the telephony culture, review the strange assumptions that the data people seem to have. Then, regardless of your background, you are prepared to go on to Chapter 2, which helps explain why telecom people think the way they do. Do remember that the telecom people have been doing this sort of thing since Morse's telegraph and Bell's telephone, and have really learned some things that are good to know!

CHAPTER

2

The Service Provider Landscape

We are the Borg. Resistance is futile. You will be assimilated.

**We are WorldCom. Resistance is futile.
You have been assimilated but may not have noticed.**
—Apocryphal, we think

**. . . I have had, of course, intimate friends among both scientists and writers. It was
through living among these groups and much more, I think, through moving regularly
from one to the other and back again, that I got occupied with the problem of what,
long before I put it on paper, I christened to myself the "two cultures."**
—C.P. Snow

**No man is an Islande, entire of itself; every man is a piece of the continent, a part of
the main; if a clod be washed away by the sea, Europe is the less, as well as if a
promontory were, as well as if a manor of thy friends or of thine own were; any
man's death diminishes me, because I am involved in mankind; and therefore never
send to know for whom the bell tolls; it tolls for thee.**
—John Donne

In Chapter 1, I introduced the idea of cultures and their effect on networking. In
this chapter I want to go somewhat more deeply and cross-culturally, and begin
to look at the total environment that has been created by the mixing of traditions. These working definitions are functional, neither marketing nor deeply
technical. They very definitely avoid the tendencies of an unfortunate number
of marketers to fall back on fear, uncertainty, and doubt (FUD). I also distinguish between a set of customer definitions and a set of provider definitions.

Among the first issues in looking at a wide area network (WAN) problem is
understanding precisely how a WAN differs from other sorts of networks. With
the advent of newer technologies, WANs have become harder to define. They
are not simply networks with greater range than local area networks (LAN).
While we usually think of networking in technological terms, the key strategy in

making useful distinctions between modern WANs and LANs is administrative, not technological. WAN implementations involve a service provider and a service consumer, which are different organizations. LANs are operated by the same organization that uses their services. Defining WANs in terms of administrative models solves some otherwise awkward definitions based on technology. Asynchronous transfer mode (ATM) is a modern high-speed networking technology with the capability of transcontinental range. Yet ATM is also a viable technology for metropolitan area and campus networks. The administrative versus technological distinction has been with us for well over a hundred years, but only recently has become blurred.

History: The Basis for WAN Regulation and Competition

WANs are not new in human history, even when physical relay networks such as the Pony Express are excluded. In the Napoleonic era, the French telegraph system began with optical networking in 1793. The optical transmitters were flags and lanterns and the receivers were human eyes. This system used a series of line-of-sight relays at which operators wrote down messages sent by the position of movable arms at other stations, and then signaled the message to the next station using their own semaphore.

The organizations that operated the semaphores were the first service providers that carried messages that were other than hard copy. Their organizational models were built on postal services. The user gave the information to the service provider, and had no direct involvement with its delivery.

Semaphore Scalability

The semaphore systems soon ran into the limits of scalability that plague all communications systems. Semaphore stations had to be within human line of sight, a distance that was limited by intervening terrain and tall buildings, weather, and darkness. Skilled operators were scarce. And only one message at a time could be sent between two stations.

When Morse invented the telegraph in 1844, it seemed that many of these scalability restrictions disappeared. As long as two stations could be linked with copper wire, the line-of-sight limitations did not apply. Still, the service soon encountered its own scaling limitations.

Telegraph Scalability

While telegraph technology allowed for transoceanic range, time zone variations came into effect. There was a desire for unattended operation while it was night in one time zone. *Message switching* was invented as a means of auto-

LEARNING ABOUT WEATHER

In the 1980s, I taught a series of basic communications courses to military organizations. The classes were filled with very smart people, both enlisted and officers. I found that a historical approach was useful, and included the equivalent of smoke signals, semaphore using flags, and drums. I would ask for volunteers to be a semaphore system, and would pick the most junior people to be the sender and receiver. They would stand at opposite ends of the room and wave their flags. I also asked the most senior officer in the room to participate, and whispered instructions to him or her. Shielding it with my body, I slipped a large sheet of posterboard to the (usually) colonel or navy captain. The signalers would innocently be waving their flags, when suddenly a senior officer would run in front of one of them and start blocking their line of sight with the posterboard. Invariably, the senior officer got thoroughly into the spirit of the exercise, leaping into the air when the junior signaler tried to raise the flag, and usually dancing around with a demonic laugh. Eventually, as the signalers became totally confused, I'd ask aloud, "OK, Colonel. Who are you and what are you doing?"

The normally dignified senior officer would give a huge grin and say, "I'm a cloud."

Then I would turn to the class and say, "That, ladies and gentlemen, is how weather is a scalability problem for simple communications systems."

matic transmission. In this system, operators would prepare punched paper tapes containing messages, splice them together onto long reels, and allow separate machines to actually transmit them. The received messages also were punched onto tape. At first, operators would listen to the received messages as convenient, but teletypes eventually printed text messages without human intervention. These text messages are the direct ancestors of electronic mail.

As traffic grew, massive and eventually impractical amounts of wire were needed between stations, because the basic technology allowed only one message to be active per medium. Many inventors sought to deal with the limitations of one message per copper medium, including a teacher of the deaf named Alexander Graham Bell. Bell's approach, called the *harmonic telegraph*, used what we today call *frequency-division multiplexing*, associating different simultaneous sessions with different tones. Like Charles Babbage's early computers, this technique was fundamentally sound but could not really be built without true electronics. Unlike Babbage's effort, it led to a practical technology: the telephone, in 1876.

Like the semaphore and electrical telegraph, telephone technology maintained a difference between end users who wrote and read messages, or who actually spoke and listened, and a service provider. The service provider maintained the wires and the switching system, which originally was the manual switchboard.

Bell himself did not want to go into the telephone business, but after his proposals were rejected by Western Union, the major telecommunications service provider of the time, he went on to create the Bell System, which was to come under the ownership of American Telephone and Telegraph (AT&T). Western Union had rejected Bell's proposal because it felt there was no business case for people talking over wires. AT&T subsequently acquired Western Union, but, after regulators became concerned that AT&T was monopolizing communications, relatively cheerfully divested itself of Western Union as part of the 1913 Kingsbury Commitment. AT&T, however, did not rename itself AT.

The Bell System made what we call *plain old telephone service* (POTS) practical. *Public switched telephone network* (PSTN) is often used as a synonym for POTS; PSTN is really the more correct term.

Telephone Scalability

With the success of telephony, new scalability issues came into effect. In the beginning, telephone companies, each with its own local wiring between the subscriber and the switchboard in the central office, proliferated. Pictures from the turn of the twentieth century show desks littered with telephones from different companies, a painful but practical necessity unless one wished to be limited to calling only other subscribers on the Bell System, the Home System, and so forth. The idea of a single telephone on every desk, or in every home, came later. But the sheer volume of this wiring became overwhelming, and the idea of a technical monopoly on local wiring soon emerged.

Another scalability problem was that if manual switchboards remained the fundamental mechanism for interconnecting callers, there were not enough people to operate the switchboards. Solutions included automatic switching, introduced in the nineteenth century, and decentralized *private branch exchanges* (PBXs) or private switchboards to connect internal enterprise users to one another, then to shared external trunks. At first, PBXs were manual plugboards, but as the automation of telephone switching progressed, PBXs began to use electromechanical and then electronic switching. The term *private automatic branch exchange* (PABX) attempted to capture the essence of technological advances in the PBX, but never won wide acceptance.

Models Evolve

No large network has ever been built without a hierarchy [Oppenheimer 1999]. Telephone networks introduced the distinction between national and international numbering plans, with additional hierarchical structures inside most national plans. These were external models seen by subscribers. Depending on

SOCIAL FACTORS AND SWITCHING

Both the original automatic switch, invented by Almon Strowger, and the eventual global transition from manual to automatic switching were driven by social as much as technical factors. Strowger, a Kansas City funeral director, had a competitor who was related to the local switchboard operator. Concerned that the operator was steering grief-stricken customers to the competitor, Strowger whittled the first automatic switch, simply to be sure that calls intended for him reached him. In other words, the motivation for a major technological advance was ensuring a proper share of the local corpses.

Automatic switching was fairly slow to be adopted by the major telephone companies. Following in the tradition set by Western Union in telegram deliveries, the telephone companies first used teenage boys as switchboard operators. This proved catastrophic for customer relations and smooth network operations. Stephen Levy points out that the boys' misbehavior, such as making comments to customers and during customer conversations, interconnecting random subscribers, and so on, may be a historical precedent for hacking: teenage male hormones and communications equipment do not mix well [Levy].

The telephone companies then, given the social conventions of the time, turned to well-mannered young women as operators. Telephone executives realized, however, that at the growth rates they saw in the network, there soon would not be enough women in the U.S. population to operate the required switchboards. Automated switching became a requirement for scalability.

the regulatory environment, provider internal structures remained hierarchical, but reflected the realities of multiprovider topology.

Some will claim that distributed peer-to-peer models such as Gnutella have no hierarchy. In practice, however, such distributed models have no organization responsible for their operation. While peer-to-peer networking can be perfectly appropriate within an enterprise, large-scale peer-to-peer networking is not sufficiently reliable or maintainable for mission-critical applications.

The Internet and its predecessors had a simple topological model in which it was meaningful to speak of a single core. Just as the telephone system has evolved to have competitive providers, market evolution has turned data topology into a complex one that allows multiple providers to flourish at many levels of the hierarchy.

Traditional Telephony Models: Organizational Aspects

Early telephony systems were too labor-intensive to grow to the size of present networks. Automated switching was as major an advance as the basic speech-over-wires technology. In a switch, the components that set up the path for a call are much more complex and expensive than the components that maintain the user-to-user call. A major advance in automated switching was to separate the control and user planes. Control components set up each call and handed it off to user switching components, then dealt with the next call. Control and user functions could thus be scaled independently (Figure 2.1). This separation has reached a high level of sophistication in the models used for asynchronous transfer mode, also called the broadband integrated services digital network (B-ISDN) model, and is continuing to evolve in the Internet Engineering Task Force (IETF), with work on separate control and forwarding planes. In contrast, early data networks did not separate control and data, even in network components such as routers. There is an increasing trend toward doing so, in devices and even in separate control management. See, for example, the work of the IETF Forwarding and Control Element Separation (FORCES) working group.

Even in today's environment, you must always be aware that any connectivity that is not preprogrammed into your switch requires expensive manual intervention. Related challenges, still not completely solved, are the broad issues of provisioning and mobility. Provisioning involves the issues of telling the switching system about the existence of subscriber equipment or connections to other carriers so that the switching system can recognize them. Traditionally, provisioning has required manual input to start the process. Large providers have invested huge amounts in automating the process once begun. Mobility, however, involves some degree of automation in starting the process.

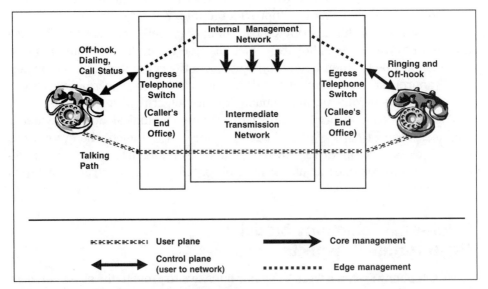

Figure 2.1 Basic control and user separation.

Cellular telephony is a very familiar model of a mobile service, in which the telephone operates in many physical locations (cells) within the territory of the cellular service provider. *Roaming* services, in which the telephone continues to operate in other providers' geographic coverage area, are more of a challenge. Roaming for data connectivity is a less developed commercial idea, but certainly is emerging, especially with text messaging on pagers and mobile phones. Indeed, messaging and advanced cellular services probably are more prevalent in Europe and Asia than in the Americas.

The Bell System concentrated on urban markets, and, even after it gained a practical monopoly there, there were certainly competitors, especially in rural areas. The Brown Telephone Company of Abilene, Kansas, was an example of what is called an *independent telephone company*, to distinguish it from Bell/AT&T.

Open access is a current concern in broadband networks. Its basic premise is that "any willing [service] provider" can contract directly with subscribers of the access service to provide content or network access. Investors in the new access networks, however, would be happiest if they could lock in subscribers to their content services, at least acting as a portal to other services so, for example, they could always present paid advertising to subscribers. To some extent, in the U.S. regulatory environment, open access is a descendant of the universal service concept introduced in 1907 by Theodore Vail, CEO of AT&T (the Bell System). In Vail's concept, every telephone should be able to establish connectivity with every other telephone. This did not mean that every individual should *have* a telephone, or that anyone other than the Bell System should provide connectivity. Indeed, Vail's approach largely assumed a technical monopoly, with technical standards to assure interoperability among regional Bell companies and those external companies not in Bell-served areas. Vail's ideas did reduce the annoying proliferation of different telephone networks, but it still took regulatory intervention, in 1913, to ensure that the Bell System would interconnect with non-Bell companies. That 1913 event, called the Kingsbury Commitment, established separate roles for local exchange carriers (LECs) and interexchange carriers (IXCs). AT&T established firm control of the long-distance IXC role. The Kingsbury Commitment legitimized the role of non-Bell LECs.

The idea of a single LEC firm in geographical area seemed, until quite recently, to be a natural, technical monopoly. It seemed undesirable to have different LECs running masses of copper wire over and under city streets. Alternatives have emerged, and today we speak of an *incumbent LEC* (ILEC) as the first LEC in a given area (that is, the one that owns the predominant copper) and *competitive LECs* (CLECs). We will discuss the details of ILECs and CLECs later on, as well as the evolution of the IXC, but the important thing to realize now is that the idea of separate organizations—of separate technologies—at the edge and core of a common network is not new.

Enterprise Network Models

One useful and popular model to describe enterprise network architecture was introduced by Cisco Systems. Any model, of course, is a guideline, and, as shown in Figure 2.2, this model has been used with both WAN and LAN cores. The model divides the network into three tiers:

1. *Access.* Contains end users and local servers. It is possible to put centralized servers in an access tier, but, when doing so, it is usually best to put the individual servers of a local cluster into the access tiers. Load distribution to these servers is at the next tier.

2. *Distribution.* Contains devices that transition between environments (for example, LAN to WAN, building to campus, or to different transmission technology). Often, the distribution tier requires the greatest intelligence for protocol conversion, buffering, and so on. The term *edge* is preferred in provider rather than enterprise use, and sometimes substitutes for *distribution* even in the enterprise.

3. *Core.* Efficiently links sites of the infrastructure. May be a collapsed LAN backbone primarily of layer 2 and inter–virtual LAN (VLAN) devices, or may be a set of routers.

One enterprise guideline is that layer 2 relays tend to have all their interfaces inside tiers, while layer 3 relays (that is, routers) and higher layer relays (for example, firewalls and proxies) tend to have interfaces between different tiers. This guideline is not terribly rigorous, as a speed-shifting switch between a workgroup and a building (or campus) core often logically straddles the top of the access tier and the bottom of the distribution tier. Large distribution networks include multiple levels of concentration.

When demand access is involved (for instance, dial-up), it can be convenient to put end hosts and access routers in the access tier, dial-in servers at the bottom of the distribution tier, and concentrating routers inside the distribution tier. Large routers link regions to a core router or complex of routers. Another

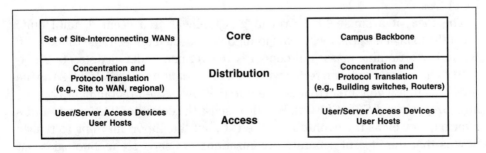

Figure 2.2   Three-layer model.

function that fits nicely in the distribution tier is that of firewalls or border routers providing connectivity outside the enterprise. (See Figure 2.3). In Figure 2.3, note that the central servers themselves are at the distribution tier, but that user connectivity to them comes through the core and that they have their own interserver links at the access tier. Having isolated links and possibly specialized hosts, such as backup machines, for large servers can keep a great deal of traffic localized and avoid negative performance impact.

This model works well for networks of medium size. Small networks may collapse certain of the tiers together, and very large networks become more like carrier networks. In the optimal use of this model, the customer access router is closest to the end hosts, customer core routers link campuses or sites, and distribution routers perform concentration and translation functions between access and core. External connectivity is generally a function of the distribution tier, although if all otherwise unknown traffic defaults to a central external router, that router might be in the customer core. The model has limitations in large enterprise networks, where there may be multiple operational levels of local, regional, and national/international corporate backbones. One approach, shown in Figure 2.4, is to apply the model recursively, where the top level of one organizational level becomes the bottom level of another organizational level. The recursive approach really does not work well, because each tier, and each of the devices that commonly straddle the tiers, has distinctive characteristics. An access device does not share characteristics with a core device in a larger network.

Another method is to create additional core layers for major geographic levels, such as national and intercontinental. Figure 2.5 shows the logical design I did for an international manufacturing company in which there was relatively little communications among the regions, but all regions had significant communications with headquarters. It was reasonable to have all inter-regional communication go through headquarters. In Figure 2.5, note that the headquar-

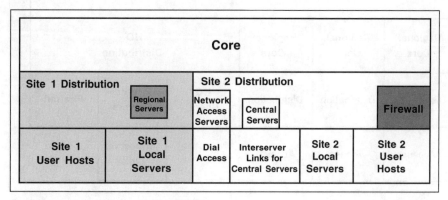

Figure 2.3 Three-layer model details.

Core
Distribution
Access
Core
Distribution
Access

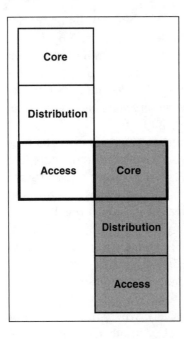

Figure 2.4 Recursive three-layer approach.

ters users and central servers are treated as a virtual region, rather than being put into the core. The core should only be used for communications and carefully selected network management devices, never for application servers.

Not every enterprise has the same requirements. Figure 2.6 shows my logical design for a worldwide transportation company that had extensive interregional communications plus an Internet connectivity requirement for each region. This

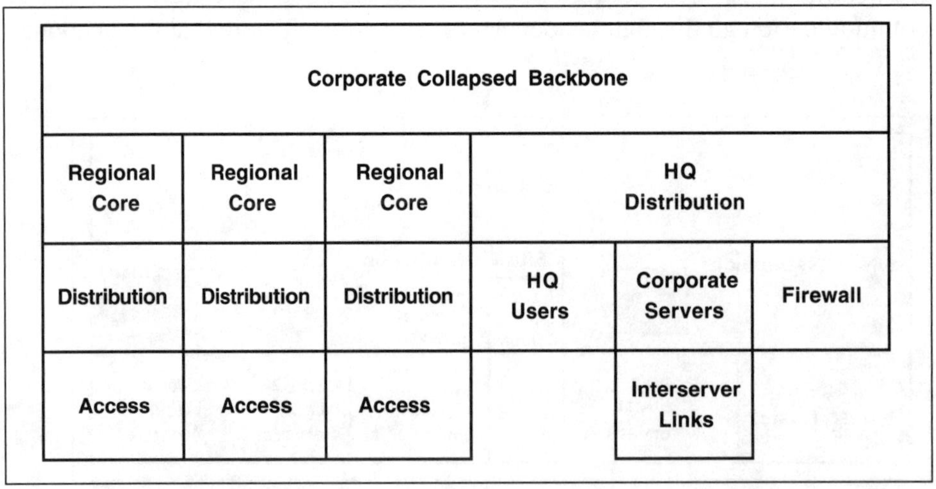

Corporate Collapsed Backbone
Regional Core
Regional Core
Regional Core
HQ Distribution
Distribution
Distribution
Distribution
HQ Users
Corporate Servers
Firewall
Access
Access
Access
Interserver Links

Figure 2.5 Multilevel enterprise core—centralized organization.

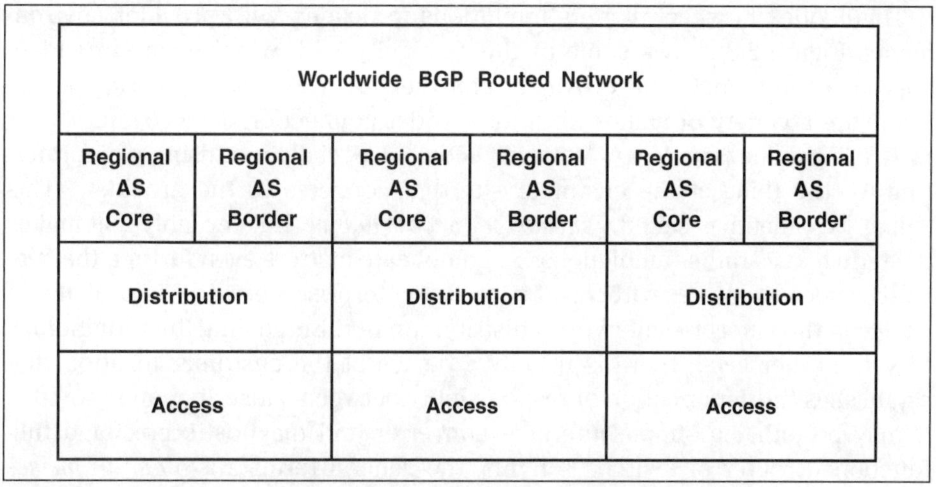

Worldwide BGP Routed Network					
Regional AS Core	Regional AS Border	Regional AS Core	Regional AS Border	Regional AS Core	Regional AS Border
Distribution		Distribution		Distribution	
Access		Access		Access	

Figure 2.6   Multilevel enterprise core–distributed organization.

model works acceptably for centrally controlled enterprises, but does not scale well for interenterprise networks such as credit card authorization. Large banks, for example, need to optimize their own cores for internal use, but need to connect to the credit authorization network. The logical characteristics of such networks fit best into the distribution tier, which becomes the place of interconnection. Interconnecting at the distribution tier allows the core to return to its original simple and fast role of interconnecting sites inside one organization. The requirement for a distribution layer function between access and core, however, does not disappear. Increasingly, network architects define two distinct sets of function at the distribution tier: the traditional one between core and access, and a *border* function concerned with interorganizational connectivity (Figure 2.7). Border functions can deal both with controlled cooperative relationships (for example, a bank to the Visa or MasterCard service networks, or to the Federal Reserve), and with access to the Internet via firewalls.

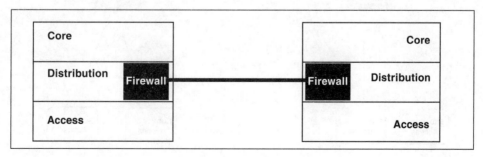

Figure 2.7   Distribution tier evolution.

This model, however, has its limitations in dealing with provider environments. Figure 2.8 shows some of the ambiguity with which many providers approach the model. The providers call their own POP *entry point access*. There are a variety of names for interprovider connection devices, but *border router* is gaining popularity. Matters become especially confusing when referring to "the thing at the customer site that connects to the provider." This "thing" is sometimes called a *subscriber access device*, but certainly that makes the term *access* rather ambiguous. To complicate matters even further, the subscriber access device, with respect to the enterprise network, is probably a device in the enterprise network's distribution tier. Entangling the terminology to yet another level, there is usually a device at the customer location that establishes the demarcation of responsibility between subscriber and provider. It may be either a simple interface converter and diagnostic box or a full-functioned router or switch. For this, the general terms *customer premises equipment* (CPE) and *customer location equipment* (CLE) have emerged, but still may contain some ambiguity. The basic assumption is that the customer owns the CPE and the provider owns the CLE, but operational responsibility may vary. For example, I own my digital subscriber line (DSL) access router, but I don't have the configuration password to it; my ISP does.

The customer, of course, may have a complex enterprise network. What we think of as CLE or CPE, however, is an increasingly intelligent interface between customer and provider. It also is a point of economic and legal demarcation at which responsibilities change and service level guarantees are monitored. The interface may contain firewall functionality, which can be either at

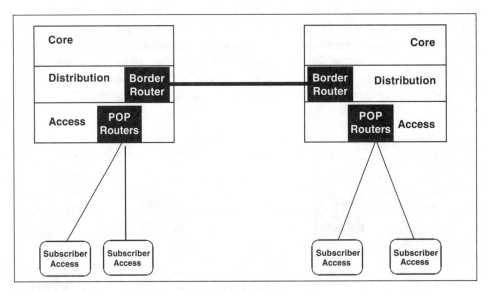

Figure 2.8 Data carrier interconnection evolution.

the customer site or at the POP. As seen in Figure 2.9, the customer edge function may contain equipment to multiplex outgoing Internet traffic, virtual private networks (VPNs), and voice over IP (VoIP) onto a broadband access facility. The provider may manage any of the edge devices; at least one device normally will be managed this way. If the provider allows the subscriber to manage its own device, the provider will have ironclad configuration settings, which are not negotiable.

Service Provider Models

The hierarchical enterprise model was useful, but did not quite fit modern service provider networks, independently of whether the provider was data- or

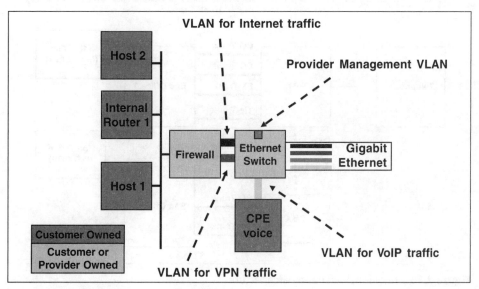

Figure 2.9   Intelligent edge—subscriber side.

voice-oriented. Particular problems came from increased competition, with competition both in the internetwork core and in the local access system.

Pure Telephony

Historical telephony gives some useful perspectives. In Figure 2.10, the PBX is equivalent to CPE in an IP services network. The PBX connects to external switches over *trunks*, also called *trunk lines*. The term *trunk* is sometimes used for a data access facility, but these are more commonly called *local loops*. *Tie trunks* connect PBX sites within the enterprise. *Central office* (CO) trunks connect the PBX to a telephone service provider. Such a provider is usually assumed to be the LEC, but there may also be *bypass trunks* that connect to IXCs. CO trunks, whether to the LEC or the IXC, can be two-way, incoming-only, or outgoing-only with respect to the PBX. Other than the very smallest, sites will need multiple trunks, which, from the perspective of the PSTN, are called *trunk groups*. A trunk group contains multiple voice channels, which can be physical analog pairs, but, for larger and more modern installations, are likely to be digital carrier facilities or Integrated Services Digital Network (ISDN) physical links. Trunk groups have some similarity to inverse multiplexing in data applications, where more bandwidth is required than can be provided with any single physical facility. The similarity becomes even more striking if we compare not the individual data streams or circuits over the set of physical media, but the fact that the set of media terminates in interfaces that carry aggregates (Figure 2.11).

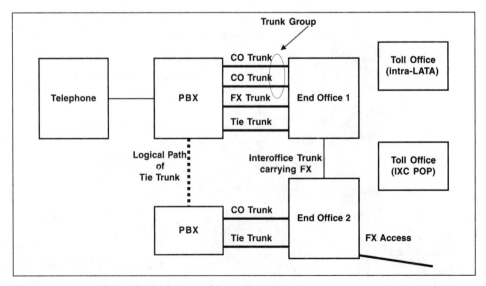

Figure 2.10   Traditional telephony architecture.

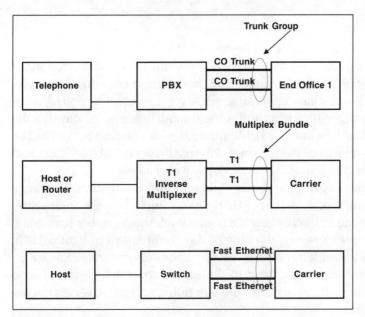

Figure 2.11 Parallels for inverse multiplexing.

A special case of a CO trunk is a *foreign exchange* (FX) trunk that connects logically to an alternate central office, so that the phone number associated with the trunk appears to be in the serving area of the remote CO. FX trunks fill a function much like that of wide area telephone service (WATS) lines, but FX trunks tend to provide service inside the LEC while WATS services tend to be provided by IXCs. Their real function is similar: Do not make the calling party pay long-distance charges. Foreign, in this case, refers to areas outside the LEC's territory. These may or may not be located within a foreign political entity.

Another special CO trunk case is *direct inward dialing* (DID), in which the central office allows individual extensions of the enterprise to be dialed from the outside. DID has signaling that tells the PBX which extension needs to be rung. There are fewer physical DID trunks than there are extensions, because the PBX is intelligent. A variant is Centrex service, in which the intelligence is in the central office switch, not at the enterprise. In Centrex service, there must be the same number of Centrex trunks as there are enterprise extensions. While Centrex trunking is more expensive than DID to an intelligent PBX, it offers the advantage that the telephone company, not the enterprise, performs the detailed management of the service. Centrex, in many respects, is the direct ancestor of what we call virtual private networks today. VPNs most commonly are data-oriented, but they offer the ability to outsource the detailed management of that network, especially in the WAN.

IP Services

ARPANET and NSFNET are direct ancestors of the current Internet, but had much simpler topologies. The early ARPANET did not have a distinct core; it was a partial mesh. The NSFNET (Figure 2.12) had a single core, to which independently operated regional networks, and several exchange points, connected. To get to another network, in the basic model, you went through the core if the destination was not reachable through your regional network. The early cores were not fast in modern terms—internal links might be 56 Kbps, and it could be both slow and unreliable to rely on the core alone.

Various institutions began to establish bilateral and multilateral exchange points, principally to reduce latency. Given slow lines, there is much less latency when traffic can be exchanged at a regional exchange, rather than going farther toward the core. A reasonable rule of thumb for speed of light delay is that networks add 6 µs per kilometer of distance. For many years, the propagation delay was insignificant compared to the serialization delay—the time to move the data off the medium and into the computer, and the reverse process on output (see Table 2.1).

The five original NSFNET exchange points were principally to establish access to specific resources, such as supercomputer centers. These were not the original exchange points (see Chapter 12 for more details). Regionalized exchange points, at 64 Kbps, could save two-thirds of the latency involved if it were necessary to backhaul traffic to a core 1,000 kilometers away.

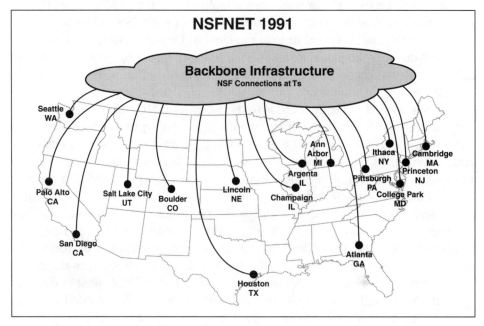

Figure 2.12   Original NSFNET.

Table 2.1 WAN Serialization Delays at Common Frame Lengths

	BIT RATE				
FRAME LENGTH	64,000	128,000	1,540,000	44,736,000	155,000,000
64	8.000	4.000	0.332	0.011	0.003
128	16.000	8.000	0.665	0.023	0.007
1500	187.500	93.750	7.792	0.268	0.077

Exchanges to reduce latency have become less important as lines become faster and serialization delay becomes smaller. They still have value in more isolated locations that may not connect to the very fastest media. While many popular discussions speak of an "Internet core," the actuality of a single, homogeneous core is long dead. Indeed, there has come to be a qualitative as well as a quantitative difference caused by the higher speeds. Contrast the speeds in Table 2.2 with those in Table 2.3; the packet training delays saved by cells are negligible.

The largest carriers do not interconnect in shared exchange points, although it is an urban legend that they do so. They might interconnect in the same building that contains the exchange point, but they do so with direct media interconnections. See Chapter 8 for further discussion of the physical aspects of bilateral interconnects and of exchange points.

Modern Models

In the contemporary environment, it is far easier to begin by tracing the life of a packet from source to destination, avoiding extensive discussion of the quite complex issues of what organization operates which component. Business and political factors will become involved here, such as the outsourcing of certain functions and the departmental responsibilities for others.

Regardless of whether the initiating end user site is a single residential subscriber or a large corporate network, there still needs to be a demarcation point between subscriber and provider responsibility. The customer premises device, regardless of ownership, can have varying degrees of intelligence. If it is not a

Table 2.2 Time to Transmit ATM Cell at Modern Optical Speeds

155 MBPS	622 MBPS	2.4 GBPS	10 GBPS	40 GBPS
2.7E-06	6.8E-07	2.1E-07	4.2E-08	1.1E-08

Table 2.3   Time to Transmit a 1,500-byte Ethernet Frame at Modern Optical Speeds

155 MBPS	622 MBPS	2.4 GBPS	10 GBPS	40 GBPS
7.9E-05	2.0E-05	6.0E-06	1.2E-06	3.1E-07

full-functioned router, it may be a modem or digital equivalent, which has a point-to-point connection to an intelligent device at the provider edge. When the customer site has its own network infrastructure, ranging from a simple household LAN to a complex campus network, more intelligent CPE/CLE is needed. Such devices are most commonly routers, although they may be layer 2 switches with capabilities of traffic shaping and separating internal data traffic, voice, and Internet/Extranet traffic onto different VLANs (as in Figure 2.9).

MULTIPLE KINDS OF DELAY

The most obvious type of transmission delay is serialization delay—the time it takes to clock the bits of one frame from the buffer of an egress interface onto a fully available transmission line. For example, it takes approximately 1.2 ms to clock a 1,500-byte Ethernet frame onto a 10-Mbit medium. In the real world, however, there are other components of transmission delay.

Propagation delay comes from the speed of light in the particular medium. One rule of thumb is that there are roughly 6 ms of propagation delay per kilometer, so sending the 1,500-byte Ethernet frame across a 1,000-km link requires 1.2 ms to get the frame into the link, 6 ms to get it through the link, and another 1.2 ms to get it off the link, for a total of 8.4 ms.

A third component is queueing delay, which occurs when the frame has to wait for other traffic queued ahead of it to be transmitted over the medium. If one identical frame were queued ahead of the frame we are discussing, there would be an additional minimum delay (not counting delays in moving frames inside the host) of 8.4 ms before transmission can start. One of the fundamental premises of ATM is that small cells do not cause as much queueing delay as long frames.

Complicating the realities of queueing delay is the phenomenon of *packet training,* in which an application sends a message that breaks into multiple frames that may be queued as a train. If a file transfer application sent a 64-Kbyte Transmission Control Protocol (TCP) burst, that would put over 40 frames ahead of the frame we are discussing—nearly half a second of queueing delay. Prioritization schemes can prevent critical traffic from being trapped behind trains of low-priority traffic, typically with a maximum queueing delay of one frame. Such schemes add complexity, and still do not help if there are trains of the same priority.

To achieve the desired speeds and ranges, new broadband services need electronics between the customer premises and the access office. Conversion from copper to optical media frequently is necessary. In multiunit buildings such as apartments and office high-rises, these conversions usually take place in an equipment room. For residential applications, they may take place in an outdoor equipment pedestal, in sealed enclosures on telephone poles, and so on. The assortment of equipment that interconnects the customer premises with the end office increasingly is called the *collector network*, and modifies the three-level hierarchy to insert a collector tier between access and distribution tiers (Figure 2.13).

A specialized access provider rather than a traditional ISP often operates the collection tier. As detailed in Chapter 7, many regulatory as well as business factors may dictate the type of firm that operates the collection tier, but it is most likely to be an ILEC or CLEC that wholesales access service to ISPs.

The model continues to evolve, with these informal boundaries:

- *First meter.* Residential or other LANs close to the CLE/CPE.
- *First 100 meters.* Building-wide LANs, including carrier distribution LANs in multitenant buildings such as hotels and apartment houses. May also include fiber from the building to a curbside pedestal.
- *First mile.* Outside connectivity to the first ILEC office.
- *Second mile.* Connectivity between the LEC and the POP of an ISP or other organization offering services beyond basic connectivity (for example, Internet access, telephony, private data networking, video content).

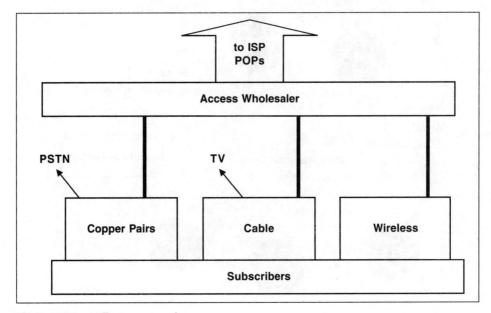

Figure 2.13   Collector network.

The Provider Edge

In modern networks, the provider edge is no longer a single device, but a set of
devices (Figure 2.14). Depending on the access technologies in use, there can
be an assortment of devices that face the subscriber. In traditional telephony,
these are the terminations of analog copper loops and the associated *channel
banks* that convert analog signals to digital. With broadband services, they may
be *DSL access multiplexers* for copper-based digital subscriber loops, or *head
ends* on cable systems. There may be large modem pools connected to Point-to-
Point Protocol (PPP) servers for dial-up users. There often will be *digital cross-
connect systems* to interconnect various digital streams inside the edge office,
bundling them into higher-speed streams. Digital-to-analog converters (DACs)
are of limited intelligence and have been designed for operation by a single
organization, for connectivity within that organization. *IP services switches*
(IPSSs) or *media gateways* (MGs) meet the needs of access wholesalers. More
intelligent DACS may be remotely programmable with such protocols as the
Generic Switch Management Protocol (GSMP).

Some content services, such as web caches, can very reasonably be placed in
edge sites. There can be multiple reasons for doing so. An obvious one in
today's environment is that a request that is serviced at the edge doesn't require
upstream bandwidth. Some optical network evangelists pooh-pooh this argument, claiming that optical bandwidth is becoming so cheap that saving bandwidth is not an important issue. Today's reality, however, is that many ISP POPs,

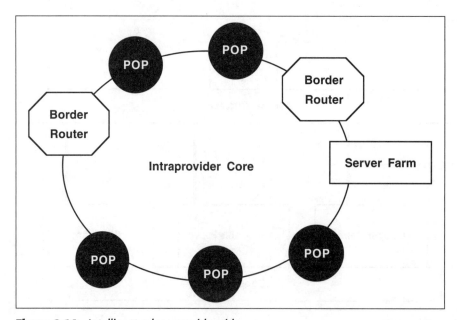

Figure 2.14   Intelligent edge—provider side.

especially in rural areas, have limited upstream bandwidth, such as a single T1, and are not likely to get more in the near term.

Another reason for edge caching includes reducing latency for retrieving Web pages that many users will access. How many technologists need their daily Dilbert fix? How many times, however, does the Dilbert page need to be loaded from United Media's site? How much better can latency be if it can be loaded locally?

Yet one more reason, still to be proven on a large scale, is that customized content, such as video pay-per-view (especially with a VCR-like function that allows rewinding) is inherently a parallel processing problem. This problem lends itself for distribution to POPs, although it may also lend itself to distribution onto set-top boxes at the subscriber location. A key determining factor will be whether the links from the POP to the customer premises are fast enough, and storage at the customer cheap enough, to download entire movies and have the VCR function be local. Otherwise, it will be necessary to maintain individual subscriber state on streaming video servers.

Provider-oriented routers can either connect edge sites into the core of the edge site operator or can be border routers that interconnect the edge to third-party IP providers. Optical economics may make it cost-effective to simply place optical multiplexers at edge locations and backhaul traffic to IP provider sites. In such cases, the optical subsystem at the edge is effectively an interface extender for the remote provider router. Note that there is a loss of intelligence at the edge with this option using current optical equipment. If intelligence is required (the separate treatment of currently multiplexed streams), it will have to be performed elsewhere.

Provider Core Strategies

One of the counterintuitive truths about routing is that routing is more scalable, not less scalable, when the amount of routing information available is minimized. An especially important place to minimize information is the intra-provider core (Figure 2.15). There will be more on this at the end of the chapter.

People still refer to the "Internet core," but it really no longer exists. Service providers, however, are very concerned with their own core. An intraprovider core is under the control of a single provider, and is used to interconnect the edge sites of that provider. Connections to other providers, to server farms, and to customers do not belong in the intraprovider core. Such cores certainly can have internal routers for aggregation and to find alternate paths. In cores of any appreciable size, an interior routing protocol is needed for path discovery. Recent interest in subsecond convergence [Alaettinoglu 2000a] is especially relevant to intraprovider cores.

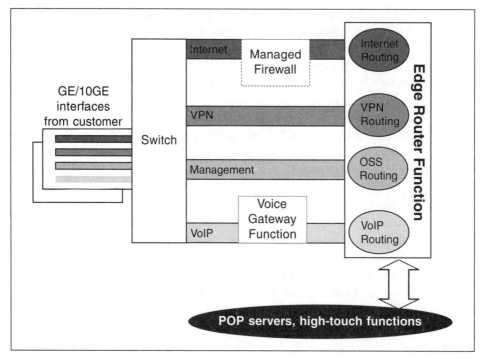

Figure 2.15   Intraprovider core.

Current Exchange Practice

"Major" exchange points, in North America and Western Europe, are most commonly peering points between lower-tier providers. Major exchange points, operated by large providers or specialized exchange operators, contrast with smaller cooperative metropolitan exchanges. Such providers still buy transit from major providers and have direct connections to their transit providers. While such connections may physically be in the same building as the exchange point, they do not go through the exchange fabric.

Even in these areas, there are a significant and growing number of metropolitan exchange points in cities that may not be on the largest provider backbones, such as Tucson, Toronto, and Baltimore. Providers and selected enterprises in these areas are interested in decreasing their bandwidth requirements to their transit providers by finding direct paths to local peers. Note the financial savings that come from not requiring as large a pipe to the transit provider.

Traditional exchanges have had a layer 2 fabric. In smaller areas, especially in developing countries where intercontinental bandwidth and local expertise in interprovider routing are limited, there has been considerable interest in layer 3 exchanges. Exchanges historically have been provider-only, but the distinctions among large content hosting centers and exchanges have been blurring. See Chapter 12 for details of pure routing exchanges, and Chapter 13 for the hybrid content/routing exchanges.

What Are All These Devices Doing?

Cross-cultural contexts require precision in terminology. We have multiple problems in that different technological cultures use the same words to mean different things. We also have the problem of running into conceptual brick walls because nonobvious principles remain unknown. Let's discuss some of these key concepts, both the commonly used ones and those underlying them.

Control Planes: IP Equivalents to SS7 Success

With the increasing separation of control and switching processing, it becomes practical to add the type of capacity that is needed. While there certainly are exceptions (for example, switches serving rock concert reservation desks or talk radio), switching and port capacity tend to be limits before a system runs out of control capacity.

Most of the work on the OSI Reference Model was done in the 1970s, although the model was formalized in 1984. A new architectural effort, Broadband ISDN (which included ATM), was begun, and one of its objectives was to clarify the control and management functions where the original OSI model was deficient. The original OSI model concentrated on user information transfer. In Figure 2.16, you will see how the B-ISDN work separated C-plane control functions (that is, from the subscriber to the provider edge) and M-plane management functions (that is, internal to the provider) from U-plane user information transfer. Outside telephony, current usage tends to merge the M and C planes and generally refer to a control plane. One of the reasons that telephony management functions are quite efficient is the use of a separate control network. See "Internal Provider Control" in Chapter 7.

IP versus Provider-Operated IP versus Public Internet

One of the great sources of mismanaged expectations is equating any provider service based on the Internet Protocol (IP) with a provider of services connected to the global, public Internet. What's the difference? Originally, the term *catenet* referred to a set of interconnected, separately administered networks—networks that were concatenated. IP emerged as a basic mechanism to use in

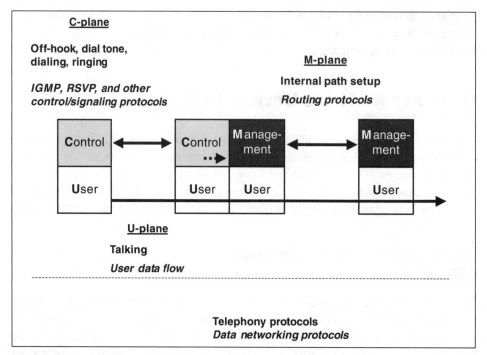

Figure 2.16   U/C/M Planes with B-ISDN and IP equivalents.

interconnected networks, and the term *internet* came into largely academic use for such networks.

The global Internet (uppercase), as we know it today, is the set of separately administered networks (specifically autonomous systems) that participate in a common addressing scheme and whose connectivity is achieved using the Border Gateway Protocol (BGP) (see the following text). Since there is no single operational authority controlling the Internet, there is no way to enforce service level agreements across it. The Internet provides many and useful functions, but it remains the largest successful anarchy in the history of mankind.

It was said of fascist powers that they at least made the trains run on time. If the trains in question are made up of packets, making them run on time—in the sense of service level agreements—does take some central authority. At the very least, it takes a set of contractual agreements among providers, who contract to provide defined levels of service for known traffic.

Routing, as Opposed to Routing: Internet versus Telco Traditions

It is rather difficult to go anywhere without knowing where you are going. You need a set of directions, a map, or a wise guide. In networks, we generally speak of the means by which directions are obtained as part of routing. Routing, however, includes many things. In many discussions, the subcomponents of routing differ in telecommunications and data contexts. On advice of my feline associate, Clifford, who believes fur is one of the essential truths, I shall refer to "furbling" rather than these overloaded technical terms, and define the architectural components of furbling. I will show that it can be approached more generally, with more software and architectural reuse, than we have been doing.

It's always a bit troubling to discuss even the cost engineering approaches of the U.S. intelligence community, for there is always the concern one will cross that threshold of "we could tell you, but then we would have to kill you." Trusting that Agents Scully and Mulder will show good sense, I will refer to refinements in the U.S. satellite intelligence collection systems. These systems originated and proliferated as "stovepipes," with all requirements driven by a particular type of information to be collected: communications intercepts, radar location and surveillance, optical imagery, and so on. This resulted in constellations of specific satellites in the same orbit, over the same targets, with incredibly expensive launch and operational costs repeated many times. Fairly recently, it was realized that the satellites proper were often characterized more by the nature of their orbit than what they collected. Some types of information are best collected from low earth orbit, such as close-look imagery and intercepts of low-power, line-of-sight signals, both communications intelligence (COMINT) and electronic intelligence (ELINT). Other types of information, such as missile early warning, are better collected from high or geosynchronous orbit. When the requirements for satellites were recategorized according to where they need to orbit, and combining sensors onto them, costs drop radically.

And so it is for what we call routing. But we may never achieve those improvements in cost and functionality if every group insists on its own terminology, or on its own definitions of words shared by other groups. Let me therefore introduce some of the things one does when one furbles.

SOME ESSENTIAL CONCEPTS

In modern relays (and more about them later in this chapter) the forwarding and control planes are separated. At a high level, remember that the routing information base (RIB) contains the assembled knowledge of the control plane. The forwarding information base (FIB) is derived from the RIB and distributed to the forwarding plane elements, where it is used to make forwarding decisions.

Topology Discovery

Topological information is no more than identifying nodal points and the arcs that connect them. As shown in Figure 2.17, topology discovery mechanisms include learning about directly connected media through hardware status and learning about distant media through information provided by dynamic routing protocols. Router **Garlic** learns about nonconnected networks through routing protocols from **Basil. Basil,** in turn, learned about distant networks from **Oregano.** The reverse path, in which **Garlic** tells **Basil** about its networks, is omitted from the drawing simply for graphic simplicity.

At the transmission system level of topology discovery, for example, we have synchronous optical network (SONET) sections, paths, lines, and knowledge of the next node on a ring. At the application endpoint (as opposed to midbox), we have knowledge of prefixes/subnets and hosts/routers on them. At the bridging level, we know about Message Authentication Code (MAC) addresses and bridge ports. In a product, we may discover this information through manual configuration, through local hardware, through the announcement/update mechanisms of certain protocols, and through directory and directory-like servers.

As part of the discovery mechanism, individual interface costs are usually learned. The general approach in IP routing is to establish a metric for a route, which is the sum of interface costs along that route (Figure 2.18). Keepalive mechanisms can detect the failure of local next hops, signal the information that a particular path is not available, and trigger fallback and/or route recomputation. Keepalives are complemented with hardware detection of errors.

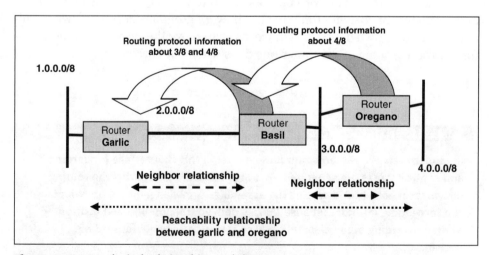

Figure 2.17 Topological relationships and discovery.

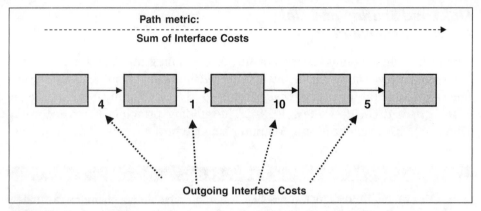

Figure 2.18 Costs and metrics.

The hello mechanisms of interior routing protocols are often the way in which link failures are detected, especially on media such as 10/100 Ethernet, which has no hardware failure detection mechanism or data-link layer keepalive protocol. Other applications for using hellos to detect failures are on individual virtual circuits in frame relay, where the physical WAN interface remains up but a virtual circuit goes down, and, for any of an assortment of reasons, the LMI does not signal the failure. In many frame relay networks, however, the layer management interface (LMI) is a reliable means of determining when a virtual circuit changes status. Simple Network Management Protocol (SNMP) notification also is a means of detecting a status change.

BANDWIDTH CONSERVATION FOR KEEPALIVES

The Open Shortest Path First (OSPF) and Routing Information Protocol (RIP) routing protocols have "demand circuit extensions," which deliberately suppress the hello function and make an optimistic assumption that links are always up unless network management (configuration or fault management) notifies the routing process of the status change. Efforts are made to pass only significant nonadjacent topology changes along demand circuits.

While demand circuits were conceived as a means of preventing excessive dial-up circuit use, where the hellos might cause dialing on demand even though there is no user traffic to send, they have found other applications. In particular, they are useful on very-low-bandwidth links, such as high-frequency radio (for example, U.S. Coast Guard ship transmitters) or where the transmission plant is very poor (for example, the former Yugoslavia). These techniques offer promise for bandwidth conservation in the wireless Internet.

Link Load Sharing and Link Failure Circumvention

One of the fundamental features of furbling is hiding information inside one layer from a layer above or below it. *Information hiding* is the computer science term, but I prefer *Schwarzenegger's Second Law.* [For my first law, see my *WAN Survival Guide* (Wiley, 1999.)] The guiding principle here, according either to Schwarzenegger or a computer science professor, is: "Lie." The com-

---

SCHWARZENEGGER'S LAWS OF NETWORKING

It seems all too little known that action star and bodybuilding champion Arnold Schwarzenegger is a very intelligent man with a wicked sense of humor. (It should be obvious that any Republican who marries into the Kennedy clan *has* to have a sense of humor!) He has a deep understanding of human psychology, which a few insightful critics realize is expressed in his sensitive, introspective movies intended for the intellectual audience, such as *Commando.*

Early in *Commando,* Arnold is captured by The Bad Guys, and put into one of those Classic Situations from Which He Cannot Possibly Escape. One of the Bad Guys mocks Arnold, who calmly replies, "You know, Solly, you are a very funny man. I like you. Just for that, I will kill you last."

Of course, Arnold escapes within minutes. After the traditional car chase, he captures his first Bad Guy, who turns out to be none other than Solly. Arnold uses modern psychotherapeutic techniques, based on rational emotive therapy, to interrogate Solly. He puts Solly in the proper environment for his counseling, which, in this case, means that he holds Solly by his foot over a thousand-foot drop. In response to Solly's defiant refusal to tell Arnold what he wishes to know, insisting what Arnold wants is not important, Arnold sagely responds, "No. Only one thing is important to you now."

"What's that?"

"Gravity."

Arnold has used a fine therapeutic technique with Solly, helping him see the rational consequences of his initial emotional response. With that help, Solly tells Arnold everything he wants. Solly then realizes he is still hanging by one foot over a thousand-foot drop, and cheerfully reminds Arnold, "Remember? You were going to kill me last?"

Arnold calmly opens his hand, saying; "I lied."

And that is Schwarzenegger's Second Law of Networking: *Lie.* If an upper layer has certain expectations of a lower layer, and the lower layer does not provide a service matching them, insert a shim layer between the two. This shim layer will tell the upper layer what it wants to hear.

In the same movie scene, Arnold also demonstrated his Third Law. Returning to the car, Rae Dawn Chong asks, "What happened to Solly?" Arnold replies, "I let him go." And that is the Third Law: do not retain resources when they are no longer needed. There are many kinds of inverse multiplexing (shown at a high level in Figure 2.19), but they all share a common property: the lie.

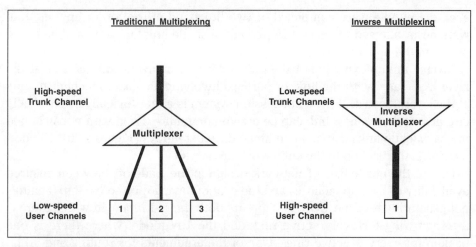

Figure 2.19 Multiplexing and inverse multiplexing.

mon property is that the layer where the multiplexing takes place lies to the layer above it, giving the impression that the upper layer is transmitting and receiving over a single link.

Inverse multiplexing obviously is a way of sharing load, of making more resources available than any individual link can provide. In addition, however, inverse multiplexing can add significant fault tolerance. If one of the links in the inverse-multiplexed "bundle" fails, and the load can be redistributed over the remaining links, the layer above will not be aware of a link failure. There might be a loss of a packet or frame, but the bundle will appear to be unchanged. Of course, if the links of the bundle are all appreciably loaded, the upper layer may notice performance degradation. A general rule in queueing theory suggests that performance begins to drop when utilization exceeds 50 percent. If, how-

MANY DISTRIBUTION METHODS

There are many ways to distribute load over multiple frame or packet links. The three main methods are round-robin per packet or per frame, per destination, and source-destination hash. Per-destination methods are the most likely to become unbalanced in bandwidth over the various links, and thus suffer the greatest impact on performance if a heavily loaded link fails. Round-robin is bandwidth-efficient, but requires significant processing and also may impact the performance of a host performance because it is especially likely to cause out-of-sequence frames. See [Berkowitz 1999] for a detailed discussion of the advantages and disadvantages of specific load distribution mechanisms by routers, and [Berkowitz 2000] for a discussion of load distribution among servers.

ever, the bundle were composed of two links and utilization of any one link were never allowed to exceed 25 percent, a single link failure would be transparent to the upper layer.

Inverse multiplexing is not the only way to circumvent link failures at the layer associated with the link, or perhaps involving a control mechanism only at the layer above it. If the transmission system is either logically or physically circuit switched, a new link can be created on failure. Even with nonswitched media, backup links can be maintained as hot standbys (Figure 2.20). The dotted ring is the backup to the solid working ring(s).

One of the challenges of network design is the trade-off between ensured availability of backup facilities and the cost of having unused backup facilities not generating revenue. SONET supports both the 1+1 mode, in which there is a backup ring for every active ring, and the 1:N mode, where there is one backup for every N active rings. One of the arguments for routing and MPLS rather than SONET-style restoration is that there are a greater potential number of alternate paths and that less capacity needs to be left idle for backup.

Circumventing Relay Failures

Relays interconnect links: routers at layer 3, bridges and WAN switches at layer 2. Much as transparent circumvention of link failure is a subtle yet important part of furbling, so is transparent circumvention of relay failure. Since relays can be complex devices, recent work has proposed means of circumventing failure of subsystems of relays as well as the entire relay.

An example of the first method, exemplified by IETF's Virtual Router Redundancy Protocol (VRRP) [RFC 2338] and Cisco's Hot Standby Routing Protocol

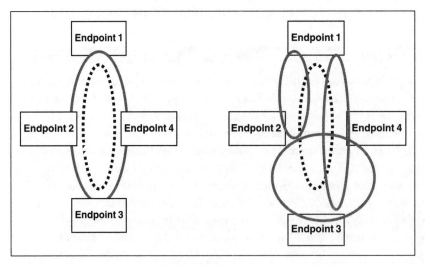

Figure 2.20   1+1 and 1:N SONET APS.

(HSRP) [RFC 2281], is a strict interpretation of Schwarzenegger's Second Law. The lying, in this case, is to hosts. The hosts are given an IP address for a default gateway router to reach destinations outside their subnet. In actuality, this is a virtual address shared among multiple routers (Figure 2.21). The actual VRRP or HSRP messages flow between the routers; the hosts do not see them. In each redundant router group there is a primary and secondary router. The primary router sends periodic "go back to sleep" messages to the secondary router. If the secondary router does not hear such a message, presumably because the primary router went down and is unable to send it, the virtual router address activates on the secondary router, and the hosts will continue sending to the virtual address, unaware of any failure. One of the nuances of these protocols is that there is both a virtual IP address and a virtual MAC address, so the Address Resolution Protocol (ARP) caches of the hosts remain valid.

Certain techniques have historically been used only with LANs, but as various techniques called Ethernet enter the carrier space, they should be considered. As you will see in Chapter 8, I consider it unwise to use the more complex topologies practical in LANs in the wide area, although Ethernet-style physical and data link standards are perfectly reasonable.

In a general LAN, the Institute of Electrical and Electronic Engineers (IEEE) 802.1d spanning tree algorithm is used to recover from link or bridge failures. Unfortunately, forwarding stops while the spanning tree topology is being recomputed. Figure 2.22 shows a technique, based again on Schwarzenegger's Second Law, for speedy recovery after failures. The spanning tree algorithm is general, searching everywhere for potential bridges that might offer useful paths. In practical LAN designs, however, the network engineer knows what

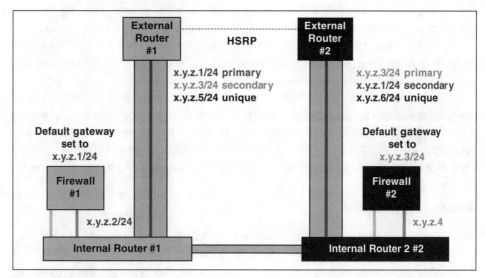

Figure 2.21 Router fault tolerance.

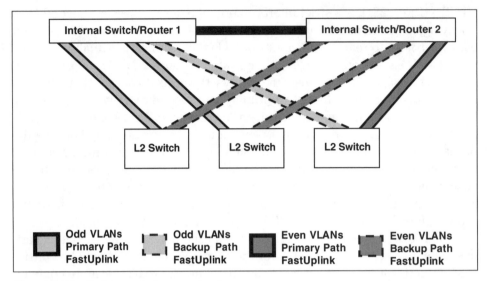

Figure 2.22   Fast recovery in spanning tree.

paths exist in the hierarchy. Using a proprietary extension to spanning tree such as Cisco's Fast Uplink feature, where spanning tree would eventually find a single backup bridge/switch at the next level of hierarchy, the hierarchically lower switches simply can be programmed with the address of the backup switch. Essentially, the switches are told by the person configuring them, "Trust me. I'm the network engineer."

There is another emerging approach entering layer 3 routing. In the real world, the routing control mechanism can fail, but what that really means is that updated information will not arrive at the router until routing control recovers. In telephony, if the SS7 control system fails, calls in progress are not dropped, but new calls cannot be made until the system recovers. These new routing approaches use much the same logic. They will continue to use the existing FIB to forward packets.

Over time, the FIB will become increasingly stale, and more and more packets will be sent to incorrect destinations, where they will be dropped. There is an underlying optimistic assumption that the routing control system will recover soon, and far less damage will be done by the few misrouted packets than would be by invalidating the entire FIB and refusing to route any packets.

Route Computation

Once a node has topological information, it can apply an algorithm that produces routes. Routes can be optimized for next hop behavior or for end-to-end connectivity. At the IP level, we have two major methods for producing routes. It is not quite appropriate here to use the term *algorithm*. While the major techniques—distance vector, path vector, and link state—are associated with certain algorithms, even without additional constraint-based routing, those algorithms are only part of the process. Distance vector is not used as the main mechanism of any carrier-class standard routing protocol. Path vector is the mechanism of the Border Gateway Protocol, used between providers. Link state, the basis for the OSPF and Intermediate System–Intermediate System (ISIS) protocols used for intraprovider cores and enterprise routing, uses modified Dijkstra algorithms to calculate intraarea routes, then uses linear methods to add interarea and external routes. In modern protocols, flexible metrics can be used at each of these levels, including multiple constraints. A constraint can have the semantics of a simple preference factor for a link (for example, bandwidth or delay), but can also involve a concept of resource reservation (for example, decreasing available bandwidth after each reservation, and, after all the resource is allocated, excluding the link from further assignment) or a qualitative policy rule. Policy rules are most important for exterior routing, and also may involve consulting the active RIB as well as the routing table generated by a particular information source.

Basic Interior Routing

For IP, link state and distance vector are used for interior routing protocols, called interior gateway protocols (IGPs) for historical reasons. Unconstrained IGPs have the following basic assumptions:

1. If you can find a single path to a destination, use it.
2. If there is more than one path to a destination, compare metrics.

   - If one of the paths has a lower metric than the others, select it.
   - If more than one of the paths have equal metrics, declare them eligible for load sharing.

3. If you have no other path to a destination and a default route is defined, use the default route.

Many additional constraints can apply to these basic rules. For example, in OSPF, an intraarea route is always preferable to an interarea or external route regardless of metric; an interarea route is always preferable to an external route; and a type 1 external route is always preferable to a type 2 external route.

In optical discussions, the term *constraint* seems to be used in a more restrictive way, often in connection with capacity. Yet there are resource-sensitive extensions to IP routing protocols, such as OSPF and ISIS with traffic engineering extensions (OSPF-TE and ISIS-TE), which add data structures for carrying reservation information. OSPF and ISIS with optimized multipath extensions (OSPF-OMP and ISIS-OMP) optimize multihop routes based on periodic sampling of utilization throughout the routing domain.

Another way of looking at constraint-based routing is that it introduces traffic management and other policies into routing protocols that originally were intended only to establish reachability.

Basic Exterior Routing

Path vector, the basic algorithm of BGP, should be considered part of a reachability protocol rather than a more general routing protocol. The sequence of events in exterior routing is as follows:

1. Listen to peers announce potential routes to a destination. Apply ingress filters to them, delete those denied by policy, and change attributes as required by acceptance policy. Store these in a per-peer or per-peer-group Adj-RIB-In.

2. Test the selected routes to see if they are preferable to your existing route, or go to new destinations. Subject to additional constraints (for

---

MPLS IS NOT A PANACEA

MPLS, and associated protocols such as Label Distribution Protocol (LDP), RSVP with Traffic Engineering (RSVP-TE), and Constraint-Based Routing LDP (CR-LDP) are neither topology discovery nor route computation protocols. Their role comes later in this discussion. Unfortunately, many people in the industry, especially those working for telephone companies or for vendors specializing in the telephone market, assume MPLS is a total replacement for IP, and that the confusing topic called IP routing will somehow go away. They are wrong, because MPLS is an overdrive to conventional IP routing. The idea of an overdrive, unfortunately, can be misleading. Originally MPLS and its predecessors were seen as faster means of forwarding than conventional router lookup. Routers (which admittedly may be called layer 3 switches by some marketers) now can have sufficient hardware assistance for route lookup, and fast enough lookup algorithms, that MPLS forwarding is not significantly faster than router forwarding.

The distinct value of MPLS is its ability to place useful equivalents to circuits between connectionless IP and a variety of transmission media. MPLS is sometimes jokingly called "ATM without cells," but one of its attractions is the ability to do the sort of traffic engineering and QoS control that is much easier with connection-oriented than connectionless services. MPLS also has features that make it useful for VPN creation, especially involving multiple providers. Another attraction of the MPLS work is its generalization into Generalized MPLS (GMPLS), which will allow a largely common control plane to control transmission systems that do not understand packets. Such systems include optical and multiplexed transmission technologies.

instance, whether you have a valid hop to the new route), replace the selected route or add it to the BGP Loc-RIB.

3. For those routes that pass both the requirements of entry into the Loc-RIB and the main RIB (see next section), store these routes in per-peer or per-peer-group Adj-RIB-Outs and advertise them to peers as specified by advertising policies.

There may be direct importing and exporting between different route computation processes, or routes may be imported from the RIB.

Route Selection

Take routes determined in route computation and compare the routes learned from different computational sources, some of which may be preferred to others. Install the selected routes in the RIB, deriving a FIB from it as appropriate (Figure 2.23). The basic process is defined in [RFC 1812], but all major vendors have extended it. Establishing preferences among various routing information sources, such as route weight in Bay RS or administrative distance in Cisco IOS, is most common. Load sharing extensions also are common. The RIB, defined as the repository of routes the router is actually using to route, also becomes part of path computation by specific protocols. BGP, for example, will not advertise a route that has a next hop that is unreachable according to the RIB.

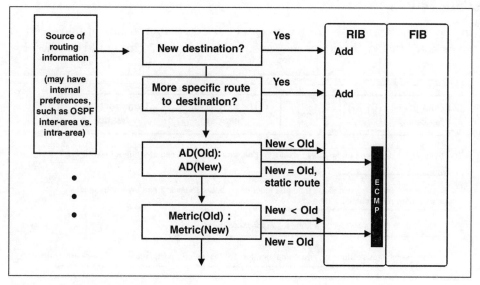

Figure 2.23   Selecting among routes.

Forwarding

Classical routers make forwarding decisions by looking up the packet header in the FIB, and—assuming a matching destination address is in the FIB—forwarding the packet to the next hop indicated by the FIB entry. Classical bridges make decisions in a different way, but still based on header information in individual frames. MPLS forwarding devices make hop-by-hop forwarding decisions based on the label in each packet, and higher-layer forwarding devices still make per-packet decisions. Figure 2.24 summarizes these decisions.

It is a fairly general trend in high performance routers to separate the forwarding plane from the management and control plane. Forwarding tends to need specialized hardware, but not huge amounts of intelligence. Routing (or furbling) control, however, is processing- and memory-intensive.

A fundamental architectural element of advanced furbling is the distribution of FIBs to line cards (Figure 2.25). Most high-performance routers do this in the internal fabric, but there are proprietary protocols that allow the control plane and the forwarding plane to be in separate boxes, such as Cisco's client/server multilayer switching control protocol. The IETF FORCES working group is exploring standardized protocols for communication between the control and forwarding planes.

In telecommunications, there has always been the ability to forward on a real or virtual circuit basis: from one switch port to another, or from one multiplexed time slot to another. The Generalized MPLS (GMPLS) initiative unifies the setup of forwarding tables for circuits and packets, which may involve path setup.

Path Setup

In certain situations, before a path can be used for forwarding, it may need to be created (that is, resources may need to be assigned). This could be a hop-by-

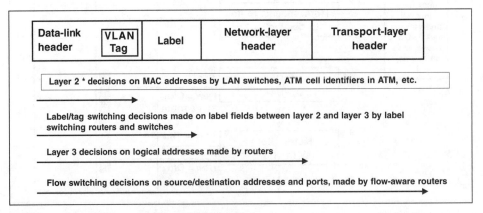

Figure 2.24 Per-data-unit forwarding decisions.

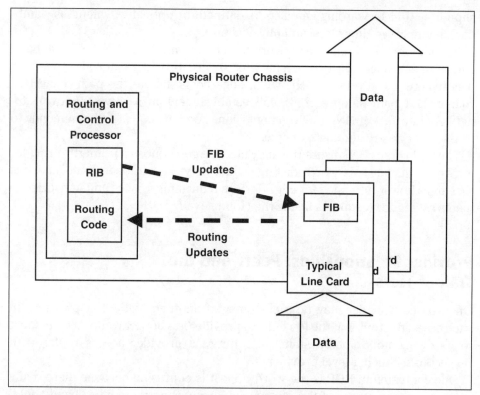

Figure 2.25   Modern router with distributed forwarding.

hop reservation of resources, a dial or equivalent virtual circuit setup, a mutual notification of directories, and so on. The emphasis in this step is deciding that end-to-end resources are available before hop-by-hop forwarding is told to use the path.

In MPLS, label distribution protocols (LDP, CR-LDP, RSVP-TE) set up paths. A variation of LDP, the Generic Switch Management Protocol (GSMP), can be used to set up paths in layer 1 cross-connects. See the MPLS discussion in Chapter 6. The original RSVP had a model of hosts initiating resource reservations for microflows (individual source-destination pairs). This approach has limited scalability. RSVP has also been used to allocate bandwidth between routers. It is worth noting that protocols conceived as host-initiated, such as RSVP, Internet Group Membership Protocol (IGMP), and so on, often use soft-state models. Most traditional path setup functions are hard-state connection establishment mechanisms. Soft-state models require periodic messages to maintain the reservation, or else it is released. Hard-state models retain a reservation until it is explicitly released.

GMPLS extends the use of MPLS setup protocols to define paths on which the forwarding decision is not on a per-packet basis. Packet forwarding is still supported, but forwarding can also be defined for optical wavelengths (lambdas), multiplexed time slots, and physical ports.

In traditional WAN terms, a network-to-network interface (NNI) or broadband carrier interconnect (BCI), when initiated by interprovider gateways, triggers a user-to-network interface (UNI) when edge hosts initiate the path request or routers and path setup. Q.2931 call establishment in a private network-to-network interface (PNNI) environment is one good example. TL/1 commands to cross-connects are another example.

The UNI versus NNI distinction may not be a good one in a primarily provider environment, but it is worth distinguishing between path setup mechanisms that are primarily intended for edge devices requesting service and network elements asking for resources inside the cloud.

Provider Relationships: Peers and the Trail of Tiers

One service provider may be a customer of another, higher-tier provider. In such cases, the router at the lower-level provider is a border router with respect to its own autonomous system (AS), but is a provider access router with respect to the higher-level provider.

One confusion in BGP is the word *peer*. It is confusing because there really are two distinct usages of the same word, one at the protocol level and one at the policy level. At the protocol level, two routers that are BGP peers simply have a BGP session running between them over a TCP connection. This is an important level, because if you don't have session-level connectivity, the higher-layer things in BGP cannot happen. BGP protocol peering is at the level of pairs of routers. The other meaning is at the policy level, and refers to a business relationship between entire ASs. In policy level peering, pairs of ASs decide either that they have the same status or that one AS is at a higher level in the food chain. When two ASs decide they are peers in the sense that they have comparable customer bases and routing infrastructure, they also assume there is a roughly equal relationship in which they have approximately the same number of customers. They decide it is to their mutual benefit that their customers reach one another. They do not pay one another for routing information, but simply advertise their customers' routes to one another. They emphatically do *not* exchange their full Internet routing tables.

In contrast, when an enterprise "buys transit" from a service provider, there is an unequal consumer-provider relationship. The consumer pays the service provider for Internet access. The consumer may choose to receive the full Internet routing table from the service provider. Another option, quite commonly used in load sharing, is to have the service provider send only those routing table entries that go to the ISP's directly connected customers.

Interprovider relationships often are stated with respect to "tiers." While there are no formal definitions of a tier, and salespeople often and meaninglessly harp on their elite tier status, there is utility to the basic idea, which places the largest providers at tier 1. Marketers for one provider whose business is interprovider connectivity and brokerage have elected themselves tier 0, but the industry, thankfully, has ignored this term. There is a regrettable tendency for the sales team of one provider to try to convince the consumer that whatever their competitor's tier, they are at a higher one.

Emphasizing that the distinctions have not been formalized, the usual definition of a tier 1 provider includes the following:

- The provider obtains all its route information from bilateral peering or its own internal routing system. It never buys transit.

- The provider either owns or operates a high-speed continental or intercontinental backbone. When the term *tier 1* emerged, such backbones needed DS3 speed, but OC-3 or faster is more appropriate today. Recently, Cable and Wireless raised industry eyebrows by requiring their peers to have a minimum backbone speed of OC-48.

- The provider has 24-h routing engineering/operation support available, at least to peer providers.

- The provider is present in at least two major exchange points, and preferably five or more. This does not preclude additional bilateral peering.

A practical, although unfortunately circular, definition is that tier 1 providers principally connect to other tier 1 providers, or to their own customers. Tier 2 providers have largely been absorbed into tier 1 providers, but they typically are regional networks differing from tier 1 providers principally with respect to geographic scope. The classical tier 2 provider was one of the original NSFNET regional networks. Things become much less clear below tier 2, although tier 3 is sometimes considered a metropolitan or similar local area provider that does have multihomed uplinks, while tier 4 is an access provider without multihomed uplinks.

An Introduction to Scalability Issues in the Modern Internet

The modern Internet is an evolution from the ARPANET, NSFNET, and its earlier implementation. Christian Huitema has commented that the Internet has repeatedly been saved by just-in-time inventions that meet the scalability problem of the day. Many of these inventions were refinements of existing methods. With the continuing growth of the Internet, it becomes increasingly clear that some of these methods have reached their limits, and new technologies are needed. One of the most basic concerns is that the original Internet exterior routing protocols dealt with a simple single-core model. The first version of BGP [RFC 1105] introduced the notion that a given autonomous system (AS) might have more than one BGP-speaking router, and that these routers needed to have a consistent view of the different ASs with which they might communicate. The basic operational assumption, however, was that each AS would announce a small number of addresses. Remember that classless addressing only was introduced in version 4 of BGP. Prior to BGP-4, ASs typically announced only one or a very small number of classful prefixes. At first, these announcements had a very simple purpose: to state that the particular AS offered to route to the announced prefix. Traffic engineering was not an objective, nor was complex and conditional alternate routing.

Several scaling problems came together in the early 1990s. One, presented as "address exhaustion," was really a shortage of the especially convenient Class B addresses. Another factor was the capability of the most widely deployed Internet core routers of the time, the Cisco AGS. This router had only 16 Mbytes of RAM, so there was difficulty in physically storing a large number of routes. Memory is not a major issue in more modern routers. See Chapter 9 for more discussion of BGP routing implementation issues.

CIDR-Style Provider Aggregation

In the early 1990s, it was realized that the classful addressing technique was at the root of the immediate problems. The classful world had a problem that appeared similar to Goldilocks and the three bears: Class A was too big, Class C was too little, and only Class B was just right. Class B, however, with its potential for 64K hosts, was really far too big for most enterprises, and wasted a great deal of space. One of the fundamental assumptions in the Classless

AUTONOMOUS SYSTEMS: THE DEFINITION EVOLVES

The current definition of an AS is introduced in RFC 1930. The key elements of this definition are that an AS consists of a set of address prefixes (and routers) and that these routers may be under the control of multiple organizations. The utterly key criterion, however, is that all of these organizations must present a single and consistent routing policy to the Internet.

Having a single and consistent routing policy emphatically does not require the AS to advertise to, or accept from, the same set of routes to every neighboring AS. Policy elements can be specified with respect to single ASs, or even single routers. It is the complete set of routing policies that must be consistent.

Inter-Domain Routing (CIDR) addressing architecture was to start allocating not on the rigid 8-bit boundaries of classful addressing, but on arbitrary boundaries. With arbitrary allocation, the amount of address space allocated was based on actual needs rather than artificial administrative boundaries.

Geographic and Other Aggregation Schemes

Provider-based aggregation is inherently anticompetitive, as it tends to lock customers in to a single provider. If a customer wishes to change providers, it needs to renumber. Consider the North American (telephone) numbering plan

---

OCTETS LEAD TO EVIL THOUGHTS

Classless allocation, however, was only one part of CIDR. Another key part was *supernetting,* a means of reducing the number of routes in the global routing table [RFC 1338]. Consider the topology in Figure 2.26. All the enterprises and local ISPs connect to the Internet via a national-level provider, AS1. The various customers of AS1 have various peerings among themselves, such as a mutual backup scheme among local providers AS111, AS222, and AS333. It is perfectly reasonable for these local providers to have specific routing policies with one another, but these policies do not need to be seen at the global level at which AS1 operates. For the sake of this discussion, assume the local providers have no upstream providers other than AS1.

It also can be reasonable to have AS1 customers (for example, AS333 and AS444) that connect to the upstream provider at several geographically dispersed edge points of presence. See Chapter 10 for a more detailed discussion of multihoming to a single provider. Since none of the AS1 customers are reachable by other than AS1, the rest of the world (ROW) only needs to see the set of addresses that AS1 can reach. AS1 certainly can have more detailed internal policies among its customers.

What addresses, however, do those customers actually have? For historical reasons, some AS1 customers may have their own provider-independent (PI) address space. As shown in Figure 2.27, their upstream has to announce their PI block if it is to have connectivity. If new customers, however, obtain provider-assigned (PA) assignments of part of AS1's space, the details of these assignments do not need to be seen outside AS1. In the absence of other factors not considered in the original BGP design, such as a desire to do traffic engineering, the ROW will work quite well if it only sees the aggregate address advertised by AS1.

For more details on address allocation and assignment, see Chapter 5, and for the applications of address aggregation, Chapters 9 through 12.

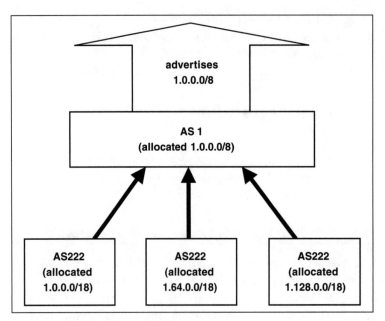

Figure 2.26 Basic provider aggregation.

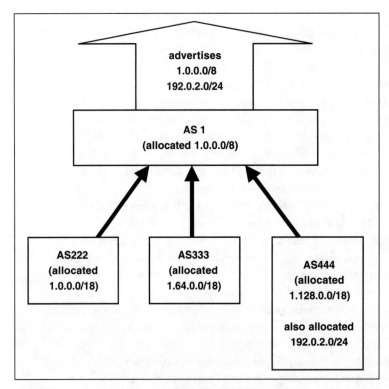

Figure 2.27 Advertising provider-independent space.

(NANP). The high-level part of a national telephone number—the area code—does not depend on the customer's telephone company. Instead, the significance of the area code, and that of the exchanges below it, is geographic. It is perfectly reasonable to devise a telephone routing plan that aggregates numbers to the level of area code, much as CIDR lets IP addresses be aggregated to the level of major providers. Unfortunately, existing IPv4 allocations have been made without concern for geographic allocation—even provider-based allocation is relatively new. Geographic aggregation is under consideration in the IPv6 addressing planning efforts, although provider-based aggregation is the main focus there.

Overloading State into the Routing System: An Introduction

Aggregation, whether provider- or geography-based, enormously helps the scalability of the global routing system. In a highly aggregated environment, there are fewer routes and the aggregated routes tend to be more stable. Reducing the number of routes decreases requirements for both memory and the amount of information to be transferred between routers. Increasing stability reduces the processing load on route computation engines.

Increasing aggregation decreases the ability of enterprises and providers to exert fine-grained control over the way traffic flows in the public Internet. The first motivation for more fine-grained control is to improve fault tolerance, by advertising alternate paths, through different providers. Multihoming for fault tolerance is consistent with some of the spirit of BGP's original design, although it is not clear to what extent continued growth in multihoming can be supported. Even more explosive scaling problems, however, may be coming from a desire to influence traffic flow. Enterprise AS888 legitimately needs to advertise its address space to both AS1 and AS2 in order to be reachable through two different providers. The fault tolerance requirement, however, would be met if AS888 advertised only one address space to both AS1 and AS2. Assume, however, that AS1 is geographically closer to the west half of AS888, and AS2 is closer to the east half. It is the desire of AS888 to go to the "best" provider for each of its hosts. Chapters 9 and 10 detail why such provider preference may, at best, be marginally achievable. The point to be made here, in the

---

BE RENUMBERING FRIENDLY

When enterprises design their IP infrastructures appropriately, renumbering need not be approached with fear and loathing. See [Berkowitz 1999] and [RFC 2072] for information on renumbering-friendly design.

context of scalability issues, is that AS888 will have to advertise three prefixes, not one, to attempt traffic control as well as fault tolerance. The less specific aggregate needs to be advertised to both AS1 and AS2 so that the entire block is always reachable, but the more specific prefixes need to be advertised to affect preferences.

Looking Ahead

In the first two chapters we have established the context for the service provider marketplace. In the next two chapters, we will discuss how providers decide which specific services to offer to their customers, and then how to translate these external service definitions into technical policies that will guide the internal provider network design.

CHAPTER

3

Services, Service Level Agreements, and Delivering Service

The best test of truth is the power of the thought to get itself accepted in the competition of the market.
—Oliver Wendell Holmes

What is truth?
—Pontius Pilate

No quality of service mechanism creates bandwith that does not exist.
—Paul Ferguson

"Letting the market decide" what it wants is all very nice in theory, but in practice suppliers need to decide what services they will offer and that they reasonably expect subscribers to buy. Subscribers, at least in their first look at the market, will do best if they buy commercially available services, demanding customization only when essential.

For the service provider, one of the most fundamental questions is whether it will be sufficient to limit user traffic at the edge and avoid complex QoS mechanisms at the core. This is not an unreasonable strategy, because economies of scale happen in large cores. Overprovisioning need not be wasteful, especially when brute force bandwidth is cheaper than precise control. You might think of this as throwing money at the problem, as opposed to throwing lots of money at the problem.

Defining Services: The Context for Policy

Policy was originally a military term [Gorlitz 1975] referring to guidance by a commander to subordinates, the goal of which was to help the subordinates make the same decision the commander would, but in his absence. It was not seen as rigid rules, but as guidance for intelligent people. The meaning has evolved over time. Most readers have encountered the surly clerk who responds, "It's not our policy," when he or she really means, "It's not our rule," or, potentially, "Stop bothering me."

Clausewitz defined war as the continuation of national policy by military means: "War, therefore, is an act of policy. . . . not a mere act of policy, but a true political instrument, a continuation of political activity by other means" [Clausewitz]. In building a modern WAN, the customer first needs to decide on the rules for continuing business policy into the geographic distribution enabled by WAN service. Network architects need to help the customer clarify confused assumptions that go into policy formulation, and then to specify a set of means that carry out the policies. A customer defines policies that represent business choices and requirements. An example of such a policy in the telephone system is selection of a long-distance carrier. The end user subscribes to a particular interexchange carrier, and it is the responsibility of the local exchange carrier to be able to reach that IXC. There will be levels of policies, and differences between the broad policy definition and the specific enforcement of a technical policy.

When you work for a carrier, you need to verify that your connectivity to the user sites (that is, technical policy enforcement for provisioning) is sufficient to carry out the business policies you agree to with your customer. At the same time, carrier staffs need to avoid providing to sites too much capacity that will go unused (or unpaid for) for the expected project lifetime. There is a delicate balance in providing facilities, however: It is extremely expensive to install new physical transmission paths of copper or optical fiber. It is considerably less expensive to install higher-capacity electronics at the ends of the path. The trend is to install upwardly compatible facilities—either fiber that will support a wide range of new optical technologies, or copper pairs that can support the higher-speed digital subscriber line (DSL) technologies.

Having vented my spleen about misuse of the term *policy*, I must note that there are some valid uses for it in modern networking. I suggest that a networking policy is most usefully considered a user objective. For example, the applications staff of an enterprise might specify a quality-of-service policy for an interactive transaction processing application, which would define the maximum latency the application needs in order to provide its response time goal.

The information technology (IT) staff of this enterprise would refine this user policy, determining the contributions of latency of the end hosts and the enterprise's local network, and then determining the maximum latency of WAN links used by the application. While the terms *quality-of-service policy* and *service level agreement* are often synonymous, a *service level agreement* (SLA) is most often a contract between the user of a service and the provider of a service. End user organizations often write SLAs with their enterprises' IT staffs, which, in turn, contract with WAN providers for WAN SLAs that will work in the context of the broader SLAs.

WAN service providers need to agree to SLAs that are achievable in the real world. Quality-of-service documents glibly speak of "best effort" versus "guaranteed service," and these terms will be discussed further in the next chapter. WAN providers offering "guaranteed service" still have to conform to reality, no matter how their sales departments plead. Providers executing a service under an SLA might be faced with a choice imposed by limited resources. Under resource constraints, the policy executor must prioritize certain traffic to achieve a performance objective. If internal network management traffic and application traffic are contending for the same limited bandwidth, an intelligent executor will prioritize the network management traffic. Not to do so is to jeopardize the continuing existence of the network. No service can be guaranteed on a broken network.

For providers and for their customers, policies must recognize the realities of budgets. The monetary cost of a service is an obvious aspect of budgeting in the network, but there are other things to budget. From a technical standpoint, any interface to a provider has a certain bandwidth. If the bandwidth budget is exceeded, something has to compensate. Some traffic may need to be delayed or dropped if it is sent beyond the budgeted capacity. Time also needs to be considered in the budget. If it takes 16 weeks to have the latest, most expandable optical fiber connection to the provider installed, but multiple copper circuits are available in 2 weeks, is the value of long-term expandability worth 14 weeks of delay in starting your connectivity? Do interim, lower-capacity methods make sense?

Do not confuse policies and mechanisms! Policies are formal definitions of the problem you are trying to solve. Chapter 1 looked at ways of identifying the problem. Subsequent chapters will discuss mechanisms for enforcing policies.

Layers of Management: TMN

Policy and management are closely related but different. A key concept in the International Telecommunications Union's (ITU's) Telecommunications Management Network (TMN) architecture is applying the well-known technique of layering to management. Services are visible to end users as a result of the behavior of elements internal to the network providing connectivity. Figure 3.1 illustrates this separation of service, network, and element management.

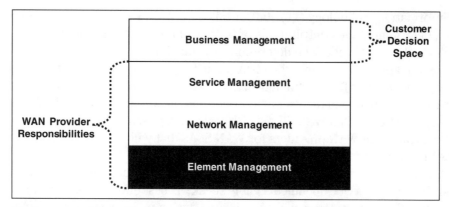

Figure 3.1 TMN model.

TMN was developed with traditional carrier models in mind, independently of IETF work. Its model fits telephony traditions. The IETF view of policy management generally corresponds to what TMN calls network and element management. Policy specification is at the network level, while policy management is element-specific. TMN breaks the management problem into four major layers, presented here from bottom up:

1. *Element management.* The direct monitoring and control of network components such as routers and switches. It includes device statistics collection, error detection, updating firmware, resetting devices, and so on. While TMN describes element management as vendor-specific, it is reasonable to generalize element management to managing the abstract devices specified with management information bases (MIBs).

2. *Network management.* The monitoring and control of functions that involve the interactions of multiple elements. From a monitoring standpoint, network management could involve viewing the network topology. Dynamic routing protocol exchange is a control function in TMN network management. Network provisioning policy to enforce a given degree of connectivity would be a good example.

3. *Service management.* The control and management functions that are visible to the network's users. Such users could be enterprises or value-added carriers. End-to-end quality of service is associated with service management, as is network accounting and user administration. WAN providers will have their own sets of policies for providing services. Typically, there will be a price associated with each policy.

4. *Business management.* Strategic and tactical business requirements. The user decision on selecting a long-distance carrier would be representative of such a requirement.

From the user perspective, policy is created at the business management layer and mapped to service definition. A practical problem definition states business objectives in a manner that can be mapped into service definitions achievable by carriers. It also includes requirements for services operated by the enterprise, such as campus networks. TMN concentrates on the lower layers of management, while the IETF policy work, although not defined in strict TMN terms, starts at the upper layers.

Public versus Private

I cannot emphasize strongly enough that not all IP applications are best served by Internet service providers, if the term *ISP* implies that the service provided is access to the public Internet. Many mission-critical functions will use the Internet Protocol, but for many reasons cannot mix their traffic with general public traffic.

While it is possible for an enterprise to operate its own VPN, doing so typically is client/server-based and not as scalable as a provider-provisioned VPN (PPVPN, defined as a VPN in which the service provider participates, or indeed controls, the provisioning and operational management of the VPN). The IETF, after many years of political squabbling, eventually decided that PPVPNs are a meaningful area of standardization. Access to PPVPNs is discussed further in Chapters 8; the overall PPVPN architecture is discussed in Chapter 13.

Bandwidth

Point-to-point dedicated lines would seem to be the most basic offering a carrier can make. The line is characterized by its bandwidth and a presumably fixed latency.

Basic IP services can involve either dedicated or switched access. While dedicated IP access might seem straightforward, a bandwidth specification is not completely meaningful. Typically, even when there is a dedicated access facility, its bandwidth refers only to the speed of the link between the customer premises and a provider POP. Oversubscription of a link means that the total of all potential inputs to the link is greater than the link capacity. For example, the physical link in Figure 3.2 is potentially oversubscribed if all the frame relay virtual circuits burst simultaneously. The reality, however, is that most network traffic is bursty, and there is a fairly good chance not all channels will want to transmit simultaneously.

Oversubscription is not evil, but the degree of oversubscription on a particular service is, at the very least, a major implementation policy on the part of the provider. Specific oversubscription levels are rarely made available to customers, although certain services differentiate in the marketplace, based in part on the level of oversubscription they use. Figure 3.3 shows the positioning of

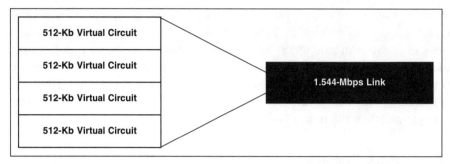

Figure 3.2 Oversubscription.

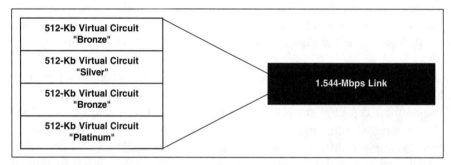

Figure 3.3 Oversubscription and services.

"bronze" (consumer grade), "silver" (business grade), and "platinum" (premium) services. In a simplistic model, the egress router checks the queues of each class of service before sending a packet. If any platinum traffic is waiting, it is serviced continuously until the queue is empty. If any silver traffic is waiting and there is no platinum traffic, a buffer up to a certain length might be checked before any bronze traffic is allowed to have a slice of the bandwidth. If platinum traffic arrives, it will wait only one frame at most before being sent.

Depending on the access technologies, there even may be oversubscription between the customer premises and the POP. IP over cable systems have shared bandwidth, just as does any technology based on shared Ethernet LAN technology. Between an access wholesaler's collection POP and the ISP POP, there is rarely enough bandwidth for every user to burst simultaneously at the full access link rate.

Availability Policies

Another important policy is the response to resource failure. It's really rather simple. Assume that you have certain resources that can handle a load L. If you want to have 100 percent backup, then, assuming duplicate resources, you cannot load either resource beyond $0.5L$.

Some applications can use an overloaded resource and still provide some degraded service. Other applications will fail completely if the resource gives inadequate performance. If your application is of the first kind, you may choose to accept degraded operation in the event of a failure, so you might load the resources to $0.75L$. You must, however, make this an explicit decision.

SLAs

We often speak of service level agreements primarily with respect to performance, but they also must consider availability. Let there be no mistake about quality of service. It is, by definition, discriminatory. On the other hand, it is discriminatory to give an ambulance the right to violate traffic regulations. Is that wrong? Or is it that the ambulance is subject to a different set of regulations, and the conceptual error many people make with respect to IP networks is that all traffic should be subject to the same regulations? Some of those people assert "equal rights" for network management traffic and routing control messages in the internal provider network; voice over IP and transaction processing in a premium-priced VPN; and Web browsing, e-mail, and Internet Relay Chat (IRC) in the public Net. From the standpoint of free market economics, these different services are apples and oranges (although my Macintosh is beige and titanium).

In many public forums, Paul Ferguson makes the comment that having QoS mechanisms does not repeal the speed of light. Unfortunately, many zealous salesdroids forget this, if they ever knew there was a limit to the speed of light. More subtle arguments are made by proponents of the theory "the Internet should be free" or "corporations should not dominate information." Let me simply say I do not propose to get into what might be considered discussions of Marxist economic theory as applied to information. The First Amendment to the United States Constitution protects your right to your press; it does not give others the right to use your press on demand.

Availability and SLAs

In the dark hours of the night, construction crews cut through a fiber cable. Alarms ring out in the local ILEC operations center, and repair technicians are dispatched instantly. Working frantically, the repair crew fixes the fault before the break of dawn.

Was the facility down? Answering this question may be as difficult as solving the old conundrum, "If a tree falls in an empty forest, and there is no one to hear it, is there still a sound?"

Whether or not the facility was down depends on the context of the availability part of the service level agreement. If the SLA explicitly applies during the prime business day, then the facility was never down. If the availability part of the SLA explicitly says that availability will be 24 hours per day, then the facility was down.

While provider contracts are often forms that cannot easily be changed, it may be a win-win situation, setting reasonable expectations for the customer and avoiding simplistic definitions of reliability.

METRICS OF AVAILABILITY?

In the early 1980s, I wrote the technical requirements for the first federal procurement of data communications services that specified performance parameters (using FED-STD-1033) rather than an explicit network technology. The procurement, done for the Environmental Protection Agency (EPA), tried to be quite realistic. One aspect of this was that it was realistic to expect providers to have immediate backups for major facilities in their core networks, but that local loops between POPs and customer premises rarely were redundant and would take longer to repair. Our vendors appreciated that we had different time-to-repair objectives for backbone and local loop failures, and we recognized that redundant local loops had to be explicitly engineered— and paid for—if a particular facility was critical. One challenge in defining these specifications was the length of the acceptable downtime interval. The EPA did not, at the time, have any life-critical hazardous material applications, so, realistically, downtime was a matter of pleasing internal constituencies.

The EPA data center manager, Don Fulford, taught me a great deal about the real-world practice of requirements analysis. When I asked him about the downtime interval, he explained that his boss, Sam Brown, was of the opinion that the data center should never run out of certain things for more than a very brief time. One of those things was printer paper. It was tolerable that the facility's truck might need an extra hour to get replacement supplies from the local warehouse, but if the outage were longer, Sam would get irate customer calls. If these calls came in the middle of the night, Sam would awaken Don.

Don explained that Sam regarded network availability as one of those things that had to be available except for brief outages. Don told me that he was willing to be awakened by Sam four times per year due to network problems. While our RFP was commended for its precision, the availability requirements really were defined in terms of the Fulford unit—a period of downtime that would cause Don to be awakened by Sam. All of our detailed numbers derived from the fundamental requirement that we were to have no more than four Fulfords per year.

It is for good reason that many informal models put the political layer at the top of the OSI stack.

QoS and SLAs

One basic way to think about QoS requirements is in terms of common applications such as:

- Network management
- Delay-critical traffic (voice and interactive video)
- Limited tolerance (video stream)
- Transaction processing
- General interactive traffic
- File transfer

You will find the basic requirements of applications covered by a relatively small number of basic parameters:

- Delay, often called *latency*
- Constant delay
- Variable delay, often called *jitter*
- Packet loss probability
- Throughput

Later in this chapter, we will propose classes of service with various combinations of these parameter values.

Absolute Latency

First, the network needs to protect itself. Routing updates, keepalive messages, and critical network management information must get through. Routing protocol time-outs are one set of limits. Real-time voice and video applications begin to suffer when the end-to-end delay exceeds 150 to 200 ms. Poor-quality conversations, reminiscent of CB radio, are still possible within 400 ms, and may be acceptable for some applications. Delay of 200 to 400 ms will remove the nuances of emotion, but one rarely needs to give poetic directions to the warehouse on what part number to pull from the shelf. People begin to notice delay at approximately 200 ms. Fast typists who key 120 words per minute press a key approximately every 400 ms, so a delay of more than 600 ms would lose the illusion of local typing.

Delay limits for transaction processing are far more subtle. Human factors studies on forms-oriented data entry have shown that productivity was not maximized by minimizing response time. For reasons not immediately apparent, clerks doing insurance data entry with a forms-oriented mainframe application were most productive when response time was between 1 and 3 s. The reason for greater productivity over significant time—on the order of an hour—is that a response time of 1 to 3 s was noticeable without being extremely annoying. When the same operators had subsecond response times, they would type quickly and send their screens without pausing to look for typing errors, relying on the host for editing and validation. Increasing the response time to 1 to 3 s was just noticeable enough that the operators would pause before entering the screen and manually correct errors. With subsecond response time, the operator might reenter the screen several times until correct, decreasing the total number of correct screens entered per hour.

Jitter

Jitter is latency that varies from packet to packet, and it can have critical impact on multimedia transmissions. As an example of the effect of jitter, compare the meaning of these two spoken phrases:

"He is a very nice man."

"He is a very [significant pause] nice [significant pause] man."

In an ideal stream of data, each packet arrives at the destination with an identical delay (for example, 100 ms). Jitter can be informally defined as the average difference from that fixed transmission delay, measured over a sequence of packets. If, for example, the first packet arrives in 50 ms and the second packet in 150 ms, the average jitter is 50 ms. The ITU has defined objectives for jitter in multiservice networks as shown in Table 3.1 [ITU 1999].

Loss Probability

While jitter causes major concern for multimedia, is a lesser problem for interactive data applications, and has little effect on noninteractive traffic, packet loss is a quite different situation. Up to this point, we have talked about delay as being composed of serialization, propagation, and queuing components. Loss, however, introduces its own delays if the application expects reliable transmission and lost packets need to be retransmitted. In classic TCP, packets are not instantly transmitted but have to wait for a timer to expire. Contrary to popular

Table 3.1   Jitter Objectives for Multiservice Networks

DEGRADATION CATEGORY	PEAK JITTER
Perfect	0 ms
Good	75 ms
Medium	125 ms
Poor	225 ms

opinion, retransmission as a means of ensuring an error-free stream is not needed or even desirable for all applications. If TCP, for example, waited for every packet to arrive before it could be passed on to the receiver, delays could become extremely long. If an alternative algorithm were used that selectively retransmitted only the packets in error, you would still be faced with a choice: either delay until all packets were received, or deliver them out of order. For a voice application, the latter choice, to use a *Star Wars* analogy, might result in the following stream: "If Yoda so strong in Force is, why words can not he in right order put?"

Multimedia applications exhibit paradoxical behavior with respect to loss. Human senses are wonderful things, and have the ability to interpolate content if part (but not an excessive part) of a stream is missing. This is a good thing, because it is impractical to retransmit lost packets belonging to a stream. Jonathan Rosenberg has reported on experimental experience with human perceptions of packet loss in voice over Internet Protocol (VoIP) [Rosenberg 1997]. These perceptions were measured by an established technique, mean opinion score (MOS), which is used to quantify telephone listeners' subjective experience (Table 3.2).

Again, this is a subjective measurement—telemarketers calling at dinnertime, even with a speech quality of 5, are very annoying and objectionable! One counterintuitive but extremely useful observation, seen in Table 3.3, is that voice quality is relatively insensitive to loss. It is far more impacted by variable delay, a major cause of distortion.

The Stanford Linear Accelerator Center (SLAC) interprets the unacceptable loss rate as corresponding to a total packet loss rate of 10 to 12 percent. Still, there is a surprisingly good tolerance for lost packets in voice, leading to the observation that it is more important not to delay or jitter voice packets than it

Table 3.2 Perceptions of Packet Loss in VoIP: MOS Levels

MOS	SPEECH QUALITY	LEVEL OF DISTORTION
5	Excellent	Imperceptible, toll quality
4	Good	Just perceptible, not annoying; toll quality
3	Fair	Perceptible, slightly annoying
2	Poor	Annoying but not objectionable
1	Unsatisfactory	Very annoying, objectionable

Table 3.3   Effect of Packet Loss on MOS

CUMULATIVE PACKETS LOST	MOS
1	4.2
2	3.2
3	2.4
4	2.1
5	1.7

Table 3.4   Voice Loss Objectives

QUALITY	SLAC CURRENT	SLAC ORIGINAL	ITU	MCI TRAFFIC PAGE
Good	0–1	0–1	<3	<5
Usable	1–2.5	1–5	<15	<10
Poor	2.5–5	5–12	25	>10

is not to drop them [Cottrell 1999]. In Table 3.4, SLAC figures reflect a current environment that includes IP telephony and X/Windows. They interpret the loss rate for VoIP by assuming the VoIP packets are spaced 20 ms apart, so 10 percent loss causes two consecutive frames to be lost approximately every 2 s, while 2.5 percent loss causes the same loss every 30 s.

VoIP runs over User Datagram Protocol (UDP). Vern Paxson was quoted by SLAC as giving the conventional wisdom that 5 percent loss rates have a significant adverse effect on standard TCP. Effects become significant for VoIP when the loss rate exceeds 3 percent.

First Class, Business, Economy, or Baggage?

I am the first to admit that much about air travel causes me to wonder if someone with a very sick sense of humor is designing that industry's business processes. For example, as I write these lines, I am making travel plans to go to the IETF meeting in London in about three weeks. It's a business-class ticket on United Airlines, in both directions, between the same two airports. Yet United insists I can have an electronic ticket in one direction but not in the other. Apparently, I am missing something.

Nevertheless, the airlines do have some useful things to teach us. One of them is to have a relatively small number of classes of service, but a very com-

Table 3.5   Classes of Service

APPLICATION	AVAILABILITY	LOSS	LATENCY	THROUGHPUT
Voice	High	Moderate (see Tables 3.2–3.4)	Very low (see Table 3.1)	Minimal
Broadcast video	High	Moderate	Very low	Very high
Mission-critical transactions	High	Low	Low	Low
General business	Moderate	Low	Moderate	Low
Bulk transfer	Moderate	Low	High	High

plex pricing system for standard packages. Because my employer has a bulk pricing contract with United I do not get to fly Virgin Atlantic with its in-flight massages.

To apply the airlines' concept, service providers should develop a relatively small number of standard services meant for different applications, using bulk pricing where appropriate (Table 3.5). Trying to set custom quantitative parameters for each customer, other than perhaps the very largest, will eat you alive in engineering costs.

Connectivity Policies 1: Load Sharing, Fault Tolerance, Multilinking, and Multihoming

When I worked as a government contractor, I learned that many of our procurement officers viewed their responsibilities in terms of not helping us carry out our mission, but of making sure that no one received one dollar more than their contract allowed. If it cost a million dollars to prevent such a shocking waste, that was in keeping with The Duty We Owed the Taxpayers. That mentality often carries into networking, where financial people want to be able to know who is responsible for transmitting every bit, so the costs of sending that bit can be charged back to the responsible organization. As with the government procurement people, it is irrelevant that the cost of microlevel accounting might be far greater than any possible costs to be charged back.

Yet another aspect of the bean-counter mentality applies when an organization has multiple transmission facilities. The principal purpose of having multiple facilities may have been to avoid a single point of failure, but the bean counters cannot tolerate the idea that a line is allowed to lie idle. They insist on

---

A WISE PERSPECTIVE

In his book *Computer Architecture,* Caxton Foster gives the best single metaphor I've ever seen for utilization. He invited an executive to look at the parking lot, filled with cars, and inquired if anyone was concerned about the utilization of those cars. Clearly, they were used perhaps 10 percent of the day.

The important thing was that the cars be available when needed. Being sure that bandwidth is available when needed is the first goal of deciding when redundant facilities are warranted. If the facilities are then loaded up to be always "doing something useful," then there is no spare capacity for contingencies.

"load balancing" among the various lines. Load sharing, a more accurate term in most cases, does have real technical merit. Load balancing implies something more precise, in which the amount of resource used is strictly controlled, regardless of the cost of such controls.

Connectivity Policies 2: Intranet, Extranet, and Internet—To Say Nothing of IPv6

To whom do your customers want to connect, and are they willing (or desirous) of having you control those connections? There are both performance and security reasons to have a private network, even a virtual private network. Whether or not that network is internally or externally managed is a business decision that reflects, in part, the technical capabilities of the customer. As a provider, you need to decide which of these markets you are in. Even if you are a traditional bandwidth provider, there is a good deal of evidence that IP VPNs are beginning to replace ATM and Frame Relay services. The VPNs tend to be more flexible and lower in cost.

There will certainly be a number of late adopters that continue to want frame or ATM, or that have equipment that requires those technologies. In many fields, there has been a profitable niche business servicing old technologies abandoned by the mass of service providers. So, your business decision as a service provider will be whether to offer VPNs, to offer bandwidth for VPNs (either to customers or resellers), or both.

Industry surveys have shown that the two major reasons customers choose to go with in-house VPNs are lower costs and better security control. You may be able to lower your costs, and thus prices, with economies of scale. Offering equivalent security, however, can be more subtle, and can be as much a matter of perception as of reality.

Customer Service

Providers really need to soul-search about how they want to present themselves to their subscribers and to partner providers [Berkowitz 2001b]. The result of such soul-searching is an understanding of how to set reasonable expectations. Chapter 6 deals with, among other things, implementing customer service; this discussion focuses on the philosophy involved. You may have multiple service offerings, but you must understand the customer types associated with:

- Minimal-cost residential/small office home office (SOHO) service
- Business SOHO
- Large-site service
- Hosting services

You must care for each of these customer types in accordance with the reasonable expectations of how the service is presented to the customer. For example, the customer that has bought a business-grade SOHO DSL service expects more responsiveness than the customer that buys a consumer-oriented service at a third the price.

Effective providers that avoid subscriber churn must provide their customers with a generally satisfactory experience that is at least perceived to be no worse than that provided by competitors. The customer experience begins with initial sales contacts and proceeds to the initial service provisioning and installation. Many adversarial relationships begin with provisioning and installation, especially in DSL environments, where it may be necessary to coordinate the activities of the ILEC, a DSL wholesaler, and one or more content providers.

Any service will have occasional failures. No reasonable customer fails to appreciate that reality. But profitable providers need to learn not to offend customers during problem reporting and resolution. As pricing moves higher and the promised service becomes more and more business-grade, there is an increasing perception that the provider needs to be proactive in customer support. Some of this may involve automated tools that look for trends that access links are becoming overloaded. Other aspects of proactivity include reasonable advance notices of planned outages.

Providers that track the quality of service delivery and make recommendations on it create win-win situations for customer and provider. Bandwidth utilization on access links is fairly easy to track and project. If the provider contacts the customer before overutilization imposes a performance penalty and explains that at current growth rates, the customer will experience problems in N months, the provider is in a good position to suggest and accept an order for additional billable bandwidth. Make this a low-key process and maintain the perception of cooperation rather than sales pressure. Bandwidth utilization, of course, does not solve problems of oversubscription. When resources are being committed on a multiuser basis, as might be seen with a VPN, oversubscription can be considered.

For the provider's own use, it is worth tracking customer downtime as well as the number of support requests placed by the customer and the typical response to them. Some customers may be experiencing excessive downtime but not reporting it, and thus may become increasingly frustrated. Others may be overwhelming the support staff with irrelevant queries, and the cost of supporting these customers may be more than it is worth.

The economics of supporting both consumer- and business-grade SOHO users can be complex. Competitive pricing simply may not be adequate for true business-grade support, and reasonable expectations need to be set. To deliver the actual support, providers need to search out support methods that are not labor-intensive. See Chapter 6 for more on customer support.

Representative Service Requirements

Examples given here will focus on IP services, but include situations that occur when the user wants the IP equivalent, in QoS and reliability, of a dedicated line. Once the problem statement is established, the initial characteristics of the solution need to be sketched out.

Case Study: Basic Internet Access: Huffle, Puffle, and Cetera

Huffle, Puffle, and Cetera, a law firm, wants unrestricted access to the public Internet for its staff librarians and its 100 attorneys. Since the firm's practice includes workers' compensation, employees occasionally need to download large medical graphics files or video files documenting accidents. While the firm has no complex routing requirements, one partner has experimented with the Internet for years, and obtained a /24 allocation for the firm. The security policy is fairly simple. No outside users are entitled to use any server at the law firm, other than to send it e-mail. There will be some secure communications, but they will be a host responsibility. There is a public Web server, but it is guest-hosted by the firm's ISP (see Figure 3.4).

The firm wants "decent" reliability, but can tolerate outages of general Web connectivity lasting up to a day, and outages of the mail system for up to 2 hours. The major concern is getting more bandwidth for image files (see Figure 3.5). In addition, the firm wants to join an extranet operated by a legal service firm in Hawaii, which is doing an excellent business of giving East Coast law

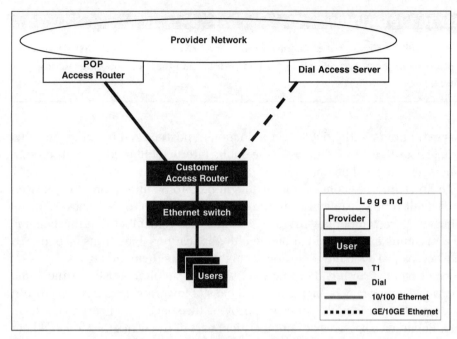

Figure 3.4 Current network of Huffle, Puffle, and Cetera.

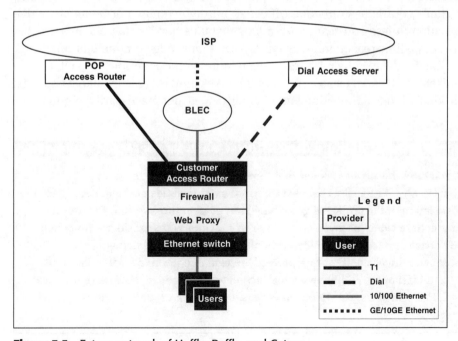

Figure 3.5 Future network of Huffle, Puffle, and Cetera.

KEY TO THE SOLUTION

This is really a simple set of requirements. Don't overcomplicate it. Just because optical technology can deliver gigabits doesn't mean that the customer needs them.

---

firms extra hours in the day to get a document postmarked by midnight. This extranet uses IPSec tunnels across the public Internet, but recommends its subscribers have more than one point of connection to the Internet.

The firm's Internet connectivity would appear to be little more complicated than default routes. You will want to monitor bandwidth to see that it remains adequate. Do remember law firms *love* to sue. Also remember that this client is not yet running extremely high-bandwidth applications. Law firms also love to sue when you've oversold them something that costs them money.

Since several firm members may be working simultaneously on the same case, web caching may be an attractive means of lowering upstream bandwidth requirements while simultaneously improving the speed of delivery to the local users. Public web services are not a critical part of the firm's mission and lend themselves to being outsourced. The main role of the firewall is to protect inside users from the outside when inside users browse the Internet.

Will there be a reason for the firm to investigate VoIP? Perhaps the most common reason for initial use of VoX applications is interoffice communications, and Huffle, Puffle has only one office, so pure voice may not be an attractive application unless you team with a long-distance carrier that accepts VoIP. A more compelling reason to investigate VoIP is facsimile communications. A fax often can be delayed by minutes or even hours without serious impact, and an intelligent VoIP service can defer sending faxes until there is available capacity. This kind of fax application, incidentally, does not necessarily require any

---

CONVENTIONAL AND UNCONVENTIONAL WISDOM ON FACILITY GROWTH

If you have the slightest belief that the client's bandwidth will grow significantly, it's usually cheapest to install extra facilities at the initial service installation. If the projected growth will not go over three to four T1s, run the appropriate cable for inverse-multiplexed T1. Otherwise, consider a fractional T3 service or dark fiber. Optical technologies, however, are changing the economics involved. It may be perfectly reasonable to run a small number of T1s. But if it appears that new construction will be needed, be sure that optical facilities, which can run T3 but have far more growth capability, will be installed.

LAWYERS DO IT IN COMPLICATED WAYS

Huffle, Puffle is located in a large office building. You have just learned that a specialized building local exchange carrier (BLEC) is planning to offer LAN-based connectivity in this building, which, for digital services, may be quite price-competitive with T1 services. The BLEC will have at least 1 Gbps and probably 10 Gbps capacity leaving the building, with capability for expansion using wavelength-division multiplexing (WDM).

This new service is just that: new and operationally unproven. It may, however, become very attractive. Be sure any routers you install have extra Fast Ethernet interfaces for WAN connectivity so they can make use of this service.

change in the analog or digital facilities leaving the premises. The server simply applies its intelligence to placing calls when capacity is available.

In planning the growth policy, understand the nature of voice performance requirements. While modern VoIP does not have high bandwidth requirements, it still has to be engineered to minimize delay. If videoconferencing becomes an issue, even more symmetrical bandwidth may be needed.

Table 3.6 sums up the firm's requirements.

Table 3.6 Summary of Requirements for Huffle, Puffle, and Cetera

Address space	Provider-independent	
Name and address management	Customer-operated DHCP	
	Provider-operated DNS	
L1/2 connectivity	Primary	T1 to POP
	Backup	Multiple dial backup for mail service (cellular available)
		Dial-up for workstations
Routing requirements	Advertise all to provider	
	Accept default from provider	
Midbox requirements	Performance-enhancing web cache	
	Firewall	

Case Study: Multihoming to Multiple POPs

Design and Dig, a design and build construction firm with four sites spread across several states, wants to reduce its network costs. Since the firm grew rapidly from mergers rather than by local expansion, the states are scattered across the country. The managing partners of all of the previous companies knew one another in architecture school. They have an existing IP network without Internet connectivity (see Figure 3.6).

The firm has an excellent reputation for its designs and the buildings it constructs. Part of its success has been based on an internally developed collaboration system that the partners want to start marketing as a service to their industry. They do not consider networking to be a core competence, only the applications running on their network. They want the provider to do most network management, and are willing to renumber into provider space to facilitate this. They insist that the renumbering effort create a renumbering-friendly environment so they can make future changes with ease [RFC 2072]. The provider is expected to manage access and firewalling to the servers of the collaboration service. The provider will also manage the switches in each office, assigning ports to internal-only, internet-capable, and VoIP categories.

Since the company's collaborative system uses computer-assisted design among their architects, the partners are concerned with bandwidth. The cur-

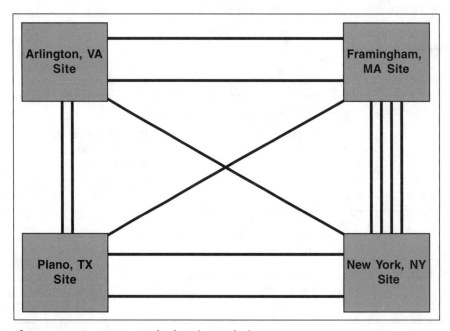

Figure 3.6   Current network of Design and Dig.

rent network has a full mesh of inverse-multiplexed T1 lines. Many of the sites using multiple T1s are using four or more, which approaches the break-even point for T3 facilities. New economics, however, affect this choice. If there are T3 optical facilities that will support WDM, the decision fairly clearly is to leapfrog T3 and probably go to Gigabit Ethernet, with the option of 10GE (see Figure 3.7).

The partners want to evolve to an intranet which will lower their long-haul communications costs. Since they are quite geographically dispersed, they want multiple points of connection to the Internet. The principal reliability concern is with their intranet. Each office does not need its own Internet connection, but it does need redundant communications to the service provider. Due to the partners' emphasis on a single point of contact for their intranet, they are quite willing to work with a single service provider, as long as that service provider can demonstrate extensive and reliable national connectivity. They understand that ensuring diverse facilities inside the carrier will involve extra cost, which they will pay—but they also want to be able to monitor the carrier's compliance. Table 3.7 summarizes the firm's requirements.

Voice over IP between the offices has some attraction to the firm, but is not a crucial requirement since most offices manage their own projects. The moderate-term bandwidth requirement leaving the offices is on the order of 10 to 20 Mbps.

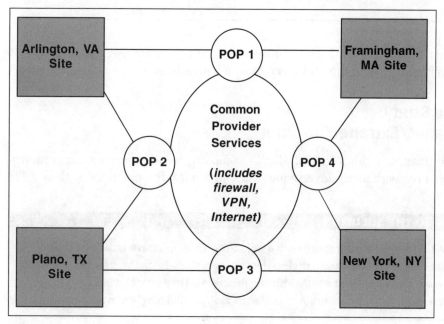

Figure 3.7 Future network of Design and Dig.

Table 3.7 Summary of Provider Requirements for Design and Dig

Address space	Provider-assigned	Individual sites have /22. Provider will aggregate to /20 and advertise to multiple points of connection to Internet.
Name and address management	Backup to customer DNS	
	Outsourced VPN management	
L1/2 connectivity	Primary	Multiple T1 or faster to primary POP InMux?
	Backup	Multiple T1 or faster to secondary POP InMux?
Routing requirements	Advertise preferred routes to primary POP, less preferred backups to secondary POP	
	Accept explicit routes to intranet and extranet locations; otherwise default	
Midbox requirements	Performance-enhancing web cache	
	Firewall	Provider-operated and redundant.

What should be the interior routing policy of the enterprise, and how should it advertise routes to the provider? At which locations?

Case Study: Intranet/Extranet/Internet

Magic Images, a video special effects company, began operations in a metropolitan area with many advertising firms, which it interconnected with an ATM

KEY TO THE SOLUTION

The client is most concerned with availability. They will have growing requirements for VPNs, and, given their potentially graphics-intensive business, are apt to grow significantly in bandwidth requirements. They do not want to manage the details of their network and prefer to work with a single service provider.

network. Prior to the firm offering this service, production studios had to send disks by motorcycle courier to the special effects house, pausing production while the special effects work was done.

Production studio time is expensive, but it is even more expensive to split up the production of a graphics-intensive commercial into several pieces that end whenever material is sent to the video specialist. Splitting the work would involve charges for setting up and tearing down the studio for each time segment. It is generally more cost-effective to let the actors enjoy the very plush buffet while video production progresses.

Avoiding the 15- to 30-minute courier delay was immediately attractive. When both the courier delay and the delays associated with copying material to removable storage disappeared, directors often gained even more efficiency, because it became convenient to have special events work done on much smaller pieces of work.

Broadcast-quality video is extremely graphics-intensive. The initial bandwidth between the studios and the special effects houses was at OC-3 (155 Mbps), but it was very clear that bandwidth requirements would continue to increase. Directors often wanted to send the output of multiple cameras, and send it at higher-than-broadcast-quality resolution. These OC-3 links provided ATM virtual circuits, not IP routing, and needed substantial manual provisioning. Given that multiple studios fed into the main special effects facility, the link from the local provider to the switch at the main facility was OC-12.

The service saw potentially contradictory issues in its growth. First, it was very clear that it could use all the bandwidth it could get. Second, the industry in its area did not work around the clock, but there were other potential concentrations of customers—California's Hollywood, India's Bollywood (Ramoji Film City, near Hyderabad), New York's Madison Avenue, Tokyo's animation studios, and Toronto's television production—around the world, in different time zones. Because Magic Images knew how to implement an ATM layer 2 network, it cloned its environment to the other major cities, with an OC-12 to each, adding OC-12 links to the main site (see Figure 3.8). With a worldwide network, very expensive video production equipment could be used around the clock. It was probably reasonable to put certain services in each major city, and for each city to have its own set of workstations. Not having to duplicate the most expensive equipment could tremendously reduce costs, as long as the long-haul bandwidth cost did not remove the profits.

Some of Magic Images' clients collaborate with one another as well as with Magic Images. Magic Images has set up LAN emulation systems for these trust relationships, as shown in Table 3.8. Note that a studio, such as LA-2, can belong to more than one cooperative group. Group 4 involves collaboration with competitors of Magic Images, who do not have Magic Images' networking skills but have unique video processing capability. Magic Images may have a

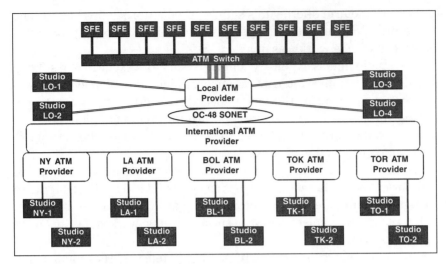

Figure 3.8 Current network of Magic Images.

business opportunity to provide communications outsourcing to its production competitors for which communications is not a core competence.

In the long term, Magic Images actually needs several kinds of worldwide networks (see Figure 3.9). It needs Internet connectivity to advertise its services. It needs an intranet to coordinate the use of its own resources. We will refer to the address space used for the intranet as VPN1. (See the discussion of VPNs in the next chapter.) Both at its own site and at customer facilities, Magic Images will not replace its ATM equipment overnight. There must be a transitional period where both ATM and Ethernet interfaces are supported (see Figure 3.10). Magic Images can, however, take advantage of new-generation optical switching in the metropolitan and long-haul environments.

A variety of security concerns affect Magic Images. It operates its own firewall at the main site for its general Internet traffic, but conventional firewalls would have difficulty operating at the graphic application speeds, and in any case may be more general than what the quite specific applications need. One way of accomplishing the security goals for video may be to have multiple

Table 3.8 Studio Groupings

Group 1	NY-1, LA-2, TO-3, LO-1
Group 2	LA-1, LA-2, TO-1
Group 3	BL-1, TK-1, LO-4
Group 4	LO-2, NY-2, Demonic, Angelic

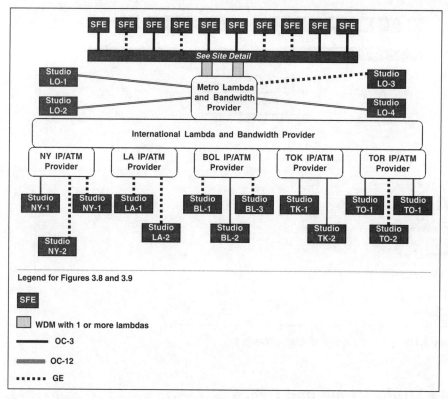

Figure 3.9   Future network of Magic Images.

address families within the overall VPN architecture—essentially having multiple independent extranets within the structure. For purposes of this example, we will assume that VPN1 is the intranet, that VPN2 through VPN4 correspond to groups 1 through 3, that VPN5 is the potential offering to Demonic and Angelic, and that individual VPNs can be set up for the individual studios that simply want to communicate with Magic Images.

For the provider, the immediate concerns are providing large bandwidth, with lots of capacity for growth, in metro areas and between metro areas. Short-reach/metro optical systems may be justified very early in the process. For long-haul operations, the firm might lease high-bandwidth links and operate its own routers, or may collaborate in provider-operated broadband video services. While security is indeed a concern, encryption hardware that operates at these high speeds may be prohibitively expensive. Television scrambling schemes do not have the overhead of strong encryption systems such as IPSec with triple Data Encryption Standard (DES), generally the industry standard for financial data.

Table 3.9 summarizes Magic Images' requirements.

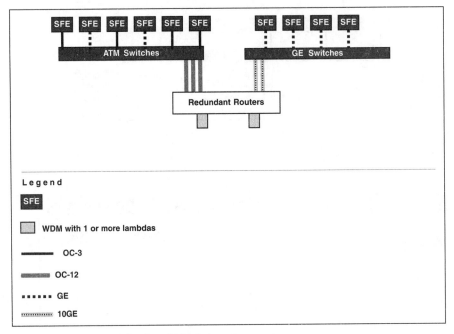

Figure 3.10 New main site of Magic Images.

Case Study: Home and Office Internet, Cooperating Local ISP and Content Providers

In the lovely town of Johnson City, advanced communications began with the city-operated cable TV system, which initially delivered only video content. Johnson City loved video, however, and the system soon began offering both locally produced content and commercial pay-per-view services. It expanded its offerings to include Internet connectivity.

Johnson City is in a remote rural location, with scenic beauty not financially attractive to national-level providers. As is not unprecedented in a rural area, it does have a major hospital, and various research organizations have spun off from the hospital. The Johnson City Medical Center's (JCMC's) information technology department (JMedNet) first provided intranet and internet services

KEY TO THE SOLUTION

It's going to be hard, in the long term and assuming success, for this firm to have too much bandwidth. Aggressive movement to fairly bleeding-edge optical technology is appropriate.

Table 3.9 Summary of Requirements of Magic Images

Address space	Provider-independent public space plus multiple VPNs	
Name and address management	Backup DNS, including VPNs	
	Customer-managed addressing	
L1/2 connectivity	Primary	Currently OC-12 to POP; GE or faster desirable. Optics should support OC-192 and/or DWDM
	Backup	Diversely routed link to alternate POP, preferably using fiber, but will consider OC-12 wireless
Routing requirements	Advertise public routes and VPN to provider	
	Accept default and VPN routes from provider	

to the Medical Center proper, then to the related researchers, then to suppliers, and eventually offered commercial services in the Medical Center area. Most of the subscribers are on dedicated fiber within a short distance of the JCMC campus, with a few free-space radio and laser links (see Chapter 8).

Once the cable TV system became profitable, the city spun it off into a not-for-profit community service, Johnson City Cable (JCC). Again, the remoteness of Johnson City dissuaded large local providers from chasing the local user base.

JCC provides IP access to its residential cable subscribers, and also handles dial-up connectivity for regional subscribers not in a cable-served area, or when cable is down. It contracts with the local telephone company to provide dial servers in remote areas, which, due to regulatory restrictions, only provide PPP connectivity; the actual IP session is between a client associated with the dial-up port and a server at JCC (See Chapter 7).

Johnson City now has two Internet service providers, each with a particular niche and generally cooperative with one another. JCC focuses on residential and SOHO applications, while JMedNet focuses on the larger commercial sites (see Figure 3.11). Both systems have policies of open access on their collector networks, but outside providers have shown little interest. As a cable TV provider, JCC does have an assortment of satellite earth stations, and has high-bandwidth downlinks and a moderate-bandwidth, high-delay uplink.

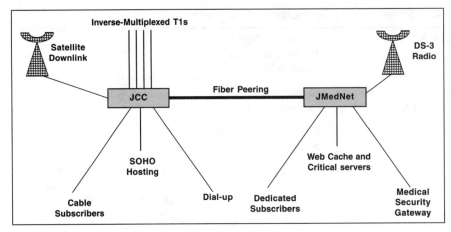

Figure 3.11 Current network of Johnson City.

The Johnson City Medical Center Foundation has received a large grant to improve communications in the area. As an interim step, the Medical Center has been connected to a DS3 microwave system leaving the area, and has received permission to allow commercial users on this system until other facilities are available. After alternative commercial facilities are available, the microwave system will stay in place as a backup for medical, research, and educational use. Communities (see Chapter 5) will be used to enforce acceptable use policies (see Figure 3.12). The city sees one of the fundamental aspects of that improvement to be connecting the external gateways to transcontinental, redundant optical facilities. SONET is one possibility, but IP over optical to dif-

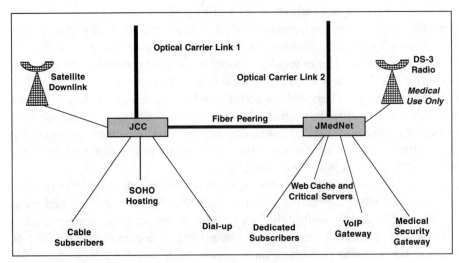

Figure 3.12 Future network of Johnson City.

Table 3.10 Summary of Johnson City Requirements

Address space	Separate blocks for JCC and JCMC	
Name and address management	JCC and JCMC handle their own addressing	
	JCC and JCMC want backup provider DNS	
L1/2 connectivity	Primary	T3 or better to POP from both using diverse connectivity
	Backup	Mutual backup between JCC and JCMC
Routing requirements	Advertise assigned space and provider-independent customer space to provider	Advertise selected routes as belonging to medical community
	Accept default from provider, with medical community routes preferred for JCC	

ferent hubs also is a possibility. The city also wants to explore cost-effective ways to bring broadband service to the more remote POPs. These will generally be beyond the range of free-space optical, and it may be worth considering radio systems rather than pulling fiber.

Table 3.10 summarizes Johnson City's requirements.

KEY TO THE SOLUTION

Take advantage of the cooperative nature of the local service providers, and be sure you take solid advantage of mutual backup and the specialties of each.

Looking Ahead

In the next chapter, we will begin translating these functional/business requirements to technical policies. Those policies, in turn, will be the basis for specific network design.

CHAPTER

4

Translating Service Definitions to Technical Requirements: Policies

Bad administration, to be sure, can destroy good policy; but good administration can never save bad policy.
—Adlai Stevenson

Advertising, in the final analysis, should be news. If it is not news, it is worthless.
—Adolph S. Ochs

The art of conversation is the art of hearing as well as being heard.
—William Hazlitt

Policies are formalizations of business goals and services in support of business goals. They bridge between business descriptions and the functional requirements for implementation discussed in subsequent chapters.

Two standards organizations, the ITU-Telecommunications sector (ITU-T) and the IETF, have been developing architectures that include policy. Their objectives have been slightly different, although I find them quite nicely complementary. The ITU Telecommunications Management Network (TMN) model, shown in Figure 4.1, starts with a top-down view of customer requirements and moves down in increasing detail until it deals with the configuration and control of specific network elements such as routers. In contrast, the IETF POLICY working group concentrates on a means of collecting and distributing policy information without specific reference to the content of that informa-

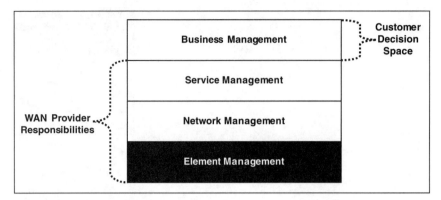

Figure 4.1   ITU TMN model.

tion. Policy rules reside in a repository and are distributed to policy enforcement points in real devices (see Figure 4.2). See the section "Service Level Policies" later in this chapter for an example of how this framework is used to distribute accounting policy. I find the two models can usefully be combined, as shown in Figure 4.3. The TMN model defines what is to be distributed and the POLICY model gives a framework for how it is to be distributed.

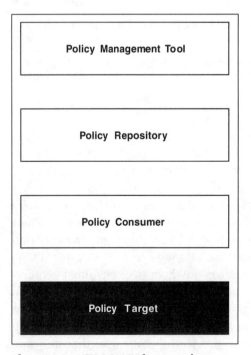

Figure 4.2   IETF POLICY framework.

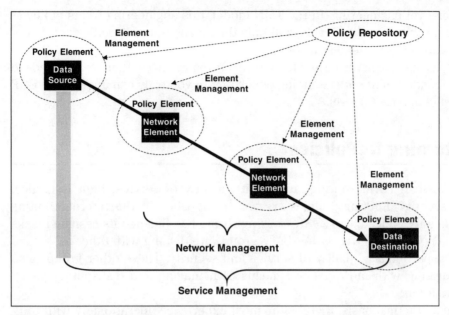

Figure 4.3 Combined TMN and POLICY.

The Delicate Balance: "But I Wanna Learn BGP!"

In this chapter, you will find that I walk a delicate line between the functionality of BGP for conveying policy-related information and the actual behavior of the protocol. This is deliberate; I am trying to defer the protocol discussion to Chapters 9 through 12. My personal experience was that I started learning BGP by studying the protocol handshakes and specific router configurations. While I was able to do a few "cookbook" things, I couldn't claim any real understanding until I began to study policy specification. At the time, the principal (and limited) policy specification technique was RIPE-181, which has been superceded by the Routing Policy Specification Language (RPSL) [RFC 2622]. RPSL itself continues to evolve.

Until rather recently, it was my claim that it was an urban legend that BGP transmitted actual policies. My claim, until recent extensions were made, was that BGP transmitted the information on which policy mechanisms inside routers could make policy decisions. These mechanisms were various combinations of pattern-matching rules (for example, filters) and actions to take when patterns were matched. The Outbound Route Filtering (ORF) extensions, introduced later in this chapter and discussed in subsequent chapters, actually exchange policy information. Until ORF was implemented—and it is still experimental and evolving—the implementation of policy began with higher-level engineering. In the TMN model, this engineering treats policy at the network or service levels, and only then maps it into specific router configurations at the element level.

So, have some patience and learn from my experience—there really needs to be a foundation of understanding policy before you truly can understand BGP specifics at a useful level.

Returning to Policies

Policies can cover routing, availability, quality of service, fault tolerance, and security. Routing policies are well established in the Internet routing community. Indeed, the RPSL Working Group has finished its assigned tasks and is no longer active. Other IETF groups are dealing with other aspects of policy, particularly quality of service and security. These other groups also are dealing with more general means of managing and distributing policy information.

On a practical basis, there is the most experience operationally with routing policies, specifically RPSL. Policies are defined with respect to individual autonomous systems. RPSL focuses on the interaction of individual AS with neighboring AS, and explicit AS-SETs made up of fixed entries. There are more complex ways to get it to work with less explicitly defined groups of ASs or groups of routes.

The sidebar shows some good and classic reasons for routing policy. Given a wider range of policy actions, additional reasons may begin to be implemented in future routers. These include security (both direct protection and detection of denial of service attacks) and advanced accounting and statistics.

RPSL is not a programming language, although router configuration language can be generated from it. Its purpose is to give network operators a formal means of specifying routing policies at different levels of the Internet. Its flexibility allows it to be meaningful at the levels of sets of ASs, of individual ASs, and of routers in an AS. It is an extensible language to which new capabilities can be added. Briefly, RPSL is the replacement for less flexible languages with the same general functions, including RIPE-81 and RIPE-181. It is an object-oriented lan-

RPSL IS EXTENSIBLE

The charter of the RPSL Working Group specifically was developing a language to describe routing policy in the public Internet. The language itself, however, is designed to be extensible. Some applications of RPSL that simply were out of scope for the Working Group include interior routing and routing policy for VPNs, both intranet and extranet, with potentially overlapping address spaces.

REPRESENTATIVE NEEDS FOR ROUTING POLICY

Juniper suggests several basic reasons for implementing a routing policy:

- You do not want a routing protocol to transfer all its routes into the routing table. If the routing table does not learn about certain routes, they can never be used to forward packets and they can never be redistributed into other routing protocols.

- You do not want a routing protocol to advertise all the active routes learned by that protocol.

- You want a routing protocol to receive active routes learned from another routing protocol. This is sometimes called route redistribution.

- You want to set the information associated with a route, such as the preference value, AS path, or the BGP community.

- You want to define BGP damping parameters.

- You want to perform per-packet load balancing.

guage that allows configurations to be generated for the policies of an AS and its constituent routers. RPSL operates in the context of a global routing policy system, which can include abstractions of relationships over classes of multiple ASs. Its outputs are not limited to router configuration; it also provides the information base for many troubleshooting and research tools, including tools that can examine proposed policies before they enter the routing systems and detect problems before they occur. It can be used to identify opportunities for better internet scaling, such as the potential for aggregating addresses, although this remains partially an area for research.

Routes are the elementary objects that routing policies control. Routes are supersets of IP prefixes in that they contain a prefix but also have additional attributes. In the context of BGP, prefixes are called *network layer reachability information* (NLRI).

A route in an interior routing table will have, at the very least, a next-hop attribute. If it is other than a static route, it will usually have a metric. Exterior routes, however, have variable numbers of attributes. They have no single "best" attribute in the sense of a metric, but carry multiple attributes that are used in a complex route selection algorithm (See Chapter 9).

Each AS has a set of advertising policies and a set of acceptance policies. Advertising policies specify the destinations for which the AS will accept traffic with the implied promise of best effort. Acceptance policies identify the destinations about which the AS is willing to learn, and to which it can send traffic. Obviously, there must be a certain symmetry between the policies of a pair of ASs for any traffic to flow between them.

There's a very common misconception about BGP: "BGP transmits policies." No. What BGP actually transmits is the information on which policy routing decisions can be made inside routers, although ORF has started to change this. See Chapter 9 for details on the BGP messages.

Policy Notation with RPSL

RPSL is the only standards-based routing policy notation. Tools have been written to generate specific router configuration statements from it. This discussion of notation is not intended as a complete tutorial on the languages involved. Rather, it is intended to give a sense of their capabilities.

Information flow in RPSL is defined with respect to *peering specifications*. Most often, peering specifications are of the granularity of AS to AS. They can, however, be refined to information flow at specific router interfaces, or broadened to define policy to multiple ASs. The most general form of the peering specification allows the possibility of exchanging information between routing protocols, although BGP is the default.

The full power of import and export expressions involves the capability of interacting among different routing protocols, not just BGP. Following is an example of import peering expression from the RPSL specification.

```
import: [protocol <protocol-1>] [into <protocol-2>]
            from <peering-1>
             [<router-expression-1>]
             [at <router-expression-2>] |
               <peering-set-name> ]
             [action <action-1>]

             . . .
            from <peering-N> [action <action-N>]
            accept <filter>
```

Most often, the <peering> will be an AS number, but it can be as coarsely grained as an AS-SET or as fine-grained as a link between two specific router interfaces. Formally, an <as-expression> is:

```
<as-expression> [<router-expression-1>]
                [at <router-expression-2>]
             | <peering-set-name>
```

<router-expression-1> defaults to all routers of all the peer AS, while <router-expression-2> defaults to all routers of the local AS. Adding filters to the peering specification defines which routes are accepted from the peer or advertised to it, such as accept {192.0.2.0/24}.

Actions specify additional things to do while importing (for instance, setting local preference) or exporting [for example, setting the multi-exit discriminator

(MED) or prepending to the AS path]. See "Influencers of Route Selection" later in this chapter.

RFC 2622 gives the following example:

```
aut-num: AS1
import: from AS2 accept AS2
export: protocol BGP4 into RIP
        to AS1 announce ANY
```

In the following example, AS1 injects its static routes (routes that are members of the set AS1:RS-STATIC-ROUTES) to the inter-AS routing protocol and appends AS1 twice to their AS paths.

```
aut-num: AS1
import: protocol STATIC into BGP4
        from AS1 action aspath.prepend(AS1, AS1);
        accept AS1:RS-STATIC-ROUTES
```

AS Expressions

AS expressions define one or more ASs as the object of the export or import clause. Single ASs, of course, can be specified by their number. You can also define symbolic names for ASs, or sets of ASs. For individual policy expressions, you can combine unitary and set AS information with the Boolean operators AND, OR, and EXCEPT.

DEFINING RPSL SETS

It's easy to define sets in RPSL. A basic AS-SET, for example, is defined as:

```
as-set: AS-FOO
members: AS2, AS3
as-set: AS-BAR
members: AS4, AS5
```

You can define sets recursively:

```
as-set: AS-FOOBAR
members: AS-FOO, AS-BAR
```

AS-SETs are not the only kind of set you can define, and you can use recursion for each type.

ROUTE-SETs include multiple prefixes. A fairly complex example is the peering set:

```
peering-set: prng-bar
peering: AS1 at 9.9.9.1
peering-set: prng-foo
peering: prng-bar
peering: AS2 at 9.9.9.1
aut-num: AS1
import: from prng-foo accept { 128.9.0.0/16 }
```

> **THE EXCEPT OPERATOR**
>
> **EXCEPT is the operator for set subtraction, and is equivalent to AND NOT. ((AS1 OR AS2) EXCEPT AS2), for example, equals AS1.**

Routes

Routes are a little more subtle than they first might appear. They will always contain a destination prefix, but also always contain the originating AS. Having at least these two components means that

```
128.9.0.0/16
origin: AS226
```

and

```
route: 128.99.0.0/16
origin: AS226
```

are two different routes. Table 4.1 shows additional elements that may be present in a route object. As well as being differentiated by their originating AS,

Table 4.1   Route Object

ATTRIBUTE	VALUE	TYPE
route	<address-prefix>	Mandatory, single-valued, class key
origin	<as-number>	Mandatory, single-valued, class key
member-of	list of <route-set-names>	Optional, multivalued
inject	See "Route Aggregation" in Chapter 5	Optional, multivalued
components	See "Route Aggregation" in Chapter 5	Optional, single-valued
aggr-bndry	See "Route Aggregation" in Chapter 5	Optional, single-valued
aggr-mtd	See "Route Aggregation" in Chapter 5	Optional, single-valued
export-comps	See "Route Aggregation" in Chapter 5	Optional, single-valued
holes	See "Route Aggregation" in Chapter 5	Optional, multivalued

routes can be treated differently at the finer granularity of routers in the local or an adjacent AS. Router expressions are used to specify such detail.

Ranges of Routes in RPSL

RPSL also has operators for specifying ranges of routes (Table 4.2). See Chapter 10 for examples of how these operators are used in real router implementations.

Route Sets, Communities, and Setting Attributes

Just as you created AS-SETs, you can create ROUTE-SETs. There are several dimensions to grouping routes. As mentioned earlier, you can specify routes as ranges.

RPSL route sets, like AS-SETs, either contain explicit route specifications or may recursively refer to other route sets. An important point, however, is that the ROUTE-SET is an abstraction. As such, it is not transmitted by routing protocols. Actually transmitted by BGP, however, is the *community attribute*. See Chapter 9 for details of the syntax and semantics of the actual protocol attribute, but, at this point, consider that there is a very strong relationship between the abstraction of a route set and the label of a group of routes transmitted as a

Table 4.2 IP Route Range Operators

RPSL OPERATOR	RPSL NAME	MEANING
	Exact match	Permit only 172.16.0.0/16, nothing longer or shorter.
^-	Exclusive more specifics	More specifics of an address, excluding the address itself. 172.16.0.0/16^- contains all more specifics, but not 172.16.0.0/16 itself.
^+	Inclusive more specifics	More specifics of an address, including the address itself. 172.16.0.0/16^+ contains all more specifics, as well as 172.16.0.0/16 itself.
^n	All length *n*	All length *n* specifics. 172.16.0.0/16^24 allows only /24 specifics of 172.16.0.0/24.
^n-m	All length *n* to length *m*	All length *n* to *m* specifics.

RPSL ACTIONS

The syntax of a policy action or a filter using an rp-attribute x is as follows:

```
x.method(arguments)
x "op" argument
```

**where method is a method and op is an operator method of the rp-attribute x.
If an operator method is used in specifying a composite policy filter, it
evaluates earlier than the composite policy filter operators (AND, OR, NOT, and
implicit or operator).**

---

community. RPSL allows communities to be set in announcements, which is our
first example of the ability to set attributes in RPSL.

Router Expressions and Peering Sets

Router expressions allow a finer level of granularity than do AS expressions.
They allow you to specify peering with respect to specific routers of another
AS, rather than simply at the granularity of the entire AS. As with AS expressions, you can combine router IP addresses, symbolic names of routers (that is,
instances of the INET-RTR class), and sets of routers (that is, instances of the
RTR-SET class) with AND, OR, and EXCEPT. Router expressions are optional.
If you do not specify a router expression, the policy will apply to every router in
the other AS. You have the options of intermediate granularities—specifying
the behavior of a subset of your routers to all routers at the other AS, or specifying the policy of all of your routers with respect to certain routers of the other
AS. If a <peering-set-name> is used, the peerings are listed in the corresponding
peering set object. Note that the peering set objects can be recursive.

Here are some examples from RFC 2622, using the topology in Figure 4.4.
7.7.7.1 and 9.9.9.1 are router interfaces in AS1. 7.7.7.2, 7.7.7.3, and 9.9.9.2 are
router interfaces in AS2, and 9.9.9.3 is a router interface in AS3. EX1 and EX2
are neutral exchanges. In the first example, AS1, at its own router, accepts the
route 128.9.0.0/16 specifically from AS2 router 7.7.7.2.

```
aut-num: AS1
import: from AS2 7.7.7.2 at 7.7.7.1 accept { 128.9.0.0/16 }
```

Slightly more complex is the example when 7.7.7.1 imports 128.9.0.0/16 from
AS2 routers 7.7.7.2 and 7.7.7.3. Since 7.7.7.2 and 7.7.7.3 are both connected to
the same exchange fabric as 7.7.7.1, there is no need to specify the individual
router interfaces in AS2.

```
aut-num: AS1
import: from AS2 at 7.7.7.1 accept { 128.9.0.0/16 }
```

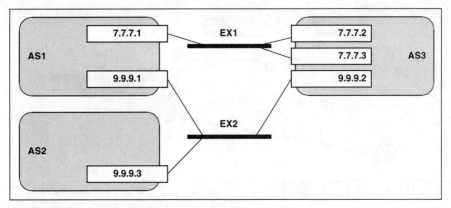

Figure 4.4 Reference topology from RFC 2622.

Influencers of Route Selection

BGP supports several attributes that influence its route selection algorithm, which is discussed in Chapter 9. We are concerned here with establishing the policies that set those attributes. Some attributes directly affect the probability of a route being selected as best. Other attributes, such as community, have multiple purposes, but may indirectly cause route selection attributes to be set. The distinction is based on scope of the attributes.

Local preference is one of the first factors considered in route selection, but its scope is that of the local AS. The multi-exit discriminator is defined with respect to multiple points of attachment to a single adjacent AS, although there are industry practices where it can be compared across multiple adjacent ASs. RPSL allows both local preference and MED to be set as actions:

```
pref = 10;
med = <positive-integer>;
med = igp_cost;   ! import metric from IGP
```

There is no generally accepted mechanism, however, for directly signaling route preference factors across nonadjacent ASs. While the idea of a destination preference attribute has been suggested many times, the reality is that all ASs in a path need to consent to the meaning of an attribute before its use is practical. ASs with no business relationship to the originator have no incentive to follow its preferences. See "Potatoes between Providers" in Chapter 10 for methods of coordinating multiple cooperating ASs.

A de facto means of influencing route selection is the length of the AS path, including techniques of artificially lengthening an AS path to make it less desirable.

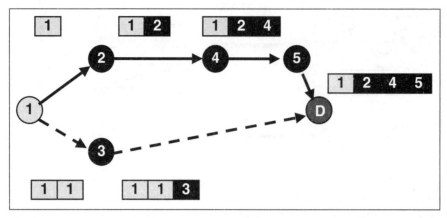

Figure 4.5   AS prepending.

AS Paths

One of the principal things associated with a route, and carried in the update, is a list of AS numbers between source and destination. Such a list is called an *AS path*. You might want to think of AS paths as having some similarity to the output of a traceroute, but as a list of ASs rather than of addresses.

Figure 4.5 shows how AS1 originates the advertisement, but each AS along the path prepends its AS number to the AS_PATH. In the most general sense, prepending, shown by the upper solid line in the figure, means that the AS inserts its own AS number in the AS_PATH, before the AS number that is currently first in the AS_PATH. Shown in the lower, dashed path of Figure 4.5, a more specialized meaning of AS path prepending is to prepend your AS number several times, which makes the AS_PATH less preferred than a shorter AS_PATH. RPSL allows the specification of AS path prepending:

```
aspath.prepend(AS1, AS1);
```

See Chapter 9 for more detail on the use of multiple prepended AS numbers, as well as the limitations of AS path prepending as a means of influencing route selection.

Routing policies are defined with respect to autonomous systems. In RPSL, an AS-object has the attributes shown in Table 4.3.

Policy and Ownership

An administrative structure is associated with the distributed routing registry that contains RPSL. This structure protects its integrity. Each AS object must first have a *maintainer* object with rights to modify policies. Human and cryptographic authentication procedures play roles in maintaining the integrity of main-

Table 4.3   RPSL AS Object

NAME	RPSL REPRESENTATION	CHARACTERISTICS
aut-num	<as-number>	Mandatory, single-valued, class key
as-name	<object-name>	Mandatory, single-valued
member-of	list of <as-set-names>	Optional, multivalued
import	import: <policy expression>	Optional, multivalued
export	export: <policy expression>	Optional, multivalued
default		Optional, multivalued

tainer objects. Maintainers may be organizational functions or specific people. Besides maintenance, there are additional functions associated with AS operations for which outside organizations may need to make contact. RPSL includes ways to identify both *person* and *role* objects. A person object is used to describe information about people involved in routing policy making and operations. Even though it does not itself describe routing policy, we still describe it here briefly since many policy objects make reference to person objects. The attributes of the person class and the complementary role class are shown in Table 4.4. The person attribute is the full name of the person. In contrast, the role object does not identify a specific person, but an organizational function involved in routing policy making or operations. Use of the role object allows continuity of operations while faced with the reality that people change jobs.

The Availability of Policies

The Internet Routing Registry (www.irr.net/) is a distributed database containing the published routing policies of ASs participating in the global Internet. The main European registry is at www.ripe.net (actually, this contains both address and routing registries). Specifically, irrd is a public domain set of routing registry tools (www.irrd.net/). Using irrd, you can set up a local mirror of the IRR on most UNIX boxes.

The actual routing table and the contents of the routing registries ideally should correspond fairly closely, but in the real world the routing registries tend only to be a subset of reality. That's quite unfortunate, because the registries are the only place where you can examine what people have defined as routing policies. Policies can only be inferred from the actual BGP table.

To complicate things further, many policies are considered sensitive proprietary information. This is most common in the bilateral peering arrangements of top-level providers, as distinct from what their announcements will be to

Table 4.4   Example of Person versus Role Object

PERSON OBJECT		ROLE OBJECT	
person:	Daniel Karrenberg	role:	RIPE NCC operations
address:	RIPE Network Coordination Centre (NCC)	trouble:	
address:	Singel 258	address:	Singel 258
address:	NL-1016 AB Amsterdam	address:	1016 AB Amsterdam
address:	Netherlands		The Netherlands
phone:	+31 20 535 4444	phone:	+31 20 535 4444
fax-no:	+31 20 535 4445	fax-no:	+31 20 545 4445
e-mail:	Daniel.Karrenberg@ripe.net	e-mail:	ops@ripe.net
nic-hdl:	DK58	admin-c:	CO19-RIPE
		tech-c:	RW488-RIPE
		tech-c:	JLSD1-RIPE
		nic-hdl:	OPS4-RIPE
		notify:	ops@ripe.net
changed:	Daniel.Karrenberg @ripe.net 19970616	changed:	roderik@ripe.net 19970926
source:	RIPE	source:	RIPE

their customers and at multilateral exchanges. Read the following extract from the IRR Web site at www.irr.net:

The Internet Routing Registry (IRR) is a next-generation database development effort with participants from many international networking organizations. Data from the Internet Routing Registry may be used by anyone worldwide to help debug, configure, and engineer Internet routing and addressing. Currently, the IRR provides the only mechanism for validating the contents of a BGP session or mapping an AS number to a list of networks.

The IRR emerged early in 1995, a time when providers worldwide were preparing for the end of the NSFNET Backbone Service and the birth of the commercial Internet. The IRR originally comprised five databases, including those operated by Merit, the RIPE Network Coordination Centre (NCC), ANS (now UUnet), internetMCI (now Cable & Wireless), and Bell Canada (formerly CA*net). There now are more than two dozen databases in the IRR.

Any ISP worldwide can register in the RADB's define RADB portion of the Internet Routing Registry. However, providers with access to a more local routing registry database are encouraged to use it instead.

Specifying Routing Policies and Actions

Just before delving into the formalisms of policy notations, it's worth thinking about the problems and solutions they solve. I like to think of the combination of matching conditions and actions as having a vague similarity to the "select one from list A and one from list B" of the classic Chinese-American restaurant, list A being the matching condition and list B being the action. Routing policy execution, however, is more complex than ordering Szechuan beef and shrimp in lobster sauce. A router of any substantial sophistication can execute more than one action per match, and it also may be able to combine matching expressions.

Let's consider a high-level view of a router and some of its components, which, for BGP, we will elaborate upon in Chapter 9. In Figure 4.6, all packets enter the router on an ingress forwarding card. Packets and events relevant to the control plane are diverted to a control engine. For this example, I will assume that the control engine is concerned with only one routing protocol, BGP.

There are two basic types of policies: *advertising* or *export* policies that define what information your AS will tell other ASs, and *acceptance* or *import* policies that specify what information your AS will accept from other, directly connected, ASs. Again, I cannot stress it strongly enough: Don't fall into the trap of thinking that the policies themselves appear in BGP protocol messages. What BGP carries is the information that is used by policy evaluation mechanisms inside your routers. ORF and some other newer mechanisms, however, do carry policies.

You can define policies at the granularity of the AS-SET, the AS, or the interface. Policy information can and should be stored in public (in the case of the Internet) databases called *routing registries*. This information can be used by an assortment of tools for network design and troubleshooting. See www.radb.net for tools.

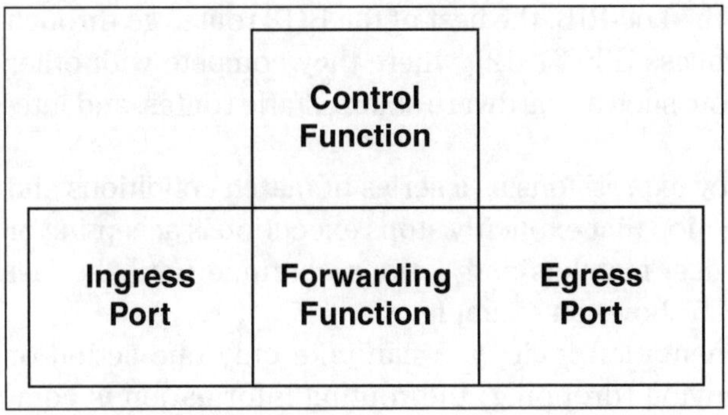

Figure 4.6 Conceptual router components.

Advertising/Export Policies

Advertising policies are the "don't ask, don't tell" of Internet routing. The way you prevent another AS from sending traffic to a destination that you can reach, but that you do not want that AS to reach through you, is not to tell that AS that you can reach the route. Even if your policy is to advertise a route, additional constraints apply before it will actually be advertised. The basic rule is not to advertise a route unless you know how to reach the next hop for that route. In other words, don't tell people that you can reach a route that is in your policy list, but that you actually don't know how to send to.

Advertising affects the way the world sees you/sends to you. Your advertising can be absolute or relative. Absolute advertising policies are the decisions to advertise or not advertise a particular route at all. Relative advertising policy manipulates various attributes of the announcement to make it more or less likely to be selected. The simplest way to state this, for non-transit ASs, is: Do not advertise any address that is not assigned to you by your ISP(s) or a registry. Transit providers may advertise addresses assigned to them, and also addresses that are assigned or otherwise valid for their transit customers. You should never advertise private address space, or address space that is associated with your internal network. It may be advisable to filter outbound packets, not just route advertisements.

For each neighbor, arriving routing updates are placed in the Adj-RIB-In, which may be a real memory structure or part of a more general table. Certain of those updates are not acceptable to the import policy and need to be dropped before they go to the next stage of processing, the Loc-RIB. Criteria for dropping them can include the prefix they carry, or other BGP attributes. The basic flow for current routers is Adj-RIB-In to Loc-RIB to main RIB, with distribution to the FIB, Adj-RIB-Out, and possibly additional tables concerned with security, accounting, and higher-layer processing. Other updates need to have attributes changed before they enter the Loc-RIB, which again may be a real or conceptual table. The Loc-RIB is the place where the BGP route selection algorithm, discussed in Chapter 9, is applied to routes that pass the import policy to find the "best" routes. From the Loc-RIB, the best of the BGP routes go through the main RIB installation process [RFC 1812], where they compete with other sources of routing information, such as hardware status, static routes, and interior routing protocols.

You can also think of policy expressions as a series of match conditions and actions on match. The only action that explicitly stops execution is accepting or denying the update. Otherwise, matches and actions continue until the last condition is reached. Table 4.5 shows an example.

Depending on the implementation logic, you can take only one action or take a series of actions. Denying (dropping) the routing information is commonly the only action taken. It is entirely common, however, to manipulate

Table 4.5 Ingress Routing Matching and Actions

SOURCE	MATCH	ACTION
Adj-RIB-In	ANY	ACCEPT | DENY
	Incoming interface	Set LOCAL_PREF
	AS path expression	Set MED
	Incoming MED	Delete community
	Community	Add community
	Next hop	Change next hop
	Origin code	Change origin
	Source address/prefix	set QoS
	Destination address/prefix	Aggregate prefix
	TOS or diffserv code point	

such things as communities and quantitative preference factors (for example, MED and local_pref). Setting QoS differs from other actions in that it establishes actions to be performed on routed traffic in the forwarding plane rather than on routing information in the control plane. See Table 4.6 for further information.

Table 4.6 Egress Routing Matching and Actions

SOURCE	MATCH	ACTION
Loc-RIB	ANY	ACCEPT | DENY
	Incoming interface	Set LOCAL_PREF
	AS path expression	Set MED
	Incoming MED	Delete community
	Community	Add community
	Next hop	Change next hop
	Origin code	Change origin
	Source address/prefix	Set QoS
	Destination address/prefix	Aggregate prefix
	TOS or diffserv code point	

General Route Installation

You can have policies that govern which updates enter the main RIB, both from the BGP Loc-RIB and from other sources of information. The basic rules for RIB installation are specified in [RFC 1812] and extended by most vendors.

Previously Unknown Route

First, when the routing table installation task receives a potential route, it will install it if the destination was not previously known. Not previously known means that the destination address matched no entry in the RIB (except for a default route, if present).

More Specific Route

If an existing entry matches the route, but is less specific, the route just received is added. Less specific means that the route in the RIB matches the destination with a lesser number of prefix bits than does the new route. Another way of putting this is that a more specific route has a subnet mask with more one bits: 255.255.0.0 is more specific than 255.0.0.0. For example, assume your routing table contains

```
10.0.0.0/8 (mask 255.0.0.0), outgoing interface S0
```

and the router receives

```
10.1.0.0/16 (mask 255.255.0.0), outgoing interface e0
```

The new routing table will contain

```
10.0.0.0/8    s0
   10.1.0.0/16  e0
```

Preference among Routing Information Sources

Most router vendors have preference factors that can be set among different sources of routing information. Cisco calls its preference an *administrative distance* (AD), which is an 8-bit number. The lower the administrative distance, the more preferable the source of information. Tables 4.7 through 4.9 show selected vendor preferences.

The basic rules for selecting routes are derived from specifications in [RFC 1812]. Most vendors have defined additional selection mechanisms, especially preferences among sources of routing information. Be aware that the additional

Table 4.7   Cisco Preferences among Sources of Routing Information (ADs)

SOURCE OF INFORMATION	DEFAULT AD
Directly connected	0
Static routes in the form interface-name	0
Static routes in the form next-hop-ip (can be manually set to 1–255)	1
EIGRP summary	5
External BGP	20
EIGRP	90
IGRP	100
OSPF	110
IS-IS	115
RIP	120
EGP	140
External EIGRP	170
Internal BGP	200
Floating static (less preferred than dynamic)	201–254
Untrusted	255

criteria for selection, particularly the preference given to different dynamic routing protocols, varies among vendors. A very common error, which I've committed many times, is forgetting that the specificity of the prefix is always preferred to the preference (administrative distance, in Cisco-speak) for the source of routing information. A summary route from the latest, greatest BGP implementation will be overridden by a RIP subnet route from an old UNIX box.

Standard BGP has no concept of multiple equal-cost paths to a destination; BGP will submit only one route to a destination to the route installation process. Metrics, therefore, will never come into play when deciding whether or not to install a route learned from BGP. Yes, there are BGP attributes called multi-exit discriminators (MEDs), which used to be called inter-AS metrics, but these are used internally by BGP route selection, not by the main route selection. Some router implementations have proprietary BGP equal-cost multipath methods for attempting load-sharing under very specific circumstances, but these are beyond the scope of this discussion.

Table 4.8 Bay RS Preferences

SOURCE	PREFERENCE
Route with highest preference value	1
Direct route with lowest cost	2
Lowest-metric OSPF intraarea route	3
Lowest-metric OSPF interarea route	4
Lowest-metric OSPF Type 1 external route	5
The BGP route with the highest LOCAL PREFERENCE value or the OSPF Type 2 external with origin of BGP and the lowest RIP metric	6
The lowest-metric RIP route or the OSPF Type 2 external with origin of INTERNAL and the lowest RIP metric	7
The static route with the least metric	8
The OSPF Type 2 external received from a Bay/Wellfleet router of RS 8.0 or earlier	9

Acceptance/Import Policies

As with advertising policies, you can make absolute or relative decisions on what routes you receive (see Table 4.10). These decisions can consider many factors, including the route itself and the source of the route. Some of the same principles apply to acceptance policies as well as to advertising policies. For example, never accept an advertisement that points to private address space. Many ISPs supplement BGP acceptance policies, which apply to the routing protocol, with more general routed packet filters at the ingress points at which customers access the ISP. RFC 2267 describes the practice of not accepting packets with source addresses that are not expected on the ingress point, and RFC 2644 provides additional protection rules. Policies can be applied to external advertisements as well as to received updates. In the BGP context, the policy rules are applied to the Loc-RIB before they reach the Adj-RIB-Out.

WHAT IS YOUR PATH?

The path you advertise is a path to you, and it is informational, not mandatory. Each AS in both directions makes decisions based on its local policies and the information it receives from all connected ASs.

Table 4.9 GateD Preferences

SOURCE	PREFERENCE
Direct connection	0
OSPF routes	10
IS-IS level 1 routes	15
IS-IS level 2 routes	18
Internally generated default	20
Redirects	30
Routes learned via route socket	40
Static routes from config	60
ANS SPF (SLSP) routes	70
HELLO routes	90
RIP routes	100
Point-to-point interface	110
Routes to interfaces that are down	120
Aggregate/generate routes	130
OSPF AS external routes	150
BGP routes	170
EGP	200

Table 4.10 Advertising Policies

SOURCE	MATCH	ACTION
Loc-RIB	ANY	ACCEPT | DENY
	Prefix expression	Set LOCAL_PREF
	AS path expression	Set MED
	Incoming MED	Delete community
	Community	Add community
	Next hop	Change next hop

Proprietary Policy Notations

Of the major carrier router implementations, Juniper's JunOS explicitly identifies the concept of a policy. Cisco's IOS certainly supports policies, but Cisco's configuration language does not include an explicit abstraction of routing policy. Indeed, what Cisco calls its policy routing feature is a quite specific mechanism that routes packets by considering source address as well as destination, and is intended primarily for enterprise routing. Juniper's JunOS makes policies much more visible than in Cisco's IOS. Juniper's key definitions [Juniper-RRP4.4] are as follows:

> When a routing protocol places its routes into the routing table, this process is referred to as importing routes into the routing table. Applying routing policy to routes being imported to the routing table allows you to control the routes that the routing protocol process uses to determine active routes.
>
> When a dynamic routing protocol uses the routes in the routing table to send a protocol advertisement, the protocol takes the route from the routing table, a process referred to as exporting routes from the routing table. Applying routing policy to routes being exported from the routing table allows you to control the routes that a protocol advertises to its neighbors. The process of moving routes between a routing protocol and the routing table always is described from the point of view of the routing table. That is, routes are imported into a routing table from a routing protocol and they are exported from a routing table to a routing protocol. It is important to remember this distinction when working with routing policy.

JunOS

JunOS has a specific policy construct that differs from RPSL, but has some of the same structured characteristics. Its syntax is consistent with the general JunOS style, which draws from FreeBSD UNIX configuration language. There are two primary ways to use policy with JunOS. Our principal focus here is on BGP acceptance and advertising policies. JunOS policy expressions, however, also can be used to control the exporting of routes out of the main RIB, into, for example, OSPF and ISIS. You write policies per routing protocol, using the policy-option construct. Most of the detailed policy matching and action conditions are in the policy-statement policy-name inside the policy-option structure, but are preceded by information about AS path, community, and damping.

```
policy-options {
  as-path name regular-expression;
  community name members [community-ids];
  damping name {
```

```
half-life minutes;
max-suppress minutes;
reuse number;
suppress number;
            }
policy-statement policy-name {
  term term-name {
    from {
      match-conditions;
      route-filter destination-prefix       match-type <actions>;
      prefix-list name;
          }
    to {
        match-conditions;
        }
      then actions;
              }
        }
prefix-list name {
  ip-addresses;
        }
```

Cisco: An Indirect Notation

Cisco's configuration language historically does not have an abstraction of policy. Policy is implicit in the filters, advertising rules, and so forth (see Figure 4.7). The original Cisco policy mechanism that applied to routing updates, as opposed to general packet traffic, was the distribute list (see Figure 4.8). Distribute lists are subcommands of the routing major command, and specify particular prefixes to accept or reject. Much more power was added with the route map (see Figure 4.9), which allows multiple actions to be taken on a routing update. While route maps are powerful and widely used, they still are what is effectively a programming language inserted into a hardware-oriented configuration language. The policy languages of all commercial router implementations require considerable expertise to use—expertise that simply may not be available. For the industry, longer-term solutions require more than productivity tools for experts. They also require tools that give limited capability to operators with limited experience. It may be reasonable to give a new operator a tool that allows a local customer to be multihomed, but it is not reasonable to give such an operator tools that can affect the global Internet. RPSL is a start on better tools, but there is no question that more work is needed. Since RPSL is object-oriented, it may very well be that computer-assisted software engineering (CASE) tools intended for object-oriented programming may be adapted to policy specification.

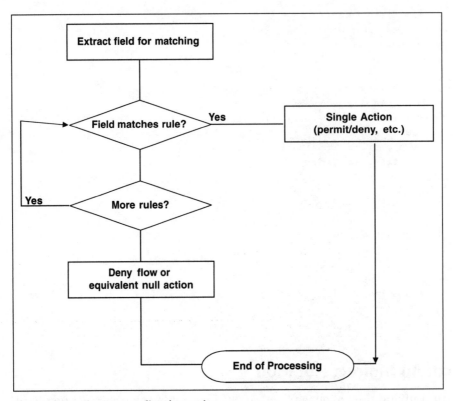

Figure 4.7 Cisco access list abstraction.

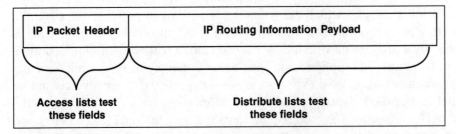

Figure 4.8 Cisco access versus distribute list abstraction.

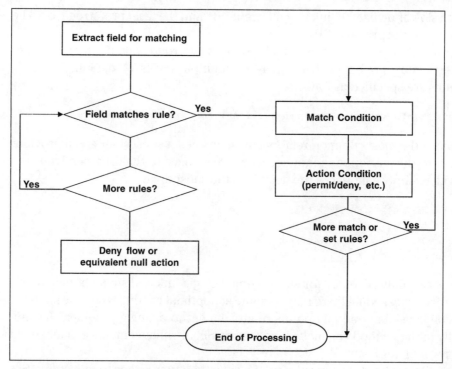

Figure 4.9   Cisco route map abstraction.

Representative Requirements for Routing Policies

Reasons for defining policies are often economic, reflecting the transit and peering relationships of the AS. They may be intended to enhance fault tolerance or load distribution for customers, or they may reflect external regulatory or legal requirements.

Defaults and Beyond

RPSL supports the notion of a default route, as do OSPF and ISIS. I like to think of default routes as somehow meeting Groucho Marx's criterion for joining private clubs: "I wouldn't join any club that would have me as a member." Less cynically, the default route is like an ancestral home, where you are always welcome. It is quite common to want to have a hierarchy of more and less preferred default routes. For example, the most preferred default might be to the ISP with which you have the fastest dedicated link; the next most preferred would be over a slower dedicated link to a different ISP; and the least preferred would be a dial-up to the primary ISP.

As mentioned earlier, the default route is the route taken when no other route is more preferred. There may be multiple levels of default. In RPSL, defaults are specified as follows:

```
default: to <peering> [action <action>] [networks <filter>]
```

One of the most common relationships between a subscriber and a provider is to have the subscriber announce its address space to the provider, while the provider simply announces the default to the subscriber.

```
aut-num:  AS1 ! the provider

aut-num:  AS2 ! the subscriber
default:   to AS1
```

This is certainly adequate for single-homed single-link and single-homed multi-link topologies. While there may be some suboptimal routing when the simplest version is used at multiple points of attachment to a single provider, the simplicity of the method can make it attractive. Slight enhancements can make the routing more efficient.

Default can be at the granularity of a specific router rather than just an AS:

```
aut-num: AS1
default: to AS2 7.7.7.2 at 7.7.7.1
```

You can, for example, set preferences among defaults. The lower the preference value, the more preferred the default.

```
aut-num: AS1
default: to AS2 action pref = 1;
default: to AS3 action pref = 2;
```

Multilinking and Multihoming

There really is no precise industry definition of multihoming, although work continues on creating one [Berkowitz 2001e; Black 2001]. Whatever it may be called, its major objectives are ensuring fault-tolerant connectivity and distribution of workload over multiple resources. Conceptually, multihoming can be implemented at almost any OSI layer, but we concentrate here on layer 3, with some discussion of layer 2.

You can have multiple physical links to the same service provider without BGP. When the multiple links go to the same ISP router, this is called *multilinking*. Multilinking can operate with layer 3 IP load sharing or with layer 2 techniques such as multilink PPP. The most common non-BGP approach is to use load-sharing default routes.

Case Study: Basic Internet Access: Huffle, Puffle, and Cetera

Returning to the case of Huffle, Puffle, and Cetera, the routing requirements are quite simple: The firm defaults to its ISP. It has multiple defaults, one over the T1 and a less preferred one over dial-ups. Since the firm has no independent routing policy, it does not need its own AS. Simply for convenience in the RPSL notation, however, I shall assign it the private AS number 64000. The AS that provides the connectivity, however, does need to advertise the firm's provider-independent /24.

```
aut-num: AS64000
default: to AS1 at T1-ROUTER action pref = 1;
default: to AS3 at PPP-ROUTER action pref = 2;
```

It's entirely plausible, for example, that Huffle, Puffle might use multiple T1 links to the service provider, inverse-multiplexed to appear as one link to routing. Of course, to get serious redundancy, the links would need to go by different physical paths that do not have significantly different delay (Figure 4.10).

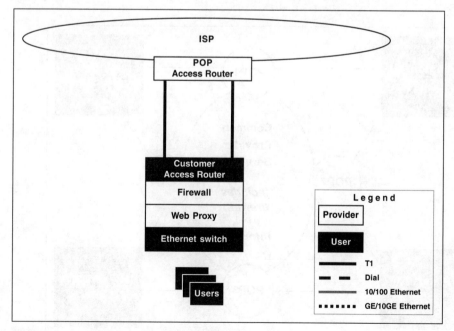

Figure 4.10 Multilinking at Huffle, Puffle, and Cetera.

In terms of general Internet routing policy, you are multihomed only when you have BGP peering with two or more ASs. Unless you are multihomed in this manner, the address registries will not assign you a registered AS number. There is a special case where you have BGP peering with more than one BGP speaker in the same ISP, as does Design and Dig in Figure 4.11. There is no definitive term to describe this method, although it frequently is called multihoming as well. Whenever you are not sure about the form of multihoming being discussed, be sure to determine which AS numbers with which you are peering.

When you have multiple connections to the same provider, and a large geographically dispersed network, it can be useful to run BGP to the ISP. As shown in Figure 4.12, you can multilink as well. BGP gives you the ability, in such cases, to tell your ISP of the best ways to reach certain destinations in your enterprise. The provider usually does not send this more detailed information to the Internet, because the rest of the Internet simply needs to know how to reach your single ISP.

Multihoming to Multiple POPs of a Single ISP

Increasingly, there is a partial exception to the rule that BGP is not useful when connecting to a single ISP. That exception exists when you connect to multiple

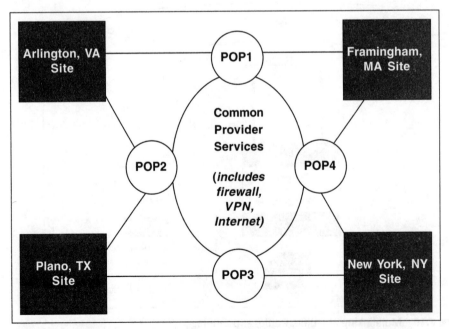

Figure 4.11 Design and Dig—multihoming without multilinking.

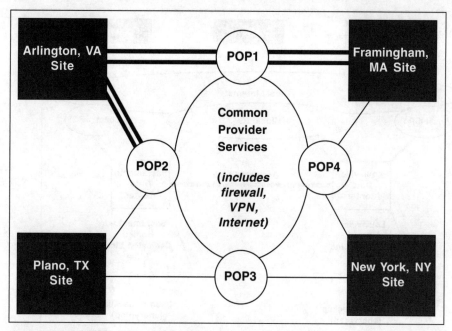

Figure 4.12   Multilinking and multihoming to a single provider.

physical routers in the ISP. It is a partial exception because even if you run eBGP, you are apt to use a private, not registered, AS number, which the ISP strips from the updates it sends to the outside, showing itself as originator. You can also use a private AS number when the addresses involved are lent to you by the provider, and only the aggregate containing your route and the routes of other customers of the ISP are advertised outside the ISP. Details of such multihoming are in Chapter 9.

One of the basic policies for multihoming to a single ISP, when the customer address space is assigned by that ISP, is described in [RFC 1998]. As shown in Figure 4.13, you export to the AS (presumably using a private AS number) the routes to which you prefer to sent at that point of route injection.

Case Study: Multisite Enterprise

With this in view, Design and Dig will need an intranet, an extranet, and Internet access. Again, for purposes of clarity in RPSL, the company will be assigned the AS number 64001, although it actually falls under the provider's routing policy. Due to the partners' concern with reliability of the intranet, each of their offices will have a link to a primary POP and a secondary POP of their provider. They will attempt a degree of load balancing by advertising their intranet address space with different preferences over the two links.

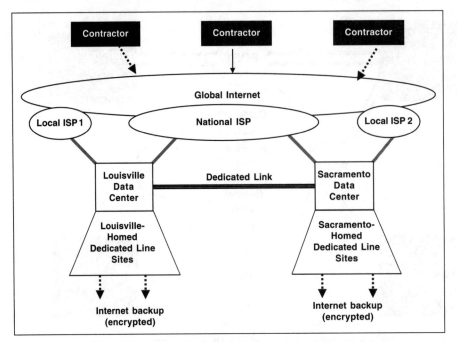

Figure 4.13   Complex enterprise multihoming.

The principle of this sort of route advertisement tends to seem very obscure, until you grasp it in a blinding flash of insight. Advertised routes are *attractors*. You advertise the route in the direction to which you want to attract traffic to that route. The advertisement is in the control plane; the traffic is in the forwarding plane. The exact techniques used to prevent the more specific internal routes from being exported to the general Internet will be discussed in Chapter 9.

Multihoming to Two ISPs

With respect to the public Internet, you are multihomed when you run BGP to more than one other AS. Multihomed ASs may be *transit* or *nontransit*. The vast majority of enterprise networks that run BGP to the outside are nontransit. For additional reliability, it is perfectly reasonable to combine multilinking, multihoming to multiple POPs of the same ISP, and multihoming to multiple ISPs.

Situations can exist where enterprises legitimately offer limited transit. They are not trying to be ISPs, but for various reasons may provide connectivity to partners. This is very common in higher education, where, for example, one campus of a state university may manage the primary connectivity for other campuses and junior colleges.

Enterprise-level transit also can have commercial applications, as shown in Figure 4.13. In this situation, there are two cases where the enterprise provides selective transit service. The first is for a manufacturing subcontractor that needs access to a second subcontractor on another continent. The main enterprise advertises the route of the second subcontractor to the first, and will not accept traffic from the first intended for any other destination. The second case involves an academic and industry cooperative research project. The enterprise is a large enough participant in the project to justify high-speed access to the dedicated research network. The acceptable use policy of that network allows only participants to access it. One of the enterprise's business partners has a limited involvement in the research project, but is too small to justify a direct connection. The enterprise has agreed to provide that partner with access to the research network through its direct connection. However, the enterprise will not go so far as to allow the partner to use the enterprise's commercial connection for backup connectivity. In other words, if the direct link to the research network goes down, the enterprise's internal researchers still will have access via the commercial ISP connection, but the business partner is on its own.

Figure 4.14 shows a situation where general Internet access is at one key corporate location, but there are special concerns for the Internet access of the corporate research lab. While this is the easiest topology to manage, it may or may

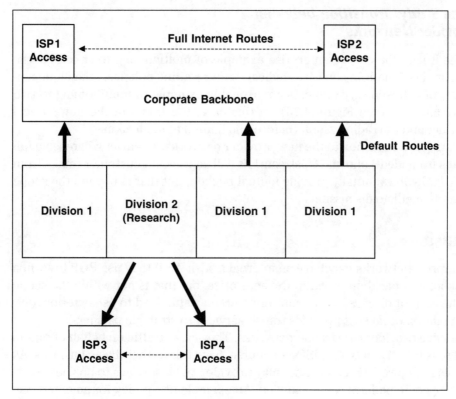

Figure 4.14 Geographically dispersed access.

not be desirable for companies that span large geographic areas, or where other factors are involved. In this case, the research lab has far more Internet experience than the operators of the corporate network. The enterprise has abundant bandwidth in the core, so while each division has multiple points of attachment to the core, the firm does not obsess about load balancing from each point. It simply makes sure that any one point of attachment can handle the load. As a result of the deliberate overprovisioning of bandwidth, the routing is fairly simple: Each divisional edge router, except for those that served the research division, announces the default route into the divisional area. The research division, however, accepts full corporate routes (with summarization) from the core, and generates its own default from its own Internet gateway. Careful filtering is used to ensure that the research default did not propagate into the core. In this manner, the research division knows how to reach intranet destinations, but defaults to its own Internet connectivity for destinations outside the enterprise.

There comes a time, however, when the designer must look at the complexity of such routing policies and ask if the enterprise is technically competent to manage them. If it is not, then an assortment of alternatives need to be considered, including outsourcing some of the management to an appropriate ISP or locating key services at a hosting center that does have the appropriate staff.

Case Study: Transition between Provider Networks

While it isn't the classic enterprise example of multihoming to two ISPs, the case study of the Johnson City Medical Center routing policies, taken independently of Johnson City Cable, is a reasonable example of multihoming to two upstream ISPs (see Figure 4.15). In this case, the ISPs are the new optical provider and the radio system (before it is limited to medical use).

During the transition to the new provider networks, JMedNet will receive full routes from MedRadio and Upstream1. It will also accept customer routes from JCC. JCC will eventually provide mutual backup, but that is beyond the scope of our immediate discussion.

Transit

Enterprise networks may have an internal transit AS if they use BGP to form a backbone of backbones within the enterprise, but that is not within the scope of the current discussion. An enterprise AS may still need to use exterior routing policies, because it provides transit services to strategic partners.

Service providers are transit networks. They carry traffic on behalf of others and pass it to the network. ISPs, of course, have this as their basic business. As shown in Figure 4.16, enterprises may provide transit services to business partners. Specific policies can be applied. An example of a policy for an enterprise transit AS would be that the AS will provide transit to the academic AS for its

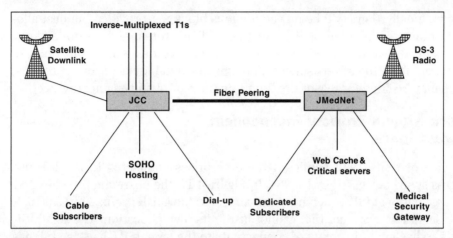

Figure 4.15   Multihoming to two ISPs: JMedNet in transition.

research partner and also for its internal researchers. If the AS link to the academic network fails, however, the enterprise will still route its internal researchers via the commercial ISP, but will not pay for the partner's access via the commercial ISP.

Transit with Provider-Independent Address Space

Transit is much less complex if all participants have provider-independent address space. In principle, all can advertise their allocated blocks to one

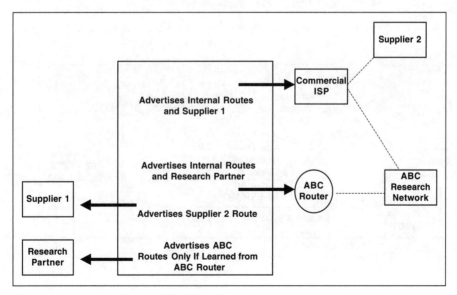

Figure 4.16   Enterprise providing transit.

another. Ideally, there will be one contiguous block per provider, but past allocation practices, mergers and acquisitions, divestitures, and so on, all may
cause a need to advertise multiple blocks. Such advertising of multiple blocks
is separate from the advertising of more specific sub-blocks of these prefixes,
which may be done for reasons of fault tolerance or traffic engineering.

Transit without Provider-Independent Address Space

The idea of transit still applies if the enterprises connected to the ISP use
address space delegated by the ISP. In Figure 4.17, the upstream provider AS1
is a large national ISP, which has been allocated the CIDR prefix 192.0.0.0/16. It
has a small ISP customer that cannot justify its own allocation. The small ISP,
however, has multiple points of connectivity to the large ISP. The large ISP has
assigned 192.0.2.0/22 to the small ISP, which in turn will assign pieces of this
space to its own customers. Also, AS1 has assigned a private AS number, 62222,
to the small ISP.

Assume that AS1 has numerous external peers, so it is immune to single failures of upstream connectivity, and it has an overprovisioned core, so there is no
real concern with AS62222 being load-balanced once its traffic is inside the AS1
core. Considering those factors, there is no reason that the more specific

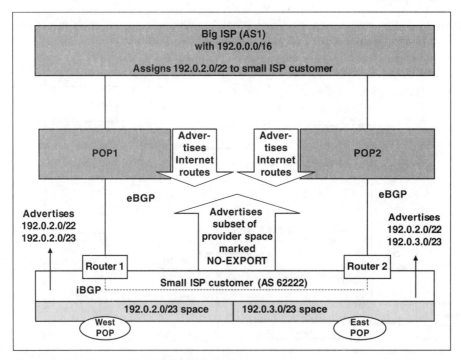

Figure 4.17 Transit with PA address space.

> ### THE OLD ONES AMONG US
>
> The provider for this example is hypothetical, but AS1 is assigned to Genuity, which traces its ancestry to BBN, GTE Internetworking, and so on, and has the motto, "AS1 and Proud of It!"

announcements of AS62222 need to be seen outside AS1. It will be more than adequate for AS1 to advertise its aggregate. The small ISP customers that are single-homed can use NAT to either POP. If a small ISP customer needs to dual-home, it can use an allocation from the east or west side of the small ISP, but will retain connectivity even if one of the small ISP's upstream connections fails.

In Chapter 10, we will explore more complex scenarios when multiple upstream ISPs are involved.

> ### HOW NOT TO DO IT
>
> Bad Things happen when you accidentally create a transit AS by doing such things as re-advertising all routes learned from one eBGP speaker to another. You really, really do not want to promise AT&T Worldnet that you will carry traffic to UUnet.
>
> Other Bad Things can happen when you rush, and when you do not deny everything not explicitly permitted. Figure 4.18 shows a perfectly functioning enterprise with multihoming to a single provider. For this example, assume it has been properly assigned 96.0.0.0/16.
>
> Figure 4.19 shows the network of another company just acquired by your own. The less clueful network designer there did not know of the existence of private address space, and so picked a "random" network number for what "would only be internal." The number picked was 3.0.0.0/8, which happens to be assigned to General Electric. Later, when that company decided it did need Internet access, its provider, AS666, set up NAT that mapped the company's address space into AS666's space. At the time of the merger, the acquired company's administrator forgot to tell you about this mapping.
>
> Your pointy-haired manager demands that you connect the new subsidiary immediately, and disconnect the AS666 connectivity to save money. Mr. Pointy Hair does know enough routing to be dangerous, and orders you to redistribute the new company's routing into yours and then advertise the combined addresses to AS1, resulting in the configuration in Figure 4.20.
>
> Assuming AS1 does not filter the routes coming from your enterprise, and re-advertises them to the general Internet, it will be a race to see if the first angry calls reaching you are from the lawyers of General Electric (to which 3.0.0.0/8 is assigned), irate customers of General Electric that are trying to reach the Internet via your enterprise, or your internal users complaining of poor performance as your links are overwhelmed by traffic arriving from outside.

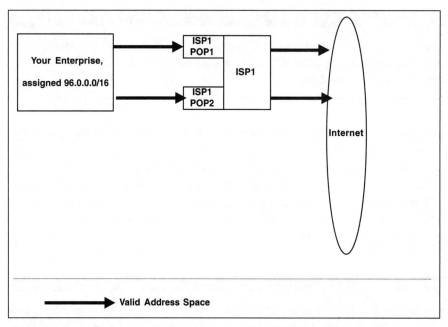

Figure 4.18 Currently clued enterprise on the path to cluelessness.

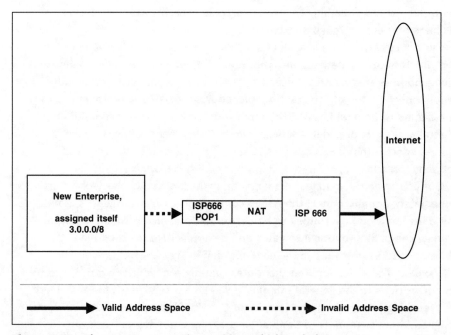

Figure 4.19 The company yours is acquiring, which, unbeknownst to your pointy-haired manager, was being saved from its sins by its former ISP.

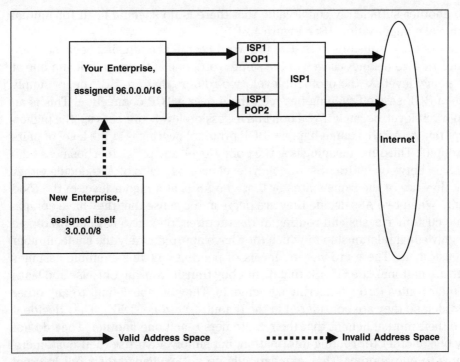

Figure 4.20 The joined enterprises, about to make substantial parts of the rest of the Internet rather annoyed.

JCC and JMedNet Joint Policies

While the relationship between JCC and JMedNet and their upstreams is a classic subscriber buying transit from a provider, the relationship between the two organizations themselves is bilateral peering. This peering is somewhat more extensive than is seen between major providers, who only exchange customer routes.

The basic logic of the relationship here is to send traffic that belongs to the partner's customers directly to the partner, and Internet traffic to the upstream(s) unless the upstream is down (so to speak). In the event of such a failure, send all Internet traffic to the partner, which will forward it to its upstream. All upstreams need to know to expect address space from their customer's partner.

Bilateral Peering among Major Providers

Interprovider peering, in the most general sense, involves the economic as well as the protocol meaning of peering. It implies a meeting of equals, who will give one another sufficiently equal value that there is no specific need for mutual financial compensation. (See Figure 4.21.)

One of the confusions in BGP is the word *peer*. It is confusing because there really are two distinct usages of the same word, one at the protocol and one at the policy level. At the protocol level, two routers that are BGP peers simply have a BGP session running between them over a TCP connection. This is an important level, because if you don't have session-level connectivity, the higher-layer things in BGP cannot happen. BGP protocol peering is at the level of pairs of routers. The other meaning is at the policy level, and refers to a business relationship between entire ASs. In policy-level peering, pairs of ASs decide either that they are of the same status or that one AS is at a higher level in the food chain. When two ASs decide they are peers in the sense that they have comparable customer bases and routing infrastructures, they also assume there is a roughly equal relationship in which they have approximately the same number of customers. There are varying levels of peering, but this example assumes both are national, "tier 1" ASs that do not buy transit from anyone else and learn all their routes through peering agreements. They do not default to any other provider, so they are considered in the default-free zone (DFZ). They decide it is to their mutual benefit that their customers reach one another. They do not pay one another for routing information, but simply advertise their customers' routes to one another. They emphatically do *not* exchange their full Internet routing tables. They also do not automatically honor service level agreements made to customers of other providers, because they are not being economically compensated to do so.

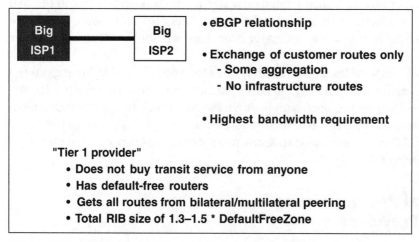

Figure 4.21 Bilateral peering.

In contrast, when an enterprise "buys transit" from a service provider, there is an unequal consumer-provider relationship. The consumer pays the service provider for Internet access. The consumer may choose to receive the full Internet routing table from the service provider. Another option, quite commonly used in load sharing, is to have the service provider send only those routing table entries that go to the ISP's directly connected customers. See Chapter 13 for more complex economic peering models.

Peering at a Multilateral Exchange Point

The basic policy at a multilateral exchange point (Figure 4.22)—a point where all participants are conceptually equal—is that participants advertise customer routes to all peers and accept all from other peers. A convention has developed at some exchanges where the multi-exit discriminator (MED), normally used to indicate preference among multiple connections to the same ISP, can also be used to indicate route quality to destinations. See Chapter 9 for the implementation-specific modifications that enable MEDs to be compared across multiple adjacent ASs. In this convention, the MED value is an estimate of the delay to the destination in milliseconds.

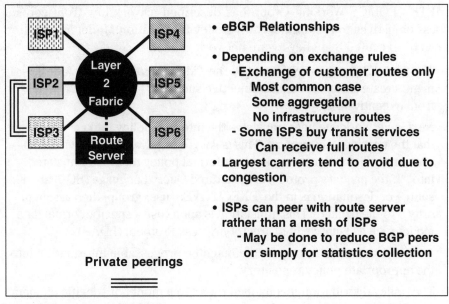

Figure 4.22 Multilateral exchange.

Security Policies

There is a subtle overloading of the term *security policy*. It clearly includes the business policies about information access, and the associated risk/benefit analysis.

Never build networks without first deciding on a security policy. A security policy is not a technical document, but should be a one- to two-page document approved by top management. The security policy both reflects requirements and provides a framework for legal enforcement. The fundamental elements of a security policy are as follows:

- Who is authorized to use resources?
- If there are different classes of users (and there should be) who should be trusted to do what with whom?
- What action will be taken if there is unauthorized use?

Very close to the policy are the domains of trust. Is the service provider trusted? The end user? Sites? I find it useful to draw a matrix of user types and resources and black out the cells where no access is permitted (Table 4.11). In the remaining cells, I then fill in the security mechanisms appropriate to the interaction between the user and the protected object.

Service Level Policies

The IETF's POLICY Working Group has described a workflow from general business objectives to build the Quality Policy Information Model information that can be executed by policy-aware network elements.

1. The first IETF step is equivalent to the TMN step of Business Management: create a human-centric objective such as, "Prioritize all queries from executives."

2. Next, a network engineer translates the informal policy into a requirement that the provider can support. This is roughly equivalent to service management in TMN. For example, the informal policy might be translated into, "If the packet's protocol is Structured Query Language (SQL) and its source or destination is in the 'EXECUTIVES' user group, then assign priority 5 to the packet." This translation is apt to use a specific formal data model such as Lightweight Directory Access Protocol (LDAP).

3. A network administrator puts the machine-processable information into the appropriate policy repository.

4. The policy distribution mechanism refers to a model of specific element capabilities and translates the machine-processable abstractions into device-specific configuration operations.

Table 4.11 Trust and Enforcement

RESOURCE TYPE (FOR EXAMPLE, PROTECTED OBJECT)	USER TYPE			
	Administrator	Cleared staff	Contractor	Public
Infrastructure	Specific location, biometrics, RADIUS, 128-bit DES			
Data entry	Specific location, RADIUS, 128-bit DES	Specific location, RADIUS, 128-bit DES		
Customer accounts	RADIUS, 128-bit DES IPSec or SSL when remote	RADIUS, 128-bit DES IPSec or SSL when remote	RADIUS, 128-bit DES I Psec or SSL when remote	
Public database	RADIUS logging	RADIUS logging	RADIUS logging	Logging of read-only access, intrusion detection

Table 4.12 Cisco QoS Policy Propagation

SOURCE	MATCH	ACTION
Ingress interface	Access lists	Set IP precedence
	BGP community lists	Set internal QoS class identifier
	AS paths	

5. Under appropriate operational controls, the configuration/distribution agent configures the elements affected.

QoS Policy Propagation

Cisco has introduced a useful proprietary feature called quality of service (QoS) policy propagation via Border Gateway Protocol (BGP). Unfortunately, this name is misleading. The feature does not propagate QoS policies between routers using BGP. It sets BGP attributes that can be used to make QoS policy decisions, but the policy itself comes from a QoS policy management host that QoS element management implements individually on a set of routers. This feature allows matching on a series of conditions and setting QoS actions based on those matches (see Table 4.12). It does not directly affect QoS, but marks packets so they can be recognized by specific QoS mechanisms, such as queuing, committed access rate (CAR) shaping, and weighted random early detect (WRED). The new IETF Outbound Route Filtering (ORF) work, for which several variations are in draft, actually does transfer policies in BGP (Figure 4.23).

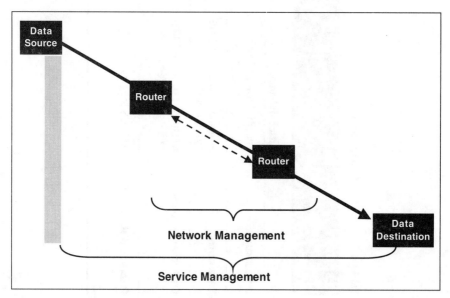

Figure 4.23 TMN and ORF.

It is intended to reduce the amount of BGP information that needs to be transmitted by exchanging the inbound filters that each BGP speaker would apply, so its peer can apply these filters to outbound traffic and not send what will, in any case, be filtered out. ORF applies only to routing packets, not to data packets.

Accounting Policies

During my days as a U.S. government contractor, I had a great deal of difficulty getting an order placed for some operationally critical equipment. In response to my pleas, the contracting officer explained, "My job has nothing to do with you getting your work done. My job is to see that the Federal Property Management Regulations are properly enforced." In other words, millions could be spent to be sure no one received one dollar more than their entitlement, but not one cent to get missions accomplished. Again and again in enterprises, I have watched with dismay as financial managers insisted on being able to track in infinite detail the usage of network resources, so they could properly charge back each user's share of resources. The fundamental problem with their doing so, however, is that the resources required for the desired level of accounting sometimes exceed the cost of the resources being used. It would be far more cost-effective for the enterprise simply to treat the network as a general overhead cost, much as the cost of mowing the lawn is treated.

Things become more complex in a service provider environment. My colleague, Francis Ovenden, observes that what you cannot measure, you cannot bill. If a provider cannot bill, it will receive no revenue and rather quickly fail.

Simple billing charges a flat rate by the speed of access facilities. But as differentiated services come into play, as different user groups share common facilities and really need costs to be allocated fairly, and so on, more powerful accounting is needed. Many of the accounting categories of interest are identifiable by some of the same patterns that were matched as part of routing policy. New actions, however, become involved for accounting (see Table 4.13). There's certainly an opportunity to extend RPSL to include accounting actions. You might declare that you want byte and packet counts on all traffic associated with a given route or community.

You need to distinguish between the collection of raw accounting information and the interpretation of it. For example, you might want to base your pricing on geographic location. It's not necessary to decide the area in real time, as long as you can correlate prefixes or communities with geographic locations in non-real-time postprocessing. In like manner, if you want different rates depending on time of day, the log of raw accounting data will usually be timestamped. To do this, RPSL needs to be understood in order to be able to specify forwarding plane actions as well as control plane actions. Today, you can have a control plane action such as AS path prepending. From [RFC 2622]:

Table 4.13 Accounting Match and Action Events

SOURCE	MATCH	ACTION
Ingress interface	TOS or diffserv code point	Create accounting bucket (with summarization period)
	Incoming interface	Count matching packet
	AS path expression	Count matching bytes
	Incoming MED	Count matching packets with specified QoS
	Community	Count errors
	Next hop	
	Origin code	
	Source address/prefix	
	Destination address/prefix	

In the following example, AS1 injects its static routes (routes which are members of the set AS1:RS-STATIC-ROUTES) to the interAS routing protocol and appends AS1 twice to their AS paths.

```
aut-num: AS1
import: protocol STATIC into BGP4
        from AS1 action aspath.prepend(AS1, AS1);
        accept AS1:RS-STATIC-ROUTES
```

But, in a different example from RFC 2622, the forwarding plane action of reverse path verification is implicit:

In the following example, AS1 imports a different set of unicast routes for multicast reverse path forwarding from AS2:

```
aut-num: AS1
import: from AS2 accept AS2
import: protocol IDMR
        from AS2 accept AS2:RS-RPF-ROUTES
```

It is my belief that the trend of separation between forwarding and control planes will continue, and needs to be made explicit in RPSL. Reverse path forwarding verification, for example, might become an action; actions may also be defined to perform accounting actions whenever an instance of a certain identifier is seen.

The IP-VPN Address Family and Routing Notation

Before discussing the specific policies for the example customers described in the previous chapter, we have to have some way to discuss the address policies associated with VPNs. Therefore I introduce some informal extensions to RPSL for dealing with these additional applications. The idea of an address family begins in RFC 1700, in which IPv4 is assigned address family identifier 1 (AFI1) and IPv6 is assigned AFI2. BGP multiprotocol extensions continue the idea [RFC 2858].

Routing Distinguishers

RFC 2547 introduces the idea of the VPN-IPv4 address family, in which 8-byte routing distinguishers (RDs) precede a regular IPv4 address. The RD disambiguates otherwise identical address assignments. In the subsequent discussions, basic IP addresses are written in the standard CIDR form of four octets followed by a prefix length, such as 1.2.3.4/8, or a prefix length range operator (see Table 4.2). When used in a VPN, the address is followed by an RD (for example, 10.1.1.1/16:RD103). Addresses without RDs can be assumed to be in the public address space. This notation is not RPSL standard, but defined for this book; RPSL extensions are being discussed by the IETF just for this purpose.

The latest draft of the evolving RFC 2547 defines two kinds of routing distinguishers. Both begin with a 2-byte type field, followed by an administrator field and an assigned number field. The type field is consistent with the address family identifier used by the multiprotocol extensions to BGP [RFC 2858], further discussed in Chapter 9. If the administrator and assigned number fields are all zeroes, the address following the RD is assumed to be a normal, globally unique IPv4 address. This is not quite the same as saying it is globally routable, because the IPv4 address in question could be from the private address space defined by RFC 1918. Using RFC 1918 addresses in global routing is usually considered a very bad idea, although certain ISPs may use them in their intraprovider networks (see Chapter 8).

In format type 0, the administrator field will be a 2-byte AS number, and the assigned 4-byte number following it is under the control of that AS. In format type 1, the administrator field is a 4-byte IPv4 address, followed by a 2-byte assigned number under the control of the authority to which the IP address has been assigned. Chapter 5 discusses the nuances of the distinction between address allocation and address assignment, but a key thing to observe here is that the IP address can be under the control of an enterprise that has no AS number of its own.

Using Routing Distinguishers in Extended RPSL

This book uses nonstandard extensions of RPSL, which may evolve into parts of the language. Remember that a route is made unique by the route prefix (an IP address with a length attribute) and the origin (an AS number):

```
route:     128.1.0.0/16
origin:    AS222
```

The problem of disambiguating routes in different VPNs relies on the routing distinguisher. If we define an additional route attribute as an RD, we disambiguate the same address in multiple VPNs managed by different ASs, using RD format type 0. Format type 1 is beyond the scope of this discussion.

Of course, to use an RD attribute for a route, we need a way to define RD names. By convention, omitting the RD gives an RD of all zeroes, which means the route is part of the public address space. Limiting the discussion to format type 0, we can define:

```
RD-NAME: <rd-name>
  Type: 0 or 1
    !if type=0, the rest of the triplet is
                      ASnumber,VPNnumber
    !if type=1, the rest of the triplet is
                      IPaddress,VPNnumber
  ASnumber: <number>
  VPNumber: <number>    ! 4 byte

RD-SET: <RD-set-name>
 members: RD-NAME1, RD-NAME2, ...
```

This allows us to refer to a route originated by an AS as ASn:RDname:route.

Complex VPN Case Study

In the previous chapter, Magic Images, as is common for customers, has actually understated its requirements. Magic Images actually needs several kinds of networks. It needs intranets both for its network management and for its purely internal services. At present, the internal network is local to its London facility, but the management intranet is worldwide. The company needs intranets both for its network management and for its purely internal services.

As shown in Figure 4.24, Magic Images needs Internet connectivity to advertise its services. For simplicity in this discussion, we will assume that all hosts with public Internet capability will have unique Internet addresses. In a real high-availability network, as we will see in Chapter 13, many servers might

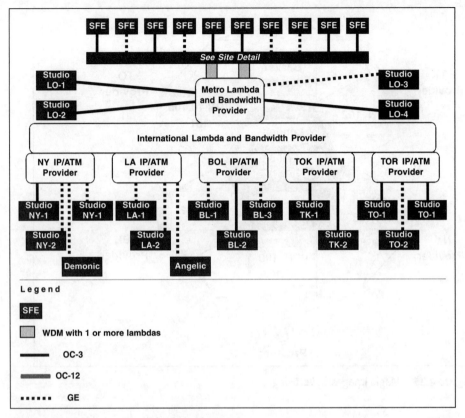

Figure 4.24   Future network of Magic Images.

actually have private addresses behind a load distribution device that advertises a virtual public address to the Internet.

The Emerging VPN Strategy

The actual customer studios need to connect to the Magic Images resources as
extranets. In some cooperative productions, it is possible that multiple customers will collaborate, so Magic Images must be able to allow certain customers to exchange data. Magic Images also must be able to ensure that
customers that are competitors cannot see one another's data. Figure 4.25
shows what routes it will advertise to selected peers.

The Real Requirements

The data in Table 3.9 involved multiple LAN emulation (LANE) domains separated by routers for better security, or actual firewalls when the clients were
willing to pay the cost of very high-speed firewall equipment. Group 1 and 3

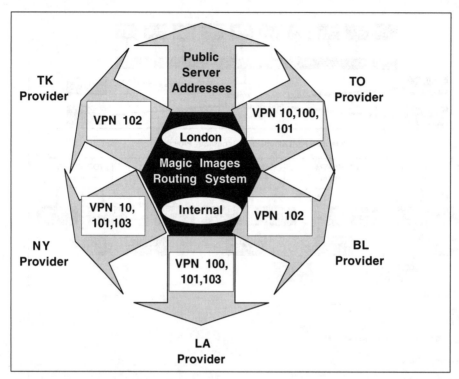

Figure 4.25 Magic Images advertising.

users were willing to accept a single emulated LAN, because they dedicated servers, or at least well-controlled server interfaces, to that application. Group 2 consisted of two locations of the same company, with a router link to the third site. Group 4 was composed of organizations that did not trust each other, but some were more distrustful than others. The large studios, Angelic and Demonic, used routers and firewalls. (See Table 4.14 for further details.) In the new design (Table 4.15), each former emulated LAN will be a VPN, but there will also be VPN extranets in which competitors can connect, but in a controlled manner. All the VPNs will use private address space [RFC 1918]. Each intranet and single-enterprise VPN will have a single address space.

A POSSIBLE ADDITIONAL DIRECTION

The VPN RD principles introduced here may be relevant to Generalized MPLS, where the unit of routing is not necessarily a packet with an address, but things such as an optical wavelength (a lambda) or a time slot in a multiplexed stream. It certainly will be possible to build high-capacity, often provider-oriented, VPNs out of such things, not replacing IP VPNs but complementing them. See Chapter 8 for more discussion of GMPLS.

Table 4.14 Detailed Existing Topology for Magic Images

EXTRANET	USERS	EMULATED LANS
Group 1	NY-1, LA-2, TO-3, LO-1	NY-1, LA-2, TO-3, LO-1
Group 2	LA-1, LA-2, TO-1	Emulated LAN for LA-1, LA-2
		Router from LA-2 to TO-1
Group 3	BL-1, TK-1, LO-4	BL-1, TK-1, LO-4
Group 4	LO-2, NY-2, Demonic, Angelic	Emulated LAN to LO-2
		Emulated LAN to NY-2
		Router and firewall from Demonic to Magic Images emulated LAN
		Router and firewall from Angelic to Magic Images emulated LAN

Handling Extranets

Each extranet will also have a single private address space, to avoid the overhead of NAT, but at increased administrative cost because human and machine effort will be needed to avoid address overlaps. For example, extranet 103 will need to be divided into four nonoverlapping address spaces, which may be further subnetted by individual subscribers (Figure 4.26).

Table 4.15 Summary of Future Topology for Magic Images

	VLAN AT HQ	VPN/RD	FORMER GROUP	PARTICIPANTS
Magic Images network management	1	1		
Magic Images Internet access	2	2		
Intranet	3	3		
Single-client extranets numbered 10–99 (10 as example)	10	10		LO-1,NY-1
Multiclient extranets numbered 100–199	100	100	1	NY-1, LA-2, TO-3, LO-1
	101	101	2	LA-1, LA-2, TO-1
	102	102	3	BL-1, TK-1, LO-4
	103	103	4	LO-2, NY-2, Demonic, Angelic

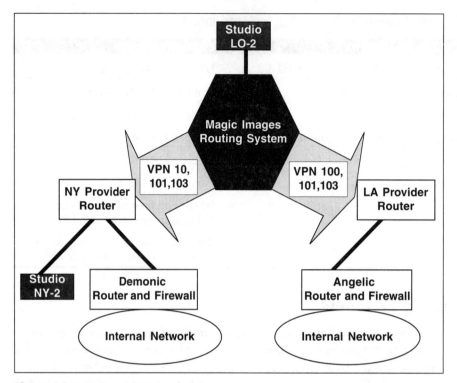

Figure 4.26   Extranet 103 topology.

Looking Ahead

The next chapter deals with the administrative mechanisms for obtaining address space and AS numbers and registering them in appropriate registries. After discussions of physical carrier characteristics in Chapters 6 and 7, and of interior routing in Chapter 8, Chapters 9 through 12 deal with the translation of routing policies into BGP implementation.

CHAPTER

5

Administration, Addressing, and Naming

Rules are always subject to interpretation.
—Ferengi Rule of Acquisition #284

Question: What is the most important machine in the hospital?

Answer: The machine that goes "ping."
—Monty Python and the Meaning of Life

The tree of addresses must periodically be watered with the blood of renumbering.
—Something Thomas Jefferson might have said about addressing

This chapter walks a delicate line, starting by presupposing that the reader thoroughly understands the structure of IPv4 addresses under classful assumptions. The real delicacy, however, comes in showing how various aggregates of addresses are created and described, giving enough information to provide the reader confidence that such address structures have value, but deferring the detailed discussion about their use to the routing technique chapters (Chapters 9 through 12).

Technical and Cultural Assumptions about Addressing

If you are from the mainframe/MIS culture, the hardest thing to understand about real-world exterior routing is that in the global Internet, no one organization is in charge. Your desire to have your traffic routed end-to-end, in the forward and reverse directions, through ISPs with which you have no financial relationships, is as relevant to the situation as are the inalienable rights of life, liberty, and the pursuit of happiness to a person drowning alone in the North Atlantic. You must understand that you can only influence, not command, in the public network, although you may be able to achieve the desired level of control using virtual private networks (VPNs) implemented by the same providers that provide public connectivity. There is no more important time to realize that you deal with IP service providers, not simply Internet service providers. When dealing with the global Internet, avoid the viewpoint of *Star Trek: the Next Generation's* Q Entity: "It's hard to be a team player when you're used to being omnipotent." You may have been omnipotent with respect to addressing in the enterprise, but you are definitely not omnipotent in the global context. No one is.

People from the LAN computing culture often fail to realize the real-world scalability requirements of the global Internet. While it is nice philosophically to have all information freely available, routing systems of this size simply cannot continue to scale unless there is significant hiding of information, and unless routers receive only the information that is significant to their role. I have seen many people from both mainframe and LAN cultures bewail that their external router is thrashing under the weight of tens of thousands of routes, when the router may only need to see one or a few routes and still operate quite nicely in the Internet.

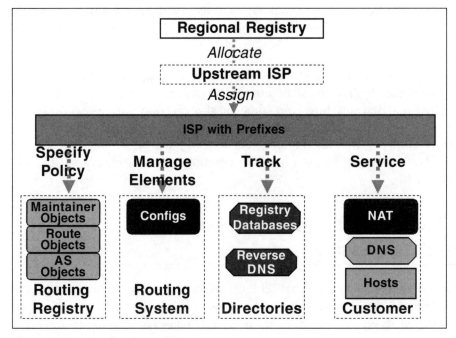

Figure 5.1 More than just addresses.

Addressing is a major part of playing in provider networks, but IP addresses are not the only kind of information that has to be managed. Figure 5.1 reminds us that the address space will be issued either by an address registry (see "Working with Registries" later in this chapter) or by a delegate of an address registry. Even if you have the address space, it may not be very usable unless you register routing policies, as introduced in the previous chapter and continued here.

From the combination of addresses and routing policies will emerge actual router configurations that need to be installed and maintained by element management. Most often this is a manual process, but there is great interest in productivity tools for this area. Some public-domain tools exist for generating router configuration statements from RPSL.

You will also need to track your use of initial and future address space, which includes linking it to DNS and other databases. There is an unfortunate amount of unfairness in the availability of address space—some organizations received large allocations because they were early players, and could not justify so much space today. There is, however, no way to take back address space that is inadequately used by old-timers. Even for new registrants, the main means of pressure is to refuse additional space until effective use of the allocation given has been made.

To service customers, you will also need administrative procedures and automated tools to tell them what addresses to use. These addresses may be in the private address space and may need to be translated to public address space.

Registered and Private Space

The IPv4 address space is divided into blocks available for allocation in the public Internet and blocks intended for use purely within enterprises or carrier infrastructures. The private address space (Table 5.1) is defined by RFC 1918. There are some additional special cases, but you will most commonly encounter the RFC 1918 space when seeing nonregistered address space.

There are some other possible blocks that you should never see in the public Internet, such as the 169.254.0.0/16 link-local block, the specification for which is buried deeply in the Dynamic Host Configuration Protocol (DHCP)

Table 5.1 RFC 1918 Private Address Space

ABSOLUTE RANGE	CIDR REPRESENTATION
10.0.0.0–10.255.255.255	10.0.0.0/8
172.16.0.0–172.31.255.255	172.16.0.0/12
192.168.0.0–192.168.255.255	192.168.0.0/16

> **YET ANOTHER SPECIAL CASE**
>
> In Chapter 4 we introduced the IPv4-VPN address family. The actual IP addresses used in VPNs are normally part of the RFC 1918 space, and the addresses themselves may appear in multiple VPNs, disambiguated only by the routing distinguisher. When you support VPNs, you must have administrative and technical machinery in place to know that this particular 10.1.1.1 belongs to VPN 30 and not to VPN 42.

specifications [RFC 2131], the networks reserved for DNS root servers and for exchange points, and so on. (See "Martian Filters" in Chapter 10.) In addition, there is a substantial amount of IPv4 space that has not yet been allocated either by the Internet Assigned Numbers Authority (IANA) or registries. In a nutshell, I recommend that service providers use registered space anywhere in their networks where an external troubleshooter might need to traceroute through it. This is a controversial position, for reasons both of address conservation and of security. There is nothing wrong with a provider using private address space for the individual real servers in a cluster, which are only reachable through a load-sharing NAT load distribution appliance that has a registered "outside" address.

As a provider, you will start operations with address space assigned to you by upstream provider(s) until you can justify a minimum allocation from the appropriate registry. Each registry has a specific request template for IP address space, but there are certain things you will need to do to prepare to fill out any of the templates. First, you must obtain globally routable address space. In general, you will need to be able to justify that you can immediately use 50 percent or more of a /20 if you are to receive a direct allocation from a registry. If you do not have this amount of space, and you plan to offer ISP services, you will need to borrow space from an upstream provider. If you terminate your business relationship with that provider, you will need to renumber.

Kinds of Public Address Space

There are two kinds of public address space: *provider-independent* (PI), often called *portable*, and *provider-assigned* (PA), also called *provider-aggregatable*. When a registry issues PI space, this part of the process is called *allocation*. When the recipient of PI space issues part of it to customers, this is called *assignment*. Allocation and assignment are frequently used as if they are synonyms, but they really are not. Address space is *allocated* to a provider, which then may *assign* portions of it to customers for their use.

Principles for Use of Public Address Space

In any routing system, addresses must be unique. Special arrangements have been made for address space that need be unique only in an enterprise, as previously discussed. Historically, IANA "owned" the public address space. As the Internet grew, it delegated detailed assignments to regional address registries (Table 5.2). When U.S. government funding of IANA ended, its function passed to the Internet Corporation for Assigned Names and Numbers (ICANN). ICANN's work in addressing has been much less controversial than its activities in the domain naming area. Registries are in the process of being opened for Latin America and Africa.

Routability

Just because you have been issued a globally unique address doesn't mean that all IP service providers are obligated to route it. From the perspective of RFC 2050 and the registries, the first goal is to allocate addresses in hierarchical blocks, to encourage aggregation. It cannot be emphasized strongly enough that having an allocation does not mean it will be globally reachable!

There is constant conflict between the ideals of routing and the realities of commerce. A typical dialogue between two respected operational engineers began on August 28, 2001, when Randy Bush wrote to the NANOG list:

> I agree that there is no "right" to have a route in someone else's router. Different providers, different policies etc. etc. However, if I choose to filter on allocation boundaries but advertise prefixes to peers that I myself would filter based on my own policy is that considered hypocritical? Bad form? Acceptable?

A response came from Pete Kruckenberg on September 1:

> Curious that this entire discussion is justified by delivering what your customers pay you for, when what is proposed couldn't be further from that.
>
> If this is about what customers pay for, then we would be discussing how to accommodate, and even encourage effective multi-homing at a more granular level. Customers pay for the network to work end-to-end. More choices mean

Table 5.2   Active Regional Address Registries

REGION	REGISTRY
North America	American Registry for Internet Numbers (ARIN)
Europe	Réseaux IP Européens Network Coordination Centre (RIPE-NCC)
Pacific Rim	Asia-Pacific Network Information Center (APNIC)

REGISTRIES AND OPERATIONAL FORUMS

It can be confusing to distinguish between the organizations that manage addresses and the operator forums where the use of addresses (among other topics) is discussed. This is especially confusing in the case of RIPE-NCC and RIPE.

Réseaux IP Européens is a nonmembership European operator forum. RIPE-NCC involves many of the same people, but is a separate membership organization. In the Americas, ARIN is the address registry but the North American Network Operators Forum (NANOG) is the operational group. Similarly, in the Asia-Pacific area, APNIC is the registry but the Asia-Pacific Regional Internet Conference on Operational Technologies (APRICOT) is the operational forum.

---

better performance, more reliability. The entire premise for this discussion goes directly against that.

Let me guess, this *is* for the good of the users, because if we don't do it the world will blow up with too many routes. Uh huh. And everyone is turning down customers who want to multi-home a /24.

I pay my network providers to reach all those multi-homed /24's quickly and reliably. Filtering devalues your network, I buy from your non-filtering competitor instead. BTW, your sales people (if you are a major carrier) are salivating over my RFP. Your CEO sweats bullets over next quarter's numbers. Filtering /24's doesn't seem important to them.

Where did the "you don't pay me, so you can't use my route table" argument come from? A multi-organizational, ubiquitous, globally-reachable, resilient network pre-

---

THE MICROALLOCATION ISSUE

While there are local differences, the minimum allocation of PI space is generally a /20. Special exceptions have always been made for the Internet infrastructure itself, such as address space for root servers and for exchange point fabrics. The problem arises for enterprise sites that actually only need a few addresses, because most of their network is behind address-translating firewalls and load distributors, but want PI space so they are not locked into one provider. At least in the IPv4 world, there is no fully satisfactory solution to this problem.

Microallocations for Internet infrastructure differ significantly from microallocations made for enterprise multihoming, because they are not intended to be generally advertised on the Internet. Access to them is either manually supplied to the participants or hard-coded into appropriate servers and files.

sumes that the majority of routes in my router are *not* my customers, and *that's* why the network is valuable.

I'm not saying there isn't a problem, or that we shouldn't be doing anything about it. But it's one thing to talk about the problem (technology needs to improve to allow individuals and small companies to have better reliability), and quite another for networks to be hypocritically preaching/enforcing the "pay or be filtered" principle while violating the principle themselves.

This goal is breaking down with increasing customer demand for multihoming and traffic engineering. As you will see in Chapter 9, to achieve multihoming to two providers, it may be necessary for the provider that assigned your space to advertise your more-specific block in addition to the larger aggregate in which it is contained.

Registration

Another goal of registry operations is establishing repositories of allocations and assignments. Such repositories, and the associated system of delegation from ICANN to regional registries to local registries or ISPs, prevent duplicate address assignment. Having accessible repositories also helps operational troubleshooting, because they provide a means of identifying the source of packets causing a problem—and an administrative means to reach a person at that source.

Spammers and other network abusers have used unassigned blocks to send out malicious traffic, and knowing what has and has not been assigned can be a basis for filtering. The major problem here is that current routers are limited in the number of address filtering rules they can enforce. There's also the minor matter of keeping those filters current as address allocations and assignments evolve.

Conservation

The first stated principle of registry allocation policy is *conservation:* "Fair distribution of globally unique Internet address space according to the operational needs of the end-users and Internet Service Providers operating networks using this address space. Prevention of stockpiling in order to maximize the lifetime of the Internet address space." [RFC 2050]

THE SCOPE OF ROUTABILITY

Even when current technologies require that you have multiple routes to achieve the desired fault tolerance and load distribution, it still does not mean these routes have to be present in every ISP router in the world.

One of the implications of the conservation policy is that very little, if any, consideration is given to the administrative convenience of the recipient of the addresses. Administrative convenience, with respect to addressing, can mean many things. It means that static addresses are not to be assigned to individual hosts that connect to the network via access servers capable of dynamic address assignment. That implies that it will be quite difficult to support servers that only have dial connectivity, although there are ways to accomplish this. It also means that network designs are expected to reflect that periodic renumbering is a reality, and they should be designed in a renumbering-friendly manner [Berkowitz 1998, RFC 2072]. Yes, this may make day-to-day operations more difficult unless prior planning is done to prevent poor performance. Essentially, the master registry policy document's response to claims that something is administratively difficult is approximately, "Life is hard, then you die."

Dynamic Address Assignment

Aspects of being renumbering-friendly include appropriate use of dynamic assignment mechanisms such as DHCP and the Internet Protocol Control Protocol (IPCP) subprotocol of PPP. (See Figure 5.2.) They include dynamic linkage between address assignment and DNS. Above all, they recognize that when certain tasks seem mind-numbingly boring and repetitive, they are mind-numbingly boring and repetitive to people. Computers experience no such frustration.

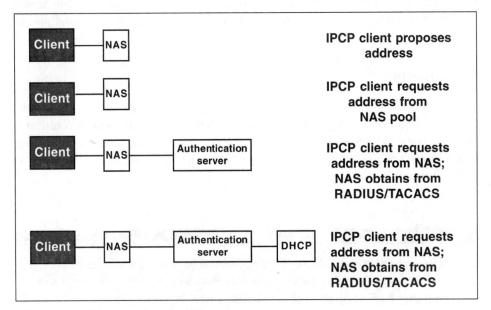

Figure 5.2 Address sources for dial-ups.

NAT and Other Midboxes

Registries assume that you will conserve address space by using NAT for appropriate customer topologies. Indeed, whether you have considered the use of private address space and NAT is one of the specific questions in RIPE-NCC's address request template (see "Representative Templates from RIPE-NCC" later in this chapter). The most common midbox is network address translation (NAT). Other types include firewalls, load distributors, tunneling functions, and so on (see Figure 5.3).

Troubleshooting Realities

Many new technologies of the midbox flavor, especially NAT, have been introduced in an effort to solve the addressing shortage, but they generally introduce operational issues that must be considered. Other address-conserving methods, such as dynamic address assignment with DHCP or the IPCP subprotocol of PPP, also introduce operational challenges. How do service providers ping, traceroute, or use other standard diagnostics for enterprise address spaces to which they do not directly connect? For enterprises themselves, when addresses are dynamically assigned, how does a troubleshooter find the specific address, at a specific moment in time, that has been assigned to the device having problems?

You must have some fixed identifier to find the device. In campus networks, it can be the cubicle or jack identifier that is wired to a specific switch, from

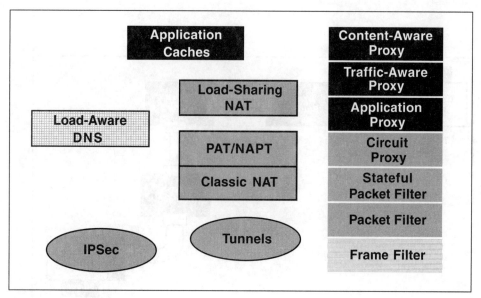

Figure 5.3   Midboxes.

which you can retrieve the active MAC address, which can be looked up in the DHCP log file. If your DHCP and DNS are dynamically linked, you may not initially need to track down the physical location. You could simply ping or traceroute to the DNS name. A similar method works if you give DNS names to your dial-in ports and have the IPCP function of PPP associate addresses and names. If midboxes or tunnels are present, you will either have to troubleshoot cooperatively with the user or to have access to both sides of the address-translating or address-encapsulating device. For example, in Figure 5.4, the white interfaces are in the carrier's address space but the black interfaces are in the subscriber's address space. Note the juxtaposed black and white interfaces at the ingress and egress to the tunnel.

If your administrative machinery is sufficiently reliable, you can print DNS name labels for hosts and stick them on the machines. Your troubleshooting, however, will rely on the stickiness of glue, the ability of the user to read the identifier to you, and the promptness with which data bases are updated, not to mention the ability to keep creative users from changing things on their own, for reasons that may even seem perfectly valid to them.

Another aspect to conservation is not assigning globally routable addresses to single-homed enterprises (Figure 5.5). Reasonable exceptions may be made for well-known servers, but NAT with port translation will work for many host-based applications. It would be considered desirable if a customer multihomed to the same provider could still use NAT, but that realistically presents a difficult challenge of synchronization and failover among the multiple NATs (Figure 5.6). Remember that a wide range of technologies fall under the general heading of NAT (see [Berkowitz 2000] for details).

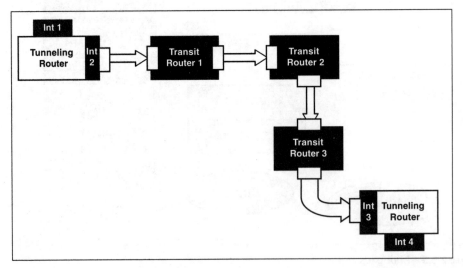

Figure 5.4 Tunneling and traceroute.

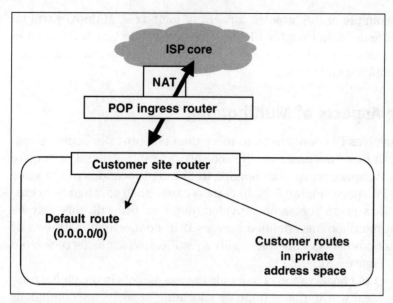

Figure 5.5 Single-homed connection with NAT.

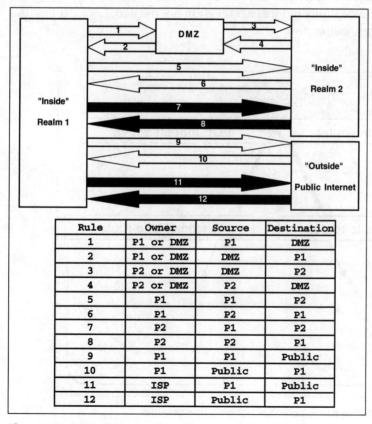

Rule	Owner	Source	Destination
1	P1 or DMZ	P1	DMZ
2	P1 or DMZ	DMZ	P1
3	P2 or DMZ	DMZ	P2
4	P2 or DMZ	P2	DMZ
5	P1	P1	P2
6	P1	P2	P1
7	P2	P1	P2
8	P2	P2	P1
9	P1	P1	Public
10	P1	Public	P1
11	ISP	P1	Public
12	ISP	Public	P1

Figure 5.6 NAT types.

NAT is one example of the broader concept of midboxes. Midboxes will be discussed in more detail in Chapter 13, but, generically, they are devices, often serving useful purposes, that violate the original IP assumption that IP addresses are significant end-to-end.

Addressing Aspects of Multihoming

Multihoming involves IP connectivity to more than one provider access point. These points can be of the same or different providers. In general, it is quite realistic to use PA space when multihoming to different locations of the same provider using PA space (Figure 5.7). In certain cases, such as when both customer connections go to the same provider router or firewall, this may be achievable, but multihoming—defined here as BGP connectivity with two or more other autonomous systems—is usually a justification for using registered address space (Figure 5.8).

Another aspect of conservation is reducing the use of slots in the global routing table. In an ideal world, this is done by allocating or assigning contiguous blocks of addresses, subnetting them as required inside the recipient's network but only announcing the aggregate to the world—and the global routing tables. In practice, many exceptions to ideal aggregation are needed. Let's explore the mechanisms of aggregation now.

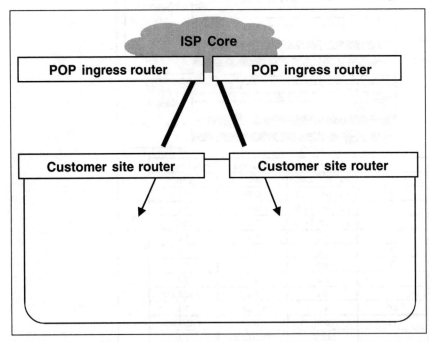

Figure 5.7 Multihoming to multiple POPs of the same provider.

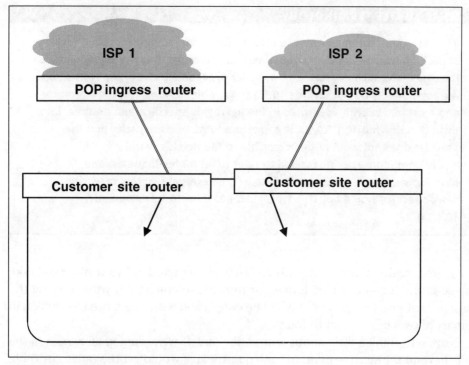

Figure 5.8   Multihoming to multiple providers.

Route Aggregation

Perhaps the major means of continuing to scale the Internet routing system is to aggregate as much as possible. Good aggregation means that you combine several more-specific routes into a less-specific one without losing information that would affect the desired routing topology.

An AS can aggregate for other ASs feeding into it. Done carelessly, this can cause significant problems, but, especially when the aggregation is done for space assigned by the AS, it can be a significant help to scalability.

Planning Aggregation Schemes

Aggregation, also called *supernetting* or *summarization*, is the process of collapsing several more-specific prefixes into one less-specific prefix by moving the prefix boundary to the left. Aggregatable prefixes are generally assumed to be contiguous, although there may be exceptions. (See the discussion of a hole in the aggregate in "Some Subtle Terminology.") For example, let us say you have the assignment 10.0.0.0/16. You want to divide it into four parts (see Table

> **SOME SUBTLE TERMINOLOGY**
>
> RPSL uses the term *aggregate* to refer to the actual route generated, such as 10.1.0.0/16 and the term *component* for the routes that are represented by the aggregate, such as {10.1.1.0/24, 10.1.2.0/24, and 10.1.4.0/24}. Notice that the components do not include 10.1.3.0/24, which is a *hole* in the aggregate and must be explicitly identified in the aggregate specification. Assume, for this example, that 10.1.3.0/24 is a provider infrastructure prefix that the provider does not want to be accessible to the outside world.
>
> The term *more-specific* is used to refer to all routes that exist and have longer, more-specific prefixes than the aggregate. In this case, the more-specifics would be {10.1.1.0/24, 10.1.2.0/24, 10.1.3.0/24, and 10.1.4.0/24}.

5.3). First, realize that the first 16 bits (10.0/16) are fixed. All your work will take place in the low-order bits. Since our immediate concern is with splitting the assignment into four pieces, we will be concerned with two more bits, which in binary allows us to count to four.

Now, let's think a little about dotted decimal. If we assumed all zeroes in the bits beyond the starting point of each quartile, we would get the ranges in Table 5.4. These differ only in the first 2 bits of the third octet—or, in other words, their first 16 bits are identical. They could therefore be aggregated into 10.0.0.0/16.

> **STAY OUT OF TROUBLE**
>
> These bits happen to be in the third octet of the dotted decimal expression, but until you are absolutely comfortable with what is happening in binary, please don't think about octets. It is an almost guaranteed source of confusion.

Table 5.3   Splitting a Space into Binary Quartiles

FIXED FIRST 18	BITS 17–18	USAGE
00001010 00000000	00	First quartile
00001010 00000000	01	Second quartile
00001010 00000000	00	Third quartile
00001010 00000000	00	Fourth quartile

Table 5.4 Dotted Decimal Quartiles

FIXED FIRST 18	BITS 17–18 AND REMAINDER	DOTTED DECIMAL EQUIVALENT
00001010 00000000	00 000000 00000000	10.0.0.0/18
00001010 00000000	01 000000 00000000	10.64.0.0/18
00001010 00000000	10 000000 00000000	10.128.0.0/18
00001010 00000000	11 000000 00000000	10.192.0.0/18

But There's an Art to This . . .

I've learned that new addressing designers sometimes try to aggregate too much. Let's say you are given a /16 assignment, and you are setting up your internal topology, which has four POPs, a server farm, and a core. You intend to use OSPF for your internal routing. Many people—and unfortunately several vendor routing courses—would immediately say, "Aha! I have four nonzero areas! I'll split my assignment into four parts!" At first, this seems reasonable. But where is the address space for area 0.0.0.0? What about the server farm? They don't belong in area 0.0.0.0. You could use a different block of private address space. That actually might be a good idea if these were registered addresses and you did not want area 0.0.0.0 accessible from the outside. But let's assume you want all your address space announced into an enterprise-wide, or provider-wide, backbone of backbones. In such a case, you might want to announce an aggregate that includes the backbone.

Berkowitz's Pessimistic Postulate of Addressing Design

When I am presented with an addressing structure that has N major "natural" divisions, such as the four nonzero areas just described, I find it good practice to break the address space into at least $4N$ (and often $8N$ or $16N$) pieces. In the real world, user populations rarely split evenly, so too much aggregation can waste space in one area while another area suffers address drought. There are pieces of address space available for specialized infrastructure functions such as NAT or firewall demilitarized zones.

Therefore, if I were responsible for an address plan in which there were four user divisions and a backbone, I'd actually use a structure like the one in Table 5.5, so I might do my initial assignments of addresses to the proposed topology as shown in Figure 5.9. Note that I assigned contiguous blocks to the main user areas but left space in reserve. In this example, I happen to know that area 0.0.0.2 is heavily populated, so I have given it extra space.

Table 5.5 Finer Granularity in Address Assignment

FIXED FIRST 18	BITS 17–20 AND REMAINDER	DOTTED DECIMAL EQUIVALENT
00001010 00000000	00 00 0000 00000000	10.0.0.0/20
00001010 00000000	00 01 0000 00000000	10.16.0.0/20
00001010 00000000	00 10 0000 00000000	10.32.0.0/20
00001010 00000000	00 11 0000 00000000	10.48.0.0/20
00001010 00000000	01 00 0000 00000000	10.64.0.0/20
00001010 00000000	01 01 0000 00000000	10.80.0.0/20
00001010 00000000	01 10 0000 00000000	10.96.0.0/20
00001010 00000000	01 11 0000 00000000	10.112.0.0/20
00001010 00000000	10 00 0000 00000000	10.128.0.0/20
00001010 00000000	10 01 0000 00000000	10.144.0.0/20
00001010 00000000	10 10 0000 00000000	10.160.0.0/20
00001010 00000000	10 11 0000 00000000	10.176.0.0/20
00001010 00000000	11 00 0000 00000000	10.192.0.0/20
00001010 00000000	11 01 0000 00000000	10.208.0.0/20
00001010 00000000	11 10 0000 00000000	10.224.0.0/20
00001010 00000000	11 11 0000 00000000	10.240.0.0/20

The RPSL Components Attribute

Before delving into this RPSL attribute, a few concepts are in order. First, RPSL understands that there can be different sources of routing information, such as BGP, IGPs, and static routes. It also understands that policy filters can be applied to the outputs of these routes, as in Table 5.6.

The components attribute identifies the more-specific routes that are combined to form the aggregate. Its basic syntax is:

```
components:
    [[<filter>] [protocol <protocol> <filter> ...]]
```

In the attribute, filter implicitly ANDs with the more-specifics from the sources of routing information, so only the routes that both come from the specified source and match the filter will be included. When there is no components attribute associated with a route, it will contain all more-specifics.

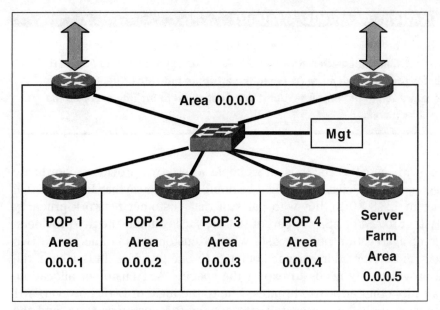

Figure 5.9 OSPF topology with fine-grained addressing.

There is, however, one more option in the components attribute specification. BGP-4 includes the ATOMIC_AGGREGATE value, which means that when it has received a set of overlapping routes (for example, less-specific and more-specific), it chooses to select only the less-specific. In other words, it chooses not to deaggregate. In the full form of the RPSL components attribute:

```
components:
    [ATOMIC]
    [[<filter>] [protocol <protocol> <filter> ...]]
```

Putting the ATOMIC tag on a component essentially means, "Do what I say, don't try to interpret it."

Table 5.6 Aggregate Route Objects

route: 128.8.0.0/15	route: 128.8.0.0/15
origin: AS1	origin: AS1
components: <^AS2>	components: protocol BGP4
	{128.8.0.0/16^+}
	protocol OSPF
	{128.9.0.0/16^+}

> ### IMPLICATIONS OF ATOMIC_ATTRIBUTE
>
> **You should be aware that the aggregation indicated for a route that is marked with ATOMIC may mean that its actual AS_PATH, as opposed to the AS_PATH attribute, goes through more ASs than the attribute indicates. The AS_PATH is still guaranteed to be loop-free, but it does not claim to include every AS the update has traversed.**

Table 5.7, from [RFC 2622], is an example where two providers coordinate their aggregation policies. They might be doing this because they have a mutual customer in 128.8.0.0/15, but with parts of that customer network primarily homed either to AS1 or AS2. No part of 128.8.0.0/15 is outside the two providers. A different aggregation policy exists when a customer is connected to two providers and all the address space belongs to one provider. In this case, the second provider only needs to export the specific AS1 customer allocation, along with its other advertised routes. Due to the logic of BGP, however, AS1 has to export both the aggregate that contains the customer route and the more-specific customer route. If AS1 did not do so, the other AS, advertising the more-specific, would be selected by all other ASs that heard its announcement.

Table 5.8 is an example of the use of the export-comps attribute in RPSL, which effectively is a filter whose output is the more-specifics that need to be exported. In RPSL, a route object can specify an aggregate route, which it does if any of the following components are used to generate it.

Table 5.7 Outbound Multi-AS Aggregation Example

```
route:       128.8.0.0/15       route:       128.8.0.0/15
origin:      AS1                origin:      AS2
components:  {128.8.0.0/15      components:  {128.8.0.0/15^-}
aggr-bndry:  AS1 OR AS2         aggr-bndry:  AS1 OR AS2
aggr-mtd:    outbound AS-ANY    aggr-mtd:    outbound AS-ANY
```

Table 5.8 Exporting a More-Specific

```
route:        128.8.0.0/15
origin:       AS1
components:   {128.8.0.0/15^-}
aggr-mtd:     outbound AS-ANY
export-comps:            {128.8.8.0/24}
```

Source: RFC 2622, Figure 31.

Aggregation Boundary (aggr-bndry Attribute)

Aggregation boundaries are at a fairly high level of abstraction in that they are defined by an AS expression over AS numbers and AS sets. When there is no aggregation boundary, the originating AS is the only boundary for aggregation. Inside the boundary, more-specifics are distributed, but only the aggregate is exported outside the boundary.

aggr-mtd

Somewhat more fine-grained than aggr-bndry, the aggr-mtd attribute specifies how the aggregate is generated but can differentiate between inbound and outbound advertisements. Its syntax is as follows:

```
aggr-mtd:
    inbound
    | outbound [<as-expression>]
```

For outbound aggregation to occur, the more-specifics must be present at the AS. The aggregates will be created just before exporting to adjacent ASs, except for ASs, that are inside the aggregation boundary. Inbound aggregates are formed just before importing. You cannot specify an <as-expression> for inbound aggregation.

Holes

Hole requirements are important and complex in the commercial reality of the Internet. The holes attribute lists the component address prefixes that are not reachable through the aggregate route (perhaps that part of the address space is unallocated or you do not desire it to be reachable by outsiders, such as your server farm). Do not confuse advertising a hole with advertising a more-specific; they do opposite things. Advertising a more-specific says the route is reachable; advertising a hole says that it is not reachable.

Table 5.9 Holes

CASE	EXAMPLE	COMMENTS
Customer contracts	A customer writes a provider contract so that normally PA space moves if the customer terminates the contract.	Discouraged
Enterprise divestitures	An enterprise sells off a part of itself and an address block is associated with that part.	

While the practice of allowing a customer to take part of a PA allocation along if changing from the allocating provider is not desirable, this is still a commercial reality (Table 5.9).

Route Injection

Aggregates can be defined on ingress or egress. It is quite common to have more-specific customer routes come into your AS, but to report only aggregates containing these routes to your peers and upstreams, assuming the customer address space is part of your allocation.

In RPSL, the inject attribute indicates which routers aggregate and when in the routing process they do so. The syntax of this attribute is:

```
inject: [at <router-expression>] ...
        [action <action>]
        [upon <condition>]
```

<action> and <router-expression> have been described in Chapter 4. If there is no <router expression>, there is an assumption that all in the aggregating AS will perform the same aggregations. Using <router expression> allows a subset of those routers to be responsible for aggregation. Actions allow you to set route attributes, such as communities or preferences. When there is no upon <condition>, an aggregate will be generated only if there is an active component in the routing table that matches the filter criteria in the components attribute. If there is an upon <condition>, the attribute is generated if and only if the <condition> is true. <condition> is generated with the logical operators AND and OR (i.e., NOT is not valid here) over the variables:

- HAVE-COMPONENTS { list of prefixes }, which must be more-specifics of the aggregate. It is true if and only if every prefix in the list is present in the active RIB of the router. This list can include prefix range operators such as ^-. If it does, at least one prefix from the indicated range must be present in the RIB.

- EXCLUDE { list of prefixes }, which requires that none of the prefixes be present in the RIB. If the list of prefixes includes prefix ranges, no prefix within those ranges can be present for EXCLUDE to be evaluated as TRUE.

- STATIC always evaluates as TRUE.

The examples in Table 5.10 are interesting both from the BGP perspective given, and also because they reflect the different approaches to OSPF summarization at area border routers used in the Cisco IOS and Bay RS. In the first case, all components must be present for the attribute to be generated. This is the Bay/Nortel approach in OSPF summarization. If all the components are not

Table 5.10 Examples of Inject

```
    route:       128.8.0.0/15              route:       128.8.0.0/15
    origin:      AS1                       origin:      AS1
    components:  {128.8.0.0/15^-}          components:  {128.8.0.0/15^-}
    aggr-mtd:    outbound AS-ANY           aggr-mtd:    outbound AS-ANY
    inject:      at 1.1.1.1                inject:      upon HAVE-
action med = 100;                     COMPONENTS {128.8.0.0/16,
                                      128.9.0.0/16}
    inject:      at 1.1.1.2               holes:       128.8.8.0/24
action med = 110;
```

present, Bay RS does not summarize at all at the ABR, but instead announces all components. In the second case, the aggregate is generated if only one of the components is present. Cisco OSPF summarization actually goes further, generating the aggregate even if none of the components is present. Both approaches, in either BGP or IGP, have legitimate applications. Personally, I would like to see the two approaches available in all router implementations.

Working with Registries

While the major registries essentially ask for the same information, their templates, for historical reasons, differ considerably. ARIN's go back to the first templates created and have a need for backward compatibility.

The regional registries are membership organizations, and their membership sets their priorities. They do listen to public comment, although people who want to comment need to have some idea of how to do so—on the appropriate mailing lists, by contacting members of the leadership, or appearing at the in-person meetings. One issue is the balance that the regional registries maintain between education and the processing of IP and autonomous system number (ASN) requests. Another issue is whether to give preference for new allocation requests or requests for additional space.

ARIN

ARIN's general model is to have organizations requesting allocations deal directly with ARIN staff. There are a few exceptions, such as national registries for Mexico and Brazil. ARIN does not have as strong a membership model as does RIPE-NCC, but operates on a cost-recovery basis. Fees are assessed for:

- Subscription for bulk IP registration services for ISPs
- Registration and annual maintenance for individual address space assignments

- Registration and annual maintenance for ASN allocations
- Registration and annual maintenance for transfers of individual address space and ASNs
- Subscription/registration and annual maintenance for public exchange points
- Membership for nonsubscribers interested in participating in ARIN

RIPE-NCC

RIPE-NCC has a different model, which places local internet registries (LIRs) as a layer between the regional registry and customers. In the RIPE service region, you must be a LIR to obtain PI space. While the need to have substantial amounts of independently routable address space is important to an ISP, operating an LIR introduces complexity, cost, and responsibility.

According to RIPE-NCC, a LIR and is responsible for making assignments in accordance with the following responsibilities:

- Making the right assignment decisions following global assignment policies (as described in the European Internet Registry Policies and Procedures).
- Keeping records of the information gathered in the assignment process (as described in the European Internet Registry Policies and Procedures).
- Storing assignment information in the RIPE database and keeping this information up to date (as described in the European Internet Registry Policies and Procedures).

Representative Templates from ARIN

ARIN has different templates for ISP and end user initial allocations. In understanding these fairly long templates, I have found it useful to split them into the subtables that follow. The first thing you will have to explain is how your AS connects to the world (Table 5.11). It will be fairly hard to justify provider-independent space unless you have at least two upstream connections, either with service providers or at exchange points.

ARIN looks more favorably on requests that return small pieces of address space, reducing overall fragmentation of the address space and thus conserving slots in the global routing table. Of course, this kind of efficient resource use does tend to require renumbering. Table 5.12 shows how you document the reassignment/return of space.

ARIN, of course, must communicate with you in processing and granting the request, so administrative information is necessary (Table 5.13).

For ISPs, ARIN's projections for address space are based on 3-month requirements (see Table 5.14). In general, you will need to show your regional registry that you have used 80 percent of an allocation before you get the next

Table 5.11 ARIN Connectivity Characteristics

INTERNET CONNECTIONS	
0a.	Directly connecting to peering points? Please list
0b.	Connectivity via service providers? Please list
0c.	Other
3.	Network name
5.	CIDR Block requested
6.	Portable (P) Non-portable (N)

Table 5.12 ARIN Reassignment

REASSIGNMENT INFORMATION	
1a.	Block
1b.	Assigned
1c.	Reserved
1d.	Available
1e.	Reassignment option

Table 5.13 ARIN Administrative Information

ADMINISTRATIVE INFORMATION: TECHNICAL POINT OF CONTACT (POC) AND ORGANIZATION	
2a.	ARIN handle (if known)
2b.	Name (last, first)
2c.	Title
2d.	Postal address
2e.	Phone number
2f.	E-mailbox
4a.	Name of organization
4b.	Postal address of organization
4c.	Maintainer ID (if known)

Table 5.14 ARIN Address Requirements Projection

HOST INFORMATION
7a. 3-month projection for dial-up customers
7b. 3-month projection for leased-line customers
7c. Additional information

Table 5.15 ARIN DNS Information

DNS SERVERS	
8a. Primary server hostname	9a. Secondary server hostname
8b. Primary server net address	9b. Secondary server net address

allocation. To get the initial allocation, you typically will need to demonstrate 50 percent immediate utilization. In calculating that initial utilization, don't forget that your infrastructure is part of it.

ARIN is quite concerned that proper DNS support will exist for your address block. From an availability standpoint, it is wise to have at least your primary or secondary DNS server outside your domain (Table 5.15).

Representative Templates from RIPE-NCC

RIPE-NCC begins by asking the requesting organization to fill in templates identifying the organization and the person responsible for the request (Table 5.16). Details of the actual address request are then required, both at a global and detailed level (Table 5.17). There is also a need to associate the request with blocks in the registry database (Table 5.18). Additional clarifying information is welcome, such as details of internal aggregation.

Table 5.16 Overview of RIPE-NCC Organization Templates

#[REQUESTER TEMPLATE]#	#[USER TEMPLATE]#
name:	name:
organization:	organization:
country:	country:
phone:	phone:
fax-no: (optional)	fax-no: (optional)
e-mail:	e-mail:

Table 5.17 RIPE-NCC Global Address Request

#[REQUEST OVERVIEW TEMPLATE]#
request-size:
Addresses-immediate:
Addresses-year-1:
Addresses-year-2:
subnets-immediate:
subnets-year-1:
subnets-year-2:
inet-connect:
country-net:
private-considered:
request-refused:
PI-requested:
address-space-returned:

Table 5.18 RIPE-NCC Network Template

#[NETWORK TEMPLATE]#
inetnum:
netname:
descr:
country:
admin-c:
tech-c:
status:
mnt-by:
mnt-lower: (optional)
mnt-routes: (optional)
notify: (optional)
changed:

SOURCE: RIPE

Managing Your Address Space

Registries (ARIN in the Americas, RIPE-NCC in Europe, and APNIC in the Pacific Rim) will ask you to justify your address space requests. Each of their Web sites has a template for the address request, and the process is discussed extensively in Chapter 9 of [Berkowitz 1998].

Once You Have the Address Space

Don't just take the allocation and hand it out randomly to your customers. If you don't manage it well, you'll have a great deal of trouble getting additional space. Figure 5.10 illustrates the continuing process of adding address space to your routing system. When you start operations, you will probably do it with PA

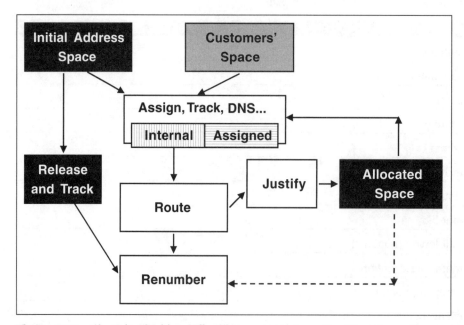

Figure 5.10 Life cycle of address allocation.

space from your upstreams. With continuing growth that you can document, you can eventually get PI space and further allocations as you need them. Registries tend to issue more space based on 3-month requirements, so you must keep your utilization database up to date.

In addition to your own address space, you may need to route PI space allocated to your customers. You may even need PA space allocated to other ISPs as part of multihoming. You will have two key areas of responsibility: working with the registries and working with your customers. Some of the key aspects of a good working relationship with your registry include keeping excellent records of your assignments downward and documenting them in appropriate databases (see Table 5.19). Registries do like to know you are using address-conserving techniques such as private address space with NAT, name-based Hypertext Transfer Protocol (HTTP), and dynamic address assignment when feasible. While not strictly a part of addressing policy, the overall registry relationship will be better if you register your routing policies, keep the registry entries maintained, and keep your forward and reverse DNS in good shape.

The first step, after you have received your allocation—which might not be as much as you requested—is to review your addressing plan. While address allocations for service providers are generally made on 3-month projections, business plans change, and the aggregation structure you planned may have changed.

When you have a substantial number of routes, you may want to use tools to explore how effectively you are aggregating. Cidradvisor, part of the routing arbiter tool set, is one such tool. However you analyze your aggregation, you will want to set up an address database, even if it is no more than a spreadsheet. The most important thing is that you keep it updated. The next most important thing about your addressing database is that it should contain more than just

Table 5.19 Berkowitz's Laws of Address Administration

Avoid entering an address more than once.	
Automate configuration updating.	Don't forget DNS, firewalls, access servers, accounting
	Trivial File Transfer Protocol (TFTP) or telnet/expect
	Replace versus merge
	Scheduled reboot
Remember "the most important machine in the hospital" (M. Python).	
Document automatically.	For troubleshooting
	For justifying address allocation

addresses. Indeed, your provisioning operations for DNS, firewalls, assignment to router interfaces, and so on, should all center on this database.

My fundamental rule of address management is: Never type in an address more than once. Every other reference should be algorithmically derived from the original entry.

Document Your Current Practice

When you are requesting the space, it is wise to categorize what space you now have assigned or allocated, and what space your infrastructure and your customers are using (Figure 5.11). *Bogus space* is address space that is assigned to someone else, but that the customer independently decided to use.

Document Infrastructure and Existing Assignments

You will certainly need space for infrastructure such as router-to-router links, management servers, WAN links to customer routers, dial-up servers, and so on. These assignments should be the easiest to document and to clean up if any improper assignments have been made.

You will need to be able to explain your topology logically (Figure 5.12). This explanation should identify aggregation boundaries and places where addresses are assigned dynamically. Registries will generally want a tabular inventory. Believe me, they also appreciate the logical drawing, but their procedures require a table such as Table 5.20.

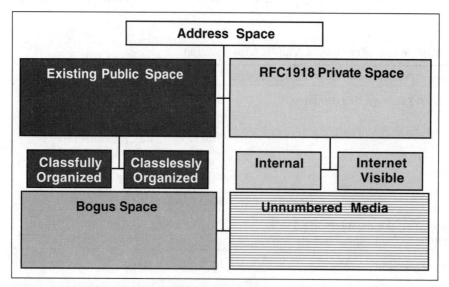

Figure 5.11   Categorizing address space in use.

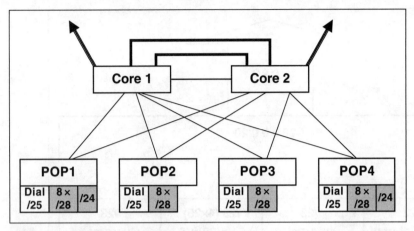

Figure 5.12   Creating a logical topology.

Once you have the logical topology in place, you need to be able to propose your actual addressing plan. Again, you will need to show 50 percent initial utilization, but this percentage can be flexible. The registries will generally understand inefficiencies due to aggregation and consider that a legitimate part of your requirements, if you give a sufficient technical explanation with your application. (Figure 5.13 shows a graphical convention for this, which was taught to me by my colleague Pete Welcher.) The addressing plan should indicate any provider-independent space your customers will continue to advertise and any provider-dependent space you will still use. Registries also like to see where you propose to conserve public address space by using RFC 1918 private address space, or at least an explanation of why private address space is not feasible for your application.

Table 5.20   RIPE-NCC Address Space Template

			ADDRESSES USED			
PREFIX	SUBNET MASK	SIZE	CURRENT	1 YEAR	2 YEARS	DESCRIPTION
Totals						

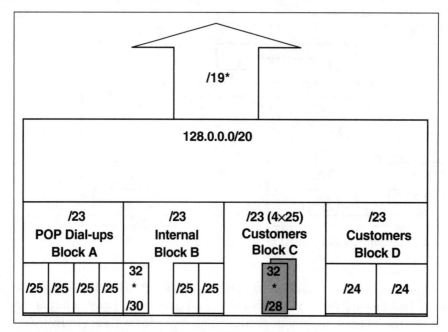

Figure 5.13   Preparing a preliminary addressing plan.

Operational Step 1: Capturing Customer Administrative Information

For your customer assignment information to be manageable, your order processing needs to begin with capturing some very basic administrative information, such as the customer billing contact and any sales or support people your organization assigns to the account. You also need to identify relevant technical contacts at the customer or explicitly recognize that the customer really has no internal technical support. In the latter case, you should have a procedure for identifying what technical support the customer will get from you without charge and what is billable. If the customer has any DNS domains assigned, you need to know what they are called and where the primary and secondary DNS servers are located.

Operational Step 2: Gathering Customer Usage Information

It has been reliably observed that the most important difference between a network sales representative and a seller of used cars is that the seller of used cars knows when he is lying. To avoid this situation, one of the first practical guidelines is to ask your customers questions that are meaningful to them, and then translate the answers into the responses the registries want. True, some customers will understand exactly what the registries need, but the average nontechnical enterprise will not. Some basic questions that nontechnical customers are likely to understand include:

- How many sites do you have?
- What is your schedule for growth?
- What are your requirements for flow among sites?

Working with customers can be challenging, because many customers simply do not want to become involved in the details of address management. Even worse, competitors' sales representatives may try to convince your potential customers that the competitor will not require the same address justification from them. Things get much more complex when the customer wants fault-tolerant connectivity, which may mean multihoming. Again, complications ensue if customers have multiple data centers or distributed processing—but such customers are much more likely to have staff people who understand at least basic IP addressing.

You should apply some reality checks to customer network descriptions. If a customer claims to have 2000 hosts in a single, nonsubnetted network, the customer has problems even more basic than Internet connectivity.

Your chief problem will tend to be the upper manager who does not want to spend any effort on renumbering or on using assigned space in a manner that in any way limits options or causes inconvenience. Thankfully, many enterprises do not need direct Internet access for many of their hosts, so address-translating firewalls may greatly simplify the situation.

Figure 5.14 shows an actual worksheet I used with a medical applications provider, which made sense to the customer and was useful in eliciting

---

WATCH OUT FOR USERS WITH SMALL PI SPACE

There's no question that users often prefer having PI space. If their address allocations are relatively small (longer than /20), however, such small blocks can cause problems. Some of these problems include having their routes be filtered out by other providers. There are several reasons this can happen. Prefix length is an obvious one, but failure by the user to have the prefix registered in a routing registry also can lead to filtering.

Some providers, once they have gained customer confidence, have been able to convince the user to renumber into PA space and return the PI allocation. They do this with more than just good will, also making a contractual commitment to give a comfortable grace period of continuing to let the user use the PA addresses if the user changes to another provider, and working with the other provider to make a smooth transition.

Figure 5.14 Think requirements, not subnetting.

	APPLI-CATION SERVER SUBNET /28	MANAGE-MENT SERVER SUBNET /28	WAN LINKS TO OTHER DATA CENTERS /30	14-USER DIAL ACCESS SERVER SUBNET /28	100-LOCAL-USER SUBNET /25	60-LOCAL-USER SUBNET /26	SMALL CLINIC (11 USERS, SERVER, ROUTER, SWITCH) /28	MEDIUM CLINIC (27 USERS, SERVER, ROUTER, SWITCH) /27
October 1999								
January 2000								
April 2000								
July 2000								

information. The row containing prefix length information, however, was not shown to the customer. Once the worksheet was filled in, it became reasonable to define an aggregation plan that considered POP-level aggregation and also included growth figures based on verifiable sales trends. You will want to encourage customers to ask for as little address space as possible, implement a renumbering-friendly design, and add address space when (and not before) their usage justifies it. Given topological details, the registries will be reasonable if the assignment efficiency is less than ideal due to issues such as POP aggregation.

Operational Step 3:
Recording Customer Assignments

Your database should have functions for assigning the next available package of types you commonly support, certainly customer and possibly POP. The function may need to be given the argument of nearest POP as well as the actual package type. For a single LAN, single-homed to you, this process should generate two variables, lanPrefix and wanPrefix. These will be used in the next step of configuration generation. See Table 5.21 for a summary of the information needed.

Operational Step 4:
Automatically Generating Configurations
for Which You Are Responsible

As the routing engineer for connecting customers, what do you need to do? Assume the basic topology with which you provide customer service is that shown in Figure 5.15. You will need to configure an access router at the customer site and a port on an aggregation/distribution router in the POP. I will assume that there is static routing between the customer and the POP and that a dedicated line connects the two. See Chapter 9 for additional details if there is dynamic routing. In addition to the routing configurations, appropriate DNS entries need to be generated. If you provide firewalling services for the customer, the appropriate rules need to be added to the firewall configuration. You might use frame relay, VLAN, or other multiplexed technologies between the customer and provider. These technologies are likely to be provisioned by a third party that grooms multiple customer interfaces, via its WAN cloud, into a high-speed interface on your POP aggregation router. If so, the provisioning process must include the administrative step of finding the logical identifier associated with your customer.

Let's look at some templates for automatic configuration generation. I emphasize that the purpose of these specific examples is to show means of

Table 5.21 Information You Need on User Space

LAN size	You may establish SOHO /29, branch /28 or so, and perhaps office /24. Larger address requests, which often mean multiple LANs are involved, need scrutiny by engineers.
Multiple LANs at site	Who is responsible for routing at the site?
Access link type	Reality check time! If the customer wants to support 250 users with a single dial-up, the customer has very unrealistic expectations unless special circumstances are involved. Although rigid rules on associating bandwidth with address space are generally frowned upon by addressing experts, it is reasonable to create a rough guideline that when violated justifies a closer look by routing engineers. /29 needs at least 128 or 384 Kb /28 needs at least 384 or 512 Kb /24 probably needs 768 or 1544 Kbps
Any existing PA addresses	If so, are they assigned from your space? Should they be renumbered into a larger block? If they are from another provider, and the customer does not plan to multihome, what is the timetable and who is responsible for renumbering? If the customer does plan to multihome to multiple providers, your routing engineering team needs to become involved.
Any existing PI addresses	Do they still need them? Will you update your routing policy to announce them? Will your upstream(s) accept them?
Confirm the site is single-homed to you	Meshes, multihoming, and discontiguous networks need special handling. You may be able to automate the assignment of multihomed links to different POPs, if the customer is using PA space from you. Manual engineering probably is needed if the customer uses PI or private address space.

automating your address management, not to show ideal routing configuration. These templates assume a simple single-homed topology from customer to POP (Figure 5.15). Figure 5.16 shows a template, using Cisco configuration language, of how the remote site router could be configured as well as the basic DNS entries for the customer. Figure 5.17 shows the equivalent part of the aggregation router configuration, which needs to be merged into an existing configuration. This configuration fragment assumes that you want DNS names assigned to all your router interfaces, which certainly can make reading traceroutes easier.

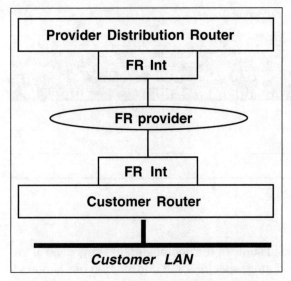

Figure 5.15 Basic topology from customer inwards.

```
int e0
ip addr (lanPrefix + 14) 255.255.255.240
int S0.rmtDLCI
ip addr (wanPrefix + 2) 255.255.255.252
ip route 0.0.0.0/0 (wanPrefix+1)
---------------------------------------
<router-e0>        IN A (lanPrefix + 14)
(lanPrefix+14)     IN PTR <router-e0>
<router-s0-DLCI>  IN A (wanPrefix + 2)
(wanPrefix + 2)   IN PTR <router-s0-DLCI>
! SOA,NS, MX, firewall, etc. as necessary
```

Figure 5.16 Remote site template.

```
ip route (lanPrefix) /mask (wanPrefix + 2)
int S0.distDLCI
ip addr (wanPrefix + 1) 255.255.255.252
! blackhole as appropriate
---------------------------------------
<distrouter-s0-DLCI>
 IN A (wanPrefix + 1)
(wanPrefix + 2)
 IN PTR <distrouter-s0-DLCI>
```

Figure 5.17 Customer delta to aggregation router.

Table 5.22 Basic Per-Router Configuration Worksheet

ROUTING PROTOCOL AND IDENTIFIER (FOR EXAMPLE, AS NUMBER)	ROUTER NAME (YOUR ADMINISTRATIVE ID)	ROUTER ID

Documentation

Tables 5.22 and 5.23 are examples of some of the documentation you will want to keep for each router. You will find more specific BGP information in Chapters 9 and 10. You might wonder what kind of policy information is appropriate on non-BGP routers. A good example is an ingress router that advertises RIP default so local hosts can find it, but does not accept any routes for security reasons.

Requesting More Space

It has been my experience that, contrary to some popular opinion, regional registries are not there to torment people. Properly filling out the forms, auditing your customer address usage, following best current practice, and supplying technical documentation with your request when you want to do something unusual all go a long way in helping you get addresses.

The registries typically have different templates for requesting additional space. One of the more challenging parts of the process can be when your main assignment is provider-dependent space from an upstream, but you are now

Table 5.23 Per-Interface Configuration

ROUTING PROTOCOL AND PROCESS IDENTIFIER (FOR EXAMPLE, AS NUMBER)			
ROUTER NAME			
BGP ROUTER ID			
INTERFACE ID AND IP ADDRESS	NEIGHBOR IP ADDRESS	ADVERTISING POLICY FOR THIS INTERFACE	ACCEPTANCE POLICY FOR THIS INTERFACE

ready to justify your own provider-independent allocation. You can't wave a flag and instantaneously renumber everything, so transition is part of the challenge. Specific multihoming requirements may still mean that you have to advertise part of the PA space from one or more upstreams. If you had a /19 today and needed more space, you'd probably get a far better reception if you asked for a /18 into which you agreed to renumber your existing space, rather than another random /19.

The principle of routability and the encouragement of aggregation is the reason the registries will not give out small allocations (typically longer than /20) unless special circumstances apply. They (and the routing community) want the small blocks to aggregate into larger blocks, and it is the larger providers that have the larger blocks.

Autonomous Systems

Once you have the address space, you apply separately for an AS number. The same registries that control address space control AS space. Templates for applying for AS numbers are found on the registry Web pages. Strictly speaking, having registered address space and a valid AS number are sufficient to participate in global Internet routing. Stopping here, however, will in practice mean that you will not be able to reach significant parts of the Internet. Many large providers automatically generate their BGP configurations to accept updates only from ASs with policies registered in a routing registry. Some providers also filter on prefix length, and will not accept a prefix longer than /19 or /20. Indeed, the actual rules may be considerably more complex: Longer prefix lengths may be acceptable if from the traditional class C space, but not from the traditional class A or B space. The filtering providers, to varying extents, keep track of when part of the traditional A or B space has been made available in CIDR blocks. Exceptions to this policy can often be negotiated when you are multihoming. See www.nanog.org for information on provider filtering, and also specifically ask your upstream provider about its filtering policies.

[RFC 1930] established a block of private AS numbers. The top 1K from 65535 down is similar to the private IP address ranges established by RFC 1918. Use these numbers for internal testing. Private AS numbers also are used in situations such as internally for enterprises that use BGP to create a backbone of backbones, such as multiple OSPF domains interconnected with BGP. Private AS numbers also are used when passing information to a single ISP that does not propagate the details of that information to the rest of the Internet. The originating AS can be stripped by a variety of methods described in Chapter 10.

The previous chapter explained how the AS is the basic building block of global routing. In your request for an AS number, the registry will expect you to provide the information listed in Table 5.24.

Table 5.24 Requesting an AS

Administrative contact	
Technical contacts	
Autonomous system name	
Router description	Hardware and operating system.
Deployment schedule	In general, you will be expected to give installation dates for two or more upstream providers.
Networks (by name) connected by the router(s)	
Internet addresses of the routers	

Registering a Routing Policy

We introduced routing policy in the previous chapter. In principle, a routing registry contains the information on your policies that will let another AS form meaningful relationships with you. A routing registry contains the information needed for other ASs to understand your eBGP. Routing registries historically have been separate from addressing registries, but ARIN and RIPE do maintain both. Again, there are several steps in registering in this kind of registry.

Reviewing from the discussion in Chapter 4, Table 5.25 identifies the minimum information you will need to register in the appropriate routing registry. Part of the administrative process of registering is securely establishing the *maintainer object*, which defines who can change your data in public registries. Different registries have different rules for validating an applicant, such as a telephone call to a listed number, a copy of a driver's license, or digital certificates. Never forget that you must maintain a variety of administrative relationships. These relationships include your organization, your upstream ISPs, the address registry, and the routing registry. DNS also plays a role.

Not all providers use registries. If you are multihomed to any that do use registries, however, you must use them. In any case, the exercise of registration is

A REGISTRY BY ANY OTHER NAME

Routing registries are primarily operated by the same organizations that operate the address registries, but address registration and routing policy registration are two distinct steps. The linkage between the two varies with the policy of the particular registry. RIPE-NCC, for example, will not assign an AS number unless a basic routing policy is registered.

Table 5.25 Information for the Routing Registry

OBJECT	
Maintainer	Mandatory
AS	Mandatory
Route objects	Mandatory
Role objects	Optional
Route sets	Optional
AS sets	Optional
Inter-AS network	Optional
Communities	Optional
Routers	Optional

a good reality check to ensure that you have gone through the steps needed to get your AS into the Internet. Other incentives are the many registry-based tools that are available as freeware.

Evolution of the AS Number

In general Internet routing, AS numbers are assigned by the same registries that assign IP addresses. With the growth of the Internet, there is increasing concern that the 16-bit AS number space may become exhausted. The growth in AS numbers is not so great that there are a large number of transit providers, but a rapid growth in enterprises that need to run BGP for multihoming or traffic engineering. A proposal to support 32-bit AS numbers in a manner generally compatible with the existing system is under way in the IETF. Chapter 9 discusses use of 32-bit AS numbers as one of the capabilities that can be negotiated.

IPv6 Address Allocation

IPv6 is the next generation of the Internet Protocol [RFC 2460]. It is not a panacea for every problem now encountered in the Internet, and emphatically does not automatically solve the problems associated with scaling the routing system. My intent here is not to present a complete IPv6 tutorial, but to deal with the operational aspects of IPv6 allocation and assignment. Unfortunately, many people perceive the much longer addresses in IPv6 as making address space "free," and having the potential to assign unique addresses to every person, enterprise, cat, and router interface in the world.

Table 5.26   IPv6 Formats

ALLOCATION	PREFIX	FRACTION OF ADDRESS SPACE
Reserved	0000 0000	1/256
Unassigned	0000 0001	1/256
Reserved for NSAP Allocation	0000 001	1/128
Reserved for IPX Allocation	0000 010	1/128
Unassigned	0000 011	1/128
Unassigned	0000 1	1/32
Unassigned	0001	1/16
Aggregatable global unicast	001	1/8
ADDRESSES		
Unassigned	010	1/8
Unassigned	011	1/8
Unassigned	100	1/8
Unassigned	101	1/8
Unassigned	110	1/8
Unassigned	1110	1/16
Unassigned	1111 0	1/32
Unassigned	1111 10	1/64
Unassigned	1111 110	1/128
Unassigned	1111 1110 0	1/512
Link-local unicast addresses	1111 1110 10	1/1024
Site-local unicast addresses	1111 1110 11	1/1024
Multicast addresses	1111 1111	1/256

IPv6 Address Structure

IPv6 addresses are 128 bits long [RFC 2373]. The format prefix, a variable number of the most significant bits, identifies the format of a specific address instance (Table 5.26). We are concerned here with the allocation of globally aggregatable unicast addresses, the 001 prefix addresses.

Table 5.27 Fields of Unicast Address Format

FIELD ID	PURPOSE	LENGTH (BITS)
FP	Format prefix (001)	3
TLA ID	Top-level aggregation identifier	13
RES	Reserved for future use	8
NLA ID	Next-level aggregation identifier	24
SLA ID	Site-level aggregation identifier	16
INTERFACE ID	Interface identifier	64

The Aggregatable Unicast Address

Aggregatable unicast addresses are designed to support the current type of provider-based aggregation, but also a new, basically geographic, type of aggregation based on exchange points [RFC 2374]. The latter is, realistically, experimental, and provider-based aggregation may remain the norm. Let's look at the overall structure of the global unicast address format in Table 5.27.

Top-Level Aggregation Identifiers

One of the goals [RFC 2460] in assigning 13 bits to the top-level aggregation (TLA) is to be certain that the default-free routing table stays within current router capabilities. A length of 13 bits allows for 8,192 TLA IDs. The idea is that a router in the default-free zone (the area within which there are no default routes; all possibilities are known) will have a RIB that contains all assigned TLAs, plus more-specific routes inside its own routing domain. (See Figure 5.18.) At the time the 13 bit TLA size was selected, the typical IPv4 DFZ routing table had 50,000 routes. While the table has roughly doubled at the time of this writing (June 2001), when the TLA was sized there were serious questions about whether 50,000 routes was above the threshold of reasonable routing stability. This concern still exists. The problem is not purely the number of "best" routes selected by the route selection algorithm (see Chapter 9), but the reality that there may be 10 to 15 instances of every route. The more instances, the more the table changes and churns, both of which put more workload on processors and cause even more bandwidth to be consumed by BGP announcements.

Designers of the initial TLA structure did think about improved routing technology that might make larger DFZ tables more practical. Remember that the Reserved field is between the TLA and next-level aggregation (NLA), so either

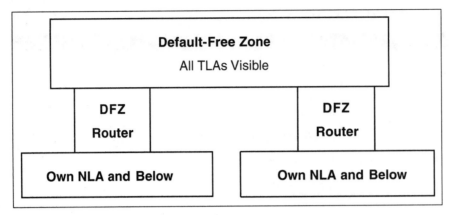

Figure 5.18 DFZ IPv6 router relationships.

the TLA field can expand to the right or the NLA field can expand to the left. The alternative to using parts of the Reserved field is to allocate additional format prefix(es) for aggregatable unicast addresses. Table 5.27 shows that many prefixes have not yet been assigned.

Besides the technical goals of keeping the top-level routing table manageable, there are other operational and organizational guidelines for the assignment of TLAs. TLAs will only be assigned to transit providers and exchanges. They are not intended as a means of creating provider-independent address space for enterprise multihoming; IPv6 has other mechanisms for that purpose. Initial allocation will be conservative. IANA will directly assign small blocks of TLA IDs to registries, and also may directly assign TLAs for experimental use or new applications such as exchange-based allocation. The registries will first assign a sub-TLA ID (see "Sub-TLAs" later in this chapter) and will only assign a full TLA when the recipient demonstrates it has assigned more than 90 percent of the space. Recipients will not need to return or renumber their sub-TLAs.

Organizations receiving TLAs will do so with the understanding that they do not own them, as is the practical case with IPv4 allocations. TLA recipients are considered the stewards of a common resource. The recipients need to meet an assortment of qualifications to keep their role of stewardship. First, they must have the will and the technical capability to offer native IPv6 transit services (for example, running IPv6 over a sub-IP or data-link protocol, not a tunnel) within 3 months of the assignment. Registries will want to see a specific plan, including details of allocation and registration procedures and the availability of a public database with this information. We are just beginning to learn the operational realities of IPv6, and we want only serious players to have TLAs. This is quite consistent with current IPv4 practice of justifying the need for addresses. It also avoids the ugly equivalent of "domain squatting" and other DNS speculation.

To be considered, the TLA applicants must already have a verifiable track record of providing IPv4 transit to other organizations. Simply being IPv4 multi-homed is not enough. It must be possible to verify the organization's transit capability with objective means such as traceroute and BGP route advertisements. TLA recipients must make their assignments available on the public Internet, although that does include their infrastructure. This both helps gain operational experience for the community and makes important information available for the troubleshooting that certainly will be needed. Recipients must periodically demonstrate to the issuing registry (for example, with logs or routing table dumps) that they are actually doing TLA routing and carrying transit traffic. The TLAs must be aggregatable (not longer than 48 bits). The combination of the TLA, Reserved field, and site-level aggregation (SLA) must be sacrosanct if the multi-homing and provider change mechanisms implicit in the IPv6 architecture are to work. A TLA recipient must pay registration fees to IANA and to the relevant regional registries, and must pay these fees before the TLA or sub-TLA is assigned. Before the recipient can get more space, it must demonstrate that it has assigned more than 90 percent of the NLA space in its earlier allocations.

Failing to show that these rules have been followed can result in revocation of the allocation. There is no specific protection mechanism established for assignees of these addresses, so users of IPv6 have a strong motivation to be sure their upstream follows appropriate registry procedures.

Sub-TLAs

Registries will receive small blocks (on the order of a few hundred) sub-TLAs. Initially, they may assign sub-TLAs to organizations that otherwise meet assignment requirements. Sub-TLA IDs are a special case of TLAs: They use part of the reserved field, but only in conjunction with TLA ID 0×0001. Organizations receiving sub-TLAs must demonstrate that they are providing native IPv6 transit service within 3 months of the assignment, or the registry can revoke the assignment.

Reserved Field

This field is not just arbitrary, but is intended to get us out of trouble if we underestimate the size required for the TLA or NLA fields. Either the TLA can expand to the right or the NLA can expand to the left.

Next-Level Aggregation Identifier

This 24-bit field is intended for use by TLA holders in creating an addressing hierarchy, including internal aggregation and the identification of sites (particularly infrastructure sites such as POPs). Again, if it becomes necessary to extend this field, the Reserved field is available. The TLA holder decides how the parts of the NLA field are used in its particular hierarchy. The assigning registry does not have to assign the full NLA space under a TLA to the TLA recipient. This is particularly logical when a sub-TLA, not a full TLA, has been assigned.

In many respects, structuring the NLA is much more challenging for a service provider than working with a TLA. You will either receive or not receive a TLA or sub-TLA, but, until you receive more than one such identifier, the TLA simply serves as the root of your addressing tree. You'll have to track its usage, but you don't directly do anything to it. Not so with the NLA, which plausibly will be segmented into hierarchical subfields that make sense for your provider topology. A caveat here is that registries may only assign part of the NLA space for a particular TLA to the organization receiving the TLA. The 90 percent rule again applies: The recipient may request more of the TLA space when it has used 90 percent of the TLA space. The idea here is to follow the "slow start" practice established with IPv4 CIDR assignments. As with any addressing plan, you will need to decide what trade-offs are appropriate for your particular business plan and technical architecture. The more hierarchical the structure, the greater the amount of aggregation, thus providing more stability, smaller routing tables, and less routing traffic. Flat assignment is easier to use but results in larger routing tables. Dare I suggest that any organization that meets the criteria to receive a TLA should be quite competent in managing an aggregation structure?

Site-Level Aggregation Identifier

A 16-bit length for this field allows 65,535 prefixes per site, which seems sufficient for all but the largest of organizations. If more prefixes are needed, additional SLAs can be obtained from the upstream provider.

A degree of wasted space was accepted when the SLA size was chosen in order to force the length of all prefixes identifying the same site to be the same (48 bits). Having a common length should facilitate changing upstream providers and developing multihoming strategies, although the latter especially are not a solved problem for IPv6.

Interface ID

Finally, the interface ID field is intended to provide unique identification for hosts. It is deliberately longer than a 48-bit MAC address, which has been used as a host address in some architectures but has proven to have limitations.

Renumbering

Startup providers are likely to need to renumber their IP space several times during the process of building their businesses. They will probably have to start with space assigned by an upstream provider, then get a minimum allocation of their own, then justify subsequent allocations. As RIPE puts it:

> When changing upstream providers, an organisation that does not operate an LIR will probably have to renumber their networks and return the formerly used address space to the LIR it was received from. Organisations operating an LIR do not depend on others for assigning address space to their own or their customers' networks. On the other hand, operating an LIR takes up considerable amounts of time and financial resources that should not be underestimated.

Allocations are not necessarily contiguous, so there may be additional renumbering into larger, contiguous spaces that provide better aggregation.

How should you renumber? First, be aware that a great many mechanisms may be affected, unless previous designers and administrators planned to be renumbering-friendly (see Figure 5.19). Second, draw on industry experience. Most people who have done major renumbering with little or no user impact agree that the key is to have a comprehensive database in place. This database, at the very minimum, contains thorough current IP and DNS information as well as the physical location of equipment and administrative and technical

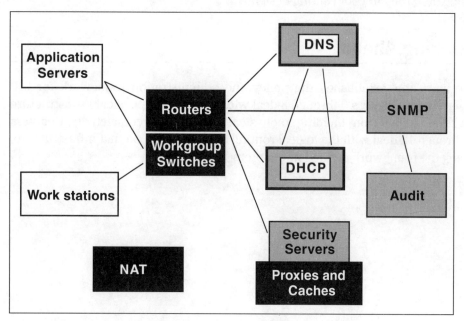

Figure 5.19 Mechanisms affected by renumbering.

contacts for it. The actual renumbering will be carried out by software running against the database.

Important in a renumbering is what I will call *dual-use capabilities*. These are tools that will work both in the current numbering and in renumbered environments. One key tool is getting all hosts to use DHCP, which should be dynamically linked to DNS. People often forget that DHCP can give extremely long or permanent leases—it isn't just used for address conservation. By getting all address assignments into DHCP servers, or functional equivalents such as remote-access servers, you greatly minimize the number of places where you have to make changes for the renumbering to be implemented.

One challenge is to find hidden IP addresses, such as IP addresses that are hard-coded into applications, into software license managers, and network management tools. These tend to be more prevalent in user applications than network infrastructure, although there is one notable case where a major network management package asked for a registered address during installation. It then generated a license key from this address and monitored the network for activity by this address. If no activity was seen for a prolonged period, the software concluded it was pirated and shut itself down.

Routers other than those in small and home offices typically have fixed addresses and do not use DHCP. In general, you will need to establish new configuration files, merge them into current configurations, and typically "bounce" interfaces down and up so the new addresses take effect. The routing domain will then have to reconverge with these new addresses—another argument for using hierarchy in your routing design.

Looking Ahead

We have now established the policy and administration framework for ISP operations. Chapters 6 through 8 deal with some of the physical infrastructure of ISPs, ranging from building to physical and data link connectivity. Chapters 9 through 12 deal with the logical routing superimposed on that infrastructure, using the framework defined in Chapters 1 through 5.

CHAPTER 6

Carrier Facilities: Getting Physical

The loftest edifices need the deepest foundations.
—George Santayana

Water runs downhill.
—Second Law of Plumbing

If it don't leak, don't fix it.
—First Law of Plumbing

Well, we are one of those small ISPs. Our company, over the past 6 years, had an association with a larger ISP. This larger ISP had customers in a Metroplex area as well as customers in South America.

If you believe in the old adage that all things are equal when everyone is running the same two programs (MSIE and Netscape) and same type of equipment, then the percentage of trouble tickets would be the same in a small ISP as it would be in a large one. On one occasion the president of the larger ISP called and asked if I could come down for a meeting. So I did. The main topic of this meeting was why we were having less customer complaints than the big boys. Both companies were handling everything the same. My answer was: We started a help desk. Every time something went wrong, I sent out an e-mail. The e-mail detailed the problem and how long I thought it was going to take to fix it.

If, during the repair, we found it was going to be longer, I sent another e-mail to our customers. Upon repair, I sent another e-mail and explained the problems, including whether the repair was a band-aid or a solid repair. I also e-mailed our group about planned outages, C&W problems, etc. Well, it has been 6 years and I am still writing the e-mails. But now, we call them "Vidnet—Alerts."

In our last poll, I asked if our customers wanted the alerts stopped. To my surprise, 100 percent of the users that replied stated, "No, keep up the good work." So I don't believe you can go wrong if you keep your customers informed. It doesn't matter if

> *you are an ISP or a software company. The more information you can supply to the customer, the happier the customer. Even if they [sic] don't understand everything in the e-mail . . .*
> *—Morris Allen, president, VidcomNet, Inc.*

Originally, there were telcos and everyone else. Today, there are a broad spectrum of carriers and carrier-like organizations. Cultures are still evolving. At a minimum, there are cultures of telephone companies, major data center providers, and Internet service providers. They complement the enterprise culture. Boundaries between carrier and customer, between telephone companies and ISPs, are blurring. As the cartoon character Pogo says: "We have met the enemy and he is us."

Carrier Business Models

I would be tempted simply to ask, "What part of money do you fail to understand?", but that is overly simplistic. Carriers are motivated by the bottom line of earnings, which has three components, two involving cost and one involving revenue:

1. *Equipment cost.* Direct costs, one-time installation and training, facility preparation

2. *Operations cost.* Maintenance (internal or vendor), provisioning, customer installations, quality monitoring

3. *Service revenue.* Attracting new customers and keeping old ones, service level delivery verification, billing systems, collection in a reasonable amount of time

Carriers want to maximize revenue. Depending on the corporate financial model, a potential carrier inside an enterprise may also obtain revenue, but as an internal funds transfer. Alternatively, a potential carrier may focus on cost reduction.

Service providers behave differently depending on whether their markets are *established, startup,* or *potential.* A potential organization is an enterprise that provides internal carrier-like services and whose users have the same expectations they would of a more traditional carrier. Electrical and gas utilities, with their own rights-of-way, often provide internal carrier services. Utilities are one part of the critical national infrastructures, and financial networks are another. Established carriers have the advantage of a continuing revenue stream provided by their installed base. Established carriers have the disadvantage that their installed base may include obsolescent components that are not fully amortized. They may be dinosaurs, but I would hate to have to be in hand-to-claw combat with a *Tyrannosaurus rex*. The reality is probably less that *T. rex* is the dominant saurian at a long-established carrier, but probably the even more dreaded *Roget's thesaurus*. Engineers often fear and loathe writing, even though they will face network carnosaurs. Startup carriers have the advantage of flexibility, like the fast little mammals that dodged the dinosaurs. However, they have the disadvantage of being low in the food chain. Of course, the grass is always greener on the other side—or, in the case of mammalian scavengers versus saurian predators, the other creature's kill is always tastier than your own. And certainly less work to obtain . . . unless you become the next kill. Startup carriers envy the revenue base of established carriers and want to have their own solid stream. Established carriers spawn new business units to go aggressively after startup niches.

Telephone competition began with alternative long-distance providers, then with competitive local exchange carriers. Both IXCs and CLECs began as traditional telephone companies. Now, however, telephony is a service offered by providers that previously offered only IP services or cable television.

Just as *VPN* and *switch* have tended to become overloaded terms, so has *carrier classness*. The term *carrier-class* comes from the telephone industry, and it has some fairly consistent operational definitions associated with it. One of the challenges for ISPs, hosting centers, and so on, is to use the shared parts of the carrier-class model, but not the parts that do not apply. For example, one tradition in telephony operations is that if a configuration fails, the device it manages will roll back to the earlier configuration. Rollback could be catastrophic to the Internet routing system if it caused an incorrect policy to be reactivated. See Chapter 13 for a discussion of the evolution of hosting centers, which have increasing similarities to, yet important differences from, exchange points.

Even within the traditional telecommunications space, there are complex issues of where equipment is placed. Traditionally, there was the end office. If the means of access to the customer premises is the original telco copper pairs, then the end office will be the termination point. With competitive LECs and xDSL service providers, however, there may be a minimum amount of equipment at the end office. There may be no more than a multiplexer at the end office, with a high-speed link to switching and other equipment either at a competitive carrier facility or at a shared *carrier hotel*.

Carrier Classness

Carrier-class and *carrier-grade* have become popular marketing buzzwords. There really is no strict definition of the overall problem. It is reasonable to say that the best of traditional telephony availability is desirable for any service.

FIVE-STAR VERSUS FOUR-STAR?

In the 1970s, the Greek company that made Metaxa brandy (an interesting beverage, quite different from French brandies), made light of French cognacs advertising as three-, four-, or five-star. The star system really wasn't defined for Greek brandies, but Metaxa offered a coupon for which they would send you a box of adhesive gold stars of which you could affix as many as you liked to the Metaxa bottle. Seven were suggested. (In the interest of full disclosure, when I am feeling flush, my preferred brandy is the French Rémy Martin XO).

Given this background, I am really surprised that no carrier or vendor to date has offered to supply boxes of gold nines, which can be affixed to equipment until the client is comfortable.

Sometimes, carrier grade is associated with a "five nines," or 99.999 percent, availability. But what does this mean? Component availability? Probability of a call being dropped?

From the enterprise perspective, a carrier cannot fix problems of availability caused by the enterprise. A central office may be nuclear-hardened, but if there is one local loop to it and a backhoe cuts the loop, the enterprise is down. If the enterprise procures bandwidth independently from two long-haul carriers without contracting one carrier to be responsible for having physically diverse paths, the enterprise has no one but itself to blame if both carriers lease capacity from a third carrier and a backhoe cuts the third carrier's medium.

There is a huge difference between failures that prevent new access to the network and failures that interrupt existing service instances. "Once up, always up" needs to be interpreted in that context. Once up, always up certainly pertains to availability, but it also means that the network must be able to grow. Scalability and maintainability mean that elements can be upgraded without interrupting current services. Beyond the level of component failover inside a network element, carrier-grade operations require failover mechanisms among network elements. Finding alternate paths, of course, has been one of the traditional strengths of IP networks, which were developed partially to find alternate paths around nuclear fireballs.

For data applications, the routing reconvergence time in well-designed networks may not be invisible to users, but reconvergence in seconds or low tens of seconds has minimal effect on transaction processing, Web browsing, and so on, as long as data are not lost. Telephony applications, however, have much more stringent requirements for reconvergence after failures. Outages of 200 ms can begin to degrade voice quality, and 2-s delays can cause calls to be completely disconnected. SONET alternate protection switching was developed because telephony needed reconvergence in the millisecond range. Yet, some of the recovery properties of SONET are needed for telephony but not necessarily for data. SONET also wastes capacity in the backup ring. See Chapter 8 for more efficient (although admittedly less proven) alternatives to SONET.

An assortment of techniques are evolving to speed reconvergence in IP networks. These techniques may be pure IP, such as equal-cost load sharing or quasi-static routes, or may involve alternate MPLS paths.

Service Provider–Vendor Relationships

Many aspects go into the process of supplier selection by service providers. These include the characteristics of working with the supplier, the characteristics of the equipment, and the nature of operating and maintaining the equipment.

Supplier Attributes

Enterprises often stress using a single vendor to whom they can outsource operations, or which at least can provide them a single equipment vendor with whom to speak. Carriers have a somewhat more pessimistic tradition in which they prefer not to have a single vendor for any given critical function. Part of the philosophy of carrier grade is psychological, taking ultimate responsibility for availability.

The reality is that any vendor, no matter how competent, will have hardware or software bugs that only appear in operations. AT&T and MCI both have had national frame relay outages caused by bugs in Lucent/Ascend and Cisco switches. I'm not singling out these switch vendors, who make excellent products. Service providers will want to know how the vendor provides technical support, both in a proactive and reactive mode. Proactive technical support includes resources for planning and implementing new installations and upgrades. It may include a continuing relationship in which the provider sends operational statistics to the vendor and receives advice on potential reliability and capacity issues. Reactive technical support includes whatever is needed to solve problems.

Equipment Attributes

Providers will look at both hardware and software aspects of the vendors' products. From a business standpoint, this examination will include initial costs of both purchase and implementation, as well as the continued cost of vendor maintenance, staff training, and spare parts. From an operational standpoint, the provider wants realistic estimates of downtime, which can be caused by in-service upgrades, failures, and preventive maintenance. Diagnostics—both hardware and software—also are important capabilities, along with problem reporting and bug tracking.

Another aspect of carrier grade is called "once up, always up" in telephony. This aspect includes the idea that cards, power supplies, and other electronics, including control processors, can be maintained or replaced without impacting the overall network element. At the level of circuit cards, rational layout of their cabling can be as operationally important as the card electronics. A hot-swappable card that cannot be swapped without disconnecting a cable to seven cards unrelated to the problem is not carrier-grade. Common components such as management processors and power supplies must be redundant and hot-swappable. In the real world, many network elements have some parts that cannot be replaced transparently, such as the backplane or midplane. Designers work hard to limit such parts to functions that are unlikely to need field maintenance, and try to remove the single points of failure. Even single points

NETWORK EQUIPMENT BUILDING SYSTEMS (NEBS)

NEBS establishes the physical environment in which a component is expected to work, ranging from temperature and humidity to heat dissipation to electrostatic discharge. There are three increasingly stringent levels of general NEBS requirements, and four levels of earthquake protection.

Meeting NEBS level 1 does not so much speak to the reliability of the network element as much as it ensures that the element does not interfere with other equipment in a carrier facility. Its focus is on safety and electromagnetic emissions. The Federal Communications Commission (FCC) did order that complying with NEBS level 1 qualifies a CLEC to collocate its equipment in an ILEC facility. NEBS levels 2 and 3 actually deal with system reliability.

Be careful to understand the realities of NEBS and the difference between compliance and certification. Compliance means that the vendor says that its product meets the NEBS requirements. Certification means that an independent third party has verified compliance. Even compliance means that the vendor has verified that the entire product—not just individual cards or shelves—meets the requirements in a practical configuration. It is less clear what certification means, because there are no formally approved testing laboratories, such as those meeting the National Voluntary Laboratory Accreditation Program, or recognized organizations such as Underwriters Laboratories. A certifying organization, such as Telecordia (formerly Bellcore), depends on its reputation.

Customers may find it acceptable to ask for the vendor's NEBS test results and have them reviewed by an expert on staff. This is not a trivial task, because the test results for a product of reasonable complexity can fill a thick notebook. Alternatively, the customer may want independent NEBS testing. Depending on the complexity of the product, this can cost from hundreds of thousands to millions of dollars.

such as midplanes will be designed not to fail totally but to degrade during operation. Once up, always up also refers to software. It must be possible to upgrade software on some processors without disturbing services.

Providers will have the key physical and environmental requirements for their equipment dictated by where they plan to install that equipment. If the equipment will be in a telephone facility, it must comply with some level of NEBS. If it will be in a classic data center, it must meet the classic data processing environmental requirements, which originate from historical IBM specifications. Components need to be scalable. Scalability factors include the minimum capacity of a piece of equipment and the extent to which it can be expanded without a "forklift upgrade." Providers need to consider the factors that affect recurring costs. These are the attributes involving element, network, and service management.

Network Attributes

Network is used here in the sense of the TMN concepts of service and network, as opposed to element, management. Network attributes affect the end-to-end behavior of the network being managed. From the financial standpoint, network attributes affect both revenues and costs. Customers are attracted to new network functions and cheaper alternatives for existing functions. They stay with a provider that meets service level agreements.

Established carriers are most concerned with controlling their operating costs and the costs of adding capacity. Network stability is next most important, since this contributes to keeping their customer bases. Supplier management is their lowest priority, because they typically have well-understood supplier relationships in place. Startup carriers want to maximize their service offerings under the constraints of deployment cost. To attract users to their new services, network attributes are most important. Operational attributes are next in importance, because ease of use is critical to rapid deployment. Potential carriers may not need some of the features that competitive vendors do, such as billing. Since their economic incentive is cost avoidance rather than revenue generation, their highest priority is operational attributes, minimizing the cost of ownership. They are next most concerned with supplier and network attributes, and least concerned with equipment attributes.

The Facility Conundrum

As they consume the fluid more essential for military aviation than jet fuel—beer—fighter pilots are apt to mutter the mantra, "I feel the need . . . for speed." The need for analog bandwidth, and then for digital speed, has been a constant in communications since Samuel Morse tapped out his first telegraph message. In today's carrier environment, there is evolution in the transport between subscribers and the provider edge, and in the provider's own core and interprovider links. While the evolving technologies can overlap, the edge layer 1 and layer 2 technologies generally are discussed in Chapter 7 and the core technologies in Chapter 8. See Chapters 9 through 12 for a discussion of the IP and related technologies that layer on top of these facilities.

Economic factors increasingly define the facility market. Typically, the first facility provider with unique connectivity or technology obtains decent market share and margins. When additional facility providers enter the same market, offering a similar service, the facility becomes a commodity and margins drop radically [Huston 2001a]. The traditional telephone company, or incumbent local exchange carrier (ILEC), owns and operates local loops. In addition, it normally owns and operate higher-capacity links between its own offices and to other carriers' points of presence. ISPs and network service providers (NSPs) may actually own national optical backbones, they may lease dark fiber and run the optoelectronics at the ends, or they may buy bandwidth from pure facility providers.

Assorted equipment vendors and operators propose solutions that may seem to differ greatly. The most fundamental difference, however, often is their assumptions about the availability and cost of optical bandwidth. When bandwidth is expensive, or simply not available, it makes more sense to put as much intelligence as possible at the carrier edge, minimizing the need for upstream bandwidth. When bandwidth is cheap, economies of scale can apply. The edge only needs enough intelligence to move bits to central locations where transit and content providers exchange or originate data. I find the cheap bandwidth–expensive bandwidth division to be an oversimplification. Certain functions may go to the edge because they work best there. The economic climate will also have a major effect. The reality is that not all areas already have massive optical fiber, and it is unclear that carriers will continue large investment when the stock market is weak.

Non-Facility-Dependent Service Providers

Any type of service provider can choose to operate facilities, but most find it more economical to subcontract facilities to specialized facility providers. There will always be exceptions, such as an ISP using free-space optical or radio communications with a nearby and critical customer. Very large enterprises may operate facilities of their own, such as Microsoft with its multiple campuses in the Seattle area, or military base communications. Dial, cellular and broadband access providers are a special category and are discussed in the next chapter.

ISPs and IP Service Providers

Unfortunately, many startup ISPs have the early mortality rate of trendy restaurants. I remain unsure of whether an Internet cafe is the combination of the best or the worst parts of the restaurant and ISP markets. Internet service providers differ in focus. The most common type offers public dial-up services to end users. Some larger ISPs specialize in business-to-business or business-to-internet access and deemphasize dial access. Others outsource their dial access to dial wholesalers (Chapter 7). Network service providers sell bandwidth to ISPs. They may also sell connectivity to enterprises, although their sales models often are geared toward customers with significant bandwidth requirements.

Content Carriers and Hosting Centers

The more things change, the more they stay the same. In my youth, large facilities that provided time-shared services were mainframe-based organizations called *service bureaus*. To a large extent, a hosting center is a service bureau that uses many servers rather than a mainframe. Of course, things are further confused by the reality that modern servers, or even workstations, have significantly more computing power than 1970s-era supercomputers.

There are three related types of business here:

1. *Hosting centers.* Run customer machines or lease machines to customers. May provide services such as backup and rebooting, but generally are not concerned with applications.

2. *Content providers.* Can range from Web hosting to extensive application service providers.

3. *Content distribution services.* Have some equipment at the data or hosting center, but put equipment at access ISPs.

Some customers operate their own data centers with multiple servers, or indeed may operate multiple data centers. These tend to be large businesses whose connectivity is a critical part of their business, such as Amazon.com or American Express. Customer-operated data centers have their place, but there are many incentives to move machines to large hosting centers. Such hosting centers are carrier-grade in the sense of environmental hardening, security, 24/7/365 staffing, emergency power, and so on. Depending on the particular policy, customers have varying levels of access to hosts. Hosts may be in private cages accessible only to the customer and the operations staff, hosts may be accessible only to the operations staff who take service requests for customers, or there may be a large open facility with both trust and verification of the individual customers. Another argument for large hosting centers is the ability to justify especially high-speed, diverse connections and large amounts of globally routed address space. It is not at all uncommon to see large centers connected to diverse OC-48 SONET rings, and OC-192 is entering the market. The problem of having globally routable address space for small numbers of servers multihomed to different ISPs is not fully solved, and a large provider may be more able to solve this problem.

It would seem reasonable that an enterprise with critical multihoming requirements would want provider independent addresses. Unfortunately, many enterprises with such requirements do not have enough Internet-reachable hosts to justify their own address space. Even if they did receive space, some large providers filter prefix advertisements longer (that is, with a lesser number of hosts) than /19 or /20. Smaller enterprises simply do not qualify for this much address space, so even if they have registered space and advertise it, it may not be globally reachable. Hosting centers, however, often have large numbers of hosts and justify globally routable address space.

The term *hosting center* generally refers to a facility shared among enterprise servers. Carrier hotels are similar except that their customers are not enterprises but other carriers. A carrier hotel, for example, may be a point of presence for several ISPs in a locality, with shared high-speed uplinks. Carrier hotels also emphasize carrier-oriented infrastructure, such as −48 V DC power. Yet another variant is the cooperative local exchange, where ISPs and enterprises may cooperate to avoid sending traffic destined across the street by way of a major carrier hub hundreds of miles away.

Traditional and Startup Telcos

Telephone companies are entering data and multiservice provider markets themselves and also providing colocation for competitive providers. After the AT&T divestiture, several classes emerged. In the established and (to some extent) startup category are:

- Long-distance carriers with national facilities
- Long-distance carriers with regional facilities (ILECs) and local independent telephone companies (ITCs)
- Value-added networks that lease facilities

Primarily in the startup category are:

- Competitive local exchange carriers (CLECs)
- Competitive long-distance providers (ICPs)

These organizations have primarily competed for voice services, but have extended their offerings into data. CLECs may lease copper from incumbent telcos, or could bypass the ILEC local loop with optical or wireless local loops of their own.

To confuse things even further, cable television providers are entering both the data and voice markets, while traditional data providers now support voice over IP. Remember that the new competitive environment sometimes, but not always, separates basic loop access from switching.

Exchange Point Facilities

Another special case of carrier-class facility is the multilateral IP exchange point. The primary intent of such facilities is intercarrier connectivity, so the main discussion of exchange points is in Chapter 12. Of course, nothing is ever completely pure. While the original exchange points were purely for IP carriers, variants are used for hosting centers, which are discussed in Chapter 13.

Carrier-Quality Installations

One of the perceived differences between carrier class and enterprise class is that carrier class installations never go down. Obviously, this is not a universal truth. Installations that approach the perception of carrier class are much more carefully engineered than many enterprise data centers, and the more knowledgeable the designer, the greater the implementation of lessons taught by experience.

The Building and Its Environs

Begin with the building itself. A major consideration is its accessibility to other relevant carriers and customers, and to the underground ducts through which fiber is pulled. Some metropolitan areas require ducts, or even dark fiber, to be part of all new construction. Others at least try to coordinate the vehicular traffic disruption caused by multiple carriers' excavations—often after bitter complaints by carriers who do not want their competitors to know where they are installing capacity.

Consider local environmental hazards. If you are in a flood area, the building should be higher than the typical flood line. In hurricane, earthquake, or tornado areas, the standard building code is merely a starting point. Remember that even if the building survives a natural disaster, it still needs connectivity and electrical power. In the event of disaster, some of your key people may be unable to leave, and you need to have some minimum "hotel" capacity for them.

A building can be operated by a pure facilities-based carrier, an access provider, an IP services provider, a content provider, an exchange point, or a content delivery service. It may contain any or all of these functions under a common technical management. There are also commercial examples of separately managed facilities in the same building. For example, major hosting companies that also qualify as ISPs have built hosting centers in the same building that contains a carrier-only exchange point. Only a short length of in-building fiber (usually diverse sets of fiber) interconnects the hosting center on one floor with the exchange point on another floor, without violating the connection policies of either the hosting facility or the exchange point.

Equipment Mounting and Physical Density Issues

A problem common to traditional and new-generation carriers is that of *footprint*, the amount of floor space taken by equipment. One way of stating the carriers' objective is optimizing the amount of equipment that can fit into a standard 7-ft rack. Even racks differ in the various cultures. Telcos traditionally have racks that take 23-in-wide equipment, while the general electronics industry assumes equipment will be 19 in wide.

The footprint problem does not only involve vertical and floor space *Footprint*, *real estate*, and *form factor* are other terms used to describe the next issue, which is the number and type of interface connectors that can physically fit onto a chassis. As network speeds grow, the internal switching fabrics of high-performance routers and switches grow in power—and cost. Interface cards that plug into the fabric must have circuitry that is compatible with the fabric's speed. If a card slot in a chassis is 7 in high, there is a limit to how many connectors it can have. The practical limit seems to be 8 to 16. Think of the waste in connecting T1 circuits to gigabit and terabit routers. A plausible T1 card could connect only approximately 25 Mbps of data. A SONET card, with connectors of similar size, could connect 10 Gbps. One workable method of providing reasonable improvement in port density is to use not a *backplane*, to which all cards connect, but a *midplane*, which has card connectors on both of its sides. Hardware designers often separate the front and back of the midplane into different functions. On the Cisco 8850, for example, switching fabric and control cards are on the front, line cards on the back. Midplane design also allows different card heights. 8850 front cards are full-height, while there are two half-height cards in most of the back slots. The half-height cards are used for line interfaces. One card deals with common logic at the media-independent part of the physical layer, and possibly the data link layer as well, while the other is specific to the physical optical or electronic interface used.

If the goal is to increase the number of ports, aggregation devices or shelves may be appropriate. Such devices can be local or remote to the physical switches. Nortel Passport WAN switch slots, for example, have at least 400 Mbps of fabric bandwidth. An 8-port DS3 card that plugs into the fabric has two physical connectors. Each connector has a cable that goes to the panel that contains the actual DS3 connectors, which are too large to allow high density on the main switch chassis.

Power, Power, I Want Power

Central offices routinely use −48 V DC power rather than 110 or 220 V AC household power. The DC voltage is protected by large banks of batteries, which are trickle-charged by utility power but backed up with generators. Do not think of these battery systems as conventional computer room uninterruptible power systems (UPSs). Think more, instead, of the last World War II submarine movie you may have seen, where a huge battery room provides all power to a submerged submarine.

There are likely to be small power distribution and circuit breaker units in each equipment rack, but one of the advantages of centralized DC power is reducing the amount of vertical space in racks taken up by AC power converters.

Power, no matter how well backed up, still can fail. If you are trying to provide a highly available service, you must consider the effects of a total power failure in a key facility. A good rule for a high-availability network device is that it should have modular power supplies that are hot-swappable (that is, that can be changed while in service without disrupting other functions). In addition, the device should have full functionality with only half of its power supplies in operation.

Uninterruptible Power Supplies: Power Conditioning and Storage

While the terms *UPS* and *backup power source* are often used interchangeably, there is an important difference. UPSs are intended to provide computer-grade power directly to electronics, hiding not only outages but noise, brownouts, spikes, and other transient disturbances. They contain significant power conditioning, which is most commonly based on batteries but may use mechanical flywheels. Depending on the design of the particular UPS, they may constantly supply power to the load from the power storage, possibly having multiple storage units for separate operation and recharging. Alternatively, they may nor-

---

HINT

When putting more conventional data equipment into a central office environment, such as hubs or switches, you will need to provide an inverter that produces 110 V AC power from −48 V DC. Ironically, many small devices then need to convert the 110 V AC to various DC voltages that they use. At the same time, be aware that unless the conventional data equipment meets at least NEBS level 1, it may not be permitted in a central office. Hosting centers, carrier hotels, and exchange points may be more relaxed about non-NEBS equipment.

mally condition utility power, but may be able to make an extremely fast switchover to the stored power.

UPS implementation can involve some subtle procedural and software issues. For example, if the main power goes down and the UPS takes over, a more intelligent UPS will send a signal to the protected hosts after its battery capacity drops to a certain level. This signal is intended to let the hosts go into a graceful shutdown. But what happens if the main power comes back on after the shutdown signal is sent? Is there—or should there be—a means of canceling the signal? After some power failures, power may return only briefly. Therefore, perhaps a cancel should only be based on the UPS batteries recharging to a certain level. And, after a graceful shutdown, are there circumstances under which the protected hosts should restart automatically, perhaps when the UPS batteries reach a certain level of charge?

Another consideration, if hosts restart automatically, is the possibility of broadcast storms. If many identical hosts power on simultaneously and send out DHCP or other service requests simultaneously, this can represent a load for which the DHCP server is unprepared. Broadcast storms can result when the clients do not get a response from the infrastructure server and retransmit at approximately the same time.

Power Sources

Diesel generators are the most common source of alternate electrical power for large installations, although small, portable generators often run on gasoline and large turbines may use kerosene or other jet fuel. Solar panels charging batteries can be an interesting alternative for small, remote sites.

You cannot just install a generator and forget about it until you need it. Generators, and their supporting elements such as fuel and starter batteries, need regular inspection and maintenance. Diesels typically should be tested weekly. Diesel fuel does not have an indefinite shelf life—3 years is a reasonable estimate—but you should seek expert advice that considers your local weather and the type of storage tank.

> Tuesday's terrorist attack on the World Trade Center has had a significant impact on Con Edison's energy infrastructure in lower Manhattan. The fire and subsequent collapse of 7 World Trade Center have permanently damaged two substations located adjacent to the building as well as major electric transmission cables. A third substation located near the South Street Seaport also lost service. Approximately 12,000 customers are currently without electric power, approximately 270 steam customers are without service and approximately 1400 customers are without gas service.
>
> There are 140 Con Edison crews working in the devastated area. We are inspecting and testing equipment, preparing work locations and are coordinating our efforts with appropriate emergency agencies.

SECURITY AND POWER GO TOGETHER

A distinguished university with extensive experience in networking went through a detailed review of its electrical power requirements. All computers and controls were designated as follows:

Class C. Utility AC power only; any backup power was the responsibility of the user.

Class B. Utility AC power with backup from the university generator.

Class A. Full UPS support. The UPS batteries were charged both by the utility and the campus generator.

One day a major power failure struck the area, and the UPS faultlessly prevented the dropping of a single bit from the critical networks. When it became obvious that the outage would be prolonged, the university rented a second generator and installed it, and the electricians attempted to connect it to the UPS.

Shall we say that the next minute was unforgettable to the computing manager? The UPS, its controls, and the power connections to it were in a separate and secure room, whose door was under the control of the electronic key card system. Unfortunately, the electronic lock on the UPS door had been assigned to electrical protection category C. Its fail-safe mode was to stay locked. Luckily, the university had a long tradition of lock-picking as a student skill, and the crisis was soon resolved.

> We are currently making arrangements to obtain generators to help speed the temporary restoration of electric service in lower Manhattan.
> —*Announcement by Consolidated Edison [New York electrical utility], September 12, 2001*

The generator itself has environmental requirements. Following the World Trade Center disaster, generators failed because dust choked their radiators, interfering with cooling. While a radiator can be washed with a hose, considerable care must be taken, because spraying water on a hot engine block can crack it.

The generator should be in a secure area, which will depend on your local building codes. Especially if it is at ground level, it is wise to keep a spare (and charged) starter battery in your office—they have been known to be stolen.

HVAC and the Carrier Environment

Heating, ventilating, and air conditioning (HVAC) are fundamental aspects of building design. Most often, the problem is getting rid of heat, but heating cannot be ignored, especially in cold climates.

From the perspective of physical facilities, two cultural traditions are most important. Traditional data culture assumes computer room conditions for its equipment, in which equipment expects to operate within fairly stringent limits established by IBM. The traditional telco culture, however, expects equipment to be tolerant of the environment, although telco facilities routinely have extensive backup power, physical security, and the like.

Yet another dimension to carrier HVAC is that many equipment locations may always be unattended in the normal course of operations (for example, remote repeater sites) or may only occasionally have people among the machines (for example, server or router rooms adjacent to operations centers).

Fire Protection, and Protection against Fire Protection

Fire protection requirements are complex. Part of their complexity comes from their multiple objectives. True, part of their goal is to extinguish fires in your equipment, hopefully with minimal damage to equipment due to the firefighting methods. But fire protection also involves protecting other organizations and people from fires starting in your area. Also, some of the less obvious aspects of fire protection standards have to do with protecting firefighters actually dealing with a fire. There are restrictions, for example, on how high in a building large storage batteries can be placed. These restrictions are to prevent corrosive battery contents from showering onto firefighters dealing with a high-rise fire. Fire protection begins by establishing

---

WHAT ABOUT FIRE EXTINGUISHERS?

Fire extinguishers are very useful in stopping a small fire (for instance, in a wastebasket), or perhaps delaying a larger fire to give more evacuation time. There's probably not a fire department in the world that would object to be called at the same time someone is using an extinguisher on a fire—they can always be told the fire is out, but fires can grow with frightening speed. Extinguishers sometimes make people overconfident. Some training in their use is appropriate, even if that is a demonstration rather than hands-on. One thing that surprises many first-time extinguisher users is that the extinguishers can be quite noisy. I have seen users lose control of the discharge because they were so surprised by the noise. There is also a technique to using them. In general, you want to aim at the base of the fire and move inward with a sweeping motion, always leaving yourself a path of escape. There is a natural tendency to aim at the top of the flames, which is not nearly as effective.

standards that restrict the sorts of things that can start fires and sustain them. It then moves to fire detectors and fire alarms, and only then to automated systems intended to quench or limit fire propagation until firefighters reach the scene.

Water is the mainstay of firefighting. If a building is thoroughly on fire, the deluge of fire hoses is familiar to all. For commercial buildings, water sprinklers have proved immensely valuable in protecting life and property while firefighters are en route to the scene. Water, however, is very bad for electronic equipment, especially when that equipment is powered on. If it is possible to avoid a sprinkler discharge onto electronics and still control the fire, immense savings are possible. There are three main approaches to minimizing water damage as a result of firefighting:

1. Non-water-based fire suppression agents.
2. Dry-pipe, precharged sprinkler systems.
3. Provisions to protect electronics from sprinkler releases elsewhere in the building, given the reality that water runs downhill.

Non-Water-Based Fire Suppression

The earliest nonwater fire suppression agent was carbon dioxide, but it is unsuitable for any facility that may be occupied by people. In firefighting concentrations, carbon dioxide will render people unconscious in seconds, and can asphyxiate them if breathed for a long period. Chlorofluorocarbons such as Halon replaced carbon dioxide. In principle, these agents will not disable people by asphyxiating them. I learned a great deal about other realities, however, when I watched a live test in our computer room at the Corporation for Open Systems. Fairfax County, Virginia, required a live test of Halon systems, which in our case meant recharging the tanks at a cost in the tens of thousands of dollars. Other jurisdictions use less expensive methods to verify system operation. In any case, there were no people inside the computer room when the Halon system discharged, but we were able to watch it through glass walls. The initial burst of gas came with a loud noise and created a storm of loose papers. As the gas continued to discharge, condensation caused a dense mist to form. Visibility in the computer room dropped to near zero, and evacuation would have been a problem for anyone not intimately familiar with the layout of the room. Halon has subsequently been banned due to environmental effects on the ozone layer and replaced with agents such as FM200.

Storage tanks for the fire extinguishing agents are not small. Since the agents are quite expensive, it's generally appropriate to put them in a purpose-built closet, possibly locked if your local fire code permits.

WHEN WATER STARTS TO FLOW

Once water starts flowing through any sprinkler, the fire protection system will sound an alarm (in addition to any prior smoke or heat detector alarms) and commonly will perform an emergency power shutdown for the sprinklered zone. If your equipment is on UPS, consult a fire protection specialist to find out requirements for UPS shutdown. It is also advisable that water flow alarms be sent to a security center or directly to the local fire department.

Water Sprinklers

There are two kinds of sprinkler systems: wet-pipe and dry-pipe. Wet-pipe systems are always filled with water, but dry pipe is just that until a heat sensor gives a first-level warning, which causes the pipes to fill with water. Individual sprinkler heads start to spray only when they are exposed to enough heat to melt a water flow plug, so with wet- or dry-pipe systems, water will not necessarily go everywhere. Dry-pipe systems, however, protect your equipment from pipe failures.

Once there is enough local heat to trigger a sprinkler head, the equipment directly under it will probably already be beyond repair. You really do want the sprinkler to spray the hot spot to prevent the fire from spreading further.

Water Protection

During my career in computing and networking, I have never had a fire in one of my equipment rooms. In my earlier days in chemistry, however, I had direct experience with laboratory fires, so I can offer some perspective from both sides: preventing damage by putting out fires and damaging equipment with firefighting methods. Luckily, I have never had a networking equivalent to dealing with budding genius organic chemists who boiled ether over an open flame or poured waste molten sodium into the sink.

In my networking career, I have had several outages caused by water-based firefighting elsewhere in the building. In the most dramatic case, our computer room was on the first floor of an office and shopping building, which the building management closed on Sundays—and turned off the heat. One especially cold Sunday, the wet-pipe sprinkler pipes froze. About 10 A.M. the next day, the pipes thawed and burst. Water sprayed everywhere, not from the sprinkler heads but directly from pipe breaks in the walls and ceiling, accompanied by a shower of damp drywall. We desperately did emergency power shutdowns, which, with some of our equipment, required pulling power plugs while standing on wet floors (we were all young at the time). Of course, our staff was far calmer than the patrons in the beauty parlor down the hall, who were being showered with their heads in electrical hair driers. Several lessons came from this experience. First, don't put your critical equipment in facilities that don't have 24/7 heating in cold climates. Second, insist on dry paper pipes.

Sprinkler flow in the actual computer room is very likely to mean that you have a real problem right there. A different set of challenges, however, come from water-based firefighting on higher floors of your building. Again, I refer you to the first law of plumbing: Water runs downhill.

When I build computer rooms from scratch, and they have a raised floor, I make a practice of installing large floor drains if they are not already present. In some buildings, it is possible to put a water-resistant drop ceiling between the floor above you and your actual ceiling and have some water drains there. If you have emergency exit doors that exit directly onto stairwells, it is good practice to give them strong gaskets and make them water-resistant. Stairwells are often the easiest exit for water at higher levels.

Physical Security

Unfortunately, we live in a world where crime and terrorism are real issues to be considered in facility design. The world is not precisely predictable, which also needs to be considered as part of the security program.

One of the first routine security decisions to be made is how visible the facility should be to the outside world. It is one thing to put the corporate name prominently on a sales facility, but many providers prefer to keep their operational facilities unmarked, and indeed not to publicize their locations or make any antennas easily visible. Entry into the operational areas of a facility needs to be controlled, possibly with a zoned system where one enters the office area but needs additional access privileges to gain access to the operations center or equipment rooms. Push-button combination locks, card keys, or biometric sensors (for example, hand geometry, fingerprint, or retinal scanners) may be used for sensitive areas. Depending on your risk assessment, it may be appropriate for your access control system sensors to support a *duress code*, where an authorized employee sends a silent alarm that the employee is under threat and is being forced to open the door.

Biometrics are valuable, but their value against certain threats is sometimes overstated. If equipment thieves or terrorists really want to enter a facility, their means of identification will not be forged fingerprints, but brute force: battering rams, automatic weapons fire at hinges and locks, or explosives. Unless you are a military facility, you realistically can only delay such attacks with sturdy construction and reliable (typically wireless) communications to law enforcement reaction forces. Do not forget that attackers with military training in urban combat prefer to attack from the roof and work downward, so roof access doors should be sturdy. Indeed, in high-risk areas, it may be appropriate to use especially heavy metal for antennas on the roof, such that they would interfere with helicopter landing.

IS THAT A TIGER IN THE TANK?

One of my clients, software development firm, has a magnificently designed campus. No expense seemed to be spared on the network or on disaster protection. Being in a hurricane zone, the client had made arrangements with a nearby hotel to have the ballroom prewired with Ethernet drops to ensure a relocation site for the programmers. The client took this even further, considering that the programmers would be concerned about not only their own housing, but that of their families, and arranged that rooms would be available both for staff and families. The campus security system reflected comparable care. Electronic card keys protected doors, and indeed established extra-sensitive zones within already protected areas. The scanners were convenient to use. A roving security force patrolled the campus, and there were red phones everywhere, providing direct connections to the security center.

Not surprisingly, this enterprise was very serious about all kinds of training. As part of that philosophy, it built what turned out to be the largest video production facility in a multistate area. This facility was sufficiently capable that it became a profit center rather than a cost center, renting out studio time to local firms. One of these video customers was an auto dealership taping a new commercial. The video featured the usual Beautiful People, but also included— without the knowledge of the production center—a live tiger. During the taping, the tiger apparently became tired and bored and wanted a nap. Spying the video control room, he broke away from his handler and rushed into it. As cats will, he looked for a high perch, which happened to be the control panel, which was *very* quickly abandoned by the video staff.

The first of many escapees to reach a red security phone gabbled to security, "There's a tiger loose in the video production building!" There was a long pause, and the security officer replied, "Riiiiiight . . . uh-uh. . . . good joke. (click)." After repeated calls, security was convinced, and quickly obtained steaks for the handler to use to lure the tiger out of the control room.

By this time, the tiger had awakened. He apparently decided the control room was a nice place, warm from the electronics. He decided, in the manner of intact male felines everywhere, to mark the room as his in the way that male cats do.

The enterprise staff told me that it was a good three months before the control room stopped smelling of tiger.

Again, as an unfortunate reality of modern life, bombs cannot be ignored. It is reasonable to have a stout wall between the loading dock or mail room and critical operational facilities, with deliberately engineered blowout panels in the exposed areas' walls or ceiling to vent the force of an explosion. It also may be appropriate to landscape your grounds so there is no parking directly next to the wall of a critical area (including your generators with their inflammable fuel) and perhaps even to put in decorative concrete planters to deflect a truck ramming into the wall. This is truly an area where you need to discuss threats with local law enforcement, and, if your organization operates internationally, an appropriate security consultant, to help in risk assessment.

There is no such thing as a truly bombproof facility when sufficient explosives and skill are available. At some point, having geographically diverse redundant facilities makes more sense than continuing to harden a single facility. This principle also holds in protecting against major natural disasters.

The Human Resource and Its Management

People tend to be your most important resource. In some respects, I am still surprised when I see Dilbert-style management driving away people with critical experience, but I suppose I have come to expect it. There are many levels dealing with operations people. One reality is that answering the support phone is stressful, and, if the person answering that phone hears the same problems too often, boring. One major carrier estimated that second- or third-level support staff would stay in the same job for approximately a year and then have to be replaced. Management practices that keep these employees' valuable experience in the firm include opportunities for training, rotation into related jobs both to gain experience and for an interesting change, and promotion. Promotion may not necessarily be into another level of operations support, but elsewhere in a related area, including sales, engineering, quality management, and so on.

Traditional carriers divide their support activities into have operations, administration, maintenance, and provisioning, which covers most of the aspects of the operations process (although the word *operations* is admittedly redundant as it does not reflect real-world workflow. In the direct operational process, sales and sales engineering create the order, administration sets up billing, and provisioning sets up the resources required to provide the service. Once sales has obtained a contract to provide service, provisioning involves the preoperational steps to be able to deliver that service. Depending on your organization, administration may need to take place before provisioning, involving such functions as establishing billing, taking any deposits required, verifying points of contacts, and so forth.

YOU SOLD THEM WHAT?

I am avoiding discussion here of the sales engineering function, where the proposed service is vetted for technical feasibility before the final proposal is made and the contract signed. For this discussion, I will assume both that sales will only sell feasible solutions and that the world's greatest expert on logistical distribution remains Santa Claus.

Provisioning: Starting the Technical Operation

Provisioning is the function of selecting and installing the carrier circuits and switch resources that underlie a customer-ordered service. Name and address assignment, discussed in Chapter 5, is one aspect of provisioning. Others include ordering the local loop to the customer (or assigning a facility if you operate the local loop), discussed in Chapter 7. Local loop connectivity involves more than just assigning the facility. It also entails assigning the physical and logical ports to which the facility will connect in your POP.

You may need to order circuits from other carriers to add needed capacity or arrange connectivity to a given geographic area. Your interior routing (see Chapters 8 and 11) will play a basic role in establishing the end-to-end path, as long as it stays completely within your facilities. Interior routing may need to involve traffic engineering if QoS is guaranteed, and traffic engineering will periodically trigger the need for additional facilities.

Operations: Trouble Reporting, Monitoring, and Problem Response

The operational functions for established services vary from company to company, but they generally include, as a minimum:

- The telephone help desk. Often called *first-level support*, this is frequently an entry-level position staffed by people with relatively little technical knowledge, who work from scripts.

- Second-level technical support is often the first level where the staff can actually do anything to correct the problem. It may be wise to establish procedures where certain customers who are known to be technically competent have direct access to second- or even higher-level support.

- Third- and higher-level support tends to deal with issues such as multivendor compatibility, design problems in the network, and so on. This function often blurs into network planning and design.

Building appropriate network operations centers (NOCs) is an important part of delivering these services.

Network Operations Centers

Network operations centers vary from company to company, but they generally include:

- The telephone help desk.

- Technical escalation (staff members who actually do troubleshooting and provisioning).

- Network health monitoring, capacity planning, and network engineering. This function often is outside the NOC proper but available to it for advanced support.

Operations staff can do rather little in isolation. They need flexible, comfortable, efficient voice and data communications.

Room Layout

There are mixed opinions on whether or not wall-sized status displays are really helpful to operations. I worked with one quite competent carrier who freely admitted that its main displays were intended primarily to impress VIP visitors, and that the *Star Fleet Technical Manual* had indeed been used as the design guide. Multiple monitors at individual technicians' workstations were the day-to-day tools. While it can be debated whether wall-sized displays of network topology are really that useful, several ISPs have found wall-mounted displays of open problems, color-coded for criticality and duration, to be quite helpful in managing problems.

Communications for Your People

Having more than one screen at an operations workstation—or at the very least a large screen monitor with excellent multiple-window capability—is quite important. It is quite common, for example, to want to be able to go back and forth among a trouble ticket, a router or other device configuration, an error log, and perhaps some topology displays. Another reason why you may want multiple monitors is that the equipment controlled may have mixed interfaces—asynchronous terminal interfaces for router consoles, UNIX workstations for operations support equipment, and Microsoft workstations for administrative systems. (For the record, this book is being written on my Macintosh G4.)

DISPLAYS YOU ALWAYS WANTED TO HAVE

The aforementioned *Star Fleet Technical Manual* shows details of the set that are too fine to be seen on television, but do amuse the cast and crew. You may remember that the medical bed on *Star Trek: The Next Generation* has a set of bar graphs over the head of the bed, but the legends are not quite readable on a television set. The bottom bar actually is labeled "Medical Insurance Remaining." I leave it as an exercise for the reader to consider what you would *really* like to measure in your network—or your upper management.

Not necessarily at each operator position, but certainly well visible in the network operations centers, should be at least one or two television sets tuned to CNN and a local news station. These can give you excellent information on large-scale disasters that might be affecting your network. Weather-band radios with automatic alarms also are appropriate.

You will need to think carefully about telephone services, especially if your services involve international connectivity. North American 800 numbers frequently cannot be dialed from other countries; a toll number should be available in appropriate intercarrier documentation and in such places as routing registries. If you have a PBX, consider what happens if it breaks or if the local telephone company has a problem. It makes extremely good sense to have at least some cellular phones in the NOC as backup.

Anyone who gives telephone support needs hands-free capability, which is usually more practical with a headset than a speakerphone. It can be useful, however, to have a small conference room adjacent to the NOC, equipped with good-quality speakerphones, when several people need to collaborate on resolving a problem. Wireless headsets, while more expensive, tend to be less fatiguing and indeed may pay for themselves after a few occasions where a corded set pulls expensive equipment crashing to the floor. Be aware of the fact that they broadcast: Eavesdropping on wireless headsets is becoming a popular form of industrial espionage, and can be done from a surprising distance.

There is a good deal of opinion, although no real consensus, about non-voice but near-real-time communications for the operations staff. A good e-mail system is essential.

Pay a great deal of attention, with consulting as needed, to the human factors of operator workstations: appropriately ergonomic furniture, lighting that does not glare off screens, and so on. Fatigued people make more mistakes. While I tend to agree that beverages have little place in equipment rooms, having coffee, tea, and soft drinks available to the staff in the network operations center (perhaps with cup/can holders built into the work areas) helps morale and concentration. Require beverages to be in covered containers (no open cups of coffee or glasses of water).

Customer Support Practices

Subscribers will be more tolerant when they feel informed. Find ways of keeping them updated with decent information, without necessarily needing to interact with each customer. Voice response is probably best here, because the user may not have the connectivity to use Web or e-mail resources. Especially for business-grade users, design your telephone support very carefully, and avoid the suggestions of image or brand identity marketing consultants who look at every contact situation as an active marketing opportunity. Recognize that a customer that is reporting a problem is already frustrated and not apt to be well disposed toward the provider. Business customers, in particular, are

"PRESS 1 IF YOU ARE CALLING TO REPORT YOUR DEATH"

An amazing number of carriers lecture people who call their trouble desks on the advisability of using Web pages or e-mail to report the problem. Does it occur to any designers of these lectures that the user may be calling exactly because e-mail and Web services are not working?

busy people and simply want to speak to a service technician or at least get a meaningful update. Music on hold, and especially recorded sales pitches or customer care platitudes, do not in any way contribute to informing the customer. They can drive the customer into complete rage during a 20- or 30-minute hold time, poisoning the interaction with first-level support when it finally takes place. A periodic, professional, "You're still in queue," preferably with a waiting time estimate, can be useful. Platitudes about "It will just be a moment" are irritating when it won't just be a moment. Even these platitudes are less irritating than the periodic recorded reassurance about how "Your call is important to us," or "Increased business has caused longer hold times." Above all, recognize that the problem-reporting service is the last place in the world to sell new products. Keep in mind the following principles:

- Don't tell the caller it will be "just a moment" if it won't.
- Never, never blather about how important the call is. If it were really that important, you would have answered it already.
- Never, never, never talk about new products on the problem reporting line.
- First-line support doesn't have all the answers.

Under the economic constraints that apply to today's providers, and a cynical but realistic appraisal of the knowledge level of a great many subscribers, the first-line support staff—those who answer the phone—have little or no technical expertise. They operate from standard scripts, which often seem to have an implicit assumption that the problem is the subscriber's fault: "Is the computer on? Are all its connections tight?" The connectivity questions are fairly legitimate, if somewhat condescending. Particularly irritating, however, are demands to reinstall software or reboot computers, which can be lengthy, error-prone processes that introduce new problems and had not even been demonstrated to be related to the specific problem.

Confronted with knowledgeable subscribers, many first-level personnel become defensive. Don't get defensive or pretend knowledge that isn't there. If you use first-level support people who really are not technical, it may be quite appropriate to give key customers and other ISPs that you know to be competent special support numbers to directly reach higher-level technical support.

Provide meaningful ways to get more detailed information. A frequently updated telephone recording is good. I'm always amused how many providers' trouble-reporting systems urge me to check their Web page. If I could reach their Web page, I frequently wouldn't be reporting the trouble!

Operational Aspects of Network Security

There are several broad classes of attacks with which a provider needs to deal. Within the scope of this chapter, I will describe some of the operational aspects of dealing with them. The legal and technical aspects of this are very complex, as are the proactive measures you can implement to help prevent certain attacks, such as the following:

- One of your IP addresses is implicated in an attack on a third party.
- One of your customers is under attack.
- Part of your network infrastructure is under attack.

TRUST ME, WE'RE WORKING ON IT

When their approaches are challenged, first-level support personnel often pretend knowledge they do not have. I remember a recent episode when I asked my service provider why I could not traceroute beyond the POP access router, and was told, "The server is down." Inquiring what server the support person was talking about, or how any server interfered with a pure routing problem, I was met with a repeated, "The server, and the technicians are working on it."

In every lifetime, we have flashes in which calm and sanity return, in which we learn that our perceptions were not warped. I remember a time when chatting with my former mother-in-law, when I quoted my ex-wife as saying she was "working on it" with respect to some financial matters. Being on good terms with my mother-in-law, I mentioned my frustration with this answer. My mother-in-law was somewhat surprised and said, "In all the years you've been married, haven't you learned that when she says 'I'm working on it,' she hasn't done anything? She's been saying that since she was a little girl."

Remembering that conversation, I felt morally re-armed to say what I should have said in the first place: "Please escalate this call." Certainly, I'm an atypical user in my understanding of a provider's infrastructure. But a good deal of customer frustration—and the potential for the provider to lose a customer— could be alleviated by the provider's management encouraging a culture in which first-level support staff are not incentivized to avoid responsibility. Responsibility includes appropriate problem escalation.

Responding to these events must first and foremost be based on legal and business factors backed by top management and with appropriate legal advice. Perhaps the most basic policy question is whether to emphasize countering the threat and continuing operations or involving law enforcement early in the process. Countering may or may not stop the problem or even act as a challenge to the attacker. However, it may—especially if you find and close a security hole you discover—end the problem quite quickly. Involving law enforcement personnel will often leave you vulnerable for a longer time, because they want to gather evidence. Evidence-gathering may jeopardize the privacy of other users. On the other hand, if they can successfully identify and prosecute an offender, it is very hard for attacks to continue if someone is behind bars. Most amateur offenders have no real economic resources, so suing them is futile. But if the attack is being performed for commercial reasons such as industrial espionage or large-scale spamming, there may be a potential for financial recovery. Regardless of your policy, good record-keeping when an exploit begins is essential to any subsequent action. You will need it to build technical defenses even if law enforcement is never involved.

More complex is the situation where you are contacted by another service provider and told that an exploit is being launched from one of your hosts, either customer or infrastructure. One of the complexities of the situation here is that the person responsible for that host may be completely innocent. It is fairly standard practice for malicious crackers to launch their exploits through a series of machines between their actual host and the host that attacks the target. You need to investigate this situation yourself to begin with and decide if your customer is cognizant of the process. If the customer is innocent, you need to try to block the path the attacker is using. If the customer is not innocent, then you need to consider terminating the customer's access for violation of your acceptable use policy (you do have one, don't you?) and decide if further legal action is appropriate. You will have to give careful thought to the legalities and ethics of responding to requests for information about your customers either from other service providers or from law enforcement. Legal advice may very well be needed, especially if a court order is involved.

Looking Ahead

In this chapter we have concentrated on physical and closely related aspects of the carrier environment, but primarily on the transmission system. Chapter 7 deals with the provider edge, principally with subscriber management functions there (in contrast with logical functions in Chapter 10). Chapter 8 deals with the logical structure inside the carrier, including IP routing and sub-IP protocols. Chapters 9 through 12 deal with intraprovider and interprovider routing.

CHAPTER

7

The Provider Edge: Layer 1, Layer 2, and the PSTN

All that Sunday I listened to people who said that the mere fact of spiking down strips of iron to wood, and getting a steam and iron thing to run along them was progress, that the telephone was progress, and the net-work of wires overhead was progress. They repeated their statements again and again.
—Rudyard Kipling

A vast pulpy mass, furlongs in length and breadth, of a glancing cream-color, lay floating on the water, innumerable long arms radiating from its centre, and curling and twisting like a nest of anacondas, as if blindly to catch at any hapless object within reach. No perceptible face or front did it have; no conceivable token of either sensation or instinct; but undulated there on the billows, an unearthly, formless, chance-like apparition of life.
—Herman Melville, assuming giant squids were used for local loops

Calling an access system Ethernet does not automatically make it successful or cheaper.
—David Thorne, Presentation to IEEE Ethernet in the First Mile group

There's an old story of a visitor to New York asking a local "How do I get to Carnegie Hall?" The New Yorker, a musician, replied, "Practice, man. Practice." In the previous chapter, we looked at the Carnegie Hall of service provider networks, the increasingly optical core. It is literally the part of the network in light. The more mundane problem remains: How do the bits get there from the subscriber locations, especially those served by elderly copper pairs?

This chapter deals with the physical facilities that directly connect to the customer—assumed here to be an enterprise—and the interconnections among various wholesalers of customer services. Chapter 9 deals with the logical aspects of the customer side of the customer-IPSP interface.

The First-Meter, First-100-Meter, First-Mile, and Second-Mile Problems

Carriers provide services to customers, who connect to the service providers via *loops*. Historically, regulators distinguished between *bearer services*, which are provided by regulated monopoly carriers, and *value-added* services, provided competitively. With the advent of competition in the local loop, this distinction has blurred. The classical bearer service is dial tone, or plain old telephone service (POTS). It now extends to basic data services, both circuit- and packet-switched.

Basic service presents subtle business challenges to those who provide it—typically incumbent local exchange carriers (ILECs), or "local phone companies." On one hand, the individual instances of basic service are low in revenue. On the other hand, when the instances are taken together, they become a dependable revenue stream. This is one of the reasons ILECs have historically been slow in moving into value-added services: They are risk-averse about anything that might divert from their core cash flow.

A service is something a customer buys, either directly or indirectly. It does something the user finds useful. Since some carriers sell capacity to other carriers, what may be a service from one perspective is a networking capability from another. From the carrier perspective, VPNs for data and Centrex for voice are applications, as are IP services beyond routing, such as DNS and DHCP. Value-added voice services such as directory assistance and voice mail are applications. It is not unreasonable to suggest that broadcast channels over cable TV are its bearer service, while pay-per-view services are enhanced services.

Historical Switching and Transmission Architecture

The Strowger switch, patented in 1891, was the first automatic telephone switch. It used the control hardware both to set up the call and to manage the connection (Figure 7.1). Incoming lines went into the center of a cylinder to which all outgoing lines connected. Dialed digits caused an internal lever to "step" in two dimensions—up/down and rotating—such that it connected the incoming line to the outgoing line. The stepping action is much like walking up a spiral staircase, and Strowger switches are also called *step-by-step switches*. Outgoing lines connected to the outside of the cylinder and had metal points on the inside that met the moving lever. A single Strowger switch could only handle the digits 00 to 99, but Strowger switches could be cascaded—awkwardly—for larger digit ranges. When the call disconnected, the search levers returned to the idle position. Otherwise, they were committed for the duration of the call, even though their logical power was idle.

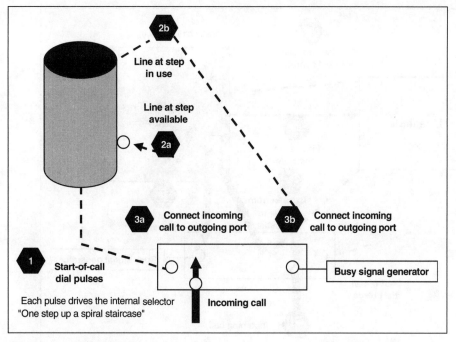

Figure 7.1   The Strowger switch.

It soon became obvious that call setup logic was far more expensive and complex than connection management. The idea of separating control and switching is not new—it appeared in electromechanical switches. The *crossbar switch* (Figure 7.2), invented in 1938, separated the functions. It assembled all lines in a matrix, with input lines in vertical rows and output lines in horizontal rows. The digit receiver needed to translate the digits into vertical and horizontal coodinates and then energize a relay to connect the two axes. Once the connection was made, the selector equipment did not need to be involved. Hanging up the connection would de-energize the relay.

As provider networks grow more intelligent, there is a distinct separation between the switching and control functions. The idea of numbers of calls that can be set up applies to controllers, conventional circuit switches, and gateways that integrate control functions. Devices that interface to customers are sized in the number of ports they can handle and the number of *busy hour call attempts* (BHCAs) that can be processed. Historically, in electromechanical switching, the cost of call setup far exceeded the cost of maintaining the connection and was the limiting factor on switch design. The economics have changed with electronic switching. They have not disappeared, but have only become more complex with distributed control networks.

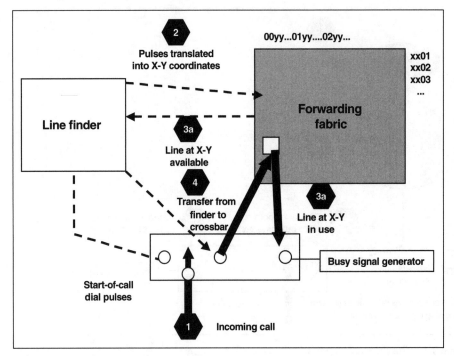

Figure 7.2   The crossbar switch.

Terminology for Separated Control and Switching

A *network service instance* (NSI) is the unit of providing service—a voice call, a data flow, and so on. *Connections* are one-way, bidirectional, or multi-directional sets of NSIs, and may be considered an association of resources. The decision on what path to take through the network is a *control plane* function. The carriage of bits of an NSI through the carrier network is a *switching plane* function. Control and switching functions do not have to reside in the same physical chassis, and it is quite common for control elements to be shared over multiple switching elements, either LAN-connected inside a CO or remotely located. Figure 7.3 shows some common telephony infrastructure functions. Note that there is no single point of failure for communications.

Every instance has a near- and far-end address, a set of signaling requirements, and a path. When the generic service has options, such as QoS, the NSI identifies a particular set of options used for the particular unit of service.

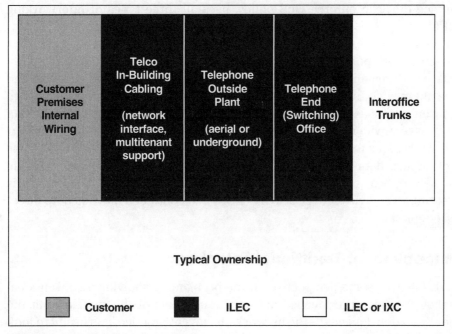

Figure 7.3   Conventional telephony.

Traditional Carrier Service Types and Interworking

Carrier switching elements move bits for several reasons: native services, service interworking, and trunking. Native services are of the same type at input and output; there are no protocol converters between the access to the service and the service proper. In other words, the originating device has the same service format as its entry point to the network. *Media gateways* convert between dissimilar networks, and are discussed further in the section "Media Gateways and the New Second Mile."

Service interworking involves dissimilar types of services, perhaps one at the customer access and another in the transport. Conversion is required, and may include one or more functions:

- Transport interworking, such as media encapsulation and conversion
- Control interworking, such as address mapping
- Application interworking, such as call screening

ISDN-to-ATM interworking, for example, uses Q.931 to access an ATM transport that uses a user-to-network interface (UNI). Frame relay to ATM, in a service that can enforce QoS policy, uses all three types of interworking [FRF.8].

Trunking services are the function of the main transport. They carry bits between access points, interworking points, and internal network switches. Trunks carry signaling as well as user information, although the signaling and user data may go by different systems within the provider network. Classical telco trunks have used time-division multiplexing (TDM) or ATM. Classical data trunks have a wider range of transports. GMPLS is likely to be the transport control technique that unifies the data and voice worlds. MPLS itself today runs over classical data transports, but these transports are themselves evolving with new optical technologies. Where ATM might be used today, there is increasing use of packet over SONET (POS) and continued movement to direct IP over optical.

Components of Traditional Telephony

Figure 7.3 gives some perspective on the problem by showing a conventional telephony architecture focused not on the internals of the switches but the major operational pieces of the network. In current practice, it is useful to look separately at particular components of the conventional architecture: the "first meter(s)" inside the customer premises; the "first 100 meters" connecting the customer with the nearest carrier facility; the "first mile" connecting the customer with the nearest copper termination point and equivalent facilities for other services; and the "second mile," which provides broadband connectivity between end offices and service providers.

The Traditional First Meter

This particular problem actually may involve cabling in the tens of meters, but the "first-meter problem" has much more flair. In traditional telephony, this problem deals with the interconnection of subscriber telephones to the demarcation point of the telephone company. In traditional telephony, this is the household or office wiring to which telephones connect, either via a PBX or directly to the telephone company.

The Traditional First 100 Meters

For residential applications, the next part of connectivity runs from the network interconnect (NI) to the entry point of the first mile. For example, this could be the aerial drop wire from your house to a splicing chamber on a nearby telephone pole.

Multitenant buildings typically have one or more wire closets per floor. In the wire closets, the pairs horizontally (that is, per floor) connecting to end

UP AND DOWN

The terms *horizontal* and *vertical cabling* are widely used in industry cabling standards.

equipment are punched down on wire punchdown blocks, to which cable bundles are connected in bundles of 25 or 50 pairs. These bundles go into a larger riser cable, which usually has 100 pairs or a multiple thereof, and then run vertically to an underground cable vault. The individual pairs are cross-connected to a cable leaving the vault and running to the central office over the first mile. Such a cable may contain hundreds or thousands of pairs.

Large buildings may have multiple cables. The sheer size and weight of multithousand pair cables is one of the drivers for today's optical local loops.

The Traditional First Mile

Traditional telephony uses twisted pairs of copper wire, bundled into large cables of hundreds or thousands of cables, from endpoints such as office building to the end office of the carrier. If these cables are relatively new, they will be suitable for emerging digital technologies such as ISDN and xDSL. Unfortunately, many performance-improving features used in the analog world are incompatible with digital transmission.

Digital end offices begin with channel banks where the analog signals are digitized. The output of the channel bank, directed to the traditional second mile, is a digital T1 or E1 stream. We have discussed T1/E1 channels as digital streams. These facilities were developed as digital carriers for voice. Formally, DS1 is a signal format and T1 is a specific transmission system that carries DS1 signals over twisted copper pairs, but the terms are interchangeable in practice. In modern terms, you can think of the basic voice-data interface device, the *channel bank* (Figure 7.4), as a set of analog interfaces and codecs under a central multiplexing control. Each analog channel converts to a 64-Kbps DS0 signal. Algorithms used by the codecs differ in various parts of the world. Canada, the United States, and Japan use μ-law, Europe uses A-law, and there are a few other algorithms such as the K-law used in Mexico. Mexico also uses E1 rather than T1 links. For end-to-end voice to work between different codecs, a gateway function will be needed.

Basic telephony multiplexing is fixed rather than statistical. It is worth noting that 64 Kbps is the basic rate at which a single voice call is digitized. North American channel banks combine 24 DS0 signals into a DS1 signal. The Consultative Committee for International Telephony and Telegraphy (CCITT)/ITU version, used in Europe, is the E1 signal.

ANALOG LEGACIES

Loading coils are components that improve the distance analog signals can travel by reducing high-frequency signals that are outside the speech range but that interfere with long analog paths. Unfortunately, the high-speed last mile technologies use exactly those frequencies.

Loading coils may be on as many as 20 percent of U.S. lines. As lines are maintained, the telephone companies are removing them. Interestingly, the original 6,000-ft spacing of T1 repeaters was selected because the most common practice for loading coil placement, called H88, placed a loading coil every 6,000 ft. T1 repeaters were designed so that they could physically go into loading coil housings.

When telephone companies cite what seems to be a long time to provide a local loop for digital access, the limiting factor is often removing the loading coils, which may be located underground or on telephone poles. Alternatively, telcos may route new loops through lines without loading coils, but that assumes that accurate records have been kept for decades—a loading coil might have been added to a link after its installation.

Wire diameter can be another analog legacy that limits local loop distance. The thinner a wire, the higher its electrical resistance and thus the shorter the range of signals that can run over it. But wire gauge is a two-edged sword: Thinner wires cost less (they need less copper), and—often more importantly— more wires can fit into the crowded ducts often seen in areas with high population density. The thinner 26-gauge wire in common use in high-density areas requires T1 repeaters every 4,000 ft.

The physical facilities over which DS1 and E1 signals are carried, called *trunks*, are high-speed links that are generally intended to contain multiplexed subchannels. Different kinds of physical links can carry these signals. T1, for example, is a specific transport technology that carries DS1 signals over twisted copper pairs. A T1 channel bank converts 24 analog channels to a single DS1 stream. Twenty-four DS0 channels occupy 1.536 Mbps of bandwidth, and the remaining 8 Kbps of the DS1 channel provides synchronization and diagnostics between the multiplexers and thus is M-plane information. User-level information, such as dialing, is also carried within the digital streams, but the details of carrying it are beyond the scope of this discussion.

The "Traditional" Second Mile: Multiplex Management

Even though we tend to speak of deregulation as relatively recent, there has been a distinction between local and long-distance carriers almost since the

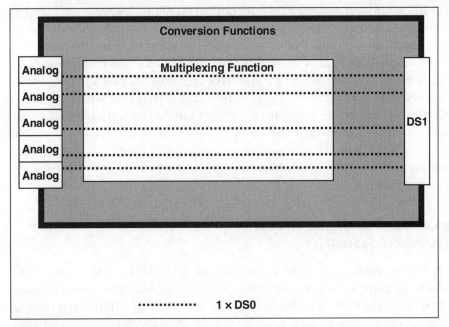

Figure 7.4 A channel bank.

beginning of telephony. The physical connections between these types of carriers have been multiplexed since the technology was available, in order to avoid the cost of large volumes of copper. Multiplexing was not limited to local–to–long distance, but also was used between central offices in a local area. Prior to the introduction of digital multiplexed carrier systems N carrier was common in local areas and L carrier for long-haul routes. T carrier was originally intended as a replacement for N carrier, and indeed the T3/DS3 rate was not meant to be used outside switching centers. Instead, it was a convenient way to connect 672-channel DS3 (obviously with some unused channels) to the 600-channel master groups of L carrier. The original DS3 inside the

I SAID TRANPORT, NOT TRANSPORT

One reliable way to confuse a conversation between data and telephony folk is to begin to refer to "transport." To the data people, this is layer 4 of the OSI model (that is, the end-to-end service). To transmission people, it is the physical high-speed medium. Creative minds can further complicate this situation. One of my colleagues, Stephen Nightingale, had vanity license plates for his car that read *OSI 4.* He explained that this clearly indicated it was his transport. Subsequently he traded in the car for a sport-utility vehicle and obtained new plates reading *OSI 4X4.*

central office ran over coaxial cable. As optical technologies were deployed, it turned out that the upper speed limit of inexpensive light-emitting diode (LED) optical transmitters, as opposed to more expensive lasers, was approximately 50 Mbps—a speed that easily accommodated DS3. While DS3 was defined and used early in the deployment of digital networks, it only became a popular WAN transmission speed with the advent of optical digital transmission.

Multiplexing was in use from the beginning of digital carrier systems. A continuing reason was to reduce the sheer mass of cable between offices, but another was to use increasingly intelligent multiplexing for circuit provisioning and management. Grooming, discussed later in this section, is a major part of such management.

Channel Bank to Digital Access Crossconnect System

At first DS1 streams did not go outside the central office or were physically patched to outgoing DS1 spans. As DS0 feeds into DS1, so higher-speed DSx signals feed into higher-speed multiplexers. The hierarchy of multiplexed rates in the United States, Canada, and Japan is called the *plesiochronous digital hierarchy*, mercifully referred to by the acronym PDH (Table 7.1). The rest of the world uses the *Synchronous Digital Hierarchy* (SDH) defined by the Conference of European Postal and Telecommunications Administrations (CEPT) (see Table 7.2). Fixed-configuration multiplexers combined channels from one level of the PDH or SDH to another. In the PDH, M12 multiplexers combined DS1 streams into DS2 and M23 multiplexers combined DS2 into DS3. As DS3 gained acceptance as a transmission technology, M13 multiplexers evolved that combined multiple DS1s into a DS3. These multiplexers, however, did not allow

Table 7.1 PDH in U.S., Canadian, and Partial Japanese Digital Hierarchy

LEVEL	SPEED	VOICE CHANNELS
DS0	64 Kbps	1
DS1	1.544 Mbps	24
DS1C	3.152 Mbps	48
DS2	6.312 Mbps	96
DS3*	44.736 Mbps	672
DS4*	274.176 Mbps	4,032

* In Europe and much of the world outside North America and Japan, a different hierarchy emerged, still based on multiples of 64 Kbps. Japan uses the DS1 and DS2 rates, but has a different hierarchy above the DS2 level.

Table 7.2 SDH in the Rest of the World

LEVEL	SPEED	VOICE CHANNELS
E0	64 Kbps	1
E1	2.032 Mbps	32
E2	8.448 Mbps	120
E3	34.368 Mbps	480
E4	139.268 Mbps	1,920
E5	565.148 Mbps	7,680

the digital streams to be reconfigured. A DS0 signal remained DS0 throughout the system; these fixed multiplexers did not allow, for example, for six DS0 signals to be combined into a 384-Kbps signal.

Digital access crossconnect systems (DACSs) are fundamental components of a carrier end office (see Figure 7.5). They are physical layer devices that accept DSx streams and combine them into DS3 and faster trunks for interoffice communications. They can demultiplex a higher-layer stream and send individual subchannels to different output ports. DACSs are the carrier building block of fractional T1 and T3. The DACS can combine multiple DS0 channels into an aggregate stream sent to the customer over a physical T1 or T3. While a

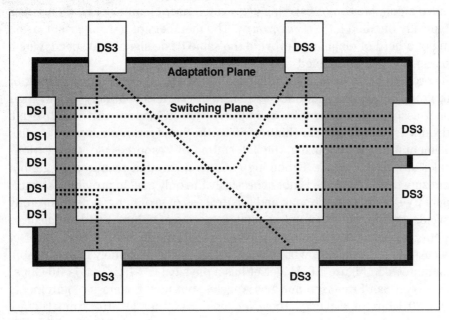

Figure 7.5 DACS.

physical T1 or T3 may be present, only the provisioned fraction is available to actually carry traffic (six DS0s, for instance, for a total available bandwidth of 384 Kbps even though 1,544 Kbps is physically present). The advantage to the carrier of installing the more capable wire is that when bandwidth demand increases, it can be met by provisioning more circuits from the excess not yet used, as opposed to running another physical installation. One of the major roles of the DACS and its descendants is *grooming*. I've never been exactly sure of the reason for the use of the term, which brings up images of dog and cat shows. A better name would probably be *trunk packing*.

Grooming

As mentioned, trunks are logical high-speed bit streams, which may have a one-to-one mapping to the physical transport (for example, DS1 to T1). Multiple trunks also may map to a single physical transport, as is quite common in optical transport systems [for example, multiple SONET signals over a single dense wave-division multiplexing (DWDM) facility]. When not attached to elephants, trunks carry user information and may carry signaling information. Trunks usually have a connotation of carrying aggregated user channels, and themselves are typically bundled into *trunk groups*. The members of a trunk group, again when not a herd of elephants, provide the same basic signal and speed, which of course may be multiplexed.

The process of provisioning trunks is not a static one in which the trunk or trunk group never changes once established. Carriers routinely groom their channel assignments to trunks to improve the efficiency with which trunk bandwidth is used. You can think of it as the bandwidth equivalent to disk defragmentation: reorganizing the allocation of resources so that various "chunks" are usable again. Grooming ensures maximum resource usage, but maximizing resource usage is not necessarily the only goal in providing service. Availability is an important goal, and the process of grooming, unless carefully managed, can increase the number of single points of failure. For example, carriers often lease additional capacity from other carriers. Assume that HugeNet has a customer, BigUser, to whom HugeNet has made extremely high availability guarantees. In Figure 7.6, HugeNet has a physical OC-192 (that is, 10-Gbps) link between San Francisco and Los Angeles, but new business requirements call for 20 Gbps of capacity. HugeNet leases another OC-192 from Dietary Fiber. HugeNet contractually requires knowing the circuit layout of Dietary

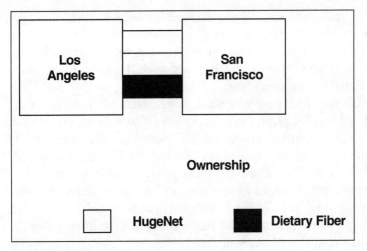

Figure 7.6 The need for extra capacity.

Fiber so that HugeNet can ensure that there is physical route diversity on the San Francisco–Los Angeles Path. HugeNet previously had a sad experience with a customer circuit, with similar availability requirements, between Los Angeles and Seattle. Since HugeNet did not have its own facilities north of Seattle, it leased bandwidth from TreeNet and JavaNet. Unfortunately, HugeNet did not know that neither TreeNet nor JavaNet had their own facilities between Portland and Seattle, and both unknowingly leased bandwidth from a common provider, FoggyNet. A single backhoe cut to the FoggyNet cable resulted in a single point of failure (Figure 7.7).

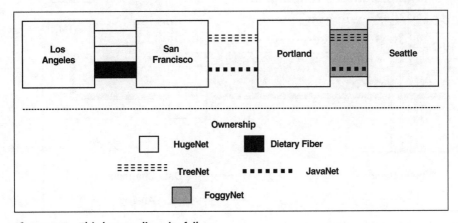

Figure 7.7 Third-party diversity failure.

HugeNet, however, has to be careful not to inadvertently introduce single points of failure on its own. As its capacity requirements grew between Los Angeles and San Francisco, HugeNet very reasonably converted the single OC-192 SONET fiber path to SONET over WDM, giving itself, initially, 10 OC-192s where only 1 had existed on the same fiber.

Naturally, HugeNet's financial planners want to minimize the cost of bandwidth leased from third parties, given the much greater internal capacity. To do this, it is completely appropriate to groom most circuits operating over third-party facilities onto the HugeNet transport. The danger is that automated grooming software, or a provisioning technician unaware of contractual requirements for diverse routing, might groom both of BigUser's paths onto the WDM facility and expose BigUser to a single point of failure. HugeNet, even if it reduces its leased bandwidth, still needs to lease some diverse links unless it builds new and diverse facilities of its own.

Sophisticated users have learned the reality that a given carrier may not always have the necessary diversity fully in place, and that ensuring that diversity is always there is a continuing process. Such users very well may want contractual authority to review their circuit layouts at intervals of 60 days or so.

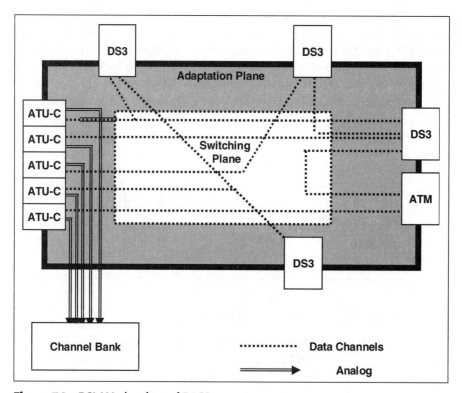

Figure 7.8   DSLAM, daughter of DACS.

Circuit layouts traditionally have been considered highly proprietary, but in today's market a carrier's willingness to allow customers to audit only their own layouts may make the sale go to the carrier that permits the audits.

DACS to Broadband Access Device

While DACSs were specifically associated with DSx technologies, a similar function arose for specific last-mile technologies. A DSL access multiplexer (DSLAM), for example, accepts customer streams, converts them to streams that are a multiple of DS0, and puts them into appropriate time slots of outgoing trunks (see Figure 7.8). As new last-mile technologies were introduced, they each had an equivalent to the DSLAM: a technology-specific termination of customer information, a switching function, and an outbound trunking function. To simplify the proliferation of different technology-specific DSLAM equivalents in the same CO, the idea of multiservice selection gateways evolved. These gateways are modular and can terminate different digital—and sometimes analog—services.

Modem Wholesaling, Virtual POPs, and the Beginning of Media Gateways

Originally, ISPs maintained their own modem pools. Some of the national providers realized that they could gain substantial revenue at relatively little incremental capital cost by expanding their modem access POPs and offering the capacity to smaller ISPs and enterprises.

Local regulatory and market conditions significantly affect the attractiveness of wholesaling. In California, for example, intra-local access and transport area (LATA) calls even between geographically close jurisdictions may involve toll charges. It is not practical for a small ISP to put a small dial access point in every area that would be needed to make everything a local phone call.

The use of wholesalers is sometimes called *creating a virtual ISP*. The ISP may maintain only its key servers and routers and outsource its access, possibly its web caching, and its long-haul connectivity (Figure 7.9).

Technical Efficiency Considerations

Modem wholesaling is not a technically trivial issue. The wholesaler, for example, might lease a given ISP 100 modems in 1 city or 10 modems in 10 cities. The group needs to be seen as one logical entity by the ISP. How does the wholesaler pass the modem traffic to the ISP? Does it terminate PPP and send IP, or does it have to encapsulate the IP? If the wholesaler terminates the PPP, how

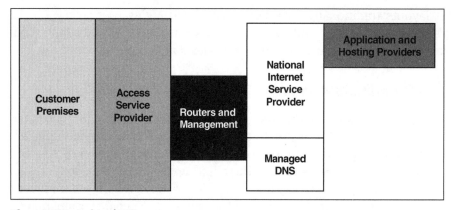

Figure 7.9   A virtual ISP.

does it verify a given user is authorized? Does it send a message to an authentication server at the ISP, or must the wholesaler become involved in knowing (and revoking) passwords?

Do not underestimate the complexity of provisioning a wholesale access point, especially when the ISP customers have any ability to view or otherwise manage the resources they lease. See "Gateway Architecture" later in this chapter for a more formal approach to virtual gateway partitioning.

Inverse multiplexing quickly presents a challenge, especially when the end user employs a bandwidth-on-demand scheme. In a large dial-up (or ISDN) access point, this becomes complicated because physical network access servers have finite numbers of user access ports (see Figure 7.10). A less common situation arises when users accept the differences in delay to different dial-in locations and use inverse multiplexing to avoid a single point of failure with respect to connectivity (Figure 7.11). Is this an inverse multiplexing procedure that will be supported? In general, it is probably better to do this with multiple IP links and some type of load sharing.

There are costs associated with bandwidth between the wholesaler access point and the ISP. Having some ISP equipment at the wholesaler location can reduce this bandwidth requirement, but at the cost of more equipment, floor/rack space charges from the wholesaler, and additional management complexity. Nevertheless, there may be justifications for putting such things as authentication, DNS, and web cache servers at access points. The wholesaler may even offer some of these services.

Regulatory Concerns

Another source of modem access is regulated ILECs, which, under the U.S. Telecommunications Act of 1996, have not been able to sell both Internet access and voice services in the same service area. They are permitted to offer the dial

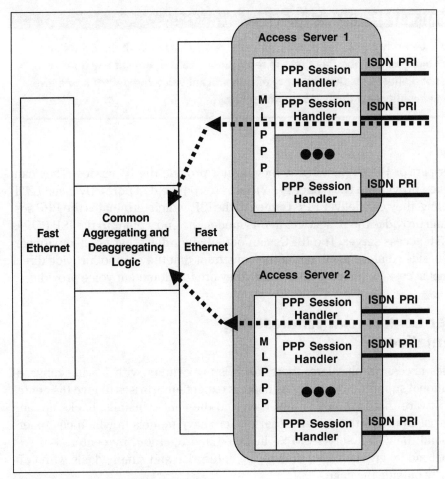

Figure 7.10 Multichassis stacking issues.

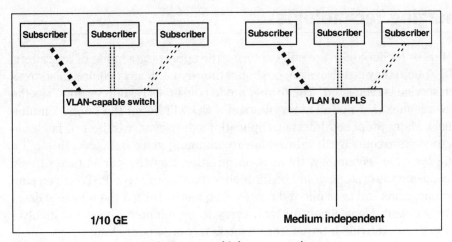

Figure 7.11 Inverse multiplexing to multiple access points.

LEGAL, NOT TECHNICAL CHANGE

ILECs are hotly contesting these regulatory restrictions in both the courts and the Congress. It is possible that the restrictions could change at any time. Also, the possibility exists that the entry of a significant voice competitor into a given market could allow the ILECs to offer Internet access.

server part of PPP/IP, as long as they do not provide the IP service. They can, however, provide an L2TP access concentrator on the dial ports. By using L2TP tunneling, they can deliver PPP frames to the ISP, which terminates the PPP session and provides the IP service. In this model, the entry point to the ISP POP is an L2TP access server. The ILECs can potentially offer other connectivity services besides dial-up, again under the constraint that they cannot provide direct Internet access in the same area where they are the dominant voice provider.

Other Commercial Wholesaling Alternatives

Besides access wholesalers, there are hosting centers with a wide range of operational support models. Some centers expect enterprises to give the center the software that is to run on a server, and the center installs, backs up, and otherwise operates the server. Other centers have models in which customers can build their own servers to be installed and operated by center staff. Yet another model gives a caged area to the enterprise and simply deals with connectivity outside the cage.

Emerging Technologies

All of these technologies are still exploring the appropriate mode of operations for IP. Should they be always on, or should they dynamically acquire an address when service is requested? The former mode conserves resources, much as the PSTN assumes that not all subscribers at a CO will be on the phone simultaneously. Many proposed Internet applications, however, will be sending content to users frequently. If television programming were delivered through a digital last-mile technology, there is no question that the percentage of customers using the system would be far higher than that for the PSTN. Even simple applications still transmit and receive frequently. During the business day, I have my e-mail client check for mail every three minutes. Given my involvement in the worldwide Internet, the business day is 24 hours long.

With frequent transmissions to all nodes, the overhead and latency involved in setting up dynamic addresses may be unacceptable. There certainly may be compromises, such as the equivalent of DHCP with very long lease times.

When we speak of last-mile technologies as using existing telephone pairs, we must realize that not all telephone pairs are usable for digital services. Each technology has a distance limitation, which in the case of ISDN is 18,000 ft. In addition, certain components and installation methods, legacies of analog transmission techniques, interfere with these technologies.

Do 800-Pound Gorillas Run at Gigabit Rates?

Most have heard the question, "Where does an 800-pound gorilla sit?" The answer, of course, is, "Anywhere he wants." At least according to high-level marketers, the networking equivalent of the gorilla is Ethernet. An increasingly broad number of technologies are called "Ethernet," although even the term is obsolete because Ethernet standards were superseded by IEEE 802.3.

I've always been amazed at the number of people who assume a 10BaseT connection gives them 10- or 100-Mbps outbound speed. Yes, that may be the speed on the connector. For years, one prominent ISP offered a "10-Megabit access" to a standard configuration consisting of a router with an Ethernet local interface and a T1 (that is, 1.544-Mbps) uplink. What is wrong with this picture?

One common use of the term *Ethernet* is to refer to the 10BaseT connector and associated 802.3 framing as the physical interface to any number of access devices, most often customer site access devices, that then connect to local loops that might be DSL, cable, or wireless. Another use is in local loops that may indeed run 802.3 framing over optical facilities. These, however, are point-to-point topologies, not the shared facility often implied by "Ethernet." 802.3, of course, is the de facto LAN standard, and certainly is appropriate for most first-meter applications. Even in those applications, you may have a 10BaseT interface to an 802.11 or other wireless shared medium.

Interfaces Other than Ethernet

The new techniques rarely displace existing technology that is generating revenue and acceptably using resources. Possible exceptions include cases where underground ducts in a metro area are filled with copper cabling. When there is older fiber, it is far more common to change the electronics and optics in the endpoints than it is to replace the fiber. New optical technologies, therefore, will have to interoperate with the older SONET/SDH technologies. At some level, they will also need to work with T1/E1 and T3/E3 equipment, although it

ISDN: MOSTLY TOO LITTLE, TOO LATE

ISDN, the first technology that provided higher-than-modem bandwidth to end users connected by telephone lines, is well proven and is now available in many parts of the world. It has decent media range of up to 18,000 ft. However, it does not have the ability to grow as do other last-mile alternatives. There will be niches, however, where it can provide useful alternatives. It also has the advantage of being old enough to be a commodity, so ISDN equipment can be reliable and cheap. ISDN's fundamental problem, in the great information technology classification, "Good, cheap, fast—pick two," is that it is slow.

xDSL services, in particular, allow use of existing analog telephony equipment simultaneously with data use. Voice over IP further lessens demand for ISDN channels.

ISDN has more optional configurations and configuration parameters than other last-mile technologies. Part of the complexity is due to the fact that the ISDN service directly connects to the PSTN, so it must have adequate signaling to do so. Even though ISDN protocols have been nationally and internationally standardized, there are still variations in the implementation in CO switches, both by manufacturer and region/country. National practice also varies as to whether the customer or the carrier controls the network termination (the ISDN term for customer premises equipment/customer located equipment). When the NT is customer-owned, it can be integrated into end equipment or PBXs. When used in this way, the external connection of the ISDN device can be the U reference point.

Telephone end office switches may have native ISDN interfaces. A more scalable approach is to bring the ISDN local loop into a DACS and aggregate the ISDN channels into at least a DS1 rate, which saves connector real estate on the end switch.

As a circuit-switched service, ISDN emulates a dedicated circuit once a connection is established. When ISDN bitstreams are concentrated, they are put onto full-capacity channels. If the call can be created, there will be capacity for it. ISDN is probably the most trustworthy of the last-mile technologies in providing guaranteed bandwidth.

may be most cost-effective not to install these interfaces on the new equipment but simply to connect to older SONET/SDH equipment that already has the appropriate interfaces.

There are challenges, however, in better serving the enterprise user. Ethernet support is a complex issue, as discussed separately later in the chapter. An interesting aspect, however, is posed by IBM-compatible mainframes, which still have important roles in massive databases, transaction processing, and data mining. IBM has defined an optical interface called ESCON, an evolution beyond the old "bus-and-tag" interface among the processor and peripherals. ESCON has sufficient range to be used in a metro area, and ESCON capability is an attractive service offering for metro carriers.

The New First Meter

As broadband service to end users becomes more prevalent, there is more and more need for an intelligent network termination and service box. Even the terminology for such a device is unclear, but one emerging distinction is customer location equipment (CLE), which is provided by the carrier, and customer premises equipment (CPE), which is provided by the subscriber. Such a device is more than a media converter between copper and optical. It is likely to need to present several legacy interfaces: video for television, Ethernet for data, and analog for telephony.

CPE/CLE is a logical point for home automation functions that do not even go to the service provider. Of course, when network connectivity exists, functions such as remote utility meter reading and energy management can be added. Network access can also offer convenience to the subscriber, with services ranging from turning on the air conditioning as one begins the commute home to baby monitoring.

Of course, some remote access functions have significant privacy implications. The CPE/CLE then becomes a very reasonable place to put a cryptographic client. Cryptographic tunneling is not the only higher-layer protocol function that logically resides in the CPE/CLE. If there is a specialized access provider that does not offer IP services, then there needs to be L2TP or PPPoE to carry the frames to the IP or other service providers. Depending on the regulatory environment, these tunneling functions may terminate at the service gateway or pass through to the service provider.

Niches for 100-Meter Services

A special niche where the ISP can manage much of the end-to-end connectivity to the end customer is in multitenant buildings, such as apartments, office complexes, and hotels (see Figure 7.12). The economics here allow the ISP to place a multiplexer or other aggregation device in a common area of the multitenant building and typically to connect to the users with LAN technology. Cable providers already have significant penetration into residential and hotel facilities, although they may lack the appropriate in-building LAN technology.

See Table 7.3 for a summary of optical access alternatives.

One possible commercial niche is the building local exchange carrier (BLEC), which provides Ethernet connectivity inside multitenant buildings and concentrates the traffic into a single, possibly diversely routed, stream that goes onto optical or high-speed wireless transport. Such firms usually design

> ### THE FIRST HUNDRED METERS (OR SO) PROBLEM
>
> **Those new technologies that operate at multimegabit rates can only travel, at best, a few hundred meters on copper facilities before they must be converted to optical facilities. This is not an issue in multitenant buildings, but it is a challenge in residential areas or areas populated by small business. The practical reality is that the end subscribers in single-tenant buildings need to connect to local copper-to-optical aggregation units, typically mounted in outdoor pedestal housings. Outdoor pedestals are already prevalent in the community antenna television (CATV) industry, even for nondata applications. They may also be used for basic telephony, especially as a means of range extension or avoiding the need for more copper pairs when the existing cables are fully utilized.**

based on massive oversubscription, with capacity requirements computed at the building, local-office, and regional levels. This can work reasonably well with typical office uses, especially when the user applications are things such as Web browsing and electronic mail. I would certainly want to get a service level agreement from the BLEC if I were going to run voice, video or critical client/server applications over their service.

Practical BLECs may very well need to rate-limit traffic at the user port level and have different service rates. They also face a chicken-and-egg situation:

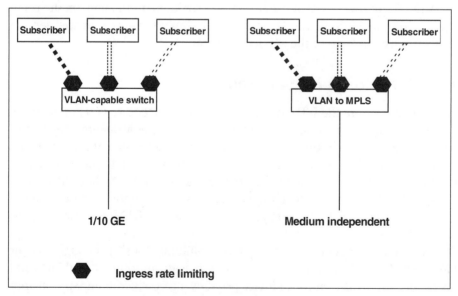

Figure 7.12 Connectivity to multitenant buildings.

Table 7.3   Optical Access Alternatives

ACRONYM	MEANING	APPLICATION
FTTB	Fiber to the building	Multitenant
FTTC	Fiber to the curb	SOHO with local copper cabling
FTTH	Fiber to the home	Optical connectivity to each subscriber

They are a reliable alternative only when they have significant market penetration into a given area, but they often have to negotiate agreements with every landlord and their deployment may be slow.

There may be niches where BLECs are especially attractive (for example, enterprises with multiunit buildings scattered in a metropolitan area, such as healthcare or educational buildings). Essentially, the BLEC takes over the role of running a campus network when there is no physical network. If tariffs permit the BLEC to provide IP services rather than raw bandwidth, BLECs may be especially viable for providing multicast services.

New First-Mile Services

Traditional copper telephone circuits are limited in the bandwidth they can provide using analog technologies or transitional technologies such as T1/E1 or ISDN. New techniques, however, provide broadband connectivity to the end user, either with new kinds of electronics on cable or with completely different media.

DSL

Digital subscriber line (DSL) is a family of technologies for high-speed transmission primarily over existing copper pairs. A wide variety of technologies, shown in Table 7.4, fall under the general DSL framework. Fiber alternatives also can be used in CATV.

ADSL places a small splitter unit at the customer premises, from which analog voice services run. However, many installers prefer to use a nonvoice pair when available. Using a separate pair eliminates the splitter cost and simplifies troubleshooting. The equivalent splitter at the CO is a function called the *ADSL transmission unit–central office* (ATU-C). DSL access multiplexers (DSLAMs) at the CO contain ATU-C functions for each customer loop, as well as DACS-like functions that transfer the customer data bits to trunks. The ATU-C also splits off the analog voice channels, which go to conventional channel banks in the CO.

Table 7.4 xDSL Alternatives

ACRONYM	MEANING	CHARACTERISTICS
ADSL	Asymmetric DSL	1.5–8 Mbps downstream; 64–800 Kbps upstream; simultaneous data and analog voice
HDSL	High-density DSL	T1/E1 replacement; no analog capability
IDSL	ISDN DSL	
RADSL	Rate-adaptive DSL	
SDSL	Symmetric DSL	Same bandwidth in both directions; 160 Kbps–1.168 Mbps
VDSL	Very-high-speed DSL	Multimegabit rates

VDSL has much less range than ADSL, HDSL, and IDSL. VDSL assumes that copper pair will connect the actual subscriber to a nearby optical network unit (ONU), which connects to the CO via fiber. Total copper lengths should not exceed 300 m. The ONU might be in an outside pedestal (fiber to the curb), inside a multiple-subscriber structure such as an office or apartment building (fiber to the building), or next to the home (fiber to the home).

Lower-speed DSL services use a pure hub-and-spoke topology, with individual copper pairs to the serving CO. As speeds increase, the medium's distance capability decreases, so remote terminals—repeaters and concentrators—will terminate end connections and concentrate them, creating a branched star. Local loops are dedicated to individual users, and, even when concentrated at remote terminals, guarantee bandwidth to the central office. At the CO, however, there may be a bottleneck. If there is no router colocated at the CO, xDSL user bit streams need to be put onto a link that will carry them to the service provider. The capacity of that link may not support simultaneous data flow from several users, or even full-rate bursts from individual users. I have seen ADSL rates in the hundreds of kilobits offered to multiple users, but with only a 384-Kbps virtual circuit from the CO to the first provider POP.

Most current systems require a CO port for each user, which is more expensive than connecting a cable to a head end. Work is going into methods of oversubscribing the DSLAM ports, much as conventional analog switches cannot support calls from all subscribers. Going to an oversubscription model would relinquish the benefit of guaranteed bandwidth and connectivity, but that might be acceptable as a consumer service.

Another practical business issue for xDSL is the role of the traditional telephone company. Traditionally, telephone companies, especially when an outside plant is concerned, have been slow to implement new technologies. Can you say ISDN? I knew you could! Telcos became comfortable provisioning ISDN at the approximate time ISDN became obsolete. ISPs, however, do not have extensive experience with local distribution. An alternative may be arising with DSL wholesalers, such as Covad. In a manner similar to modem pool wholesalers, these companies handle the DSL access for multiple ISPs and have the volume both to maintain an experience base and to gain economies of scale when installing equipment in COs. Of course, most of them are in Chapter 11 bankruptcy, if not Chapter 7. ILECs can be very strong competitors when roused. See Figure 7.13 for an example of how a wholesaler connects the ISPs.

Many xDSL providers differentiate between consumer and business use. Consumer services are cheaper, but may share bandwidth from the CO to the ISP. Consumer services also may implement the ATU-R as a card internal to a PC, lowering costs further. SOHO business applications tend to have higher quality of service and to have an external box that may combine the ADSL transceiver unit–remote (ATU-R), an Ethernet hub, and a router. Using SDSL in such an implementation is the primary way I connect externally from my home office, although I do have a more complex internal structure with additional routers and firewalls. My needs are more complex than those of most SOHO users.

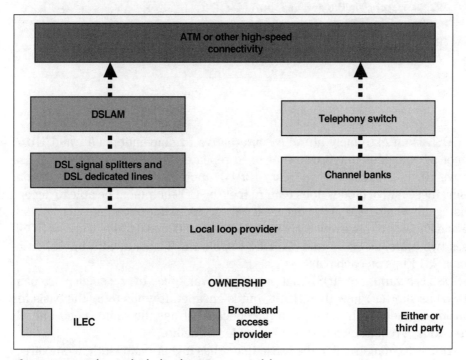

Figure 7.13   Telco and wholesaler DSL connectivity.

TRUST ME, I'M FROM THE TELCO [BERKOWITZ 2000A]

When I first tried to order DSL service, I called the ILEC and went through a strange dialogue, which is quoted here to the best of my recollection.

Howard: "I'd like to order ADSL service."

Telco Representative #1: "Whaaat?"

H (referring quickly to the marketing materials): "Oh . . . Infospeed service."

We progressed, until the question was asked:

TR1: "What kind of computer will you be using?"

H: "Why should you care? You're a bit pipe to me."

TR1: "I need to know what kind of computer, sir."

H: "I won't be plugging in a single computer, but a hub or router. I don't want to install an additional Ethernet port so I can still get to the printer."

TR1: "Sir, if our installer sees a router, he will immediately leave."

H: "What if I put a software router in a PC? How can the installer see it?"

TR1: "Ummm . . . sir, I need to escalate this call."

I reached Telco Representative #2, who nattered on about needing to know the PC type. Eventually, I told her to stop referring to the PC type, because my main machine is a Mac.

TR2: "I'm sorry, sir. We don't support Macs."

H: (deep sigh) "Why?"

TR2 (and this really, really is a direct quote):   "Because Macs don't have MAC addresses."

HDSL is an extremely attractive alternative to conventional T1 and E1. A major advantage is that it does not need repeaters on most lines if it can use native HDSL 2 binary 1 quaternary (2B1Q) modulation and rate adaptation. Using these native modes does require that the CO equipment be able to accept this signal, which it may not because it only speaks a line encoding such as AMI. T1 and E1 need to have repeaters installed every 4,000 to 6,000 ft. Current HDSL uses two pairs, as do T1 and E1. HDSL splits the T1 bandwidth into bidirectional 784 Kbps on each pair.

SDSL is a variant of HDSL that provides lower speed over a single wire pair. SDSL has shorter range than HDSL, but is cheaper. It tends to be the basis for "business-grade" DSL services, in part because it has the same speed in both directions, a requirement for two-way video or audio.

ADSL is asymmetrical in the sense that it has higher bandwidth in one direction than another. This is quite appropriate for such applications as video on

H: "Hey, if nothing else, the address of this Mac is 5012 South 25th Street. Are you referring to Medium Access Control?"

TR2: "Ummm . . . sir, I need to escalate this call."

Reaching Telco Representative #3, I asked, "What do you mean that Macs don't have MAC addresses? What do you think they use on an Ethernet?"

TR3 (somewhat technically): "Ah, but the MAC address doesn't activate until the IP stack comes up. So we can't ping you if IP isn't up."

H: "If IP wasn't up, how could you ping me with or without a MAC address?"

TR3: "Ummm . . . sir, I need to escalate this call."

TR4 apologized for the runaround and was rather sympathetic. He explained: "We note your MAC address during the installation. When you come out of the DSLAM, you go into an Ethernet switch that permits only known source MAC addresses."

H: "OK. That makes some sense." Then I thought for a moment. I could deal with that. "But what if your average Joe Sixpack PC user has a failed NIC changed, and his MAC address changes? What happens to his access?"

TR4: "Oh, easy. Joe Sixpack will note the new MAC address, call the operations center, give it to them over the phone, and they will reprogram the filter."

H: (in my best impression of Bill Cosby in his "Noah" skit) "R-i-g-g-g-h-t-t-t."

demand or Web browsing, where the majority of bytes are sent to the customer in response to customer requests.

Cable

The late-1940s technology introduced as *community antenna television* (CATV) had modest goals when it came on the scene. In geographic areas where terrain masked the path from broadcast stations to the residential antenna, a tall antenna that could reach over the blocking hills was connected to the head end. The head end then distributed television signals over coaxial cable.

CATV did not really become a substantial industry until satellites became widely used to distribute entertainment content. Cable then began to offer far more diverse programming to homes. Cable operators also offered video-on-demand pay-per-view services. These entertainment networks were optimized for one-way transmission from the head end to the subscribers, possibly with intermediate amplifiers.

Data was not an original CATV goal. Data applications on cable generally are a shared medium emulating an Ethernet, although it is possible to establish high-capacity dedicated-line equivalents by giving them their own frequency. In the great information technology classification, "Good, cheap, fast—pick two," cable is less than good when it becomes heavily loaded. Good cable system designers have to plan very carefully to be sure the medium does not become overloaded. Competitors to CATV include xDSL for data and potentially video-on-demand services, direct broadcast satellite (DBS) for entertainment access, and local wireless.

As mentioned, basic single-cable systems were limited in the applications they delivered. Their ability to carry bidirectional signals was limited. Bidirectional cable systems, which separate the cable frequency band into upstream and downstream sets of channels, do exist. The next generation is *hybrid fiber coax* (HFC), which continues to use coaxial cable to the end user but uses optical fiber for the main distribution path from the head-end to the *optical node* that converts photonic signals into electronic ones, and onto the final coaxial *drop cable* into the residence.

Cable systems have amplifiers or digital repeaters between the customer premises and the head end. The topology, however, is definitely a branched star. Connections to telephone end offices, ISP gateways, and so on, will be made at the head end.

CATV service providers face both short- and long-term demands to upgrade the technology of their installed base. Two-way services are one immediate demand. The real question is how and when cable operators will upgrade to optical technology, be it HFC, fiber to the curb (FTTC), or fiber to the house (FTTH).

Security is a real concern when a medium is shared, as are coaxial trunks. At present, some cable data providers offer limited firewall and packet filtering services, the latter especially for protecting broadcasts.

IMPACTS OF DIGITAL AND HIGH-DEFINITION TELEVISION

As digital TV and HDTV—which consume far more bandwidth than regular television—enter the marketplace, the lifetime of coaxial cable systems comes more and more into question. Digital encoding of conventional television actually requires less bandwidth than analog encoding, but HDTV requires much more bandwidth.

Existing cable systems may be able to cope with a few HDTV channels, but the idea of 500 HDTV channels absolutely demands optical connectivity.

Fixed Wireless

Cellular phones are a blessing and curse of our time. In the Washington, D.C., area, many restaurants are creating cell-free as well as smoke-free zones. Sidewalks containing both cellular callers oblivious to the world and crazed bicycle messengers are frightening. Of course, crazed bicycle messengers using cell phones takes us into a new level of fear.

Fixed wireless, while it may use some of the transmission technologies of cellular telephony, is not intended to have moving endpoints. Cellular telephony has definitely lowered the cost of some previously unaffordable wireless technologies. Applications of fixed wireless include serving geographically isolated customer sites and providing diverse local loops to enterprise in urban areas. Eastern Europe is experiencing explosive telecommunications growth, but in cities like Budapest, founded in the Middle Ages, there are no underground cable ducts and few telephone poles. In such cities, it has been found cost-effective to go directly to wireless local loops, skipping the entire generation of copper distribution. There are several alternatives to fixed wireless transmission (see Table 7.5). Stepping outside the residential and normal business environment, there are microwave and optical systems that handle special

Table 7.5 Alternative Wireless Services

TECHNOLOGY	ADVANTAGES	DISADVANTAGES
Direct broadcast (geosynchronous) satellite	Established for TV	One-way orientation
Fixed cellular	Flexible topology in built-up areas	Low speed
Local multipoint distribution service (LMDS)	Extremely high speed	Line-of-sight with short range; impacted by weather
Free-space optical	Extremely high speed	Line-of-sight with short range; impacted by weather
Low-earth-orbit satellite	Lower latency than geosynchronous earth orbit satellites	Cost and complexity of telephones; need for large numbers of satellites for complete coverage
Multichannel multipoint distribution service (MMDS)	Lower installation cost than cable TV; bandwidth comparable to DBS	Line-of-sight with moderate range; one-way orientation

---

WELL, YES, THERE IS COMPETITION . . .

Not to be forgotten, as any of these technologies go into wide deployment, is the "clue level" of real-world providers and installers. After two years of trying to convince the then-incumbent cable provider that I really, truly, had paid my bill, I gave up. Happily, they have been replaced by a new and responsive cable provider.

The Not In My Backyard (NIMBY) syndrome may limit the places where antennas can be installed, if for no other reason than esthetics. Actually, backyards themselves can be a problem. As an alternative, I tried to obtain DirectTV service to my home from my local telephone company. When the installer arrived, he took one look and said he couldn't install the antenna because there were trees on the south side of my property. I sigh at provider ads that offer "free professional installation" of home antennas, for I was unable to get the installer to understand that putting the antenna on a mast would provide a line of sight *over* the trees.

Clearly, there is local competition. Unfortunately, it is often between accounting incompetence and installation incompetence.

---

requirements, such as pay telephones in remote areas. Fixed wireless usually connotes a terrestrial system, often line-of-sight but sometimes cellular. In some applications, satellites may be an alternative to terrestrial.

Media Gateways and the New Second Mile

With the advent of broadband services, often implemented by specialized wholesale providers, the "second-mile problem" arose. While economics of dial wholesaling had reduced the growth of ISPs running their own modem access server pools, it was still possible to function that way. With cable, DSL, fixed wireless, and other new services, it was fundamentally impractical for the ISP to have a wire or fiber connection to more than a tiny proportion of switched access subscribers. The second-mile problem is the problem of information flow between subscriber aggregation points of specialized access provider and the IPSP, and possibly providers of other service such as voice and video.

As new last-mile technologies enter the market, or as new data services are added to existing CATV or other providers, new gateway devices furnish first- and second-mile providers with a cost-effective way of setting up subscriber connectivity. These gateways concentrate individual subscriber connections in the first mile with high-speed aggregates to service providers in the second mile. Gateways of this sort are descendants of the large dial-up management tools used by POP wholesalers. Just as dial servers can either be operated by wholesalers or by a service provider, so can gateways.

The operator of a gateway, commonly a broadband wholesaler or CLEC, has to manage tens or hundreds of thousands of subscriber accesses as well as sort out the aggregate data streams from these subscribers and send them to the operator's own customers, which are ISPs and other service providers. Efficient human interfaces and interfaces for carrier-specific scripts are essential for commercial success. *Service selection gateways* (SSGs) connect data subscribers to ISPs and other data providers. A more general term, *media gateways* (MGs) also provide conversion to and from nondata services such as voice and video. MG is the more general term.

According to RFC 2805, MGs map or translate "the media mapping between potentially dissimilar networks, one of which is presumed to be a packet, frame or cell network." The most obvious MG application is between telephony *switched circuit network* (SCN) facilities, such as local loops, trunks, and channel banks, and an IP packet network. Note that MG functions are perfectly applicable to situations where all interfaces are packetized, such as digital conference bridges.

Never forget the song lyrics from *Cabaret:* "Money makes the world go 'round." Reducing the labor cost of circuit provisioning is the first motivation for service gateways. Once gateways were introduced, it quickly became

GATEWAYS AND THE INTELLIGENT EDGE

In addition to the simple conversion and management of services, gateways may themselves provide "high-touch" application services in a context often called the *intelligent edge*. *High-touch* means that the gateway looks deeper into packets than do typical routers, and considers application layer content. High-touch functions tend to fall into two categories: those that are primarily concerned with application session establishment and those that involve inspection of every packet.

Web caching, content-based redirection to servers, and possibly assignment of traffic to VPNs are session-oriented. Firewalling, virus scanning, interactive voice response, encryption, and voice/video conferencing involve every packet. An obvious application is placing a multicast server at the edge to service video users in a local area.

High-touch services usually require specialized server cards in the gateway or directly attached to it. A gateway that performs high-touch services will also need to retain much more per-user state than a router, requiring much more memory and greatly complicating failover. In other words, high-touch services are user-oriented rather than address-oriented.

obvious that they were natural homes for value-added data and voice services. Another realization is that a gateway is most flexible when it is agnostic to the particular access technology. Gateways can be modular devices that can accept dial access, ISDN, or broadband access technologies such as xDSL, cable, fixed wireless, free-space optical, and cellular. Be aware that traditional layer 2 techniques connecting the access provider to the ISP are not necessarily the most flexible now available. See "Scalability with MPLS" in Chapter 10.

Gateway Architecture

Grooming can certainly be part of the functionality of a gateway, as can routing. These gateways, however, have more functionality than either traditional DACSs or traditional routers. Standard routers are connectionless, while the very essence of a service gateway is that it monitors connection state. Conventional routers do not need to keep track of individual users and individual user sessions.

The Multiservice Forum (MSF) has been established to deal with implementation issues for distributed switching systems including backbones of ATM, frame, and IP, and access technologies including analog, TDM, xDSL, wireless, and cable. Its architecture is layered into five planes (Figure 7.14). The planes are discussed later in this section, along with certain functions that span planes. One of the issues the MSF architecture deals with is scalability, and one of the fundamental approaches for making gateways scalable is separating control and management from switching. As long as there is sufficient redundancy for carrier-grade reliability, there need not be full management on every data-processing element.

STATES

Communications protocols can be hard-state, soft-state, or stateless. A hard-state protocol (for example, Q.931 or TCP) has explicit connection and disconnection phases, during which resources are committed. A soft-state protocol (for example, IGMP or RSVP) has an implied connection setup in the sense that the first message sent in the protocol creates a connection. The resources affected by the protocol monitor the connection for periodic retransmissions of the protocol message, and, if no messages are received before a timer expires, they assume a disconnection and release resources. Stateless protocols (for example, IP or UDP) do not imply any resource commitment. Protocol messages are handled by processing elements, which retain no knowledge of having handled previous knowledge. A processing element, however, must retain knowledge of the existence of a connection established by a hard- or soft-state protocol.

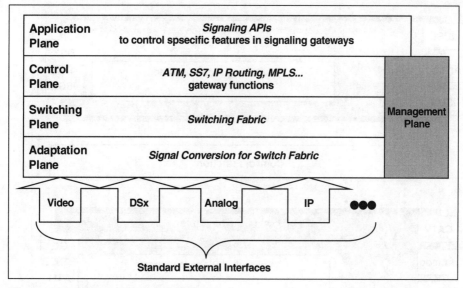

Figure 7.14   MSF architectural planes.

Figure 7.15 shows one aspect of the MSF architecture, in which one controller can supervise multiple physical switches. The architecture does not preclude multiple controllers being used as part of a fault tolerance scheme. This graphic shows the physical relationship. In contrast, Figure 7.16 shows a logical view of the service as seen by ISP or enterprise customers of an access service provider. Each customer has the impression of having its own switch, even though it may physically exist in multiple locations. Other customers may use parts of the same resource, but the customer flows are secure from one another. The MSF

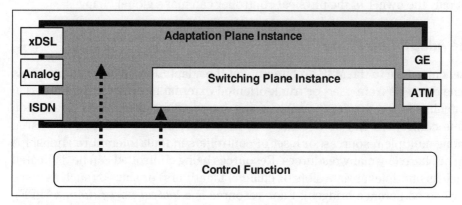

Figure 7.15   Examples of MSF control and switching separation.

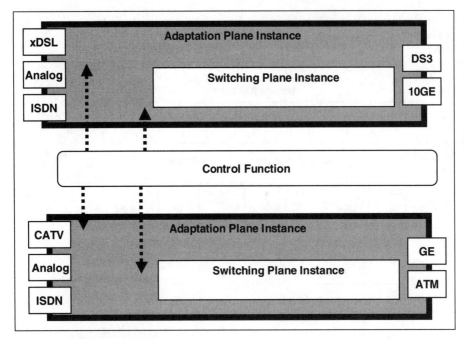

Figure 7.16 A virtual switch.

defines a *virtual switch function* (VSF) as a subset of resources on one or more physical access switches. The defining characteristic of a VSF is that it is controlled by a single virtual controller. The *partitioning function* (PF) spans the adaptation and switching planes and specifies the resources assigned to a specific VSF. A virtual controller may be a subset of the physical controller provisioned such that it controls only the resources of one customer. Virtual controllers can be set up so that the customer may manage its own resources, but only the owner of the physical controller can make global changes.

The Adaptation Plane

Users interface to the MSF architecture at the adaptation plane boundary. This plane converts from user- or trunk-oriented external interfaces to the internal switching fabric format, possibly using intermediate interfaces. Adaptation plane controllers can be dedicated to resources, a controller can be shared among multiple resources, or a set of controllers in fault-tolerant relationships can be shared by many resources. Resources being controlled can be dedicated (such as multiplexer time slots or channel identifiers) or shared (such as voice or video conference bridges). Each resource is a *logical port function* (LPF). LPFs are allocated and deallocated by the control plane. *Terminators* are entry or exit points of flows. Examples of terminators, or *bearer points*, are DS0s, ATM VCs, 4-KHz analog channels and so on. *Media resources* include the codecs that convert voice to and from bitstreams, modems, audio conference bridges, interactive voice response systems, and so on. The devices at terminators send edge signaling to the core. ISDN Q.931, ATM UNI, FR, and X.25 are all edge mechanisms. A *signal gateway* (SG) will relay, convert, or terminate these signals in a manner compatible with the switching plane.

Gateway adaptation functions include:

- Interfacing between the telephone network and a voice over IP network. In practice, these often are split into gateways for user streams and for signaling information.

- Traditional modem or primary rate interface (PRI) line interfacing to a Voice over IP network.

- L2TP or PPPoE devices that can connect an access device, such as a modem or a cable TV set-top box, to a subscriber circuit and link it to an IP services provider. For regulatory reasons, the actual modem is often connected to an L2TP access concentrator (LAC) at a wholesaler and the PPP session terminates at the ISP.

The Switching Plane

User traffic enters and exits the MSF architecture at the adaptation plane, but moves between edges using the switching plane. Routing in the switching plane is defined by the control plane. The requirement for virtual switching functions makes the switching plane more complex than a traditional layer 1 or 2 switching system.

An ATM cell switch is completely inside the switching plane. The adaptation plane presents it with frames, for which it performs the necessary segmentation and reassembly. The ATM switch and ATM network are responsible for

---

OLD FUNCTIONS IN NEW TERMINOLOGY: CHANNEL BANKS IN THE ADAPTATION PLANE

Channel banks historically were the devices in which conventional voice was converted to T-carrier digitized voice. In modern terminology, they are one specific case of adaptation function.

The adaptation function, in general, converts services visible to the user (e.g., voice, video, files) into formats that the switching plane can process and move between switching ports. It also provides service-specific roles such as queue management.

"backbone" functions such as traffic management, handling point-to-multipoint circuits, and path merging.

The Control Plane

Where the adaptation plane contains the on and off ramps to the MSF highways of the switching plane, the control plane is the traffic cop. The control plane is responsible for all aspects of routing, including the allocation of switching and adaptation resources. Not only does it set up paths in the traditional routing sense, but it is also responsible for managing labels, including GMPLS labels, ATM virtual path and virtual circuit identifiers, and Frame Relay data link connection identifiers (DLCIs).

Five functions make up the control plane. They are variously concerned with managing LPF instances, virtual switch control, bearer control (that is, control of end-to-end paths), network service instance control, and signaling gateway control. Not all these functions will be present in every service provider environment.

The *signaling gateway function* (SGF) interfaces between different signaling protocols such as SS7 and H.323. RFC 2805 defines it as a function that "receives/sends SCN native signaling at the edge of a data network." SGF can perform this interface function using tunneling or translation. It is intelligent, and can decide to block a particular request if its policy so indicates.

The Application Plane

MSF looks at applications as including user-visible services involving voice, video, and data services. Messaging services include voice mail and electronic mail. Another class of applications is *directory enabled services* ranging from

---

"PULL OVER, SIR. I'M MEGACOP."

The architecture for communication among the elements of a physically decomposed MG is being developed in close cooperation between the IETF and ITU-T. The actual protocol for this communication is called MEGACOP [RFC 3015] in the IETF and H.248 in the ITU-T. It makes no functional distinction between a decomposed gateway, with distributed subcomponents potentially on more than one physical device, and a monolithic gateway such as described in H.246. MEGACOP does not define the application plane functions of the elements it interconnects, simply the means of transferring commands among them.

> ### REMIND YOURSELF: IT'S THE SPECIFIC PROGRAMMING, NOT THE TECHNOLOGY IN GENERAL
>
> I recently spent several minutes with an "advanced" speech recognition system of an appliance repair firm, trying "air conditioner," "cooling," and quite a number of other options before I realized it wanted to hear "heating and cooling." The reason I was calling for repair was that the temperature in my house was already 85 degrees. After that interaction, my internal temperature had also climbed.

toll-free number translation to personal number portability. Hybrid application services are developing and include voice-enabled Web applications, call centers, and so on. Directory assistance is closely associated with this category.

Advanced applications, in the telephony industry, have been called Custom Local Area Signaling Services (CLASS), and include such things as directory assistance, conference bridging, credit card billing, and so on. Enhanced telephony services such as call forwarding, three-way calling, and the dreaded call waiting are also applications. There are processing applications as well, including automated credit card processing and the even more dreaded intelligent voice recognition, be it "Welcome to 911. Press 1 if you are reporting a murder (pause). Press 2 if you are being murdered," or the more advanced speech recognition systems.

Long-Haul Niches

Optical transmission systems with niches for satellites are clearly the future of long-haul transmission. There are qualitative differences between optical systems built for metro areas (tens of kilometers) and long-distance systems with hundreds or thousands of kilometers between repeaters. Ultra-long-reach systems (for example, transoceanic cables), may form a distinct category.

Roles for satellites include serving remote areas that cannot justify their own optical connectivity or terrestrial cellular radio infrastructure. Satellites are also quite appropriate for point-to-multipoint, one-to-many applications such as distributing video, news, stock quotations, and software updates. Many-to-one applications, such as environmental telemetry, real-time tracking of vehicles, and so forth, also lend themselves to satellites.

Third-generation cellular networks offer considerably more data capability than existing cell phones, but are still inherently a metropolitan or regional technology, providing access to the long-haul networks.

PSTN Integration

With all the industry hype about voice over IP (VoIP) and related services, the reality remains that there is a huge worldwide investment in pure voice equipment. As or more important is that there are a great many vendors and network operators that think in telephony, not data, terms. There have been many attempts to define a term that properly shows the movement toward commonality of voice, video and data networks. *Convergence* is one popular term that I personally hate, because it becomes confused with routing convergence. *Succession*, Nortel's term, has merit because it recognizes that this movement must be evolutionary rather than revolutionary. No term, however, has gained general acceptance. Whatever this effort is called, you should realize that several major technical disciplines are involved: They are complementary, but they are sufficiently complex that each needs its own significant work.

A basic discipline, of course, is converting analog speech and video to and from digital form. Another aspect deals with the interaction between end user equipment, including between telephones directly connected to service providers using VoIP, telephones to PBXs, and PBXs to providers. Yet other aspects are concerned with the internal management of service provider networks and the setup of paths carrying user information through multiple service providers' networks. In all of these, remember that a service request can start from a traditional telephone that at some point needs to convert to IP formats, or an IP device that at some point will have to interface with existing telephone facilities.

Edge Control for Individual Subscribers

Analog telephones, not surprisingly, use analog signaling for their control communications with the edge office. There are three major parts to telephone control:

1. Local loop control.
2. Dialing, call progress, and ringing.
3. Voice digitizing.

Conventional telephones use a single wire pair (two insulated wires twisted around one another) to the central office. Analog trunks between PBXs and COs may use one or two pairs; analog trunks between COs always use two pairs.

Local Loop Control

In conventional analog telephony, there are two kinds of devices that connect to copper loops from the subscriber premises to the central office: telephones and PBXs. A telephone has a *foreign exchange station* (FXS) interface and expects to connect to a *foreign exchange office* (FXO) interface. A PBX presents an FXO interface to local telephones, but, especially with smaller PBX, will present an FXS interface to the end office. As a person from a data background who has learned to be bilingual in voice, the analogy that helps me is to think of FXS as similar to a data terminal equipment (DTE) interface. FXO is analogous to the data circuit-terminating equipment (DCE) point of demarcation to the carrier.

Actions on the FXS interface trigger the sending of dial tone to your telephone. Normally, when the handset is in the cradle, it is considered *on-hook*. Lifting the handset causes the spring-loaded handset buttons to rise and complete a circuit to the FXO interface. The telephone is now in the *off-hook* condition. It may appear that this produces dial tone, but actually several things happen before dial tone is present. The off-hook signal, part of what is called *loop-start signaling*, tells the CO/PBX that the local loop is in use.

A slightly different form of signaling, variously called *ground start* or *wink start*, is used in CO/PBX device (for instance, FXO to FXO) interfaces on two-wire local loops. Higher-quality trunks between CO and/or PBX devices run over four-wire loops, and a different signaling protocol called *E&M* is used there. To be honest, there is no absolutely accepted definition of what E&M stands for—definitions include "Ear and Mouth," "rEceive and transMit," "earth and magneto," and others.

Dialing and Call Progress

The true dial, which sends low-speed pulses, is obsolete in most developed countries. The term has stayed with us, even though analog telephones signal the number to which they want to connect with tones sent along the same circuit as the user talking path. The technique used is called dual tone multiple frequency (DTMF). Pulse and tone signaling are only present on the local loop. When they reach the CO, signaling information is diverted to the control plane, which initiates management plane actions to attempt to make the

BUT ISN'T THE DIAL TONE IN THE TELEPHONE?

Lots of people have trouble with this concept, and occasionally ask, "How do I know it isn't there if I haven't lifted the handset?" The teaching analogy I use is, "Is the light in your refrigerator on if the door is closed? How do you know?" A student once answered me with supreme confidence, "No. It is off." When I inquired from my lofty instructor position how he could know, he responded, "It burned out and I never replaced it."

desired connection. While the call is progressing, you may hear "bleepity-beep" tones that let you know that the call is being processed, and eventually, you will hear tones you associate with the remote telephone ringing or being busy. Other potential responses include what is commonly known as "fast busy" but properly is called *reorder*, which means that network resources are busy.

ISDN and VoIP phones actually send messages. In the case of ISDN, call signaling travels as Q.931 protocol messages over the D channel, which are mapped to appropriate SS7 messages at the CO. Whether the actual telephone is analog or digital, control/management information separates from user information at the edge office.

When the remote telephone answers, either by going off-hook if analog or sending appropriate messages if digital, the telephone network commits the user connection and also begins billing for its use. If either telephone is analog, the end office channel banks convert the internal digital signals to analog. If the telephone is digital, it can receive the digitized voice information directly.

Perspectives on Digitizing User Signals

While the increased use of optical transport, according to its advocates, makes bandwidth almost free, not every signal flows over optical transport. Wireless media remain bandwidth-limited, especially in such applications as shipboard high-frequency radio or cellular telephony.

In legacy telephony systems, the standard digital equivalent per analog channel is 64 Kbps, known as the DS0 signal. Even before bandwidth enters the discussion, there is an issue of the digitizing algorithm used by the coder-decoders (codecs). Essentially, there are two pulse code modulation (PCM) digitizing algorithms used to produce digital streams: μ-law and A-law. μ-law is primarily used in the Americas and Japan, while the rest of the world uses A-law. Conversion logic needs to be in the codecs if one end is encoded with one algorithm but the other end uses the other algorithm.

More efficient bandwidth utilization becomes an issue when dealing with legacy data systems over which VoIP is used or inherently bandwidth-limited systems such as wireless. Table 7.6 shows the bandwidths associated with different ITU-T standards.

Telephone System Capacity Planning

In the PSTN, there are separate capacity measures for the number of calls that can be set up and the number of calls for which a switch can pass user traffic. For many years, call setup was the limiting factor. Very high rates of calls can overwhelm the call setup of a switch that would actually have sufficient capacity to carry the traffic.

Table 7.6   ITU-T Standards and Bandwidth

ITU-T STANDARD	BANDWIDTH (Kbps)	CODING DELAY	REMARKS
G.711	64	1 ms	The standard
G.723.1	5.3/6.3	30 ms	Part of H.324
G.726	40, 32, 24, 16	1.25 µs	Most use 32
G.728	16	2.5 ms	Low delay
G.729	8	15 ms	Cellular personal communications

Increasing capacity can call for adding different sorts of resources, including the number of physical ports, the call setup capacity, and the user traffic through the switch. Capacity has to be considered on a network basis, not a network element basis—what good is it to improve the port capacity of a switch so that it can accept 622 Mbps of bandwidth, but then to give it only 155 Mbps to the next level of the switching hierarchy? Actually, there can be a very good reason: Traffic analysis may indicate that only 155 Mbps will leave the switch. The remaining 467 Mbps will flow between customers of the switch. In other words, the switch primarily sets up calls between its local users rather than servicing long-distance calls.

Call Setup

If the goal is to increase the BHCA capability, it may be necessary to add processors to the device implementing the control function. In systems with high availability requirements, it is usually best to add additional processors rather than to increase the speed of the existing main processor. In a "carrier-grade" implementation, it must be possible to add processors without interrupting service. However, many older carrier devices required system downtime when changing processors. These systems, however, would usually continue to handle pre-established calls.

Established Call Capacity

To increase the established call capacity, many switches allow switching fabric resources to be added. This is another motivation for midplane design, because it is rather difficult to replace a backplane without interrupting service when all cards are connected to the backplane. One of the reasons that control functions are quite efficient is the use of SS7 as the internal signaling architecture.

Internal Provider Control:
SS7 Connectivity to the PSTN
(ISP as CLEC or IXC)

Demand for telecommunications service always has increased. In the original telephony model, the dialed digits went from the telephone to the switch and from switch to switch until the destination was reached. A 4-kHz analog circuit, or its DS0 digital equivalent, passed no user information while setup was in process. As long as the signaling information passed through the same channels as user information, channels were inefficiently used. In common channel signaling, of which SS7 is one example, there are separate trunks for user traffic and for signaling.

Call setup is time consuming and does not involve much data volume. Prior to common channel signaling, traffic trunks had to be committed from the initial off-hook to the network's decision about reachability of the destination. When call setup took 10 s, that was 10 s when billable traffic could not be carried by that trunk. If user channels were committed only after SS7 had discovered that the called destination was not busy or otherwise unable to accept a call, utilization of the traffic trunks would become much more efficient.

Once digital signaling information existed, a wide range of applications became possible. Toll-free numbers, for example, actually are aliases for real telephone numbers. Special billing rules apply to these numbers. When an end office receives a call request to a toll-free number, it sends a request over the SS7 network to a network control point, which returns the translation, routing, and billing information. The end office then places the call to the real number.

Other specialized billing makes routine use of SS7. These include credit and prepaid calling cards, 900 services, and collect calls.

SS7 is capable of conveying short messages, such as caller ID or paging, using TCAP, an application protocol in the SS7 stack. It is not the intention of SS7 designers, however, that the main SS7 signaling network carry significant amounts of user data. As it has been said that war is too important to leave to the generals, SS7 trunks are far too important to network availability to leave them open to the possibility of congestion due to user traffic.

The SS7 Stack

SS7 has its own architectural stack, shown in Figure 7.17. It certainly has similarities to the OSI reference model, but is not specifically OSI-compliant. In SS7 terminology, the upper layers are called *parts*. The *ISDN user part* carries information used for creating, maintaining, and terminating ISDN calls. *The*

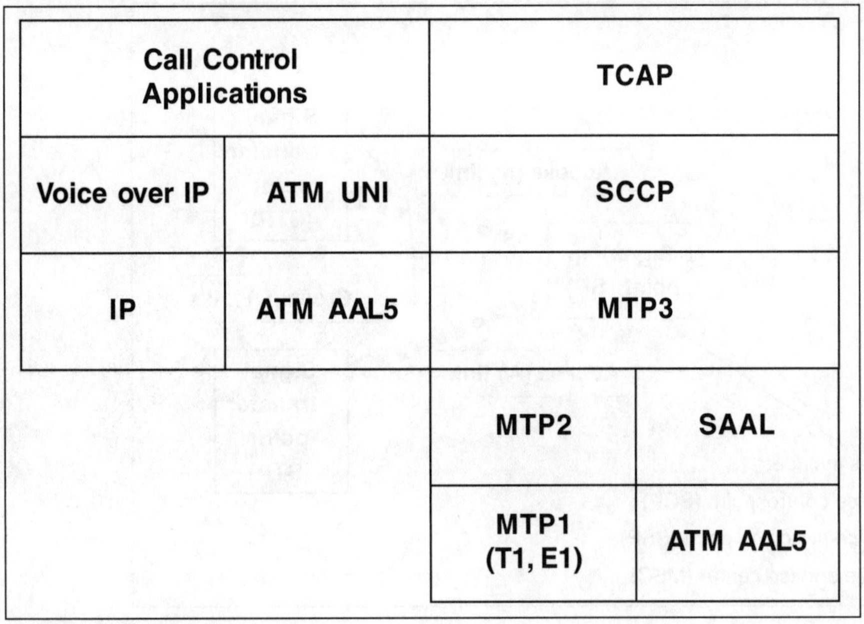

Call Control Applications		TCAP	
Voice over IP	ATM UNI	SCCP	
IP	ATM AAL5	MTP3	
		MTP2	SAAL
		MTP1 (T1, E1)	ATM AAL5

Figure 7.17 SS7 protocol layers.

transaction capabilities application part (TCAP), as its name suggests, carries transactions across SS7. Typical transaction databases include SCP directories, mobile access points, and so on. The *message transfer part level 3* (MTP-3) manages routing, traffic, and links in digital transports.

The higher layer parts can be carried over various lower layers. The message transfer part level 2, or Service Specific Connection Oriented Protocol (SSCOP), transports payloads across point-to-point links. In contrast, the ATM signaling adaptation layer carries payloads across ATM transports. The signaling connection control part carries payloads across arbitrary connectionless and connection-oriented transports.

SS7 Points and Links

Signaling transfer points (STPs) are analogous to standalone path determination processors in routers and switches or in multiservice selection gateways. In the PSTN, they tell the voice switches how to make connections. The generic term for the forwarding elements controlled by STPs is *signaling points*. Access (A) links connect the controlled devices to STP pairs.

Signaling points (SPs), addressed in the SS7 network with *signaling point codes* (SPCs), are the working parts of SS7, roughly corresponding to forwarding

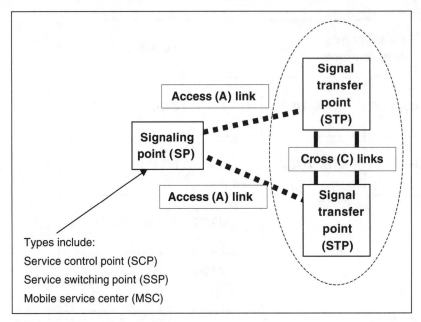

Figure 7.18 Basic SS7 functions.

engines in IP. SPs also include directory functions such as 800 number translation at *service control point* (SCP) SPs. A general voice switch is a *service switching point* (SSP). *Mobile service centers* (MSCs) provide connectivity to the PSTN for mobile telephone users. Figure 7.18 details basic SS7 functions.

As critical components, individual STPs in the SS7 network are redundant. This redundancy does not mean that there are pairs of side-by-side STPs that are vulnerable to the same fire, flood, or errant backhoe. Instead, the STPs of a pair are geographically separated but with redundant communications links between them. The links between STPs in the pair are called *cross (C) links*. See Figure 7.19 for details on flat routing in SS7.

Diagonal (D) links interconnect STPs at different hierarchical levels (see Figure 7.20), in contrast to bridge (B) links, which interconnect STPs with other STPs at the same hierarchal level of the SS7 network. Additional redundancy at the same level can be provided through Extended (E) links, which are very similar to B links except that they go to additional STPs, farther away from the current STP pair.

There may also be reasons to share information among only certain STPs, as in a software-defined enterprise network. This also might be done for traffic engineering. Fully associated (F) links are those that interconnect nodes that have some administrative association with one another.

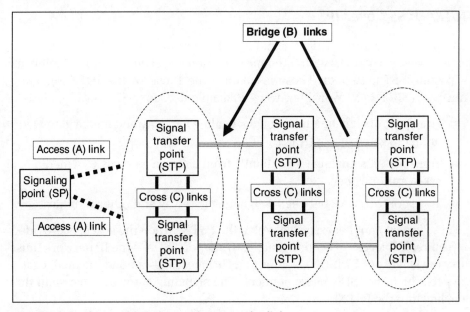

Figure 7.19 Flat routing in SS7 with A, B, and C links.

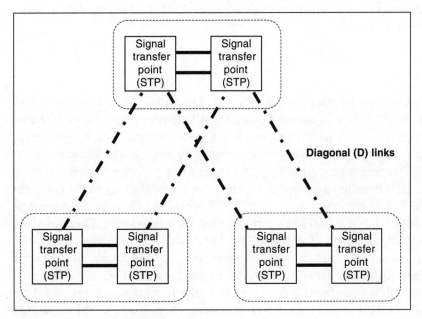

Figure 7.20 Hierarchical routing in SS7.

SIGTRAN: SS7 over IP

As networks integrate, critical signaling information of the PSTN needs to be carried over IP networks with the same performance, security, and reliability as in existing SS7 networks. These issues are the focus of the IETF Signaling Transport (SIGTRAN) Working Group. Plausible uses for SS7 over IP include:

- Transport of signaling between a signaling gateway and media gateway or media gateway controller

- Transport of signaling ("backhaul") from a media gateway to a media gateway controller

- Transport of TCAP between a signaling gateway and other IP nodes

These uses do not necessarily involve the PSTN. When the services provided do require SS7 access—as, for example, to support ISDN—the IP network must carry the Q.931 or SS7 ISDN user part (ISUP) messages among the media gateways to which the ISDN users connect. The signaling gateway must send this signaling into the PSTN.

Interprovider Control

As telephony control and management traffic moves onto IP networks rather than physically separate networks, there is a need for protocols to convert between the user VoIP environment, new carrier VoIP, and existing digital carrier management networks.

IPTEL

There are two major protocols for VoIP control in primary user systems, ITU-T H.323 and IETF Session Initiation Protocol (SIP). Both protocol architectures include the requirement to have a device that converts the "lightweight" internal control protocols to the format of the carrier system, and to know where to send the carrier messages. In H.323, this intermediary device is called a *gatekeeper.* In SIP, it is called a *proxy.* IETF's IP Telephony (IPTEL) Working Group defined the Telephony Routing over IP (TRIP) protocol to handle the exchange of local routing information between external VoIP providers. This function, however, is only one part of the problem. TRIP deals with interprovider management. It does not, however, deal with signaling between customer gateways and the ingress provider servers. The requirement here is called *gateway registration,* and allows the provider's server to make routing decisions based on information the server has about user gateways. Proprietary solutions to this problem exist, but IPTEL is working on a standard protocol for the purpose.

> ### HAVE WE BEEN SLIMED?
>
> When I first saw the H.323 terminology, it seemed vaguely familiar, but I couldn't quite place it until I heard a discussion of encrypted voice in an H.323 environment. Not only did that secure environment have a gatekeeper, but it had a master key server—a *keymaster.*
>
> The gatekeeper and the keymaster. *Ghostbusters,* anyone?

SPIRITS

Another aspect of integrating the IP and voice worlds is the focus of the IETF Services in the PSTN/IN Requesting InTernet Service (SPIRITS) Working Group. SPIRITS deals with how entities in the telephony intelligent network (IN) or the traditional PSTN can request services from elements of the IP network. A SPIRITS client sends a PSTN/IN service request to an IP network, while the SPIRITS server either decides not to honor the request or to execute it. Remember that the SPIRITS server and the PSTN/IN requesting system are in the IP environment, so some complex trust modeling problems need to be solved to make this architecture one of production quality.

How could SPIRITS be useful? A good example is Internet call waiting, in which a telephone user who uses analog access to the data network can be informed of incoming electronic mail. Another example might be sending call forwarding requests from an IP terminal. SPIRITS defines the signaling events; the ITU-T defines the actual service.

Looking Ahead

This chapter deals with physical connectivity among customers, wholesalers, and providers. In the next chapter we will examine connectivity inside a single provider. Chapters 9 through 12 recapitulate this customer-to-provider-to-interprovider approach, but from the logical routing standpoint.

CHAPTER 8

Transporting the Bits: The Sub-IP and Physical Intraprovider Core

As of now, I am in control here, in the White House, pending the return of the vice president and in close touch with him.
—*Alexander Haig*

I could carve out of a banana a man with more backbone than that.
—*Theodore Roosevelt*

What can go wrong, will.
—*Murphy's law*

When you consider that most of the edge traffic of a provider will enter the provider's core variously to go to other edge points, to border routers connecting to other providers, or to hosts inside the carrier, it is reasonable to assume that the intraprovider core has the highest bandwidth requirements of the carrier. Less obvious, however, is that the topology of a well-designed core may be simpler than the edge.

A great deal of current provider core practice, and expectations about practices in the relatively near future, comes from the constant evolution of high-capacity transmission media. There are several key requirements for an interprovider logical core, although they differ depending on the particular business of the provider:

- Fault tolerance and rapid reconvergence
- Traffic engineering, both for premium services and for general capacity planning
- Efficiency of facility usage

Basic Layer 1 Resilient Media

We have another ambiguous use of *layer* here. Even rather elderly media types, such as T1 lines, have provisions for automatic failover to a backup. At the simplest, a channel service unit (CSU), the demarcation point between carrier and subscriber, can terminate a primary and a backup line and automatically switch to the backup if the primary fails (Figure 8.1). Observe that the two T1 lines are in different binders, which at the very least are different bundles in the same cable and ideally are separately routed cables. Depending on how you contract with the local loop provider—or whether you are the local loop provider—this kind of backup often will be cheaper than a hot standby backup, because only one line will actively transfer data at any given time, and thus only one line will consume upstream bandwidth.

This example shows the failover at the endpoint. *Alternate span switching* can also be used in the outside plant. The T1 repeater housings, spaced every 4,000 to 6,000 ft, can contain logic that detects a failure in one line and switches its traffic to another line physically accessible to the same repeater. A different alternative will incur costs, but may very well be worthwhile in terms of reliability. It is an excellent example of the concept of *graceful degradation*. Assume you have 48 voice channels, 24 of which are more critical than others. Normally, channels 1 through 24 are serviced by T1 A, while

---

CRITICAL ASSUMPTIONS FOR THE READER

Chapter 11 discusses the details of both IGP and BGP within provider cores, as well as the use of MPLS and other tunnels. In this chapter, we make the assumption that IGP information is available to the sub-IP protocols.

Be very, very sure you understand that this is an editorial assumption and not a technical one. Technologies such as MPLS absolutely require IP routing to exist before they can reach their maximum effectiveness. Essentially, MPLS and many of these other new sub-IP technologies are "overdrives" or "optimizations" on the topologies that IP routing would create. These optimizations may provide better traffic engineering, faster restoration, or more efficient resource use in specific technologies.

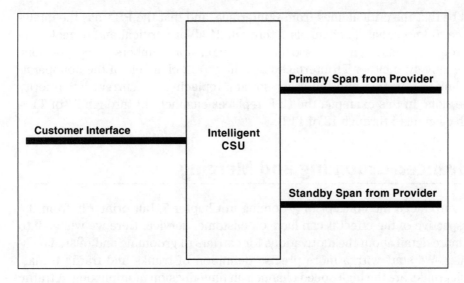

Figure 8.1 Basic T1 failover.

channels 25 to 48 are serviced by T1 B. You will have to provision your channel assignments such that all the critical lines can be serviced by one T1 interface or that the critical services will be the first 12 time slots on each interface (see Figure 8.2).

One strategy, which needs to be cooperative between the subscriber and the provider, protects against line failures. Assume that T1 B fails. One alternative requires the failure to be sensed at the central office and the PBX, but the result

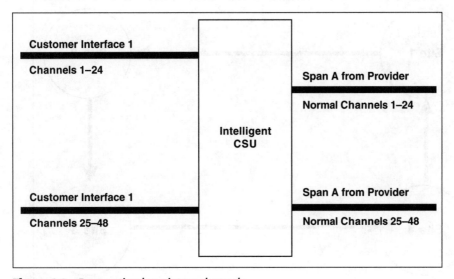

Figure 8.2 Preempting by primary channels.

will be that the critical lines from B interface, and that the PBX has the intelligence to know that its channels 1 through 24 all are critical and to make the appropriate changes in the association of extension numbers with time slots. Alternatively, if either T1 interface fails, the top 12 channels of the nonoperating link are merged into the other stream, replacing the current low-priority time slots. In this example, the CPE replaces channels 13 through 24 of T1 A with channels 1 through 12 of T1 B.

Advanced Grooming and Merging

We introduced the concept of grooming in Chapter 7, but primarily from the perspective of the effect it can have on customer service. Here we will go into far more detail about the motivations for carriers of grooming and related techniques. We start with a more precise definition of trunks and traffic trunks. Basic trunks are the high-speed channels in time-division multiplexing. A traffic trunk is a logical or physical facility that carries all traffic of a single service class between two endpoints. It is a meaningful concept in both basic layer 2 networks and in label-switched networks.

In this chapter, the emphasis is on grooming or merging multiple slower streams into a stream that is more efficiently carried on a higher-speed link or path. Chapter 11 deals with the use of trunking in traffic engineering.

Trunking can offer resilience as well as efficient resource use. Potential topologies for trunking include:

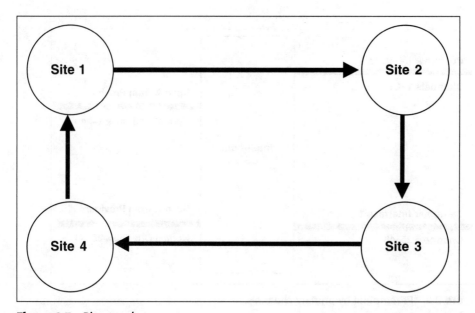

Figure 8.3   Ring topology.

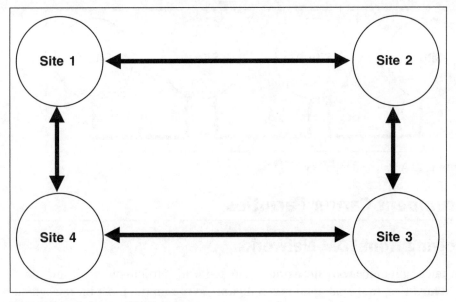

Figure 8.4   Point-to-point topology.

- Two-fiber hubbed ring (Figure 8.3)
- Point-to-point (Figure 8.4)
- Meshed (Figure 8.5)
- Add-and-drop multiplexer (ADM) chain (Figure 8.6)

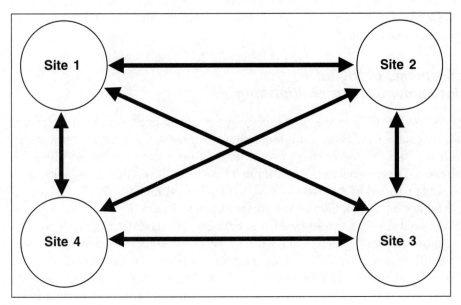

Figure 8.5   Mesh topology.

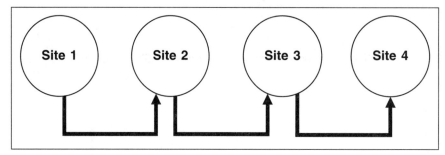

Figure 8.6 ADM chain topology.

Incumbent Carrier Facilities

Evolving from TDM Networks

The telecommunications network originated with circuit-switched and dedicated facilities, first analog and then digital. To obtain the most basic scalability, dedicated lines needed to be multiplexed onto high-capacity trunks in the carrier backbone.

Basic Digital Telephony Multiplexing

Traditional voice signals are digitized into 64-Kbps streams called DS0. Much more bandwidth-efficient forms are available and are used in services such as VoIP, but the world's telecommunications networks are made up of multiples of 64-Kbps digital streams, plus transmission overhead specific to the medium type. DS0 signals combine into the higher rates of the PDH or SDH introduced in the previous chapter.

Refinements of Digital Telecommunications Multiplexing

Since a DACS is DS0-aware, new services were developed to exploit this awareness. Originally the DS0 streams were simply routed among carrier trunks. The DACS function, however, began to extend to both multiplexed and inverse-multiplexed user services. In fractional T1 service, however, some multiple of DS0 was provided to a customer over a T1 physical facility. This is a physical layer bitstream, not an interleaved service such as Frame Relay.

Fractional services worked well, and have been extended to T3. They may be even more attractive there than with T1 services, since the crossover point where a T3 is more cost-effective than multiple T1s may be as low as 6 or 7 T1s, while a T3 can carry 28 T1 equivalents. Installing the T3 local loop gives far more growth capacity. T3 services are most commonly run over optical fiber.

Originally fiber was used as a simple range extender for a high-rate bitstream. At first, the appeal of optical networking was its range—the long distances possible between repeaters. Soon, however, it became much more than a means of range extension. It offered the highest available bandwidth and the possibility of switching nodes far faster than pure electronics could achieve.

Backhaul

There are definite economies of scale in transmission equipment. The cost per transmitted bit is far less on a wavelength-division multiplexed optical facility with multiple 10-Gbps channels than on a standard repeatered copper T1 line. Given these economies, a straight line may be the shortest distance, but not necessarily the cheapest. *Backhaul* (see Figure 8.7) is the technique of moving data to potentially more distant but higher-capacity facilities that have the lowest transmission cost.

The classic objection to backhaul is that it increases propagation delay. As optical transmission facilities grow faster and faster, their reduced per-bit transmission times may make up for the increases in distance-sensitive propagation. Many historical workarounds to backhaul were developed when fast data lines ran at 56 Kbps.

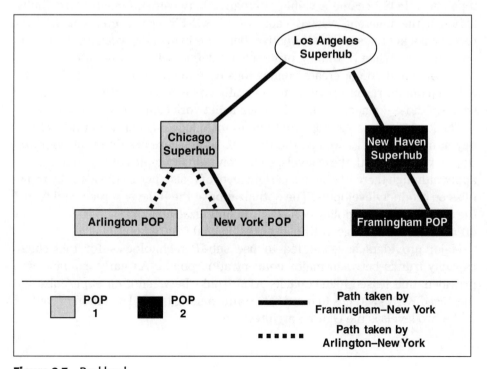

Figure 8.7   Backhaul.

Layer 2 Overlays

Trunking has long been a feature of the internals of service provider networks, even before MPLS. It was fairly common practice for large carriers to build "superhubs" linking high-capacity ATM or SONET/SDH links, and then to overlay their IP networks onto these layer 2 networks. See Chapter 11 for further distinctions of the use of native VPN technologies such as ATM LANE and MultiProtocol over ATM (MPOA).

ATM over SONET was the basic approach, but PPP over SONET became even more attractive due to its greater efficiency. These models still continued the basic inefficiency of the underlying transport, which generally needed to be configured manually. ATM did have PNNI dynamic routing available, but this did not help with POS. Indeed, some light traffic flows, such as frame relay from POPs, might come in using frame relay. Another alternative was to use a bandwidth- or facilities-based provider to groom dedicated and FR circuits into high-bandwidth links that reduced interface count.

While ATM offered a standard means of obtaining high bandwidth, it was still subject to the "cell tax." There is a constant philosophical debate among high-bandwidth transmission architects as to whether the increase in bandwidth available from a technology obviates whatever overhead it may have. Packet over SONET eliminated the cell tax, although it was limited to point-to-point topologies. POS became a viable alternative between sufficiently large hubs, although the inherent wasted capacity of SONET was a concern. IP over resilient packet rings is one alternative that helps in avoiding wasting capacity in backup rings. While IP routing protocols do define paths, those paths are truly hop-by-hop and do not create connections or commit resources. Sub-IP protocols do commit resources and are generally connection-oriented, although the scope of those connections may be a single network element such as a DACS.

The long-term answer appears to be to introduce a general routing technology into the sub-IP as well as the IP level. While there are different optimizations involved in both these levels, some common principles of dynamic routing apply, although there has been a certain level of resistance to the ideas by transmission product developers. The optimization at the IP level is reachability and the ability to impose policy controls; the optimization at the sub-IP level is for efficient resource usage, traffic engineering, and fast restoration.

Major providers have tended to use sub-IP technologies for their high-capacity trunks between major concentration points. An early example was providers that leased high-capacity ATM trunks between their superhubs and then used WAN switches to distribute traffic among them. The union of routing at the two levels is the GMPLS architecture.

Where Does Ethernet Fit in All This?

Although used very imprecisely, *Ethernet* is a popular buzzword in the optical product space. There are very significant differences between the original Ethernet II specification and early IEEE 802.3 specifications, and references to "optical Ethernet" in the service provider marketplace. To illustrate this, observe that a minivan and a Boeing 777 are both transportation systems. They both seat passengers. They both may even have meal service. But the differences in range, speed, cost, and complexity are profound.

In this chapter, the emphasis is on carrying Ethernet frames over media appropriate for a provider core. The next chapter, which focuses on the lower-layer aspects of the provider edge, deals with customer Ethernet interfaces and Ethernet local loops. Let's review some characteristics of classic Ethernet and discuss how the usage of Ethernet in the WAN differs.

Ethernet and the basic IEEE 802.3 standards were established for environments with "local" distance limitations—up to 500 m, and often less. The basic media for these environments was multiaccess and broadcast-capable, having potentially 1,000 devices on a single medium. For a variety of reasons, primarily associated with the speed of the early media, the frame length was limited to a payload of 1,500 bytes. Many modern applications, discussed in the next chapter, would be happier with a much longer frame length.

These environments often supported IEEE 802.1d spanning tree bridging, which was often pushed far beyond the reasonable limits of devices. Good practice does not put more than 500 to 1,000 IP hosts into a single broadcast domain, but there are many horror stories of enterprises that pushed broadcast domains over 10,000 devices, and whose networks died most painfully in a broadcast storm. Spanning tree topologies are not especially robust when reconverging after failures. They do not support parallel paths between two nodes, although there are both proprietary and IEEE methods for inverse multiplexing Ethernet in a manner that is invisible to 802.1d.

The intended applications of VLANs have gone through several evolutions. First, in the IEEE 802.10 effort, they were intended as a means of enforcing LAN security, including encryption at the data-link layer. Their second generation came with IEEE 802.1q, where they added flexibility to installations by allowing high-speed trunks to carry traffic from different broadcast domains.

In the wide area context, *Ethernet* has a much more restricted meaning. First, its topology is restricted to point-to-point or nonbroadcast multiaccess (NBMA). When the topology is NBMA, it is imposed with an active hubbing device, not a shared medium. Second, it implies that the basic 802.3 frame is used to encapsulate packets. Third, it is quite common for the 802.1q extension to be used as a convenient means of sorting out different user streams on the same fiber. In other words, 802.1q serves as a frame-level multiplex identifier, rather than the time slots of SONET or SDH. Therefore, in this chapter, the emphasis regarding Ethernet over advanced optical facilities is on identifying and discussing those facilities that can accept such frames. Using Ethernet as the subscriber interface is a topic for the next chapter.

To date, most vendors have focused on using LAN-oriented equipment to carry Ethernet over dedicated fiber. As of late 2000, Nortel does have alternatives in addition to its LAN-oriented 8600 switch. The two alternatives are Ethernet interfaces on DWDM products and Ethernet interfaces on the SONET-oriented Optera add-drop multiplexer, which can connect both to SONET and to IEEE resilient packet rings.

Inverse Multiplexing

Inverse multiplexing is a technique that allows high user data rates to be provisioned using multiple slower, but available, physical facilities. The basic idea of inverse multiplexing is to combine several carrier streams into one faster stream delivered at the customer interface. It complements basic layer 1 resilience.

You can multilink at different layers, although I hesitate to associate these with specific OSI layers because the layering is often specific to the transmission system. With low transmission speeds (for instance, multiple DS0), bit-level inverse multiplexing can make sense. Techniques include the BONDING method of combining six DS0 streams into a 384-Kbps aggregate often used for videoconferencing, but not for data. Another bit-level method uses multiple modems to provide speeds in the low hundreds of kilobits to sites that cannot access residential broadband or that need to be portable. However, data-link multiplexing with multilink PPP is more common than bit interleaving in these modem applications. At higher speeds, the technique of *inverse multiplexing for ATM* (IMA) [ATMF af-phy-0086] can be used to create ATM connectivity when only DS1 physical facilities are available. The inverse multiplexing equipment spreads cells over multiple DS1 facilities.

Evolution to First-Generation Optical Facilities

Optical transmission media came into use as alternatives to copper, often at the same speed but with longer range and lesser requirements for repeaters. The increased ranges possible with optical transmission, especially on the longer-reach systems that do not need repeaters, have major economic benefits for most carriers.

In many cases optical networking has replaced satellite networks. There are still many applications for satellites, especially involving broadcasting or remote areas. However, nowhere does the distance capability of optical systems impact an application as it does transoceanic cables. Shall we say that it is not tremendously convenient to pay a service call on a malfunctioning repeater that is under several thousand feet of the stormy North Atlantic? Current optical systems have demonstrated unrepeatered range of 4000 kilometers.

Optical networking has moved beyond transmission alone. Now, intelligent gateways and cross-connects make some decisions at the true optical level, without the need to convert optical signals to electronic signals, manipulate them, and convert them back.

ATM was a major driver for optical networking. At speeds above 100 Mbps, ATM cells actually flow over synchronous optical network (SONET) or synchronous digital hierarchy (SDH) in Europe. SONET has a three-layered architecture:

1. Paths interconnect optical service endpoints.

2. Lines interconnect optical service multiplexers.

3. Sections interconnect optical media and repeaters. (In SONETspeak, repeaters are called *regenerators.*)

In the IETF's framework, an optical subnetwork is a set of optical cross-connects (OXCs) that supports end to end networking of optical channel trails providing functionality like routing, monitoring, grooming, and protection and restoration of optical channels. It may have an OMS and/or OTS underlying it. (See Table 8.1 for a comparison of optical transport networking (OTN) and SONET terminology. Carriers expect that any practical optical network architecture will be able to operate hundreds of OXCs with thousands of wavelengths or physical ports per OXC. There can be hundreds of parallel fibers between OXCs, each with hundreds of wavelengths.

SONET serves as today's gold standard for protection/failover mechanisms. These will be discussed immediately after this section on SONET/SDH basics, and we will return to their principles in Chapter 11 on higher-layer cores. To be viable in applications such as telephony, IP and MPLS cores have to be able to provide the high availability of SONET.

Table 8.1 OTN versus SONET Terminology

OTN	SONET
Optical channel (OCh)	Path
Optical multiplex section (OMS)	Line
Optical transmission section (OTS)	Section

SONET Architecture

Path terminating equipment (PTE) connects to the user of the SONET service, such as a router with a SONET interface or a telephone circuit switch. Line terminating equipment (LTE), such as DACSs and ADMs, terminates a physical SONET transmission facility.

ADMs are not new concepts in telecommunications, having been used in DSx TDM. In SONET, however, they have additional capabilities. ADMs can be configured in stars or rings. Basic SONET ADMs have synchronous in and out SONET connections and a synchronous or asynchronous connection to their site. Only those subchannels relevant to the site are dropped to that site; the rest of the channel passes through unchanged (Figure 8.8a). If the site link is asynchronous, it can rate-adapt from a lower edge speed to a standard speed. Due to the synchronous nature of SONET, the ADM does not have to demultiplex the

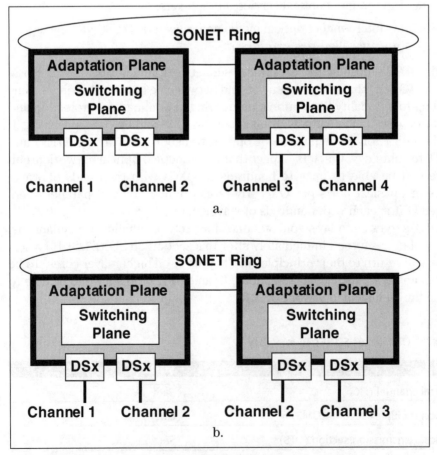

Figure 8.8   (a) Add and drop, (b) drop and repeat.

entire aggregate stream, but can simply extract the channel of interest. The synchronous master clocking lets an ADM extract a channel in a specific time slot rather than having to demultiplex the stream, extract the channel, and regenerate the stream.

A variant on ADM is *drop and repeat* (Figure 8.8b), which is essentially a multicast technology. With drop and repeat, a subchannel drops off to a site, but the ADM passes the same signal on to the next site. This is especially useful for video distribution or large audio conferences. Section terminating equipment is either the terminations of an optical link at PTE or LTE, or the connection a link to optical regenerators. Optical regenerators are comparable to repeaters in data networks.

SONET Speed Hierarchy

Like the PDH and CEPT hierarchies, SONET has its own hierarchy of speeds. These speeds, shown in Table 8.2, include SONET overhead. While SONET overhead is not as heavy as the ATM cell tax and the ATM adaptation layer (AAL) tax, the full SONET rate is not available to user traffic. The 51.84 Mbps STS-1 rate is the basic building block of SONET. You can draw the analogy that STS-1 is to SONET as DS0 is to the PDH; it is the basic quantum of speed. It is slightly faster than a DS3, so it can encapsulate DS3 or slower links into what are called *virtual tributaries*, as shown in Table 8.3.

Table 8.2   SONET Hierarchy

OC LEVEL	SPEED
OC-1	51.84 Mbps
OC-3	155.52 Mbps
OC-9	466.56 Mbps
OC-12	622.08 Mbps
OC-18	933.12 Mbps
OC-24	1.244 Gbps
OC-36	1.866 Gbps
OC-48	2.488 Gbps
OC-96	4.976 Gbps
OC-192	9.953 Gbps (usually called 10 Gbps)
OC-768	39.813 Gbps (usually called 40 Gbps)

Table 8.3   Multiplexing into an STS-1 Bitstream

SERVICE	SPEED	CARRIES
VT 1.5	1.728 Mbps	DS1
VT 2	2.304 Mbps	CEPT1/E1
VT 3	3.456 Mbps	DS1C
VT 6	6.912 Mbps	DS2
VT 6-Nc	$N * 6.912$ Mbps	$N * DS2$
Asynchronous DS3	44.736 Mbps	DS3

Packet over SONET

PPP over SONET has better bandwidth efficiency than ATM with any AAL type. If the optical link carries IP between two routers, the bandwidth between those routers is guaranteed—what else can use it? ATM's QoS capabilities are of no use in this situation. If ATM is delivering end-to-end virtual circuits, it does have a role. But for intercarrier router links, it is hard to justify ATM in preference to POS.

SONET has become a transitional technology, just as ATM/SONET was an evolutionary step beyond TDM. Due to the large and effective SONET installed base, newer technologies must support SONET. A difference between SONET and some of the newer technologies is that an intermediate level of frame- or packet-to-bit conversion is necessary before information can go onto the SONET facility. The one exception is that there are a substantial number of products that put PPP frames onto SONET. PPP, however, is less useful than Ethernet framing.

Models for Survivability

The networking corollary to Murphy's Law is, "Murphy was an optimist." There will be failures in any real-world network. One of the fundamental properties of "carrier-grade" networks is that they plan for automated recovery from failure. This planning involves both providing spare resources and mechanisms for detecting failures and invoking appropriate spare capacity. *Survivability* describes the ability of a particular network to maintain service—possibly degraded service—after faults occur. Survivability has to be engineered into the network using such techniques as protection and restoration.

RESTORATION PRIORITY

The term *restoration priority* includes both a specific network design principle and an important administrative mechanism for carriers in the United States and certain other countries. In network design, it specifies the order in which failed resources can take over a backup resource.

The U.S. National Communications System has a set of rules for how carriers are to restore facilities in national emergency facilities. For example, nuclear command and control have higher priorities than local emergency response services, which have higher priorities than banking facilities.

Protection and Restoration

Several concepts go into survivable, self-healing networks. In an ideal world, there are always spare resources. *Protection* techniques automatically substitute a backup resource for a failed resource, and assume a resource will be pre-designated and available. *Restoration* techniques may have to locate spare resources before the failed service can be put back in service. Another way of regarding healing is that protection depends on the preallocation of facilities, while restoration involves some level of routing intelligence to find resources.

Preemption and Extra Traffic

In the real world, there may be more failures than backup components. *Preemption* methods establish policies where resources in current use may be taken away from their current user (that is, a user of extra traffic) and reassigned to a use with higher priority. Extra traffic is not protected. For example, the control system of a network *must* protect itself if any recovery is to take place. Resources are assigned *preemption priorities* to determine the order in which they can be preempted by more critical services.

1+1 protection is the most expensive protection model, because it duplicates all resources, including signal sources, transmission systems, signal receivers, and logic to know which is the active stream. It can be justified only for the most critical resources, such as the fundamental control and management system of networks. SS7 frequently uses 1+1 protection. Indeed, the U.S. nuclear war command and control networks use 1+1+1. . . . up to some classified number of ones. 1:1 takes longer to recover from failures than does 1+1, but at lower cost. As in 1+1, there must be a mechanism to select the active link, but 1:1 is simpler because only the link needs to be selected, not the data stream. 1:1 also offers the potential to use the backup link for preemptible traffic.

PROTECTION SWITCH AND RESTORATION TIME

The metric for protection is the time from detection of a fault to completion of the protection facility activation. This time includes fault detection, control overhead, and the time to complete the switchover. Restoration time is the time from the occurrence of a fault either to the complete restoration of the service or to the time no resources are determined to be available either as spares or by preemption.

One of the differences between packet and TDM networks is that packet, especially MPLS packet, can establish potential backup paths but not commit resources to them. In physical networks where the control and transmission paths are integrated, this is not possible.

The next step in economy among protection architectures is 1:n, where a single resource backs up n active resources. Again, the backup resource could be used for preemptible traffic. As soon as you go to 1:n, or to 1:1 when the backup path is carrying preemptible traffic, you deal with the problems of restoration priority and restoration time.

m:n is a more complex yet more economical model, where m active resources are backed up by n backup resources. This model has generally been too complex for physical systems, but may be emerging in the MPLS environment.

Reversion and Regrooming

After a fault recovery action is taken to protect a working service, what should happen after the fault is corrected? The basic alternatives are *reversion* and *regrooming*. In reversion, once the original working circuit is repaired, the traffic on the protected circuit moves back to the working circuit in a nondisruptive, "make before break" manner. Reversion, of course, assumes the original circuit is available.

Regrooming, or *non revertive mode*, applies when there is no preferred circuit to which to return the service. The original resource failure might have been due to physical destruction, and it may or may not ever be available again. Regrooming, which often involves dynamic routing, entails a search for new resources from which the functional equivalent of the original resource can be created. There may be no transfer of the current working service; the new resources may simply be designated as a protection facility for the current facility. Nonrevertive mode is the default behavior for facilities whose backup alternative is more complex than 1+1 or 1:1.

SONET Recovery

Just because you are SONET-connected does not mean that you have automatic backup. You must explicitly have *Automatic Protection Switching*, a SONET high-availability technology. In the original version, SONET LTE connects to a primary and backup SONET medium. The specific SONET terminology used is the working and protection ring. APS supports 1+1 and 1:n models.

In APS, only the working ring actually carries user traffic. A management protocol, however, runs over both rings. The APS Protect Group Protocol detects failures and triggers ring switchover. SONET, however, has been extremely reliable, and duplicating all rings is very expensive. In the 1:n variant shown on the right side of Figure 8.9, one protection ring covers four units of LTE. When a failure occurs, the protection ring is activated only between the endpoints affected by the actual failure. A key emerging extension is that SONET does not need to run over its own physical fiber, but can run on a wavelength of DWDM. This allows links in multiple protection rings to run over the same fiber, with due regard not to put both links of the same ring over the same physical fiber.

Some people think of ATM as providing rapid recovery from failures, but it is SONET, not ATM, that provides 50-ms restoration. If alternate paths are statically provisioned, ATM can use them as soon as it detects a failure, but IP routing is equally able to use alternate static routes without waiting for routing protocols to reconverge. Dynamic ATM call establishment is not instantaneous.

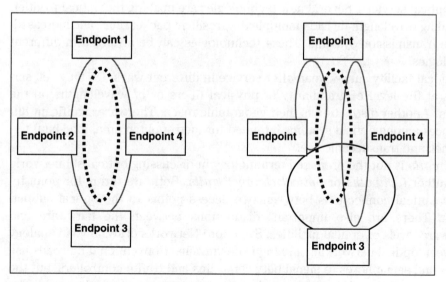

Figure 8.9   SONET protection example with 1+1 and 1:4 APS.

What Are Carrier Goals for New Optical Technologies?

Carriers interested in next-generation optical transport networking (OTN) see the various technologies combining to create an environment of automatic switched optical networking (ASON) technologies (G.ASON). ASON is not just an interesting group of technologies, but presents a set of business values to carriers. It will increase their flexibility and decrease their operating cost by using standard protocols for end-to-end provisioning. The availability of standard protocols that support more complex topologies also will give better resource utilization than current SONET/SDH. Use of standard protocols will also drive down costs of both operational software and equipment, since interoperable products can compete against one another.

Increased flexibility includes the ability to respond to market changes and new user signals. Not only will staffing costs go down, but the flexible topologies will reduce the cost per transmitted bit by allowing better resource utilization. SONET-style 1+1 backup is very inefficient from a resource perspective. In other words, ASON will provide active traffic engineering at the optical layer in a manner that allows network resources to be dynamically allocated to meet changing requirements.

Optical Service Offerings

A separate issue from the actual technology is how facilities-based providers sell optical services. Several new technologies are pushing the optical frontier, including wavelength-division multiplexing, resilient packet rings, and increased-range transmission systems. These technologies can be arranged in different topologies.

Optical facility carriers can offer service in different ways. Do they sell services at the level of granularity of physical fibers or of wavelengths on the fibers? Another distinction is their geographic reach: There are significant differences among optical systems intended for metropolitan area, long-haul terrestrial, and transoceanic use.

Circuits is not the preferred terminology in discussing optical subnetwork, but rather *lightpaths* or *optical channel trails*. Both are terms for point-to-point optical connections between two access points to the optical subnetwork. There are also important distinctions between the hardware and software levels of optical facilities. Sycamore Networks draws a vivid analogy between optical networking and high-speed trains: Conventional railroads use lights and semaphores to signal between trains and traffic controllers, but the Japanese and French "bullet trains" are too fast for mechanical signals. The hardware innovation that made these trains practical was infrared signals, but this hardware was not really practical until software in the train's onboard computer could interpret the signals' significance and detect possible dangers. In like manner, Sycamore refers to as the physical components, such as transmitting lasers, optical receivers, and optical instrumentation, as *hard optics*. *Soft optics* control these components and make it possible to reconfigure services without dispatching technicians for expensive and slow physical equipment changes.

Yet another paradigm becomes involved when resilient packet rings and Ethernet-based services are considered in the transport. If they use DWDM, they may have multiple aggregates. Within aggregates, however, the granule is the frame or packet.

Characteristics and Constraints of Optical Networks

Flow

In an optical network, a flow is the smallest unit of a data stream, much like a single TCP connection. A flow may map to a wavelength or a time slot in the transmission system.

Granularity

The original TDM systems broke channel capacity into granules of bitstreams of constant or even different rates. Their basic unit of information, however, remained the bit. At any given instant, the channel was passing a single bit from one of the data streams in the trunk. Even though an individual fiber could carry a great deal of data, the original production-quality systems, using SONET/SDH, carried single digital streams. These streams were multiplexed and demultiplexed electronically and transmitted optically. In other words, their granularity remained at the bit level over a single aggregate trunk.

Wavelength-division multiplexing is a valuable yet disruptive technology that breaks the assumption that there is a single data stream per fiber. It can be meaningful to assign at the level of granularity of:

- Fiber (offered as managed fiber services)
- Wavelength on fiber (offered as managed wavelength services, also called managed lambda services)
- Digital multiplex within wavelength

Reach/Range

Optical transmission systems have several ranges of reach, as shown in Table 8.4.

Table 8.4   Ranges of Reach of Optical Transmission Systems

TYPE	REACH	APPLICATION
Very short	Hundreds of meters	Host to access device; interoffice connectivity
Metro	Tens of kilometers	Local loops
Long haul	Hundreds to low thousands of kilometers	Long distance along accessible paths
Ultra-long	4,000 km or more	Long distance along inaccessible paths (for example, underseas, the Himalayas, trans-Siberia)

Facilities-Based Services

Table 8.5 shows leasing alternatives for facilities-based services.

Managed Wavelength Services

The provider of managed wavelength services controls the fiber itself but leases full lambdas to its customers. The customer can decide how to multiplex the lambda, or not to multiplex it at all (for instance, 10-Gbit Ethernet). The customer's multiplexing can use SONET/SDH, resilient packet rings (RPRs), or other methods—they are literally transparent to the fiber operator. Managed

Table 8.5   Leasing Alternatives

	PDH/SDH	MANAGED FIBER	MANAGED WAVELENGTH
Capital cost	Low (assuming existing plant)	High	Moderate
Cost per bit	High	Lowest	Low
Capacity	50 Mbps	Highest	High
Topological flexibility	High	Low	Low to moderate
Scalability	Not implicit*	Highest	Substantial
Protection	Not implicit	Optional	Optional
Service activation	Slow	Moderate	Fast

* If the service is provisioned with a facility that has additional capacity, such as having several DS1s multiplexed from a single DS3 physical facility, adding capacity may simply be a matter of reprovisioning the multiplexers.

wavelength service will not have the massive economy of scale per unit of bandwidth that a managed fiber service can offer, but most applications do not need such massive bandwidth. Managed wavelength service does offer greater flexibility in pure topology, offering the potential of grooming multiple wavelengths onto a central fiber or protected fiber. The capital cost is lower than for managed fiber.

In metro environments, the increments available are OC-3 to OC-192, and OC-48 to OC-192 (or more) in long-haul systems. The bandwidth is adequate to offer business opportunities for reselling lower-speed increments. Different grades of protection are available, from the <50-ms restoration characteristic of dual-ring SONET, to intermediate backup, to unprotected but not preemptable, to preemptable.

Managed Fiber Services

A managed fiber service offers an entire medium to its customer, and the customer can decide how many wavelengths to put on it. There may be capabilities for automatic protection switching to other fibers. Optical transmission facilities can run directly between customer facilities, if the physical topology of the sites permits. It is more common that they will take multiple optical hops through optical provider facilities.

Connection-Oriented Services

Connection-oriented services keep control of the wavelength or fiber with the service provider. They include managed bandwidth services, static provisioned bandwidth (SPB) service, and bandwidth-on-demand (BOD) service.

Managed Bandwidth Services

The traditional facilities-based service provider supplies bandwidth to its customer, from fractional T1 to OC-192. Carrier charges are independent of usage. One of the criticisms of such services is that there may be substantial delay in provisioning additional capacity. Another criticism is that the managed bandwidth technologies may not have the automatic failover capabilities of newer technologies such as SONET.

One of the interesting aspects of providing efficient managed bandwidth is the capacity of the local loop. In North America, the point at which fractional T3, or even full T3, service becomes more cost-effective than multiple T1s typically is at the bandwidth equivalent of six or seven T1s. The provider, when provisioning the initial local loop for a customer needing only one or two T1s, needs to ask whether the customer's requirements are likely to grow to the point where a T3 local loop would have reasonable utilization and a lower capital cost than multiple T1s. Indeed, many facilities-based providers are running OC-3 or faster SONET to suburban office parks, installing a provider-owned ATM switch or SONET add-drop multiplexer there. This puts the provider in a position to be quite responsive to subscriber requests for more capacity. Use of dual-ring SONET to connect to such locations also offers a great deal of confidence in availability, including protection against the dreaded backhoe fade. Direct optical links can be quite reasonable in metropolitan areas. There are many reasons, however, why enterprises and IP service providers do not install the fiber themselves. Perhaps even more complex than the actual laying of the fiber is arranging rights-of-way, coordinating with local authorities when roads need to be disrupted, managing the chaos of digging, and so on.

SPB Service

SPB service falls between physical dedicated facilities and on-demand services. Bandwidth cannot necessarily be changed in real time, and changing it may require manual intervention by the carrier. Charging is usage-independent. However, the service concept does include the concept of the customer requesting changes in bandwidth provisioning via an enhanced UNI, or, more likely, a customer-specific web interface into the provider's provisioning system. Obviously, the ability to point and click to reprovision services would lower carriers' internal provisioning expense.

SPB extends the equivalent functionality to the customer, but limited to the capabilities of physical facilities they have installed. For example, if 1-Gbps Ethernet, of which the customer pays for 500 Mbps of bandwidth, serves the user, the user could use SPB procedures to change its bandwidth to 300 or 800 Mbps. The user could not, however, use SPB to get 2 Gbps, since that is physically not available from the facilities.

BOD Service

Customer financial people absolutely hate paying for resources they are not using. Sometimes this hatred leads to silly behavior, as when the costs of tracking resource use or creating on-demand resource provisioning is greater than the potential savings. In other cases, the concern is warranted, and BOD has been defined to meet those cases. BOD involves connections initiated by an edge (user device) and automatically implemented by the network. A practical setup time goal should be well under 1 s, which implies that there is a permanent physical connection between the edge equipment and the service entry point. Think of the conventional telephone call and you are quite close to describing the service. Charging for BOD is based on connection time. The actual charges can vary with such things as time of day, requested quality of service, and so forth.

Equipment using BOD needs to have enough intelligence to operate a UNI. That means that for legacy equipment optical BOD is either not an option or requires an intermediate converter box. BOD has different implications for traffic engineering than for virtual private lines, since the connections will last for less time (have a shorter holding time) than soft permanent connections in the SPB service. BOD imposes more work on the network switching elements. Just as with telephone calls, the service request might be denied if resources are not available. A BOD service, however, may include a feature by which future service reservations can be made.

Optical Virtual Private Networks

Current concepts of VPNs are that they are implemented as tunnels over some underlying transport, which can be IP or a sub-IP layer such as MPLS. VLANs and LANE are usually considered outside the scope of VPNs, the key differentiator being that "native VPN" networks that are limited to a medium, but VPNs can go over any topology supported by IP.

The next distinction in VPNs is whether they are customer-provisioned or provider-provisioned. The service provider may be completely unaware of a customer-operated VPN using, for example, IPSec tunnels. Provider-provisioned VPNs (PPVPNs) use several models, including BGP/MPLS [RFC 2547], multiple virtual routers, and optical VPN. There is also a specific concept of an optical VPN (OVPN). OPVN service creates a dedicated optical transmission system under the customer's control. This system is a subset of the carrier's resources. Only sophisticated users that understand optical networking may make effective use of OPVNs, but that market does include local and specialized carriers and very large content providers. The carrier charges not for bandwidth usage, but for the resources for the time that they are committed to the customer. The customer is expected to manage admission control and other traffic management; the service provider is not responsible for congestion. OVPN customers certainly will have a view of the actual facilities in use, and may have awareness of backup resources.

New Facilities

The ability to manage multiple wavelengths on the same fiber and on sets of fibers is the basis of the emerging optical technologies. By sets of fibers I mean the ability to cross-connect different wavelengths without an intermediate stage of conversion to and from electronics.

> ### SOME TERMS CAUSE DOUBLE TAKES
>
> An optical network where the signal remains optical from end to end is called a *transparent optical network,* in contrast to an *opaque optical network,* which requires conversions between electrical and optical domains. Ignoring the reality that the wavelengths used for optical transmission are in the invisible infrared spectrum, the idea of transparency, is that you could look through one end of the fiber and see the invisible signal source at the other end. Actually, you wouldn't see it, but you'd be very likely to suffer eye damage.
>
> Has anyone tried recently to explain "you may be blinded by an invisible force" to a primitive shaman being educated that spirits and curses don't exist in the world of science?

WDM

Returning to the physical aspects, SONET/SDH is no longer the speed champion of optical networking, if speed is considered the aggregate of all bits on a fiber. Wavelength-division multiplexing (WDM) can carry multiple SONET/SDH channels over a single fiber. In WDM, individual channels are carried in different wavelengths (frequencies) of light. DWDM advocates tend to call these wavelengths *lambdas,* after the Greek character λ, traditionally used in physics to represent wavelength. Deployed products offer up to 32 OC-192 channels per fiber, and research and development demonstrations show 240 or more channels. OC-768 channels have also been demonstrated; the question here is more the nature of current requirements for multiple 40-Gbps channels rather than multiple 10-Gbps channels. Research continues, however, and 80-Gbps channels are in development.

The multiplexed channels need not all be the same speed or even format; there are many commercial WDM installations that support both OC-48 and OC-192 over the same fiber. WDM becomes dense when it carries a large number of wavelengths per fiber. In the near term 160 or more are expected to be commercially available, and even more dense prototypes are being tested. Another way to think of this is that it will be quite practical to have in excess of a terabit of aggregate bandwidth per fiber (for instance, 160 * 10 Gbps)—and when a fiber cable is installed, it usually contains lots of individual fibers.

The range and capacity of WDM are affected by a number of interacting factors. Avoiding limiting combinations of these factors is the goal of what optical specialists call *constraint-based routing,* such as optimizing for paths where individual flows do not have to change wavelength. This is called preserving the wavelength continuity property.

Another constraint is avoiding the need to go through optical-electronic-optical conversion. The major factors [IETF Optical Framework] are:

- The number of wavelengths on a single fiber.

- The serial bit rate per wavelength.

- The physical type of fiber.

- The amplification mechanism. Erbium-doped fiber amplifiers (EDFAs), for example, do not require conversion of the optical signal to electrical format before it can be regenerated or amplified.

- The number of nodes through which the signal passes before it reaches the egress node or before regeneration.

DWDM has different market drivers for local exchange versus long-haul carriers. In the local market there is a strong desire for "transparency" that can flow over a lambda dedicated to a user or to competitive carriers. The user would have total control over the traffic mix on the lambda, even though that traffic might only be a few hundred megabits on a gigabit-capable lambda. In the local market, DWDM means bandwidth becomes almost free. DWDM has to be compared, however, to the cost of running additional fibers.

Local exchanges were not the original goal for DWDM, which was introduced to reduce the crunch on long-haul optical networks. Bandwidth is not free in transcontinental or intercontinental networks. In long-haul DWDM, the most important cost factor is regeneration. Long-haul providers will be reluctant to commit expensive regenerator capability to underused lambdas carrying transparent traffic.

Resilient Packet Rings (RPRs)

RPRs are a metro-oriented technology intended to be more data-friendly and cost-effective than SONET/SDH. They are primarily being developed by the IEEE 802.17 Working Group, although there is a coordinating IP over RPR working group in the IETF's sub-IP area and an industry forum, the RPR Alliance, is being formed. One of the major goals of RPRs is to have the fast protection switching of SONET, but using the capacity of the alternate ring for traffic rather than merely for backup. Of course, if one ring fails, either some low-priority traffic will be dropped or the ring's performance will degrade.

The actual RPR technology is a layer 2 Medium Access Control protocol, which can operate over the same physical facilities as SONET, but also 10-Gigabit Ethernet and new physical media. With respect to SONET, it replaces the framing and the protection mechanisms. As opposed to Ethernet, it offers protection switching at SONET speeds. Metropolitan area networks (MANs), and RPRs in general, are intended to smooth some of the disconnects between enterprise-oriented LANs and long-haul SONET/DWDM [Vijeh 2000]. RPR technology is agnostic of the specific underlying transmission technology. The

---

RINGS ARE GOOD ROUTING BACKBONES

I have consistently found that rings with redundant equipment at their nodal
points make excellent OSPF backbones for enterprises. They can still scale by
going to ring-of-ring or star-of-ring topologies.

---

granularity of the specific RPR technology is optimized for carrying Ethernet
frames rather than bitstreams.

Rings, rather than meshes, are more efficient topologies given the physical
plant realities of metro areas. Rings are far more deterministic than meshes,
which gives a considerably greater level of comfort to providers who want to
offer service level agreements.

Free-Space Metro Optical

When *metro* truly means a small geographic area, open-air or free-space links
that do not use fiber at all can be quite useful in appropriate niches. Compared
with fiber-based systems, free-space links are quick to install, can service locations that might not be reachable with buried cable, and can be much cheaper
while providing the same service. They do require a line of sight between locations that will not be blocked by building construction, foliage, or protected
birds building nests in front of the lens. Various topologies are possible, ranging
from point-to-point to full mesh. One creative alternative is to use a point-to-
point link to another building that is served by a different local loop and central
office.

The typical eye-safe open-air optical system, such as the Nortel OPTera 2400, is
not intended for long distances. Link ranges of 200 to 500 m are typical, with an
OC-12 rate. In properly chosen campuses or business districts, these ranges may
be entirely appropriate when considering linking a group of buildings, and especially extending high-speed connectivity to an access point to a fiber network.

Broadband Wireless Radio

While the microwave towers of the past have not quite qualified as national historical monuments, fiber optics have replaced them in most applications. Many
towers have been demolished, while others have been converted to cellular
telephony use. There remains, however, a reasonable set of niche applications
for nonoptical free-space transmission media. They often act as the on-ramp to
the optical core superhighway, but also serve as feeders from individual wireless telephony cell sites, for television distribution among studios and transmitters, and so on. These systems are capable of longer range than typical
free-space optical systems. They may be cheaper to install along a right-of-way

when the owner of the right-of-way already has towers installed, such as in the case of utilities and railroads. Since the signal-carrying beam of a radio system is physically wider than an optical system, there is somewhat more flexibility in the definition of line of sight.

Evolution or New Species? Circuits without Resources, ATM without Cells, and GMPLS

I think of MPLS as an overdrive for packet switching. IP routing information is used to create label-switched paths (LSPs). LAN emulating label edge routers (LERs) use packet header information to assign packets to forward error controls (FECs) and LSPs, and LSPs along the path use per-packet shim information to make forwarding decisions. Recently, the MPLS architecture has been expanded to Generalized MPLS (GMPLS) [Kompella 2001a–c], in which the forwarding decisions of LERs or LER-like elements may not be based on per-packet information. The alternative information on which forwarding decisions is made includes time slots in TDM streams, wavelengths in WDM channels, or physical ports (for example, on cross-connects). Traditional MPLS, within the GMPLS context, is the packet switch–capable (PSC) subset.

The idea of a label persists, but simply is not bound to a packet. Labels now can be associated with time slots, lambdas, and ports, without radical changes to LSP setup protocols. These setup protocols do have to evolve, however.

There is a basic change in the topology of LSPs. A traditional LSP begins and ends on an LER—a layer 3 aware device. GMPLS simply requires the LSP to begin and end on the same type of device. To some extent, this has already been the case with ATM label-switching routers (LSRs), which do not recognize packets but make decisions based on cell headers.

In GMPLS there are four LSR types:

1. *Packet switch–capable (PSC)*. This is the regular MPLS kind of LSR that makes decisions on per-packet labels.

2. *Time-division mux–capable.* This type of GMPLS-controlled device is much more like a physical layer cross-connect (for instance, DACS) than a traditional router. Devices such as add-drop multiplexers could perform a kind of LSP merge.

3. *Lambda switch–capable.*

4. *Fiber switch–capable.* Interfaces that forward data based on the position of the data in the real-world physical space. An example of such an interface is an interface on an optical cross-connect that can operate at the level of a single fiber or multiple fibers. Such interfaces are referred to as fiber switch–capable (FSC).

THE FUNDAMENTAL RULE OF GMPLS

An LSP must start and end on the same type of LSR.

In GMPLS, payloads are not limited to packets, but can include Ethernet or SONET/SDH frames. Indeed, the payload need not even be a discrete unit such as a packet or frame, but can be bit streams—pure bandwidth. The number of labels on a non-PSC link is likely to be far lower than on a PSC link.

Issues of non-PSC LSRs

Dealing with non-packet paths has additional implications. Regular MPLS LSPs are unidirectional. When the tunnel does not involve per-packet decisions, there must be the ability to set up bidirectional LSPs. There is no reason why bidirectional LSPs might not be used in PSC environments when doing so would simplify setup and recovery. Another difference is that label values have no inherent meaning in PSCs. They are effectively random numbers. When the label in a lambda switch LSR corresponds to a particular position of a mirror, the choice of the label value can significantly influence the setup time of the LSR. GMPLS adds the capability for an upstream node to suggest label values that will minimize its setup time. GMPLS also concerns itself with the range of labels that can be selected by a downstream node. When labels are associated with wavelengths or ranges of wavelengths, controlling the label value helps in maintaining the wavelength continuity property, or at least in selecting wavelengths within the capability of the particular node.

GMPLS Requirements for LSP Identification

In setting up LSPs, GMPLS must identify the nature of the LSP in the LSP setup messages. This is not the nature of the underlying link. The LSP, for example, might use Ethernet framing but be carried over an OC-192 lambda. A given link might support more than one LSP type. For example, an optical link might encode some LSPs at the lambda level and others at a level requiring optical-electronic-optical conversions to obtain framing information. Table 8.6 gives details of LSP encoding types.

Special Considerations for Lambda Switch–Capable (LSC) LSRs

An LSC LSR switches individual wavelengths under GMPLS control. It is an optical cross-connect (OXC) that accepts optical interfaces and switches wave-

Table 8.6 LSP Encoding Types

VALUE	TYPE
1	Packet
2	Ethernet V2/DIX
3	ANSI PDH
4	ETSI PDH
5	SDH ITU-T G.707 1996
6	SONET ANSI T1.105-1995
7	Digital wrapper
8	Lambda (photonic)
9	Fiber
10	Ethernet 802.3
11	SDH ITU-T G.707 2000
12	SONET ANSI T1.105-2000

lengths among them. LSC LSRs may be used for distributing wavelengths or aggregating them onto higher-speed links.

Current (pre-GMPLS) OXCs can provide optical restoration using SONET protection switching. SONET restoration is faster than restoration using the OXC, but cannot handle as much capacity as the OXC. OXCs may serve as protocol converters between ATM and pure optical, as long as the individual speeds match.

Another related element is the *optical domain service interconnect* (OCSI), which allows on-demand creation of switched virtual circuits. It is analogous to an ATM UNI for DWDM. At the speeds of DWDM, of course, the user will, in many cases, be a carrier.

IP over Optical

IP over ATM over SONET has always been distasteful to large, bandwidth-hungry providers due to the ATM cell tax. ATM's ability to contain individual circuits is extremely useful in telephony, but is of very limited value in point-to-point connections between major carrier sites.

The first significant alternative to retaining the advantages of SONET speed while casting away the cell tax was to run the Point-to-Point Protocol (PPP) directly over SONET media. Doing so meant that the endpoints directly sent variable-length frames instead of cells, and the cell tax went away. Carrier attention now turned to SONET itself, and the implicit bandwidth waste of protection rings.

There are alternative means of sending IP directly over optical media and still having protection functions, but without the overhead of SONET. Many of these assume some form of optical multiplexing on the facilities, with fast, computer-controlled OXCs that can reprovision a failed circuit over different wavelengths or time slots. OXCs are the purely optical equivalent of DACSs. OXCs can be all-optical or involve optical-electrical-optical conversion. In either case, an OXC is a port-oriented, space-division switch.

Identifying and provisioning these alternate paths, and sending control messages to the OXCs, needs further work. A good deal of this work is taking place in the IP over Optical (IPO) Working Group of the IETF sub-IP area. This group's draft framework states:

> There is general consensus in the industry that the optical network control plane should utilize IP-based protocols for dynamic provisioning and restoration of light-paths within and across optical sub-networks. This is based on the practical view that signaling and routing mechanisms developed for IP traffic engineering applications could be re-used in optical networks. Nevertheless, the issues and requirements that are specific to optical networking must be understood to suitably adopt the IP-based protocols. This is especially the case for restoration. Also, there are different views on the model for interaction between the optical network and client networks, such as IP networks. Reasonable architectural alternatives in this regard must be supported, with an understanding of their pros and cons.
>
> Thus, there are two fundamental issues related to IP over optical networks. The first is the adaptation and reuse of IP control plane protocols within the optical network control plane, irrespective of the types of digital clients that utilize the optical network. The second is the transport of IP traffic through an optical network together with the control and coordination issues that arise therefrom.
>
> This draft defines a framework for IP over optical networks covering the requirements and mechanisms for establishing an IP-centric optical control plane, and the architectural aspects of IP transport over optical networks. In this regard, it is recognized that the specific capabilities required for IP over optical networks would depend on the services expected at the IP-optical interface as well as the optical sub-network interfaces. Depending on the specific operational requirements, a progression of capabilities is possible, reflecting increasingly sophisticated interactions at these interfaces. This draft therefore advocates the definition of "capability sets" that define the evolution of functionality at the interfaces as more sophisticated operational requirements arise.

Looking Ahead

Cynical industry old-timers speak of much of networking as using smoke and mirrors. Optical routing, however, really does deal with mirrors, as well as other components for manipulating wavelengths of light. Incoming lambdas are beamed at electronically tunable reflectors, which bounce them to an optical receiver for an appropriate output port. In other words, the switching function is optical but the control function is electronic. Other optical components can change lambdas between the input and input port, much as a DACS can move a DS0 channel from one DS1 time slot to another. Optical splitters can create multiple copies of incoming lambdas, optically implementing multicasting.

A strong trend is to use MPLS setup protocols, such as constraint-based LDP, for dynamically configuring the optical routing tables. MPLS, in turn, depends on IP routing protocols to discover the routes over which label switched paths can be established. The next four chapters deal with IP routing protocols in the carrier context.

Basic BGP and the Customer Side of Exterior Routing

If it scales, everything else will follow.
—Mike O'Dell

BGP converges worse than RIP.
—Craig Labovits

BGP is intended to manage external routing, not merely facilitate it.
—Annlee Hines

Interdomain routing is the problem of conveying routing information between building blocks, called *autonomous systems* (ASs), with individual routing policies. These building blocks most commonly are ISPs and enterprises in the public Internet. We established the context of policy information in Chapter 4 and discussed the administration of ASs in Chapter 5. In this chapter we go into the structure of the Border Gateway Protocol, version 4 (BGP-4 or simply BGP), the only protocol used for interdomain multicast routing.

Interdomain routing is used in an assortment of lowercase internets. As a generic term, a *lowercase internet* is a set of interconnected networks that cooperate in some ways but have some level of independence. It is perfectly reasonable to have lowercase enterprise internets large enough to need the capabilities of BGP and to be split into multiple ASs. Interdomain routing mechanisms may be used to communicate VPN reachability information among customers and providers. Also, there are perfectly legitimate interdomain networks that need to be isolated from the public Internet, such as classified military networks. Military networks are sufficiently large that it is impractical to manage them centrally (even if the army did trust the navy). Splitting a common military network into ASs allows a substantial degree of delegation of operations.

Financial networks for banking and for credit card processing, large companies such as worldwide shippers and automobile manufacturers, and others commonly link together business partners. I hesitate to use the term *extranet* here, because it often connotes the assumption that virtual private network technology is being used.

BGP Never Stands Still

The Exterior Gateway Protocol (EGP) was the first widely deployed Internet exterior routing protocol [RFC 0827]. EGP assumed all user ASs were connected to a single Internet core (Figure 9.1). The original 1987 model of BGP (see Figure 9.2) was a relatively small increment from the EGP that preceded it. BGP-1 did allow for the possibility of intermediate hierarchical levels between the "core" and edge ASs, and was designed to be extensible. It was not designed to support a large number of routers. It did accept the possibility of having multiple cores, as quickly became the case with separate routing for commercial versus government-subsidized academic and research traffic. Even in the early days of the Internet, there were special cases where academic institutions would interconnect directly to avoid the latency of a 56-Kbps core. These were the ancestors of today's exchange points (see Chapter 12).

With the massive growth of the Internet, more and more changes have been made to basic BGP. Where an AS might have had only one BGP-speaking router, it now may have hundreds of internal BGP routers and thousands of external BGP interfaces. Commercial requirements, such as traffic engineering and

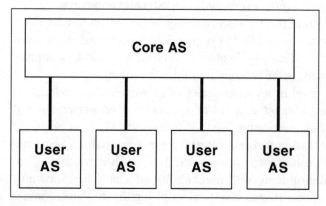

Figure 9.1 EGP model.

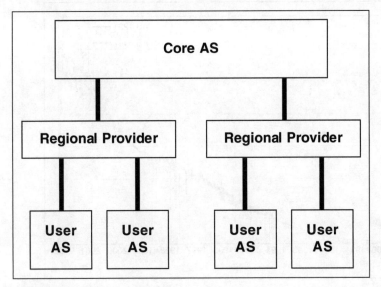

Figure 9.2   1987-vintage BGP.

VPNs, are being implemented with BGP due to its flexibility, but many of these requirements go against the grain of the fundamental architectural assumptions of BGP. There is a growing consensus that we can continue to tune BGP and related operational practices for 5 to 7 years, but eventually we will need to look at new paradigms for exterior routing [Doria 2002, Huston 2001a].

Scaling BGP is a constant battle of trade-offs between such things as stability and fast convergence, more fine-grained control and more resources required for routing, and so on. We do not truly know what governs BGP convergence at the level of the Internet as a whole, at the level of an individual AS, or at the level of individual routers. There is considerable research on these issues, especially the first [Labovits] and third [Berkowitz 2001a, d, e]. The current BGP specification [RFC 1771] is badly out of date with respect to current operational practice, and is under active revision [Rekhter 2001b]. With luck, a new BGP RFC may be available at, or soon after, the publication of this book. We are monitoring growth patterns in the number of prefixes (Figure 9.3) and AS numbers (Figure 9.4) in the Internet. The growth in prefixes seems due to multihoming and traffic engineering. The growth in AS numbers, if broken into end versus transit ASs, suggests that end user multihoming is driving the increase. It is uncertain whether this is the true cause, and experimentation is under way to obtain better information [Berkowitz 2001e]. Today's Internet topology is, to put it gently, chaotic (Figure 9.5). It is "flattening" with respect to hierarchy, which jeopardizes the scalability assumption of prefix aggregation.

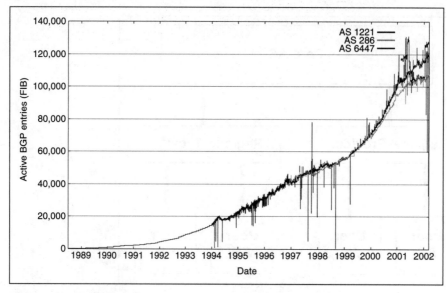

Figure 9.3 Prefix growth.

BGP, iBGP, and eBGP

There is only one BGP, although you will see the terms *internal BGP* (iBGP) and *external BGP* (eBGP) used extensively. The same protocol is used in both, but iBGP runs between BGP speakers in your AS, while eBGP connects your AS to an AS with a different AS number (see Figure 9.6).

As discussed in Chapter 4, routing policies control the information that BGP advertises and accepts. Think of them in these terms. Any routing update that includes a reachable route, is, in the words of noted routing engineer Avi Friedman, "a promise to carry traffic [to that route]." In Figure 9.7, AS1 promises AS2 that it will carry traffic to blocks A and C. AS1, however, only offers block A traffic to AS3 and AS4, and does not offer connectivity to block B to any outside AS.

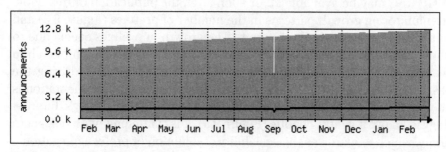

Figure 9.4 AS growth.

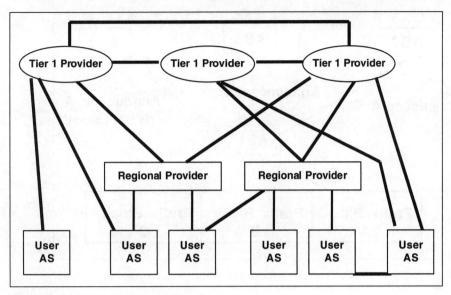

Figure 9.5   2001-vintage Internet.

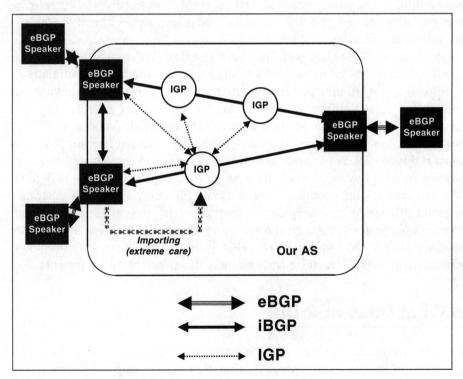

Figure 9.6   eBGP and iBGP.

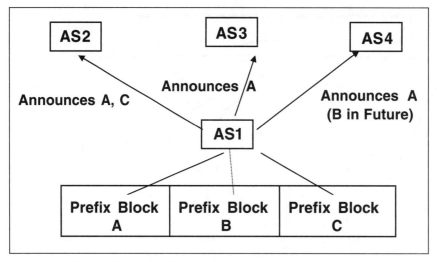

Figure 9.7   Don't ask, don't tell: BGP routing policies.

The simple way you indicate to other ASs that you do not want to transport traffic to some specific destination is not to tell them about it. You can be selective in telling or not telling different ASs different things. *Advertising policies* specify what promises you will make. *Acceptance policies* specify promises from others to which you will agree.

Don't confuse BGP policy with BGP protocol flow. Figure 9.8 shows several ways in which policy information flows over different media between pairs of AS. You can specify routing policy down to the router interface level, but it is not required. The three configurations in Figure 9.8, while using different physical connectivity, would use the same routing policy. In general, policy is defined between ASs, not IP addresses. A single physical connection to a single ISP, as shown in Figure 9.9, is certainly one you may create in the lab, but is rarely needed in actual practice. It would be quite unusual to justify running BGP to an ISP if you have a single connection to it. Some ISPs may expect the customer site to run BGP simply as a keepalive so they know that the site is up. In general, however, ISPs prefer to have customers avoid running BGP unless it is actually necessary. In fact, ISPs may control a BGP router at the customer's premises, because errors in BGP can have wide-ranging effects on the entire Internet.

So What Does BGP Do?

BGP is the means of passing routing information among ASs. Since the major application of BGP is interprovider routing, there is a strong need for interoperability among different vendors' implementations. While individual imple-

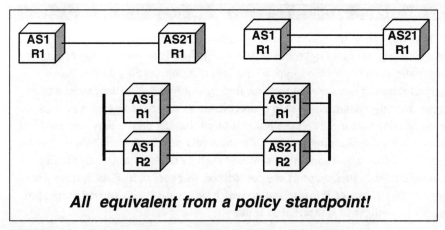

All equivalent from a policy standpoint!

Figure 9.8 Logical, not physical, connectivity defines BGP relationships.

mentations contain many BGP policy tools inside the router, the protocol itself does not generally have vendor-specific extensions. The protocol is fairly simple, but the information it carries is not. Even more complex is the policy evaluation configuration that lives inside BGP-speaking routers.

BGP is intended to be extensible for special applications, and there are multiprotocol extensions to BGP for carrying the routing updates of address families other than public IPv4. The principal other families carried today are IPv4 addresses for virtual private networks (VPNs) and interdomain multicast, and IP version 6 (IPv6) addresses. When the protocol is used to carry multiple address families, it is called MP-BGP [RFC 2283].

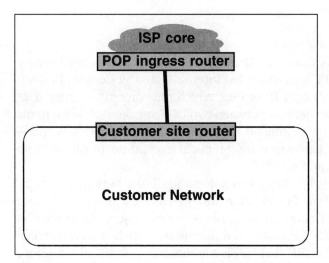

Figure 9.9 Single physical connection to single ISP.

READ MY LIPS

BGP isn't the entire answer to Internet routing. It's one piece. The biggest beginner misunderstanding about BGP is that its job is to pick the best route to a destination, from the standpoint of the organization sending traffic. While enterprise routing does concentrate on finding optimal paths, the goals of the Internet routing system are first to protect itself, and second to find a path to the destination that meets all the policies of all the ASs on the way. The next common misunderstanding is that "BGP transmits policies." While this may not be strictly untrue when some new features such as Outbound Route Filtering (discussed later in this chapter) are considered, in general, BGP itself does not carry policies. It carries information on which policy decisions can be made, but the policy intelligence is internal to routers.

While BGP transmits routes rather than information about links, it is not a classic distance vector protocol. BGP uses its own algorithm, called *path vector*, which prevents loops by applying rules to the AS path. The essential element of this algorithm is that when an AS that receives an update finds its own AS is in the path, a loop must exist and the update is not used. The BGP route selection process, detailed in Chapter 10, uses these sequences and other information to choose among multiple routes to the same destination. BGP route selection is one application for AS_PATH information; loop avoidance is another. BGP is a relatively simple protocol with respect to the actual handshakes. Most of its complexity comes from the way in which it selects the NLRI it will accept or advertise.

The BGP Stack

BGP runs on top of TCP, as shown in Figure 9.10. This contrasts to interior routing protocols such as OSPF and Extended Interior Gateway Routing Protocol (E)IGRP, which run directly over IP, or ISIS, which runs directly over the data-link layer. BGP sessions are defined between two BGP speakers. A session runs over TCP Port 179. There is an implicit assumption that both speakers will be on the same subnet, but there are many practical exceptions to this assumption. See "NEXT_HOP (Type Code 3):".

There's a Scottish proverb, "Why keep a dog and do the barking yourself?" BGP's principal authors, Tony Li and Yakov Rekhter, along with the IETF Inter-Domain Routing Working Group, chose to obtain as many services as possible from existing protocols. EIGRP, OSPF, and ISIS all have their own retransmission mechanisms. IGRP, EIGRP, and OSPF run directly over IP, with no inter-

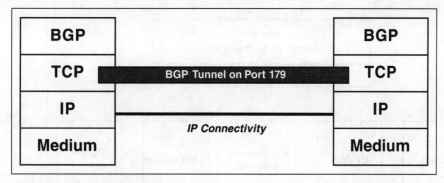

Figure 9.10   The BGP stack.

vening transport layer. RIP runs over UDP. Standard ISIS runs directly over the data link layer, although there are proposals to have it run over IP. TCP handles reliability, but even more importantly makes the details of IP routing between the endpoints invisible to the BGP session. This allows transparent multilinking but not multihoming.

When two BGP processes form a connection, they transfer the entire routing table, subject to policy restrictions. A keepalive subprotocol runs to ensure connectivity. After initialization, in which the BGP routing table is transferred, only incremental updates are sent, along with notification messages on an as-needed basis. On a T1 line, it can take between 2 and 8 min to transfer and synchronize a full routing table. Once the routers are initialized, typical times to propagate a change through the entire Internet run from 90 s to 3 min. Problems in the global routing system can significantly increase BGP convergence time. BGP's convergence time is one of the reasons real-world ASs use both IGPs and BGP. The convergence time of modern IGPs, such as OSPF, EIGRP, or ISIS, is far shorter than that of BGP.

Protocol Interactions

BGP has a relatively simple protocol state machine compared to OSPF or EIGRP. There is no explicit OPEN confirmation. OPEN is confirmed implicitly with a KEEPALIVE. Carried in a TCP data field are four BGP message types, but a fifth type, ROUTE REFRESH, is being added. Since use of the latter is negotiable, see the section "Negotiable Capabilities." The maximum size of any message is 4,096 bytes; the smallest is 19 (the header only). The common header is shown in Figure 9.11. A new feature, capabilities advertising, allows the peers to exchange information on optional BGP capabilities at the time the connection is established.

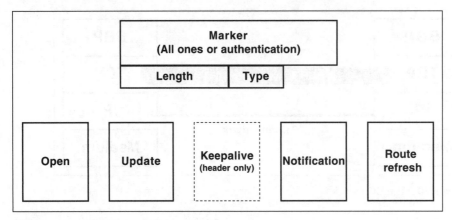

Figure 9.11 Overview of BGP message types.

BGP Session Management: OPEN, KEEPALIVE, and NOTIFICATION

OPEN messages establish initial BGP connections. The two BGP speakers need to agree on the hold time value and the values of any optional parameters or authentication if the connection is to be established. Hold time is the BGP time-out. The BGP speaker will terminate the connection if it fails to receive either an UPDATE or KEEPALIVE before the timer expires. Setting hold time to zero, however, tells the BGP speakers not to time out.

BGP does not use TCP to check whether peers are reachable, but uses its own KEEPALIVE mechanism. A BGP speaker sends a KEEPALIVE to each peer, typically at an interval of one-third of the configurable hold time and no more frequently than once per second. Setting a hold time of zero at connection establishment time can turn off KEEPALIVE. These messages consist only of a 19-byte header.

BGP signals fatal errors with the NOTIFICATION message. After a BGP speaker sends this message, it immediately closes its BGP connection.

WHEN WILL WE DISCUSS PACKET AND RELATED FORMATS?

In general, we won't, because this is a book about network design, not protocol design or operational troubleshooting. We will talk about the kind of information that is in protocol information, and occasionally about encoding when encoding is relevant to understanding the hierarchy of options for a particular parameter. I will also mention sizes, because they may have an effect on bandwidth. In general, however, if you need the exact layouts, it is best to go to the appropriate RFCs so you have complete information.

Authentication

BGP has a rather limited ability to authenticate messages, and better alternatives are being studied as means of improving the security of the routing system against denial-of-service attack. The actual authentication field in a BGP packet is based on a Message Authentication Digest 5 (MD5) digest produced from the TCP pseudoheader (including selected IP header fields), the TCP header with options excluded, the TCP segment (containing the BGP message), and a key known to the two parties to the session. While MD5 authentication has been deployed operationally, it is not considered a particularly strong cryptographic hash algorithm. It is entirely possible that a stronger algorithm may be adopted, or that IPSec might be used for BGP security.

Capabilities Advertisement

As the complexity of the Internet has increased, so have the capabilities of BGP. Older routers do not necessarily support all these capabilities. The installed base of older routers, however, cannot be made obsolete, so any new capability must be implemented with backward compatibility. To make these capabilities available with minimum impact, a relatively small change has been made to the BGP OPEN message, adding a parameter called *capabilities*. The parameter, when present, lists the capabilities supported by the sender of the OPEN. If the receiver of the OPEN does not support capabilities advertisement, it will not recognize the optional capabilities parameters and will refuse the connection with a NOTIFICATION message bearing the unsupported parameter subcode. It is now the choice of the original sender whether to send a new OPEN with no capability parameter. If the receiver does support capabilities advertisement, but not the specific capabilities being proposed, it will again refuse the connection with a NOTIFICATION message with the unsupported optional parameter code. Again, it is the decision of the originator whether to retry the session setup without that parameter.

UPDATE Message

Actual topology information, both at initialization and subsequent to it, is carried in UPDATE messages. A message may contain either new routes, routes to be withdrawn, or both. The rule for including multiple new routes in the same UPDATE is they have to have the same attributes (for example, next hop and AS PATH). When an update is intended to announce a more or less specific route than one already in the table, the same message should carry both the withdrawal of the previous route and the announcement of the new route.

Multiple routes can be withdrawn in the same UPDATE message. Unfeasible routes are analogous to poisoned reverse routing advertisements. If the value of unfeasible routes length is zero, no routes are being withdrawn from service. If the length field is nonzero, the withdrawn route field is a list of address prefixes in length/prefix form. Note that these are not necessarily 32-bit prefix fields. As opposed to the length of the overall withdrawn routes field, prefix lengths apply to specific routes. A length of zero here implies the default route. The prefix field proper contains an octet-aligned prefix. Trailing fill bits are ignored.

Negotiable Capabilities

While the previous section introduced the mechanism of capabilities negotiation, it did not deal with the capabilities that can be negotiated. Since capability negotiation has been introduced, more and more features use it. Indeed, the flexibility given by capabilities negotiated at session establishment time has led to a proposal for dynamic capability negotiation. Dynamic capability negotiation allows a capability to be negotiated after the session has been established.

As with all features, increasing flexibility increases the complexity of configuration and troubleshooting. There's a classic sign in all-you-can-eat buffets that should be read by anyone considering a new feature: "Take what you want, but eat what you take." That sign really is but a starting point. Before taking a feature from the BGP buffet, be clear what problem it solves, and that you have or expect to have that problem. If the feature proves unreliable—the newer ones are being implemented quickly—or proves not to solve the problem, don't be afraid to roll it out of your configurations.

Multiprotocol Extensions

One of the first features to use capability negotiation was the multiprotocol extensions to BGP. This feature allows BGP to carry routing information for protocols other than IPv4. Its use with a specific peer must be negotiated, and that negotiation includes which address families the BGP speaker is willing to support.

The underlying assumption of the multiprotocol (MP) extensions to BGP (BGP-MP) is that relatively little of the basic information it carries is IPv4-specific. The main IPv4-specific items are:

- NEXT_HOP
- AGGREGATOR
- NLRI

Some newer capabilities, such as extended communities [RFC 2558], also have optional IPv4 content.

To support additional protocol families, we minimally need a way to associate the appropriate address family with the NLRI and NEXT_HOP. The basic way of doing this is to signal during capability advertisement that multiprotocol extensions are supported. There is a capability code that says MP extensions are supported, and, within that parameter, a capability value that identifies the particular address family supported. The parameter may support multiple address families.

Route Refresh

The Adj-RIB-In conceptually contains all BGP routes received on an interface. When the speaker at the other end is sending all or a substantial part of the global routing table, per-interface memory requirements can become quite large. A fairly straightforward workaround was to keep the Adj-RIB-In conceptual. As routes were received, acceptance policy rules were applied to them, and only those that survived the input policy were sent to the Loc-RIB. This seems reasonable, until you change an acceptance policy rule. At that point, how do you know that one of the rejected routes would not pass the new policy and belong in the RIB?

The first operational solution was to bounce the BGP session up and down, resulting in the neighbor resending its entire Adj-RIB-Out. Especially on slower links, this could take significant bandwidth and introduce a noticeable delay. If BGP rules were followed, all routes whose next hop was to the neighboring router would now be invalid, and would have to be readvertised to all other neighbors, causing a cascading bandwidth and processing requirement on other routers, potentially across the entire Internet.

The next implementer approach was to have the router store the entire Adj-RIB-In, rather than only those routes in it that passed filtering criteria and went to the Loc-RIB. If the acceptance policy then changed, the information was already there to refilter. While this improvement avoided the need to do a full reconvergence, it was both memory- and processor-intensive.

The next step was to negotiate a soft refresh [Chen 2000] between pairs of BGP speakers. When both routers advertise the route refresh capability, a speaker whose policies change can send a ROUTE REFRESH message to the neighbor (see Figure 9.12). On receipt of that message, the neighbor will readvertise the appropriate Adj-RIB-Out, which the local speaker will refilter and send the surviving routes to its Loc-RIB.

Even though soft refresh improved the situation, there was still the real-world problem that the sender of the Adj-RIB-Out might very well send routes that would be filtered by the receiver, wasting bandwidth and receiver processing time. Outbound Route Filtering was a new way to deal with this problem.

Outbound Route Filtering

I have long maintained that BGP doesn't transmit policies, but sends the information on which policy decisions are made based on information configured into the router by element management. Outbound Route Filtering (ORF) has

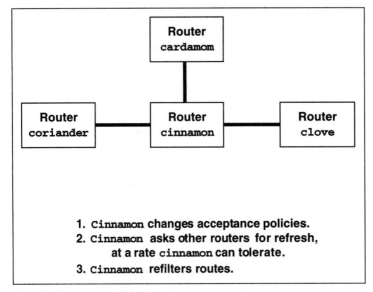

Figure 9.12 Route refresh.

forced me to modify that position, giving a final (if qualified) victory to a long-running debate between myself and Sue Hares, cochair of the IDR Working Group that develops BGP. At the next IETF we attend, I owe Sue a drink.

The idea of ORF is that it can be of mutual benefit to a pair of routers to exchange their acceptance policies, so a router about to send its Adj-RIB-Out can prefilter it, thus requiring only the bandwidth for the updates the receiver will really use (see Figure 9.13).

Several independent proposals have been made for the policies that can be exchanged, and there is an attempt in the Inter-Domain Routing (IDR) committee to come up with a unified proposal that contains the three filtering criteria suggested:

1. Prefix expression for NLRI.

2. AS path expression.

3. Community.

These are a subset of the policy options available on commercial routers, but cover the great majority of cases. Like soft refresh, ORF is an optional capability that must be advertised and agreed to between peer BGP speakers.

Graceful Restart

In the real world, things break. Operational experience has shown that the control plane of a router may crash, breaking all routing protocol sessions and

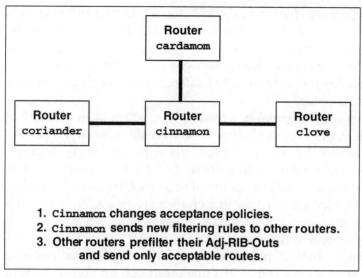

1. `Cinnamon` changes acceptance policies.
2. `Cinnamon` sends new filtering rules to other routers.
3. Other routers prefilter their Adj-RIB-Outs
   and send only acceptable routes.

Figure 9.13 Outbound route filtering.

stopping updates to the RIB, but the FIB and forwarding plane may remain operational. The BGP graceful restart capability takes an optimistic view of the FIB contents: that it is more useful to continue forwarding while the routing system recovers, accepting the possibility that some FIB entries may have become obsolete, than to stop forwarding altogether until routing works properly again.

Graceful restart capabilities also are being developed for ISIS and OSPF, and it is arguable that BGP graceful restart makes little sense if the BGP speaker does not also implement IGP graceful restart. When the IGP does support graceful restart, it is good practice for BGP to wait until the IGP converges to begin route selection.

When the routing system on a highly connected router in the Internet's default-free zone (DFZ) fails, strict interpretation of current BGP practice can impact the Internet as a whole. Remember that when a BGP speaker loses connectivity to a route, it must withdraw the route and propagate the withdrawal to all peer speakers to whom it previously advertised the route. It may advertise a new route with a different next hop, but it must withdraw the failed route. The graceful restart capability provides a way to avoid a flood of withdrawals and announcements, on the assumption that the routing control subsystem can be restarted and the router can keep forwarding while its BGP is reinitializing. Specifically, advertising this capability tells peer speakers that the router advertising the capability can retain its FIB during a BGP restart. It is not intended for use when the speaker explicitly terminates the session with a NOTIFICATION message.

Optimism can be a great character trait in humans, but network engineers have to pay homage to Murphy's Law. For the graceful restart capability to be plausibly fault-tolerant, it must have safeguards against its optimism being unjustified. More deployment experience is needed to determine the optimal timer values, or possibly the need for other safeguards, to prevent excessive blackholing or route flapping.

In the capabilities advertisement is a restart time, which is an estimate in seconds of the time it will take the BGP session to reinitialize after a restart. If the timer expires and the router that advertised the capability does not return, its peers can declare it down faster than they would if they had to wait for the BGP session to time out. One feature of this capability, which could be useful beyond the original intent of the graceful restart capability, is the end-of-RIB marker. The presence of this marker in an update indicates that all routes have been sent, and, if the interface has been batching any routes, full convergence can begin. Indeed, it has been recommended that as long as a BGP speaker can generate an end-of-RIB marker, it can be useful for it to advertise the graceful restart capability even if it cannot retain its FIB during a BGP restart. Once the receiving speaker receives the end-of-RIB marker from all peers that have indicated they are restarting, it can begin to run route selection on the received routes. Assume the situation in Figure 9.14, where router cinnamon is restarting. Until it receives an end-of-RIB marker from all its peers for a given address family, it has not built its Loc-RIB and thus has no routes to advertise.

After route selection, the FIB is updated and any previously marked stale data is removed. The reason stale data must be removed at this time is to avoid the effects of multiple restarts. One of the complexities of graceful restart is properly handling multiple restarts. The solution involves the restarting speaker marking its existing routes as stale. Stale routes are not treated differently from other routes in the forwarding process. A router with this capability optionally may include a stale route retention timer and flush these routes if the timer expires. It must support a timer that can be configured as to how long to

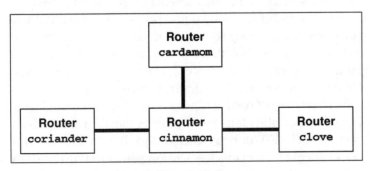

Figure 9.14   Advertising during graceful restart.

defer the start of route selection. Since a BGP speaker may only advertise routes in its active FIB, only at this point can cinnamon begin advertising.

Thirty-two-bit AS Numbers

While we are not at a crisis level, there is an increasing trend of allocating AS numbers to end users who multihome, which is increasing the rate at which the AS number space is being exhausted. Well before there is a crisis in AS numbers, the IETF has defined mechanisms for using upwardly compatible 32-bit AS numbers [Vohra 2001]. In the IETF work, a BGP speaker that supports the 32-bit (4-octet) AS numbers is called a NEW BGP speaker, while one that does not is called an OLD BGP speaker. A NEW BGP speaker must tell its neighbors that it supports 32-bit AS numbers. It does so during the capability negotiation part of session establishment, so, rather obviously, a NEW BGP speaker must support optional capability negotiation. A BGP speaker sends its AS number in several protocol messages:

- OPEN: the my autonomous system field
- UPDATE attributes
- AS_PATH
- AGGREGATOR
- COMMUNITY

Each one of these messages needs a way to deal with 32-bit communities. For OPEN, this is fairly easy, as the 32-bit community capability advertisement contains a 4-octet my autonomous system number. It is necessary to introduce a new attribute, NEW_AS_PATH, to carry path information with 32-bit AS numbers. This attribute is generated only by NEW BGP speakers.

Attributes

The intent of this book is to teach about how to use protocols, rather than design them. Nevertheless, there are aspects of BGP that need to be well understood before you can use it effectively. Some of these aspects are at a high level, such as having a deep appreciation of one of the differences between IGPs and BGP—the amount of additional information associated with routes. IGPs have a prefix, a metric, and perhaps some additional information such as a tag or an OSPF metric type. BGP routing updates, however, have the potential of carrying many more attributes.

A simple routing protocol like RIP carries a few attributes, such as metric and next hop. More complex routing protocols, such as OSPF, use additional information, such as intraarea/interarea/external status. BGP, however, has the ability to attach many attributes to a given route. The minimum set is the source of the update (that is, ORIGIN), the next hop to reach the route, and the AS path.

Categories of Attributes

While there are common and required attributes, there can be many different sets of attributes. Each attribute has a type code and several bits that describe its usage. You need to know about the usage bits to understand how an update flows among AS.

One attribute bit does not pertain to the propagation of attributes: the extended bit. By setting the extended length bit, you can create attributes longer than 255 bytes. Table 9.1 shows bits in the attribute field.

The presence of the optional flag means that all well-known attributes must be passed along to downstream peers after appropriate updating. The high-order bit (bit 0) of the attribute flags octet is the optional bit. It defines whether the attribute is optional (if set to 1) or well-known (if set to 0).

The standard does not require all implementations to support all options. The transitive flag specifies how implementations handle options they do not recognize. If the transitive flag is set on an incoming option, then the option must be passed downstream if not recognized. If the flag is not set on an option, then the option is ignored and not passed downstream. All well-known attributes are transitive.

Some optional attributes can be set by AS along the path, as distinct from the originator. If an intermediate AS adds or changes an attribute, it must set the *partial bit* (bit 2 of the attribute flags field). There are several meaningful combinations of the bits that you should recognize. Each attribute will fall into one of the categories in Table 9.2.

The Attributes Themselves

Some attributes appear in every BGP update. Others variously appear only in iBGP or eBGP. We usually say that iBGP and eBGP are the same protocol with differences only in the peering points, but the differences in attributes are one of the few areas where iBGP and eBGP can be thought of as different protocols.

Table 9.1 Bits in the Attribute Field

0	Optional
1	Transitive
2	Partial
3	Extended length

Table 9.2 Attribute Categories

CATEGORY	OPTIONAL	TRANSITIVE	
Well-known mandatory	0	1	Must be present; must be supported; must be preserved
Well-known discretionary	1	1	May or may not be present; must be supported; must be preserved if present
Optional transitive	1	1	May or may not be present; may not be understood, but must be preserved
Optional nontransitive	1	0	May or may not be present; need not be preserved if not supported

Again, iBGP peers between speakers in the same AS, while eBGP peers between speakers in different AS.

This section will not go into details of the use of attributes in route selection; for that, See Chapter 10. It does, however, identify the attributes themselves. This listing is intended to establish a vocabulary rather than go into great detail of how the attributes are used.

ORIGIN (Type Code 1)

ORIGIN, a mandatory attribute, tells the receiver the type of the original source of the NLRI information. This information will be used as a midlevel tiebreaker in the BGP route selection algorithm. The BGP standard defines the values and meanings of this well-known mandatory attribute as shown in Table 9.3.

AS_PATH (Type Code 2)

A well-known mandatory attribute, AS_PATH is composed of a variable-length series of AS path segments (Figure 9.15). Each path segment is a triple composed of a type, length, and value. The path segment type (see Table 9.4) is a 1-octet-long field with the following values defined either in the base BGP standard or in the BGP confederations document [RFC 1965]. See Chapter 10 for a discussion of confederations in POP design. The path segment length is a

Table 9.3 BGP Route Origin Codes

VALUE	MEANING
0	IGP—the originating AS learned about this NLRI from its own IGP.
1	EGP—the AS transmitting this NLRI first learned about it from eBGP.
2	INCOMPLETE—NLRI was learned by some other means, such as static routes redistributed into BGP.

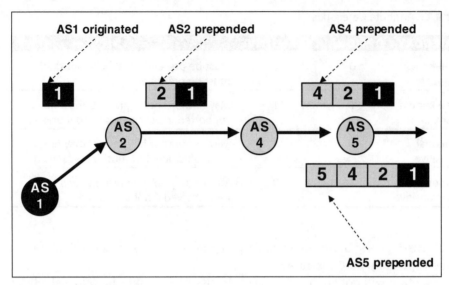

Figure 9.15 AS path.

1-octet-long field containing the number of ASs in the path segment value field. The path segment value field contains one or more AS numbers, each encoded as a 2-byte field.

AS_PATHs on routes received from other BGP speakers are only modified by eBGP speakers that advertise the route outside the local AS. Such eBGP speakers prepend their own AS numbers as the last element of the path vector (the leftmost position). If the first element of the received path is of the AS_SET type, the prepended sequence should be of the AS_SEQUENCE type. When a BGP speaker originates a route, it should include its own ASN in UPDATEs sent to other AS, but should include an empty AS_PATH attribute when advertising

Table 9.4 AS Path Types

VALUE	MEANING
0	Not defined.
1	AS_SET—unordered set of ASs that a route in the UPDATE message has traversed.
2	AS_SEQUENCE—ordered set of ASs that a route in the UPDATE message has traversed.
3	AS_CONFED_SET—unordered set of ASs in the local confederation that the UPDATE message has traversed.
4	AS_CONFED_SEQUENCE—ordered set of ASs in the local confederation that the UPDATE message has traversed.

to iBGP speakers in its own AS. The reason for this is the iBGP loop avoidance rule that tells it to ignore any route learned from an iBGP peer.

NEW_AS_PATH has the ability to carry 32-bit AS numbers through OLD BGP speakers. There is a restriction that AS_CONFED_SEQUENCE and AS_CONFED_SET [RFC 3065] cannot be parts of a NEW_AS_PATH attribute. Backward compatibility for NEW_AS_PATH is ensured by mapping current 16-bit AS numbers into 32-bit AS numbers with the high-order 16 bits set to zero.

NEXT_HOP (Type Code 3)

NEXT_HOP is well-known mandatory attribute defining the IP address of the next-hop router to be used for the next hop for all destinations listed in the NLRI field of the UPDATE message. This attribute is used both in iBGP and eBGP. Any iBGP speaker can advertise any internal router as the next hop, provided the IP address of the iBGP border router is on the same subnet as the local and remote BGP speakers. In other words, in the iBGP mesh, one router can act as "announcement proxy" for another on the same subnet. According to the standard, a BGP speaker can also advertise any external border router as the next hop, providing:

- The IP address of the proposed next-hop router was learned from one of the advertising router's peers.

- The interface for this router is on the same subnet as both the local and remote BGP speakers, unless the eBGP_MULTIHOP configuration is used.

There are two common special cases in configuring the next hop, which are present in major implementations but not required by standards. When two eBGP speakers need to peer across more than one subnet, use eBGP Multihop. A common example of such usage is shown in Figure 9.16, where the physical connectivity between two eBGP speakers runs over multiple load-shared links.

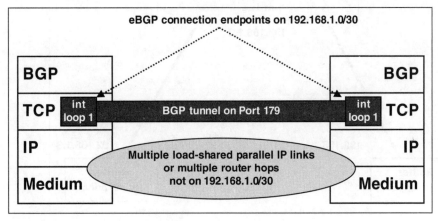

Figure 9.16 Using eBGP multihop.

You do not need to configure multihop if both BGP speakers are in the same AS, speaking iBGP.

The other special next hop case has various applications, the most frequent of which is routers on a single point-to-multipoint nonbroadcast multiaccess (NBMA) medium such as Frame Relay or ATM. Especially in provider environments, using a separate /30 subnet on point-to-point subinterfaces may not scale, because existing router operating systems can support only a finite number of interfaces. In Figure 9.17, router **bay** advertises a route that it learned from router **anise**. That route contains the next hop of **anise**. **Coriander**, however, does not have a virtual circuit giving it connectivity to **anise**. **Coriander** cannot send directly to **anise**. By using NEXT_HOP_SELF, you force **bay** to put its own address, rather than that of **anise**, into the update. Since **coriander** does have a virtual circuit to **bay**, everything will then work.

The underlying reason for the formal standard's restriction on NEXT_HOP is avoiding loops. A BGP speaker must not:

- Advertise the address of a peer as the NEXT_HOP of a route the current speaker is originating to that peer

- Install a route that has itself as the next hop, unless the NEXT_HOP_SELF configuration option is used

MULTI_EXIT_DISC (Type Code 4)

Originally called the INTER_AS_METRIC in BGP-3, this is used only in eBGP. Officially it is used to compare otherwise identical eBGP routes to the same directly connected AS. The lower the MED value, the more preferred the route

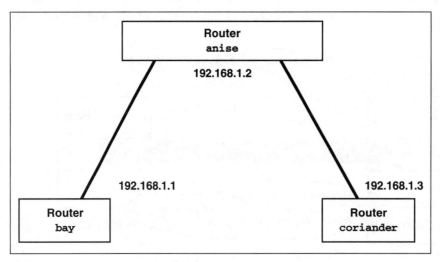

Figure 9.17 Using NEXT_HOP_SELF.

will be. Industry practice has introduced additional applications for the MED, where, under certain circumstances, it can be used to compare routes from different but still directly connected ASs.

LOCAL_PREF (Type Code 5)

Local preference is a route preference attribute with a scope of a single AS, so it is used only in iBGP. It is well known and discretionary. The higher the local preference value, the more preferred the route. Remember that the rule for preference is opposite between MED and LOCAL_PREF. Routes with high LOCAL_PREFs but low MEDs are preferred.

ATOMIC_AGGREGATE (Type Code 6) and
AGGREGATOR (Type Code 7)

Both these attributes deal with address aggregation. The first indicates that an AS, for policy reasons of its own, is passing a less specific—rather than a more specific—route. ATOMIC_AGGREGATE is well-known, discretionary, and of length 0. AGGREGATOR is an optional transitive attribute 6 bytes in length, which contains the last AS number that formed the aggregate route (encoded as two octets), followed by the IP address of the BGP speaker that formed the aggregate route encoded as four octets). NEW BGP speakers generate the AGGREGATOR attributes with the AS information encoded as 32 bits.

COMMUNITIES (Type Code 8) and EXTENDED
COMMUNITIES (Type Code 16)

A given route can belong to one or more *communities*, which are routes that share some common property. For example, an academic network that handles both academic and commercial traffic under an acceptable use policy might set a community attribute on the university updates; this community attribute value would indicate that the route meets the acceptable use policy. The same route can be tagged with more than one community. A given route, for example, might belong to both the U.S. Energy Department ESnet and the European high-energy research network Conseil Européen pour la Recherche Nucleáire (CERN). An excellent term occasionally used for communities is that they *color* routes. Think of policies where you could simply say, "Advertise all red routes to AS1, advertise no blue routes to AS-SET 3, and accept only green routes from router 1.2.3.4 of AS2."

ROUTE SETS VERSUS COMMUNITIES

Both RPSL route sets and BGP community attributes identify groups of routes. The route set name, however, is an abstraction, while the community identifier actually travels with the route.

Community attributes are optional, transitive, and variable in length. Current communities are 32 bits long, structured as two 16-bit fields. By convention, the first 16 bits are either zero, denoting a well-known community known to the Internet, or the AS number that "owns" the community value. The second 16 bits are meaningful either as defined by the owning AS, or, in the case of well-known communities, by the IETF. A new attribute, extended community, was introduced as a part of virtual private network definition but is proving to have multiple applications. First, the 16-bit AS-specific field was becoming a scarce resource for large ISPs. Second, it is structured so that a community can be owned by other than an AS, which can be quite important in situations where an enterprise is part of a provider's public AS, but still needs enterprise-unique community functions.

The new extended communities are still optional and transitive. Each is encoded as an 8-byte string, but there are different formats for this encoding. The first 2 bytes always are a type field. Types 0x0000 through 0x7FFF are controlled by IANA, while types 0x8000 through 0xFFFF are vendor-specific. When the high-order octet of the type field is 0x00, the extended community is defined with respect to a 16-bit AS. The remaining 6 bytes are split into a 2-byte administrator field, which is a 16-bit AS number, and a 4-byte assigned number field under the control of the administrator. If, however, the high-order octet is 0x01, the extended community is defined with respect to an IP address. The next 4 bytes of the value field contain an IPv4 address, and the last two contain a 16-bit assigned number under the control of the organization that controls the IP address. A high-order type field octet of 0x02 means that the extended community is defined with respect to a 32-bit AS number. The first 4 bytes of the value field are the AS number, while the last 2 bytes are an assigned number under the control of that AS.

ORIGINATOR_ID (Type Code 9) and CLUSTER_LIST (Type Code 10)

These attributes support the route reflector feature used for scaling iBGP meshes, a technique detailed in Chapter 10. Both attributes are optional and nontransitive. ORIGINATOR_ID is 4 bytes long, and CLUSTER_LIST is variable length. Briefly, route reflectors are a technique for setting up clusters of iBGP peers in a client-server manner that avoids the needs for full mesh inside the cluster. Individual iBGP routers are defined either as route reflectors, which participate in the full mesh, or as route reflector clients. Route reflector clients only have iBGP peering with the route reflector(s) in their cluster. There can be more than one route reflector per cluster. The ORIGINATOR_ID identifies the source of routes, and the CLUSTER_LIST is a mini-AS_PATH used to detect updates that are looping inside the cluster.

Multiprotocol Reachable NLRI (Type Code 14) and Multiprotocol Unreachable NLRI (Type Code 15)

These two attributes used in the multiprotocol extensions to BGP are both optional and nontransitive. The multiprotocol reachable NLRI attribute identifies a newly reachable route in an address family other than global IPv4, while multiprotocol unreachable NLRI identifies a route that has been withdrawn.

Multiprotocol extensions to BGP are now used for IPv6 and for RFC 2547 VPNs. These attributes are still carried in BGP UPDATE messages, of which the ORIGIN and AS_PATH pertain to the native IPv4 BGP communications that carry the message. When multiprotocol extensions are in use, it makes sense that the advertisement of destinations is useful only when the next hop for these destinations is reachable. Since not all BGP speakers support multiprotocol extensions, it makes for a cleaner environment if the advertisements and withdrawals of other than IPv4 are grouped in their own updates. A router that does not support MP can simply drop the entire update. From the standpoint of compatibility, it also makes sense to group the unreachable routes—the withdrawal. These two new attributes were introduced to ease introduction of multiprotocol extensions.

A First Look at iBGP

When you introduce more than one eBGP-speaking router, you introduce the need to coordinate their activities. This is done with iBGP connectivity. The basic setup of iBGP is simple. You need to declare neighbors inside your own AS (Figure 9.18). In small to medium ASs, all BGP speakers should be fully

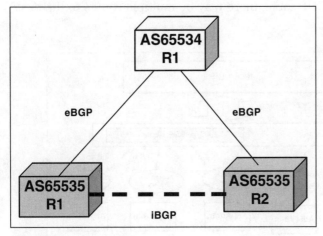

Figure 9.18   Basic iBGP.

meshed with iBGP. Full meshing does not necessarily mean there is a physical link between them, but there must be a full mesh of BGP sessions among the BGP speakers. iBGP full meshing, however, does not scale to large size, and only the smallest ISPs can run it.

As the iBGP topology becomes more complex, you are likely to need to reduce the number of sessions on any one router. There are two basic techniques for doing so, both of which introduce hierarchy into iBGP. These techniques, discussed in Chapter 10, are route reflection and confederations.

RIBs and Routes

The interaction of BGP with general IGP routing is sufficiently complex that it is easiest to look first at the process of installing routes when there is only one BGP route to each destination. Mechanisms for selecting among multiple BGP routes are discussed in Chapter 10.

BGP does not replace IGPs. BGP is primarily concerned with the reachability of destinations outside the AS, while IGPs deal with the reachability of internal destinations. iBGP relies on IGPs to find the various BGP speakers in an AS. An especially important aspect is the use of IGPs to discover the topology over which label-switched paths can be established in an intraprovider core (see Chapter 8).

Once BGP is running, there will exist at least two routing tables in the router. The BGP table shows the set of routes received via BGP that are accepted by the acceptance policy and whose next hops are reachable through the main routing table. Some of the routes in the BGP table may indeed be the best to a particular destination, and may be installed as well in the main routing table. (See Figure 9.19.) In the BGP table, there may be multiple routes to the desti-

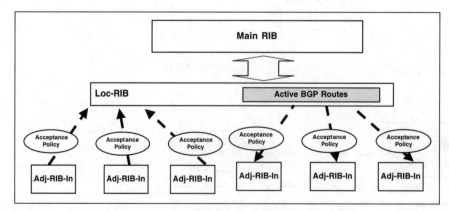

Figure 9.19   Relationships among BGP tables and main RIB.

nation. Only the best of these routes, however, is passed to the routing table installation process in standard BGP.

Acceptance Policies and BGP

Acceptance policies apply to routes that the local router receives from another router. The most common way to implement acceptance policies is to test each incoming BGP update against a pattern-matching expression, and, if the update matches the expression, take one or more actions. Such actions obviously include dropping the update, but they may also include setting parameters on the update message that will subsequently be used in route selection or to convey information to downstream BGP speakers. Another potential input action is to create an accounting category related to some information on the update.

Yet another category of acceptance policy does not deal directly with isolated updates, but rather with updates in some context. One context is the total number of routes received from a particular neighbor. Performing such a test is a reality check. You would not, for example, typically expect to receive more than 10 or so routes from an enterprise BGP router. If you receive thousands, something is likely to be wrong. Another contextual policy is to penalize routes that are rapidly flapping up and down.

Conceptually, updates arrive at a BGP router and are placed in a per-neighbor data structure called the Adj-RIB-In (see Figure 9.20). Those updates are then tested against acceptance policies, and, if they pass those policy tests, go into a per-router structure called the Loc-RIB. Policy tests for updates may involve details not seen in the main table. As they go into the Loc-RIB, updates are tested against other routes already present in the Loc-RIB, and a best route to each destination is selected. This testing is called the *BGP route selection algorithm* and is distinct from the process the router will use to install routes in its main RIB.

Routes in the Loc-RIB are submitted to a process that decides which routes should be installed in the router's main routing information base (RIB). The RIB

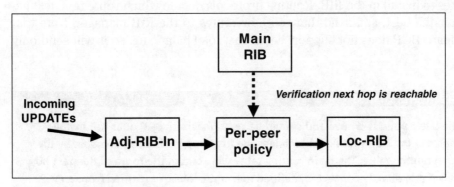

Figure 9.20 Acceptance policy.

contains the best routes selected from all sources, and uses yet another selection algorithm to select routes from those offered by interior routing protocols, hardware interface status associated with directly connected routes, static routes, and exterior routing protocols.

A RIB is optimized for updating by routing protocols. It complements the forwarding information base (FIB), which is optimized for high-speed destination lookup. Depending on the router implementation, some FIBs are simply lookup-optimized tables in main memory, and others are in hardware-assisted lookup chips. High-performance routers often have multiple FIBs, which are distributed onto line cards.

BGP Route Selection Algorithms: IETF and Variants

BGP uses a number of steps in selecting routes (see Table 9.5). Most of these steps involve evaluating attributes associated with each route. At this point, let's focus on the algorithm itself. There are 10 steps in the original algorithm, but there are also a few additional steps widely used in the industry but not part of RFC 1771.

General Route Installation

It is worth reviewing several parts of the basic RFC 1812 algorithm for route installation, focusing on the parts that BGP will encounter (see Figure 9.21). There are two principal interactions of BGP with the main routing table. The more obvious one, of course, is that routes learned by BGP may be added to the main routing table. The less obvious one is that BGP will not advertise a route to other ASs unless that route is reachable based on the main routing table. In other words, the next hop address for the BGP route must be reachable in the main routing table.

It is the RIB manager, not any specific routing protocol, that decides which routes to install in the RIB. Routing protocols decide which route to a destination is the best, and send that route or routes to the RIB manager. Note that standard BGP does not support equal-cost load balancing, so it will send only

---

DON'T MISS THIS!

The latter point is critical and should be reemphasized. BGP does not install routes in the BGP routing table unless the next hop is already reachable by the main routing table. The main routing table will contain the route to the next hop only if it is directly connected, defined in a static route, or learned from an IGP.

Table 9.5 BGP Route Selection

IETF-SPECIFIED RULE	COMMON INDUSTRY EXTENSION
Discard any route whose next hop is unreachable.	
	If the next hop is accessible, prefer the route with the highest weight. Weight is a Cisco-specific parameter that is not transmitted in BGP updates, but is a manually configured parameter local to the current router.
Prefer the route with the highest local preference attribute.	
Prefer routes originated on the current router.	
	A widely used criterion that is not part of the IETF specifications is to prefer the route with the shortest AS_PATH (that is, the least number of ASs in the path).
If routes have the same AS_PATH length, prefer interior to exterior to incomplete origin.	Cisco interprets confederation routes as interior, but the algorithm prefers confederation exterior to confederation interior.
Of paths with the same origin, prefer those with the lowest MED value.	In the absence of a specific IETF interpretation, Cisco's default was to assume routes without an explicit MED have a MED of zero. Recently, the IETF clarified the expected behavior, which is the opposite of Cisco's interpretation. This clarification specifies that, when presented with routes that either have MEDs or do not, the routes without MEDs should be less preferable than a route with an explicit MED of any value. Also, the BGP specification states that MEDs should be compared only between connections to the same adjacent ASs. There are applications such as multilateral exchange points, however, where it can be very useful to compare MEDs between multiple adjacent ASs. See Chapter 12.
If the MEDs are equal, prefer routes with external rather than internal sources.	Some implementations reverse the order of this and the next step.
Prefer the path through the closest IGP neighbor (that is, lowest IGP metric).	
Otherwise, select the path with the lowest originating router ID. Since router IDs must be unique, this will be a final tiebreaker. Router ID is selected by the same algorithm used to select the OSPF router ID.	The BGP specification does not support equal-cost multipath, but several vendor implementations have proprietary extensions for doing so. If multiple paths are enabled, add the current route if both the current best route and the new route are external and come from the same adjacent AS. Cisco supports up to 6 load-shared paths.

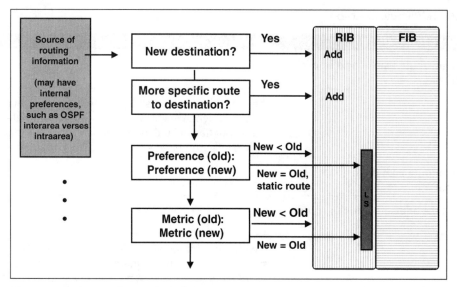

Figure 9.21 General route installation.

one route unless proprietary sharing is in use. To review, the rules for general route installation are:

1. If the route is not in the current RIB, install it. This includes situations where the route is a more-specific of an existing route—the new route is added but the less-specific is not deleted.

2. If the route is from a source of routing more preferred (see preferences in Chapter 4) than a current route of the same specificity, replace the existing route.

3. If there is an existing route of the same specificity and the same source, and the source uses metrics:

    —If the new route has a better metric, replace the old route.

    —If load sharing is enabled and the new route has the same metric, add it to the table and mark the set of equal-cost routes eligible for load sharing.

Advertising Policies and BGP

Advertising external policies requires BGP to send to external ASs updates that contain the route for which your AS is willing to accept responsibility for traffic delivery. You do not need to announce the same set of routes or route attributes to all of your neighboring ASs.

Customer Configuration Requirements Overview

You read a list of representative policy requirements in Chapter 4. Now let's examine the customer-side BGP setup to achieve those comments, along with the administrative agreements the customer will need from the provider(s). Establishing basic BGP routing, as in a simple enterprise homed to two ISPs, is somewhat more complex than setting up interior routing. With both interior and exterior protocols, you establish a routing process and indicate what networks it can advertise. With BGP, you also need to specify the peers. Peers are not automatically discovered. This is a matter of intentional protocol design, not a limitation. It goes with the previous comment that you need not advertise the same routes to all peers.

Like OSPF, BGP needs a router ID. In practice, this ID is the IP address of the loopback interface. In contrast to OSPF, the loopback interface is commonly used as an active part of protocol exchange.

Before trying to configure BGP, you need a clear idea of the BGP routing system. For every BGP router, you must know the items listed in Tables 9.6 and 9.7.

Table 9.6   Per-Router BGP Configuration Worksheet

AS NUMBER	ROUTER NAME (YOUR ADMINISTRATIVE ID)	BGP ROUTER ID

Table 9.7   Per-Interface BGP Configuration

AS NUMBER			
ROUTER NAME			
BGP ROUTER ID			
BGP INTERFACE ID AND IP ADDRESS	NEIGHBOR IP ADDRESS	ADVERTISING POLICY FOR THIS INTERFACE	ACCEPTANCE POLICY FOR THIS INTERFACE

Multilinking and Multihoming: The Customer Side

Always remember to keep in mind what is the problem you are trying to solve. If your goal is increasing availability, that doesn't necessarily equate to increasing redundancy. Uncontrolled increases in redundancy lead to uncontrolled increases in complexity, and may actually decrease availability (see Figure 9.22).

Multihoming, a not especially well-defined term, can feel like quicksand unless you are clear what problem you are trying to solve. Simply to improve availability in Internet access, consider what threats concern you, and decide if the countermeasures in Table 9.8 are cost-effective. The shaded issues are not soluble with BGP.

Multihoming, however, involves multiple BGP connections. In terms of general Internet routing policy, you are multihomed only when you have BGP peering with two or more ASs. Unless you are multihomed in this manner, the address registries will not assign you a registered AS number.

The main reason to run BGP is to have external IP connectivity. The main motivation for multilinking and the various flavors of multihoming is to avoid a single point of failure in your external IP connectivity.

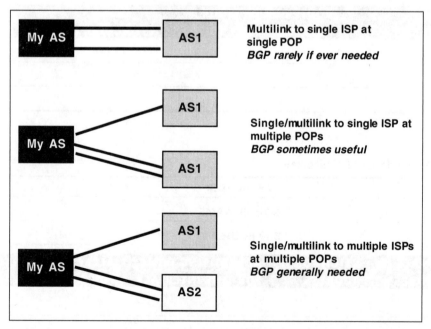

Figure 9.22 Multilinking, single-provider multihoming, and multiple-provider multihoming.

Table 9.8 Faults and Countermeasures at Lower Layers

THREAT	ALTERNATIVE COUNTERMEASURES
Media failure of a single IP subnet to the ISP	1. Inverse multiplexing with multilink PPP, fast/ gigabit Etherchannel over optical transmission, SONET
Failure of a single IP interface on a single customer or ISP router	2. Run BGP over load-shared IP using multiple interfaces
Failure of a single customer or ISP router	3. Install multiple customer routers interconnected to each other with iBGP and to the ISP with eBGP
Failure of the ISP's BGP routing system	4. Connect to multiple ISPs with eBGP
Failure of the ISP's BGP routing and failure of physical components	5. Apply countermeasures 1–4 in combination

Motivations for Multilinking

You can have multiple physical links to the same service provider without BGP. When the multiple links go to the same ISP router, this is called *multilinking*. The most common non-BGP approach is to use load-sharing default routes.

Let's look at a variant of our Huffle, Puffle case study, in which the firm has only one router but wants to protect against failure of a single link or interface. One approach, discussed in Chapter 8, is to use an external inverse multiplexer. Another approach, which again can either be in an external device or on the router, is to inverse-multiplex at the data-link layer using multilink PPP (MLPPP). When you do the inverse multiplexing on the router, you certainly simplify the hardware involved and the potential troubleshooting. The major disadvantages of MPPP are that it can take appreciable CPU resources and that it is limited to a round-robin load-sharing method. A third approach is to use IP equal-cost load sharing. Round-robin load sharing will be comparable in resource consumption to MLPPP, but, depending on the specific routing implementation, there may be more intelligent load-sharing algorithms available. In general, the best load sharing is based on source-destination pairs.

Non-BGP Multihoming

If BGP is impractical, you still are not limited to static default routes or RIP for multihoming at the network layer. OSPF can support some load-sharing and primary backup policies, although these are likely to have greater asymmetrical routing than properly configured BGP. For load sharing, assume you have two autonomous system border routers in backbone area 0.0.0.0. Each has a static default route to a different ISP POP. When you import these routes into OSPF, you must configure the router such that they are imported as type 1 external routes. The two routes must have the same metric at the point of importation.

A type 1 external route has an OSPF cost that is the sum of the external metric and the internal metrics to reach the autonomous system boundary router (ASBR) advertising the route. As long as you have multiple type 1 defaults, outbound traffic will go to the closest exit point from the OSPF domain. If failure(s) cause there to be only one exit point, all traffic will move automatically to that exit point. If you have two ISPs in the role of primary and backup, or if perhaps you have a fast and a slow link to the same ISP, you normally want to use only one exit point. In that case, you must import the defaults into OSPF as type 2 external routes, with higher metrics set on the backup interfaces. OSPF considers only the external cost in choosing between type 1 and type 2 metrics, so traffic will go out the lower-metric interface unless that interface goes down.

You can combine these methods and come up with configurations such as two equal-cost exits to one ISP and a backup to another POP of the same or different ISP.

Motivations for BGP Multihoming to One Provider

There are many applications where it makes sense to have BGP peering with more than one BGP speaker in the same ISP. There is no definitive term to describe this method, although it frequently is called multihoming. Whenever you are not sure about the form of multihoming being discussed, be sure to determine the number of ASs with which you are peering.

When you have multiple connections to the same provider, and a large geographically dispersed network, it can be useful to run BGP to the ISP. As shown in Figure 9.22, you can multilink as well. BGP gives you the ability, in such cases, to tell your ISP of the best ways to reach certain destinations in your enterprise. The provider usually does not send this more detailed information to the Internet, because the rest of the Internet simply needs to know how to reach your single ISP. BGP connections to a single provider can be over layer 2 or layer 3 multiplexing. Layer 3 multiplexing is most common.

One of the nuances of multiple links to the same provider router is the need to have peering between loopback interfaces, not the physical interfaces of the routers. BGP makes the basic assumption that peers are on the same subnet, so, depending on the implementation, you may need to configure eBGP-multihop for BGP tunnels to work.

Motivations for Multihoming to Multiple Providers

By multihoming to multiple providers, you gain some protection against failures in any given provider's routing system. This is not pure protection, because there are many cases where a problem in one provider's routing system propagates itself to multiple ISPs. Still, there have been cases where the entire BGP system of a large provider failed.

Multihoming to multiple providers may or may not protect you against media failures. Obviously, if you reach the ISPs through a single cable to your end office, a single cable cut defeats the added reliability of any multihoming. It is also possible that multiple ISPs share a common upstream facility that can disable them all.

Once you are running BGP, you can multihome to multiple providers. The more routing information you accept from these providers, the more intelligent the choice you can make about the best exit—you can even influence the entry point for incoming traffic. The more routing information you accept and influence, however, the more resources you will need in the control plane of your router.

One common compromise is to designate one ISP as your primary, and point your preferred default at it. In this scenario, you also accept the customer routes, and possibly the directly connected AS routes, of the other provider. In the vast majority of cases, you can reasonably assume that if an ISP advertises a path as directly connected or internal, it will be the best path to the destination. This, of course, will not necessarily be true if the same destination is multihomed to both your ISPs.

Starting Simply: Defaults

RPSL supports the notion of a default route, as do OSPF and ISIS. I like to think of default routes as somehow meeting Groucho Marx's criterion for joining private clubs: "I wouldn't join any club that would have me as a member." Less cynically, the default route is like an ancestral home, where you are always welcome. Or, at least, people have to act as though you are.

It is quite common to want to have a hierarchy of more and less preferred default routes. For example, the most preferred default might be to the ISP with which you have the fastest dedicated link; the next most preferred would be over a slower dedicated link to a different ISP; and the least preferred would be a dial-up to the primary ISP. Preference might also depend on pricing structures and the minimum units for which you must pay once a link is activated.

This is certainly adequate for single-homed single-link and single-homed multilink topologies. While there may be some suboptimal routing when the simplest version is used at multiple points of attachment to a single provider, the simplicity of the method can make it attractive.

Asymmetrical Routing

A consequence of the independent policies of Internet AS is *asymmetrical routing*. Assume your AS has connections to two ISPs, AS1 and AS2. If you send out a query through AS1, there is no guarantee whatsoever that the response will not return through AS2. In fact, rough industry estimates suggest that with two equal ISPs, 30 to 40 percent of your responses will return through a different ISP than the corresponding request.

You need to know about asymmetrical routing for several reasons:

1. When you troubleshoot, do not assume that anything is broken when you see asymmetrical routing.

2. Delay is unpredictable when you do not know the path that will be taken. As a consequence, delay-sensitive applications should avoid the general Internet and be run over physical or virtual private networks with service level agreements.

3. You cannot allocate "just enough" bandwidth on one ISP access, assuming the load will be equally distributed.

Let's return to Huffle, Puffle and Cetera for some examples of how load sharing can make routing simple. Assume the firm changes its backup strategy so that there are two T1 lines from the main router to the ISP. The firm has contracted for facility diversity for these lines. If IP or MLPPP is used to define the default as including the bundle of two T1s, and if either fails, the load will shift to the remaining T1. There will be performance degradation, but no other effect on routing. Static routing will suffice.

There really is no need for the provider to run BGP to Huffle, Puffle and Cetera since the provider has assigned the address space. The ISP can create static routes to Huffle, Puffle and import them into its own routing system. If Huffle, Puffle still wants to use two routers, one for PPP backup, an IGP will be needed between the routers. The PPP router needs to generate a default route with a higher metric than the T1 bundle. In other words, the two routers must be interconnected and the T1 (or dual T1) default must be advertised into Huffle, Puffle's domain until the link goes down. As long as the T1 default is present, traffic routed to the PPP router will take another hop to the PPP router. Only if that default disappears will the PPP link activate and advertise default into the domain.

Multihoming to Multiple POPs of a Single ISP

Increasingly, there is a partial exception to the rule that BGP is not useful when connecting to a single ISP. That exception exists when you connect to multiple physical routers in the ISP. It is a partial exception, because even if you run eBGP, you are apt to use a private, not registered, AS number, which the ISP removes from the updates it sends to the outside. You also can use a private AS number when the addresses involved are lent to you by the provider, and only the aggregate containing your route and the routes of other customers of the ISP are advertised outside the ISP.

Multihoming to a Single Provider using PA Space

The technique for multihoming to multiple POPs of a single ISP using address space assigned by that provider is defined in RFC 1998. To understand this scenario, assume that the ISP announces a single large address block to the rest of the Internet (Figure 9.23). Let's look again at Design and Dig, who we met in Chapters 3 and 4. The company's ISP assigns it the address block 96.0.4.0/21, which is split into four /23 sub-blocks for each office, and the private AS number 64001. Each office is connected to two POPs of the provider (see Figure 9.24).

Load Sharing Using More-Specifics

Each office has an internal addressing policy that assigns a /24 to IP interfaces to the first floor and the second floor offices. All of these are still part of the provider's address plan, so there is no value to the rest of the world in seeing them as long as the provider aggregate is being announced.

Now we are ready to begin BGP announcement, but there are some subtle rules. To achieve a degree of load sharing, each office would like to advertise half its addresses to one of the POPs to which it is connected and half to the other POP, with the caveat that either POP should be able to accept all routes in the event a POP or the link to it fails (see Figure 9.25). It is in the interest of the global routing system that these routes, which are of no value to any provider outside the immediate one, do not leak into the general Internet. The routes, therefore, need to be tagged with the well-known NO-EXPORT community.

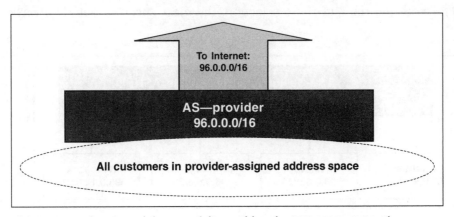

Figure 9.23 The ISP and the rest of the world under RFC 1998 assumptions.

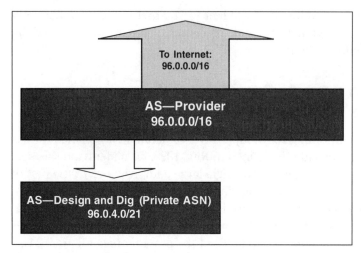

Figure 9.24   Customer address plan, RFC 1998.

Remember a community is an attribute in the BGP update that means that the route should not be advertised outside the current AS. The solution is not finished, however. This multihoming approach will work quite nicely—as long as nothing breaks.

Design and Dig's goal is that as long as both POP links are up, the ISP will send traffic to the optimal first-floor or second-floor router. If one link fails, its more-specific advertisement will disappear, and all traffic will flow over the other link. Unfortunately, things don't really work this way. If the customer only advertised the more-specific /24 routes, and the second-floor router went down, how would the provider know that the other /24 was still reachable through the first-floor router?

The answer to this problem is that both the first-floor and second-floor customer routers have to advertise both the /23 and /24 (see Tables 9.9 through 9.11). Under the rules of route selection, the most specific route is always

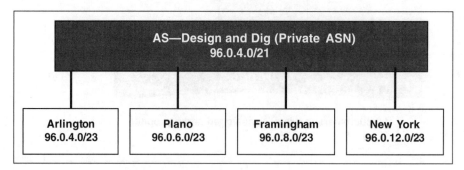

Figure 9.25   Basic RFC 1998 advertising.

Table 9.9 Per-Router BGP Configuration Worksheet for Design and Dig Office 1

AS NUMBER	ROUTER NAME (YOUR ADMINISTRATIVE ID)	BGP ROUTER ID
64001	DD-ARL-1	192.168.1.1
64001	DD-ARL-2	192.168.1.2

taken. In practice, the ISP will advertise default plus routes to the other Design and Dig offices. Since Design and Dig will only get routes from its ISP, it doesn't really need to filter them but simply can accept whatever is sent. The customer used a private AS number to advertise its routes to AS1. It does not justify its own AS number, because it has no routing policy that differs from that of its upstream provider.

Load Control with MEDs

For the original purpose of multi-exit discriminator (MED) attributes, assume advertising AS1 has multiple connections to the directly adjacent AS2 (Figure 9.26). The attribute will not propagate to AS3; it is only for the guidance of AS2 by AS1. AS2 is free to set its own MED to AS4, but this MED has no relationship to the MED set by AS1. AS1 advertises multiple instances of the same route, but with different MEDs. The lower the MED, the more preferred the route instance (see Tables 9.12 and 9.13).

Chapter 12 shows some new applications of MEDs that involve multiple providers. The original intention of the MED was only to show preference among the routes advertised to a single AS. In the case of Design and Dig, MEDs give us an alternative to using more and less specific routes for load sharing with failover.

Table 9.10 Per-Interface BGP Configuration, Design and Dig Office 1, Router 1

AS NUMBER 64001			
ROUTER NAME DD-ARL-1			
BGP ROUTER ID 192.168.1.1			
BGP INTERFACE ID AND IP ADDRESS	NEIGHBOR IP ADDRESS	ADVERTISING POLICY FOR THIS INTERFACE	ACCEPTANCE POLICY FOR THIS INTERFACE
Serial 0 96.255.0.1/30	96.255.0.2/30	Announce 96.0.4.0/23 with NO-EXPORT, 96.0.4.0/24 with NO-EXPORT	Accept ALL

Table 9.11 Per-Interface BGP Configuration, Design and Dig Office 1, Router 2

AS NUMBER 64001			
ROUTER NAME DD-ARL-2			
BGP ROUTER ID 192.168.1.2			
BGP INTERFACE ID AND IP ADDRESS	**NEIGHBOR IP ADDRESS**	**ADVERTISING POLICY FOR THIS INTERFACE**	**ACCEPTANCE POLICY FOR THIS INTERFACE**
Serial 0 96.255.0.5/30	96.255.0.6/30	Announce 96.0.4.0/23 with NO-EXPORT, 96.0.5.0/24 with NO-EXPORT	Accept ALL

RFC 2270

A different case than RFC 1998 involves enterprises that have existing provider-independent address space, typically addresses that they have had for years. To have their provider advertise their block, however, means that either they must advertise it with BGP to the provider, or the provider must define it statically and redistribute it.

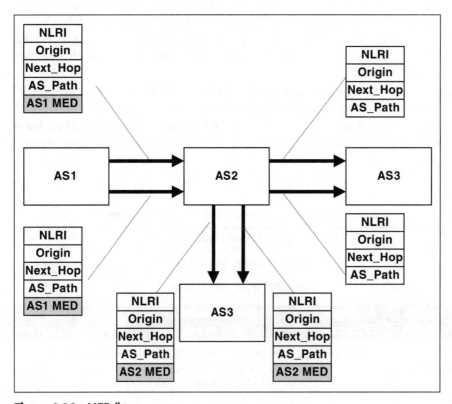

Figure 9.26 MED flow.

Table 9.12 Per-Interface BGP Configuration, Design and Dig Office 1, Router 1 Using MED

AS NUMBER 64001			
ROUTER NAME DD-ARL-1			
BGP ROUTER ID 192.168.1.1			
BGP INTERFACE ID AND IP ADDRESS	NEIGHBOR IP ADDRESS	ADVERTISING POLICY FOR THIS INTERFACE	ACCEPTANCE POLICY FOR THIS INTERFACE
Serial 0 96.255.0.1/30	96.255.0.2/30	Announce 96.0.4.0/24 with NO-EXPORT and MED = 100, 96.0.5.0/24 with NO-EXPORT and MED = 200	Accept ALL

[RFC 2270] proposes a mechanism to allow multihoming to a single provider without wasting a registered AS number (see Figure 9.27). The service provider assigns the same private AS number to each enterprise it services. At the ingress routers to the provider, however, the private AS number is stripped, so the advertisement will appear to the Internet as being originated by the service provider. The feature that allows the private number to be stripped is called *private AS path manipulation*. Using this mechanism does save AS numbers, but also imposes some restrictions, which, however, should not be onerous in practice. One requirement is that the customer must default to the ISP. The next restriction is that the customer AS cannot receive full routes from the ISP, because BGP would reject routes with the ISP's AS number in the AS path. This means that customers X and Y cannot receive direct routes to one another. However, since both customers X and Y have the same ISP as their only upstream, default routing should suffice for connectivity between X and Y. This method, incidentally, does not preclude multihoming to multiple POPs of the ISP.

If the customer adds an upstream ISP or changes its upstream, the customer

Table 9.13 Per-Interface BGP Configuration, Design and Dig Office 1, Router 2 using MED

AS NUMBER 64001			
ROUTER NAME DD-ARL-2			
BGP ROUTER ID 192.168.1.2			
BGP INTERFACE ID AND IP ADDRESS	NEIGHBOR IP ADDRESS	ADVERTISING POLICY FOR THIS INTERFACE	ACCEPTANCE POLICY FOR THIS INTERFACE
Serial 0 96.255.0.5/30	96.255.0.6/30	Announce 96.0.4.0/24 with NO-EXPORT and MED = 200, 96.0.5.0/24 with NO-EXPORT and MED = 100	Accept ALL

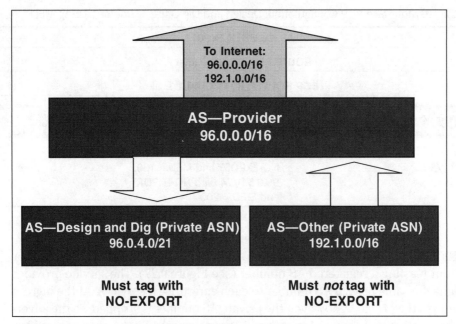

Figure 9.27   RFC 2270 multihoming (customer side).

must either change to a registered AS number or to a private AS number agreed to by all upstream providers. The former method is preferred, but the latter is also used in practice. When all ISPs use the same private AS number, which they then strip, it appears that more than one AS is originating the same prefix. According to the BGP specification, this is a violation, generally referred to as an *inconsistent AS*. In practice, it may make troubleshooting somewhat more difficult, and can interfere with route filters that are autogenerated from routing registry data. There are workarounds to this problem, which involve not depending solely on the RPSL origin code for deciding on the correct originator. A community, for example, can identify legitimately inconsistent AS origination.

The RFC 2270 method is somewhat more flexible with respect to addressing than is RFC 1998. RFC 2270 does not require the customer address space to be assigned by its upstream. If the customer address space is provider-independent, or assigned by a different provider, you do not want to tag the routes with the NO-EXPORT community. If you do assign the customer address space, however, it is appropriate to use NO-EXPORT.

Private AS manipulation is not yet standardized. The discussion here refers to Cisco's implementation. The neighbor x.x.x.x remove-private-as per-neighbor command strips private AS numbers, subject to the constraints of Table 9.14.

Table 9.14   Rules for Private AS Stripping

PRIVATE AND PUBLIC?	CONFEDERATION PRESENT?	CONTAINS AS NUMBER OF NEIGHBOR?	ACTION
Private only	N/A	N/A	Private AS removed
Private and public	N/A	Yes	No effect
Private and public	Yes	N/A	Removes private after confederation part
Private and public	No	No	Error

Multihoming to Two ISPs

With respect to the public Internet, you are multihomed when you run BGP to more than one other AS (see Figure 9.22). Multihomed ASs may be *transit* or *nontransit*. The vast majority of enterprise networks that run BGP to the outside are nontransit. For additional reliability, it is perfectly reasonable to combine multilinking, multihoming to multiple POPs of the same ISP, and multihoming to multiple ISPs.

Assuming equal-capacity links to the two ISPs, it is fairly natural to desire to share load across them. To have any real chance of accomplishing reasonable load balancing, you need to understand the capabilities and limitations of BGP. Many of these limitations are a result of the scalability design principles of modern routing protocols.

Scaling Potatoes

Routing protocol design follows Darwinian principles. The first priority is survival—of the local router and of the routing system as a whole. Just as the first priority of hippopotamus reproduction is for the hippos to look good to other hippos, the first priority of routers is they work well with other routers.

Optimal routing is not the first priority in making a robust routing system. Indeed, route optimality may mean different things at different times. For a given application, minimizing latency is optimal. For a different application, maximizing throughput is optimal. Survival often means maximizing closest-exit routing and minimizing routing table churn. The latter depends significantly on maximizing route aggregation, which causes a loss of detail.

In any hierarchical routing system, there is a very basic issue of routing policy, variously called closest exit versus optimal exit or hot potato versus cold potato (see Figure 9.28). The hot potato assumption, which is the default in

---

CHURN MAKES MORE THAN BUTTER

In dairy operations, you churn cream with repetitive motions, pumping the handle until the butter precipitates out. In routing, *churn* is a repetitive processor operation that may or may not produce useful output.

When routing churn comes from the addition of new destinations on the internet, it is normal and desirable, because it gives users more capabilities. When churn results from links bouncing up and down, causing routers to go through repeated flap cycles of announcements and withdrawals, the overhead can lead to routers crashing—and even more withdrawals associated with their failure.

---

modern routing protocol, means that a router wants to get rid of a packet as quickly as possible. "Getting rid" means selecting the path that will cause the packet to exit the BGP AS or IGP area as quickly as possible. This may not be the best end-to-end path, but it is the most conservative of local resources. Cold potato routing accepts less efficient resource utilization in the interest of finding the best end-to-end path. For example, ISPs that offer service level guarantees often use cold potato routing for their premium traffic. By keeping packets inside their AS as long as possible, they can control the quality of the majority, if not all, of the paths the packets traverse.

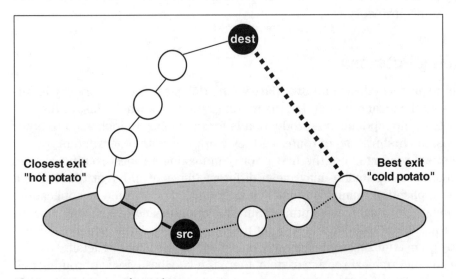

Figure 9.28   Potato alternatives.

Minimizing Local Information

Especially in IGPs, hot potato routing minimizes the amount of routing information that enters an area. In BGP, hot potato routing also may minimize the routing information received. Minimization includes aggregation and the use of default routes.

It may seem counterintuitive, but making a routing process aware of more routes does not help it, unless there are distinctly different ways each route will be processed. In the terms used in MPLS, you want to reduce the number of routes to the number of forwarding equivalence classes that will be present in the local environment—the number of ways a packet can leave that environment, both topologically and with quality of service. When you reduce the amount of routing information, you decrease the memory and CPU needed on edge routers and increase local stability by decreasing the potential for routers to have to respond to flapping routes.

An OSPF Example

OSPF stubby areas are examples of hot potato policies, with the extreme case being Cisco's totally stubby area, which only receives the default route. In a totally stubby area, the only metric that is important in sending traffic to a destination outside the area is the intraarea metric to the available bit rate (ABR) or ABRs. Totally stubby behavior, incidentally, is the default behavior for an ISIS nonbackbone area. If you have two ABRs (let's call them East and West), the traffic from internal routers in the eastern part of the area will go to ABR East, and traffic from internal routers in the western area will go to ABR West. This will be true even if an eastern interior router wants to send to a destination to which ABR West has a better path in area 0.0.0.0.

In stub areas, interarea routes can be leaked into the stubby area, so if one ABR has a better path to some other area, and the cost internal to the current area does not make the total cost more than that of going through the other ABR, traffic will go to the first ABR. It can, in fact, be based on total cost.

In regular areas, the potential exists to leak all external information into nonzero areas and let them pick the absolutely best path to the destination. Taking this to extremes, if you had multiple Internet connections, each ASBR would inject a full 100,000-plus Internet routes into OSPF—or even more when aggregated customer routes of your providers are considered. In addition, any redistributed static or IGP routes would add to the table. This isn't scalable.

The goal of most good designs is to give each nonbackbone router to a reasonable, redundant path to a high-powered router that has lots of information. It is that router that makes most decisions. Let's say you have two nonzero areas and area 0.0.0.0. Areas 0.0.0.1 and 0.0.0.2 each have two ABRs. Link speed in all areas is not constant. Router Interior.1.1 in area 0.0.0.1 wants to send to destination 2.1.1.0 in area 0.0.0.2. The sum of interface costs from router 1.1 to ABR1.1 is 50. The sum of interface costs to router ABR1.2 is 100. Each ABR connects to a separate backbone router, which has links of different speeds to ABRs entering other areas. Assume the sum of interface costs from ABR1.1 through backbone 1 to ABR2.1 is 200, and the sum of interface costs from ABR1.2 to backbone 2 to ABR.2.2 is 100. Further, assume the sum of interface costs from ABR2.1 to 2.1.1.0 is 100, and the sum of interface costs from ABR2.2 to 2.1.1.0 is 50. Therefore the optimal end-to-end path with respect to the OSPF metric is ABR1.1 to backbone 2 to ABR2.2 (100 + 100 + 50 versus 50 + 200 + 100). If, however, area 1 is totally stubby, it can't see the area 0 and 0.0.0.2 routes. Area 1 routers can only consider the costs inside area 0.0.0.1.

Special cases emerge with OSPF and ISIS. With the totally stubby area, or the basic ISIS level 1 area, you will not get end-to-end optimization. You will get the benefits of stubbiness and its smaller routing tables and workload, and you will get an optimal path from the source to the area 0.0.0.1 exit—not beyond it. You will get closest-exit routing and no extra added attractions.

Optimal routing requires the ingress router know about the area 0.0.0.0 and 0.0.0.2 paths so it can select the best end-to-end path. But to have the information for the ingress router to make this decision, you may hit it with lots more routes and potentially overload it.

BGP Potatoes

From the perspective of a basic customer who defaults to an ISP, the customer is doing closest-exit routing. Most ISPs do closest-exit routing to other ISPs, except when providing service with multiprovider service level agreements (See Chapter 12). A customer AS that receives only default, even at multiple points, is the BGP equivalent of an OSPF totally stubby area.

AS Path Expressions

One of the ways to signal requirements for multiprovider cold potato routing is to use only certain ASs in which you have confidence. In the real world, you would also negotiate communities with them, but let's explore how you can select paths associated with different ASs. To do this, you specify AS path filtering with UNIX-style regular expressions (regexp), a method of specifying patterns to be matched. Patterns that can be described with regular expressions are far more complex than those that can be specified with a bit mask. If you haven't spent a fair amount of time as a UNIX programmer, regular expressions seem

> **REALITY CHECK**
>
> If a customer has its own AS and has not told you it is doing transit, all the BGP advertisements that customer sends you should originate with its AS number. The source addresses of all the customer's packets should be in address ranges advertised to you with updates.

strange and challenging. If you have spent a fair amount of time as a UNIX programmer, you know regular expressions *are* strange and challenging.

Exact Matches

An AS number in a regular expression, written without any special pattern-matching characters, will match only that AS number. When you code an AS number without any qualifiers in a regular expression, only that AS number will be matched. The regexp 789 only matches AS789. The regexp 666 only matches AS666.

You may code multiple exact matches. 789 666 matches only a path that contains AS789 and AS666, in that order. 666 followed by 789 will not match. Neither 666 nor 789 alone will match.

Special Matching Characters

Think of the preceding example, 789 666. What if you wanted to accept any path that contained the sequence 789 666, but really didn't care whether other AS preceded or followed them? There are several ways you can specify only part of a sequence using regular expressions (see Table 9.15). Assorted symbols operate on groups of pattern-matching character. In one of these capabilities, you specify a range with square brackets. [1,3,7] will match 1, 3, or 7. [1-7] will match 1,2,3,4,5,6, or 7. Combining ranges with other matching characters, [1-3]99 will match 199, 299, and 399. Another capability with regular expressions is to show alternate choices. 1 | 2 will match either 1 or 2, but not both.

Selecting and Influencing Outbound Paths

When you have multiple external connections, you have different degrees of control on the path your outgoing traffic takes to the outside and the path that externally generated traffic takes to enter your AS. This makes sense, because you are making the primary decision on outbound routing, although your decision will be influenced by the amount of information available to you.

Table 9.15   Symbols for Regular Expressions

SYMBOL	NAME	MATCH CRITERIA
.	Period	Any single character, including space
^	Caret	The start of the string (for example, an anchor on the left)
$	Dollar	The end of the string (for example, an anchor on the right)
*	Asterisk	Zero or more sequences of the pattern
?	Question mark	Only zero or 1 occurrences of the pattern
_	Underscore	Comma, left and right braces, left and right parentheses, beginning and end of the string, or white space
+	Plus sign	One or more sequences of the pattern

The Keep It Simple Case

Some conventional wisdom about selecting outbound paths actually is an artifact of experience with old equipment. When the random access memory (RAM) of an edge router was limited to 16 Mbytes, it was impossible to accept a full routing table and simply let BGP pick the best exit. More modern yet inexpensive routers now have enough memory to hold one or more views of the full routing table.

Figure 9.29 shows an example from one of my clients, which needed fairly powerful routers simply for its input/output capacity. Either router could handle the full Internet load of the enterprise. Router **oregano** was connected to ISP1, router **garlic** was connected to ISP2, and **oregano** and **garlic** were interconnected with iBGP. Both ISPs sent full Internet routing tables plus their customer routes. Both ISPs were sufficiently well connected that we achieved a roughly equivalent amount of load sharing without further tuning. At the same time, we did monitor traffic to see if any particular destinations were taking up inordinate amounts of bandwidth on one link.

A Little More Redundancy

The incremental cost of adding an ISP2 link to **garlic** and an ISP1 link to **oregano** (dashed lines in Figure 9.29) will probably be small, and doing so will protect against a simultaneous failure of a link to one router and a crash of the second router. If you do this, try very hard to get diverse local loop facilities to the POPs of the two ISPs.

My client was in a suburban office park, which, as is increasingly common in new construction, was on a dual SONET ring that gave redundant communica-

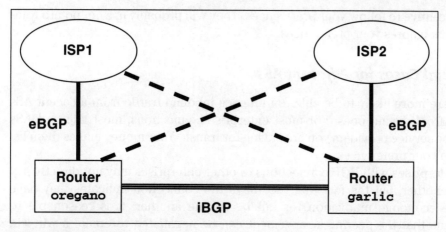

Figure 9.29 Let BGP sort it out.

tions to the two POPs. If this had not been the case, and if the ILEC did not have the park homed to multiple central offices, I would next have looked into business-grade CATV as a backup, then into wireless connectivity to a separate CO.

The Direct-Customer-Is-Better Strategy

In this example, my client connected to two large ISPs and had the router capacity to accept full routing. A different approach, which is especially common when routers have limited memory, is to treat ISP1 as your primary carrier and ISP2 as a backup, but with the exception that you want to use ISP1 as the primary carrier to its direct customers (that is, in its address space) or to those ASs that are directly connected to ISP1.

```
accept:          from AS1 default pref=2
                 from AS2 default pref=3
                        ^+          pref=1
```

This policy will take the primary default from AS1 and use the AS2 default only if you lose default from AS1. Indeed, you don't even need to take any routing from AS1 other than the default.

Selecting and Influencing Inbound Paths

It is far more difficult to influence the path inbound traffic takes to you than it is to control how traffic leaves your AS. The fundamental issue here is economic: Service providers with which you have no economic relationship have no incentive to follow your preferences. They will probably use hot potato routing that ignores your preferences.

Special Cases for Adjacent ASs

You are more likely to be able to influence inbound traffic from adjacent ASs than from distant ones. For most enterprise connections, most adjacent ASs will be service providers you are paying for transit. Your money makes them listen to your preferences.

Enterprises with BGP connections to other enterprises may not directly pay one another, but the fact that they have the connection indicates they have some economic motivation for talking to one another. It is reasonable to assume that the peering arrangement can be negotiated to create a win-win topology for both sides. It's far less likely that tier 1 providers will care very much about the preferences of other tier 1 providers' customers. When there is a need for controlled quality of service between major providers, the best strategy is usually to contract with one provider for a VPN and make that provider responsible for the interprovider economic incentives to make other providers care about your QoS requirement.

AS Path Prepending and Its Limits

I find it ironic that the most popular way to make a route less desirable for incoming traffic depends on a route preference factor that is not part of the BGP specification: AS path length. *AS path prepending* is a technique in which you insert your AS number more than once into the AS path (Figure 9.30). In principle, the longer the AS path, the less desirable the route. The basic limitation of AS path prepending is that you have no control over the update as it moves through multiple ASs. By the time your updates arrive at the destination, the less preferred path may have a shorter AS path length than the more preferred path.

There have been periodic proposals to introduce a BGP attribute (destination path attribute) that conveys an absolute preference of the originator for which incoming path to take. Unfortunately for its proponents, there are simply no economic motivations for its adoption. Since you do not control the path your update takes beyond your directly connected ASs, as in Figure 9.30, your less desirable path actually is more desirable at the destination. This will lead to asymmetric routing.

Communities and Service Level Agreements

When there are economic motivations to enforce an end-to-end SLA, a VPN certainly is one answer. Another approach that often is useful is tagging routes

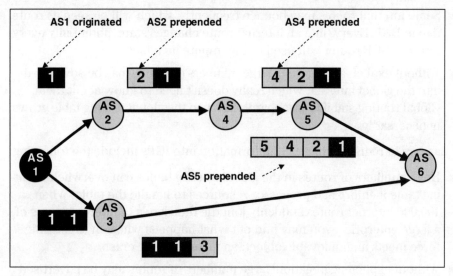

Figure 9.30 AS path prepending and its limitations.

with a community string and making sure that every AS along the preferred path accepts the meaning of that community. This has been reasonably common practice in academic and research networks.

Assume you have a set of universities that cooperate on a research project that requires minimal latency. All the participants agree to treat traffic associated with that project in the desired manner, probably because they all receive research funding from the same organization. One of the universities creates the community. Assume the university is AS6666 and that routes associated with the joint academic VoIP project will be marked with the community 6666:1000. Each participant in the project agrees to recognize this community. Each AS decides how to implement the desired QoS. The AS might set a local preference based on the community, assign the packets to a MPLS tunnel, set type of service bits in the IP header, and so on. Remember that there is a difference between a signal (the community attribute) and the response to the signal.

Importing and Exporting among Routing Protocols

It is possible to import and export routes between BGP and IGPs. Things can go awfully wrong, however, if a routing error causes another AS's routes to be blackholed, if you redistribute a flapping route, and so on. The dangers of redistributing IGP information into BGP include the following:

- Some internal routes may bounce frequently, which will be seen as route flap in BGP. Every time an internal route changes state, potentially every Internet BGP router will need to recompute its tables.

- Without explicit aggregation, large numbers of routes may be advertised into the global internet, which really doesn't need to know about them. Global routing stability is jeopardized when the global routing table grows unnecessarily.

The dangers of redistributing BGP information into IGPs include the following:

- Huge numbers of routes in the global routing tables can overwhelm routing table memory and processor resources to handle the table. When 100,000 internet routes suddenly join the thousands of internal routes of a large enterprise, you may find out what happens when an irresistible force meets an immovable object: an inconceivable crash.

- Without explicit aggregation, large numbers of routes may be advertised into the global internet, which really doesn't need to know about them. Global routing stability is jeopardized when the global routing table grows unnecessarily.

If you redistribute, you should filter such that only desired routes are permitted. The basic criteria for filtering are:

- Accept only packets whose source addresses are reachable from entries in your routing table.

- Reject packets from external protocols whose source addresses are inside your AS.

Importing Default into an IGP

While this is the easiest procedure to manage, it may or may not be desirable for companies that span large geographic areas. There may be specific organizational concerns, such as a research lab with far more Internet experience than the operators of the corporate network. While the focus of this chapter is BGP, it is worth noting that appropriate enterprise IGP design can be an important part of the solution. Figure 9.29 showed the real-world situation of a large enterprise client of mine that appropriately wanted a main point of Internet connectivity for most of its divisions. This main point would be logical, and actually had geographic diversity, firewalling, and other high-availability features. At the time of the implementation, the dual T3 lines to different ISPs seemed more than adequate (see Figure 9.31).

One corporate division, the research laboratory, had been involved in Internet research since the beginning of the ARPANET and already had extremely

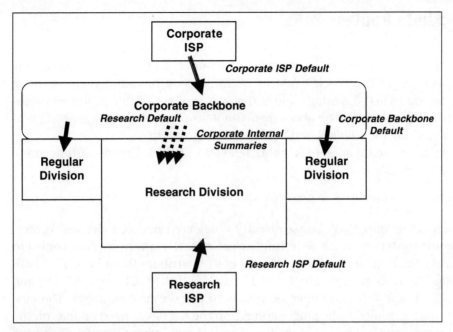

Figure 9.31 Special default.

well-managed external connectivity. Indeed, the department's link, had more bandwidth than the corporate link. This division wanted to access the rest of the corporation, so totally separating it was not an alternative. The solution here had distinct similarities to the problem discussed earlier in "Non-BGP Multihoming," except it also required BGP.

In this case, you still have two autonomous system border routers. One connects to a BGP speaker in the corporate backbone, while the other connects to your existing ISP. You do import default from both, as type 2 external routes, and set a higher cost on the router to area 0.0.0.0. The difference from the previous example is that you accept full corporate routes from the backbone. As long as the nonbackbone router is up, however, you will prefer its default route for other than the more-specific corporate routes. In the event the nonbackbone ASBR fails, all external traffic will default to the backbone ASBR. If the backbone router fails, under the policies stated, all traffic will try to reach its destination via the nonbackbone router.

You may know that certain corporate destinations are not reachable from the Internet, so you might implement a policy to prevent such traffic from going outside. This can be done either with destination address filters on the nonbackbone router or with blackhole routes on that router. These blackhole routes must not be imported into OSPF.

Blackhole Routes

In practice, *blackhole routes* are very commonly used in ISP operations. The static route is announced to the general Internet, and attracts traffic to any address in your CIDR block. Once the traffic reaches the router, there are more specific routes in the routing table of that router. If any of those internal routes go up or down, information about them is not propagated into the general Internet, increasing the stability of the global routing system.

Here is an example. An ISP is assigned 10.1.0.0/16. Create a static route (using Cisco notation):

```
ip route 10.1.0.0 255.255.0.0 null0
```

and import it into BGP. Using directly connected and IGP-derived routes, make the router on which BGP runs aware of active, more specific routes to other destinations in the block, but do not redistribute them into BGP. BGP assigns four customer blocks, 10.1.0.0/24, 10.1.1.0/24, 10.1.2.0/24, and 10.1.3.0/24, and has more specific routes to these four customers. The customers are assumed to be single-homed, so the /24 never need appear on the Internet as long as the /16 is visible. The ISP only advertises the /16 to the Internet. If any of the sub-blocks go down, the failure is not advertised, thus avoiding forcing the other routers on the Internet to recompute their routing tables. The other routers still send traffic to, for example, 10.1.1.0/24 to the ISP boundary router. If that router has a specific route to 10.1.1.0/24, it sends the traffic there.

Assume, however, that the path to 10.1.1.0/24 happens to be down. On receiving a packet to this route, the router will find its route to 10.1.0.0/16 to be the best match, better than the default route. It will forward the packet to the next hop for the black hole, which will silently discard the packet. In other words, whenever a sub-block of the ISP's allocation becomes unreachable, the ISP will handle the issue gracefully (not air its dirty laundry to the world) and simply discard the traffic because it knows the problem exists. If 10.1.1.0/24 becomes unavailable, the rest of the Internet still sends to the border router, which silently discards traffic to the sub-block. No Internet Control Message Protocol (ICMP) or BGP withdrawals are generated. Eventually, either the sending application will realize the specific destination is down, or routing will come up and connectivity will automatically be restored.

Perhaps even more important than avoiding ICMPs, having the blackhole route allows your router a useful default route. If you did not have the blackhole route, the packet would match the default route to your upstream and be sent to the upstream in a loop that would end only when IP time to live was exceeded. Incidentally, if you traceroute to the destination, the traceroute will fail at the border router.

Looking Ahead

Once you learn to work with attributes, you can create intelligent multihoming. The next levels go into transit networking, first with full iBGP meshes (Chapter 10) and then with scalable iBGP using confederations or route reflectors (Chapter 11). Chapter 10 will also discuss customer multihoming strategies in which the proper solution involves both internal changes to the customer network and provider actions. Such strategies include mutual backup among multiple enterprises.

CHAPTER

10

Subscriber to Provider, and Subscriber to Subscriber Edge: IP

Ferguson's Law of Engineering: No amount of magic knobs will save a sloppily designed network.
—Paul Ferguson

186,000 miles per second. It's not just a good idea. It's the law.
—Seen on a button

In this chapter we are primarily concerned with getting user traffic into your POPs and with considerations regarding the placement of POPs. We will touch on some design and optimization techniques for POPs, but not the interconnections of your POPs by your intraprovider core or your connections to other providers. The provider also will need management communications to run its own services, and perhaps the closely related functions of outsourced customer management and web hosting or other value-added services.

Let's say you are a local provider filling a niche in a remote area. It is not a poverty-stricken area by any means, but simply far from major cities. Due to low labor costs, you have some enterprise customers of substantial size. You also support an assortment of residential and small business customers, including a few information-intensive teleworkers. Your community has local information resources, including a junior college and an endowed political think tank.

Telco patterns and geography dictate that you will need to concentrate access into several points of presence. The focus of this chapter is designing the POPs and associated capabilities. There will be significant discussion about protecting your infrastructure from customer errors or malicious attacks from the customer side.

Chapter 9 presented the customer side of the edge interface. Subsequent chapters will examine your intraprovider core and your connections to other providers. But what do your customers need? Their needs fall into several categories:

1. Residential and SOHO customers needing single IP addresses

2. SOHO customers with single subnets

3. Enterprise customers with basic access requirements for single or multiple prefixes

4. Enterprise and other customers with high-availability requirements, potentially including small ISPs

Let's start the process with the most basic kind of user and the first step in provisioning that user—taking the service order and converting it into a checklist of technical steps to be carried out. We will then examine the process for more complex user types.

Taking Orders

Orders originate in sales, and describe some form of user visible service—dial-up low-speed access, Internet connectivity for a single LAN, Internet and VPN connectivity for a complex enterprise, and so forth. You will need to make sure that a physical or virtual connection exists between the user and an appropriate POP(s). You must ensure that ports on routers or other devices in the POP are available and allocated to the user. To make a profit, and to avoid destruction, your accounting and security services must recognize the user and deny invalid users. For value-added services such as content caching, you must provision the desired higher-layer services.

A COMMON CUSTOMER MISUNDERSTANDING

It is unfortunately common for customers to complain that they don't see "full routes" at a point where they expect to do so. There can be many good reasons they do not, and they do not understand because they do not understand the theory and practice of BGP.

First, as part of the loop prevention design of BGP, a BGP router only passes on the routes it is actually using. The route the customer expects to see may indeed be known to a BGP speaker in your AS and available as a backup route, but may not be passed along to customer routers because it is not in active use. This is completely correct behavior. Second, the routes the customer is expecting may be present implicitly as parts of aggregates.

Provisioning

Before any data can flow, resources need to be assigned, passwords or other identifiers need to be distributed, and accounting needs to be set up. This general process is called *provisioning*. From Goralski & Kolon, *IP Telephony* [2000]—discussing OAM&P—"When asked about the *P* for Provisioning, a Bell Labs engineer replied, 'Provisioning determines when a customer can be billed for the link, so it's important enough to deserve its own letter in this country.' "

Single-Address Users (Type 1)

Assume you are a basic ISP with dial-up access and a single upstream provider. At a minimum, you will have to assign user identifiers and passwords to your users and give this information to the users—making sure you are giving it to the real users.

Even when users establish connectivity through Ethernet broadband access, the ISP will almost certainly see PPP frames delivered for each user. The IP Control Protocol part of PPP handles the basic login management and address assignment. For some providers, the alternative to PPP is to use DHCP to assign the address, but I generally find PPP coupled with Remote Authentication Dial-In User Service (RADIUS) to be more scalable and flexible. I freely agree that this can be a judgment call in some networks. See "AAA and Security Functions in the POP" later in this chapter.

You will need to enter the user identifier and password information into your authentication server(s), which will also perform the *authorization* function: specifying what the user is permitted to do. For example, as part of anti-spamming efforts, many dial access providers will not accept Simple Mail Transfer Protocol (SMTP) traffic from a dial-up user unless its destination is a mail server under the control of the provider or some other form of authentication has validated the user right to use SMTP.

It's quite reasonable to make basic user provisioning a standard procedure, with, at a minimum, paper forms. Building an automated order-taking interface usually gives a very substantial return on your investment by reducing the cost of training order-takers and improving the efficiency of their work.

SOHO (Type 2)

Things become more complicated when provisioning service for SOHO and large enterprise customers. For one thing, security policies become more complex. A given SOHO user may need access to both the public Internet and one or more VPNs. Again, standardized procedures can form the basis for many of these customer provisioning functions. A rather basic function needed for dedicated, but not switched, access is to identify the customer's connection and associate it with an appropriate interface on one of your POP routers. This connection could be a physical link such as a T1, a physical multiplex channel (either TDM or optical), or a logical connection such as an L2TP tunnel. If the latter, see Chapter 7.

Assigning users to physical or logical ports is a function that lends itself to being automated in order to speed workflow and avoid errors. Having broadband wholesalers (for example, cable or DSL) between the ISP and the end customer introduces at least one, and possibly more, levels of administrative coordination. Wholesalers rarely deal with the end user, so you will have to send the appropriate wholesaler a request to connect the end user to your service. Depending on the technology involved, the wholesaler may directly determine the feasibility of connecting to the user. This would be the normal practice for IP over cable. If the end user already has cable service, the hookup can be very fast—indeed, many cable providers support *self-installation*, in which the cable provider simply ships a cable modem to the end user along with instructions on how to connect it to the existing television cable. If the user does not have existing cable service and it is not available in the neighborhood, there may be construction delays or the wholesaler may decline the service. Different broadband providers have different practices. I recently installed IP over cable after finally giving up on DSL as far too unreliable. The cable provider did bundle an ISP service with the connectivity service, but did not object to me using my primary ISP. Giving credit where credit is due, Comcast of Arlington, Virginia, did an excellent job. While my main cable entrance is in my living room, my data equipment is primarily in another room. The technician was quite willing to run additional coaxial cable so the modem could be installed where it was needed, rather than making Ethernet connectivity to the modem my problem.

When DSL is involved, the DSL provider may, in turn, need to order a local loop from the ILEC. Even if the DSL service is provided under the corporate umbrella of the ILEC, the divisions may be quite separate from an administrative standpoint. A potential nightmare for ISPs is when the first-mile provider uses the CPE MAC address for authentication. Especially when this MAC address is on a computer network interface card (NIC) and the NIC is changed, you may see a sudden security shutdown of the service. To make matters worse, since you, as the ISP, do not have physical access to the CPE, you have no way to know the MAC address has changed. Higher-layer authentication functions tend to be far more flexible.

Single-Homed Enterprise Access (Type 3)

In this context, *single-homed* does not preclude enterprises that have multiple sites connected to you. The restriction of single homing here is that any given site has only one way to reach a single service provider. Enterprises of

ORIGINATING DEFAULT

In nonmultihomed situations (possibly excluding single-homed large enterprises) the ISP normally will act as the external gateway. There may be an on-site router that points to the ingress provider router; or, if the customer simply has layer 2 connectivity, the provider router will originate default.

When the customer uses DHCP, DHCP is quite capable of telling the customer what default router address to use. But the default router is not necessarily equivalent to the default route distributed into an enterprise customer network. Assuming the provider has a BGP connection to the customer site router, the ISP certainly can originate BGP default. However, a key thing to remember is that the BGP default need not be the same as the IGP default. Indeed, there can be multiple levels of IGP default in hierarchical customer networks. For example, a very reasonable customer router configuration, might use the provider BGP default as its own default but have explicit routes to other customer sites reachable by dedicated circuits. That customer router simply advertises the default route into the enterprise cloud. Other enterprise routers do not need to know if the external gateway router uses a higher-level default learned from BGP or explicit routes to other sites.

In Figure 10.1, the ISP advertises default to the enterprise gateway. That gateway router also has static routes to specific extranet partners. As long as the more-specific static routes are available, the traffic will go via the dedicated path, not the Internet. If the enterprise uses OSPF, you can develop fairly sophisticated multihoming by using different default route types (for example, external type 1 versus external type 2) and different default route metrics.

any appreciable size will need dedicated connectivity of a bandwidth appropriate to their requirements. Even at a single site, they are apt to have more than one IP subnet, so a routing function will be needed even if outsourced to the provider.

When the connectivity uses a medium that supports layer 2 separation of subnets, such as metro Ethernet VLANs, it may be cheaper in customer site equipment and easier to administer if the CPE/CLE is a VLAN-aware switch and the actual routing is done at the POP. If you do customer internal routing at the POP, prudence dictates that the customer-specific routers be separate from the main ISP routers, although virtual routers may meet this requirement.

Our basic assumption is that the enterprise connects to you for Internet access. Intranet and extranet VPNs are discussed in Chapter 13. If the customer already has address space, you need to include it in your routing system and administrative address management (see Chapter 5). Customers may want you to run addressing or naming servers. Depending on the technical experience

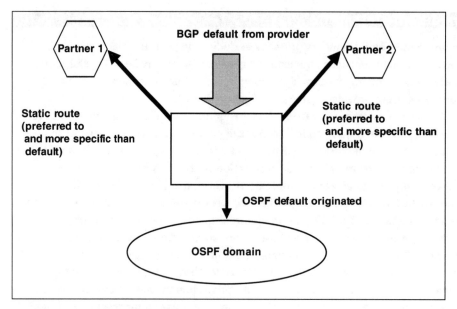

Figure 10.1   Internal and external default.

and staffing of the customers, the servers they are most likely to want you to run, in order of highest to lowest preference, include:

1. Primary DNS.

2. Secondary DNS.

3. DHCP, possibly with dynamic DNS linkage.

Having the ISP run such servers does not eliminate the necessity of having backup servers at the customer site, to ensure that the customer's internal operations do not stop if it loses connectivity to you.

Multihomed Enterprise Access (Type 4)

In this discussion, *multihoming* means that individual customer sites have more than one way to reach either multiple POPs of the same ISP or POPs of different ISPs. Provisioning this sort of user simply does not lend itself to automation, and the engineering considerations are detailed later in this chapter in many case studies.

You will still have basic provisioning functions, such as assigning a given user circuit to a specific router port in a POP. The routing aspects of such users, however, will need careful design. From a business standpoint, consider the costs of this engineering time, and whether it should be charged to cost of sales or be billed to the customer.

AAA and Security Functions in the POP

Authentication, of course, is the first part of *authentication, authorization, and accounting* (AAA). One of the first requirements of the access point—be it a dial port in a POP, a port in a wholesaler media gateway, and so on—is to authenticate that a given connection attempt actually comes from a legitimate user. This is especially important for services involving mobile users, such as dial and cellular services. It is still a consideration for shared-medium services such as cable, and even may be needed for services, such as xDSL, that have hard-wired local loops. The latter is needed for the same reason that a telephone subscriber can have service canceled, but the LEC does not tear out the copper pairs to the subscriber location. Just checking whether service is authorized is sufficient.

Authentication

With the standard IETF mechanism, the RADIUS architecture is used for authentication. While there are definitely IETF standards for RADIUS, there also are many proprietary extensions, so be careful that you do not create interoperability problems with "added features."

RADIUS deals with the login, authentication, and authorization of user access to a protected resource. As shown in Figure 10.2, the host accessing the resource begins by submitting a login request containing a user identifier. Conceptually, the access server forwards the user ID to the RADIUS server, which responds with a challenge for authentication. In practice, the login message often contains both factors of the authentication process. If authentication succeeds, the RADIUS server sends a permission message for the access server to grant access. Access may be a simple permit/deny, or include authorization information—more fine-grained detail on what the user is allowed to do.

TWO-FACTOR AUTHENTICATION

The best current practice in authentication is to use what security experts call *two-factor authentication.* The first factor is who the user purports to be, and is usually a logon ID. The second factor is "something you know," "something you are," or "something you have." Things you know are most commonly passwords, which may be reusable or one-time. Things you are include biometrics (for example, fingerprint or retinal scans) of the user, or perhaps the location associated with dedicated access (which does not, of course, imply that the authorized user is making the access). Things you have include hardware-generated authentication tokens such as Security Dynamics' SecurID product, or a list of one-time passwords.

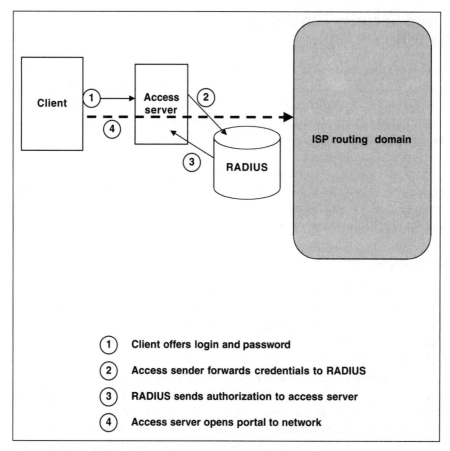

Figure 10.2 Authentication flow.

Dynamic Address Assignment

While IPCP can assign or confirm an address assignment, it cannot send the default router or DNS address, subnet mask, maintenance termination unit (MTU), and so on. This additional information can come from DHCP or RADIUS. IPCP packets have a client address field into which the client either places an address it proposes or the value 0.0.0.0 to indicate it wishes the PPP remote-access server (RAS) to assign an address for this particular connection (see Figure 10.3). As part of the PPP connection negotiation, the RAS can authenticate the requesting user's ID. In practice, this authentication uses the Challenge-Handshake Authentication Protocol (CHAP) subprotocol of PPP. CHAP sends a random challenge string to the requesting client, which the client encrypts and sends back to the RAS, along with the user ID. If the RAS, or a RADIUS server to which it acts as a proxy, correctly decrypts the encrypted challenge, the connection is permitted.

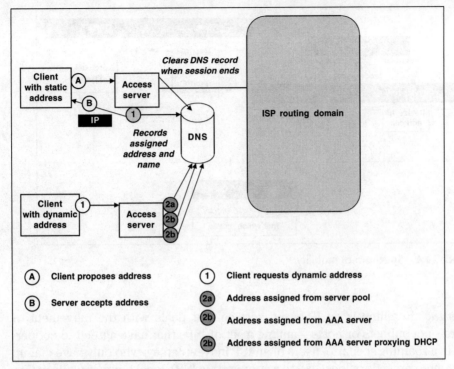

Figure 10.3   How PPP clients get their addresses.

Mobility

Mobility spans a wide range of requirements, some of which are appropriate POP services and some of which are not. The simplest possible illustration is one of your dial-up users calling into a local POP. Figure 10.4 shows a range of additional mobility services. Even within the simple dial-up function, there are several possible mobility mechanisms:

1.   Simple terminal applications, such as credit card authorization, which do not have general IP capability. The terminals connect, possibly via the PSTN, to a purpose-built application gateway.

2.   Remote access to workstations, as with PC/Anywhere or Timbuktu. The user appears at the IP address of the workstation.

3.   Entry into the full enterprise network as an IP host with a dynamically assigned address.

We have already discussed basic authentication, with the added complexity that the authentication server may not be physically at an access wholesaler POP. However, there are higher layers of mobility, the first of which is called

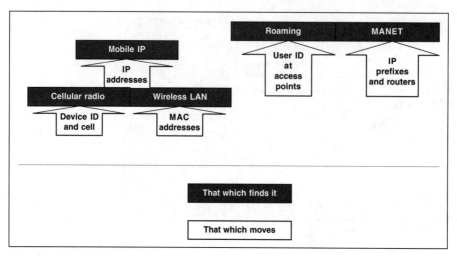

Figure 10.4 Spectrum of mobility.

roaming. Roaming is an IP-based service that deals with the movement of users—not subnets or hosts—among a set of ISPs that have agreed to cooperate. In a roaming scenario, users of an ISP in New Jersey, who only have dial-up accounts, can make a local call to a cooperating ISP's local number while in California. The California ISP forwards the authentication request to the home ISP, and, based on the home ISP's response, grants or denies access. The remote ISP may also cut accounting records if roaming access is subject to a surcharge. Practical roaming services have *phone book servers* from which roaming users can retrieve lists of local access numbers.

Even more advanced mobility services, the needs for which are still emerging, include wireless LANs, third-generation wireless, and mobile routers.

Additional Security

Users may want to go through mutual authentication with servers in order to ensure that they are not talking, for example, to an unknown server masquerading as their bank. Two-factor authentication can obviously go in the other direction. Another related area is authenticating indirectly through encryption. If a user can establish public key communications with a service, and the service can verify the user's public key and identity through a trusted public key infrastructure, that effectively authenticates the user.

It is quite natural, as long as authentication has been done, to provide other value-added security functions at the access point. Such services include provider-operated firewalls, encryption of Internet services, and VPNs (see Chapter 13).

Accounting and Billing

At the very least, the accounting function of AAA should record login attempts (both successful and unsuccessful). The most common means of recording this information is the UNIX-derived syslog protocol.

How much information about the login attempt should you record? How much information should you record about what the user does once logged in? The answers to these questions quickly involve legal and ethical as well as technical questions and often differ on a country-by-country basis. Users generally have an expectation of privacy, but, as a service provider, you have a right to maintain information that may help you troubleshoot your services. Troubleshooting can include detection of malicious hackers. Law enforcement may have additional expectations, especially in view of rapidly changing legislation to deal with threats such as terrorism. A distinction is usually made between simple login/logoff records and recording the content of the user interaction. Even the latter includes distinctions such as capturing e-mail headers only versus capturing e-mail content. Providers must be familiar with their local rules for what is generally termed "lawful interception," including what can be requested with and without a police order.

Some European legislation proposes that service providers retain logs (or even traffic) for some period of months, so law enforcement can look for clues after they become involved. From a purely technical standpoint, such requirements may impose huge mass storage requirements for providers, with the appropriate degree of redundancy.

Accounting and billing include more benign business functions. When users are billed for connection time, you obviously need to track their connections. If connection cost is distance-sensitive, you need to track user destinations. If you have (or face upstream) tariffs that differ by time of day, they must be tracked and separated into the appropriate categories as well. Accounting also can be very useful in capacity planning. Analysis of traffic logs, even on dedicated lines, can suggest when the user has too little or too much bandwidth, and you can work cooperatively with the user in tuning bandwidth requirements. This may be an integral part of service level agreements, especially those that are valid only at certain volumes of user traffic.

POPs and Layer 2 Switches

A modern POP is quite likely to contain layer 2 switches as well as routers. Of course, many commercial products contain both routing and bridging functions. In metropolitan Ethernet environments or wholesale broadband access with Ethernet interfacing, it is quite common to use VLANs simply to separate customers multiplexed onto Gigabit or 10-Gbit Ethernet (see Figure 10.5).

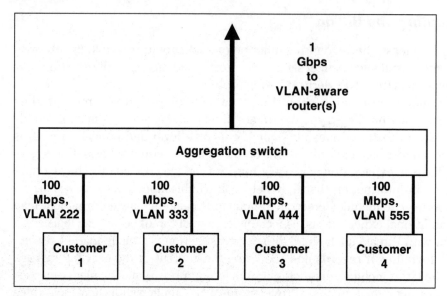

Figure 10.5 Metro Ethernet.

The switch used for this demultiplexing may be the same as the switch used for internal connection within the POP, or may be a different switch. You may need multiple switches simply to get enough ports, or because the port speed mixtures differ between the access problem (for instance, 100 Mbps concentrating to 1 or 10 Gbps) and the internal POP problem (for instance, primarily 1 or 10 Gbps).

A concern sometimes mentioned is that traffic from one user VLAN can somehow "leak" into the VLAN of another user. This is not plausible as a protocol error, but could happen due to misconfiguration. A well-tested automatic provisioning process should make this sort of configuration error extremely unlikely, but manual configuration can give me security jitters.

Demultiplexing Layer 2 Access Services

WAN switches (for example, ATM or Frame Relay) may be appropriate for demultiplexing from a groomed local provider cloud (see Figure 10.6) or for interconnections either in the core or to other providers. POPs are likely to contain multiple routers, as well as infrastructure servers for AAA functions, DNS and possibly content caches, and access servers. Interconnecting these components is a good application for a layer 2 switch, especially with VLAN capability. Indeed, multiple switches may be needed, even ignoring the requirement for failover.

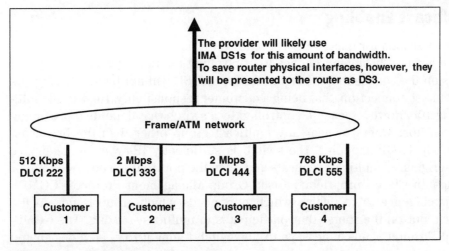

Figure 10.6   Groomed subscriber access.

POP Internal Backbone

Layer 2 switches can be very useful in interconnecting components in the POP, even if their intelligence is no greater than that of a remotely programmable patch panel. Switches can be quite appropriate because concurrent transfers are quite common. Consider, for example, the AAA flow in Figure 10.7. One access server may be accessing the AAA server for authentication, but also accessing a core aggregation router for a different flow. Switching can give the impression of simultaneous communication with both "upstream" devices, the AAA server and the router.

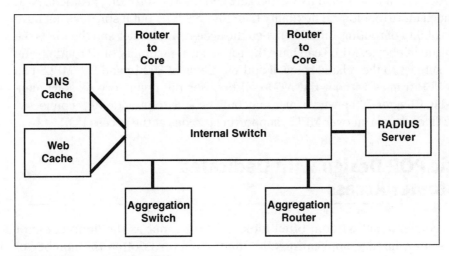

Figure 10.7   Intra-POP switches.

Multicast Enabling

Another reason for using switches at the POP is controlling multicast flows. There are two basic approaches to controlling multicast traffic to different hosts on the same subnet. In most cases, the ISP will not be involved in the direct host connection, that being a customer responsibility. Host-level multicast traffic, however, can be controlled by a switch that defaults to assuming that no host wants to hear any multicast group other than the broadcast group. In IGMP snooping, the switch is sufficiently IP-aware to recognize host-originated multicast requests and open the port to that specific group or groups. In Cisco's proprietary Cisco Group Management Protocol (CGMP), the intelligence to recognize which port needs which group is not on the switch, but on the router that participates in multicast routing. The CGMP-enabled router sends a message to the switch telling it to open a designated port to a designated multicast group.

Scalability with MPLS

It is also quite possible to have a switch encapsulate VLANs into MPLS. Broadband and modem access wholesalers traditionally used Frame Relay or ATM, with one subscriber per virtual circuit, to connect customers to ISPs. With the increased use of metro Ethernet, VLANs appear to be a functional replacement for these virtual circuits, but they have some limitations. The VLAN identifier field in 802.1q is slightly larger than the DLCI identifier field in Frame Relay, but is considerably smaller than the ATM virtual path identifier (VPI)/virtual circuit identifier (VCI) field. VLANs also are a flat address space and do not have the merging capability of ATM.

Through techniques such as VP merging and the PNNI routing protocol, ATM has much more topological flexibility than FR or 802.1q, but it still does not have the flexibility of routing. MPLS between the access wholesaler and the ISP is the technique of choice. MPLS can have the topological flexibility of IP routing, and is not subject to the relatively small address fields of 802.1q and FR. MPLS can carry PPP frames without the ATM cell tax. For the regulatory reasons mentioned in Chapter 7, the wholesaler may only be able to provide PPP connectivity. L2TP can also run over MPLS, supporting proxies at the access POP.

Basic POP Design with Dedicated Customer Access

While conventional wisdom often looks at throughput as the limiting factor for a router, in edge applications the limiting factor is often the number of interfaces the router supports. The first level of interface limitation is physical: the simple number of ports that can fit on the router chassis. It might seem that being able to groom traffic onto physical interfaces would alleviate the problem, but current router operating systems still cannot deal with huge numbers of software-defined interfaces. Using NBMA, point-to-multipoint topologies can help, but the reality is that, to have thousands of interfaces available at a POP, you will need to have multiple router platforms and connectivity among them.

Once IP packets arrive at the edge routers, they can be routed into a much smaller number of interfaces that connect across the provider core, to other providers, or to hosts (including caches) at the POP. Given that there will be multiple routers in the POP, and potentially traffic that stays local to it, there will usually need to be routing whose scope is limited to the POP. Such routing can use an IGP or BGP. While small POPs can use full mesh iBGP, there are an assortment of reasons to use iBGP scalability techniques such as route reflectors and confederations. Let's examine the general topic of iBGP scalability and then discuss IGP routing that is appropriate for POPs.

Intra-POP Routing

It is common practice to run an IGP—usually ISIS or OSPF—in the POP, as well as running iBGP. The purposes of the IGP include fast convergence within the POP, route summarization, and making fine-grained decisions on metrics. POPs and the ISP core generally communicate with iBGP, although each POP and the core may also be independent IGP domains. Some designs either use two-level IGP hierarchy completely inside POPs or treat the core as an IGP backbone. See Chapter 11 for considerations of core routing.

IGPs for POPs

In networks of reasonable size for POPs, ISIS and OSPF can reconverge in times on the order of low numbers of seconds. By adjusting timers and other parameters, they can often be tuned to converge in 3 s or so, which is often adequate for enterprises running timing-sensitive protocols such as IBM System Network Architecture (SNA).

While ISIS historically is more popular in the core (see Chapter 11), OSPF has offered some features that are attractive for POP applications. Recent updates to ISIS may make the difference less important, and we may see a trend toward making OSPF the primary enterprise IGP and ISIS the primary ISP IGP. OSPF has some functionality that can be quite useful in complex enterprise routing, whereas ISIS has demonstrated excellent scalability in the ISP environment. Especially when multihoming involves complex intra-enterprise routing as part of the solution, definitely encourage customers to use appropriate

OSPF features such as type 1 and type 2 externals. See Chapter 9 for non-BGP multihoming strategies.

RIP has limited utility for small customer networks. With respect to the POP, it is really a signaling protocol to help the customer hosts find their default gateway. Generally, I discourage the use of RIP in any way between customer and provider, but you may be forced to use it in some accounts. See "Routing Security Branches from Inappropriate Use of RIP" later in this chapter for some security holes that RIP can produce. I cannot think of any justification to use RIP as the intra-POP routing protocol.

iBGP in the POP

iBGP does not scale well, because both TCP and per-peer policy are processor intensive. Depending, of course, on the processing power of the routers, conventional routers tend to dislike more than 20 to 30 busy BGP sessions and to become extremely upset at 100 (see Figure 10.8). There are two main ways to improve iBGP scalability: route reflectors and confederations. The peer group technique, discussed in "Peer Groups" later in this chapter, is sometimes useful in scaling iBGP. A related scalability feature is whether or not to enable synchronization. Chapter 11 discusses the use of route reflectors and confederation in the provider core that interconnects POPs. The emphasis here is on POP applications.

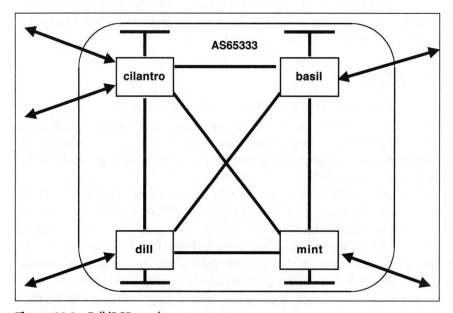

Figure 10.8   Full iBGP mesh.

Route Reflectors [RFC 2796]

Route reflectors are one of two basic approaches for reducing the number of iBGP peers internal to an AS. Traditionally, iBGP speakers peered in a full mesh, which does not scale well beyond 20 to 30 peers per router. With route reflection, a given router either is a route reflector client or a route reflector. Clients, typically edge routers, peer only to the route reflector(s) inside their cluster. A cluster can contain more than one reflector for reliability; the reflectors must connect to each other.

Implementing Basic Route Reflectors

A cooperating set of route reflectors and clients is called a *cluster*. The clients should establish iBGP peering only with the reflector(s) in their clusters, not with all iBGP speakers in the AS. For the topology in Figure 10.9, you must be sure that the clients have iBGP connectivity to the reflector but not to each other. Both the clients and the reflector are free to have eBGP connectivity with any outside AS.

BGP generally uses the path vector algorithm to reject updates that contain loops. It does so by dropping any eBGP update that arrives containing its own autonomous system number as part of the AS path in the update. Additional mechanisms are needed to prevent loops in route reflection. For the basic case of a single reflector, routes generated by the reflector contain an *originator ID* attribute, which contains the router ID of the reflector. The reflector will discard any routes it receives that contain its own originator ID.

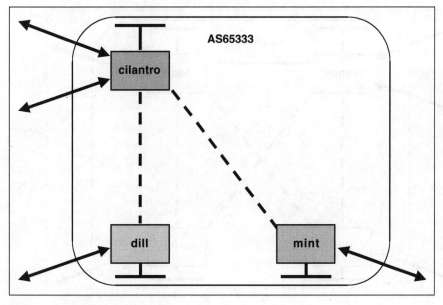

Figure 10.9   Basic route reflection.

> ### A CAUTION FOR ROUTE REFLECTION
>
> **Route reflectors summarize the routing information they gather, and only give their clients what the reflector believes to be the best path. It is possible, therefore, that the route given to a client is not the optimal route that the client router would find if it were not in a cluster but was fully iBGP meshed. In practice, this may not be a significant problem, as long as there are no routing loops. See [RFC 2796] for a discussion of alternative ways to make reflected route selection consistent with full mesh selection.**

Multiple Reflectors and Cluster IDs

To avoid a single point of failure, a cluster can have more than one reflector (Figure 10.10). Loop prevention then becomes more complex, because a reflector needs to drop an update received from outside the cluster if the update originated with another reflector in the same cluster. Cluster lists are the additional loop prevention mechanism needed in a cluster that has more than one reflector. All reflectors in the cluster need to have the same cluster ID.

Confederations

Communities define sets of routes. *Confederations* (Figure 10.11) define sets of ASs, but with the additional connotation that all but one AS are hidden

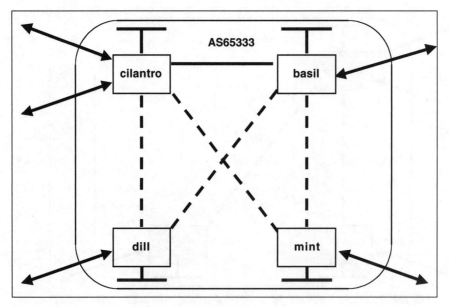

Figure 10.10   Multiple reflectors in a cluster.

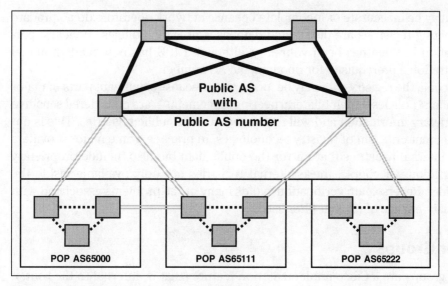

Figure 10.11   Confederations used for POPs.

from the Internet. In Chapter 9, we introduced well-known communities used for scoping advertisements. Confederations use an additional well-known community, LOCAL-AS, which has the well-known meaning that the route is not to be advertised outside the local AS. In other words, it has a more restrictive scope than the NO-EXPORT community, which specifies that the route is not to be exported from the confederation.

POP Design for Dial-up and Other Switched Access

As we discussed in Chapter 7, the user connection terminates either directly on an access server you operate or on an access server operated by an access wholesaler.

Scalability Issues: Protecting the Routing System

Registry Level

Routing registries have long been controversial as operational components of the global routing system. There are two principal concerns. First, the registry data may be inaccurate or incomplete because network operators do not update it. Routing registries are distributed databases of RPSL policies. Typically, participation in them has been voluntary, although RIPE has now made minimal registration a prerequisite for obtaining an AS number.

Second, the registry data may be incomplete because significant parts of major providers' policies—their bilateral peering agreements—are considered sensitive proprietary information and will not be recorded in public registries. This is not an inherent criticism of registry technologies. In practice, some major providers have internal registries that mirror the public data but also include proprietary information. Of course, these internal registries are only available inside the provider. Reverse path verification avoids many of the problems associated with the maintenance of explicit filter lists.

Peer Groups

Peer groups are a Cisco implementation feature (that is, internal to the router, not a protocol extension) that have benefits for both configuration and performance. Let's say you are an ISP with a group of customers, and you have the same policies with all of them. If you repeated the policies for each interface, you would need to traverse the policy information base each time you sent updates to your customers.

Conceptually, to advertise, the router must traverse the BGP Adj-RIB-Out for each interface, even though many Adj-RIB-Outs may be identical. Doing so costs memory for storing multiple copies of the same information and costs processor resources for computing the same update multiple times.

A side benefit of using peer groups is that the policies only need to be written once. Of course, nothing is free. The updates computed for a peer group will contain the same next-hop value, so peer groups only make sense when you have several peers on the same interface. Topologies that meet this criterion are more likely to be found in eBGP than iBGP.

Routing Security Breaches from Inappropriate Use of RIP

Bad ISPs, however, do not filter. Really terrible ISPs not only do not filter, but also announce your routes to the rest of the Internet. Figure 10.12 shows a truly terrible, yet real-world, example of what happens when ISPs are not careful to filter—and, even worse, when enterprises are not careful when using RIP as a tool for router discovery. This enterprise has an Internet access policy that requires the approval of three vice presidents before a firewall account will be set up for an employee. Ivan has such an account, but Toshiro does not. Both Ivan and Toshiro use UNIX workstations that are connected to their local router

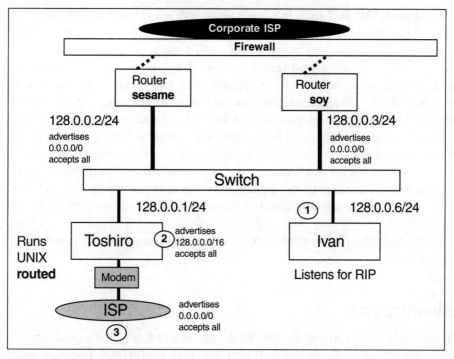

Figure 10.12 Dangers of RIP.

by Ethernet, and these workstations run *routed*, the UNIX RIP daemon, as part of the standard configuration (one of the dangers of blindly using the default installation). The corporate backbone, which uses RIP routing, is on Gigabit Ethernet and the firewall connects to the corporate network with an OC-3 POS. Ivan routinely gets excellent performance on Internet access.

Toshiro's pointy-haired boss orders Toshiro to have a project done in one week or be fired. The nature of the project requires Internet access, but two of the three VPs will be on vacation all week. To save his job, Toshiro personally purchases a cheap modem and an ISP account and connects his workstation to his ISP without disconnecting from the Ethernet.

Ivan, at point 1, is the first to realize that something, somewhere, is wrong. The standard behavior of most UNIX systems is to become a RIP router as soon as a second interface is enabled unless routed is specifically configured as passive. Ivan's workstation sees Toshiro's router advertising one hop to Internet destinations, while the path to the corporate firewall has three hops. Under RIP's rules, Ivan's workstation goes to the closest router, which has a dial-up-speed Internet access rather than an OC-3.

At point 2, Toshiro's router is advertising the corporate network to his ISP. Without filtering, even if the corporate network uses private address space, other customers of Toshiro's ISP have a backdoor entrance to Toshiro's enterprise, bypassing the firewall. If Toshiro's ISP, at point 3, redistributes RIP into BGP, it now tells the world in general that it promises connectivity to Toshiro's enterprise. These problems would be prevented if Toshiro's ISP filtered routes advertised to it, accepting only the prefix associated with Toshiro's dial-up. (This is an example of ingress route filtering.) Another point is that the backdoor access is inside the firewall, meaning an enormous security breach. This incident (and I have no doubt at all it has happened in the real world) confirms that intelligent cooperation is the key to effective security. Even among secret intelligence agencies, you will find philosophical differences. The CIA tends to stress employee understanding, while the NSA operates more on the assumption that "if we want your opinion, we'll tell you what it is."

Lack of understanding why leads to expedient workarounds with catastrophic consequences.

Authentication

BGP supports MD5 authentication. While this is not the world's most cryptographically strong authentication, it still provides protection. You may make the decision that all external routing announcements need to be authenticated, which puts the MD5 function on routers at the POP or interprovider border router (Chapter 12). Keeping authentication out of the core may minimize the workload and control complexity of core routers. The trade-off, of course, is that once a piece of traffic is inside your perimeter, it will not face further examination.

Prefix Limit

At the POP, the value of prefix limiting protects against malicious hacking involving the routing system, and also protects against configuration errors by multihomed enterprises. This approach is discussed in the interprovider context in Chapter 12.

Outbound Route Filtering and Graceful Restart

Outbound route filtering, introduced in Chapter 9, reduces both the bandwidth and acceptance processing loads on cooperating routers. In turn, this reduces the overall resource requirements for eBGP, helping avoid router crashes and inopportune withdrawals. Graceful restart also reduces the potential for inopportune withdrawals and the load on the overall eBGP system.

Scalability Issues: Protecting Routed Traffic

One hallmark of attempted malicious hacking is that the source address of hostile packets is spoofed, to prevent tracking the packets back to their real origin. Crackers rarely attempt denial-of-service attacks from their own hosts. Commonly, they dial into an ISP, insert code that then cracks another machine used as a launch pad, and repeat the process until the malicious code is on a machine with excellent high-speed connectivity. The actual attacks come from that machine. Even on the attacking host, however, crackers usually use a bogus source address to make finding the attacker more difficult. But that self-protective measure is a clue that an attack is under way.

Let's say the cracker breaks into a customer of yours that does not offer transit services. The customer uses the PA space of 96.1.0.0/23. No packet should originate from that customer that does not have a source address in 96.1.0.0/23.

Ingress Filtering and Reverse Path Verification

Let's distinguish between a security goal and alternate ways of implementing a solution for that goal. Ingress traffic filtering, in which an ISP accepts only those packets with source addresses in the range administratively associated with their customer, poses interesting philosophical problems. Such filtering does not directly help the ISP filtering on source addresses. If most or all ISPs filter on customer source address, however, the Internet as a whole gains considerable immunity to denial-of-service attacks by malicious hackers. Such an address prevents ISP defenders from tracerouting back to the attack source. Ingress source filtering will block these forged packets. Obviously, you could use basic packet filtering and deny any packet coming in on your interface to a customer that does not have a plausible source address. Depending on your router design, doing so may present scalability problems, both administrative and with regard to routing processing power.

If customers get additional address space assignments, your administrative process must include creating new filters that pass valid packets. Also, per-packet explicit filtering can be processor-intensive. A more scalable approach is called *reverse path verification*. In this method, you do not need to create explicit filter lists. Consider that a router routinely looks up the destination address in the routing table. In many router designs, it is relatively simple to add a function in the fast path where the router also looks up the source address in the routing table. If there is no path to the source address via any interface, you are almost certainly dealing with a bogus packet.

Especially when multihoming is involved, reverse path verification can get more complex. There are scenarios where the destination may be reachable through a different interface than the ingress interface. If the router uses distributed forwarding tables, it is possible that the particular interface might not have the reverse path. See Chapter 12 for a discussion of interprovider filtering.

Rate Limiting

If your router looks into the IP packet at least as far as the protocol type, you may see traffic types that if they occur in high volume, usually mean someone is up to no good.

The Role of Firewall Services

Firewalls should play little or no role in routing. Indeed, they should function as an "air gap" between internal and external routing (Figure 10.13). I'm often asked how to get routing protocol packets to pass through a firewall, but I'm very rarely presented with a plausible scenario as to why this is either useful or wise.

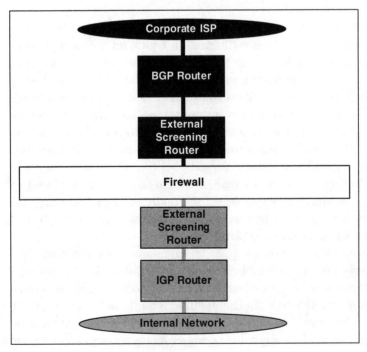

Figure 10.13   Firewall and routing.

IPv6

Do not assume IPv6 will be a panacea on the routing system. While the underlying structure of IPv6 address allocation could indeed improve aggregation among major providers, IPv6 customer multihoming is not a solved problem.

The Provider Side of Basic Customer Requirements

This section deals with an assortment of real-world requirements where the customer sites only connect directly to the provider. A later section will discuss cases where the customer has internal links that are integral to the overall fault tolerance solution.

Single Homing, Single Link

Your major requirement is being aware that the link is up, and, while it is, announcing the appropriate customer route into your POP. If it is PA space, you'll want to aggregate it in the POP before announcing it into your core.

If it is PI space, remember that it must be advertised to the Internet if it is routable. Unless the customer has its own autonomous system number, you will want to register the customer address space as a route object under your AS in a routing registry.

Single-Homed Multilink

Huffle, Puffle, & Cetera, if it accepts the proposal with two T1 lines, is a good example of this technology. There are no special IP routing considerations when using layer 2 multilinking. As the provider, however, you may need to consider the effect of multiple multilink bundles on your router resources, and possibly use alternatives.

On many commercial router implementations, multilink PPP is quite processor-intensive. Indeed, some implementations limit MLPPP to one bundle per router, which may be perfectly acceptable for the enterprise but decidedly not acceptable in the POP. If you have multiple bundles entering the POP, carefully evaluate the effect on the router.

Alternatively, there are various commercial outboard devices that aggregate multilink bundles and present a Fast Ethernet or DS3 interface to the router. Different bundles may be identified with different MAC addresses or Frame Relay DLCIs, so you can keep the different customers separated. As yet another alternative, you may use IP equal-cost load balancing among the various circuits. There are a number of algorithms for doing this, and their efficiency, processor load, and other effects vary with the router implementation. See the discussion of equal-cost load sharing in [Berkowitz 2000].

Multihoming to Single Provider Using PA Address Space: Provider Side

You'll want to aggregate the route advertisement associated with this customer. When you start planning your aggregation, however, you must be sure to distinguish the level of aggregation that is appropriate inside your network, as distinct to the aggregates you want to advertise to the Internet at large. Distinguish between customers being multihomed to multiple POPs and the interconnection (internal multihoming) of your POPs in relation to one another and to your core. If your POPs are multihomed in your core—and generally they should be—you should not aggregate too much when leaving the POP. By doing so, you may confuse your routing system about how to find an alternate path to the POP. It may be perfectly reasonable to aggregate customer addresses.

Multihoming to Single Provider Using PI Address Space: Provider Side

It's plausible that you would aggregate PI space as it leaves your AS, but you probably do not want to aggregate at the POP level. There are legitimate exceptions. For example, you might want to aggregate all the address space at a POP that is associated with dial-up servers. Such servers are unlikely to be involved in multihoming schemes. The Design and Dig case study, in fact, has an addressing plan that deliberately makes it impractical to aggregate at a given POP, whether it uses PA or PI space. Consider the Figure 10.14 variant of Design and Dig's setup. If each POP aggregated into your core with only the Design and Dig aggregate, the sites would not know how to reach one another, much less fail over.

Multihoming to Multiple Providers, Customer Uses Your PA Space

In this situation, you must announce the more-specific customer block as well as your main aggregate (Figure 10.15). You also should do some administrative coordination with the other providers involved and verify that all providers register the route object in their routing registries. Prudence dictates that you document the agreement, if any. Even if the customer has its own ASN, you will still generally want to specify it as part of your announcement policy. In any event, if you fail to advertise the more specific, none of your customer's traffic will return to you (Figure 10.16).

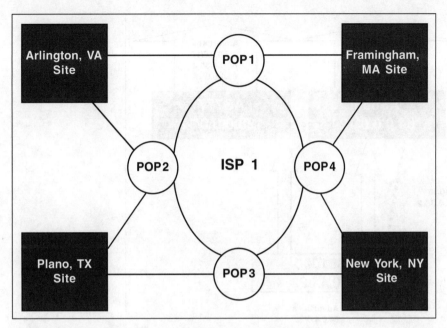

Figure 10.14 Inappropriate aggregation to a single provider.

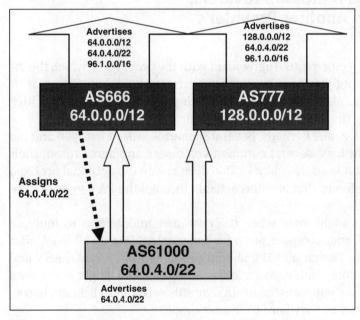

Figure 10.15 Multiprovider multihoming with your PA space.

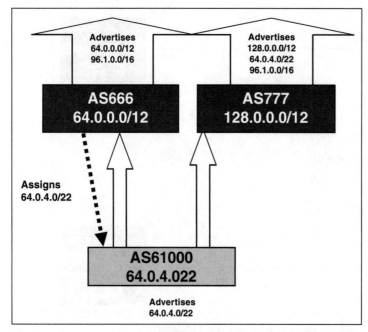

Figure 10.16 Inappropriate aggregation by one of a set of multi-homed providers.

Multihoming to Multiple Providers, Customer Uses Another Provider's PA Space

You should have a specific written agreement with the provider to which the PA space connects, giving you permission to advertise a more-specific on it. It would be wise to put this in your registered routing policy, perhaps even with a comment explaining the multihoming relationship.

Can you aggregate at all? Perhaps. Several scenarios arise. First, you and the other provider might have several common customers and agree to put their space in an aggregatable address block. This does create the potential problem of blackholing a customer that is still reachable through the PA owner (Figure 10.17).

Another situation might arise when the customer multihomes to multiple POPs of both the PA address space provider and your AS (Figure 10.18). Under these circumstances, Design and Dig should probably have its own ASN and register the policy. Conceivably, you and the other provider might agree on a private AS strategy that supports the desired multihoming, but I hesitate to recommend that as it may be very hard to troubleshoot.

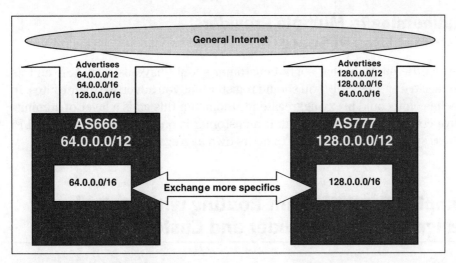

Figure 10.17   Mutual aggregation.

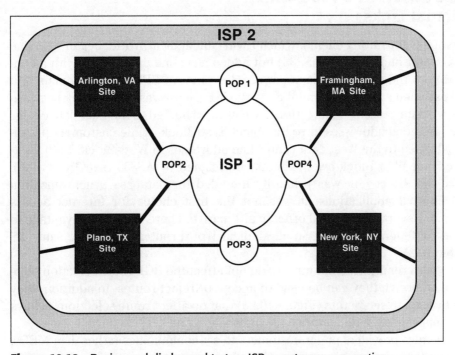

Figure 10.18   Design and dig homed to two ISPs: upstream aggregation.

Multihoming to Multiple Providers, Customer Uses PI Space

There's little question that such a customer should have its own ASN and its own registry entries. Still, you should register that you advertise their routes. In principle, you could proxy-aggregate for them, but this adds a layer of administrative complexity I would avoid. If a customer is qualified for an ASN and PI address space, it should be able to do its own aggregation.

Complex Fault-Tolerant Routing with Mutual Design between Provider and Customer

Up to this point, the external connectivity in our enterprises has always gone to the ISP. There are many situations, however, where internal enterprise links, and indeed BGP, may become an important part of the overall fault tolerance strategy.

Case Study: RFC 1998 with Internal Links

One of my consulting clients, which I will call Medical World, began with one data center and one ISP (AS333) but added a second data center with a connection to the same ISP. Each data center ran an OSPF routing domain and was assigned a private AS number by the ISP. There was a direct link between the two data centers (Figure 10.19). Customers homed to the East data center were assigned addresses in route object East-Block, while customers principally homed to the West data center had addresses in West-Block. Both East-Block and West-Block are in PA space assigned by AS333 (see Table 10.1). Since the direct link was primarily intended for database synchronization and internal applications, it was not the first choice for Internet access backup. Nevertheless, it did offer an alternative. There is no real advantage to using confederations here, so all Medical World routers are in the same AS (Table 10.2).

Just as a reminder, communities do not affect the BGP route selection algorithm, although they can be used to accept or reject routes. In addition, they can be used to set factors (Figure 10.20) that do affect route selection. Always remember that not all factors have the same scope.

Generally, providers prefer customers to set communities rather than MEDs, because the provider can set internal preferences as it desires rather than accept

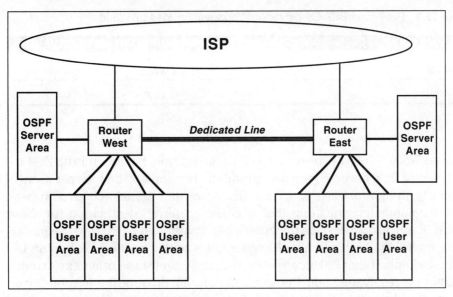

Figure 10.19   Medical world topology.

a numeric value from a customer. Especially in intercarrier operations, there may be specific conventions for values, as discussed in Chapter 12.

Let's see Medical World's logical interface configuration for enforcing the desired policies (Table 10.3), which uses communities to the outside and local preference inside. It could have used MEDs to the outside, but, again, most providers feel a loss of control from customer MEDs.

Router East has the mirror-image configuration of Router West and is not shown here. Some of the interesting things to note in Router West's policies are that local_pref is used on iBGP, and on eBGP information once it is accepted, but communities are used on eBGP. AS333, the provider, defines its community 100 to mean "set local preference to 100" and its community 500 to mean "set AS333 local preference to 500." The backup strategies for

Table 10.1   Policy Overview with Direct Link and One Provider

	INTERNAL		EXTERNAL	
DATA CENTER	**PREFERRED**	**BACKUP**	**PREFERRED**	**BACKUP**
East	Direct	ISP1 to West	ISP East POP	ISP West POP to Direct
West	Direct	ISP1 to East	ISP West POP	ISP East POP to Direct

Table 10.2   Per-Router BGP Configuration Worksheet for Medical World

AS NUMBER	ROUTER NAME (YOUR ADMINISTRATIVE ID)
64001	West
64001	East

Medical World's Internet users, as well as the Internet backup for the East-to-West server link, become increasingly subtle. Backup for the Internet users is relatively straightforward. Each site advertises its Internet access addresses with a community indicating that it is the preferred destination for these routes. Each also advertises the other's block, but with a much worse preference. Internally, each site has the other site's router as the next hop on the dedicated link. If that link goes down, the next hop for the other site's routes will not be resolvable, and the site will stop advertising the less preferred other side addresses. Backing up the link is more complex. Each site can advertise that it can reach the server farm at the other site, but its advertisements will show the private AS number as its origin. Without the provider stripping the AS number such that the carrier AS shows as the origin, the other Medical World site would reject the advertisement as containing its own AS in the path, a violation of BGP loop detection rules.

Private AS stripping is not standard, although available on several vendors' products. Another strategy might be to give different private AS numbers to both sites, although that certainly would interfere with an RFC 2270 strategy by the carrier.

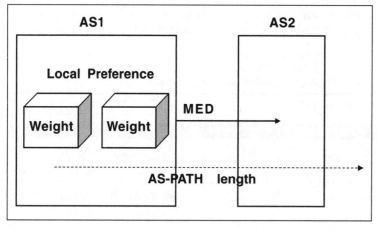

Figure 10.20   Scope.

Table 10.3 Per-Interface BGP Configuration, Medical World Router West

AS64001			
ROUTER WEST			
BGP INTERFACE ID AND IP ADDRESS	**NEIGHBOR**	**ADVERTISING POLICY FOR THIS INTERFACE**	**ACCEPTANCE POLICY FOR THIS INTERFACE**
Serial 0	ISP West POP	West-Block, communities 111:100, NO-EXPORT	Default
			East-server with private AS stripped, local_pref=200
		West-Server 111:100, NO-EXPORT	
		East-Block, communities 111:500, NO-EXPORT	
Serial 1	ISP East POP	West-Server, local_pref=500	East-Block, local_pref=100
			East-Server, local_pref=500

Case Study: Enterprise Providing Basic Transit

Assume you are Medium State University (MSU), AS111, with a limited role as a service provider to other state educational institutions. You have the connectivity in Figure 10.21, in which a commercial service provider, AS333, is the first choice for all external traffic. However, you do not want to offer transit to other customers of AS333. You can reach 96.0.0.0/16 in AS222, an ISP that connects to a corporate research facility with which you cooperate. The actual research facility has addresses in the 96.0.0.0/23 block, but its more specific addresses are not advertised to the public. In addition, you have a reciprocal backup agreement with AS444, another state's university. Finally, you are the primary service provider for AS555, another campus within your state system. You only want to provide connectivity for your own campus to AS222, although you would like to provide AS555 with 96.0.0.0/23 specifically through your direct connection to AS222. You are a little reluctant to provide connectivity to AS444, so you want to make the routes you advertise to AS444 less

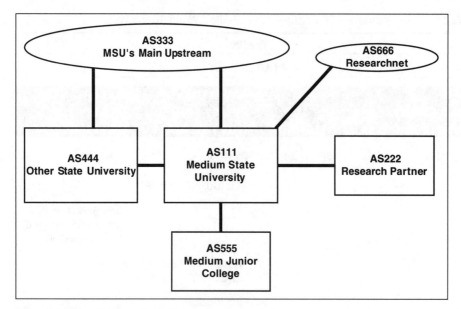

Figure 10.21 Medium State University connectivity.

desirable than routes to the same destination that AS444 can reach through its own link to AS333.

Table 10.4 shows details of these policies.

Note the conditional advertisement using the AS path expressions ^RES-AS* and RES-AS111 $. The start-of-path caret (^) means the route must be originated by a member of the set of ASs participating in the research community RES-AS. The terminal * is a wild card that means that acceptable paths include any that start in a RES-AS member. 111$ means 111 must be just before the end of the path.

To Confederate or Not to Confederate

Communities define sets of routes. Confederations define sets of ASs, but with the additional connotation that all except one AS are hidden from the Internet (Figure 10.22). They have applications both in complex enterprises and in POPs. Confederations have additional configuration information that distinguishes among the three kinds of peers:

- iBGPs.
- Confederation eBGPs.
- Regular eBGPs.

Complex enterprise topologies may need neither BGP nor confederations. My general experience is that confederations are more useful than route reflectors

Table 10.4 Per-AS Policies, MSU

		AS111	
		MAIN ROUTER	
CONNECTION	**DESCRIPTION**	**ADVERTISING POLICY FOR THIS INTERFACE**	**ACCEPTANCE POLICY FOR THIS INTERFACE**
AS333	Upstream	All 111 routes All 555 routes All community 666:1 ^RES-AS$	Accept all
AS222	Research partner—access to your customer routes	Community 666:1 ^RES-AS*	Accept community 111:1
AS444	Mutual backup, also AS333 customer	Advertise AS333 prepended Advertise own routes	
AS555	General access plus access to AS222	Advertise ALL	
AS666	Research net available to 111, 222, and 555 666 access available to 222 only via direct 666 link	Advertise research routes, community 666:1	Research routes, community 666:1

in enterprise backbone applications, but that the reverse is true for providers. The difference is that once you are inside an ISP core, you probably do not have a great many restrictions on what goes where.

Case Study: Intercontinental Enterprise without Confederations

It is wise to know when complex BGP is not the correct solution. This case study and the next deal with large multicontinental enterprises with different traffic models. They both needed backbones of backbones, but the complexity of the backbones differed radically.

Consider the case of Panacea Products, a pharmaceutical company (Figure 10.23). The enterprise operated in a very hierarchical manner. Regions had substantial internal traffic and communicated with the corporate headquarters.

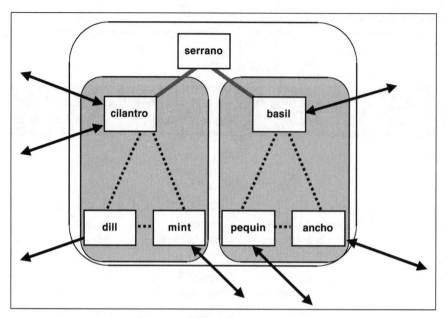

Figure 10.22 Confederation relationships.

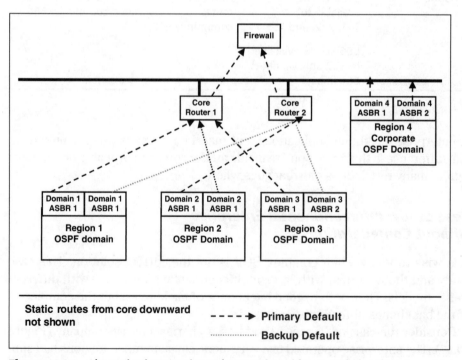

Figure 10.23 Alternative intercontinental enterprise without confederations.

The limited traffic exchange among regions could reasonably be accomplished on the headquarters backbone. The corporate data center and corporate site were treated as a separate domain that connected to the backbone, although they were at the same location. This was done to localize the substantial traffic inside the corporate site and to simplify the backbone. Alternate paths to corporate came from primary dedicated or frame relay links, with quasi-static ISDN routes for backup (see Table 10.5). This design will not be practical unless great care is taken to allocate addresses with a model based on regional aggregation. So, the routing became quite simple (see Table 10.6). Each region had two default routes, a dedicated link to one headquarters router and an ISDN link to a different headquarters router. The central site routers, in turn, had static routes to the regional routers. The central site always initiated the ISDN calls after detecting the failure of a dedicated link. This created a need for an IGP between the two central routers, so the router with the dedicated link to a given region could tell the dial-on-demand router when that link went down.

At this point, you may ask, reasonably, "But the customer solved the multihoming problems by itself. Why is this in a provider-oriented book?" The answer is that I did this design not directly for the customer, but for a major international provider. That provider could get major revenue simply for the dedicated and ISDN links required. By not trying to sell the customer complex provider routing that was not needed, the provider gained credibility and made the sale.

Table 10.5 Panacea Private Address Plan

REGION	ADDRESS RANGE
Headquarters and infrastructure	10.0.0.0/14
Americas	10.4.0.0/14
Europe	10.12.0.0/14
Asia-Pacific	10.16.0.0/14

Table 10.6 Static Routing for Panacea Headquarters

AGGREGATE	DEDICATED	ISDN
10.4.0.0/14	Router 1	Router 2
10.12.0.0/14	Router 2	Router 1
10.16.0.0/14	Router 1	Router 2
10.0.0.0/14	Router 2	Router 1

Case Study: Complex Long-Term Relationships

A different customer, an international shipping company I will call Rebel Express, really did have decentralized operations on several continents. There was a partial mesh of intercontinental links with different bandwidths and loading factors (see Figure 10.24). The company wanted considerable control over the intercontinental backup links taken. The degree of control Rebel Express wanted over backbone backup, plus the reality that the company connected to ISPs on different continents, necessitated BGP in the backbone. Route reflectors did not lend themselves to the desired degree of control, so this became an excellent application for confederations (see Table 10.7).

The enterprise really had redundant routers in each location, but these are omitted for clarity in understanding the underlying routing strategy. First, let's look at just the connectivity of the most highly connected router in the North American East site (Table 10.8).

Transcontinental North American and intercontinental Western Hemisphere bandwidth is cheaper than transoceanic bandwidth. Rebel Express wants the primary backups to follow the cheapest path, but still wants to ensure high availability even if a less desirable backup needs to be used. But this is the physical connectivity, not the order of preference in choosing paths. Assume

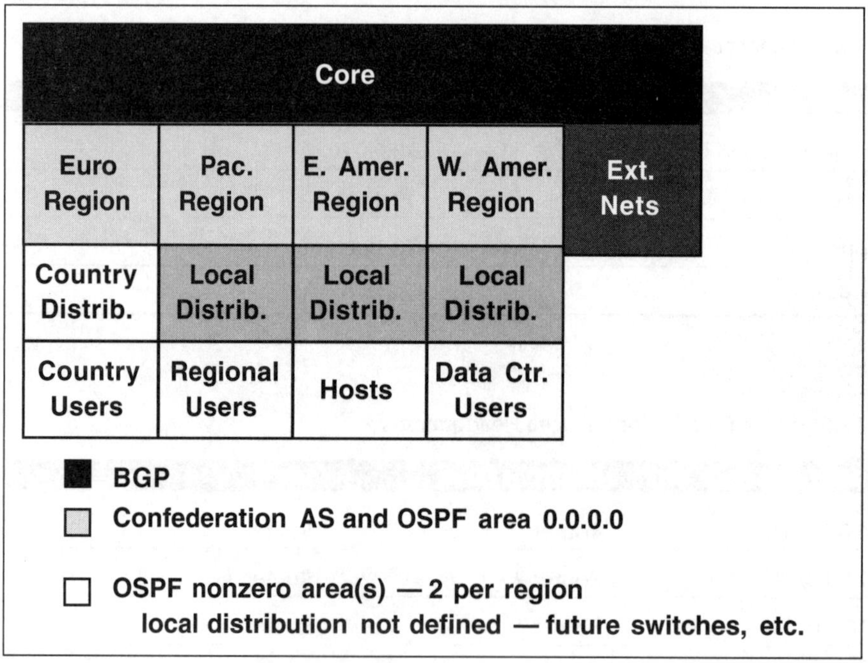

Figure 10.24 Rebel Express backbone.

Table 10.7   Autonomous Systems in Rebel Express Routing

AS NUMBER	MEANING
888	Registered AS
65001	European confederation AS
65002	Asia-Pacific confederation AS
65003	North America East confederation AS
65004	North America West confederation AS
65005	Latin America confederation AS
333	Western Hemisphere ISP
111	Eurasian ISP

there are no security concerns in routing traffic through the Internet, and see the goal in Table 10.9. How do we implement this goal? AS65004 tells its basic preferences to its neighbors using AS path prepending (Table 10.10). This is not the only way this could be done; communities could be used as an alternative, but this is meant as an example for the use of AS path prepending inside confederations.

Case Study: Confederations for Transition

For a different customer, which I will call Cosmopolitan Cosmetics, I recommended confederations be used as a transition mechanism after a merger. Each of the premerger companies had had its own ISP and private AS number (see Figure 10.25). Conveniently, the two private AS numbers were different. Both companies had /16 PI address spaces in the traditional Class B space. After the merger, Cosmopolitan still wanted to be homed to two ISPs. It also wanted to be flexible in the way it assigned addresses—no limitations of classful address space.

Table 10.8   Per-Interface BGP Configuration, External 1

BGP INTERFACE ID AND IP ADDRESS	NEIGHBOR
Serial 0	AS333
Serial 1	AS65001 (Europe)
Serial 2	AS65004 (North America West)
Serial 3	AS65005 (Latin America)

> **AN AUTHOR'S OBSERVATION**
>
> Would you really have expected me to have assigned the same private AS to both hypothetical companies if it made the case study more confusing?

The first step was to create an internal backbone, invisible at first to either ISP, and link the two ISPs by BGP (Figure 10.26). This first step was overseen by a manager who lacked a full understanding of the problem. It seemed like a good idea, and it worked quite well for the former Company A to reach Company B, and vice versa. Cosmopolitan thought it would automatically get mutual backup this way, but soon found this not to be the case, because it had not coordinated with the ISPs. Both ISPs involved did ingress filtering both on address and AS number (see Table 10.11). AS333, for example, only accepted 128.0.0.0/16 source addresses from AS64001 on its connection, so it rejected announcements and packets from the former Company B. AS666 did the equivalent to the former Company A addresses. Still, the basic Company A connec-

Table 10.9   Logical Order of Preference to North America West

BGP INTERFACE ID AND IP ADDRESS	NEIGHBOR
Serial 2	AS65004 (North America West)
Serial 0	AS333
Serial 3	AS65005 (Latin America)
Serial 1	AS65001 (Europe)

Table 10.10   Policies for North America West

BGP INTERFACE ID AND IP ADDRESS	NEIGHBOR	ADVERTISING POLICY FOR THIS INTERFACE
Serial 2	AS65004 (North America West)	AS65004 routes
Serial 0	AS333	AS65004 routes with AS65004 prepended once
Serial 3	AS65005 (Latin America)	AS65004 routes with AS65004 prepended twice
Serial 1	AS65001 (Europe)	AS65004 routes with AS65004 prepended three times

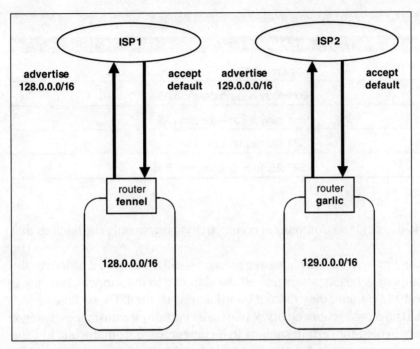

Figure 10.25 Cosmopolitan's topology before the merger.

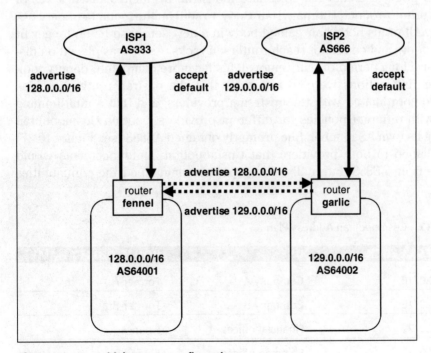

Figure 10.26 Initial merger configuration.

Table 10.11   Autonomous Systems in Cosmopolitan's Routing

AS NUMBER	MEANING
999	Registered AS
64001	Company A confederation AS
64002	Company B confederation AS
333	ISP1 AS, former Company A ISP
666	ISP2 AS, former Company B ISP

tivity worked, as did the Company B connectivity—it was only the backup that did not.

One of the first operational changes was to move all the financial offices to the former Company A headquarters and all the shipping to the former Company B site (Table 10.12). Again, they did not coordinate with the ISPs, so finance and shipping had no outside connectivity. While under certain circumstances, it might be a security benefit for certain subnets to be unreachable from the outside, the situation here was that Cosmopolitan had its product shipping, accounts receivable, and accounts payable cut off from the world.

At this point, a somewhat fortunate industrial accident caused a vat of Cosmo's prime product, Ultimate Hair Body, to spill on the incumbent network manager. All of his body hair gained body in a new sense, so he no longer fit through doors and could not reach routers in racks. As he was placed on disability for a long period of hair removal, his far more competent deputy took over. Her first actions were to recognize that the desired routing policies had to be coordinated with the upstream providers, and that a multihoming system with different policies for different providers justified Cosmopolitan obtaining its own AS number. She promptly obtained AS888 (see Figure 10.27) and explained to both providers that Cosmopolitan announcements would originate from AS888. Internally, Cosmopolitan maintained the communities

Table 10.12   Cosmopolitan Address Plan

ADDRESS BLOCK	USE	ROUTE OBJECT NAME
128.0.0.0/16	Company A	Former-A
129.0.0.0/16	Company B	Former-B
128.0.4.0/22	Financial offices	Finance
129.0.8.0/21	Shipping offices	Shipping

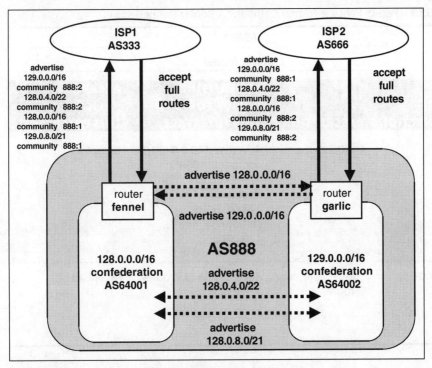

Figure 10.27 Proper confederation use with ISPs.

for the old classful blocks. Shipping and finance moved directly into the new registered AS.

A considerable amount of administrative coordination was necessary for the ISPs to handle the addressing changes. Cosmopolitan established community 888:1 to designate a primary route and community 888:2 to be a backup route, and suggested the ISPs set appropriate local preferences based on these communities (see Tables 10.13 and 10.14).

Service Level Classification and the ISP Challenge: When to Oversubscribe, When to Overprovision

Let's look again at Medical World. When the company added VoIP applications, it also added the complexity of ensuring that real-time traffic received priority handling in its provider backbone, at least when the provider linked it among its own sites and its customer sites. Medical World did not expect the provider to guarantee QoS to arbitrary Internet destinations.

Table 10.13   Per-AS Policies, Former Company A Router (fennel)

| | | AS888 | |
| | | **Router fennel** | |
CONNECTION	**DESCRIPTION**	**ADVERTISING POLICY FOR THIS INTERFACE**	**ACCEPTANCE POLICY FOR THIS INTERFACE**
AS333	Upstream 1	Advertise 129.0.0.0/16 community 888:2; 128.0.4.0/22 community 888:2; 128.0.0.0/16 community 888:1; 129.0.8.0/21 community 888:1	Accept all
AS64001	Former company B routes	Advertise AS333 routes; 128.0.0.0/16 community 888:1; 129.0.8.0/21 community 888:1	Accept all

Table 10.14   Per-AS Policies, Former Company B Router (garlic)

| | | AS111 | |
| | | **Router garlic** | |
CONNECTION	**DESCRIPTION**	**ADVERTISING POLICY FOR THIS INTERFACE**	**ACCEPTANCE POLICY FOR THIS INTERFACE**
AS333	Upstream 1	Advertise 129.0.0.0/16 community 888:1; 128.0.4.0/22 community 888:1; 128.0.0.0/16 community 888:2; 129.0.8.0/21 community 888:2	Accept all
AS64001	Former company A routes	Advertise AS333 prepended; advertise own-routes	

In this case, Medical World and its provider agreed on a community to mark the high-priority traffic. Initially, the community was used with the Cisco BGP policy propagation feature to set type of service (ToS) bits and use conventional router queuing mechanisms that recognized ToS. Eventually, the community became the identifier by which an MPLS label edge router assigned priority traffic to the appropriate traffic trunk. See Chapter 11 for a discussion of traffic trunks in the core.

Forwarding Equivalence Classes

Forwarding equivalence classes (FECs) are central to the (G)MPLS architecture, but I find them very useful in general routing design as well. Think of a FEC as a condition under which traffic can leave your routing domain. At a minimum, this will be a specific router interface. Huffle, Puffle, for example, has two FECs: the dedicated line and the PPP switched backup.

Another way to distinguish among FECs at a common physical interface is the QoS requirement for the traffic. In practice, this has to involve some sort of "coloring" of the traffic, such as a BGP community or settings of the Type of Service bits in the IP packet header. If Huffle, Puffle had some high-priority VoIP traffic that only could go out over the dedicated outline, the firm would have three FECs:

1. VoIP high priority on the dedicated router interface
2. Normal-priority data on the dedicated router interface
3. Normal-priority data on the switched router interface

Evaluating the traffic color, avoiding congestion, and so on are computationally intensive functions that do not lend themselves to core routers, whose main effort is forwarding. Classifying traffic into FECs is especially attractive as an edge function, because a practical topology of distributing POPs inherently creates a distributed processing environment. Many router processors can work in parallel to classify traffic. Once traffic is classified, an MPLS label edge router (LER) can assign it to an appropriately colored label-switched path (LSP). Not surprisingly, the edge of the provider network is in the POP, so that is the logical place for LERs to live.

The greatest impact of (G)MPLS appears to be in traffic engineering. Traffic engineering, however, is only one part of ensuring SLAs. Even the SLA is not the total answer to user-perceived performance, which certainly can be affected by enterprise network and host behavior. [Berkowitz 2000] contains a much deeper discussion of the enterprise-controlled aspects of this problem, but let us review some aspects here as a part of understanding what portions of quality are reasonably within the service provider scope. We also need to review where the provider should implement these parts. At the very least, some parts are appropriate to the edge while others are appropriate to the core. At the edge, we are often concerned with traffic policing, connection admission control, and so on. In the core, we are especially concerned with per-hop behavior (PHB).

What Interferes with Quality?

The user-oriented trade press, and much of enterprise router training, focus on the mechanisms of quality enforcement, such as queuing. This emphasis often leads to inadequate requirement specification or to specifying requirements that are unnecessarily expensive. Paul Ferguson [Ferguson 1999] has correctly observed that no QoS mechanism can repeal the speed of light. The speed of light in particular media, as well as the clocking rates of transmission interfaces, are basic physical phenomena. They lead, respectively, to *propagation delay* and *serialization delay*. In the presence of these physical delays, multiple devices contending for a common resource (for instance, the physical link between enterprise and provider) can produce congestion. Congestion causes *queuing delay*. When congestion causes traffic to be dropped, or if traffic is lost due to transmission errors, congestion can become even worse if the host response is to retransmit.

A medium's capacity is expressed in bandwidth (the number of bits per second it can carry). Media are not perfect. Bits do not move instantaneously across media, and media may have transmission errors that cause some bits to be lost. Often, the serialization delay in clocking bits onto the medium is the most significant, and most overlooked, part of total latency. Once the bits are on the wire, they must move along the wire to the destination. This propagation delay is the product of the speed of light in the specific medium and the length of the medium. For most terrestrial facilities, the propagation delay can be approximated as 6 ms per kilometer of airline distance between two reasonably distant points.

Remember that a fundamental principle of IP architecture is to place intelligence in the end host. TCP flow and error control, for example, do not directly interact at all with the router network. Relays (routers or switches) can buffer either on input (before the routing decision is made) or output. This discussion focuses on output buffering that takes place when the output WAN interface is busy (that is, the associated medium is congested). The time that a packet waits to be sent out a medium that is busy with other traffic is queuing delay. Queuing delay adds to transmission and propagation delay.

Buffering, or queuing, mechanisms have two parts. First, a *queuing algorithm* defines when traffic is placed in a queue rather than being sent to the original resource (for example, the output interface). A *scheduling algorithm* defines when to take traffic from a queue, and which queue to select if there is more than one. The closer they are to the end user, the more benefits buffers can provide. Interactive applications are *bursty*. There is human "think time" between queries and responses. Buffering can smooth these bursts, so by the time the combined traffic of many users hits the provider, the aggregate traffic stream is statistically much more regular.

I consider it consistent with this IP design principle to concentrate on buffering in customer side routers rather than in the POP. It's a matter of economy of scale—relatively little additional memory may be needed in the customer router, but if provider edge routers had to have significant buffering for all of the customer interfaces, memory cost might rise astronomically. See [Berkowitz 2000] for a discussion of buffering in customer hosts and routers.

Provider Management of Incoming Traffic from the Subscriber

Often, the reality is that the physical medium connecting a dedicated-access subscriber to the POP has a much higher potential bandwidth than does the service the user ordered. For example, most frame relay implementations with speeds greater than 64 Kbps but less than 1.536 Mbps are connected by a standard 1.544-Mbps T1 line. Metropolitan optical Ethernet generally uses Gigabit Ethernet.

There is nothing wrong with using faster facilities, which indeed give the provider a great deal of flexibility if the user wants to upgrade service. Another advantage is the absence of rate-limiting requirements. If the bandwidth is lightly used (for instance, below 50 percent), it is quite likely no link-level congestion will occur and packets will never queue. The potential downside, however, is that the user may be able to send a burst at the speed of the link. Consider Figure 10.28, where, if all the users simultaneously sent at full burst rate, the upstream links of the POP would be overwhelmed. In a metropolitan area it may be very convenient to install Gigabit Ethernet links, but somewhere you will need to rate-limit.

There is a great deal of debate about where burst control should be placed in the customer network. Obviously, the safest method for the provider is to put rate control in the CPE/CLE. The disadvantage of doing this is that it increases the complexity of the CPE/CLE, and thus increases the cost of a widely deployed component.

If the high-speed links run directly between the user and a port on the provider's POP equipment, rate control can reasonably be implemented there, with decent economies of scale. When Ethernet is used, you very well may find front-end routers with cheaper switches that still can rate-control based on flow information.

Things become much more complex if you have an intermediate second-mile provider grooming traffic to you. In this case, the rate control realistically has to be in the CPE/CLE or in the access provider equipment. The access provider can rate-control at the local loop interface, or, less desirably, can oversubscribe its connection to you and drop traffic whenever capacity is exceeded. More

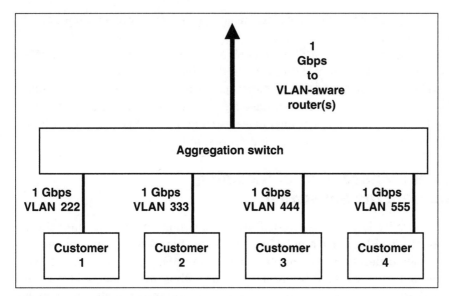

Figure 10.28 Bad burst business.

recent implementations, however, add capabilities of rate-limiting and traffic shaping, in which the fastest possible delivery is not the principal goal. The goal is for traffic to comply with a traffic specification (Tspec); if it is arriving faster than the Tspec, it needs to be slowed.

Scheduling Outgoing Traffic to the Core

Networking offers a great many opportunities for economies of scale. One of these tends to be core bandwidth. It often makes the best sense to overprovision bandwidth of core links in the interest of greatly simplifying the core routers.

As the industry moves toward specialized services, the trend is to traffic-engineer different MPLS LSPs for different service requirements. The LSPs terminate on different POP interfaces, or even different POP routers. By separating the service types, you avoid the complexities of mixed buffers for different grades of service.

Figure 10.29 shows a representative POP of one of my clients, which ran Fast Ethernet or sometimes Gigabit Ethernet to switches at its customers that were VLAN-aware. Each service (for example, the VoIP PBX or the customer Internet router) plugged into a different switch port and was assigned to a different VLAN. The POP switch aggregated VLANs of the same type and sent them to an appropriate label edge router. The LSPs leaving the POP and going toward the core were 10-Gbps Ethernet.

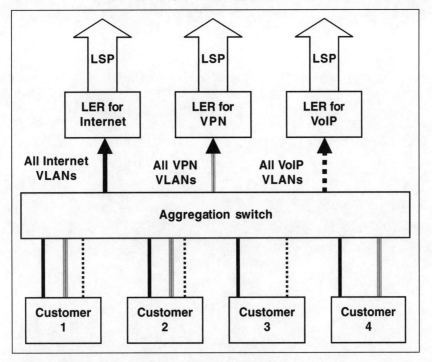

Figure 10.29   VLANs for different grades of service.

Looking Ahead

This chapter began with the problem of introducing edge traffic into the core or getting it to other providers that may not be connected to the same POP. It ends with the challenge of providing different grades of service for traffic leaving the POP for the core. The next chapter deals with the design of that core, as the core serves as the mirror for the POPs and interprovider border routers that connect to it.

The Intraprovider Core: IP/MPLS

Entities should not be multiplied unnecessarily.
—William of Occam

**Traffic engineering is the ability to move trunks away
from the path selected by the ISP's IGP and onto a different path.**
—Tony Li and Yakov Rekhter [RFC 2430]

**MPLS brings connection-oriented paths to connectionless IP, including
constraint-based routing, "automagic" tunnels and traffic engineering.**
—Kireeti Kompella

William of Occam was very wise. "Occam's Razor" has many translations from the Latin, but a generally accepted one is that the simplest solution that explains a situation is the most likely. In more recent times, this has evolved into the KISS rule: "Keep it simple, stupid."

As George Orwell observed in *Animal Farm*, "All animals are equal but some animals are more equal than others." He also observed the typical generality, "Four legs good, two legs bad." The parallel here is that not all routers and routerlike devices are equal. There is the distinct difference, generally not well understood by vendors or their carrier customers, that core and edge devices have fundamentally different requirements. Core devices should emphasize performance, efficiency, and simplicity. Edge devices should emphasize flexibility, functionality, and the ability to fit into a complex routing system that eventually feeds into the core.

The chief role of the core is data transfer. Current trends are to build the core from devices that have excellent forwarding capability, but not necessarily a great deal of control plane intelligence. Another trend is separating the control and forwarding planes. In other words, you want to minimize the amount of state in the core to that which is needed to manage the topology, and, if you support QoS, to enforce traffic engineering.

A fundamental assumption in developing TCP/IP is that most intelligence is in edge hosts, with their responsibility for error and flow control. The IP routed core was optimized for routing. Unfortunately for current requirements, conventional routing itself was not optimized for consistent quality of service and predictable reliability. This thinking has continued into another generation, in which much of the routing intelligence is in edge routers that set up relatively simple paths across the core. These paths use Multiprotocol Label Switching (MPLS) or Generalized MPLS (GMPLS), which were introduced in Chapter 8. The idea of simplifying the core with respect to the edge, however, is not dependent on MPLS. It has been done with L2 overlay networks (see Chapter 8), and with good practice using a mixture of conventional IGPs and BGP.

To be competitive, modern cores have to be scalable and survivable and support different service classes. I believe a general discussion of the goals of a modern core should begin with a discussion of the modern concepts of trunks and forwarding equivalence classes in carrying data, staying at first agnostic to the underlying technology used for transmission along the paths.

There is no single optimization that makes a network scalable. While control plane scalability is essential, so is having scalable bandwidth in the core. Exten-

NUCLEAR WAR AND OTHER NETWORKING URBAN LEGENDS

It is often suggested that the first packet-switched networks were developed with the specific goal of high reliability under nuclear attack, but that is not the reality. As military communications planners learned the capabilities of packet networks, they certainly added them to the variety of ways that critical messages could be sent. The fundamental war-fighting networks, however, were primarily different systems in many parts of the radio spectrum, which, in the extreme case, only needed two antennas to survive.

Traditional routing is reliable in the sense that it can use many alternate facilities, but the conventional routing protocols do not have systematic means of being used in the design of highly survivable networks with predictable quality of service.

There are many urban legends, some of which preceded networking but have been disproven by it. Many have suggested, for example, that if a million monkeys were placed in front of typewriters, they would eventually produce Shakespeare. That experiment has been tried. It was called the Internet. No Shakespearean text was produced.

sive functionality is certainly nice for your sales force, but scalability enters into your capability to provision and maintain the functions sold by sales. The saving grace for bandwidth is that optical technologies make huge bandwidth available at low cost, and, in many cases, overprovisioning is reasonable both for avoiding congestion and providing survivability. Things will get much more complex in developing countries where there is no high-bandwidth infrastructure, but there are still relevant techniques such as satellite links.

As networks evolve, the bandwidth bottleneck is more likely to be on the edge than in the core. While vendors speak glibly of massive Metro Ethernet optical bandwidth, inspecting ISP mailing lists will show that rural POPs often have only a DS1 or multiple DS1 uplink and that broadband access providers massively oversubscribe their connections to their ISP customers. That small DS1 uplink, also called a *hose*, has become a popular approach to capacity planning.

Developing Requirements: Pipes, Hoses, and Trunks

It was said of one political patriarch that he told his operatives to buy the election in a given state, but that he didn't want to pay for one vote he didn't actually need. And so it is with Internet traffic engineering: It is the art and science of ensuring adequate performance and availability while minimizing idle capacity elsewhere in the network. In other words, satisfy your users and remain competitive at the least cost. The same goes for bandwidth to a customer site. The customer doesn't want to pay for one bit of bandwidth that isn't actually needed. The provider has a somewhat more complex problem, because it may be wise practice to provision the capability for more access bandwidth than the customer initially needs so that there is little delay in upgrading the link if that becomes a requirement. Carriers have found the ability to quickly allocate bandwidth to be extremely popular with users, and to be a valuable competitive differentiator.

Terms that have become useful to describe the user and provider views are *pipes* and *hoses* [Duffield 1999]. Pipes are the end-to-end user view of a service; hoses are the provider view of the connection to the customer site (Figure 11.1). A good ISP will help its long-term customer relationships by monitoring bandwidth utilization and periodically telling the customer when the customer appears to need more or less bandwidth or when trend prediction suggests that more bandwidth may be needed. Be willing to tell the customer when reducing bandwidth will save money. The temporary loss of revenue will be more than made up for in long-term relationship values.

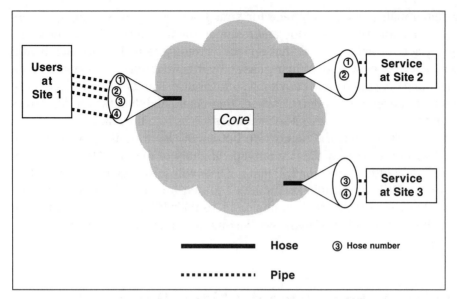

Figure 11.1 Hoses versus pipes.

Both hoses and pipes carry flows. What's the difference? I'm vaguely reminded of the saying, "Friends help you move. Real friends help you move bodies." In the case of pipes and hoses, the litmus test that decides which is which is the endpoint. Pipe endpoints are in the user domain, while hose endpoints are some interface in the provider domain.

Hoses can be oversubscribed or overprovisioned. In oversubscription, the sum of potential user flow bandwidth exceeds the capacity of the hose. Remember that the user interface to the hose may have enough capacity, but some point along the end-to-end hose may not be able to handle the full simultaneous burst of all signal sources. Hoses can be overprovisioned by providing more capacity than the sum of all users can produce. Overprovisioning often makes a provider more attractive in that adding bandwidth (up to the physical capacity of the link) to a given hose is merely a software matter. To avoid economic abuse, the provider will generally need to enforce rate-limiting.

STOP AND THINK

Is there a significant difference between a hose and a traditional access link? It depends. A Frame Relay access link that has a guaranteed burst tolerance is, in fact, a hose. If there are no guarantees when the customer sends a burst of traffic, even if those guarantees mean that anything over the guaranteed bandwidth will be dropped; you have a "stupid" access link. Hoses are predictable.

Hoses are easier to allocate than pipes. When there are no solid performance measurements at the start of a service, a safe approach is to look at the burst capability of all hosts at the site, limited by the capability of internal links and routers, and provision the hose to support that bandwidth. This is their *egress burst capability*. Continued performance monitoring can adjust the actual amount of bandwidth to be charged for, but you now have an adequate physical facility in place.

You will find that pipes and hoses are an excellent basic planning mechanism, but the proper, reliable distribution of traffic flows among pipes and hoses also requires network design using trunks. Using trunks requires additional protocol mechanisms to supplement conventional routing.

Applying Pipes and Hoses

Let's walk through a very simplified pipe and hose provisioning exercise. You are a small ISP with two POPs and one upstream (Figure 11.2). Your customers do have bandwidth guarantees to the upstream, which connects to you with a POS OC-192 (see Table 11.1). Physically, the OC-192 is provisioned for 8 Gbps of bandwidth and has an identical physical backup link.

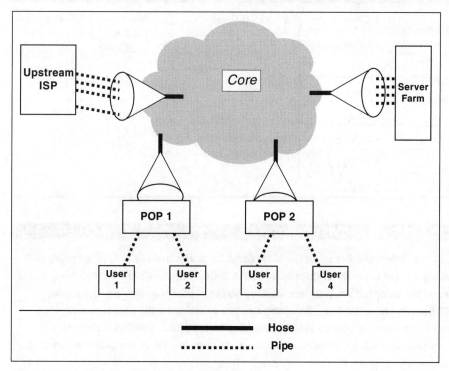

Figure 11.2   Pipes and hoses in a small ISP.

ECONOMIES OF SCALE ARE ECONOMIES OF SCALE

In these provisioning models, I have chosen to use typical optical speeds. The same principles of economies of scale hold with other technologies. For example, in most of North America, the break-even for ordering a full DS3 comes when you are about to order a sixth or seventh DS1. The full DS3 has the capacity of 28 DS1s, so you essentially get 20 or more DS1s free, less any cost for new router interfaces, and so on. Even more dramatic savings may be possible with fractional DS3 or frame relay over DS3. There are many routers that have DS3 physical interfaces but that would be overloaded if they actually had to handle 44.736 Mbps of bandwidth. The vendors of these routers are not doing anything wrong. They are providing a perfectly reasonable access device to a DS3 facility whose bandwidth will only be partially used.

Table 11.1 Bandwidth and Media versus Pipes and Hoses (Single Point of Failure)

CUSTOMER	BANDWIDTH	POP	POP PIPE TO UPSTREAM	IMPLEMENTATION (ACCEPTING SINGLE POINT OF FAILURE FROM POP TO UPSTREAM)
1	1 Gbps	1	5 Gbps	Minimum 2 OC-48s (at 2.5 Gbps) or 1 OC-192
2	1 Gbps			
3	2 Gbps			
4A	1 Gbps			
5	1 Gbps	2	3 Gbps	Minimum 2 OC-48s (at 2.5 Gbps) or 1 OC-192
6	500 Mbps			
7	500 Mbps			
4B	1 Gbps			

PLANNED OVERPROVISIONING

Note the difference between physical capacity and bandwidth. While an OC-192 has a physical capacity of approximately 9.5 Gbps of user bandwidth, this carrier has adopted an overprovisioning strategy of not assigning more than 8 Gbps to a given OC-192. When the OC-192 is loaded with that capacity, the carrier considers it time to install an additional OC-192. This 8:9.5 ratio is hypothetical; each carrier should develop its own model of the point at which a new facility is needed.

Motivations for Traffic Engineering

Traffic engineering includes aspects of both traffic and resource performance. In practice, it also includes survivability. One list of motivations [Donnell 1999] looks at problems that traffic engineering might solve:

- Managing expenses by deferring a circuit upgrade
- Utilizing excess bandwidth as it becomes available
- Managing large volumes of bandwidth from a single source
- Eliminating congestion on a specific circuit
- Improving customer service in rapidly growing regions

Full-scale MPLS and even dynamic reservation protocols may not necessarily be needed for some of these goals, especially when the goal applies to an exception case in your network. See, for example, "An OSPF Manual Traffic Engineering Workaround," later in this chapter. Traffic engineering does not require (G)MPLS, but most new implementations use label switching. There are traffic engineering extensions to the major IGPs, although the trend is to use the IGP-provided information to set up label-switched paths (LSPs) rather than to provide the direct topology for forwarding traffic with service level agreements (SLAs). Whatever the mechanism, it can be reactive or proactive. People with enterprise backgrounds tend to think first of reactive methods such as queuing and selective discard, whereas people from telecommunications backgrounds think of possibly cumbersome proactive methods such as connection admission control. As with most polarized arguments, the optimum lies somewhere around the middle. One of the reasons for this is that traffic engineering should properly take place simultaneously at multiple layers. Installing more bandwidth at the physical level, for example, is cumbersome but necessary. It often takes months for high-speed circuits to be physically installed and provisioned at both ends of the circuit. Changing routing policy and tables can take hours to minutes for making the changes and minutes to seconds for the information to propagate. The actual per-packet decisions such as traffic policing must take place at packet rates, which can easily be in nanoseconds.

Let's reexamine our small ISP, with the constraint of no internal single point of failure (see Table 11.2).

Core and Interprovider Hierarchy

Large-scale routed networks are inherently hierarchical, so hierarchy plays a role in their fault tolerance that does not exist in such things as SONET/SDH. Current thinking defines the issues of intradomain or horizontally oriented fault tolerance, as well as interdomain or vertically oriented fault tolerance. In both

Table 11.2 Bandwidth and Media versus Pipes and Hoses (No Single Point of Failure)

CUSTOMER	BANDWIDTH	POP	POP HOSE	IMPLEMENTATION (NO SINGLE POINT OF FAILURE)
1	1 Gbps	1	5 Gbps	Minimum 2 OC-48s (at 2.5 Gbps) No single point of failure 4 OC-48s* or 2 OC-192s
2	1 Gbps			
3	2 Gbps			
4A	1 Gbps			
5	1 Gbps	2	3 Gbps	Minimum 2 OC-48s (at 2.5 Gbps) No single point of failure 3 OC-48s or 2 OC-192s
6	500 Mbps			
7	500 Mbps			
4B	1 Gbps			OC-48 or 2 OC-192s

* You'll need four OC-48s because, while a single OC-48 can handle half the aggregate, no single OC-48 can handle the bandwidth of customer 3 and any other customer, assuming that no load sharing splits the customer 3 workload.

cases, the role of hierarchy is to increase abstraction and decrease the amount of state per abstraction that must be retained, leading to scalability.

Do not let the term *horizontal* suggest to you that we are dealing with flat topologies. The horizontal-versus-vertical distinction is more one of administration and control, expressed in different levels of abstraction. A vertical hierarchy involves the interaction of multiple technologies at different layers, such as IP routing control and MPLS. While the terms are popular in new IETF documents, be aware that they are not always used with ideal precision. Most often, horizontal hierarchies involve the same layer and usually the same technology. Vertical hierarchies most often involve going between technologies. But the terms are sometimes and not consistently, used to show administrative boundaries—vertical being between organizations, and horizontal in the same organization. I can only advise reading carefully to determine the context in use.

A horizontal hierarchy involves the same technology in all participating entities. Indeed, it could very well extend to multiple IGP domains linked by a BGP backbone, as long as they are all under the control of the same administration. A horizontal hierarchy can certainly include scalability methods appropriate to the protocol method, such as BGP confederations, MPLS merging, and so on. It includes the ability to operate in networks whose topologies are learned by IGPs that have at least two levels of hierarchy (for example, ISIS and OSPF backbone and nonbackbone areas).

A vertical hierarchy hides information in the lower technology from the higher-layer technology, as in hiding optical wavelength detail from IP routing.

SDH/SONET APS and other restoration mechanisms are invisible to the layers above. Restoration may take longer using vertical than horizontal hierarchy, due to needs for convergence before aggregated information can flow.

Arguably, trunks are a method of vertical hierarchy, since they are an overlay onto a lower-layer technology. Trunks do not necessarily have a one-to-one correspondence with lower hierarchical layers, especially when the trunks are end-to-end and the lower layers are hop-by-hop.

From the Edge to the Core

As introduced in Chapter 9, most routing, be it interior or exterior, follows what is variously called a *closest-exit* or *hot potato* policy. This type of routing lets you minimize the resource load on your domain by getting off the packet as quickly as possible, as in the child's game of tossing a hot potato to someone else. The crux of the issue is that the practice among large ISPs has been to focus first on integrity of both the global and their local routing systems, and second on route optimality (for example, minimum latency). Within their ASs, there can be multiple routing domains, such as the routing in POPs as distinct from their intraprovider cores.

In contrast, a *cold potato* or *best-exit* strategy keeps the packet on paths over which the ISP has control until it can be passed to the closest routing domain to the destination. This may enable the packet to actually arrive at its destination faster, though at suboptimal cost to the provider. Obviously, there must still be business agreement and technical coordination for this work. We will get into more detail on multiprovider QoS in Chapter 12.

Core Routing Scalability

Individual routing domains using IGPs historically do not scale to the number of routes that BGP can handle. That is neither an insult to IGPs nor an all-purpose endorsement of BGP; the protocols are optimized for different purposes. The Internet should be seen as a set of IGP domains linked by BGP.

In practice, to achieve scalable and predictable quality of service and survivability, routing protocols have to be supplemented with label-switching technology. In this section of the chapter, let's first deal with pure routing scenarios, as we set the background for introducing label-switching extensions.

One of the major objectives of an IGP is fast convergence within a relatively small set of topological elements. Indeed, for voice applications, there is significant interest in millisecond-range convergence. To achieve such fast convergence, one needs very fast failure detection and propagation of new topological information [Alaettinoglu 2000]. If these mechanisms were scaled to the size of the Internet, incredible instability would be likely to result. Different sets of scalability problems relate to traffic engineering and QoS. Since current IGPs do not consider either reservations for or usage of bandwidth, their metric computations may cause an extremely overloaded link or links to be regarded as the best path for multiple flows.

A second, related problem occurs when a single stream is routed through a link or router with insufficient bandwidth to handle it, although there is sufficient bandwidth available in parallel links or interfaces. There truly can be available bandwidth, analogous to the announcement, "Interstate 395 is congested leading to the Beltway, but you can divert via the Edsall Road exit." It can also be a condition where you must not divert traffic: "Memorial Bridge is empty, but that's because it's closed for the Marine Corps Marathon." To some extent, this second problem can be alleviated, but not necessarily solved, by widespread use of equal-cost load sharing. Equal-cost load sharing may actually make matters worse if local optimization to a neighbor puts traffic onto a second hop that is more congested [Berkowitz 1999]. Congestion-aware routing that looks at the entire path is more likely to be helpful, although the trend has been to use routing less for congestion response and more as the topology input to capacity-controlled bandwidth allocation.

Interior BGP Routing Scalability

Originally, iBGP speakers peered in a full mesh, which doesn't scale well beyond 20 to 30 peers per router. In conventional routers, the limits on connections come from the overhead of maintaining per-router sessions (for example, TCP and BGP header checking/authentication) and the workload of per-peer policy processing. The two basic scalability measures for iBGP are route reflectors and confederations. Route reflectors tend to be more common in ISP practice.

When the routers also are well-connected with respect to your IGP, they can also gain substantial processing load from recomputing IGP routes. This leads to an important planning consideration: Don't assume that iBGP scalability measures will be enough to let your core scale infinitely. You may also need IGP scalability measures. While single ISIS areas of a thousand routers are known

---

THE BIG CHOICES

Should you aim for a BGP-free core? (See "BGP-free Cores" later in this chapter.) Should you have a core with BGP, but use route reflectors or confederations to scale it? Should your POPs be full mesh, reflector clusters, or confederations? Should you be driving aggressively for a completely traffic-engineered core (and even POPs), or should you use traffic engineering selectively?

to work in well-managed ISP environments, I emphasize that the ISP must be well managed. Well-managed networks have a minimum of link failures.

OSPF tends not to support as many routers per area. With either case, depending on many factors including the processing power of the router control processors and the number of external routes that must leak into your IGP, you may need to use IGP hierarchy as well as iBGP scalability measures.

Full Mesh and Migrating from It

A small core with no reflectors or confederations is a *full mesh* (Figure 11.3). It may very well work for a small ISP, but eventually it will fail to scale. It is entirely reasonable, however, to full-mesh inside a POP, although that may set a limit to the size of the POP. If you already have a full-mesh iBGP network and are starting to develop performance problems, it is much cleaner to migrate to route reflectors than to confederations. Confederations, even though they are more labor-intensive, may be worth the effort if your performance problems are related to a merger or acquisition of another ISP.

Before we go into iBGP scalability alternatives, let's review a basic protection mechanism for BGP connections, both internal and external.

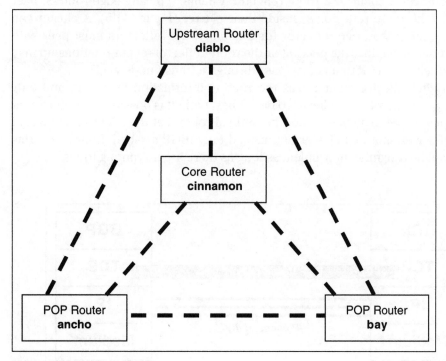

Figure 11.3 Full-mesh iBGP.

Protecting BGP with BGP Tunnels

A common technique is to run BGP over multiple load-shared IP links, with the endpoints of the tunnel associated with software interfaces, usually called *loopback*, inside the router (Figure 11.4). If a link in the load-shared bundle goes down, the TCP remains up and the link failure has no direct impact on the BGP session. Obviously, if BGP's performance assumed the full bandwidth of the bundle, there will be a degradation.

You must be careful about the load-sharing algorithm used among the various links. If a destination or source-destination cache is used for load sharing, remember that the source and destination addresses of all BGP packets in the session will be the same, so traffic will tend to use one link. Essentially, with two links, these load-sharing methods will produce a case of 1:1 backup with preallocated capacity. Of course, if you implement some of the more powerful label-switched protected paths discussed later in this chapter, they can play this role.

Route Reflectors in the Core

Route reflectors are one of two basic approaches for reducing the number of iBGP peers internal to an AS. With route reflection, a given router either is a route reflector client or a route reflector. Clients, typically edge routers, peer only to the route reflector(s) inside their cluster (Figure 11.5). A cluster can contain more than one reflector for reliability; the reflectors must peer with each other. Note that the peering or the route reflector–client relationship may be indirect; the TCP tunnel may pass through a transit node via IP.

A route reflector summarizes the routing information it gathers and only gives its clients what it believes to be the best path. It is possible, therefore, that the route given to a client is not the optimal route that the client router would find if it were not in a cluster but instead fully iBGP meshed. In practice, this may not be a significant problem as long as there are no routing loops.

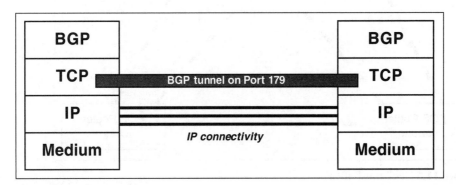

Figure 11.4 BGP tunnel.

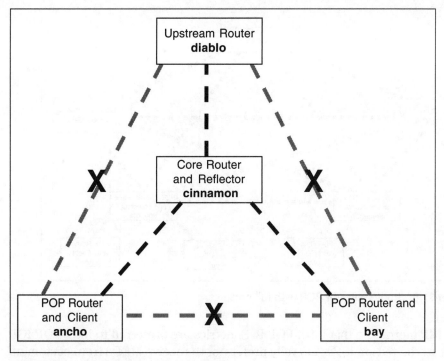

Figure 11.5 Migration to route reflectors.

Not all routers in an AS need to participate in route reflection. The key aspect is that the reflectors need to be fully meshed with the reflectors of other clusters and with any other iBGP speakers that are not part of a cluster (Figure 11.6). With respect to route reflectors, those iBGP speakers are called *conventional BGP speakers*.

Like all powerful features, route reflectors provide powerful ways to get your network in trouble. One of the most common problems is when a provider uses them in a POP and does not carefully set BGP preferences and imported IGP metrics such that an intra-POP route is always preferred to an inter-POP route. This is done for the same kind of loop prevention reasons that intra-area routes are always preferred in ISIS and OSPF. There is no protocol-level reason why a router that is a reflector in one cluster can't be a client in a higher level cluster. By building a hierarchy of clusters, there is no need ever to have a huge number of iBGP peers (see Figure 11.7).

Again, this can get you in trouble, if, for example, a lower-level client is pointed to a higher-level reflector. You also must make sure that each cluster has a unique cluster ID. Remember how BGP prevents loops by rejecting incoming AS paths that contain the local autonomous system's AS number? The same principle is used in clusters: If an incoming route contains the equivalent of the cluster ID in a path, it is assumed to be a loop. To avoid loops, manipulate

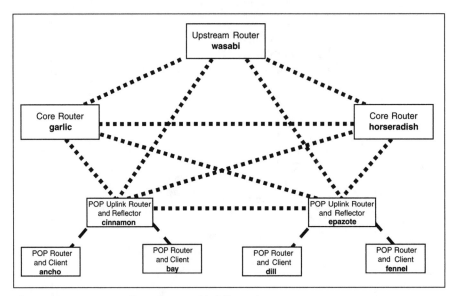

Figure 11.6 Route reflector POP with full mesh core.

your IGP metrics so that intra-POP IGP metrics are preferred to inter-POP IGP metrics. The reason ISPs generally prefer not to receive MEDs from customers closely relates to this issue of potential loops, because the MED value exported from the customer could be totally incompatible with that used by the provider. For example, what if the customer used RIP as an IGP metric and exported the hop count as the MED?

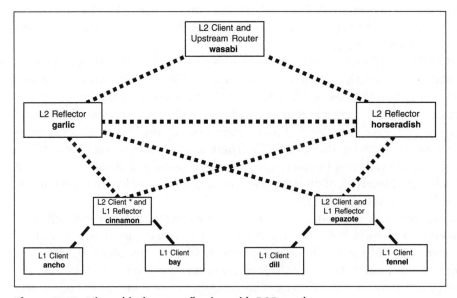

Figure 11.7 Hierarchical route reflection with POPs and core.

Confederations in the Core

Confederations have tended to be used less than route reflectors in most ISPs, because the additional level of control they can give simply isn't a requirement for an essentially homogeneous ISP. In the previous chapter we saw applications in complex enterprise strategies where this level of control was a necessity. A case where confederations may be very useful is when ISPs merge and not all their policies are consistent. Some ISPs, however, either started with confederations or don't want to change something that works, or have their own reasons for needing control.

Within the POP, you normally have a full mesh of BGP speakers. It is conceivable that you could have a route reflector inside the confederation AS, but the value of doing so is not obvious. In Figure 11.8, observe that a full mesh of BGP connections is not required among the confederation ASs. They run a special case of eBGP, so iBGP connectivity rules do not apply between the confederation autonomous systems. Also note in this figure that some POPs may speak eBGP to external ASs, while others may simply provide non-BGP customer access.

Some of the guidelines for pure BGP confederation POPs (that is, not using label switching) include using private AS numbers for the POPs themselves and, usually, having full meshes within POPs. Some large POPs might need route reflector internal structures, but if a POP approaches the complexity where that makes sense, it may be easier to create a new confederation AS.

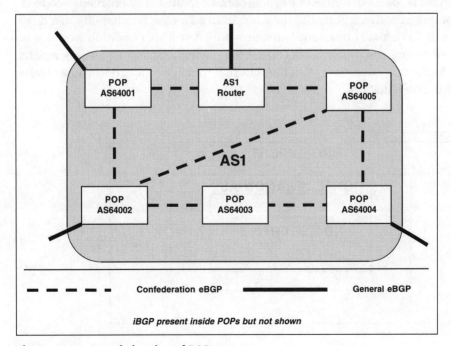

Figure 11.8   A confederation of POPs.

There is no reason why you could not have more than one confederation AS at the same physical POP.

Local preference values should be consistent among POPs, although not necessarily transmitted between confederation ASs. While some BGP implementations will allow LOCAL_PREF to be propagated between confederation ASs, it is generally more flexible and vendor-neutral to rely on communities for signaling such information between POPs. MEDs do make sense between POPs and between POPs and the core, since their scope of adjacent ASs only makes them relatively easy to track.

For ISPs, as opposed to enterprise POPs, AS paths can get extremely complicated and are best avoided as means of influencing route selection. Inside the confederation, or if confederation AS numbers are not stripped on exit, you can see odd AS paths such as 65001 65002 666 from AS666. There is a well-known community that limits the propagation of confederation AS routes, which complements other well-known communities (Figure 11.9).

Synchronization

The synchronization rule says that BGP must not advertise a route until all routers inside the AS have learned that route. Synchronization is not essential in nontransit networks, and disabling synchronization may improve performance in such networks. In transit ASs, however, either all routers must run BGP (that is, pervasive BGP) or synchronization must stay enabled. Not to do one of these creates a potential for your AS to advertise reachability to a destination that it actually does not know how to reach. This condition would arise because an ingress router learns about the destination and advertises reachability to the outside before either an internal transit or an egress router learns about that destination.

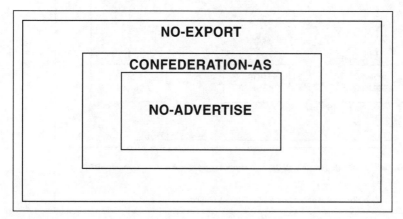

Figure 11.9 Scope of well-known communities.

My colleague, Peter van Oene, pointed out to the Cisco Groupstudy mailing list on February 20, 2000:

> Synchronization in my opinion seems often misunderstood. Essentially, this feature is relevant when a transit AS (one that passes traffic for which it is neither the source nor destination) chooses not to use a full iBGP mesh. Hence, if routers A, B, C, and D were connected in series, consider that only A and D are iBGP peers and are providing transit between multiple ISPs. For this to work, an IGP would have to have full prefix awareness, or said another way, the IGP table and the BGP tables would need to contain the same routes. Hence, it could be said that the tables would need to be synchronized. For protection, the BGP routers will not advertise a prefix outbound via eBGP to other AS's until their internal IGP table has the prefix installed. This means that likely the other IGP routers in the domain also have the prefix and thus traffic will not be black holed.
>
> In practice, no one does this! Redistributing 100k routes into an IGP is not a good thing :) All transit providers fully mesh with iBGP (with the exception of traffic engineered cores over MPLS). Synchronization is thus always turned off. In fact, Juniper does not even offer a synchronization knob.

IGP Scalability Issues

Several considerations go into IGP scalability. The first is the performance of the IGP itself, which may require building an IGP hierarchy. When such hierarchy is used, it often mirrors the hierarchy of the edge and core (that is, POPs and core in BGP) in order to minimize the processor loads from route flapping and the load of the core. There may need to be IGP hierarchy in POPs. Another aspect of IGP scalability, however, involves the limitations of current IGPs with respect to traffic engineering. IGPs with traffic engineering capability have to be able to transport additional information necessary for constraint-based routing, such as the amount of bandwidth allocated on a link.

The new routing paradigm becomes *constrained shortest path first* (CSPF), which extends existing link state paradigms to include traffic engineering, optical, and user/business constraints. CSPF produces explicit routes that meet the constraints, and then generates MPLS signaling (for example, RSVP-TE) to set up the LSPs corresponding to the explicit routes. If the link is fully reserved, it must drop out of the routing computation no matter how good its basic metric is. Current IGPs differ in their extensibility for carrying additional constraints. OSPF, for example, has packets that are relatively hard to modify, but it has the alternative of the opaque link state advertisement (LSA) packet for carrying

MIKE O'DELL ON CONSTRAINT-BASED ROUTING

"Make declarative topological statements and let computers join the dots."

EXTENSIBILITY AND IGPS

OSPF and ISIS had different design goals with respect to protocol extensibility. OSPF's design emphasized putting information onto fixed boundaries (for example, 32-bit) for speed of processing, while ISIS accepted more processing overhead for the benefit of the ability to chain future type-length-value triplets of arbitrary meaning. To meet evolving requirements, the opaque LSA was introduced. Opaque LSAs are intended to allow OSPF to evolve [RFC 2370]. They have a standard LSA header, followed by application-specific information consisting of type and ID.

One of the reasons ISIS was used for the first traffic engineering experiments was that it is easier to extend. Another reason was that the ISPs that would beta-test TE already ran ISIS as their IGP.

additional information. ISIS is more extensible and has probably been used for more of the early IGP traffic engineering experiments.

Another problem in QoS routing is managing the additional protocol overhead. If you are going to build end-to-end paths that consider bandwidth availability, potentially you will have many more routing announcements when links become more or less busy or when reservations are applied or removed. Trying for the most up-to-date possible route can lead to oscillation in the routing system. The most scalable approach is first to determine the routable topology in the absence of traffic engineering constraints and then apply as many constraints as possible and determine what best-effort and reservable capacity is left. When new end-to-end controlled paths are required, let them be created as explicit paths with appropriate backup and reservation, and do not constantly try to tune them based on changing conditions. Perfection is the enemy of excellence.

Does Interior Routing Need to Be Dynamic?

Interior routing need not be strictly limited to dynamic routing information exchange. There can be a definite role for static or quasi-static routes. *Quasi-static routes* are static routes to the same destination but with different preferences or different conditions under which they are invoked.

RPSL does provide a mechanism for describing quasi-static routes. The relevant syntax is:

```
inject: [at <router-expression>] ...
        [action <action>]
        upon static
```

the <action> could be setting a metric, a next hop, and so forth. Static routes may be particularly useful for parts of your topology that will not change without administrative action, such as customer access or interprovider links.

Generic Traffic Engineering Enhancements to IGPs

Both ISIS and OSPF have been extended for TE and (G)MPLS. Your POP designs, the vendors you select, and the features of their implementations will affect your specific choice of an IGP more. With that in mind, let's review both router-oriented and link-oriented functions of both extended protocols. There will be differences in the detailed implementation of the feature depending on the protocol, but the general functionality will be clear (see Table 11.3).

Table 11.4 shows some of the basic link information used by IGPs for TE and GMPLS. MTU size and other "vanilla" parameters are not listed to help focus on the new capabilities. Table 11.5 shows general link protection information. In Table 11.6, note there are distinctions among GMPLS types that are not in the core GMPLS specifications. Adding these types is prudent, because it may be necessary to imply additional capabilities such as border router capability. OSPF-TE does so with various settings of option bits.

OSPF Enhancements

OSPF has always had a richer set of functions for limiting the scope of propagation of routes than ISIS has had. Some of the recent standardized, proposed, and proprietary extensions to OSPF concentrate more on improving its scalability and enabling it to distribute traffic engineering and other additional information. Standardized extensions include demand circuits, not-so-stubby areas, and the opaque link state advertisement. Some newly suggested extensions deal with conditions under which nonbackbone areas can communicate directly.

An OSPF Manual Traffic Engineering Workaround

Consider Figure 11.10, where there is expected to be heavy traffic flow between the client in area 0.0.0.1 and the server in area 0.0.0.2. A dedicated link has been installed for the traffic between these two hosts, and it is also desirable that if this link goes down, backup is possible via area 0.0.0.0. OSPF's rules of hierarchy do not now permit direct interarea routes that do not traverse area 0.0.0.0. Extensions have been proposed, which are now implemented in Cisco and IBM routers, to create direct routes between nonbackbone areas [Zinin 2001]. But these extensions are not available in every implementation, and other interim measures can be effective workarounds. In the longer term, MPLS tunnels may be an acceptable alternative to these and other workarounds. Since in the long term we will also all be dead, it is worth reviewing the technique involved.

Table 11.3 Generic Router Information for TE (OSPF)

TE capability	
Ability to provision bandwidth on interfaces	
Support of constraint-based shortest past first algorithms	
Shared risk group	Group ID
Extended IS Reachability	Even for general use and certainly for TE, the ISIS reachability type length value (TLV) needs to be extended. Its chief limitation is the small size of the metric field, rather than the "wide" metric needed in large networks. OSPF has always had a larger metric field than ISIS. The current metric field also contains type of service bits (for example, delay, monetary cost, and reliability) that are not used in current practice and indeed have been removed in recent OSPF standards. The intra-area metric of the new extended-reachability sub-TLV is encoded as a 24-bit unsigned integer. The metric field in the new extended IP–reachability TLV is encoded as a 32-bit unsigned integer.* Metrics greater than the maximum 24-bit value must not be considered during intra-area SPF calculation. In other words, it is perfectly acceptable to have a 32-bit end-to-end metric whose components include 24-bit values.
Administrative group (color)	OSPF previously had the ability to add administrative tags to routes, as does RIPv2. Originally intended for BGP-OSPF interaction but never used for the purpose, a color, tag, or administrative group is roughly similar to a BGP community.
IPv4 interface address	While it should be obvious that conventional routing needs the IP address to be announced, this appearance in sub-TLVs is TE specific. There can be multiple-address TLVs for different kinds of service.[†]
IPv4 neighbor address	This sub-TLV contains a single IPv4 address for a neighboring router on this link. This sub-TLV can occur multiple times. If a router implements basic TLV extensions, it is free to add this sub-TLV to or omit it from the description of an adjacency. It must do so if it implements TE.[‡]
TE router ID	The need for a stable router ID long has been recognized in OSPF, ISIS, and BGP without traffic engineering. TE, however, introduces both additional applications and constraints on the router ID. The router ID should be identical in all the protocols used by the router.[‡]
Interface switching capability	See Table 11.6

* Encoded in 32 bits in IEEE floating point format.
[†] Units are bytes per s.
[‡] While it is not uncommon in general IP routing to advertise a /32 prefix for this address in routing protocols, this must not be done when TE is used. Doing so can cause routing loops.

Table 11.4 Generic Link Information for TE

GENERIC LINK INFORMATION FOR TE (OSPF)	COMMENTS
Maximum link bandwidth	Physical limit of bandwidth on the link.*,†
Maximum reservable link bandwidth	Maximum amount of bandwidth that can be reserved in this direction on this link. TE supports oversubscription, so this value can be greater than the maximum link bandwidth of the link.*,†
Unreserved bandwidth	Amount of bandwidth still reservable on this direction on this link. Since TE supports oversubscription, this value can be greater than the value of maximum link bandwidth.*,† In ISIS, this sub-TLV contains 8 bandwidth values, 1 per setup priority. For stability reasons, rapid changes in the values in this sub-TLV should not cause rapid generation of LSPs.
TE default metric	This is a 24-bit unsigned integer consistent with intra-area metrics. If a link is advertised without this sub-TLV, traffic engineering SPF calculations must use the normal default metric of this link, which is advertised in the fixed part of the extended IS reachability TLV.
Bandwidth availability	Maximum bandwidth, available bandwidth, reserved bandwidth for later use, and so on. This TLV may also describe the data-link layer protocols supported.
Reliability of link	
Color assigned to link	Similar to the SRLG TLV, in that an autonomous system may choose to issue colors to link based on certain criteria. This TLV can be used to specify the color assigned to the link within the scope of the AS.
Cost of bandwidth usage on link	This indicates the link usage cost—bandwidth on link unit, unit usage cost, LSP setup cost, minimum and maximum durations permitted for setting up the TLV, and so on, including any time-of-day constraints.
Membership in a shared-risk link group	List of shared-risk link groups the link belongs to.
Link supports TE	
Link protection type	See Table 11.5.
Link GMPLS type	See Table 11.6.
Database synchronization permitted on this link	Implies PSC.

* Encoded in 32 bits in IEEE floating point format.
† Units are bytes per s.

Table 11.5   General Link Protection Information

TREATMENT OF TRAFFIC ON LINK
Extra traffic
Unprotected
Shared
Dedicated 1:1
Dedicated 1+1
Enhanced

The router operating system must support static routes that are more administratively preferred than any OSPF route. Bay RS, for example, does not have such a capability. To implement the workaround, put a static route in each router along the path, which forwards to the next hop toward the destination on the special path. You can even have backup special paths if the router operating system supports static routes with multiple levels of administrative preference. You must not allow these static routes to be advertised into OSPF. Given that constraint, if the static route becomes unreachable, an OSPF inter-area route between the two hosts will activate as a backup. At such time as the static route reenters service, it will displace the OSPF route in the routing table only for the affected routers on the explicit path. This requires careful manual configuration at each hop along the path.

OSPF Protocol Extensions for Traffic Engineering

OSPF traffic engineering extensions define a new router capability: traffic engineering. Defining a new router capability is consistent with the work done

Table 11.6   General GMPLS Router Types

Packet switch–capable-1 (PSC-1)
Packet switch–capable-2 (PSC-2)
Packet switch–capable-3 (PSC-3)
Packet switch–capable-4 (PSC-4)
Layer 2 switch–capable (L2SC)
Time-division multiplexing-capable (TDM)*
Lambda switch–capable (LSC)
Fiber switch–capable (FSC)

* Encoded in a 4-octet field in the IEEE floating point format.

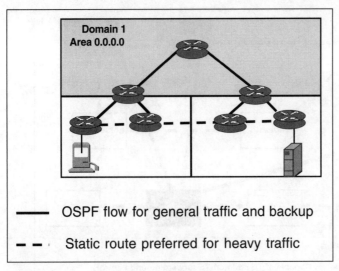

Figure 11.10   OSPF traffic engineering workaround.

for multicast OSPF (MOSPF) capable routers, although MOSPF was not widely deployed. A router may be multicast-capable or not; it may be able to originate multicasts only, receive multicasts only, or originate and receive multicasts. A router may be TE-capable or not; it may be able to originate TE traffic only, receive it only, or send and receive it. With both MOSPF and TE, OSPF routers that do not support their functionality can still play a part in distributing topological information that is used to determine multicast and TE routes. In other words, the set of all OSPF routers carries control information for TE, even though some of those routers may not be capable of TE forwarding.

To support GMPLS, the control network must be able to advertise the state of interfaces that are not packet-capable. Obviously, a nonpacket router cannot have a link state database of its own that can be synchronized in the usual OSPF manner. OSPF-TE thus requires proxy routers for non-PSC interfaces. The need for separation between OSPF and OSPF-TE topologies, which may be inside an area, means that opaque LSA enhancement doesn't quite fit. There are needs to flood to "all TE routers within an area," which are not within the subnet, area, and domain scopes of the defined OSPF opaque LSA. OSPF-TE–capable routers have two link state databases, the standard one and the TE topology. You can think of the standard database as a control plane database for TE, although it still has its conventional role with respect to non-TE traffic. There are separate adjacencies for the general OSPF and OSPF-TE databases. To have TE in an area, a router must establish adjacency with another TE router in the area, but the two routers need not be on the same subnet. Each subnet in a system supporting TE, however, must have at least one router that runs OSPF-TE on at least one of its interfaces (see Figure 11.11).

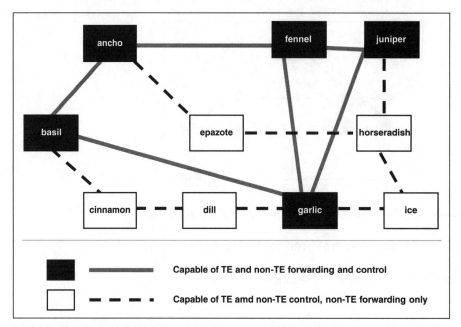

Figure 11.11 OSPF-TE subtopology.

A new option bit setting in OSPF identifies TE versus non-TE OSPF routers. TE LSAs are exchanged only with neighboring TE routers. The challenge comes when flooding to non-neighbor TE nodes. The current opaque LSA scopes do not quite match the requirements of TE—for example, there is an opaque LSA scope of "area-wide," but there is not a scope of "only TE routers in the area." Flooding in an area or routing domain introduces considerable overhead, and flooding TE-specific information over routes that contain no TE devices causes needless overhead. Optimized flooding in TE environments is not a totally solved problem, and you should closely evaluate how vendors implement their solutions until an industrywide consensus emerges.

Table 11.7 shows OSPF additional per-router information for TE and GMPLS.

A New Link Type: Positional Ring

OSPF-TE recognizes that SONET and RPR rings have some fundamental differences from other media, and adds support for them (see Table 11.8). With the exception of the following, no additional changes will be required to this LSA for TE compatibility.

- The LSA format and flooding scope remains unchanged from the existing type 2, except that the order of announcement is significant.

- To provide for non-PSC routers, the node announcements for a subnet must start with the PSC gateway to the ring.

Table 11.7 OSPF Additional Per-Router Information for TE and GMPLS

TE selection criteria	The values can be a series of resources that may be used as the criteria for traffic engineering (typically with the aid of a signaling protocol such as RSVP-TE or CR-LDP). ■ Bandwidth-based LSPs* ■ Priority-based LSPs[†] ■ Backup LSP[‡] ■ Link cost
Constraint SPF algorithms— support TLV	List all the CSPF algorithms supported.
Label edge router capability	Can also be an OSPF ABR and/or ASBR.
Interface switching capability descriptor	See Table 11.6.
STA bit	Label stack depth limit TLV follows. This is applicable only when the PSC flag is set.
SIG bit	MPLS signaling protocol support TLV follows.

* Bandwidth criteria are often used as metrics for PSC and TDM nodes, although the unit of bandwidth is apt to be vendor-specific.

[†] Priority-based traffic switching is relevant only to PSC nodes. Nodes supporting this criterion will be able to interpret the EXP bits on the MPLS header to prioritize the traffic across the same LSP.

[‡] Backup criteria refer to whether or not the node is capable of finding an automatic protection path if the originally selected link fails. Such a local recovery is specific to the node and may not need to be notified to the upstream node.

New Information for Border Routers

Summary LSAs, originated by area border routers, need to be enhanced to indicate the reachability of TE networks in the area being summarized. Summarization of TE changes and restricting the detailed change scope to the area considerably reduces overhead on other areas. As distinct from the non-TE

Table 11.8 OSPF Positional Ring Additional Information

CONNECTION TYPE	LINK ID	RING ID*
Point-to-point connection to another router	Neighboring router's router ID	Number of elements in the ring (ring neighbors)
Connection to a transit network	IP address of designated router	Ring bandwidth
Connection to a stub network	IP network/subnet number	Ring protection
Virtual link	Neighboring router's router ID	IP address of interface
Positional ring type	IP network/subnet number	Ring type (2 versus 4 fiber, SONET/SDH)

* Unlike the broadcast type, the sequence in which the network elements are placed on a RING network is pertinent. The nodes in the ring must be described clockwise.

summary LSA, the flooding scope is throughout the OSPF domain, while conventional summary LSAs flood only into area 0.0.0.0. The role of TE-capable ABRs and ASBRs is the same as in the non-TE situation, other than that the TE-capable border routers can convey additional information. Table 11.9 shows external link TE flags.

A point of caution in operating TE networks is that the reservation of capacity (that is, dynamic traffic pinning) may lead to many more changes than the usual range of up/down conditions. To minimize the impact of changes, a new LSA, *TE-Link-Update*, will be the only thing advertised when a link state changes due to TE. There are nuances to the detailed design of this LSA to minimize the number of times it is updated. The reality that not all network elements are packet switch–capable leads to the need for another new LSA, *TE-Router-Proxy*. This LSA is sent by a packet-capable router to represent such things as lambda routers.

ISIS's New Trends: ISNT?

ISIS has historically been a lean and mean protocol, with less feature creep than OSPF. The benefit of keeping it simple has definitely led to efficient resource usage. There are far more examples—primarily in carrier environments—of very large single ISIS areas than there are of single OSPF areas. As traffic engineering becomes more important, however, many of the simplifications of ISIS become severe restrictions on the topologies that can be built. In particular, the classic ISIS level 1 area can only do closest-exit routing. Extensions to ISIS therefore focus more on flexibility than performance, extending the controls on the propagation of interarea information, widening the range of media over which it can operate, and so on.

Table 11.9   External Link TE flags

LINK TE FLAGS	
Link TE TLVs	The TE attributes of this route. These fields are optional and are provided only when one or more preengineered circuits can be specified with the advertisement. Without these fields, the LSA will simply state TE reachability information.
Forwarding address	Data traffic for the advertised destination will be forwarded to this address. If the forwarding address is set to 0.0.0.0, data traffic will be forwarded instead to the LSA's originator (that is, the responsible AS boundary router).
External route tag	A 32-bit field attached to each external route. This is not used by the OSPF protocol itself. It may be used to communicate information between AS boundary routers; the precise nature of such information is outside the scope of this specification.

Conventional ISIS packets have a fixed header and some number of TLV tuples. ISIS with TE extensions adds a new object, the sub-TLV, which is found inside regular TLVs. TLVs add information to ISIS packets. Sub-TLVs add information to specific TLVs in a packet. TLVs can hold multiple instances of the related data, such as the amount of reservable bandwidth in different service classes. Remember that ISIS supports fewer media types than does OSPF. Early ISIS-TE only deals with point-to-point links, or the special case of a broadcast multiaccess link to which only one device connects.

Extensions for Controlled Violations of Hierarchy

The original ISIS specification [RFC 1195] took a straightforward approach to loop prevention, only allowing prefixes to propagate from nonbackbone areas to the backbone, not in the other direction. This unfortunately introduces the problem that the backbone cannot tell nonbackbone areas about interarea and external routes. If a nonbackbone area has multiple level 2 routers, the area does not have the information to pick the best exit (that is, cold potato). It can only do closest-exit (hot potato) routing. To allow ISIS to implement best exit, the new extended-IP-reachability TLV contains a new up/down bit [RFC 2966]. When a new prefix first enters ISIS, the up/down bit is set to 0. While the value of this bit is 0, it can be sent from a higher level to a lower level. Once in the lower level, the bit is set to 1. Prefixes with the up/down bit set to 1 can never readvertise the prefix back up in the hierarchy. This mechanism can be extended to possible future versions of ISIS with more than two levels of hierarchy. If a prefix is also advertised from one nonbackbone area to another, the up/down bit also needs to be set to 1. Some additional information is needed for ISIS to support GMPLS. TE LSAs need one more TLV, the shared-risk link group identifier. Hello protocol data units (PDUs) also need an interface ID TLV.

Core Design Issues in Transition

If I were to worship at the shrine of the Seven Commandments, I could say that core design needs to consider issues at OSI layers 1 through 3. Since OSI architects themselves have lost blind faith in those layers, I will instead deal with a more modern view. That more modern view includes definite separation between data and control planes, which exist at multiple layers. These layers do not necessarily correspond to the original layers, and indeed split into a greater number than the original three layers.

Is Explicit Routing a Step Backward?

When I teach introductory routing design classes, I often tear at my limited hair when my students persist in wanting their routers to have as much routing information as possible "so they can find alternate routes." Several fundamental fallacies arise here. Definitely in enterprise networks, and even in provider access networks, the majority of routers have very few physical links that more abundant routing information would help them choose. When I redesigned the corporate network of an enterprise that originally claimed to have 2500 routers, a detailed analysis showed that only 400 had other than a default and perhaps a dial backup path. Hierarchical structures suppress detailed information propagating everywhere, which increases stability and the ease of troubleshooting. Well-managed static routes are not necessarily maintenance-intensive or inflexible. Even beyond that, explicit routing is not quite the same as static routing, because the explicit routes that are instantiated as LSPs are set up dynamically.

The Role of Sub-IP

The focus of this chapter is on how layer 3 routing mechanisms determine the core topology, do core-related classic routing, and communicate with intelligent sub-IP mechanisms.

Chief among the sub-IP technologies is GMPLS, which, in turn, communicates with physical technologies such as SONET/SDH, resilient packet rings, and so on (see Figure 11.12). A packet will travel through many relays (layer 2 switches

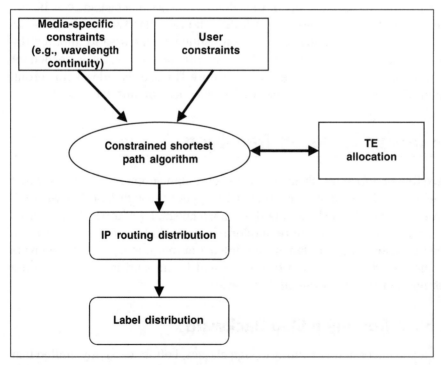

Figure 11.12 IP routing and (G)MPLS.

or layer 3 routers) along its path. The QoS implementation needs to influence the per-hop behavior (PHB) of each router or switch along the path. That doesn't mean—and generally should not mean—that every relay should be aware of the detailed service level agreement (SLA) for a given customer.

In complex networks, classification and marking should be done on the ingress devices. It is generally impractical to classify traffic in a high-speed path. Core relays are optimized to be big and fast, but not necessarily extremely intelligent. At each hop in the path, traffic can be buffered or dropped. Buffering can simply be intended to manage bursts, or it can use complex scheduling schemes to prioritize certain traffic and to stabilize the rates of other traffic types. In dealing with congestion, the broad problem is congestion control. A subset of congestion control is flow control, which assumes a connection-oriented model in which the receiver has a known reverse channel by which it can restrain the source. Where hosts and edge routers use flow control and buffering to deal with congestion, the proper approach for the core is congestion avoidance. Things happen too fast for reactivity to work; the core must be designed to be proactive. Part of being proactive is not to oversubscribe core capacity.

Traffic Trunks

We introduced the idea of trunks in Chapter 8, within the context of time-division multiplexing. One of the first steps in understanding modern trunks is to know that they carry multiple streams of information. As with many technologies, the idea of trunks has evolved. The first trunks, such as DS1 aggregates, handled a single type of information: digitized voice. The second generation of trunks, still often associated with physical instantiation, mix information types. The third generation of *traffic trunks* carry one kind of traffic, but there is an understanding that there will be multiple trunks for different kinds of traffic, and the multiple trunks will map onto an underlying transmission structure. Modern trunks have similarities to virtual circuits and to IP-routed paths, and may indeed have one-to-one correspondence to them. An important thing to realize, however, is that one-to-one mapping is not required, and other mappings may be quite desirable.

Trunking is essential to the modern understanding of scalable cores. Trunks are abstractions, although they can and should be detected and monitored to "allow the overhead in the infrastructure to be decoupled from the size of the network and the amount of traffic in the network. Instead, as the traffic scales up, the amount of traffic in the trunks increases not the number of trunks." [RFC 2430] When the amount of traffic increases, the trunk topology need not change. It can simply have more bandwidth provided to it, as by rerouting it over a higher-capacity medium or letting it load-share over additional media.

STOP AND THINK

Assuming all traffic is of the same class, is there any practical difference between a path to an aggregate of conventional IP routes and an MPLS trunk? Why? If not, why not?

Recent Background

Loosely speaking, trunks are end-to-end and carry flows. As we will see, the core design goal of simplification often involves the merging of trunks, so the ingress trunk may not have a one-to-one mapping to the egress trunk.

In an ideal world, the transport network would provide a precisely tuned path for every individual flow. In a real world, there is too much overhead associated with tracking flows to make large scale per-flow handling a practical solution. Realistically, flows can be aggregated into service classes that have similar characteristics. Another way to look at grouping of flows that go to one exit point, such as the WAN connection of an enterprise site, is that they belong to the same forwarding equivalence class (FEC). FECs are the key idea of Multiprotocol Label Switching (MPLS). Within a MPLS context, Li and Rekhter [RFC 2430] introduced the abstraction of a traffic trunk as an aggregation of flows that are placed inside the same LSP. All traffic in the trunk belongs to a common service class.

The differentiated services (diffserv) architecture defines *behavior aggregates* as "a collection of packets with the same codepoint crossing a link in a particular direction." [RFC 2474]. Traffic trunks can be routed, much as are virtual circuits in Frame Relay and ATM. While LSPs and trunks are often informally equated, there are actually important differences between them [RFC 2072]. In fact, you will find that the idea of trunking makes sense with an underlying MPLS, conventional IP routing, or other underlying structure.

MPLS has been called "ATM without cells." It is an inherently connection-oriented technology, but it does not replace IP routing. Rather, it is dependent on IP routing to discover the topology over which (G)MPLS can create its quasi-connections, label-switched paths (LSPs). LSPs lend themselves to traffic engineering and sophisticated failover techniques that connectionless IP routing lacks. One of the tricks of minimizing the amount of state associated with traf-

---

MPLS COMPONENT TERMINOLOGY REFRESHER

A label edge router (LER) can assign labels to traffic and also route traffic based on labels. It can run routing protocols and route using conventional IP routing. A label-switched router (LSR) can only route based on labels. It cannot create paths, only new labels, although it can merge paths based on labels.

Table 11.10 Traffic Engineering with ATM Overlay, Conventional IP, and (G)MPLS

FEATURE	L2 (ATM OVERLAY)	IP ROUTING	(G)MPLS
Allows circuit-switched models	Yes	No	Yes
Connection admission control	Yes	No	Yes
Traffic shaping and policing	Yes	Yes	Yes
Supports connectionless service	No	Yes	Yes
Explicit paths	Manual or PNNI	Source routed	Yes
Traffic trunking	Limited*	Extremely limited[†]	Yes
Attributes associated with trunks	Limited*	Limited[‡]	Yes[§]
Overhead	Worst	Moderate	Best
Constraint-based routing	Limited or vendor-specific	With protocol extensions	Yes
Aggregation and deaggregation	VP level	Aggregation only	Yes

* Attributes are associated more with virtual circuits than virtual paths, the latter being the best equivalent of a trunk. If all the circuits merged into a path have common attributes, then such association is possible.

[†] Load-sharing algorithms, generally vendor-specific, can approximate this. Aggregate routes also create something equivalent to a trunk.

[‡] With communities or IGP tags.

[§] Involves the underlying enhanced routing protocol.

fic engineering is suitable aggregation of flows at the edge ingress to the core, and deaggregation at the egress. The aggregated flows tend to be associated with MPLS tunnels (see "Tunneled Trunks").

Why is (G)MPLS more attractive than the L2 overlays discussed in Chapter 8? ATM is the most popular L2 overlay. Its Q.2931 and PNNI protocols meet most of these objectives, especially when soft permanent virtual circuits (PVCs) are included. Concerns about using ATM include the cell tax and the lack of support for connectionless communications. See Table 11.10 for a feature comparison, remembering that IP routing and GMPLS are used together and complement one another.

The Almost-Worst and Worst Cases

Let's change the business assumptions in the small ISP that we used for the pipe and hose example to those in Table 11.11. The company's Internet access cus-

Table 11.11 Bandwidth and Media versus Pipes and Hoses (Two Upstreams)

CUSTOMER	BANDWIDTH	POP	POP HOSE	IMPLEMENTATION (NO SINGLE POINT OF FAILURE)
1	1 Gbps	1	5 Gbps from POP to each upstream	8 OC-48s or 4 OC-192s
2	1 Gbps			
3	2 Gbps			
4A	1 Gbps			
5	1 Gbps	2	3 Gbps from POP to each upstream	3 OC-48s or 2 OC-192s
6	500 Mbps			
7	500 Mbps			
4B	1 Gbps			

tomers now connect to two POPs, either in single- or multihoming topologies. Every customer must have access to both upstreams, as shown in Figure 11.13. Topologically, this is only the almost-worst case because it only involves one class of service—basic Internet access. Still, there will need to be one trunk from each ingress router to each egress router, or $[R*(R-1)]$ trunks, where R is the number of routers and you assume unidirectional trunks.

Consider how this influences the requirements for POP routers that enter the core. If your survivability policy requires no single point of failure, or a single router or link cannot provide enough bandwidth, the number of routers and trunks must go up (Figure 11.14). This is the real problem in the ISP we are looking at. OC-48s aren't quite fast enough to meet the POP1 requirement with a single backup. Things get even worse when there are multiple service classes, such as a low-delay service for VoIP and a general Internet service. When you add different classes of service, you get much closer to the worst case, which involves $\{[R*(R-1)]*C\}$ trunks, where C is the number of classes of service. In Figure 11.15, your additional service classes only go between the POPs and the hosting server farm, so you might even be able to handle that connectivity purely within your IGP. Without traffic engineering, however, it is probably wise to configure separate trunks for the premium service.

However, there is a light at the end of the trunk tunnel, even if you don't use optical media. The first major simplification of trunks lies in trunk merging. Trunks that have the same exit point can be merged into a single trunk to the egress. Formally, the structure of many ingress paths leading to one egress point is called a *sink tree*. Borrowing from multicast terminology, it is the

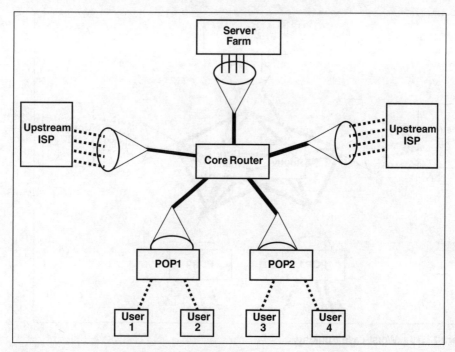

Figure 11.13 Almost-worst-case trunking.

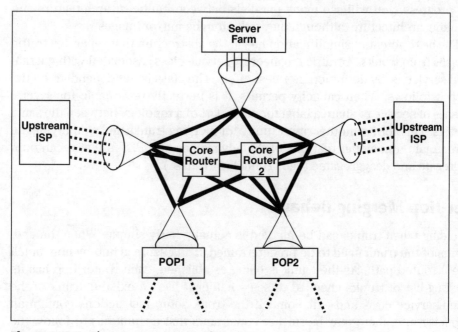

Figure 11.14 Almost-worse case getting worse.

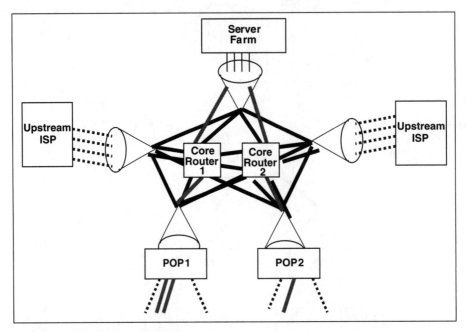

Figure 11.15 Worst-case trunking.

reverse of a *source tree*, with one source *S* and many members of the tree *G*. As we progress, you will see many parallels between multicast architecture and trunking architecture, although they will often be mirror images.

The next potential simplification lies in the abstraction that separates traffic classes from trunks. A traffic engineering service class associated with guaranteed service is, by definition, not best effort. The class is not dependent on the path it follows. When capacity permits, it is perfectly reasonable for several classes of service to share a label for all or part of a topology between the same routers. This forms another opportunity for merging trunks and simplifying the core. Again, remember that one of the advantages of MPLS is that it can both aggregate and deaggregated (see "Tunneled Trunks").

Per-Hop Merging Behavior

Deciding when trunks can be merged is actually fairly simple. While the endpoints of the trunk need to be predetermined, trunk setup is hop-by-hop, much like a routed path. As the trunk is being established, each router hop has its existing list of trunks checked to see whether it has an existing trunk of the same service class and exit point. If the trunk setup instructions contain an explicit route, there may be further constraints that a trunk has to follow the same predetermined explicit route to the destination—think of IP strict source routing versus loose source routing, or an ATM PVC, though where each hop is specified may vary (hop-by-hop versus all at ingress). If these constraints are satisfied, the trunks can merge. In MPLS, this means that while their traffic arrived with different labels, they can leave with the same outbound label. With maximal merging, the number of trunks reduces to $R*C$ sink trees (see Figure 11.16).

Let's reexamine the ISP we have been considering, with a temporary assumption that the merging router can be a single point of failure (see Table 11.12). Also, in Figure 11.17, assume that the merged facilities do not support different classes of service. MPLS label-switched routers do not necessarily need full routing information to merge paths or to protect or restore with alternate paths. The knowledge of routing does need to be at an LER that creates the path. There does have to be sufficient knowledge at every node, including LSRs, to select the next hop during path creation/recreation (on link failure).

In IP routing, aggregation can often be equivalent to merging. Assume, in Figure 11.18, that all the customers are single-homed and use your PA space, so aggregation at the POP level is appropriate. The difference is that an IP router, on receiving an aggregate, cannot deaggregate the packets without external information such as a routing policy in a routing registry.

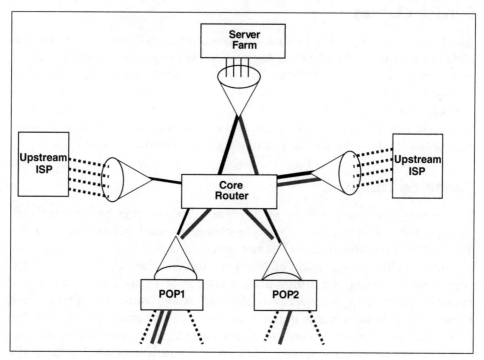

Figure 11.16 Benefits of merging.

Table 11.12   Bandwidth and Media versus Pipes and Hoses (Two upstreams, Single Merge Point)

CUSTOMER	BANDWIDTH	POP	POP HOSE	POP TO MERGE POINT	MERGE POINT TO UPSTREAM
1	1 Gbps	1	5 Gbps from POP to merge point	4 OC-48s or 4 2 OC-192s	2 OC-192s to each upstream
2	1 Gbps				
3	2 Gbps				
4A	1 Gbps				
5	1 Gbps	2	3 Gbps from POP to merge point	3 OC-48s or 2 OC-192s	2 OC-192s to each upstream
6	500 Mbps				
7	500 Mbps				
4B	1 Gbps				

Merging with Multiple Service Classes

Another consequence of TE being an alternative path determination mechanism to what the basic IGP would discover is that there is not necessarily a reason to create LSPs for best-effort (BE) traffic—simply use the path found by routing and don't use MPLS for BE. Your overall capacity planning, however, might be helped by assigning BE to LSPs. By doing so, you can predict when you might run out of capacity for BE services. Remember that BE trunks are aggregates of all BE flows. You would never need a trunk for each BE flow.

Tunneled Trunks

Trunks are tunnels, and tunnels can be encapsulated in other tunnels. In MPLS, we aggregate trunks by pushing a new label onto the stack of labels on a packet. This sort of aggregated trunk is just as much a trunk as the other types we have examined (with the exception of elephant trunks). The rule is that any two trunks can be aggregated if they share a portion of an underlying LSP. If you examine Figure 11.19, you will see that the aggregated trunk can carry different classes, because the class is in the inner label. At any point, popping off the outer label and sending the constituent trunks on their separate ways can deaggregate the trunk. Other trunks can back up aggregate trunks, and it is generally easier to plan backup for the lesser number of trunks that are aggregates. See "Survivability Mechanisms," later in this chapter.

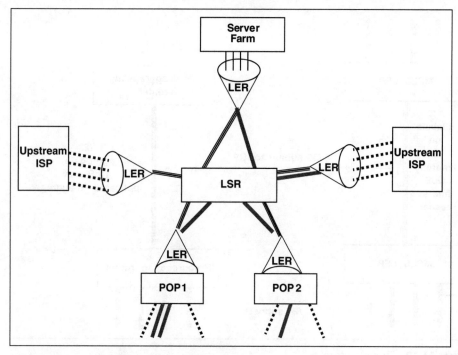

Figure 11.17 Merging with MPLS components.

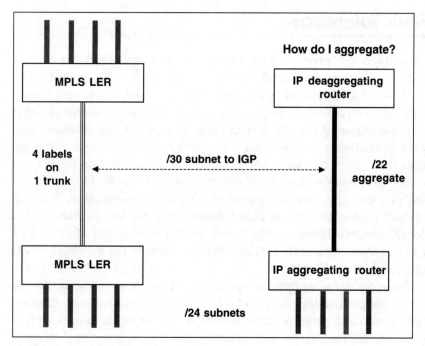

Figure 11.18 Merging and aggregation.

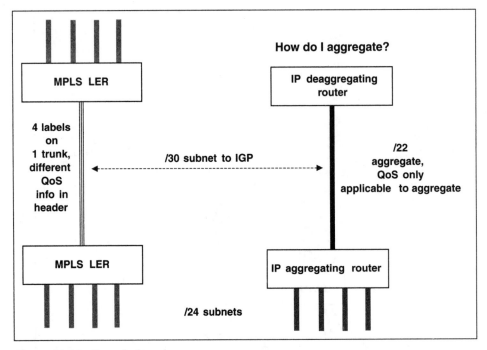

Figure 11.19 Tunneled trunks.

Core Fault Tolerance

Chapter 8 defined the primitives of protection and restoration, including topologies achievable with essentially hardware-based networks. As we look at a routed core—and a MPLS core is routed; the *traffic* is switched—additional mechanisms become possible. Other strategies include *local restoration* around the fault, or restoration of the entire path using source routing. However, you must always remember why you want a particular level of survivability and build against the defined requirements. For example, depending on the control system in use, you must restore VoIP control connectivity in 140 ms to 2 s before calls may drop. The 50-ms cutover of SONET is conservative. You may support special protocols such as IBM System Network Architecture (SNA) without local acknowledgement, which will drop a connection after 14 s of inactivity. Other protocol families that are timing-critical by nature include DEC Local Area Transport (LAT).

You may have real-time applications such as telepresence, telemetry, and so on that must have predictable delay. Delay may also be a commercial differentiator for competitive offerings of mission-critical business applications such as automatic teller machines, credit authorization, and transaction-based Internet commerce. Fault tolerance is not the only issue in horizontal hierarchy. Multi-area traffic engineering is not yet a well understood problem, even within a single provider.

What Can Go Wrong?

The first goal of the MPLS Recovery Draft [Sharma 2001] is to deal with "backhoe failures" of peer interoffice (provider core) connections. While the focus of this goal is on the transmission links themselves, it is easy enough to generalize it to include interface and router failures on those connections. The second and third failure types can be modeled as groups of link failures. Drop-side interfaces, as between a customer and an end office or between providers, may or may not be subject to the protection of the initial model. Levels of hierarchy inside a horizontal protocol model (for instance, metro to core) also may or may not be protected.

MPLS recovery cannot deal with all failures. If the LSP is being maintained by a soft state control protocol, a routing failure can bring it down. Mechanisms such as graceful restart (see Chapter 9) may make existing LSPs more robust as long as the control messages keep getting through. Congestion is not considered a failure to be recovered from, but something to be dealt with in the broad context of capacity planning and traffic engineering.

Survivability Concepts and Requirements

We introduced the broad issue of survivability in Chapter 8. We are concerned here with protection and restoration, not fault detection mechanisms or long-term repair, although we will consider the time taken by fault detection and its effect on overall survivability. The broad objective after a failure is *normalization*, which means the network returns to a preferred state after repair. The process of normalization includes protection and restoration, but goes beyond them. It also includes the choice of whether the "preferred state" after repair is necessarily the same topology as when the fault occurred. Revertive mode, for example, is a special case where the traffic must be returned to the original failed resource.

Not all services in a network need the same degree of normalization. Normalization involves two distinct objectives, possibly with different optimizations. One is the contractual SLA for a user service, and the other is the provider's engineering estimate of the criticality of internal resources.

See Table 11.13 for failure detection timers.

Table 11.13   Failure Detection Timers

FAILURE OR DEGRADATION TYPE	MPLS DEFINITION	IP ROUTING DEFINITION
Path failure (PF)	Recovery mechanisms have decided the LSP has totally lost connectivity.	BGP or IGP route withdrawal.
Path degraded (PD)	Recovery mechanisms have decided the quality of the LSP is unacceptable.	No equivalent in non-QoS IP routing.
Link failure (LF)	MPLS recovery mechanisms have been informed of a lower-layer total failure.	Typically implementation-specific, although OSPF does have a specific notification abstraction, especially for demand circuits. Usually associated with an SNMP trap.
Link degraded (LD)	MPLS recovery mechanisms have been informed of a lower-layer quality degradation.	Typically implementation-specific, although OSPF does have a specific notification abstraction. Usually associated with an SNMP trap if thresholds are defined.
Fault indication signal (FIS)	A fault along a path has occurred—passed along the path until it reaches an LSR capable of initiating recovery. Retransmitted periodically.	BGP or IGP withdrawal route. Generally considered poor practice to announce periodically.
Fault recovery signal (FRS)	A fault along a working path has been repaired.	BGP or IGP reannouncement of previously withdrawn route.

Shared-Risk Groups

Shared-risk groups (SRGs) [Dharanikota 2001] were not discussed in Chapter 8, because, while they abstractly model many of the layer 1 and 2 survivability schemes, their full potential only comes with the availability of (G)MPLS control plane functionality. We often speak of single points of failure, and that is exactly what an SRG defines—a set of network elements that will be affected by the same fault. SRGs are not a complex concept. At the link layer, a shared-risk link group (SRLG) is the set of links that can be taken down by a single backhoe cut. A shared-risk group of routers might be all of those on a common electrical power supply. A given resource can belong to multiple SRG's.

Survivability in Horizontal Hierarchies

In a horizontal hierarchy containing comparable resources under common administrative control, the principal goal is protecting a set of end-to-end connections between endpoints. These endpoints may be completely inside the administrative domain (for instance, internal trunks) or between external border routers. Each connection in this end-to-end set may have additional, area-specific protection mechanisms. Some connections will run between network elements that participate both in the horizontal (intraprovider) and vertical (interprovider) administrative domains. Other connections may run between different protocol layers in the same administrative domain.

When end-to-end protection is built on area-specific protection, success or failure of a restoration action at the area boundary will need to be signaled. Looking at this pessimistically, if there is a currently unrecoverable failure in one area, there is no need for the next area to try to find a working connection to the failure area.

Survivability in Vertical Hierarchies

In a vertical interprovider hierarchy, there must be a fail-safe recovery based on nested timers that, as long as they do not expire, do not trigger recovery mechanisms. Also, there certainly needs to be interprovider fault notification mechanisms, and extensive administrative and operational procedures that are worked out in advance of problems (see Chapter 6). When a lower layer cannot self-repair, the upper layer must be able to begin its own fault recovery. For example, if there are underlying point-to-point media, a self-healing medium such as SONET/SDH, IGP, or BGP needs to detect the failure, find an alternate path or signal the creation of one, and, where applicable, transfer LSPs to it. There also may need to be transfer to alternate providers, although this can cause a great deal of complexity in billing among the providers.

Survivability Mechanisms

Competitive near-term IP and MPLS networks need to be able to demonstrate the kind of survivability that exists in SONET/SDH transmission systems. The same kind of survivability is not necessarily expected in all-optical networks, because they remain in a prototype phase. In fact, fault notification is the first step, more important than automatic restoration.

The term *head end* is often used to describe the network management element that is responsible for survivability actions. When a head end attempts a recovery or restoration action, it ideally should create new connections that are as diversified as possible with respect to shared risk. Head ends, therefore, need SRG information. They also need to know if service restoration should be revertive or not. For nonrevertive protection, they need to be able to designate the new resource as working, using a "make-before-break" capability before releasing the old working resource. If the provider policy indicates the newly working resource should also be protected, the head end needs to find a new protection resource, typically through IP rerouting.

1:1 and 1+1 Restoration with Pre-established Protection Capacity

For the most critical applications, there needs to be an equivalent to 1:1 (generally not 1+1) SONET/SDH path protection with a pre-established protection resource. This does not preclude having preemptible traffic on the protection path. If the underlying transport is not packet-based, 1+1 protection may be appropriate.

1:1 and 1:n Restoration with Preplanned Protection Capacity

Subtly different, and appropriate for less critical traffic, is 1:1 path protection with preplanned (rather than pre-established) protection. With preplanned capacity, the protection resource can be shared among various active paths. If the active paths all have different restoration priorities, the restoration is still 1:1, but with the chance of preemption. If the active paths have the same restoration priority, this mechanism really becomes 1:n. This method is more resource-efficient than 1:1 with pre-established capacity, but is more complex. Local restoration may be a good compromise between the two methods.

Local Restoration

If one link in a multilink, end-to-end path, fails, it should be intuitive that if that link fails but can be restored transparently to the end-to-end mechanism, restoration will be faster (see Figure 11.20). Much as link-level retransmission is more efficient than end-to-end in certain specific situations, local repair is appropriate in some but not all networks. One of the main concerns is that local restoration may lead to suboptimal end-to-end paths, and path-level regrooming should be scheduled in a timely but nonintrusive way. Another consideration is whether all types of traffic are eligible for local restoration. If only guaranteed service traffic is eligible, it is possible that the local restoration link could be set up with less bandwidth with the general link.

The applicability of local repair is clearest for the failure of link SRGs, but local repair of relays is certainly possible as long as the relay's routing tables are current.

STOP AND THINK

How is this different, on a single hop, from multilink PPP provisioned so that either link can carry the entire load?

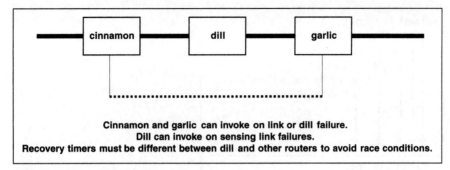

Figure 11.20   Local repair.

Path Restoration

This is the case in which a new potential path needs to be found using dynamic routing. It is slower than protection schemes, but much more resource-efficient.

Understanding Recovery Time

The MPLS recovery model does not cover every MPLS path. In the model, certain LSRs have special functions. A path switch LSR (PSL) is responsible for switching (1:1) or replicating (1+1) protected traffic between working and recovery paths. A path merge LSR (PML) receives the recovery path traffic and either puts it back into the working path or delivers it to the destination when it is the terminal LSR. Intermediate LSRs have neither a PSL or PML function. The recovery mechanism applies to path groups, which are bundles of working paths routed identically between a PSL and a PML. Only the protected path groups between the PSL and PML receive protection, since the PSL and PML are regular LSRs that also might receive best-effort traffic.

Recovery Cycle Model

In the recovery (Figure 11.21) and reversion (Figure 11.22) cycles, some timers are primarily of concern to the implementer of the recovery mechanism. Table 11.14 presents the operationally interesting timers. Other timers exist, but are primarily of interest to router developers [Sharma 2001]. The most operationally interesting timers are wait-to-restore and traffic restoration times. Do not overly emphasize making these extremely fast; make the underlying methods very reliable. Since these timers apply only when both working and protection paths are available, stability is more important than raw speed.

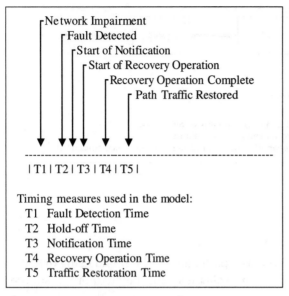

Timing measures used in the model:
T1 Fault Detection Time
T2 Hold-off Time
T3 Notification Time
T4 Recovery Operation Time
T5 Traffic Restoration Time

Figure 11.21 MPLS recovery cycle.

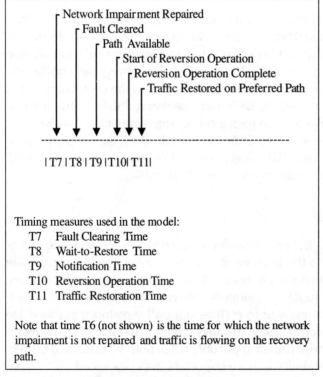

Timing measures used in the model:
T7 Fault Clearing Time
T8 Wait-to-Restore Time
T9 Notification Time
T10 Reversion Operation Time
T11 Traffic Restoration Time

Note that time T6 (not shown) is the time for which the network impairment is not repaired and traffic is flowing on the recovery path.

Figure 11.22 MPLS reversion cycle.

Table 11.14   Key Recovery and Reversion Cycle Timers

Fault detection time	Starts with the occurrence of a network impairment and ends with the time the fault is detected by recovery mechanisms. Lower-layer protocols may affect this very strongly.*
Hold-off time	The configured waiting time between the detection of a fault and taking MPLS-based recovery action, to allow time for lower layer protection to take effect. May be zero. In several IP routing protocols, this is called *holddown time*, but, unfortunately, there are several meanings of *holddown time* in different routing protocols and implementations.
Traffic restoration time	The time between the last recovery action and the time the traffic (if present) is completely recovered. This interval is intended to account for the time required for traffic to once again arrive at the point in the network that experienced disrupted or degraded service due to the occurrence of the fault (for example, the PML). Reversion is the time between the last reversion action and the time the traffic (if present) is completely restored on the preferred path. This interval is expected to be quite small since both paths are working and care may be taken to limit the traffic disruption (for example, using "make before break" techniques and synchronous switchover).
Fault-clearing time	The time between the repair of a network impairment and the time that MPLS-based mechanisms learn that the fault has been cleared.*
Wait-to-restore time	The configured waiting time between the clearing of a fault and MPLS-based recovery action(s). Waiting time may be needed to ensure the path is stable and to avoid flapping in cases where a fault is intermittent. May be zero.

* May be highly dependent on lower-layer protocols. Some lower-layer protocols give hardware failure indications in ms, while others have to wait for keepalives to be lost.

Dynamic Recovery Cycle

The autumn of falling resources is followed by the winter of lost connectivity. But we can always look forward to the spring, when faults are fixed and connectivity reconnected in an optimal way. Every spring is different, and the optimized network will not necessarily have the same characteristics after failure as before failure. New flows may have been assigned to old resources. Routing reconvergence may consider new resources. The old flow or trunk may or may not return to its original path. If it does so, this is called *reversion* following a fault (Figure 11.22). Alternatively, the routing system may find a better path for the old traffic. Dynamic reversion can be overlaid onto recovery (Figure 11.23), reversion, or both. Table 11.15 shows key timers in dynamic recovery.

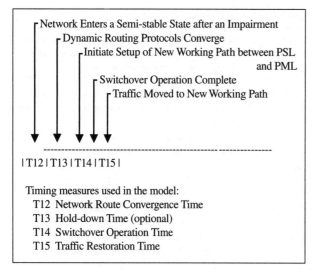

Timing measures used in the model:
 T12 Network Route Convergence Time
 T13 Hold-down Time (optional)
 T14 Switchover Operation Time
 T15 Traffic Restoration Time

Figure 11.23   Dynamic recovery cycle.

Reversion Cycle Model

I live in the great Commonwealth of Virginia, once home to George Washington, Arthur Ashe, and Thomas Jefferson. It is said that it takes three Virginians to change a light bulb: one to replace the failed component, and two to discuss how good the old one was. I am amazed, therefore, that revertive protection switching was not developed in my home state. Revertive protection switching switches the protected traffic back to the original preferred path when the original fault is corrected. Reversion normally takes place after recovery.

Table 11.15   Key Timers in Dynamic Recovery

Network route convergence time	The time taken for the network routing protocols to converge and for the network to reach a stable state. For BGP, see [Berkowitz 2001c].
Holddown time	A configured time for which a recovery path must be used.
	Experience with routing protocols and things as basic as dial backup show that restored working paths may not be stable when they first seem to return to service.
	Holddown timers prevent switching back to the restored path until there is high confidence that it is stable, reducing excess flapping.
Switchover operation time	Interval between the first and last switchover actions, which may include message exchanges between the PSL and PML.

Sub-IP Core Technologies

Major providers have tended to use sub-IP technologies for their high-capacity trunks between major concentration points. An early example was providers that leased high-capacity ATM trunks between their superhubs and then used WAN switches to distribute traffic among them. Routing among the WAN switches started out as a manual operation by skilled routing engineers, perhaps assisted by analytical models and performance measurements. Packet over SONET (POS) eliminated the ATM cell tax, although it was limited to point-to-point topologies. POS became a viable alternative between sufficiently large hubs, although the inherent wasted capacity of SONET protection rings remained a concern. IP over resilient packet rings is one alternative to avoid wasting capacity in backup rings.

While IP routing protocols do define paths, those paths are truly hop-by-hop and do not create connections or commit resources. Sub-IP protocols do commit resources and are generally connection-oriented, although the scope of those connections may be a single network element such as a DACS.

The IETF established a sub-IP temporary area to deal with methods for creating and managing forwarding paths, which are not IP but are critical to operation of new transmission systems. The control protocols for sub-IP will be IP-based.

CCAMP

While groups such as the IEEE, ITU-T, and so on develop the structure and protocol of the actual transmission techniques being controlled, the IETF, in its Common Control and Measurement Protocols (CCAMP) Working Group, is dealing with unifying these protocols. Requirements that CCAMP will examine include ensuring that signaling and management protocols are agnostic to electrical, optical, and optical-to-electronic hardware techniques, and to software tunneling techniques such as MPLS and Generic Routing Encapsulation (GRE).

A goal is to separate the control and measurement protocols so that different applications can use one without using the other. For example, measurement protocols might be very useful to billing applications that exert no control (other than that of the almighty dollar). Truly general control protocols will need media-independent ways to describe links and paths, as well as link and path protection.

MPLS

MPLS is the first major area of sub-IP protocol development, and it has accomplished a great deal. Commercial implementations are available, although multivendor interoperability issues have not been solved completely. MPLS, a software technique, is providing the basis for many of the control protocols for the more hardware-oriented techniques. There has been a recognition that it is worth looking systematically at a common control plane (telling it what to do) and measurement plane (finding out what it is doing) for all the sub-IP protocols. MPLS connectivity is defined by an IP control plane.

LSP Setup: LDP, RSVP-TE, CR-LDP

In MPLS, the protocols used to set up LSPs are not themselves routing protocols. They signal link state routers about how to match a label with a path. The information used to define the LSP and find the LSRs along it that need label information largely comes from routing protocols. Let me restate this, because it is a terribly important point. MPLS does not replace the path determination part of conventional routing. It complements it.

Bindings of labels to resources can come from automatic recognition of certain data patterns or from explicit control messages. The first category is *data-driven*, while the second is *control-driven*. Most (G)MPLS-related binding is control-driven, using the various setup protocols such as LDP, RSVP-TE, or CR-LDP. I find that data-driven mechanisms tend to be more appropriate for the edge and the user side than the intraenterprise core. For example, dial backup of a dedicated line is triggered by the loss of data on the primary link. The scalability problems of data-driven methods tend to be associated with timing. For example, for what period do you need to see a pattern before you trigger a resource allocation event? For how long can the pattern not be present before the binding should be torn down?

Control-driven mechanisms are more complex, but more predictable and thus more scalable in large, capacity-planned networks. MPLS architects initially made the decision to go with greater scalability from the beginning.

Label-Based Forwarding

It is not my goal to provide a detailed tutorial on MPLS forwarding. Nevertheless, some principles are relevant. Attaching labels to traffic gives a level of path setup and forwarding control that simply is not possible with traditional routing models that make decisions based on destination address only.

At each LSR, the label is looked up in a label information base and the next hop is determined. If the LSR is non-PSC, the label needs to be obtained from databases or external input, or fixed bindings such as label to port (or wavelength and port). At the egress, the new label is swapped for the old. Again, true label swapping applies only to packet MPLS; non-PSC links need to use an equivalent mechanism. Since labels can be stacked to create aggregate trunks/

traffic tunnels, the switch always makes its first decision on the top label in the stack. If deaggregation is called for, additional decisions may be made in the LSR.

So, a scalable trunking mechanism needs to support explicit paths, both administratively specified by operator action and dynamically created by mechanisms such as RSVP. MPLS is an attractive mechanism for specifying explicit routes. In moderately sized networks, alternatives could include non-real-time generation of static routes that are automatically configured into routers.

GSMP

GSMP provides the functionality needed to control a connection- and port-oriented device such as a DACS. Its current capabilities go beyond simple port configuration, and include statistics and event reporting as well as traffic engineering. It does, however, lack some additional capabilities needed to control optical or optical-electronic-optical (OEO) switches. These include the ability to process labels associated with lambdas or other optical identifiers and to be extended to include parameters associated with ports for optical services.

GSMP developers have become aware of increasing requirements to partition switches, much as the media gateways in Chapter 7 need to be partitioned and distributed to support open access for virtual POPs and similar open-access applications. GSMP currently assumes a static switch under the control of a single administrator, and work is under way to understand if it should be extended to include partitioning as in the MSF architecture. If GSMP is extended in this manner, existing mechanisms such as MIBs and/or policy information bases (PIBs) would be used to the greatest extent possible, although GSMP protocol extensions are possible.

Traffic Engineering Deployment

[Donnell 1999] presents a superb tutorial on gaining familiarity with recognizing problems, LSP setup, and traffic engineering applied to solve a problem. In the case in Figure 11.24, due to the IGP metrics in the congested network, more than 155 Mbps of traffic is being routed onto the **horseradish-juniper** link. To understand that MPLS does not inherently work miracles, build LSPs that follow the IGP-derived routing. You can do this by enabling RSVP signaling but not enabling (yet) constraint-based routing. When you create the Figure 11.25 network, monitor it and decide what traffic needs to move to alleviate congestion. Now, create a simple explicit route to move congestion of bandwidth off the horseradish-juniper link (Figure 11.26).

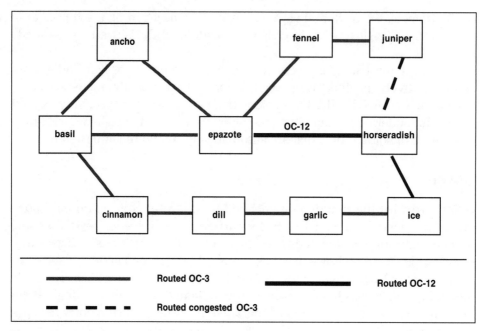

Figure 11.24 Lab network with congestion.

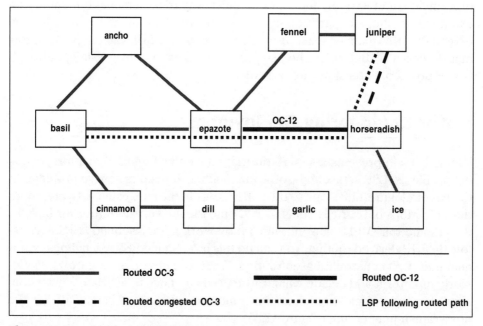

Figure 11.25 Creating non-TE LSPs.

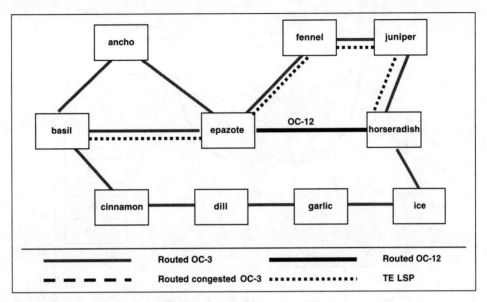

Figure 11.26 Adding TE to alleviate congestion.

Once you understand the role of manual explicit route creation in alleviating congestion, you can begin gaining experience with other MPLS features, such as fast rerouting by local repair (Figure 11.27). It is also wise to gain experience with how your network management tools see these links, routers, and other components both logical and physical.

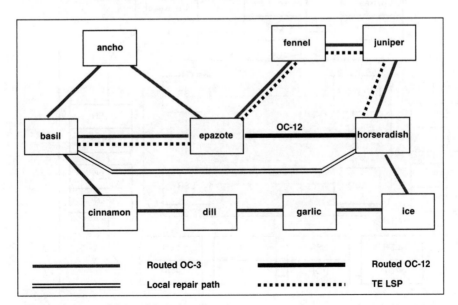

Figure 11.27 Additional functionality.

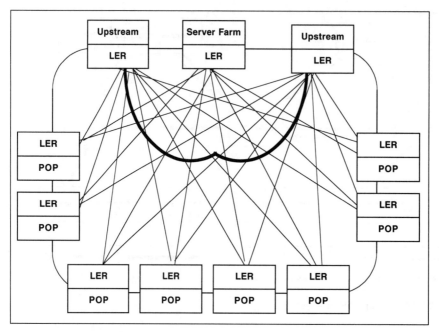

Figure 11.28   Basic BGP-free core.

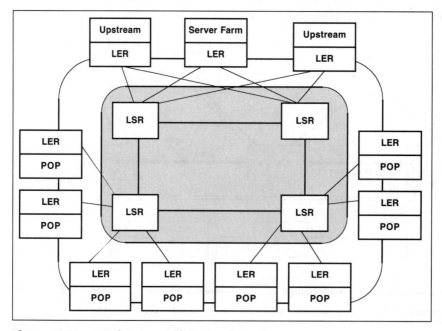

Figure 11.29   BGP-free core with regional merging.

BGP-free Cores

If all the POP egress routers also are MPLS LERs, the core really does not need BGP at all. A fault-tolerant core design might have two or more intermediate LSRs, connected to each other, that interconnect all POPs, server sites, and external border routers (Figure 11.28). The core should be preprovisioned with backup LSPs as part of traffic trunks. If new trunks are needed, they should be initiated at the edge, with the interaction of management, routing protocols, and MPLS path setup. You could also have additional intermediate LSRs, again being careful about single points of failure, to do regional merging. A BGP-free core, however, should not be IGP-free (see Figure 11.29). Without an IGP, MPLS setup protocols cannot discover the changing topology onto which MPLS will create LSPs.

Looking Ahead

Merging also may combine all the traffic meant for another provider. Hold that thought, as the next chapter focuses on interprovider connectivity.

CHAPTER 12

The Provider-to-Provider Border

Oil and Big Telecom. The oil and ISP industries are the only two major industries I know of where your biggest competitors are quite often also your biggest customers.

In the oil industry, you see it all the time with the company-owned retail stores versus the dealers—but who do the dealers buy from? Right.

It makes for some rather interesting business relationships. . . .
—*Steven J. Sobol, NANOG Mailing List, July 27, 2001*

A number of differing objectives exist as to why the ISP is entering the market, and the business plan should reflect such motivations.
—*Geoff Huston*

"XXX's Internet backbone includes redundant equipment and diverse routing to ensure the highest reliability. Leveraging XXX's advanced SONET network, we have specially engineered our network to take full advantage of SONET reliability. In addition, XXX uses the YYY routers in its backbone, which translates into greater response time and reliability for your users."
—*A real major provider sales pitch, in which sales forgot to get technical checking, names deleted to protect the guilty*

A fundamental principle governs commercial interprovider relationships: Everyone must either make a profit, or, if they pay for service, cover their costs. Major technical challenges often derive from economic imperatives.

Before certain readers bring up arguments that "the Internet should be free" or "there should be free access so as not to create have-nots," let me change the subject to physiological addiction. Not to addiction to opioids—that would be far too easy—but addiction to oxygen. Yes, you heard me correctly. Oxygen is far more addictive than heroin, crack cocaine, or barbiturates. Do any of those drugs addict with 100 percent certainty? Will virtually all of those drug addicts fight violently if they are deprived of a dose for mere seconds?

Money is the oxygen of the Internet, with both its life-giving and its addictive properties. True, governments, academic institutions, and so on subsidize some Internet participants, but money still remains the root of all Internet good and evil. When you examine any interprovider relationship, you must ask the classic question of the detective or lawyer: "*Qui bono?* Who benefits?" For any relationship to be viable, all participants must have a sense of benefit. Economists say that, for a transaction to occur, it must be perceived to be mutually beneficial (even "your money or your life" presents a choice, and we take the more beneficial choice).

The cost of providing Internet services includes the cost of subscriber access, the cost of connectivity to other providers, and possibly the cost of providing content. If your local model will accept these costs, plus a reasonable profit margin, you may succeed.

Chapters 7 and 10 discuss the technologies of access. To focus more on the cost component, [Huston 1999] identifies a set of factors that go into costing the access service:

- Characteristics of the access service
- Duration of access
- Volume of data passed
- Distance through the network
- Quality of the service
- Value-added service

These are factors that pertain only to the cost of entry into your network. When your customer wants general Internet access, extranet access to sites not directly connected to you, or perhaps access to its own sites in areas you do not serve directly, you will incur interprovider costs.

Interprovider Economics: The Most Important Part

The focus of this chapter is interprovider connectivity, for which cost is a major consideration. You learn routes from your enterprise customers, but other than the stray mutual backup arrangement, you will not learn the bulk of your routes from them.

A provider relatively low in the food chain can default to a higher-level provider. Simple defaults, however, will become less and less optimal as the lower-level provider grows. If you are homed to multiple upstreams, you really need to know routes from each of them to pick the best path and give the best service to your customers. "Best," of course, can be a subjective choice containing operational, economic, and service-level components. There are three basic ways to connect to another provider: buying transit, peering at an exchange point, and private peering. All assume different economic relationships between the providers. Each will be discussed in detail, but see Table 12.1 for a basic comparison.

The Trail of Tiers

The largest service providers interact using an economic model called *peering*. Do not confuse this usage with the use of *peering* as a synonym for an arbitrary BGP connection. The usage discussed here is economic. Specifically, economic peering means that the participants do not exchange money for service, with possibly a narrow exception for covering the costs of common functions (for example, transmission lines) owned or operated by one of the participants.

ISPs and NSPs often are called tier 1 through tier 5. Unfortunately, these categories have no universal meaning, although marketers in the larger providers tend to define tier 1 as whatever they are and their competitor is not.

Table 12.1 Basic Interprovider Alternatives

BUYING TRANSIT	PEERING AT EXCHANGE	PRIVATE PEERING
Provider-customer	Equals	Equals
Line cost to upstream*	Access cost to peer	Line cost[†, ‡]
Guaranteed bandwidth	Potential congestion	Guaranteed
Router cost[§]	Portion of router cost	Portion of router cost
Incremental router port cost	Incremental router port cost	Incremental router port cost
Simple	More things to go wrong	Simple

* The faster the link, the lower the cost per bit.

† With one line, peers split the cost. It is quite common to have two links for diversity, each provider paying for one.

‡ There can be direct physical connections between the participants' equipment at exchange points. Such connections are dedicated media, usually but not always of minimal cost, and are not subject to third-party congestion.

§ While this becomes less and less a requirement as you move up the hierarchy of tiers, some large providers may require you to use a dedicated router they specify.

Tier 1 and the Default-Free Zone

When you have a router in the default-free zone, its routing table contains no default routes. You have sufficient routes, learned through many possible sources, to get to any plausible Internet destination without defaulting to any other provider. This definition does not preclude a customer, especially a multihomed customer, from being in the DFZ. When we speak of "tier 1 providers," however, we are referring to providers that do not pay any other provider for transit. (See Figure 12.1.) All routes are obtained through bilateral agreements.

General usage suggests that a tier 1 provider have a national or international backbone with at least OC-3 rates. Some providers are asking for OC-12 or OC-48 backbones before they will exchange routes. In addition, such a provider has a presence at several regional exchange points, and may have private peerings—usually, the more the better—with other providers high in the food chain.

Another way of describing tier 1 providers, although unfortunately a circular one, is that tier 1 providers primarily connect with other tier 1 providers. Their connectivity is primarily mutual peering; they do not buy transit. Their peering and core routers are treated as utterly default free (Figure 12.2).

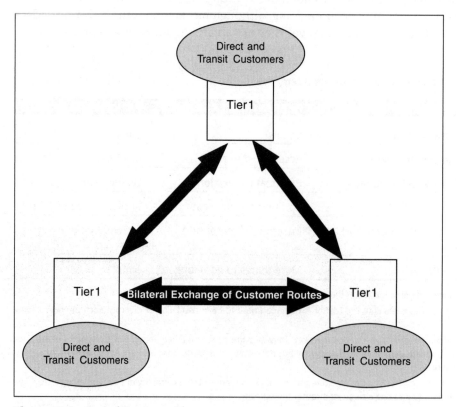

Figure 12.1 Typical tier 1 provider.

```
PLEASE NOTE - THIS ROUTER SHOULD NOT HAVE A DEFAULT ROUTE.

It is used to connect to AS with reciprocal peering arrange-
ments.

Such AS MUST NOT be able to default to us.

The configuration for this router does NOT conform to our corpo-
rate backbone standard.

For information, or to make changes, contact Core Network
Engineering at 555-1234.
```

Figure 12.2 Sample banner from peer router.

Lower Tiers

Tier 2 providers are something of an endangered species, but they can be considered organizations with a broadband backbone limited to a geographic region. Regional providers were an important part of the original National Science Foundation Network (NSFNET) design, but mostly have been acquired by larger providers. They buy transit for connectivity outside their regions and are well connected to exchange points within their regions.

The idea of a tier becomes increasingly hazy as you move down the hierarchy. One definition of a tier 3 provider is a metropolitan area provider multihomed to at least two higher-level providers. This is a plausible scenario for a local telephone company or other access provider that meets the regulatory requirements for providing direct Internet connectivity to customers. Below tier 3, you are increasingly approaching the level of the Internet cafe or the dial-up aggregator in a garage.

Basic Economic Models

There are relatively few models for commercial communications charging. Here we will discuss bilateral settlements, transit fees, and sender keep all (SKA).

Speak Telco to Me: Bilateral Settlements

The telephone industry has long used the bilateral settlement model, in which telephone companies are compensated both for terminating and originating calls. For a number of reasons, this works for connection-oriented but not connectionless packet services. Typical settlement models involve long-distance carriers compensating local carriers for the costs of originating and terminating local calls. Local telephone companies with many retiree customers sometimes generate more revenue from settlements than they do from direct charges to their subscribers. The local telephone company doesn't care if the adult children are calling their parents due to guilt or to love; it's all settlement revenue.

There are technical problems in using a settlement model for packet-based, connectionless communications. The most fundamental is the volume of accounting information. For a given telephone call, records are created at the time the call starts and the time it ends. In other words, the switching system deals with the call as the basic unit of information. In a packet-based system, however, the basic unit of information is the packet. A voice over IP (VoIP) conversation may generate thousands or millions of packets per call. Where are these packets counted and where is the billing information sent? If these calls go over the public Internet, counting them at the ingress and egress routers is inadequate. Packets within the same call may go through different ASs on their path to their destination, and each router in each AS handling the packet conceptually should be compensated. Another problem is that packet delivery is not guaranteed, but the failure to deliver can occur anywhere along the path, after the packet has consumed resources in intermediate ASs. In Figure 12.3, should AS2 and AS3 receive compensation? If they receive compensation, from whom do they collect? The originating AS, the destination AS, the AS that gave them the packet, or the AS that dropped the packet and cost them revenue? Geoff Huston has defined the problem space as follows: "Can two providers interconnect without the implicit requirement to cast one as the provider and one as the supplier?" [Huston 1999]. Remember that this sort of interconnection involves far more than two providers. Given the history of success with connection-oriented services, it may actually work for VPNs.

Feudal Loyalty Runs Up and Down: Transit Fees

To get connectivity outside their local areas, most ISPs buy transit service from one or more providers with national and/or international coverage. The transit

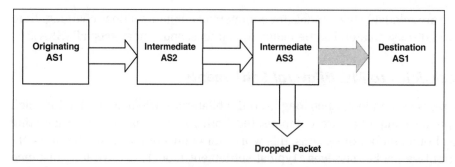

Figure 12.3 Intermediate resource consumption.

A FUTURE MODEL: CHARGING FOR ANNOUNCEMENTS

An idea that periodically resurfaces is to base a settlement-like approach on slots in the routing table. While this makes technical sense and indeed identifies a key economic resource, there has never been a viable proposal for how to collect and distribute for globally advertised routes.

provider normally charges by the speed of the access link, and will offer various alternatives of the routes it sends to the subscriber. Common route offerings include:

- All known routes, including the transit provider's customer routes
- Customer routes only
- Default routes

Don't necessarily assume that getting customer routes only from a large upstream will let you load-share without the memory impact of full routes. Major national ISPs, however, often have tens of thousands of routes in their customer table.

We Can Live in the Commons: SKA

SKA is definitely the model among the largest providers, but while often thought to be the basic model of Internet pricing, it works only with providers of roughly equal size. It assumes that each service provider bills its customers for the cost of traffic origination, but that there is no financial compensation between providers. The underlying assumption is that participants in SKA relationships originate approximately the same amount of traffic, and that it would be more cost and trouble than it would be worth to try to come up with a more precise accounting.

SKA is the model used among tier 1 providers and providers lower in the hierarchy that consider themselves of approximately equal size. SKA is a perfectly reasonable approach for a local exchange, as long as the common cost of the local exchange is covered by membership fees.

Bilateral Private Peering Arrangements

In bilateral private peering (Figure 12.4), the two participants agree they have a roughly equivalent amount of information to exchange, and do so without explicit compensation. If they have one physical link, they will share the cost. Frequently, they use two links to avoid creating a single point of failure, and each provider orders or provides one link. Both providers cover their own router costs. The link(s) are treated as BGP inter-AS links. While the addresses can come from either party, the address space is not normally advertised. If the address space is part of an aggregate, external access to the link from other than the two providers' space should be restricted.

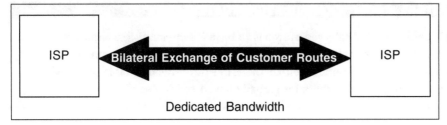

Figure 12.4   Bilateral private peering.

Bilateral Exchange Peering Arrangements

In bilateral peering at an exchange point (Figure 12.5), each provider negotiates a separate peering agreement with each other provider with which it exchanges routes. The difference between private peering and exchange peering is that in private peering only one router and access link runs from the provider to the exchange point. The routing exchanges are done through a common fabric. The exchange fabric forwards traffic between them based on MAC address or VLAN identifier. Depending on the rules of the exchange, one provider may actually sell transit to other peers and be accessed through the fabric. In such cases, the subscribers can point default at the transit provider. It is extremely bad form to point default at an arbitrary provider at a multilateral exchange.

Multilateral Exchange Peering Arrangements

At a multilateral exchange, the rules of participating in the exchange require you to exchange customer routes with all other participants. Physical connectivity may be identical to that in the bilateral exchange peering arrangement (see Figure 12.6). Generally, the lower in the food chain the exchange, the more likely it is that the exchange rules will require multilateral peering of customer routes among all participants. This does require a full mesh of BGP connections unless a route server is used, which potentially can be a problem with small routers.

At a multilateral exchange, participants do not and should not advertise default to one another unless one is a direct transit customer of the other. Even in that case, it is generally much cleaner to provide transit through a bilateral

THINGS CAN GET VERY BLURRY

Private bilateral peering physically can be no more than a piece of cable or fiber between equipment racks at the premises of an exchange point. The exchange operator staff may even run the cable. But this sort of connectivity is not bilateral exchange peering unless the connectivity traverses the shared exchange fabric.

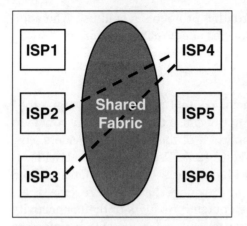

Figure 12.5 Bilateral exchange peering.

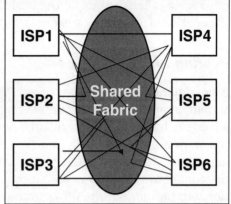

Figure 12.6 Multilateral exchange peering.

private peering cable. There may be individual arrangements where equal-level providers provide conditional default to one another as part of mutual backup arrangements. At larger multilateral exchanges, some upper-tier providers will advertise their customer routes to some or all participants.

Special Cases

Private peering consisting of a cable between equipment racks at an exchange is one special case. There are others involving either unusual economic relationships or facility types that are not pure interprovider exchanges.

Subsidized Networks

Especially in academic and research ventures, you may want your provider to send you routes belonging to special research networks. Communities usually identify such networks. If you can carry some of your traffic on a link or network that is subsidized, it is certainly to your advantage to have all applicable traffic take the special path. We have seen examples of this in the Johnson City Medical and the Medium State University case studies.

VPN Routes

Interprovider VPN routes that are not implemented using a sub-IP protocol will generally be identified with communities, especially extended communities (see Chapter 13). Since the path taken by an explicitly provisioned cold-potato VPN is known, a settlement model can make sense. The whole idea of QoS-sensitive routing also hits on this. Traffic engineering, by definition, picks paths on criteria other than those the basic routing protocols would use. The additional criteria generally consider QoS policies and possibly utilization.

Peering for Content

A continuing controversy surrounds major content providers that argue they should be eligible for bilateral peering not because they have many routes to advertise, but because a very large proportion of the network providers' customers want to reach their sites (see Figure 12.7). Especially at a mixed hosting/intercarrier site, carriers may peer with providers. Far more routes go from the connectivity providers to the content providers than in the reverse direction, but far more traffic flows from the content providers to the connectivity providers. Participants in such an arrangement believe that a satisfactory degree of equality exists.

There have been cases where major connectivity providers withdrew route peering from a major content provider, insisting that the content provider did not advertise enough routes and that the content provider should buy transit. Another case is the content distribution network (CDN), which pays access ISPs to put content caches at their POPs or elsewhere in their network relatively close to the end user. The advantage to the content provider client of the content distribution network is improving latency, while there are two benefits to the access provider: direct revenue from the CDN and reduced upstream bandwidth requirements. Indeed, access ISPs may unilaterally decide to install web caches to reduce their upstream bandwidth requirements, especially reducing bandwidth-based charges from transit providers.

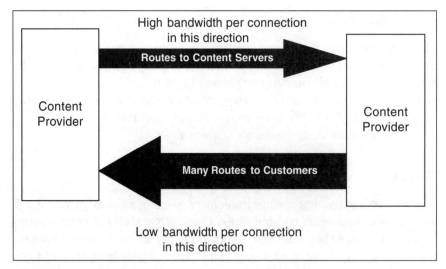

Figure 12.7 Content peering.

Interconnection Strategies: The Second-Most Important Part

Once you understand your economic model, you know how you get oxygen into your interprovider relationships. The next priority is getting food for your interprovider and customer relationships. This has several aspects: the BGP-enforced policies on route exchange, the actual pipes and hoses over which traffic is carried, and the protection of your routing system and the routing system in general.

Providers interconnect primarily with point-to-point links, or in a common switching fabric at exchange points. Aside from the ever growing technical challenges, they have to interconnect in a means that makes economic sense. With the growth of the public Internet, there are serious technical challenges to the integrity of the global routing system. There are overlaps between VPNs and the public routing system, or at least overlaps within providers.

Potatoes between Providers

To understand interprovider relations, you have to understand the economics associated with the various temperatures of potatoes. People used to enterprise networking, where a single manager controls all resources, are accustomed to having enforceable expectations of performance, and routing of traffic. In the Internet, however, unless you have a business relationship with every service provider in the end-to-end path, you have no way to control how traffic will be routed. The route taken will depend on the individual routing policies of each provider along the path. You can influence, but not control, the routing decisions of other providers.

Hot potato does need to recognize reality. In Figure 12.8, even though having a direct link between POP1 and POP4 would give a closer exit, your standard topology would not include a direct link between the two POPs. Instead, it is least resource-intensive to backhaul the packet to the first common merge point to which both POPs have access. That point is the core router. If the service objective is to provide controlled QoS, the provider will either:

1. Keep the packet inside the network it controls until it is as close as possible to the packet's destination.

THE FIRST PRIME DIRECTIVE

By minimizing the amount of resources you need to move the packet from ingress to egress, you minimize your cost. Unless you have a financial incentive to maximize control, hot potato is the most rational strategy.

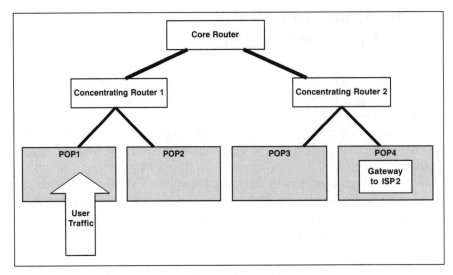

Figure 12.8 Reality and hot potato.

2. Transmit packets of the service only to providers with which it has an economic relationship and whose behavior it has the financial power to control (for instance, by giving preferred QoS to traffic marked with a mutually agreed community).

In current practice, to influence the entrance strategy of other ASs, the ISP has to advertise more-specific routes (that is, a larger number of them) to give other providers the information to choose entrances based on customer address. Adding routes to the table, however, is contrary to the broader goals of Internet scalability. Other techniques that use either some form of BGP signaling (especially communities) or MPLS are under active discussion.

For interprovider routing without QoS, conventional BGP with hot-potato routing is quite adequate. As SLAs for high availability begin to enter the picture, there is still a reasonable amount of SLA enforcement that is possible with appropriate business models, interprovider signaling with communities, and reliable design by each provider. The model chills to cold potato. It becomes harder—but not impossible—to do interprovider routing with QoS guarantees, again signaling primarily with communities. MPLS begins to have more and more advantages here, especially considering that it is possible to nest MPLS tunnels by stacking labels.

THE SECOND PRIME DIRECTIVE

Cold potato is the most rational strategy for premium services where quality of service is more important than minimizing cost.

Mutual Backup

Providers can be competitors, but the more serious the situation, the more they tend to help one another. There are many industry stories from September 11, 2001, about how providers in the New York area made resources available to one another:

> *PAIX and Abovenet (both subsidiaries of MFN) have space, power and various forms of connectivity available at 111 8th [New York City]. Anyone who was impacted by the WTC disaster and who needs a place to set up an emergency network node should get in touch w/ me (I'll intro you to MFN or to Abovenet if PAIX can't help.)*
>
> *—Paul Vixie, NANOG Mailing List, September 12, 2001*

During less massive catastrophes, there is still a good deal of cooperation, and some indeed may be preplanned. One of the most common examples is the exchanging of secondary DNS services. Exchanging bandwidth becomes more complex from a business strategy standpoint. The motivations tend to be saving money on upstream links, and possibly providing better performance on connectivity within the serving area.

One basic motivation involves two local ISPs that are customers of the same upstream national provider. The two local ISPs connect to different POPs and can establish reasonably diverse local connectivity between one another. The upstream has to agree that the local market reality is that the two local providers will go elsewhere if the upstream insists that each provider pay multihoming fees to the upstream. See, for example, the discussion of Medium State University in Chapter 10. A different model exists when local providers have a fair number of common customers, or customers that want to reach a server on the other local provider. The emphasis here is less on upstream connectivity than connectivity at the same hierarchical level.

Let's look at Johnson City in the interim period where general users can use the medical radio link. Upstream 2 has not yet been implemented (see Figure 12.9). After the radio network is limited to medical use, look at the entire Johnson City environment, in which JCC and JMedNet provide mutual transit (see Figure 12.10).

What Should You Advertise and Accept?

With our current understanding of global Internet routing behavior, reducing the number of routers in the default-free table improves stability and scalability for many reasons.

An aggregate is often a black hole and hides changes within its AS. One of the major scaling problems occurs when the total number of routes is less than the

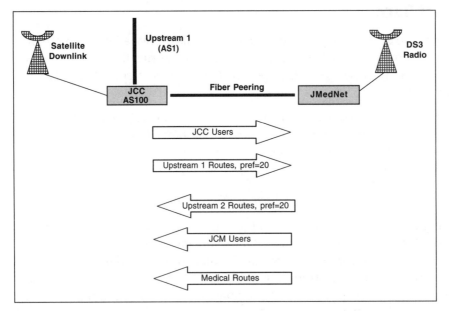

Figure 12.9 Johnson City, pre-Upstream 2.

amount of change within the routing table. So, unless there are overriding reasons for sending more specifics, you are particularly interested in sending the smallest number of routes to another provider. Your multihomed customers expect that you will advertise in a manner that makes their alternate routing visible throughout the Internet. Unfortunately, this may not be a realistic assumption. Again and again, we return to the basic principle that a participant

THE SWAMP AND THE TOXIC WASTE DUMP

As mentioned, the swamp is the original class C space. At one point, before CIDR was introduced, swamp routes filled approximately half the slots in the global routing table. The location of the swamp is arguable, but there is much more consensus about the location of its pit of horrors, the toxic waste dump (TWD). The TWD is that part of the swamp that contains prefixes, advertised internet-wide, that are longer than /24. In pre-CIDR days, it occupied about a quarter of the routing table.

Having been born in Newark, New Jersey, which Nietzsche probably had in mind when he wrote, "That which does not destroy me makes me the stronger," I believe the TWD is somewhere in northern New Jersey. Canadians, with two significant exceptions, believe the TWD is in the United States. Residents of Calgary, however, believe it is in Edmonton, and vice versa. There is not much love lost between these two Albertan cities!

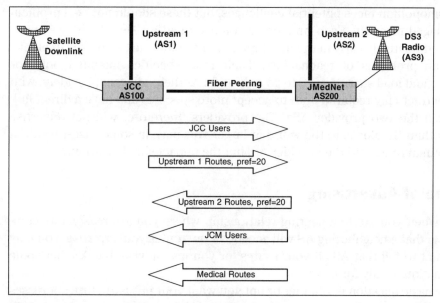

Figure 12.10   Johnson City, post-Upstream 2.

can expect control over routing only to the extent that the customer pays for control. In other words, once a customer's advertisement is propagated to an AS that is not paid for transit, that AS is under no obligation to carry detailed route information. It may do so, but it has its own acceptance and readvertising policies that are not set by you or by your customers.

Let's look at some of our customers. Huffle, Puffle, which has the simplest configuration, has the greatest likelihood of encountering reachability problems if it continues to want to advertise its small amount of PI space. There may be a saving factor: ISPs are generally more tolerant of /24s in the traditional "swamp." The swamp is the original assignment block for Class C addresses: 192.0.0.0/8. Realistically, however, the longest prefix with a good chance of universal reachability is a /20.

Design and Dig, Medical World, and Panacea Products will have no problems because their address space is completely contained in their provider's. Their more-specifics are not exported outside their provider. Medium State University has a sufficiently large address block to ensure reachability. Magic Images probably will not have problems, although its address space requirements may not justify a significant PI block. The key is that its general Internet connectivity is through its provider's block, and the provider is responsible for its VPN connectivity to other providers. Luckily, Magic Images' interprovider links have large enough bandwidth requirements to generate significant revenue for all carriers involved, which are likely to pay significant attention to connectivity. Each continental region of Rebel Express is sufficiently large to justify a /20 or shorter PI address space. This company should have no reachability problems.

Cosmopolitan faces potential challenges, but these should not be a problem if managed properly. Each premerger company had a Class B address space assigned relatively early in the development of the Internet, so these /16 blocks have no problems of reachability. Their more-specifics intended only for failover and load sharing need to go only as far as their adjacent providers, who are contractually required both to accept more specifics and have a direct link between the two provider ASs. The providers, therefore, will not advertise longer than /16 blocks to the world at large. This may, in some cases, result in suboptimal routing to the provider AS, but the impact should be minimal.

Scope of Advertising

Even when you are in a peering relationship where you are reasonably comfortable that a neighboring AS will accept all the routes you advertise, you may not want to tell that AS all your routes, or you may advise that AS that some information is only for its use.

One basic question is whether or not you want your infrastructure addresses directly accessible from the outside. In Figure 12.11, is there a reason why the dashed subnets should ever be accessed by an outside entity? Not having them directly accessible does not mean they won't show up in a traceroute, but outside hosts will not be able to ping them.

A way to control what is accessible is to have your principal advertisements be blackhole routes and to advertise only more-specifics whose advertising serves some specific purpose (see Figure 12.12). When you receive a route marked with the NO-EXPORT community, you can distribute it within your AS, but, if you honor the intention of NO-EXPORT, you must not advertise it to

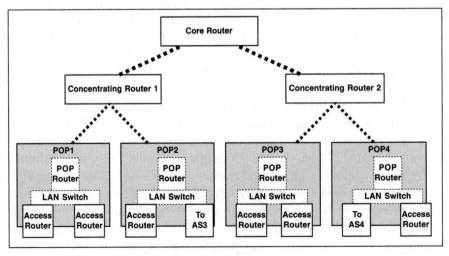

Figure 12.11   Infrastructure subnets.

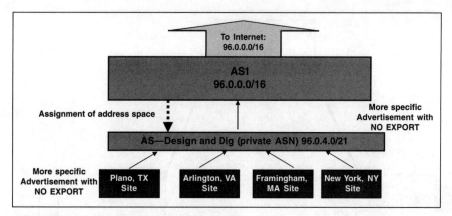

Figure 12.12   Black holes and NO-EXPORT.

other AS. The general purpose of NO-EXPORT is to provide information that is useful to a single AS or a pair of adjacent ASs, but not the Internet in general. If a customer becomes multihomed to multiple providers, the NO-EXPORT will need to be removed. Otherwise, the provider advertising the more-specifics will attract all traffic.

Weird and wondrous things can happen in multihoming. I don't use *wondrous* here necessarily to refer to goodness, but to protocol behavior that fills one with wonder about how routing can get so tricky. See Figure 12.13, to which Mr. Murphy (of Murphy's Law) appears to have given special attention. AS100, customer of AS1 and AS2, believes it has Internet-wide multihoming. In this case, it has the illusion of such. Part of the illusion comes about when AS100 tests its multihoming by disabling the link to AS1 (Figure 12.14). AS100 pings host B in AS2 and gets a normal response. In this specific case, AS2 knows how to send to AS100 because AS100 is a direct customer and has made specific arrangements for AS100 routes to be accepted and readvertised. When AS100 tests connectivity to host C in AS3, the ping succeeds (Figure 12.15), but in a somewhat strange manner. AS3 does not know how to reach the AS100 address, but it knows how to reach the less-specific of AS1. In this particular case, there is a direct link between AS1 and AS2. AS1 knows it cannot reach AS100 by its usual link, but it knows how to reach AS100 because AS2 has advertised the AS100 route to AS1. AS2 advertises the AS100 route because AS100 is a direct customer of AS2. If there were no link between AS1 and AS2, the ping would fail (Figure 12.16). Assume that AS2 and AS3 are mutually peering, not in a provider-consumer relationship. You might question this, because there is an indirect link through AS3. The problem here is that even if AS2 advertises the /24 of AS100 to AS3, AS3 happens to have a policy of not accepting routes longer than /20 from noncustomer ASs. AS3 does forward the echo request to AS1 because it knows that the host A address is in AS1's aggregate,

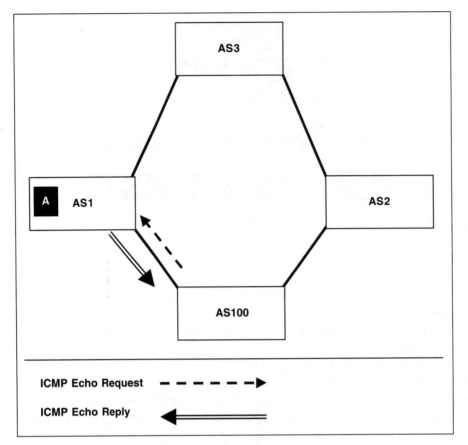

Figure 12.13 Starting multihomed configuration.

but AS1 does not know where to send the ping response because its own link to AS100 is down, and AS3 is not re-advertising the route it learns from AS2.

One of the proposals for using BGP to control preferential routing without cluttering the global routing table with unneeded more-specific routes is the addition of a well-known transitive community, NOPEER [Huston 2001a]. In Geoff Huston's proposal, route advertisements tagged with NOPEER propagate only as far as the economic relationships among specific ASs. Once the advertisement reaches a boundary of economic peering, where one provider has no financial controls over the other, the advertisement is dropped. This community prevents the propagation of the more-specific route beyond a point where it will have any effect on the path taken by traffic. It reflects the reality of SKA economics versus transit provider-customer economics.

Huston's motivation is an analysis that more than half of the global routing table entries may be there not to improve reachability of new prefixes, but to affect the

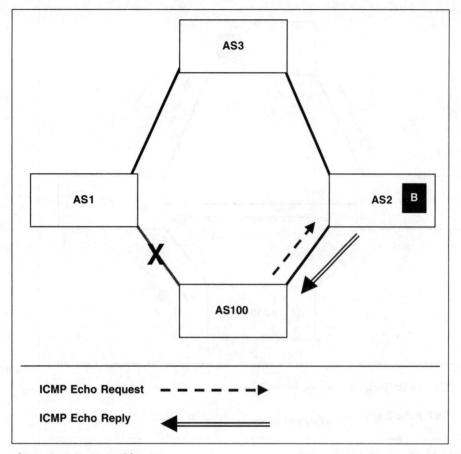

Figure 12.14 Test with AS2.

way in which existing prefixes are reached. In other words, there are present both an aggregate route and a set of more-specific routes to the same destination set. Typically, these preferred ways include fault tolerance, load balancing, or both. There are several proposals to implement this behavior. Another approach involves explicit listing of ASs to which further distribution of the more-specific route is not desirable. The problem of this approach is one of maintenance.

I have proposed a related approach [Berkowitz 2001h] with a slightly different goal, the "supercommunity." Whereas the NOPEER attribute is exclusive and tells an AS not to propagate certain information, the supercommunity advises a group of participating ASs that some particular traffic attribute should be honored. How is this different from any other community? It would typically be under the administrative control of an exchange point, which often does not have an AS number of its own. The supercommunity and the NOPEER attribute may very well be complementary.

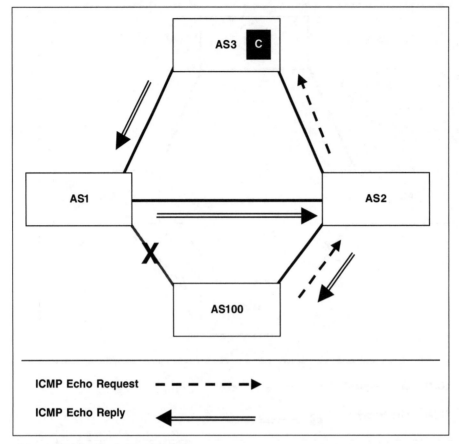

Figure 12.15 Direct AS1-AS2 link.

With the advent of extended communities, there is no longer the requirement to base the community identifier on an AS number. An IP address allocated to the exchange could be quite adequate to ensure uniqueness.

From Whom Do You Get Routes? When Should They Be Re-advertised?

While you often want to minimize the number of routes you receive, you also often want to get those routes from as many sources as possible. BGP, however, will only select what it considers the best route of those available, to be sent to the main RIB. Other, potential routes sent to the BGP router are *route instances*, and variously go as far as the Adj-RIB-In or further to the Loc-RIB.

Why do you receive less desirable routes? The principal reason is that they provide backup. They also may be routes for which you pay a transit provider. Providers will not send you routes unless they have economic motivation to do

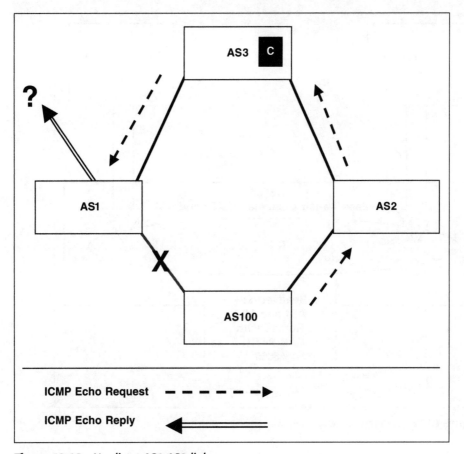

Figure 12.16   No direct AS1-AS2 link.

so. The most basic principle there is that no sane provider gives away free Internet-wide transit. Insanity, however, cannot be legislated out of existence, and some of the worst cases of insane routing have been by proxy—lower-level providers doing extremely unwise things with their upstreams and downstreams. For example, one midlevel provider accepted routes from its upstream and imported all the external routes into its IGP, which managed not to crash. It then exported the IGP routes to its downstream BGP peers with an origin type of IGP and itself as the originating AS (Figure 12.17). This had catastrophic effects on the global system, because the mid-level ISP was now offering shorter AS paths to the tier 1 provider routes. In the language of chaos theory, it became an attractor to ASs that never should have been sending to it, and that had perfectly valid routes to the common upstream.

It is to the advantage of other providers that they hear your direct customer routes, and possibly your directly connected AS routes, from you, and exchange the same information with you. In this situation you are quite possi-

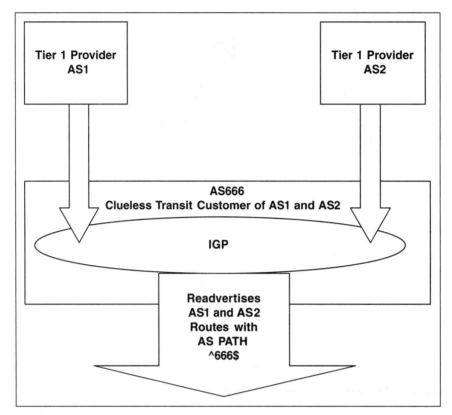

Figure 12.17 Strange attraction.

bly getting more direct routes between your mutual customers, avoiding the delay that may occur in complex backhaul and quite possibly reducing the bandwidth requirement on your links to upstreams—and thus the upstream cost to you.

Describing Aggregation in RPSL

Aggregation is a critical part of Internet scalability. Today's routers are less concerned with the memory required to hold routing tables than with the processing load in dealing with changes to those tables. While RPSL does have mechanisms for describing how an AS aggregates, check your specific router implementation to see how it operates. Different implementations, for example, may or may not announce an aggregate if all the components of that aggregate are not present in their routing table.

In principle, aggregates are announced only if an AS routing policy explicitly specifies aggregation. The default behavior is to export all routes. When explicit aggregation is defined, the more-specifics of the aggregate are suppressed from further export, unless explicit configuration tells the AS to advertise more-specifics as well. More-specifics are commonly exported as part of fault tolerance and load balancing. The more-specifics that can be advertised are specified on an AS level in the RPSL attribute aggr-bndry and at a prefix level in export-comps.

Again citing RPSL, rather than all router implementations, there may be times when a proper aggregate cannot be formed, because some of its more specific components are not present in the exporting AS's routing table. These may be due to holes created by policy, or simply because some of the more-specifics are down. Depending on the explicit policy of the AS, either nothing can be exported, the flawed aggregate can be exported (that is, it contains black holes), or only the more-specifics are exported.

Consider Figure 12.18, drawn from the RPSL RFC, and note especially the way in which routes are filtered twice before exporting, once at the AS level and once at the route level. We begin by defining the routes:

```
route:        128.8.0.0/16    origin:    AS1
route:        128.9.0.0/16    origin:    AS1
route:        128.8.0.0/15    origin:    AS1
aggr-bndry:   AS1 or AS2 or AS3
aggr-mtd:     outbound AS3 or AS4 or AS5
```

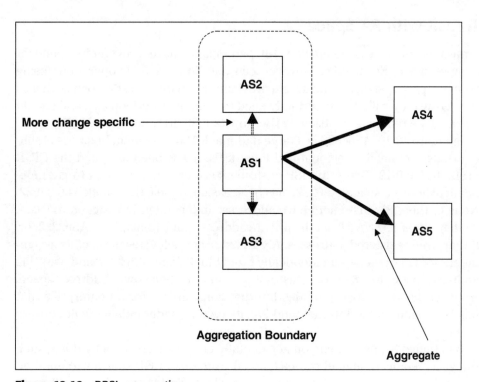

Figure 12.18 RPSL aggregation.

We have now defined the AS boundary from which the routes can be exported. Before actually exporting them, in this example, we need to know we have all the components of the aggregate.

```
components:   {128.8.0.0/16, 128.9.0.0/16}
inject:       upon HAVE-COMPONENTS {128.9.0.0/16, 128.8.0.0/16}
```

Had we been willing to export an aggregate containing holes, we would not have needed to check components.

```
aut-num: AS1
export:  to AS2 announce AS1
export:  to AS3 announce AS1 and not {128.9.0.0/16}
```

AS2 and AS3 are inside the aggregation boundary. As a result, both components, but not the aggregate, may be exported to AS2. Only one component may be announced to AS3.

```
export:  to AS4 announce AS1
export:  to AS5 announce AS1
```

Now, we export at the AS level, outbound-aggregating only to AS4 and AS5.

Transit with PA Space

Transit is much less complex if all participants have provider-independent address space. Small ISPs, however, can and do start their operations using address space assigned by upstream providers. Such ISPs must recognize that as they grow they will almost certainly need to renumber periodically, and should design to be renumbering-friendly [Berkowitz 1998; RFC 2071; RFC 2072].

In Figure 12.19, AS63333 is a large national ISP whose main business is selling transit to smaller regional and local ISPs. It has been assigned the CIDR prefix 64.0.0.0/12. Two of its ISP customers are not large enough to get independent address space. AS62222 has been assigned the CIDR block 64.0.0.0/22. None of this AS's customers have addresses independently assigned to them, so they either use NAT from the private address space to map into AS62222, or, if they need registered addresses, AS62222 further delegates parts of its assignment. AS61111 receives an identically sized block from AS63333, and uses this address space for its new customers without their own address space. AS61111, however, also provides Internet connectivity for an enterprise that has long been on the Internet, and has its own provider-independent address block.

Bad things happen when you accidentally create a transit AS by doing such things as re-advertising all routes learned from one eBGP speaker to another. You really, really do not want to promise AT&T WorldNet that you will carry traffic to UUnet.

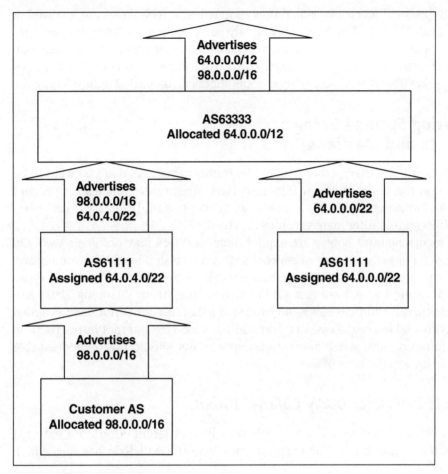

Figure 12.19   Transit with PA address space.

eBGP Scalability and Survivability

eBGP and iBGP both share the scalability limitation that a router cannot support an infinite number of peers. eBGP, however, has additional constraints that protect the local AS from errors or hacking from other, separately managed ASs. Several areas need to be considered:

- Completely legitimate workload, the totality of which overwhelms available equipment.
- Clearly illegal traffic whose intent is to cause disruption.
- Traffic that inherently is licit, but that is being sent at an abnormal volume that could cause damage. Such floods can be deliberate attacks or simply due to accident.
- Major disruptions in physical facilities.

Both protocol mechanisms and operational/design techniques are involved in scaling eBGP. Route flap dampening and dynamic route refresh are standard protocol mechanisms. Peer groups and interface prefix restrictions are implementation techniques used in Cisco routers. The use of route servers at exchange points and Martian filters for reasonability are operational methods that reduce workload.

Filtering Strange Beings: Smurfs and Martians

When you do run BGP, you announce the routes in your AS that you want to be visible on the Internet. Good ISPs also have acceptance policies that accept your announcements of only routes that belong to you. [RFC 2267] describes how ISPs should filter ingress routes and traffic.

As mentioned in Chapter 10, explicit ingress filters may not scale well. On high-speed links, a mixture of reverse path verification, blackhole routes, and minimum number of explicit filters may work much better. What should these explicit filters be? A basic list (Table 12.2) comes from [Manning 2001] and includes private address space, address space that has either not been assigned or has special historical caveats, and address space for Internet infrastructure. That infrastructure space needs to be unique, but should not be addressable outside its specific area of use.

Smurfs and Other Oddly Colored Threats

One of your challenges will be that there will be different criteria for external and internal interfaces. For example, the "Smurf" malicious hacking attack

Table 12.2 Special Use Address Space

BLOCK	REASON FOR RESTRICTION
0.0.0.0/8	Historical meanings, may be used as broadcast
127.0.0.0/8	Loopback/null address
192.0.2.0/24	Test space
10.0.0.0/8	Private address space
172.16.0.0/12	Private address space
192.168.0.0/16	Private address space
169.254.0.0/16	Link-local with DHCP
192.88.99.0/24	RFC 3068 IPv4 to IPv6 relays
all D/E space	

sends pings to the directed broadcast address of each subnet it can reach, causing massive responses and denying the use of bandwidth. There is really no reason why external organizations should be sending directed broadcasts to your subnets, so it is reasonable to block such requests from outside interfaces. This sort of blocking using explicit filtering, however, could very well necessitate a filter for every one of your subnets, which is hardly scalable. A much more scalable approach that also protects against a variety of other attacks is to deny all packets coming from the outside that have a source address in your own address space (see Figure 12.20). This might interfere with some specialized tunneling arrangements, but in general produces no operational problem. Since directed broadcast is dangerous even from the inside, you should disable it by default. On interfaces where it is needed, you can enable it, along with a packet filter that denies all packet with external source addresses. When you need directed broadcast for an application such as host autodiscovery by a network management package, permit it as narrowly as possible.

Martian Filters

One of the fundamental principles of the Internet is, "Be conservative in what you send, be liberal in what you accept." That principle, however, does not map

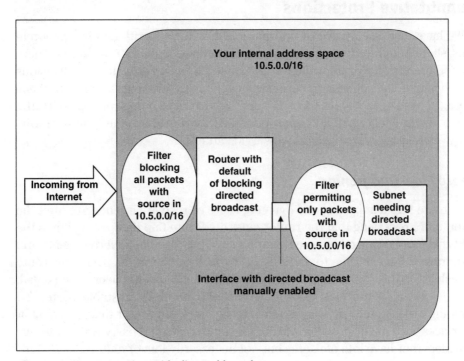

Figure 12.20   Protection with directed broadcast.

to best current practice in Internet operations, where the rule is more like, "Be conservative in what you send, be paranoid about what you accept." This sort of practical paranoia involves extensive filtering. The simplest rule for a provider is to accept only those customer routes that advertise destinations known to be assigned or allocated to that customer [RFC 2827]. The rule may be relaxed for peering with other providers that are known to apply the same filtering rules to all of their customers.

Even between providers, it is often wise to filter what are called *Martian routes*, a name that comes from the principle that such routes are so implausible that they must be from Mars. Typical Martian routes include the RFC 1918 private address space and addresses assigned to carrier resources such as the fabric at an exchange point.

Source-Routed Packets

Cutting to the chase, don't accept arbitrary source-routed packets from outside your network. They have some value for troubleshooting, but they create so many security exposures that they should only be worth considering as an internal tool. Arguably, IP source routing is obsolete, given the availability of MPLS. MPLS can set up disciplined source routes with substantial protections.

Quantitative Protections

We have discussed types of information that, for security and integrity reasons, should not be allowed into your network or sent to other networks. There is another category of information for which no binary permit/deny decisions can be made. The decision to permit the traffic depends on its volume, perhaps averaged over time. In other words, a few occurrences of a given type of traffic may be completely valid and appropriate. A flood of the same type of traffic, however, may represent a denial-of-service attack.

Route Flap Dampening

Both route flap dampening and dynamic route refresh are intended to limit the amount of processing that the router must do. Route flap dampening limits the load that can be caused by a route rapidly cycling through advertisements and withdrawals, due either to failures or to misconfiguration. Dynamic route refresh limits the load caused when the policies for a specific peer are changed.

You want to damp close to the source of potentially unstable routes, so damping on customer interfaces tends to be more important than damping at interfaces with major providers. Still, things can really get nasty with midrange providers that have lots of routes but not necessarily lots of clue.

Originally, BGP protected itself from the effects of flapping by setting timers to large values, so that the router ignores flap. To damp flapping, however, would require timers of minutes to hours, unacceptably slowing convergence for routes that are not flapping. Flaps occur when a route goes through the cycle of withdrawal and readvertisement several times within a predefined period. For each route, the router maintains a number that reflects its history of flapping. In Cisco's implementation, when a route flaps, the *penalty* value of 1000 is added to the numeric value. Once a penalty has been applied, the router divides that value by 2 whenever a period of *half-life time* goes by and the route has stayed up. If the flap number exceeds the *suppress limit*, the route is damped or *suppressed*. A suppressed route will appear in the local BGP table, but it will not be advertised until the numeric value drops below a *reuse limit*. In other words, once a route has been suppressed, the router believes it less and less. To return to the good graces of the input/output supervisor (IOS), once a route has been flapping, it needs to behave longer than a route that has not been flapping.

Adequate Resources for Routing Updates

Route flapping certainly is one pathology. But a sudden increase in the rate of route announcements after initialization may indicate a problem such as inappropriate deaggregation—a filter or configuration error just having taken place. Another protective measure can be to rate-limit the maximum number of updates per unit time that will be accepted by your router. The router implementer should provide an optional bypass to this mechanism to allow efficient transfer at BGP session establishment time.

There may be cases where providers, such as in mutual backup schemes, exchange full default-free routing tables. In such cases it is probably advisable that there be no rate limits, due to the large amount of data that must be transferred. For such peering relationships, you must be sure to provide sufficient bandwidth between the routers to avoid excessive queuing, and sufficient control plane processing power to handle the mass of updates.

Interface Prefix Restrictions

There have been some spectacular routing failures in the Internet due to midlevel ISPs inappropriately deaggregating routes they receive and suddenly adding thousands of routes to the Internet routing table. The routing architect of an AS can form reasonable expectations of the number of prefixes that an AS expects to receive from another AS. These expectations can come from a routing registry or from administrative agreements between the peers. For a typical customer of an ISP, the maximum number of expected prefixes is probably under 10. If you are a tier 1 provider connecting to a peer, you will probably receive on the order of 30 to 50 percent of the default-free routing zone. Typically, bandwidth rather than route processing limits routers in this application. When an ISP buys transit, it may receive 130 to 150 percent of the DFZ from each of its upstreams. See Tables 12.3 and 12.4 for more information.

Rate Limiting

A warm, tingling bubble bath is a delight; a tidal wave is definitely to be avoided. And so it is with network traffic. A few ICMP queries are quite normal. A flood of pings represents an error at best and a deliberate attack at worst. Known ping-based attacks include simple flooding, smurfing, and the "ping of death." There are any number of protocol messages that, at either customer or interprovider interfaces, should be limited to a plausible rate.

Minimizing Churn

Remember that routing policies are actually internal to the router, and are not part of the update. Import policies apply to updates received in the Adj-RIB-In, and only those that are acceptable under the policy filters go into the main RIB. In like manner, RIB information goes through advertising policies before it is placed in the Adj-RIB-Out to be advertised to neighbors. It is not unreasonable, therefore, to assume that when a policy changes, policy filters need to be reapplied to determine the acceptable policies. The trend in minimizing churn due to policy changes is to implement a combination of soft refresh and outbound route filtering.

The trend in minimizing churn involving partial failures of routers involves graceful restart and outbound route filtering. Traditionally, when a policy changed, the interface(s) were reset to force reexamination of the relevant peer RIB. A hard reset of an interface, however, can result in the need to transfer and filter an entire Internet routing table, which can take several minutes and impose significant central processing unit (CPU) demands (see Table 12.5).

Table 12.3   Typical Upstream Advertisements to Customer Edge

FRACTION	UPSTREAM ADVERTISES
10%	1.3 D
20%	0.3 D
70%	Default

Table 12.4   Typical Edge Advertisements to Upstreams

FRACTION	UPSTREAM ACCEPTS
50%	Aggregate and a more-specific route to the ISP edge router
20%	Advertise 10 or more routes to the ISP edge router
30%	Single route to the ISP edge router

How do you use these soft reset commands? Between a local router and a neighbor, when both support route refresh, you can use dynamic soft inbound refresh. When not all routers support route refresh, and you want to avoid the convergence delays associated with hard reset, you can use neighbor soft reconfiguration. The drawback to this method is that it is memory-intensive. It should not be surprising that the command that dynamically resets outbound peerings is called *outbound soft refresh*.

Exchange Point Design and Operation

In the most general sense, an exchange point is a place where ISPs exchange routes and traffic without settlements or transit provider payments. There are costs to connect the ISP to the exchange point location, and there are usually shared costs for operating the exchange.

The first exchange points were quite informal. In an era when the high-speed EGP core used 56-Kbps lines, considerable delay could come from backhauling to the core. Several academic institutions established routing nodes (commer-

Table 12.5   Hard and Soft Reset Operational Implications

TYPE OF RESET	GOOD NEWS	BAD NEWS
Hard	Minimal memory requirement	Forces total refresh of table and potentially long reconvergence
Outbound soft	Simple, low CPU, and low memory	No effect on inbound
Dynamic inbound soft	Minimal effect on convergence, low CPU, and low memory	
Configured inbound soft	Usable when one or both routers do not support dynamic reset, and does not have the impact of hard refresh	Memory-intensive, needs preconfiguration

---

WHAT ABOUT COMMERCIAL IXPs?

There has never been a real profit potential in the Internet exchange point (IXP) process proper [Greene 2001]. Facility and telecommunications providers that make an IXP part of their offering can make profit. A specialized case comes from hosting providers that support a colocated IXP, which attracts business to their hosting services.

---

cial routers did not yet exist) to minimize the delay in communicating with each other. Today's major reason to participate in an exchange point is saving money. When an ISP's only external connectivity is via a transit provider, it pays in full for the bandwidth needed to exchange routes and traffic with that provider.

At an exchange point, some type of shared switching or routing lowers the cost of bandwidth, and also shares the expense of exchanging routes. Per unit of user bandwidth, it is cheaper to interconnect at exchange points. However, exchange points have restrictions such that they complement, and will not replace, transit providers. Exchange points today, like the first exchanges, also minimize latency from backhaul. Especially when backhauled circuits commonly run from Asia to the West Coast of the United States, delay, even on broadband media, still is a concern.

Route Servers and the NSFNET

Not all methods for managing eBGP scaling are strictly protocol mechanisms. Some very important ones involve operational practice and design. At the time of the NSFNET's introduction, router processors still were quite limited. In a parallel to the iBGP use of route reflectors to minimize the number of peers, route servers were set up as non-forwarding routing protocol speakers. The participant routers needed to peer only with the route servers, but perform their data transfer across the layer 2 exchange point (Figure 12.21). They were introduced as part of the NSFNET, with the intention that major providers would interconnect via high-speed layer 2 fabrics at the exchange points, which in turn would be linked by high-speed pipes.

At exchange points, eBGP scales better because the ISP routers only need to peer with the route server rather than with one another. Not all participants necessarily agree to exchange traffic with one another (such as ISP3 and ISP4 in Figure 12.21). Most public exchange points run route servers using the route server daemon (RsD) (www.gated.edu) code on UNIX servers. An exchange point commonly has more than one server, and the different servers deliberately run on different server platforms (for instance, Sun and Alpha) so a bug (or a virus or a worm) in one platform or operating system does not cause a total routing failure. Route servers do not actually forward any traffic, although

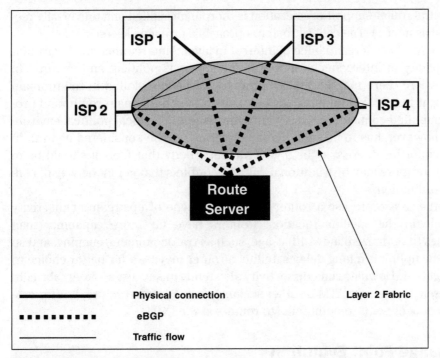

Figure 12.21   NSFNET exchange point.

they peer with routers. The actual forwarding at an exchange is via the layer 2 fabric, from router to router. You may learn of a given destination from the route server, but you are likely to need to set a next hop to the address of the egress router for that destination, not the next hop of the route server interface.

Layer 3 versus Layer 2 Exchanges

One of the first major exchange points, the commercial internet exchange (CIX), was a centrally managed router. CIX had the mission of interconnecting providers to carry traffic that did not meet the acceptable user policy (AUP) requirement of the NSFNET. Subsequent exchange points have used layer 2 fabrics. It has been observed, however, that layer 2 fabrics, especially with separate route servers, are operationally more complex than simply connecting to a central router—if

THINGS GET BLURRED

The line may blur between provider and exchange operator. You will see the term *layer 3 regional hub* used, especially in the Asia-Pacific area, but these tend to be, in fact, regional transit providers.

the central router support organization is thoroughly skilled and universally recognized as neutral. The central router approach is probably less scalable.

There has been a resurgence of interest in layer 3 interconnections. Part of it is simplicity of interconnection, but another part is political and cultural. In areas where there may be limited numbers of people skilled in interdomain routing, it may make the most sense for them to run the main router and provide simplified connectivity to lower-tier providers. The local political environment, however, has to be such that a core team will be considered neutral. In many countries, there may be a governmental body that feels it should be in control, or there may be traditional cultural conflicts that get in the way of central coordination.

Another reason to use a router fabric is the type of upstream connectivity available in the specific location. Routers have far more capability than switches to optimize bandwidth usage, such as traffic policing, queuing, and so on. If the uplink is a long-delay satellite, a router may be a far better choice to connect to it. Downstream connectivity also tends to suggest a router fabric. In the absence of a large ATM or other scalable layer 2 infrastructure, it is far easier to connect point-to-point links to routers at the IXP.

Exchange Point Evolution

As the Internet grew, the switching fabrics at the exchange points, typically single or parallel 100-Mbps fiber distributed data interface (FDDI) or OC-3 ATM, became congested, and the largest carriers bypassed them with *private peerings* (direct links with bilateral agreements to exchange customer routes; see Figure 12.22). Today's exchanges usually interconnect participants with Ethernet, most often at 100 Mbps but increasingly at the gigabit rate.

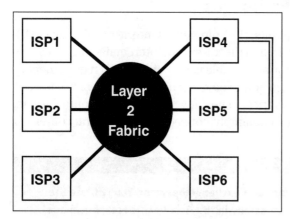

Figure 12.22   Private peering at an exchange.

Contemporary exchanges may provide an assortment of shared services not directly concerned with routing. In many exchanges, the route server has evolved to be a statistical collection point rather than an essential part of the operation. Other plausible shared services include routing registry mirrors, DNS servers, Network Time Protocol (NTP) references, and news [Network News Transport Protocol (NNTP)] servers. Private peering is more a North American than a European or Asian practice. Vendors are not building products optimized for the exchange market, perhaps because it is too small, perhaps because they do not understand it. RIPE has produced a "wish list" of desirable features for exchanges [Hughes 2001].

The shared costs of neutral exchanges are associated with the facility, not the cost of transmission. Private peerings do reflect transmission costs, although the participants may decide that no direct reimbursement is needed.

Local Exchanges

Local exchanges are increasingly popular. The first generally known local exchange started in Tucson, Arizona. In a local exchange, local providers and significant enterprises share either a small switch or a distributed layer 2 subnet, and have a small router or route server that does peering on behalf of the local organizations. It is not uncommon to find a provider in a local area that will offer a switch and rack space for other providers' routers. There may be cost recovery, or the hosting provider may feel that its upstream bandwidth savings are sufficient to pay for its overhead. Alternatively, a local exchange can be distributed, with a mesh of frame relay or ATM virtual circuits among the participants. A distributed design is probably the most reasonable approach for Vegetable Valley (see Figure 12.23). The router at the exchange needs to have enough RAM to afford several views of the global routing table. Individual AS routers, however, may not need to hold many external routes. **Daikon**, **cabbage**, and **zucchini** simply need to receive default from their upstream carrier, and customer routes from the other participants in the exchange.

By using a local exchange, you can actually go across town rather than being backhauled across half a continent to go between major providers (Figure 12.23). In Figure 12.23, **broccoli** buys transit from **asparagus** and the national provider, Light Side. Light Side has its closest superhub in Seattle, but traffic has to flow from there to Chicago, to the primary interconnect with **cabbage**'s

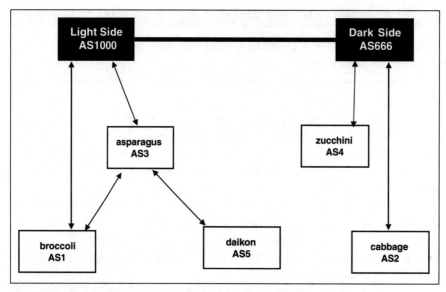

Figure 12.23   Backhaul.

ISP. However, **cabbage**'s primary ISP's national provider, Dark Side, feeds Vegetable Valley from Dallas. Traffic between **cabbage** and **broccoli**, therefore, goes via Seattle-Chicago-Dallas, or even further in the event of provider network failures or congestion.

ISPs and content providers in Vegetable Valley have banded together to form a local exchange in order to avoid sending local traffic halfway across the continent (see Figure 12.24). Since **broccoli** is connected to two upstream providers as well as to the exchange, its router(s) probably need to be able to hold full routes.

Layer 2 Alternatives

Even when the connectivity is layer 2, there are two basic approaches to achieving it: central and distributed. Centralized exchange points are more common. At a centralized exchange point, each participant is responsible for installing a router and arranging connectivity from the router to the participant's main operations facility.

Fully Distributed Exchanges

In a distributed exchange point (Figure 12.25), there is either no central location or a central location with limited functionality. The pioneering distributed exchange points use ATM and provide virtual circuits to the participants at the

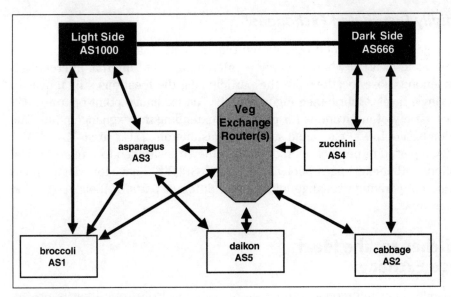

Figure 12.24   Local exchange.

participants' own facilities. There may be an ATM switch dedicated to the exchange service, or the ATM switching function may simply be a carrier capability. The central location contains dedicated switches, route servers when they are used, and any value-added servers. Local exchanges have been deployed with Frame Relay connectivity, in areas where the bandwidth requirements can be met with that speed. It is reasonable to assume that metropolitan optical Ethernet is also an option for local exchanges.

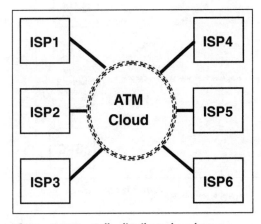

Figure 12.25   Fully distributed exchange.

Partially Distributed Exchanges

Exchanges may have good operational requirements that there be more than one physical location where customers interconnect, but internal interconnections among those locations. To the participants, the locations still appear to be a single layer 2 fabric (see Figure 12.26). The exchange point operator can have a variety of motivations for physically extending the exchange point. The London-based LYNX exchange and the Washington, D.C., area MAE-EAST needed a period of parallel operation while they transitioned to larger physical locations. Other exchanges, such as the French SPHYNX, have found it useful to provide cooperating exchange locations in different parts of their geographic service areas.

Switches for the Ideal Large Exchange

Exchange point interconnection is more common in Europe than is private peering, so it is no surprise that the most intense work on exchange point requirements goes on in the European Exchange Point forum in RIPE, the European operational forum.

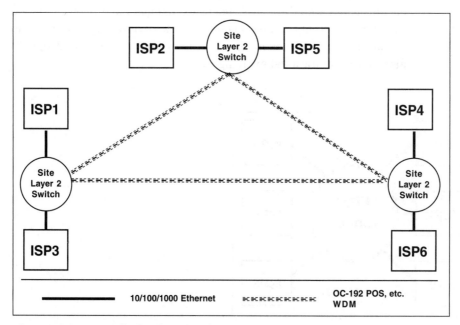

Figure 12.26 Partially distributed exchange.

REALITY CHECK

Can you think of a reason why an arbitrary user of the Internet should be able to send traffic directly to an interface in an exchange? Remember that the address space of the exchange is registered and appears in reverse DNS, so it is quite identifiable in a traceroute.

I can't think of a good reason. Yes, it is possible that a research organization might want to monitor exchange performance, but this is appropriately done with the knowledge and consent of the exchange point. Indeed, many exchanges have explicit monitoring equipment—frequently passive—installed. Would RFC 1918 space be appropriate for an exchange? If it were used, how could you interpret a traceroute going through multiple exchanges?

Topology Control

Exchanges assign exchange-specific, registered IP addresses to the components connected to their fabrics. The prefixes containing these addresses are deliberately not advertised to the general Internet, although they will show up in traceroutes. While IP addresses are assigned, much of the actual topology control and forwarding decisions use MAC addresses, not IP addresses. Layer 2 topology enforcement is critical to most exchanges. There are several aspects to such enforcement: at the specific address level and the shared medium topology level.

Enterprise switches, quite appropriately, use the IEEE 802.1d spanning tree algorithm and protocol for their topology discovery. They also make use of IEEE 802.1q VLANs, essentially as a multiplexing method (Figure 12.27). Spanning tree, however, has turned out to be less than desirable in most exchanges, where the exchange wants to control the information flow in a way that 802.1d tries to automate. Exchanges frequently disable spanning tree and configure everything manually.

Among the most basic problems is that a participant might leak 802.1d information into the exchange point. Exchanges want the ability to disable 802.1d completely on a per-port basis or enable it with per-port filtering and possibly rate limiting. Such filtering includes the ability to limit the number of MAC addresses learned at a given port and to replace previously learned addresses only on a last-out-first-in basis to prevent overwriting attacks. Most exchanges that control this at all do so by periodic manual inspections of the number of MAC addresses per port. Exchange point operators would like to examine alternatives to 802.1d, but there is no specific proposal under active consideration other than the IEEE 802.1w rapid spanning tree enhancements. The special problems of spanning tree include slow convergence with no forwarding during

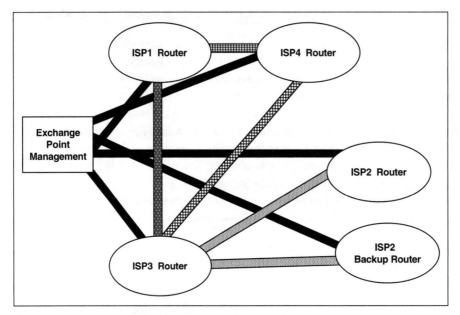

Figure 12.27   VLAN applications in an exchange point.

reconvergence, inefficient use of redundant resources (no inherent traffic sharing), and so on.

In the short term, it is probably worthwhile to treat routers in an exchange as
spanning tree end stations, which do not participate in root bridge selection.
Declaring ports as end stations only is a common configuration option in many
commercial switches. In the longer term, some type of link state algorithm
using MAC addresses may be appropriate. It also might be appropriate to use
layer 3 routing to set up MPLS tunnels among the exchange routers. IEEE
802.17 resilient packet ring is another possibility.

Forwarding

Operational scalability limits the ability of a layer 2 exchange point that uses
the bilateral agreement model to look at the layer 3 logic of exchange. There are
simply too many routing policies involved. Route servers with rigorous enforcement of policies in routing registries have some chance of operational enforcement, but have not been popular. While no exchange point working group
exists in the IETF temporary sub-IP area, it is entirely reasonable that
exchange-specific techniques may be taken under consideration. There is considerable exchange-specific work in RIPE and other European organizations.

As mentioned, exchanges may involve multiple sites. They may also involve
multiple switches, either for port density or bandwidth. Especially between
switches, multilink aggregation may be necessary to obtain the adequate band-

width. The aggregation should be standards-based, using IEEE 803.3ad. Another alternative is to use OC-192 WDM interfaces between switches, or more likely between lambda switches "front-ending" the Ethernet switches.

There are other exchange point considerations in load sharing. In enterprise networks, MAC addresses tend to vary widely, given the diversity of host and network equipment vendors. At an exchange point, however, the MAC addresses tend to be much more similar, beginning with the vendor codes of major router and switch vendors and often ending with a standardized slot/port number. Enterprise-based switches tend to use source/destination MAC address hash or round-robin load sharing. There is enough source/destination diversity in enterprise networks to make it a reasonable algorithm. Address similarity found in exchanges can cause significant asymmetry in load sharing if the source/destination hash, as is not uncommon, only considers part of the MAC address. Switches intended for exchange use should consider the whole address when calculating the hash.

Exchanges may need to examine packets in the fabric at line rate, examining layer 2 or layer 3 headers. One of the principal applications is monitoring ARP exchanges to ensure that devices connected to the fabric only use IP addresses assigned by the exchange.

Protection against broadcast storms also is critical. Operational exchanges have also noted that the load-sharing algorithms in use may send all broadcasts or multicasts out the same port, when they optimally should be spread across ports. As well, exchanges often want to restrict the presence of control protocols not essential to exchange operations, such as IGPs and Cisco Discovery Protocol. In these cases, the concern is usually less with the absolute volume of these protocols than the possibility of leaking proprietary information—or, even worse, live control information—into another participant's networks.

Multicast Issues in Exchanges

Multicasting ties well to a layer 2 exchange point, with its inherent capability for multicasting and broadcasting over a shared medium. Still, many larger exchanges that support multicasting use separate switches for the multicast traffic, if for no other reason than to learn more about a new technology and protect against unexpected problems. Such exchanges may ask the participants to use separate router interfaces for multicast and unicast traffic. Alternatively, they could accept multicast as one more VLAN, and route it differently at layer 2.

While most switches have features such as IGMP snooping or Cisco Group Management Protocol, the implementation of this remains vendor-dependent and can lead to interoperability problems. An even more fundamental problem for exchanges is that routers do not originate IGMP, only multicast routing protocol. The long-term solution may be to incorporate Personal Information Management (PIM) snooping into the switches.

Special Connectivity

In a substantial part of the world, high-speed terrestrial connectivity is not available at reasonable (or sometimes any) cost. Other applications inherently go to many destinations at high speed (think of television), so that a high-speed point-to-point service is not appropriate. In many of these situations, the answer is using satellite communications. This becomes much more complicated if the communication must be reliable. Thankfully, a reverse path for reliability (for example, TCP acknowledgments) does not need the speed of the primary channel. Other alternatives for reliability include forward error correction.

You should understand the implementation of asymmetrical communications in interprovider requirements. The speed ratio between the high-speed content and the low-speed control channel is often 16:1 or greater. Satellite channels used for these applications often have DS3 interfaces, which can carry a standard broadcast channel without requiring extensive compression.

Do not restrict your thinking about asymmetrical communications to the communications link alone. Especially when TCP is involved, there are various host settings that significantly affect performance. Neither bandwidth nor delay alone significantly affects TCP, but the product of bandwidth and delay does. The higher-speed extensions to TCP, such as selective acknowledgment, should

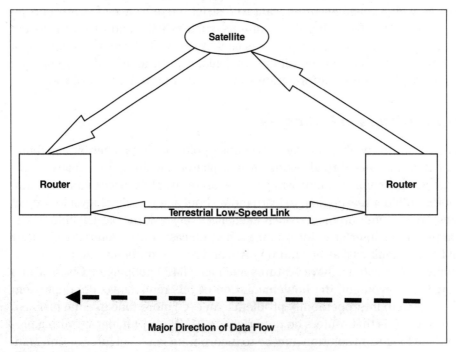

Figure 12.28   Point-to-point BGP control for high-speed link.

be implemented [RFC 2018; RFC 2883]. For server-specific parameters, see, for example, www.psc.edu/networking/perf_tune.html.

One possibility is to run the "forward" BGP path over the satellite link and the "reverse" over the terrestrial link. You may need to do this if the two links truly are simplex. Another alternative, however, is to use a bidirectional terrestrial link for BGP and announce the availability of the high-speed link using the terrestrial link (Figure 12.28).

Point-to-multipoint is common in asymmetrical applications, since the application may involve delivering the same content to multiple destinations. In this case, you have the choices of BGP over the satellite link or Internet-tunneled BGP connections to make your AS aware of connectivity over the high-speed link. In general, it is worth having a bidirectional terrestrial link for various control purposes. Send the BGP announcements over the satellite link and the TCP/BGP announcements over the terrestrial link. In the IETF, this problem is being generalized by the Unidirectional Link Routing (UDLR) Working Group [RFC 3077].

Looking Ahead

We have discussed the structure of means to carry VPN control information, but have not yet discussed VPN service offerings by carriers. That is the focus of Chapter 13, along with some host colocation scenarios that blur with exchange points.

CHAPTER

13

VPNs and Related Services

Question: What is the answer to any networking problem?

Answer: "It depends."
—Anonymous

Attachment is the great fabricator of illusions; reality can be attained only by someone who is detached.
—Simone Weil

The important thing about a dog walking on its hind legs is not how well he does it, but that he does it at all.
—Samuel Johnson, who might have been talking about VPNs.

In our industry, it seems a truism that the rate of growth of networks, and of enterprises using networks, is faster than the rate of growth in the number of competent networking people. Current business models also emphasize enterprises staying close to their "core competences" and outsourcing less critical functions. Not all companies, of course, regard networking as outside their core competence, even though their perceived products are not data networking. FedEx, General Motors, and Boeing are good examples of major companies with extremely strong internal networking capabilities. Academic institutions often have strong networking associated with their research missions. But it is a commercial reality that many enterprises would like to outsource at least some part of their networking operations. This desire becomes a business opportunity for service provider. The opportunity can take the form of managing an existing customer network or providing varying levels of turnkey virtual private networks. When I speak of varying levels, I am thinking of a range from managing site-to-site connectivity to actually managing LAN resources in those sites.

CRITICAL MASSES FOR SKILLS

When I worked as the network management architect for then-GTE Telenet, in the early 1980s, the largest private network that used our equipment, a telephone company, was about 25 percent the size of our public network. Certain equipment failure modes were rare, and might be seen only once every six months or more per 1,000 routers managed.

In discussions with our customer, we discovered that its staff turnover rate was such that it was unlikely anyone would have seen some of these rare problems before they took a new job. Our public network operations center, however, had formed a critical mass, so that it was likely we would have someone who had seen the problem before and did not have to research how to correct it.

Outsourcing can provide more benefits than simple economies of scale. It can apply greater expertise and speed problem correction.

To be a service provider, an organization inevitably needs to have a network operations center and provisioning staff. It will also develop a valuable human resource in the people who are skilled in operations. The incremental cost of adding responsibility for a customer network often is fairly small when compared to an enterprise cost of initially establishing, maintaining, and staffing a 24/7 operations capability.

When Management Is Outsourced

Having the provider manage multiple customer networks is not a simple signoff and turnkey operation. The provider NOC needs to be able to keep track of separate networks, yet operate them with a common group of people. There must be no danger of data leaking between the networks. The carrier also must, if it is contractually responsible for network reliability, prevent the customer from making changes that are not coordinated. Of course, the carrier needs access to all relevant devices in the customer network, regardless of the address space in which they operate.

A carrier-managed router, for example, needs to have addresses in the customer address space if it is to be able to route. Carriers are hesitant to take responsibility when they do not have control of the network devices they manage. While a device may be in the customer address space, it may have management passwords or other access controls that, routinely, are known only by the service provider, although the customer may want to make provision for emergency access to these passwords. Access and network providers have gone into financial collapse too often for enterprises to be completely out of control should the management provider shut down.

It may also be useful for the carrier to establish a management network, which might, in the enterprise, be on VLANs to which user devices do not have access. Packet filters on the enterprise side of VPN access devices might prevent enterprise-initiated packets from reaching the management interface of the border router.

When key operational functions are outsourced, it can become rather confusing to decide where to call for support. In a VPN, tunneling can make it impossible for one support center to do end-to-end troubleshooting.

Evolution from Outsourced Management to VPNs

As mentioned previously, it is a logical progression from outsourcing management to having the provider operate at least the WAN, and possibly the entire customer network. Since many enterprise networks primarily need internal connectivity, virtual private networks become an attractive approach. In general, a VPN is an IP network that operates over provider facilities shared with other customers. This is really no different from a private line network, where the customer traffic becomes channels in the provider's TDM backbone. It is also possible for customers to operate VPNs over shared resources such as the PSTN.

Any viable VPN will have very clearly defined responsibility for equipment, especially at customer sites. A service provider may place service provider–operated equipment at a customer site, and present a LAN or serial interface to the customer. Anything beyond the provider device is contractually a provider responsibility, but it cannot be directly controlled by the customer.

A PERSPECTIVE ON VPNS

I have long held that since a VPN is not real, it is a delightful thing for the sales force to offer. They don't have to offer vaporware; the true product arguably is vaporware! Less cynically, VPN technologies are quite real. But, as you will see again and again in this chapter, many existing protocols being used in provider-provisioned VPNs lack some field needed for generalized VPN use, or standardization of the function is pending. Many VPN approaches are now vendor-specific. Be very careful in picking early implementations that you believe offer a good chance of multivendor interoperability.

Endpoints and Midboxes

The first question of access is, "What is accessing the VPN?" The VPN may see the smallest unit of access as an individual user machine, a specific LAN, or a site with routers and multiple media. An individual host or physical site can be a member of more than one VPN, and may also be able to access a real corporate intranet and the Internet. Access policies need to be determined very early in the process and to interact tightly with your security policy.

Customer Domains

A basic definition for a customer domain is the set of network resources whose operation the customer contracts to you. A given customer organization, of course, may have multiple domains with different requirements and characteristics, billed under one master contract. A good example of differences in requirements involves Internet access. Figure 13.1 shows a multisite corporate network where the real servers use private address space but the virtual servers are on the public Internet. This is a very real-world situation, although the terminology might seem a little strange. If you think of the public Internet as real and the intranet as virtual, then, in this example, the real servers are on the virtual network and the virtual servers are on the real network.

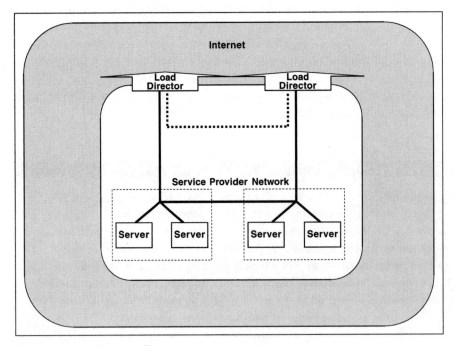

Figure 13.1   What is real?

In this example, the customer domain has two sites of its own, plus two external gateways/load directors offered by the provider. The VPN includes two server clusters at two two-host sites. As a value-added service, the provider operates an intelligent DNS that directs traffic to the least loaded server. A separate internal emulated LAN allows synchronization among the servers (see "Emulated LAN Service" later in this chapter). In any event, the customer domain will contain one or more sites, which contain one or more hosts. Some sites may be virtual, and some hosts may actually be operated by the provider.

Customer Sites

As shown in Figure 13.2, a site is a collection of hosts that use a common connection to the provider. The connection runs from a customer equipment (CE) device associated with the site to a provider equipment (PE) device associated with a provider POP. In the VPN context, a site may involve more than one physical location, as long as the VPN provider is not responsible for intersite connectivity (see "Virtual Sites"). That connection may support different VPN and Internet connectivity requirements, as well as connections to voice and other integrated services (see Figure 13.3).

Virtual Sites

For site-oriented VPNs that use encryption, if a new site or router can authenticate itself with a certificate, it can be assumed to be part of the membership. It is not much of a mental stretch to think of a virtual site as a set of hosts that pass the authentication criteria of an access wholesaler, with that access provider linking all these hosts to the VPN provider through a single connection. Any host that can reach the CE is a member of the virtual site in Figure 13.4.

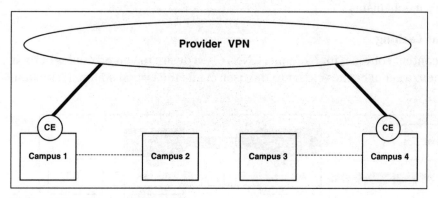

Figure 13.2 Site concept for VPNs.

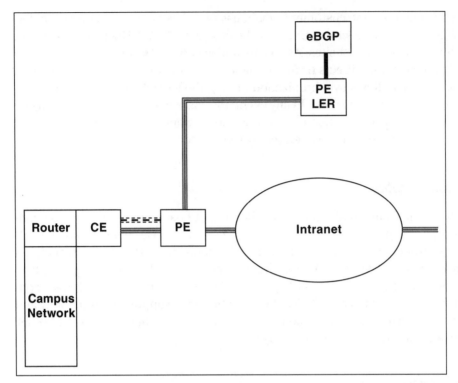

Figure 13.3   Site with VPN and Internet access.

Customer-Operated Hosts

A *customer host* may be a single physical machine with a single IP (or other protocol) address, one of several addresses on a single physical machine, or the "outside address" of a server cluster. The VPN sees hosts as IP addresses. A given customer host is associated with a single customer site. The contents of this host, however, may be distributed into content caches and use content delivery mechanisms.

Content Caching

Large content sources (for example, CNN) often desire to spread copies of their content to a set of caches closer to the user. While the virtual source (for exam-

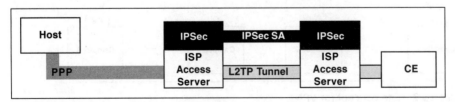

Figure 13.4   Host accessing a virtual site.

ple, www.cnn.com) appears to be on the public Internet, there may very well be a VPN interconnecting the content source to local caches it preloads with content. There is communication back to the source to keep it informed of hit rates and other usage statistics.

Content providers, however, are not the only organizations that may want to implement content caches. ISPs can often both minimize upstream bandwidth requirements and improve customer access time by installing web caches at their POPs, or at least inside their infrastructure. These reduce bandwidth by reducing the total number of content requests that must go to the end server, and improve access time by reducing the latency of the customer's access to data.

Provider-Operated Hosts

Service providers may operate hosts—real or virtual—on behalf of the customer. Such providers may support the hosting function, the network, or both.

CE and PE Devices

In Chapter 7, we introduced customer premises equipment (CPE) and customer location equipment (CLE). Both establish a point of demarcation between the subscriber and the provider; the difference is that the CPE is customer-controlled and the CLE is provider-controlled.

VPN discussions feature two seemingly similar terms, originally introduced in [RFC 2547] but now generally used in all VPN architectures (Figure 13.5).

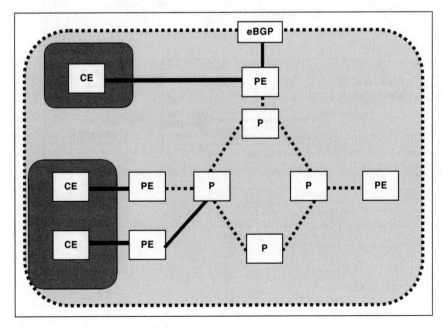

Figure 13.5 Generic VPN infrastructure components.

There is a customer edge (CE) function and a provider edge (PE) function. There is a P function that provides backbone interconnection among the PE. All these functions will be detailed later in this chapter.

Some architectures define a one-to-one relationship between CE functions and sites. If a physical site requires no single point of failure and thus requires multiple CE, it is treated as multiple VPN sites in such architectures (see Figure 13.6). Another CE approach is to use a firewall product that supports secure VPNs. Many such products do, and, even if you are not connecting externally, they tend to have well-developed administrative tools.

Aggregation optimizes the use of high-speed interfaces on high-performance carrier routers. If, for example, the customer connectivity uses Fast Ethernet, an aggregation device such as an 802.1q-capable Ethernet switch aggregates Fast Ethernets into a Gigabit Ethernet compatible with high-speed router interfaces. Also note that 802.1q is useful to multiplex different services between the customer site and the POP.

P Devices

P devices interconnect PE, although PE can directly interconnect with an intervening P device. P devices are completely unaware of the actual user VPN. A P

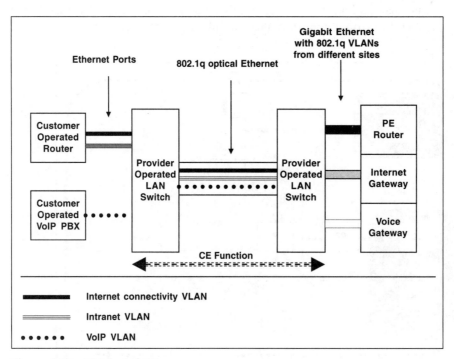

Figure 13.6 Distributed CE.

device usually will be an MPLS core router, in the sense discussed in Chapter 11. As shown in Figure 13.7, P devices can be arranged in hierarchies, with paths being merged and deaggregated as needed. The shaded P devices are the second level of a hierarchy. Not all provider VPN implementations will necessarily use P devices. Some implementations may have a partial or full mesh among the PE, so there may be a single point of failure, typically at the leaf nodes.

User Perception of VPN Types and Capabilities

VPNs broadly fall into two categories: customer-provisioned and provider-provisioned. Another way of categorizing them, not necessarily mutually exclusive with the provisioning, is dedicated versus on-demand (see Table 13.1). Where the on-demand service is more akin to the public telephone network, the dedicated VPN is sometimes called a *virtual leased-line service*. Vendors defining products can prepare feature checklists against this section, with the perhaps idealistic hope that not all features are appropriate for every product and that sheer number of features does not make one product better than another.

1. Who are to be the VPN's members? In other words, what does it connect? Individual users to servers? Sites to sites? This is the membership

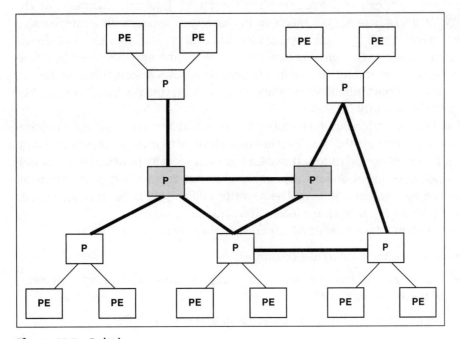

Figure 13.7   P devices.

Table 13.1   VPN Types and User Perception

| | PROVISIONING | |
OPERATING MODE	CUSTOMER	PROVIDER
Demand	PSTN and other dial-up, usually using PPP and/or L2TP	L2TP
Dedicated	IPSec	multiple virtual routers (MVRs), RFC 2547, L2VPN

problem. Security pervades all aspects of a VPN, but must first be considered as part of defining membership.

2. Who has operational responsibility for the VPN? The enterprise? A service provider? Some mixture of the two?

3. What kind of data does the network carry? Are there service level agreements for the data?

Membership and Security Policy

At the highest level, membership defines the customer hosts, sites, and domains that interconnect to form a VPN. Membership also includes other networks to which the VPN can connect, including the public Internet, extranets, or the PSTN. At a lower level, the mechanisms involved in controlling membership may involve signaling to tell the provider that a given customer element should be given connectivity. Signaling may need to be secure, and there may be different levels of trust among VPN elements once data flows among them. Of the various VPN transport/tunneling mechanisms (see "Carrying the Data"), only IPSec has inherent security functions.

Another way to look at the membership problem, from the customer requirements perspective, is that it will rather quickly need to involve a security policy. Never build networks without first deciding on a security policy. A security policy is not a technical document, but should be a one- to two-page document approved by top management. The security policy both reflects requirements and provides a framework for legal enforcement.

The fundamental elements of a security policy are:

- Who is authorized to use resources?
- If there are different classes of users (and there should be) who should be trusted to do what?
- What action will be taken if there is unauthorized use?
- Who will judge if a use is unauthorized and, if so, determine the consequences?

Very close to the policy are the domains of trust. Is the service provider trusted? The end user? Sites?

When the VPN provider is responsible for security functions, there still needs to be a distinction between edge and core requirements and functions. It will be quite common for providers to implement dial-up and other end user access control mechanisms, and the provider might also furnish security services for sites and servers (for example, IPSec tunnels among firewalls).

Where to Implement Security Mechanisms

Clear distinctions must be made for the responsibility and positioning of security mechanisms. Some security mechanisms, such as IPSec transport mode, are host-oriented and will normally be transparent to VPN providers. In particular situations, the maintenance of such mechanisms might be outsourced to the provider organization, but such maintenance will often require a different skill set (that is, host and LAN operating system administration) than general VPN support. The user organization has final responsibility for the legal and management aspects of the security policy. In some cases, the policy may preclude outsourcing certain security functions, in that outside organizations are not trusted to manage these functions.

Security is not encryption alone. In VPNs, security must consider the authentication of changes that could create a tunnel that might leak data. Virtual routers and virtual routing instances, by their basic architecture, do isolate different VPNs. As soon as the capability to have an extranet, or to have Internet access, is added to the VPN capability, there are more chances to leak data.

Situations Where the Provider Is Untrusted

The most basic question is whether the customer trusts the provider. When the customer does not trust the provider to secure content, the role of the provider becomes one restricted to packet transport. Encryption and authentication are customer responsibilities. In Figure 13.8, the customer uses the VPN for security between hosts, not trusting intermediate security gateways. Figure 13.9

A SIDE NOTE ON IPSec

The existing IPSec specification assumes that a security association (SA) will use authentication, encryption, or both. It does not assume one would use IPSec with neither capability, but the capability of doing so may actually be useful in some VPN applications. IPSec supports multiplexing and tunneling, which may be all that is needed for some VPNs, and it is certainly easier to modify a protocol to turn off existing features than to add new functionality.

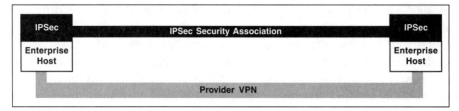

Figure 13.8 Customer security.

shows a typical application in the financial industry, where separate X3.17 encryptors are well-established. The tunnel need provide no security.

Trusting the provider may be more subtle than it would first appear. The customer might very well not trust the provider to do the actual encryption, but might be willing to use a public key infrastructure (PKI) certification authority (CA) operated by the provider. CA operation can be quite complex logistically, yet having a third-party CA does not necessarily compromise the security of user traffic as long as the user maintains the secrecy of private keys.

Situations Where the Provider Is Trusted

Over the years, I have never failed to be amused when customers begin to worry about the "security" of frame relay and ATM because "they share facilities with other customers." At such times, I'm often tempted to ask them to pull on their dedicated line in Chicago and ask the Dallas office whether the other end moved. The information on the dedicated line, of course, becomes a multiplexed channel on shared facilities once it leaves the telephone end office.

A VPN that runs completely over carrier facilities has comparable security to frame relay or ATM. If the data carried is sufficiently sensitive that it would be reasonable to encrypt it on a dedicated line, then it is reasonable to encrypt it on a VPN. If the customer has an unshakable perception that "IP isn't secure," it may be a practical necessity to encrypt. In most cases, the best place to encrypt is at the CPE/CLE or in devices in the customer network before it connects to the CPE/CLE. By doing so, the traffic is protected in the local loop, where it is generally most vulnerable to wiretaps. Once beyond the local loop, the inherent

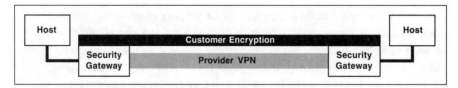

Figure 13.9 Security gateway.

difficulty of accessing and invading carrier layer 2 networks and private IP networks deters casual intruders. The additional overhead of adding encryption to a physically protected optical network may overprice the service without a real improvement in security. The service provider may manage encryption devices and/or firewalls at the customer site. Of course, when this is done, the control channels to the security devices must themselves be secure.

User connectivity may be defined to include security using a variety of security mechanisms, including IPSec, L2TP, and so on. These various mechanisms may provide other services, such as connectivity. L2TP can provide per-user authentication, or may have no security functions. Security may be requested on a discretionary basis by end user hosts, or the VPN may enforce a mandatory security policy. Cryptographic protections may be under the control of the enterprise, using host-to-host or host-to-security gateway methods, or the infrastructure may be trusted to provide encryption. The responsibilities for user authentication, device authentication, encryption, logging, and audit must be specified as part of the design of any practical VPN.

Operational Policy

To ask the fundamental question of operational policy, think of the theme song from the movie *Ghostbusters:* "Who ya gonna call?" If you do not define clearly who has responsibility for adding hosts and sites to the VPN, troubleshooting the VPN and applications on it, and doing continuing capacity planning, your VPN will be haunted by evil spirits. Operational responsibilities can be assigned to the enterprise, service provider(s), or consultants. The provider may place equipment under its control at the customer sites, or the VPN boundary may start at a provider POP. Those VPNs accessed through the bandwidth provider are purely customer-operated from the VPN standpoint; the telephone provider is unaware of their existence.

Another aspect of the model is whether clients are aware of the VPN and whether provider access components are aware of it. In principle, a client could attach to a generic ISP, establish an encrypted tunnel to a destination host, and operate transparently to the ISP. The VPN provider may be the ISP. In such cases, the VPN provider's responsibility is to provide logins and connectivity. The login might specify a class of service to be used in the provider network.

Addressing and Naming

Having addresses is not optional. *Managing* and *assigning* customer addresses are optional capabilities of a VPN service. The VPN may provide address assignment, presumably with DHCP or proxies used with IPCP or L2TP. VPNs most commonly use private addressing. When Internet connectivity is needed, the firewall has both inside and outside addresses. DNS services may be associated with the VPN, and operated by the enterprise or the service provider. When the VPN provides dynamic addressing, the dynamic address server (DHCP, IPCP, and so on) should dynamically update the DNS zone seen by the members of the VPN.

Addressing becomes more complex with extranets. It may be desirable to use registered addresses, perhaps with the restriction that they do not need global Internet routability. Address registries may be somewhat relaxed in their assignment rules when the requesting organization makes clear that it does not expect global routability and is willing to renumber if global routability becomes a need. When pointy-haired bosses demand the instantaneous interconnection of several enterprises' intranets, crying, "Ready! Fire! Aim!", it is entirely common to find that the intranets all use the [RFC 1918] private address space and some of the addresses overlap. Routing with overlapping addresses, if I remember correctly, is in the fifth or sixth circle of Dante's nine-ringed hell.

Availability and Quality of Service

When a network is down, its quality of service is by definition unacceptable. The enterprise may specify availability requirements for the infrastructure and for VPN gateway services. The implementer of the VPN needs to translate these user requirements into requirements for underlying fault tolerance mechanisms.

The VPN may provide quality of service support. It may either accept QoS requests from end users signaled with RSVP, IP precedence bits, and so on, or internally assign QoS requirements to be mapped to the transmission infrastructure. For quality of service to be effective, either the infrastructure must support explicit quality of service requests or there must be a high level of confidence that the infrastructure consistently provides adequate QoS. Assumptions about QoS need to be stated as part of any VPN design.

Requirements for QoS will restrict the transports that can be used for your VPN. VPNs based on the public Internet, and to some extent those based on the PSTN, inherit the unreliable QoS properties of their transports.

Kinds of User Information Carried

While the emphasis of this taxonomy is on VPNs that support IP, the VPN may provide mechanisms for encapsulating non-IP protocols for transmission over an IP infrastructure. Techniques for doing this include NetBIOS over TCP [RFC 1001; RFC 1002], IPX over IP [RFC 1234], GRE [RFC 1702], and so on. PPP, of course, is intended to be multiprotocol.

IPSec does not now have a protocol identifier field, but there are several reasonable approaches to identifying protocols. For example, Internet Key Exchange (IKE) could be extended to carry a per-SA field such as the Logical Link Control (LLC)/Sub Network Access Protocol (SNAP) or GRE protocol identifier. As non-IP protocol market share declines, and there are well-defined IP encapsulation methods for most non-IP protocols, it may be simplest for providers to accept the overhead of IP encapsulation and only offer IP VPNs. With IP, however, there may be requirements to deliver frames or packets in sequence. In addition, there may be a requirement to efficiently support larger MTUs than the provider might normally handle.

L2TP and GRE both have sequencing fields, which are now used for antireplay checking but could be adapted to guarantee sequenced delivery. IPSec also has a sequence field that could be used. Again, these protocol extensions are not now available, and sequencing is apt to add latency. If IP fragmentation is to be avoided when the infrastructure has an MTU that is less than the length of a full payload packet plus tunnel and delivery header, manual MTU limitations on end hosts or dynamic MTU path discovery need to be used. Alternatively, a tunnel segmentation and reassembly mechanism, such as those used in the ATM adaptation layer or in multilink PPP, could be developed but is not now available.

QoS Enforcement

If a customer is using the VPN to replace dedicated lines, and the customer applications include QoS-sensitive services such as VoIP, it is certainly reasonable to expect that the VPN can deliver QoS guarantees. A rather basic requirement for doing so is to use a TE-capable tunneling mechanism and/or traffic management at the encapsulation points.

There are several places where QoS enforcement could take place:

- At entry to or egress from tunnels
- In the tunnel transport (less QoS enforcement than traffic engineering)
- In the tunnel

Of the tunneling protocols, only L2TP directly has any mechanisms for congestion control, and even these are only for the control channel. It is not clear, however, that it makes sense for the tunneling protocol to have any congestion control mechanisms. Remember that endpoint mechanisms to enforce flow control, such as TCP windowing, are not affected by VPNs.

VPN Internal Services

To meet a given set of user requirements, the designer needs to specify who belongs to the VPN, how the VPN is mapped on to the underlying transport, and the characteristics of the transport. The combination of these technical requirements produces two basic types of provider provisioned VPNs: virtual router (VR) and piggybacking. Layer 2 VPNs and customer-operated VPNs are special cases of piggybacking. The fundamental difference between the two architectural models is the way in which reachability information is distributed. In VR models, reachability information propagates using a per-VPN end-to-end routing system. In piggybacking, there is a clear demarcation between the customer routing system and the backbone routing system of the provider.

Membership and Its Relationship to Signaling

Before a member of a VPN can have traffic routed to it, it must be defined as part of the VPN. Such definition can be a static configuration or can be negotiated dynamically. The definition can be at the level of a user, an address, or a site.

Early in the process, list fixed servers and sites that will belong to the VPN. Estimate how many computers will attach to it. Provisioning a VPN that can have 10,000 dynamic members is different from provisioning a VPN with 100 dynamic members.

The second question of access is, "How does the VPN know an access attempt is valid?" When the VPN is aware of individual users, one approach to defining membership without preconfiguration is to assume that any user who can connect through security mechanisms at an access point is a legitimate member. Once the membership is established, tunnels need to be created to allow the desired connectivity among the members.

Interactions with Customer Routing

Part of the confusion here comes from glib statements of, "We (or our customer) need/want to 'support' RIP, OSPF, etc." But what does such support mean? It is a reasonable constraint, very consistent with current Internet address allocation policy, that most enterprises running intranets, even with Internet access through a single provider, are expected to use private address space. Appropriate routing information about site reachability should arrive in the appropriate VPN routers. Too much routing information exchange between provider and customer, however, consumes resources, jeopardizes security, and may decrease availability.

Given that one of the major motivations to use VPNs, in the perceptions of many enterprises, is to outsource as much management as possible, it should not be a major constraint for the provider to assign CIDR blocks of private space on a site-by-site basis. There is no question that CIDR needs to be used if registered space is involved. So, the provider knows the range of addresses at each site. Even if there were a huge routed enterprise network behind the customer router, there is only one intranet subnet for each VPN leaving the site. There may be an additional subnet for Internet access. The larger routing system gains absolutely no useful information from knowing about details of routes behind the customer router. Let us focus on the real requirements.

Reachability

The provider routing system needs to know how to reach the CIDR blocks inside the VPN. When address space is reused, the duplicate addresses need to be disambiguated. RFC 2547 shows a way to do so by prefixing addresses with routing distinguishers.

Each site with Internet access needs to know how to default to the ISP. That does not preclude having pure customer routes that do not go outside the provider, only that either the ISP is the default or explicitly is not the default. In general, it will be preferable to default to the ISP and let any special cases be handled by more-specific routes inside the site.

Fault Detection

For management purposes, we should be aware when connectivity to a site is lost. If the layer 2 connectivity provides a keepalive, loss of reachability to the static route to the site may be sufficient. With Ethernet or other layer 2 mechanisms with no fault notification, we need at least a lightweight layer 3 hello protocol to keep the PE informed of reachability. The most general solution to these problems is the use of lightweight routing between customer and provider routers. Assuming coherent addressing, lightweight routing needs to advertise only one route in each direction.

- 0.0.0.0/0 from provider router to customer router
- The assigned CIDR block from customer router to provider router

Several major routing protocols, such as RIP and BGP, do not have fast convergence properties. On the other hand, if fast recovery mechanisms exist in the transport (see Chapters 8 and 11), the speed of routing reconvergence may not be an important issue. The role of the routing protocol may be much more a matter of advertising initial reachability than failure recovery.

Signaling versus Lightweight Routing

Another approach is to use signaling protocols to convey both reachability and availability information to the provider routing system. A signaling protocol is capable of declaring the existence of a member, requesting connectivity for the member, and declaring the continued reachability of the member, but it is not capable of picking the best path for carrying the data. The latter is the responsibility of the provider routing system.

Carrying the Data

The VPN exists to carry data. Tunnels interconnect user nodes, but the tunnels usually need protocols for their own operation. Most tunnels need some sort of encapsulation of user data before they can carry it.

It is now fair to say that all serious proposals for provider-provisioned VPNs are based on some kind of tunneling. Dial-up VPNs involve the provider, but are really customer-provisioned. There are a variety of tunneling protocols available today, all of which were developed for purposes other than VPNs (see Table 13.2). Some of these protocols may need extensions to make them more VPN-friendly. Think of a tunnel as a simulated layer 2 link onto which the VPN imposes its IP. That the tunnel itself uses IP internally is irrelevant to the VPN user. To create any tunnel in a VPN environment, the appropriate protocols need to be aware of:

- The endpoint IP addresses of the tunnel
- Any specific constraints on the tunnel, such as security

The specific means by which end user views of the VPN are mapped onto the shared infrastructure generally involves tunneling, virtual circuit setup, or the establishment of a set of labels. When tunnels are used, they may provide no security (GRE), authentication (L2TP), or a wide range of security services (IPSec). Security services may also be provided by hosts, and a less secure tunnel mechanism used to carry host-encrypted data.

When the VPN seen by the user appears to be multicast-capable, but the infrastructure is connection-oriented, provisions need to be made for supporting multicast. Techniques might involve point-to-multipoint circuits or the use of multicast replication servers.

Tunnel Establishment via Management Operations

Tunnels can be created as part of a carrier provisioning process rather than dynamically by the user. While such an approach may seem slower, it is also generally less error-prone. Customers may be given controlled access to certain parts of the provisioning system to create tunnels within their domain. For equivalents in non-VPN applications, see "SPB service" in Chapter 8. Provisioning information could go via SNMP to an appropriate, tunnel-technology-specific MIB. Where QoS policy and other appropriate information is also to be defined, other management mechanisms such as Common Open Policy Service (COPS) may have important roles.

Tunnel Establishment via Signaling Protocols

Signaling protocols (Table 13.3) essentially create the tunnel with in-band management. Using signaling protocols will generally reduce the management workload. They are especially appropriate for part-time or mobile nodes in a VPN.

Table 13.2 VPN Tunneling Protocols

	ENDPOINTS	TRANSPORT	POTENTIAL FOR MULTIPLEXING	SECURITY	MAY BE COMBINED WITH
L2TP	1. Host 2. Access server	PPP to access server; UDP/IP between access servers	Yes (tunnel ID and session ID)	Access proxy	IPSec
IPSec transport	Host	IP	Yes (security parameter index)	Authentication and/or content encryption	
IPSec tunnel	Router	IP	Yes (security parameter index)	Authentication and/or content encryption	
MPLS	Router	Any L2	Yes (label)	No	
GRE	Router	IP	Yes (key field)	No	
IPIP	Router	IP	No	No	

Table 13.3   Signaling Protocols

PROTOCOL	TUNNEL
Q.2931	ATM*
L2TP	MPLS
IPSec/IKE	IPSec
GRE	GRE
CR-LDP	MPLS
RSVP-TE	MPLS

VPN mechanisms built directly upon ATM tunneling mechanisms do not qualify as VPNs in the sense that they are not lower layer–agnostic.

* For comparison only; sets up true layer 2 VCs rather than VPNs.

In VPN operation, there is a requirement that the signaling protocol be able to carry a VPN ID. Not all tunnel-specific signaling protocols have this capability, and work on extensions is under way. The signaling protocol may or may not convey information about the use of the tunnel. It may, as Q.2931 does for ATM, merely indicate how the tunnel is to be set up. L2TP is not aware of what the PPP frames in the tunnel carry.

Layer 2 Access and Multiplexing

Layer 2 access connects the customer site to the POP. There are at least three refinements of layer 2 access: multiplexing and protocol identification, aggregation, and layer 2 multihoming. Those of you who have worked with frame relay and ATM should remember that there is a basic issue in handling multiprotocol traffic on connections. There is a choice between either carrying a protocol identifier header at the start of a frame or dedicating a virtual circuit to each protocol. We face an extension of this problem in VPNs, in that we may have to identify both protocols and multiplexed traffic within access facilities or tunnels. This identification may be out of band and associated with the circuit, or in band and associated with the frames.

The connection from the customer may or may not have multiple virtual layer 2 functions multiplexed onto it, such as multiple 802.1Q VLANs or ATM VCs. Alternatively, just as Freud once suggested that a cigar may be just a cigar, the layer 2 medium may simply map to a single subnet. Our abstraction should cause each VPN instance coming from the site to have at least one layer 2 identifier associated with it, so that N layer 2 identifiers map to N layer 3 prefixes.

We also should allow for the possibility of inverse multiplexing—allowing multiple tunnels to combine into one tunnel of higher bandwidth. Protocols do exist for doing this, such as multilink PPP, multilink Frame Relay, and inverse-multiplexed ATM. The topological models for this involve having arbitrary relationships between N layer 2 identifiers and M layer 3 identifiers, as covered in the latest evolution of the Interface Group MIB [RFC 2863]. There may also be multiple VPN tunnels between a pair of IP endpoints, when the tunnels map onto the IP delivery mechanism but deliver payloads in different VPNs. Again, this requires a multiplexing field.

RFC 2685 defines a standard VPN identifier that can be inserted either into in-band headers (for instance, with MPLS) or in out-of-band control packets.

In Figure 13.6 we saw how this provider offers VPN, Internet, and voice services. The customer site router separates Internet versus VPN traffic into different VLANs, while a third VLAN connects the PBX to the voice network. A fourth VLAN allows the provider to control provider equipment at the customer site, and a fifth may be used for outsourced management of customer equipment.

Tunnel Maintenance

Tunnel establishment is distinct from tunnel maintenance. One of the challenges is detecting the failure of a specific tunnel within some trunking mechanism that carries multiple trunks. To accomplish this, some sort of per-tunnel keepalive mechanism is needed. Such a mechanism can be part of the tunneling protocol itself, such as the optional L2TP keepalive. Alternatively, the provider can send pings or other test traffic across the tunnel. Especially in multiple virtual router schemes, routing protocol traffic can be useful as a keepalive. When the routing information is outside the tunnel, as in BGP/MPLS VPNs, other mechanisms are preferable.

Tunnels may be established using hard-state or soft-state mechanisms. The hard-state approach can still establish a lifetime for the tunnel, as with the key lifetime field in the IPSec security association. A soft-state approach takes down the tunnel after no traffic has passed for some predefined period of time. Tunnel establishment can also be triggered by a provisioning process.

Interprovider Connectivity

It may be necessary to provision the VPN infrastructure through multiple service providers. In such cases, the providers will need interprovider provisioning and VPN identification. Much as a BGP confederation presents a single AS number to the outside but contains multiple internal ASNs, a multiprovider VPN identifier may map to a set of publicly visible ASNs. While BGP may be used to convey VPN reachability information among providers, the actual destinations may be prefixed with VPN IDs and carried using the BGP-4 multiprotocol extensions. When VPN IDs are used in this manner, the routes carried need not be visible on the global Internet, but may simply be used to exchange information between ISPs with bilateral agreements.

Provider-Provisioned VPN Technologies

Three basic models of PPVPN have emerged: BGP/MPLS, multiple virtual router, and L2 VPN (see Table 13.4). They differ in the signaling interface presented to customers, the customer data encapsulation method, and the per-VPN routing logic. While early proposals suggested additional types to meet additional security requirements, today's trend is to use specific tunneling methods to provide security when needed.

Multiple Virtual Routers

Multiple virtual routers are most appropriate when the customer has an existing routing system with a decent IGP implementation (see Figure 13.10). Essentially, the VPN appears as an extension of the existing enterprise network, using the same routing protocols. The difference is that some or all of the WAN routers are now physically at provider sites and share both hardware and transmission links to reduce costs. A virtual routing instance distributes reachability information among a set of VPN routers. The virtual routing information can come from static provisioning or conventional routing protocols on the CE. The customer can use any routing protocol that the provider routers support. While no routing protocol extensions are needed, remember that Cisco's EIGRP protocol is proprietary and the provider routers might not support it unless they are (all) Ciscos. Cisco does not emphasize the MVR approach, but it is still possible to have multiple instances of EIGRP or OSPF on the same physical router and achieve equivalent functionality. Cisco does not support multiple instances of RIP or BGP.

The virtual routers themselves can be interconnected via direct links, or by aggregated links through some other tunneling mechanism (see Figure 13.11). The first kind of interconnection can go over either physical or multiplexed L2 facilities, real or virtual. The second kind implies a next level of provider hierarchy for carrying the traffic over a set of virtual routers that carries customer

Table 13.4   PPVPN Models

METHOD	SIGNALING	ROUTING	TUNNELS
2547bis		BGP	MPLS
MVRs	Customer IGP	Customer IGP/BGP	Any
L2 VPN	Emulated VP specific	Any	Any

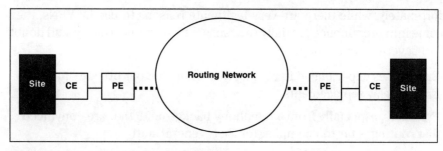

Figure 13.10 MVR customer connectivity.

VR traffic. An advantage of using hierarchy is that parts of the hierarchy can be in different provider networks. Of course, the more interprovider connectivity involved, the greater the need for BGP as the routing protocol. It is quite plausible to have a first level that uses customer virtual routers running an IGP and a higher level running BGP/MPLS.

L2 VPNs

L2 VPNs are another demonstration of Schwarzenegger's Second Law (see Chapter 2). The term L2 VPN is a bit misleading, because the provider does not actually provide a VPN to the customer. The customer sees L2 links over which it does its own routing. The L2 VPN actually is inside the provider network.

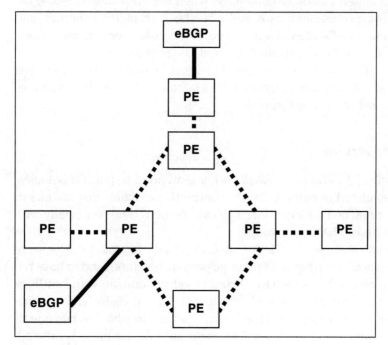

Figure 13.11 MVR PE and inter-PE connectivity.

Unfortunately, while there are very legitimate reasons to use L2 VPNs, they have come into prominence partially to assuage the fear, uncertainty, and doubt (FUD) of several communities:

- Enterprises experienced in routing that want cheaper private line or Frame Relay replacements

- Providers, especially from a telephony background, that are convinced that routing is far too complex for their general staff

- Enterprises equally terrified of routing that typically want everything to look like one big LAN

One of the great attractions of the L2 VPN is that it requires minimal changes to existing enterprises built on ATM, Frame Relay, or even wide area Ethernet. It is an irony that these provider technologies are themselves virtualizations onto the transmission system—a leased line, beyond the shortest distances, is not a real piece of copper but a virtual time slot in a TDM network.

To gain your first understanding of L2 VPN, focus on its use as a virtual private line service. For the provider to be able to make money on the service, the provider will have to emulate many private lines over a core offering economies of scale. The ability to multiplex VCs into the core tunnels is therefore critical. The multiplex identifiers are attributes of the tunneling delivery protocol, not the payload protocol of the VC.

Using signaling protocols to set up emulated VCs is not just an architectural necessity, but an added customer capability. When the customer site–to–POP connectivity is overprovisioned, as it will often be with metro Ethernet, and bandwidth economies of scale exist in the core, the customer can set up new VCs far faster than traditional private lines could be provisioned.

Since emulated VCs will share tunnels, they must be multiplexed. The need for encapsulation and multiplex identifier information indicates the setup protocol must be tunnel technology–specific.

Emulated LAN Service

Providers can offer L2 VPNs that provide other than point-to-point topologies. The idea of an emulated or extended LAN is attractive to many customers, but it needs to be approached with caution. The caution here is not especially with the VPN, but with basic LAN technology.

It is no accident that the first letter of *LAN* stands for *local*. LANs were designed to be of local size (that is, of minimal propagation time) and to have relatively small numbers of hosts (100 to 200 per broadcast domain with NetBIOS/ NetBEUI). Making a customer network one large LAN can easily lead to situations where there are too many host broadcasts. Contrary to what has become an urban legend, broadcast and multicast frames do not take up more bandwidth than any other frames. Where broadcasts can take up bandwidth is when misbehaving protocols, hosts, or network design result in broadcast storms (many hosts broadcasting simultaneously). When a broadcast storm occurs, it can make bandwidth unavailable, but even infinite bandwidth does not necessarily solve the problem. Each broadcast represents another interrupt to the host processor, so large numbers of broadcasts can overwhelm hosts. Customer-oriented LAN switches may rate-limit broadcasts on individual host ports, but emulated LAN interconnection devices may not do this.

Some LAN protocols, such as DEC LAT, also have short time-outs and may be adversely affected by long speed-of-light propagation times in extended LANs. In L2 VPNs, which are typically built from point-to-point tunnels, the broadcast and multicast support required for LAN emulation often requires a broadcast replicating server, which adds complexity and is potentially either a single point of failure or a source of gratuitous broadcasts.

My general rule for evaluating the feasibility of a LAN is to consider its worst-case requirement as the condition immediately following power restoration after a campus power failure, so all hosts simultaneously issue ARP, DHCP, and so on.

L2 VPN Architecture

At the originating site, a CE connects by an "attachment VC" to a PE (see Figure 13.12). There is no strict requirement that the two customer sites have the same layer 2 interface, but then there must be an interworking function somewhere in the service. From the PE, provider routing creates a tunnel capable of carrying L2 traffic between CE1 and CE2 (see Figure 13.13). Assuming each CE connects to a different PE, the minimum topological definition of an emulated link is the triplet <CE1-PE1, PE1-PE2, PE2-CE2>.

Make sure to distinguish between the emulated VC and the PE-PE tunnel that carries one or more emulated VCs. The L2 VPN architecture is agnostic to the tunneling mechanism, and there are clear applications at least for MPLS, L2TP, and IPSec. The tunneling protocols will probably need extensions to carry L2

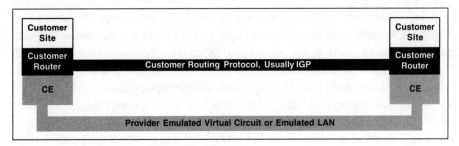

Figure 13.12   L2 VPN customer connectivity.

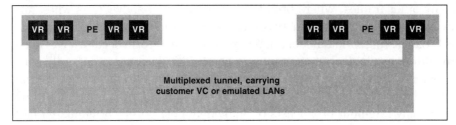

Figure 13.13 Inter-PE L2 VPN connectivity.

VPN–specific information. Current proposals suggest extensions of MPLS signaling to insert the emulated VC ID into the multiplexing field. There is no requirement that either all emulated VCs between two PEs or two CEs travel through the same tunnel. This, in fact, may be undesirable, as it creates a shared-risk group (see Chapter 11).

RFC 2547: MPLS/BGP Virtual Transport Service

L2TP is less attractive as a basic mechanism for interconnecting enterprise sites because it supports only a point-to-point topology, whereas services based on RFC 2547 can support any topology. Because 2547's bulk transfer mechanism inside the carrier network is MPLS, it has much less tunneling overhead than does L2TP. While its transfer mechanism is MPLS, its routing control plane is BGP, for which some extensions will be needed. (See "RFC 2547 and BGP.")

Multiprovider VPNs are in their infancy. Nevertheless, the RFC 2547 approach seems the consensus solution, although there is a resurgence of interest in multiple virtual router architectures. Layer 2 VPNs are not directly comparable with either of these architectures. In non-MPLS networks, connectivity might be provisioned with virtual circuits. It can be useful in an assortment of ISP business models, ranging from turnkey remotely managed enterprise networks to VTN service with the demarcation point at the CE to wholesale VTN service offerings to other ISPs.

Internet access is part of what the enterprise customer can see from a centrally managed service, although Internet access is not a function of the service core but an alternate path taken at the edge. For Internet access, some globally routable addresses need to be associated with the customer sites, although NAT, address-translating firewalls, application layer gateways, and so on can help the enterprises minimize their public address space and maximize their use of private address space [RFC 1918]. When customers are being connected to the ISP, the ISP is strongly advised to implement [RFC 2267] ingress filtering, which, when applied as routine in the global Internet, will help protect both enterprises and ISPs from denial-of-service attacks.

Extranet applications managed by the ISP are certainly possible and practical, with the major caveat being that the different enterprises that compose the extranet must have nonoverlapping address space. If any of the enterprises comprising the VPN have Internet connectivity, the security implications of such connectivity need to be evaluated on a case-by-case basis.

Enterprise customers access VPNs through customer edge (CE) devices at customer sites. The definition of a site is flexible. From the RFC 2547 standpoint, multiple physical sites linked by customer-operated facilities appear as one RFC 2547 site (Figure 13.14). Alternatively, as in (Figure 13.15), the CE may be distributed between the physical customer site and the POP. CE connects to one or more provider edge (PE) routers operated by the service provider. The PE routers connect to other PE and P functions. As seen in Figure 13.15, CE components can be, but do not need to be, routers.

CE may be managed by the enterprise or by the service provider. Most commonly, the CE is a non-BGP-speaking router that points default at one or more PEs. According to RFC 2547, CE does not have awareness of all routes in its VPN; that knowledge is on the set of PE that supports the CE's VPN.

PE Functions

PE routers are aware of VPNs and map them to LSPs. A given PE has knowledge of only those VPNs that are connected to it. On each PE is a *virtual routing/forwarding instance* (VRF), which it is a RIB/FIB specific to some set of one or more interfaces on which one or more VPNs are defined. Each VRF has a set of

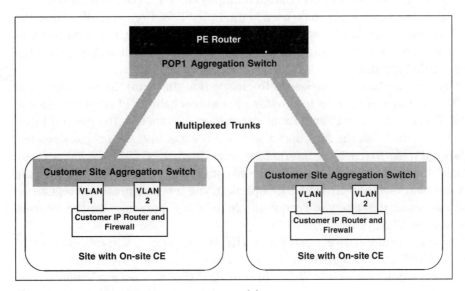

Figure 13.14 MPLS/VPN customer connectivity.

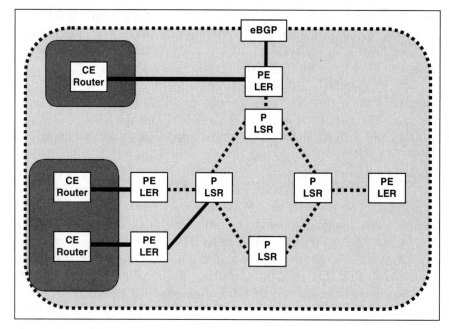

Figure 13.15 RFC 2547 components.

import and export policies appropriate to the VPNs associated with the RIB. Implementation of the VRF is conceptual and may be part of the main RIB of the physical PE router. Cisco's implementation always includes a FIB, in the form of a Cisco Express Forwarding table.

A given physical router may contain multiple VRFs. Part of the reason for this is to allow the same prefix to be used in multiple VPNs. Conceptually, it is at the VRF where the binding is made between the interface on which a packet was received and the route distinguisher that is associated with addresses on the VPN for that interface.

Why have a VRF? Its purpose is to ensure that there are the necessary and sufficient number of routes to provide mutual reachability of sites in the same VPN. These routes can belong to an intranet, an extranet, or the general Internet. Remember that the fact that a site or VPN has Internet access does not mean that it has to reach the Internet gateway via the RFC 2547 service. A vastly simplifying assumption is that CE will have multiple logical uplinks, one to the Internet and one to each VPN. The uplink to the Internet must use registered address space. It is likely to read multiple default routes, one for the Internet and one per VPN.

The relationship between sites and VRF is complex. A site can connect to only one VRF, even though it may belong to more than one VPN. A VRF can contain information on multiple VPNs. To start RFC 2547 in most implementations, you will need to configure several pieces of information on each participating router. Conceptually, there is no reason you could not create RFC 2547 VPNs on a set of cooperating virtual routers, but that makes my mind melt. At this point, I'll simply mention the parameters to be configured; see the discussion of 2547 and BGP later in this chapter for more details of these parameters:

1. Allocating the VRF and giving it a name to be used in configuration.
2. Associating a route distinguisher with the VRF.
3. Associating a list of target communities from which the VRF is to receive routes.
4. Associating a list of target communities to which the VRF is to advertise routes.

Depending on the implementation, there can be more than one VRF per physical router.

So far, you have tied the VRF into your routing system (Figure 13.16). It now needs to be tied to customer sites by associating a VRF with specific interfaces in the interface configuration statements, resulting in the relationships in Figure 13.17. The target communities you specify for the VPN restrict the topology reachable from a particular VRF. Even though some destinations may be in the same VPN, they may not be reachable from certain routers. This adds both the ability to create powerful configurations and the ability to create configurations that require divine intervention to troubleshoot.

Another way to look at the VRF is that it contains the information on all sites that are "owned" by the VRF, but not necessarily on the entire VPN. Membership in a VPN does not mean that members of a VPN can reach all of its other members; there may be closed user groups and partial mesh topologies. For example, you might want the sites connected to router **fennel** in Figure 13.18 to be able to reach the intranet sites connected to **garlic** and to **horseradish**, but not the Internet gateway at **mustard**. You would therefore apply appropriate filtering so **mustard** has a target community that is not exported to **fennel**. Whether or not the communities are ingress- or egress-filtered is not critical as long as the appropriate logic is defined. However, outbound route filtering, described in Chapter 9, makes this process much more efficient.

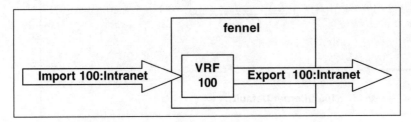

Figure 13.16   VRF and the routing system.

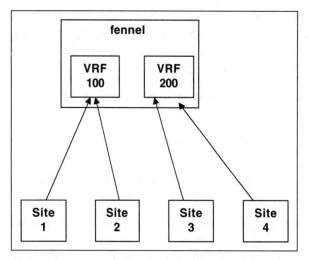

Figure 13.17 A VRF and a set of sites.

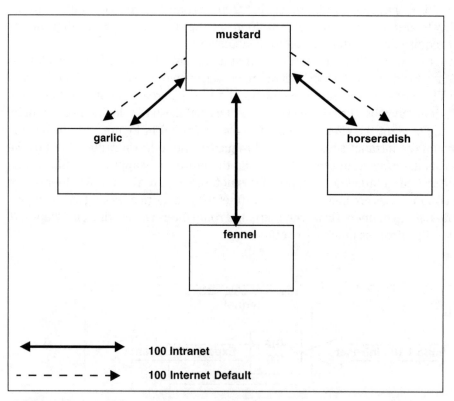

Figure 13.18 Special topologies in an RFC 2547 VPN.

RFC 2547 and BGP

RFC 2547 describes a method for using BGP and MPLS for PPVPNs. It has been deployed by several vendors, and an update generally called 2547bis is in draft. It is most common for people to refer to it simply as 2547, as the formal name is a bit awkward.

In the RFC 2547 architecture, PE routers communicate routing information via iBGP. To support RFC 2547 requirements, BGP needs to be extended in several ways. Some of these extensions form the base product, while others are intended to improve scalability or to signal QoS. Connection establishment needs to use capability advertisement to agree with the potential peers that both support multiprotocol extensions to BGP. The basic extension mechanism is defined by multiprotocol extensions to BGP, which allows the extended addresses of this service to be treated as an address family separate from IPv4. RFC 2547 also must use extended communities.

RFC 2547 allows there to be multiple VPNs that may reuse the same IPv4 address space. To avoid ambiguity, an RFC 2547 router sees IPv4 addresses as prefixed with a 12-byte route distinguisher (RD). Each RD is associated with a VPN. The most common usage will assign a RD to each customer. Customers certainly can have multiple VPNs, and thus multiple RDs, if multiple VPNs are a better fit with their administrative policies. With extranet VPNs, a given VPN may include several customers, but there must be clear "ownership" of a specific RD for the extranet.

RFC 2547 proposes a significant number of enhancements to basic BGP routing, such as closed user groups and VPN-specific routes (that is, from one site) to the same destination. The key assumption that simplifies implementation is that the PEs are fully meshed with MPLS tunnels, and the VPN-specific information is needed only at the ingress PE (see Figure 13.19). RFC 2547 requires iBGP routing between the set of PE, and routing information for MPLS path

---

A BIT OF CONCERN, AND PERHAPS AN ALTERNATIVE

As RFC 2547 continues to evolve, it offers an incredibly rich amount of functionality. At times, I wonder if it has grown too complex for mortals to manage, and for existing BGP routers to process the additional BGP state information. During a recent NANOG meeting, in an open forum on BGP scalability, a respected audience member commented "If this [that is, RFC 2547] is the answer . . . it must have been a pretty stupid question."

PEs normally are at a POP. With currently available routers, it may make good sense to separate at least the PE and Internet access functions, and possibly to devote a separate router or routers to manage core connectivity.

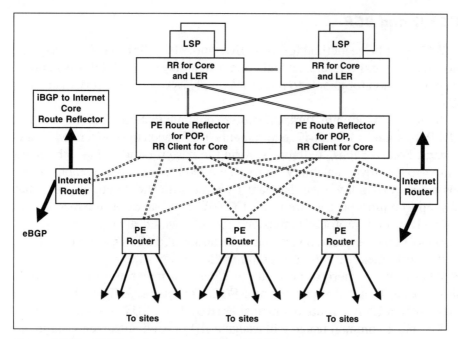

Figure 13.19 Distributed routers for BGP scalability.

setup among P and PE routers. At the core of this service is the ability to create iBGP-interconnected PEs that have VRFs for each VPN to which they are connected, and to create MPLS LSPs among P routers that interconnect the PEs. Creation of a VRF on a specific PE is a matter of configuration. Population of this VRF may be static or dynamic. Once the VRF is populated, its contents need to be propagated to other PE that supports the same VPN.

Target VPNs

The idea of the target VPN, conveyed as an extended community (see the following text), was conceived as a scalability mechanism. BGP scales better with a lesser number of routes, each with multiple attributes, than a larger number of routes without as many attributes [RFC 2547]. They propose that the latter alternative could be met with more RDs, but that such an approach would be less scalable. While a route can only have one RD, it can have multiple target VPNs.

How does a PE determine which target VPN attributes to associate with a given route? There are a number of different possible ways:

- Configure the PE to associate all routes that lead to a particular site with a particular target VPN.

- Configure the PE to associate certain routes leading to a particular site with one target VPN, and certain other routes with another.

- Have the CE router, when it distributes these routes to the PE, specify one or more target VPNs for each route. This shifts the control of the mechanisms used to implement the VPN policies from the SP to the customer. If this method is used, it may still be desirable to have the PE eliminate any target VPNs that, according to its own configuration, are not allowed, and/or to add some target VPNs that according to its own configuration are mandatory.

RFC 2547 uses two extended communities, *route target communities* and *route origin communities:*

- Route target communities identify one or more routers that may receive a set of routes (that carry this community) carried by BGP.

- Route origin communities identify one or more routers that inject a set of routes (that carry this community) into BGP.

- The intersection of a route target community and a route origin community defines a target VPN.

A General BGP-Based Autodiscovery Function for PPVPNs

[Ould-Brahim 2001] describes a multivendor proposal to use BGP to provide VPN-specific information to PE. This proposal is applicable both to 2547bis and VR VPN architectures. For 2547bis, BGP carries VPN-specific routes, which the PEs exchange with iBGP. For VR models, BGP conveys the VR addresses as well as the membership of specific VR instances in different VPNs. Once a 2547bis router receives this information, it uses 2547bis-defined iBGP to exchange information with other 2547bis PEs. Once a VR receives it, it uses the VR VPN routing protocol to exchange routing information. It is not hard to see that this method could also be used to establish interworking between VR and 2547bis VPN implementations.

In both models, the necessary information is carried in BGP multiprotocol extensions [RFC 2283]. For 2547bis, the route target extended community carries the routes belonging to the VPN, and the next hop attribute carries the endpoint address for the VPN tunnel. In the VR model, the VPN ID [RFC 2685] is contained in the route distinguisher field, carried by the new VPN-ID extended community. Another extended community, VPN topology information, carries information that allows both hub-and-spoke (that is, nonbroadcast multiaccess) as well as full-mesh topologies to be constructed.

P Router Functions

PE connects to provider (P) backbone routers, which are interconnected with MPLS LSPs. P routers are unaware of the VPNs traversing them. They only see LSPs, to which the PE has mapped VPNs. P routers are MPLS label-switched routers, usually without the ability to create or stack paths.

Case Study: VPN Connectivity Strategy

In Chapter 4 we discovered that Magic Images, as is common for customers, understated its requirements. Magic Images actually needs several kinds of networks. It needs intranets both for its network management and for its purely internal services. At present, the internal network is local to its London facility, but the management intranet is worldwide. It needs intranets both for its network management and for its purely internal services.

Magic Images needs Internet connectivity to advertise its services. This would appear to be a requirement at the headquarters site alone, but maximizing robustness and minimizing latency suggest distribution makes sense. All hosts with public Internet capability will have unique Internet addresses. The public servers will actually be server clusters behind load distribution devices; the "outside" interface of the load distributor will have a registered address, but the "inside" addresses will be in private address space.

For disaster protection, a mirror of the server cluster exists at each of the regional ISPs used by Magic Images. A content delivery VPN interconnects the mirroring servers, preloading them with content. This VPN will also link to DNS servers at the regional sites, which will resolve requests for the public server to the nearest functioning local cluster.

The Emerging VPN Strategy

The actual customer studios need to connect to the Magic Images resources as extranets. In some cooperative productions, it is possible that multiple customers will collaborate, so Magic Images must be able to allow certain customers to exchange data. Magic Images also must be able to ensure that customers that are competitors cannot see one another's data.

The Real Requirements

While Table 3.8 described LANE domains, we will now treat the LANE domains as VPNs. These domains were separated by routers for better security, or by actual firewalls when the clients were willing to pay the cost of very high-speed firewall equipment. Group 1 and 3 users were willing to accept a single emulated LAN, because they dedicated servers—or at least well-controlled server interfaces—to that application. Group 2 consisted of two locations of the same company, with a router link to the third site. Group 4 was composed of organizations that did not trust each other, but some were more distrustful than others. The large studios, Angelic and Demonic, used routers and firewalls. (See Table 13.5 for details on Magic Images' existing topology.)

In the new design (see Table 13.6), each former emulated LAN will be a VPN. There will also be VPN extranets in which competitors can connect, but in a controlled manner. All the VPNs will use private address space [RFC 1918]. Each intranet and single-enterprise VPN will have a single address space.

Handling Extranets

Generally, it is administratively best to use registered address space for extranets. This can be justified because it involves different ASs with different routing policies. If address space is a problem, you may need to use double NAT to avoid address overlaps [Berkowitz 2000].

Potential Technical Solutions for Magic Images

Magic Images could build a reasonable VPN environment using any of the PPVPN technologies. Considerations in selecting a technology include the assumption that Magic Images will continue to have its own routing staff and the desired level of investment protection for its existing routers and ATM gear. Another factor is

Table 13.5 Detailed Existing Topology for Magic Images

EXTRANET	USERS	EMULATED LANS
Group 1	NY-1, LA-2, TO-3, LO-1	NY-1, LA-2, TO-3, LO-1
Group 2	LA-1, LA-2, TO-1	Emulated LAN for LA-1, LA-2 Router from LA-2 to TO-1
Group 3	BL-1, TK-1, LO-4	BL-1, TK-1, LO-4
Group 4	LO-2, NY-2, Demonic, Angelic	Emulated LAN to LO-2 Emulated LAN to NY-2 Router and firewall from Demonic to Magic Images emulated LAN Router and firewall from Angelic to Magic Images emulated LAN

Table 13.6   Summary of Future Topology for Magic Images

	VLAN AT HQ	VPN/RD	FORMER GROUP	PARTICIPANTS
Magic Images network management	1	1		
Magic Images Internet access	2	2		
Intranet	3	3		
Single-client extranets numbered 10–99 (10 as example)	10	10		LO-1, NY-1
Multiclient extranets numbered 100–199	100	100	1	NY-1, LA-2, TO-3, LO-1
	101	101	2	LA-1, LA-2, TO-1
	102	102	3	BL-1, TK-1, LO-4
	103	103	4	LO-2, NY-2, Demonic, Angelic

the corporate structures of its international ISPs. If some of those ISPs are owned by the same company and coordinate their regional backbones, some technologies are easier when multiprovider support is not required.

An L2 VPN Solution

The use of L2 VPNs is the simplest solution in the sense of minimal impact on the existing routers, which are already connected by VPNs. It may lack flexibility, but if Magic Images continues to maintain a sophisticated routing staff, it may be an adequate solution.

Each ISP used by Magic Images would provide L2 VPNs to replace the existing L2 facilities used by Magic Images' routers. As long as moving to an IP infrastructure lowers the ISPs' cost of providing service, there are potential savings for Magic Images.

An MVR Solution

Multiple virtual routers allow Magic Images to reduce some of its cost by converting dedicated physical routers at ISPs and possibly customer sites to VR

A LIMITATION OF CURRENT ROUTERS

Routing performance competition has generally been aimed at forwarding bandwidth, but with Internet growth, and the proliferation of VPNs, control plane performance may be a limiting factor for complex topologies.

Depending on workload at specific sites, the providers might connect the VRs to real Internet access routers.

instances. As long as the real routers have sufficient control plane processing capabilities, this may produce economies of scale. One possible concern is that MVR implementations tend to emphasize IGPs, while Magic Images already uses BGP. Of course, as long as the virtual routers are BGP capable, this is no problem. Another potential advantage of MVRs for Magic Images is that this is better supported than RFC 2547 by several prominent ATM switch vendors such as Nortel and Lucent. Magic Images already uses ATM switching from an undefined vendor.

A BGP/MPLS Solution

The advantage of an RFC 2547 solution is that Magic Images already uses BGP, and may need considerable flexibility in its trust models. RFC 2547 might allow it to implement more customized security than can L2 VPNs or MVRs. Vendor support might enter into the calculation, as Cisco and Juniper have emphasized RFC 2547 over MVRs. Magic Images is large enough that P routers might even be dedicated to its traffic, with PE routers in each of its regional locations. If the ISP with which Magic Images contracts actually owns some of the regional ISPs, RFC 2547 becomes more attractive because the operation of MPLS tunnels across a single administrative domain is better understood than multivendor MPLS.

Conclusion

We have seen how a service provider evolves from a perceived market need, develops increasingly specific customer connectivity requirements, and abstracts them into technical specifications (Chapters 1 through 5). We then became familiar with the operational environment and the physical characteristics of bandwidth and data link services (Chapters 6 through 8). Next we superimposed a carrier routing system onto those services (Chapters 9 through 12), with increasing levels of abstraction as we created hierarchical routing. In this chapter, we have gone to a new level of abstraction and virtualization, mapping the customer networks to our routed infrastructure.

References

[Abul-Majd 2002] O. Abul-Majd et al., "Advanced Switched Optical Network (ASON) and Its Related Protocols," Work in Progress, IETF, 2002.

[Alaettinoglu 2000] C. Alaettinoglu, V. Jacobson, H. Yu, "Towards Millisecond IGP Convergence." NANOG, www.nanog.org/mtg-0010/igp.html, December 2000.

[ATMF af-phy-0086] ATM Forum, "Inverse Multiplexing for ATM (IMA) Specification/Version af-phy-0086.001." 1999.

[Berkowitz 1998] H. Berkowitz, *Designing Addressing Architectures for Routing and Switching.* Indianapolis, IN: Macmillan Technical, 1998.

[Berkowitz 1999] H. Berkowitz, *Designing Routing and Switching Architectures for Enterprise Networks.* Indianapolis, IN: Macmillan Technical, 1999.

[Berkowitz 2000] H. Berkowitz, *WAN Survival Guide.* New York: Wiley, 2000.

[Berkowitz 2001a] H. Berkowitz, E. Davies, L. Andersson, "An Experimental Methodology for Analysis of Growth in the Global Routing Table." Work in Progress, IETF, 2001.

[Berkowitz 2001b] H. Berkowitz, A. Retana, S. Hares, P. Krishnaswamy, M. Lepp, "Benchmarking Methodology for Single Device BGP Convergence." Benchmarking Methodology Working Group, IETF, 2001.

[Berkowitz 2001c] H. Berkowitz, "Customer Satisfaction 201." Presentation at NANOG, Atlanta, GA, 2001.

[Berkowitz 2001d] H. Berkowitz, A. Retana, S. Hares, P. Krishnaswamy, M. Lepp, "Terminology for Benchmarking External Routing Convergence Measurements." Work in Progress, IETF, 2002.

[Berkowitz 2001e] H. Berkowitz, "Re: [netz] There is a need for online discussion of new DNS NAS Commmittee." Posting to the netizens mailing list, March 31, 2001.

[Berkowitz 2001f] H. Berkowitz, D. Krioukov, "To Be Multihomed: Requirements and Definitions." Work in Progress, IETF, 2001.

[Black 2001] B. Black, V. Gill, J. Abley, "Requirements for IP Multihoming Architectures." Work in Progress, IETF, 2001.

[Chen 2000] E. Chen, "Route Refresh Capability for BGP-4." <draft-ietf-idr-bgp-route-refresh-01.txt>, 2000.

[Clausewitz 1968] C. von Clausewitz, *On War*, Middlesex, NJ. Penguin Books, 1968. (Originally published 1832)

[Cottrell 1999] L. Cottrell, W. Matthews, C. Logg, "Tutorial on Internet Monitoring & PingER at SLAC." Stanford Linear Accelerator Center, www.slac.stanford.edu/comp/net/wan-mon/tutorial.htm, 1999.

[Dharanikota 2001] S. Dharanikota, "Inter-domain Routing with Shared Risk Groups." <draft-many-ccamp-srg-00.txt>, July 16, 2001.

[Donnell 1999] A. Donnell, "Deploying MPLS Traffic Engineering." Juniper Networks Application Note 350000-01, 1999.

[Doria 2002] A. Doria (ed.), "Future Domain Routing Requirements, Group B Contribution," Work in Progress, IETF Internet Research Task Force, 2002.

[Duffield 1999] P. Duffield et al., "A Performance-Oriented Service Interface for Virtual Private Networks." Work in Progress, IETF, 1999.

[Ferguson 1998] P. Ferguson, Networld+Interop '98, Paris, 1998.

[FRF.8] Frame Relay Foundation, *Frame Relay/ATM PVC Service Interworking Implementation Agreement*, February 2000.

[G.ASON] M. Mayer (ed.), "Architecture for Automatic Switched Optical Networks (ASON)," ITU G.8080/Y1304, V1.0, October 2001.

[Goralski 1999] W. Goralski, M C. Kolon, *IP Telephony*. New York: McGraw-Hill, 1999.

[Gorlitz 1975] W. Gorlitz, *History of the German General Staff, 1657–1945*. Westport, CT: Greenwood, 1975.

[Greene 2001] B.R. Greene et al., "Internet eXchange Points (IXP), Peering, and ISP Interconnection: the Keystone of Internet Economics," version 3.1. Cisco Systems, 2001.

[Hughes 2001] M. Hughes, "Internet Exchange Point Switching Wishlist." RIPE European Internet Exchange (EIX) Working Group, April 2001.

[Huston 1999] J. Huston, *ISP Survival Guide*. New York: Wiley, 1999.

[Huston 2001a] G. Huston, "NOPEER Community for BGP Route Scope Control." <draft-huston-nopeer-00.txt>, August 13, 2001.

[Huston 2001b] G. Huston, Presentation to Internet Society Advisory Council, June 2001.

[ITU 1999] International Telecommunications Union, "General Aspects of Quality of Service (QoS)." No. DTR/TIPHON-05001 V1.2.5 (1998-09) Technical Report, 1999.

[JuniperRRP4.4] Juniper Networks. Configuration Guide for Routing and Routing Protocols, release 4.4, 2001.

[Kompella 2001a] K. Kompella, "Generalized MPLS." Networld+Interop, 2001.

[Kompella 2001b] K. Kompella, "MPLS in Perspective." NANOG, October 2001.

[Labovitz] C. Labovitz, A. Ahuga, Z. Farnam, A. Bose, *Experimental Measurement of Delayed Convergence*, NANOG.

[Levy 2001] S. Levy. *Hackers: Heroes of the Computer Revolution*. New York: Penguin, 2001.

[Manning 2001] B. Manning, "Documenting Special Use IPv4 Address Blocks." <draft-manning-dsua-07.txt>, October 29, 2001.

[Oppenheimer 1999] P. Oppenheimer, *Top-Down Network Design*. Indianapolis, IN: Cisco, 1999.

[Ould-Brahim 2001] H. Ould-Brahim et al., "Using BGP as an Auto-Discovery Mechanism for Network-based VPNs." <draft-ietf-ppvpn-bgvpn-auto-02.txt>, Work in Progress, IETF, 2001.

[Papadimitriou 2001] D. Papadimitriou, "Inference of Shared Risk Link Groups." <draft-many-inference-srlg-01.txt>, July 24, 2001.

[Rajagopalan 2002] B. Rajagopalan et al., "IP over Optical Networks: A Framework." Work in Progress, IETF, 2002.

[Ramachandra 2002] S. Ramachandra, "Graceful Restart Mechanism for BGP," Work in Progress, IETF, 2002.

[Rehkter 2001a] Y. Rekhter, D. Tappan, S. Ramachandra, "BGP Extended Communities Attribute," <draft-ramachandra-bgp-ext-communities-08.txt>, January 3, 2001.

[Rekhter 2001b] Y. Rekhter, The current RFC is 1771, but the draft clarifies some points. www/ietf.org/internet_drafts/draft_ietf_idr_bgp4_09.txt, 2001.

[RFC 0827] E. C. Rosen, *Exterior Gateway Protocol (EGP)*. 1982.

[RFC 1001] *Protocol Standard for a NetBIOS Service on a TCP/UDP Transport: Concepts and Methods*. NetBIOS Working Group in the Defense Advanced Research Projects Agency, Internet Activities Board, End-to-End Services Task Force. March 1, 1987.

[RFC 1002] IETF, *Protocol Standard for a NetBIOS Service on a TCP/UDP Transport: Detailed Specifications*. NetBIOS Working Group in the Defense Advanced Research Projects Agency, Internet Activities Board, End-to-End Services Task Force. March 1, 1987.

[RFC 1105] K. Lougheed, Y. Rekhter, *Border Gateway Protocol (BGP), Version 1*. 1989.

[RFC 1142] D. Oran, *OSI IS-IS Intra-Domain Routing Protocol.* February 1, 1990.

[RFC 1195] R. W. Callon, *Use of OSI IS-IS for Routing in TCP/IP and Dual Environments.* December 1, 1990.

[RFC 1234] D. Provan, *Tunneling IPX Traffic through IP Networks.* 1991.

[RFC 1338] V. Fuller, T. Li, J. Yu, K. Varadhan, *Supernetting: An Address Assignment and Aggregation Strategy.* 1992.

[RFC 1700] J. Reynolds, J. Postel, *Assigned Numbers.* October 1994. [Obsoleted by RFC 3232, which points to an online database]

[RFC 1702] S. Hanks, T. Li, D. Farinacci, P. Traina, *Generic Routing Encapsulation over IPv4 Networks.* October 1994.

[RFC 1812] F. Baker, *Requirements for IP Version 4 Routers.* June 1995.

[RFC 1918] Y. Rekhter, B. Moskowitz, D. Karrenberg, G. J. de Groot, E. Lear, *Address Allocation for Private Internets.* February 1996.

[RFC 1930] J. Hawkinson, T. Bates, *Guidelines for Creation, Selection, and Registration of an Autonomous System (AS).* March 1996.

[RFC 1965] P. Traina, *Autonomous System Confederations for BGP.* June 1996.

[RFC 1998] E. Chen, T. Bates, *An Application of the BGP Community Attribute in Multi-Home Routing.* August 1996.

[RFC 2018] M. Mathis, J. Mahdavi, S. Floyd, A. Romanow, *TCP Selective Acknowledgement Options.* 1996.

[RFC 2050] K. Hubbard, M. Kosters, D. Conrad, D. Karrenberg, J. Postel, *Internet Registry IP Allocation Guidelines.* November 1996.

[RFC 2071] P. Ferguson, H. Berkowitz, *Network Renumbering Overview: Why Would I Want It and What Is It Anyway?* January 1997.

[RFC 2072] H. Berkowitz, *Router Renumbering Guide.* 1997.

[RFC 2131] R. Droms, *Dynamic Host Configuration Protocol.* March 1997.

[RFC 2267] P. Ferguson, D. Senie, *Network Ingress Filtering: Defeating Denial of Service Attacks Which Employ IP Source Address Spoofing.* May 2000. [Replaced by RFC 2827]

[RFC 2270] J. Stewart, T. Bates, R. Chandra, E. Chen, *Using a Dedicated AS for Sites Homed to a Single Provider.* January 1998.

[RFC 2281] T. Li, B. Cole, P. Morton, D. Li, *Cisco Hot Standby Router Protocol (HSRP).* March 1998.

[RFC 2283] T. Bates, R. Chandra, D. Katz, Y. Rekhter, *Multiprotocol Extensions for BGP-4.* February 1998.

[RFC 2338] S. Knight, D. Weaver, D. Whipple, R. Hinden, D. Mitzel, P. Hunt, P. Higginson, M. Shand, A. Lindem, *Virtual Router Redundancy Protocol.* April 1998.

[RFC 2373] R. Hinden, *IP Version 6 Addressing Architecture.* July 1998.

[RFC 2374] R. Hinden, S. Deering, M. O'Dell, *An Aggregatable Global Unicast Address Format.* July 1998.

[RFC 2430] T. Li, Y. Rekhter, *A Provider Architecture for Differentiated Services and Traffic Engineering (PASTE)*. October 1998.

[RFC 2439] C. Villamizar, R. Chandra, R. Govindan, *BGP Route Flap Damping*. November 1998.

[RFC 2450] R. Hinden, *Proposed TLA and NLA Assignment Rule*. December 1998.

[RFC 2460] S. Deering, R. Hinden, *Internet Protocol, Version 6 (IPv6) Specification*. December 1998.

[RFC 2474] K. Nichols, S. Blake, F. Baker, D. Black, *Definition of the Differentiated Services Field (DS Field) in the IPv4 and IPv6 Headers*. December 1998.

[RFC 2547] E. Rosen, Y. Rekhter, *BGP/MPLS VPNs*. March 1999.

[RFC 2558] K. Tesink, *Definitions of Managed Objects for the SONET/SDH Interface Type*. 1999.

[RFC 2622] C. Alaettinoglu, C. Villamizar, E. Gerich, D. Kessens, D. Meyer, T. Bates, D. Karrenberg, M. Terpstra, *Routing Policy Specification Language (RPSL)*. June 1999.

[RFC 2644] D. Senie, *Changing the Default for Directed Broadcasts in Routers*. 1999.

[RFC 2685] B. Fox, B. Gleeson, *Virtual Private Networks Identifier*. September 1999.

[RFC 2702] D. Awduche, J. Malcolm, J. Agogbua, M. O'Dell, J. McManus, *Requirements for Traffic Engineering over MPLS*. 1999.

[RFC 2730] S. Hanna, B. Patel, M. Shah, *Multicast Address Dynamic Client Allocation Protocol (MADCAP)*. December 1999.

[RFC 2796] T. Bates, R. Chandra, E. Chen, *BGP Route Reflection—An Alternative to Full Mesh IBGP*. 2000.

[RFC 2805] N. Greene, M. Ramalho, B. Rosen, *Media Gateway Control Protocol Architecture and Requirements*. April 2000.

[RFC 2827] P. Ferguson, D. Senie, *Network Ingress Filtering: Defeating Denial of Service Attacks Which Employ IP Source Address Spoofing*. 2000.

[RFC 2858] T. Bates, Y. Rekhter, R. Chandra, D. Katz, *Multiprotocol Extensions for BGP-4*. June 2000.

[RFC 2863] K. McCloghrie, F. Kastenholz, *The Interfaces Group MIB*. June 2000.

[RFC 2865] C. Rigney, S. Willens, A. Rubens, W. Simpson, *Remote Authentication Dial In User Service (RADIUS)*. 2000.

[RFC 2883] S. Floyd, J. Mahdavi, M. Mathis, M. Podolsky, *An Extension to the Selective Acknowledgement (SACK) Option for TCP*. 2000.

[RFC 2966] T. Li, T. Przygienda, H. Smit, *Domain-wide Prefix Distribution with Two-Level IS-IS*. 2000.

[RFC 3015] F. Cuervo, N. Greene, A. Rayhan, C. Huitema, B. Rosen, J. Segers, *MEGACO Protocol Version 1.0*. November 2000.

[RFC 3065] P. Traina, D. McPherson, J. Scudder, *Autonomous System Confederations for BGP.* February 2001.

[RFC 3077] E. Duros, W. Dabbous, H. Izumiyama, N. Fujii, Y. Zhang, *A Link-Layer Tunneling Mechanism for Unidirectional Links.* 2001.

[RIPE-178] T. Barber, S. Doran, D. Karrenberg, C. Panigl, J. Schmitz, *RIPE Routing—WG Recommendation for Coordinated Route-Flap Damping Parameters.* 1995.

[RIPE-229] C. Panigl, J. Schmitz, P. Smith, C. Vistoli. *RIPE Routing—WG Recommendations for Coordinated Route-Flap Damping Parameters.* 2001. [obsoletes RIPE-178]

[RIPE-230] E. Bretherick. O. Ruimwijk, *Guidelines for Setting up a Local Internet Registry at the RIPE NCC.* 2001.

[Rosenberg 1997] J. Rosenberg, "Error Recovery for Internet Telephony." Voice over Networks Conference, 1997.

[Sharma 2001] V. Sharma et al., "Framework for MPLS-based Recovery." <draft-ietf-mpls-recovery-frmwrk-03.txt>, 2001.

[Vijeh 2000] N. Vijeh, "Metropolitan Area Networks (MAN) and Resilient Packet Rings." IEEE 802 Resilient Packet Ring Study Group, Interim Meeting, May 22, 2000.

[Vohra 2001] Q. Vohra, E. Chen, "BGP Support for Four-octet AS Number Space." www.ietf.org/internet_drafts/draft-ietf-idr-as4bytes-03.txt. 2001.

[Zinin 2001] A. Zinin, A. Lindem, D. Yeung, "Alternative OSPF ABR Implementations." <draft-ietf-ospef-abr-alt-04.txt>, September 2001.

Index